One World,

Many Cultures

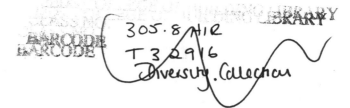

D0815644

One World, Many Cultures

Sixth Edition

STUART HIRSCHBERG

Rutgers: The State University of New Jersey, Newark

TERRY HIRSCHBERG

PEARSON

Longman

New York • San Francisco • Boston
London • Toronto • Sydney • Tokyo • Singapore • Madrid
Mexico City • Munich • Paris • Cape Town • Hong Kong • Montreal

Senior Sponsoring Editor: Virginia L. Blanford
Production Manager: Stacey Kulig
Project Coordination, Text Design, and Electronic
    Page Makeup: Pre-Press Company
Cover Designer: Wendy Ann Fredericks
Cover Photo: Hollingsworth Studios, Inc.
Photo Researcher: Chrissy McIntyre
Senior Manufacturing Buyer: Alfred C. Dorsey
Printer and Binder: R.R. Donnelley and Sons
Cover Printer: Phoenix Color Corporation

For permission to use copyrighted material, grateful acknowledgment is
made to the copyright holders on pp. 501–506, which are hereby made part
of this copyright page.

Library of Congress Cataloging-in-Publication Data
One world, many cultures / [compiled by] Stuart Hirschberg, Terry Hirschberg.
-- 6th ed.
    p. cm.
  Includes bibliographical references and index.
  ISBN 0-321-35564-4 (alk. paper)
    1. College readers. 2. Pluralism (Social sciences)--Problems, exercises, etc.
3. Ethnic groups--Problems, exercises, etc. 4. English language--Rhetoric.
5. Readers--Social sciences. I. Hirschberg, Stuart. II. Hirschberg, Terry.

PE1417.O57 2007
428.6--dc22   2005032285

Please visit us at http://www.ablongman.com

ISBN 0-321-35564-4

2 3 4 5 6 7 8 9 10—DOC—09 08 07 06

For Mick Jagger and the Rolling Stones
Thanks for the music!

Contents

Introduction   1

1 *The Family in Different Cultures*   27

5   Race, Class, and Caste   277

6 *Social and Political Issues*   *336*

7 *The Other*   389

8 *Customs, Rituals, and Values*   441

Rhetorical Contents

Preface

This sixth edition of *One World, Many Cultures* is a global, contemporary reader whose international and multicultural selections offer a new direction for freshman composition courses.

In eight thematic chapters, consisting of fifty-nine readings, twenty-three of which are new to this edition, by internationally recognized writers from twenty-two countries, we explore cultural differences and displacement in relation to race, class, gender, region, and nation. *One World, Many Cultures* also reflects the emphasis on cultural studies and argumentation that has become an integral part of many college programs.

The selections challenge readers to see similarities between their own experiences and the experiences of others in radically different cultural circumstances. Compelling and provocative writings by authors from the Caribbean, Africa, Asia, Europe, and Latin America reflect the cultural and ethnic heritage of many students. The fifty nonfiction selections include speeches, essays, autobiographies, and prison memoirs. These and the nine short stories encourage readers to perceive the relationship between a wide range of experiences in different cultures and corresponding experiences of writers within the United States. The sixth edition of *One World, Many Cultures* continues to provide a rich sampling of accounts by writers who are native to the cultures that they describe, allowing the reader to hear authentic voices rather than filtered journalistic reports.

New to this Edition

- Twenty-three selections (including two new works of short fiction) are new to this edition. Many have never been previously anthologized.
- We have added a new section ("Writing Your Essay") to the Introduction that emphasizes rhetorical modes and argumentation in the writing process.
- Web sites for further research on authors, topics, and cultural issues for half the selections are included under the new end-of-selection category "Extending Viewpoints through Writing and Research."
- We have added sixteen illustrations (cartoons, photographs, and other images) that enhance the impact of the themes and selections.
- We have broadened the emphasis of Chapter 4 to include environmental issues and Chapter 6 to include social issues in America.

- Key search terms are provided for each author.
- Selections are arranged from here (and most familiar) to there (distant and least familiar).
- In the Rhetorical Contents, twenty-six arguments are classified into the four categories traditionally used by teachers of writing.
- Each chapter is preceded by a thought-provoking quotation.

Chapter Descriptions

The eight chapters move from the most personal sphere of family life through various turning points, questions of sexual identity, the relationship of work in various environments, and conflicts of class and race to the more encompassing dimensions of citizenship, immigration, and social customs.

Chapter 1, "The Family in Different Cultures," introduces families in France, Iraq, India, and China, and within the United States, an African-American family, and a Chinese-American family, among others. These selections illustrate that the "family," however defined (as a single-parent household, a nuclear family, or the extended family of an entire community), passes on the mores and values of a particular culture to the next generation.

Chapter 2, "Turning Points," provides insights into both formal and informal rites of passage, initiation ceremonies, and moments of discovery in the lives of a Chinese-American girl, a young boy in Ireland, a young girl in Lebanon, a student in Germany, an adventurer in Borneo, a student in China, and an Australian-born writer.

Chapter 3, "How Culture Shapes Gender Roles," explores the role of culture in shaping sexual identity. Readers can gain insight into how gender roles are culturally conditioned rather than biologically determined. The extent to which sex-role expectations, both heterosexual and homosexual, differ from culture to culture can be seen in societies as diverse as those in Puerto Rico, Lebanon, Saudi Arabia, India, and Japan.

Chapter 4, "Work and the Environment," explores work as a universal human experience through which we define ourselves and others. The role of culture in shaping attitudes toward work can be seen in the different experiences of a minimum-wage worker and a Mexican-American rock blaster. We can share the work experiences of a disillusioned Japanese corporate employee, the different styles of assertion of men and women in the workplace, the insights of a commentator on water use in California, the experiences of a Swedish activist in the Himalayas, and the disillusion of an upwardly striving couple in Singapore.

Chapter 5, "Race, Class, and Caste," takes up the crucial and often unrecognized relationships between race, identity, and social class through readings that explore positions of power and powerlessness. Selections include Martin Luther King Jr.'s stirring summons for racial equality, Itabari Njeri's account of reshaping her identiy as an African American, and Mahdokt Kashkuli's story of a family in modern-day Iran who must place one of their children in an orphanage. The voices heard are those of men and women of many races in several nations, including Viramma's account of her life as an "untouchable" in south India. Unusual perspectives on class issues are provided by Mary Crow Dog's account of her experiences in a government-run school for Native Americans, Richard Rodriguez's narrative on losing contact with his Mexican heritage, Raymonde Carroll's investigation of the different cultural values that define success in America and France, and Kate Chopin's story of race and class in turn-of-the-century Louisana.

Chapter 6, "Social and Political Issues," looks at the emerging trends in popular culture and political currents in regimes as diverse as those in Mao Tse-Tung's China, contemporary Pakistan, Cyprus during the British colonial rule, and Chile under Pinochet's dictatorship.

Chapter 7, "The Other," explores the condition of all those who are estranged politically, linguistically, or culturally. The need of those who are caught between two cultures (whether actually or psychologically) and are at home in neither is the theme explored by Temple Grandin, Gloria Anzaldúa, Poranee Natadecha-Sponsel, Gino Del Guercio, Ngũgĩ wa Thiong'o, Kyoko Mori, and David R. Counts.

Chapter 8, "Customs, Rituals, and Values," focuses on the role that ritual, religion, and popular culture, East and West, play in shaping social behavior. The decisive influence of cultural values is explored through an analysis of footbinding practices in ancient China, the wearing of the kimono in Japan, the meaning of fiestas in Mexico, and the role of shopping malls in America. We gain insight into the role rituals play in a hitherto unknown tribe in North America, the place of revenge in Bedouin society, the importance of the sun dance for the Lakota tribe in the United States, and the communal satisfactions derived from *The Nutcracker* ballet.

Editorial Apparatus

The introduction covers the important aspects of critical reading, keeping a journal, and responding to the text, and includes a sample selection by Edward T. Hall ("Hidden Culture") for students to annotate. Chapter introductions discuss the theme of each chapter as related to the individual selections. Biographical sketches preceding each reading give background information on the writer's life and identify the cultural, historical, and personal context in which the selection was written. Relevant background information is provided for unfamiliar ethnic groups before the selections. Prompts ("Before You Read") that precede each selection alert students to an important cultural idea expressed in the selection.

The questions that follow each selection are designed to encourage readers to discover relationships between personal experiences and ideas in the text, to explore points of agreement and areas of conflict sparked by the viewpoints of the authors, and to provide ideas for further research and inquiry.

The first set of questions, "Evaluating the Text," asks readers to think critically about the content, meaning, and purpose of the selections and to evaluate the author's rhetorical strategy, voice projected in relationship to his or her audience, evidence cited, and underlying assumptions.

The questions in "Exploring Different Perspectives" focus on relationships between readings within each chapter that illuminate differences and similarities between cultures. These questions encourage readers to make connections between diverse cultures, to understand the writer's values and beliefs, to enter into the viewpoints of others, and to understand how culture shapes perception and a sense of self.

The questions in "Extending Viewpoints through Writing and Research" invite readers to extend their thinking by seeing wider relationships between themselves and others through writing of many different kinds, including personal or expressive as well as expository and persuasive writing and more formal research papers.

At the end of each chapter "Connecting Cultures" challenges readers to make connections and comparisons among selections within the chapter and throughout the book. These questions provide opportunities to consider additional cross-cultural perspectives on a single issue or to explore a particular topic in depth.

A rhetorical table of contents, a pronunciation key to authors' names, an index of key search terms, a geographical index, an index of authors and titles, and a map of the world identifying countries mentioned in the selections are included to allow the text to accommodate a variety of teaching approaches.

Instructor's Manual

An *Instructor's Manual* provides guidelines for using the text including teaching short works of fiction, supplemental bibliographies of books and periodicals, suggested answers to discussion questions in the text, relevant background information on countries from which the selections are drawn, a filmography, as well as optional discussion questions and classroom activities.

Acknowledgments

We want to acknowledge our appreciation for the encouragement and enthusiasm of our editor, Virginia Blanford, and our gratitude to all those teachers of composition who offered their thoughtful comments and gave this sixth edition the benefit of their scholarship and teaching experience. We would very much like to thank James Burns, University of Delaware; Joanna Chrzanowski, Jefferson Community College; Eileen Ferretti, Kingsborough Community College; Len Fox, Brooklyn College; Anne Stockdell-Giesler, University of Tampa; and Jennifer Wall, St. Cloud University; who suggested changes for this edition.

For their dedication, skill, and good humor, we owe much to Longman's able staff, especially Rebecca Gilpin, assistant editor, and Abigail Greshik at Pre-Press Company. We also thank Chrissy McIntyre for obtaining permissions for the visuals and Celeste Bates for the texts.

STUART HIRSCHBERG
TERRY HIRSCHBERG

Introduction

---◆---

Critical Reading for Ideas and Organization

One of the most important skills to have in your repertoire is the ability to survey unfamiliar articles, essays, or excerpts and to come away with an accurate understanding of what the author wanted to communicate and how the material is organized. On the first and in subsequent readings of any of the selections in this text, especially the longer ones, pay particular attention to the title, look for introductory and concluding paragraphs (with special emphasis on the author's statement or restatement of central ideas), identify the headings and subheadings (and determine the relationship between these and the title), and identify any unusual terms necessary to fully understand the author's concepts.

As you work your way through an essay, you might look for cues to enable you to recognize the main parts of the argument or help you perceive the overall organization of the article. Once you find the main thesis or claim, underline it. Then work your way through fairly rapidly, identifying the main ideas and the sequence in which they are presented. As you identify an important idea, ask yourself how this idea relates to the thesis statement you underlined or to the idea expressed in the title.

Finding a Thesis

Finding a thesis involves discovering the idea that serves as the focus of the essay. The thesis is often stated in the form of a single sentence that asserts the author's response to an issue that others might respond to in different ways. For example, the opening paragraphs of "The Little Emperors" presents Daniela Deane's assessment of an important aspect of Chinese society:

> The one-child campaign, a strict national directive that seeks to limit each Chinese couple to a single son or daughter, has other dramatic consequences: millions of abortions, fewer girls and a generation of spoiled children.

1

This thesis represents the writer's view of a subject or topic from a certain perspective. Here, Deane states a view of China's one-child policy that will serve as a focus for her essay. Writers often place the thesis in the first paragraph or group of paragraphs so that the readers will be able to perceive the relationship between the supporting evidence and this main idea.

As you read, you might wish to underline the topic sentence or main idea of each paragraph or section (since key ideas are often developed over the course of several paragraphs). Jot it down in your own words in the margins, identify supporting statements and evidence (such as examples, statistics, and the testimony of authorities), and try to discover how the author organizes the material to support the development of important ideas. To identify supporting material, look for any ideas more specific than the main idea that is used to support it. Also look for instances where the author uses examples, descriptions, statistics, quotations from authorities, comparisons, or graphs to make the main idea clearer or prove it to be true.

Pay particular attention to important transitional words, phrases, or paragraphs to better see the relationships among major sections of the selection. Noticing how certain words or phrases act as transitions to link paragraphs or sections together will dramatically improve your reading comprehension. Also look for section summaries, where the author draws together several preceding ideas.

Writers use certain words to signal the starting point of an argument. If you detect any of the following terms, look for the main idea they introduce:

> since, because, for, as, follows from, as shown by, inasmuch as, otherwise, as indicated by, the reason is that, for the reason that, may be inferred from, may be derived from, may be deduced from, in view of the fact that

An especially important category of words is that which includes signals that the author will be stating a conclusion. Words to look for are these:

> therefore, hence, thus, so, accordingly, in consequence, it follows that, we may infer, I conclude that, in conclusion, in summary, which shows that, which means that, and which entails, consequently, proves that, as a result, which implies that, which allows us to infer, points to the conclusion that

You may find it helpful to create a running dialogue with the author in the margins, posing and then trying to answer the basic questions *who, what, where, when,* and *why,* and to note observations on how the main idea of the article is related to the title. These notes can later be used to evaluate how effectively any specific section contributes to the overall line of thought.

Responding to What You Read

When reading an essay that seems to embody a certain value system, try to examine any assumptions or beliefs the writer expects the audience to share. How is this assumption related to the author's purpose? If you do not agree with these assumptions, has the writer provided sound reasons and evidence to persuade you to change your mind?

You might describe the author's tone or voice and try to assess how much it contributed to the essay. How effectively does the writer use authorities, statistics, or examples to support the claim? Does the author identify the assumptions or values on which his or her views are based? Are they ones with which you would agree or disagree? To what extent does the author use the emotional connotations of language to try to persuade his or her reader? Do you see anything unworkable or disadvantageous about the solutions offered as an answer to the problem the essay addresses? All these and many other ways of analyzing someone else's essay can be used to create your own. Here are some specific guidelines to help you.

When evaluating an essay, consider what the author's purpose was in writing it. Was it to inform, explain, solve a problem, make a recommendation, amuse, enlighten, or achieve some combination of these goals? How is the tone or voice the author projects toward the reader related to his or her purpose in writing the essay?

You may find it helpful to write short summaries after each major section to determine whether you understand what the writer is trying to communicate. These summaries can then serve as a basis for an analysis of how successfully the author employs reasons, examples, statistics, and expert testimony to support and develop his or her main points.

For example, if the essay you are analyzing cites authorities to support a claim, assess whether the authorities bring the most timely opinions to bear on the subject or display any obvious biases, and determine whether they are experts in that particular field. Watch for experts described as "often quoted" or "highly placed reliable sources" without accompanying names, credentials, or appropriate documentation. If the experts cited offer what purports to be a reliable interpretation of facts, consider whether the writer also quotes equally trustworthy experts who hold opposing views.

If statistics are cited to support a point, judge whether they derive from verifiable and trustworthy sources. Also, evaluate whether the author has interpreted them in ways that are beneficial to his or her case, whereas someone who held an opposing view could interpret them quite differently. If real-life examples are presented to support the author's opinions, determine whether they are representative or whether they are too atypical to be used as evidence. If the author relies on hypothetical examples or analogies to dramatize ideas that otherwise would be hard to grasp, judge whether these examples are too farfetched to back up the claims being made. If the essay depends on the stipulated definition of a term that might be defined in different ways, check whether the author provides clear reasons to indicate why one definition rather than another is preferable.

As you list observations about the various elements of the article you are analyzing, take a closer look at the underlying assumptions and see whether you can locate and distinguish between those assumptions that are explicitly stated and those that are implicit. Once the author's assumptions are identified, you can compare them with your own beliefs about the subject, determine whether these assumptions are commonly held, and make a judgment as to their validity. Would you readily agree with these assumptions? If not, has the author provided sound reasons and supporting evidence to persuade you to change your mind?

Marking as You Read

The most effective way to think about what you read is to make notes as you read. Making notes as you read forces you to go slowly and think carefully about each sentence. This process is sometimes called annotating the text, and all you need is a pen or a pencil. There are as many styles of annotating as there are readers, and you will discover your own favorite technique once you have done it a few times. Some readers prefer to underline major points or statements and jot down their reactions to them in the margin. Others prefer to summarize each paragraph or section to help them follow the author's line of thinking. Other readers circle key words or phrases necessary to understand the main ideas. Feel free to use your notes as a kind of conversation with the text. Ask questions. Express doubts. Mark unfamiliar words or phrases to look up later. If the paragraphs are not already numbered, you might wish to number them as you go to help you keep track of your responses. Try to distinguish the main ideas from supporting points and examples. Most importantly, go slowly and think about what you are reading. Try to discover whether the author makes a credible case for the conclusions he or she reaches. One last point: Take a close look at the idea expressed in the title before and after you read the essay to see how it relates to the main idea.

Distinguishing between Fact and Opinion

As you read, distinguish between statements of fact and statements of opinion. Statements of fact relate information that is widely accepted and objectively verifiable; facts are used as evidence to support the claim made by the thesis. By contrast, an opinion is a personal interpretation of data or a belief or feeling that however strongly presented should not be mistaken by the reader for objective evidence. For example, consider the following claim by Edward T. Hall in "Hidden Culture," an essay we include below to encourage you to try your hand at critical reading and annotation.

> Each culture and each country has its own language of space, which is just as unique as the spoken language, frequently more so. In England, for example, there are no offices for the members of Parliament. In the United States, our congressmen and senators proliferate their offices and their office buildings and simply would not tolerate a no-office situation.

The only statement that could be verified or refuted on the basis of objective data is "In England . . . there are no offices for the members of Parliament." All the other statements, *however persuasive they may seem,* are Hall's interpretations of a situation (multiple offices and office buildings for U.S. government officials) that might be interpreted quite differently by another observer. These statements should not be mistaken for statements of fact.

A reader who could not distinguish between facts and interpretations would be at a severe disadvantage in understanding Hall's essay. Part of the difficulty in separating fact from opinion stems from the difficulty of remaining objective about statements that match our own personal beliefs.

Take a few minutes to read and annotate the following essay. Feel free to "talk back" to the author. You can underline or circle key passages or key terms. You can make observations, raise questions, and express your reactions to what you read.

A SAMPLE ESSAY FOR
STUDENT ANNOTATION

Edward T. Hall

Hidden Culture

◆

1   A few years ago, I became involved in a sequence of events in Japan that completely mystified me, and only later did I learn how an overt act seen from the vantage point of one's own culture can have an entirely different meaning when looked at in the context of the foreign culture. I had been staying at a hotel in downtown Tokyo that had European as well as Japanese-type rooms. The clientele included a few Europeans but was predominantly Japanese. I had been a guest for about ten days and was returning to my room in the middle of an afternoon. Asking for my key at the desk, I took the elevator to my floor. Entering the room, I immediately sensed that something was wrong. Out of place. Different. I was in the wrong room! Someone else's things were distributed around the head of the bed and the table. Somebody else's toilet articles (those of a Japanese male) were in the bathroom. My first thoughts were, "What if I am discovered here? How do I explain my presence to a Japanese who may not even speak English?"

2   I was close to panic as I realized how incredibly territorial we in the West are. I checked my key again. Yes, it really was mine. Clearly they had moved somebody else into my room. But where was my room now? And where were my belongings? Baffled and mystified, I took the elevator to the lobby. Why hadn't they told me at the desk, instead of letting me risk embarrassment and loss of face by being caught in somebody else's room? Why had they moved me in the first place? It was a nice room and, being sensitive to spaces and how they work, I was loath to give it up. After all, I had told them I would be in the hotel for almost a month. Why this business of moving me around like someone who has been squeezed in without a reservation? Nothing made sense.

3   At the desk I was told by the clerk, as he sucked in his breath in deference (and embarrassment?) that indeed they had moved me. My particular room had been reserved in advance by somebody else. I was given the key to my new room and discovered that all my personal

6

effects were distributed around the new room almost as though I had done it myself. This produced a fleeting and strange feeling that maybe I wasn't myself. How could somebody else do all those hundred and one little things just the way I did?

4   Three days later, I was moved again, but this time I was prepared. There was no shock, just the simple realization that I had been moved and that it would now be doubly difficult for friends who had my old room number to reach me. *Tant pis*, I was in Japan. One thing did puzzle me. Earlier, when I had stayed at Frank Lloyd Wright's Imperial Hotel for several weeks, nothing like this had ever happened. What was different? What had changed? Eventually I got used to being moved and would even ask on my return each day whether I was still in the same room.

5   Later, at Hakone, a seaside resort where I was visiting with friends, the first thing that happened was that we were asked to disrobe. We were given *okatas,* and our clothes were taken from us by the maid. (For those who have not visited Japan, the okata is a cotton print kimono.) We later learned, when we ventured out in the streets, that it was possible to recognize other guests from our hotel because we had all been equipped with identical okatas. (Each hotel had its own characteristic, clearly recognizable pattern.) Also, I noted that it was polite to wave or nod to these strangers from the same hotel.

6   Following Hakone, we visited Kyoto, site of many famous temples and palaces, and the ancient capital of Japan.

7   There we were fortunate enough to stay in a wonderful little country inn on the side of a hill overlooking the town. Kyoto is much more traditional and less industrialized than Tokyo. After we had been there about a week and had thoroughly settled into our new Japanese surroundings, we returned one night to be met at the door by an apologetic manager who was stammering something. I knew immediately that we had been moved, so I said, "You had to move us. Please don't let this bother you, because we understand. Just show us to our new rooms and it will be all right." Our interpreter explained as we started to go through the door that we weren't in that hotel any longer but had been moved to *another* hotel. What a blow! Again, without warning. We wondered what the new hotel would be like, and with our descent into the town our hearts sank further. Finally, when we could descend no more, the taxi took off into a part of the city we hadn't seen before. No Europeans here! The streets got narrower and narrower until we turned into a side street that could barely accommodate the tiny Japanese taxi into which we were squeezed. Clearly this was a hotel of another class. I found that, by then, I was getting a little paranoid, which is easy enough to do in a foreign land, and said to myself, "They must think we are very low-status people indeed to treat us this way."

8   As it turned out, the neighborhood, in fact the whole district, showed us an entirely different side of life from what we had seen before, much more interesting and authentic. True, we did have some communication problems, because no one was used to dealing with foreigners, but few of them were serious.

9   Yet, the whole matter of being moved like a piece of derelict luggage puzzled me. In the United States, the person who gets moved is often the lowest-ranking individual. This principle applies to all organizations, including the Army. Whether you can be moved or not is a function of your status, your performance, and your value to the organization. To move someone without telling him is almost worse than an insult, because it means he is below the point at which feelings matter. In these circumstances, moves can be unsettling and damaging to the ego. In addition, moves themselves are often accompanied by great anxiety, whether an entire organization or a small part of an organization moves. What makes people anxious is that the move usually presages organizational changes that have been coordinated with the move. Naturally, everyone wants to see how he comes out vis-à-vis everyone else. I have seen important men refuse to move into an office that was six inches smaller than someone else's of the same rank. While I have heard some American executives say they wouldn't employ such a person, the fact is that in actual practice, unless there is some compensating feature, the significance of space as a communication is so powerful that no employee in his right mind would allow his boss to give him a spatial demotion—unless of course he had already reached his crest and was on the way down.

10   These spatial messages are not simply conventions in the United States—unless you consider the size of your salary check a mere convention, or where your name appears on the masthead of a journal. Ranking is seldom a matter that people take lightly, particularly in a highly mobile society like that in the United States. Each culture and each country has its own language of space, which is just as unique as the spoken language, frequently more so. In England, for example, there are no offices for the members of Parliament. In the United States, our congressmen and senators proliferate their offices and their office buildings and simply would not tolerate a no-office situation. Constituents, associates, colleagues, and lobbyists would not respond properly. In England, status is internalized; it has its manifestations and markers—the upper-class received English accent, for example. We in the United States, a relatively new country, externalize status. The American in England has some trouble placing people in the social system, while the English can place each other quite accurately by reading ranking cues, but in general tend to look down on the importance that Americans attach to space. It is very easy and very natural

to look at things from one's own point of view and to read an event as though it were the same all over the world.

11   I knew that my emotions on being moved out of my room in Tokyo were of the gut type and quite strong. There was nothing intellectual about my initial response. Although I am a professional observer of cultural patterns, I had no notion of the meaning attached to being moved from hotel to hotel in Kyoto. I was well aware of the strong significance of moving in my own culture, going back to the time when the new baby displaces older children, right up to the world of business, where a complex dance is performed every time the organization moves to new quarters.

12   What was happening to me in Japan as I rode up and down elevators with various keys gripped in my hand was that I was reacting with the cultural part of my brain—the old, mammalian brain. Although my new brain, my symbolic brain—the neocortex—was saying something else, my mammalian brain kept repeating, "You are being treated shabbily." My neocortex was trying to fathom what was happening. Needless to say, neither part of the brain had been programmed to provide me with the answer in Japanese culture. I did have to put up a strong fight with myself to keep from interpreting what was going on as though the Japanese were the same as I. This is the conventional and most common response and one that is often found even among anthropologists. Any time you hear someone say, "Why *they* are no different than the folks back home—they are just like I am," even though you may understand the reasons behind these remarks you also know that the speaker is living in a single-context world (his own) and is incapable of describing either his world or the foreign one.

13   The "they are just like the folks back home" syndrome is one of the most persistent and widely held misconceptions of the Western world, if not the whole world. There is very little any outsider can do about this, because it expresses views that are very close to the core of the personality. Simply talking about "cultural differences" and how we must respect them is a hollow cliché. And in fact, intellectualizing isn't much more helpful either, at least at first. The logic of the man who won't move into an office that is six inches smaller than his rival's is *cultural* logic; it works at a lower, more basic level in the brain, a part of the brain that synthesizes but does not verbalize. The response is a total response that is difficult to explain to someone who doesn't already understand, because it is so dependent on context for correct interpretation. To do so, one must explain the entire system; otherwise, the man's behavior makes little sense. He may even appear to be acting childishly—which he most definitely is not.

14   It was my preoccupation with my own cultural mold that explained why I was puzzled for years about the significance of being

moved around in Japanese hotels. The answer finally came after further experiences in Japan and many discussions with Japanese friends. In Japan, one has to "belong" or he has no identity. When a man joins a company, he does just that—joins himself to the corporate body—and there is even a ceremony marking the occasion. Normally, he is hired for life, and the company plays a much more paternalistic role than in the United States. There are company songs, and the whole company meets frequently (usually at least once a week) for purposes of maintaining corporate identity and morale.

15   As a tourist (either European or Japanese) when you go on a tour, you *join* that tour and follow your guide everywhere as a group. She leads you with a little flag that she holds up for all to see. Such behavior strikes Americans as sheeplike; not so the Japanese. The reader may say that this pattern holds in Europe, because there people join Cook's tours and the American Express tours, which is true. Yet there is a big difference. I remember a very attractive young American woman who was traveling with the same group I was with in Japan. At first she was charmed and captivated, until she had spent several days visiting shrines and monuments. At this point, she observed that she could not take the regimentation of Japanese life. Clearly, she was picking up clues, such as the fact that our Japanese group, when it moved, marched in a phalanx rather than moving as a motley mob with stragglers. There was much more discipline in these sightseeing groups than the average Westerner is either used to or willing to accept.

16   It was my lack of understanding of the full impact of what it means to belong to a high-context culture that caused me to misread hotel behavior at Hakone. I should have known that I was in the grip of a pattern difference and that the significance of all guests being garbed in the same okata meant more than that an opportunistic management used the guests to advertise the hotel. The answer to my puzzle was revealed when a Japanese friend explained what it means to be a guest in a hotel. As soon as you register at the desk, you are no longer an outsider; instead, for the duration of your stay you are a member of a large, mobile family. *You belong.* The fact that I was moved was tangible evidence that I was being treated as a family member—a relationship in which one can afford to be "relaxed and informal and not stand on ceremony." This is a very highly prized state in Japan, which offsets the official properness that is so common in public. Instead of putting me down, they were treating me as a member of the family. Needless to say, the large, luxury hotels that cater to Americans, like Wright's Imperial Hotel, have discovered that Americans do tenaciously stand on ceremony and want to be treated as they are at home in the States. Americans don't like to be moved around; it makes them anxious. Therefore, the Japanese in these establishments have learned not to treat them as family members.

Keeping a Reading Journal

The most effective way to keep track of your thoughts and impressions and to review what you have learned is to start a reading journal. The comments you record in your journal may express your reflections, observations, questions, and reactions to the essays you read. Normally, your journal would not contain lecture notes from class. A reading journal will allow you to keep a record of your progress during the term and can also reflect insights you gain during class discussions and questions you may want to ask, as well as unfamiliar words you intend to look up. Keeping a reading journal becomes a necessity if your composition course will require you to write a research paper that will be due at the end of the semester. Keep in mind that your journal is not something that will be corrected or graded, although some instructors may wish you to share your entries with the class.

TURNING ANNOTATIONS INTO JOURNAL ENTRIES

Although there is no set form for what a journal should look like, reading journals are most useful for converting your brief annotations into more complete entries that explore in depth your reactions to what you have read. Interestingly, the process of turning your annotations into journal entries will often produce surprising insights that will give you a new perspective. For example, a student who annotated Edward T. Hall's "Hidden Culture" converted them into the following journal entries:

- Hall's personal experiences in Japan made him realize that interpreting an action depends on what culture you're from.
- Hall assumes hotels should treat long-term guests with more respect than overnight guests. "Like someone who had been squeezed in without a reservation" shows Hall's feelings.
- What does having your clothes replaced with an okata—cotton robe—have to do with being moved from room to room in a hotel? The plot thickens!
- The hotel in Hakone encourages guests—all wearing the same robes—to greet each other outside the hotel in a friendly, not formal, manner.
- Hall says that in America, size of office = personal value and salary. Hall compared how space works in the United States in order to understand Japanese attitudes toward space.
- Thesis—"culturally defined attitudes toward space are different for each culture." Proves this by showing how unimportant space is to members of Parliament in England when compared

with the great importance office size has for U.S. congressper-
sons and senators.

- Hall is an anthropologist. He realizes his reactions are instinc-
  tual. Hall wants to refute the idea that people are the same all
  over the world. Says that which culture you are from determines your attitudes and behavior.
- He learns from Japanese friends that workers are hired for life
  and view their companies as family. Would this be for me? In
  Japan, group identity is all-important.
- Hall describes two tour groups, one Japanese and one American, as an example of Japanese acceptance of regimentation,
  whereas Americans go off on their own.
- The answer to the mystery of why he was being moved: moving
  him meant he was accepted as a member of the hotel family.
  They were treating him informally, as if he were Japanese: a
  compliment, not an insult. Informality is highly valued because
  the entire culture is based on the opposite—regimentation and
  conformity.

SUMMARIZING

Reading journals may also be used to record summaries of the essays
you read. The value of summarizing is that it requires you to pay close
attention to the reading in order to distinguish the main points from
the supporting details. Summarizing tests your understanding of the
material by requiring you to restate, concisely, the author's main ideas
in your own words. First, create a list composed of sentences that express in your own words the essential idea of each paragraph, or each
group of related paragraphs. Your previous underlining of topic sentences, main ideas, and key terms (as part of the process of critical
reading) will help you follow the author's line of thought. Next, whit-
tle down this list still further by eliminating repetitive ideas. Then formulate a thesis statement that expresses the main idea behind the
article. Start your summary with this thesis statement, and combine
your notes so that the summary flows together and reads easily.

Remember that summaries should be much shorter than the original text (whether the original is one page or twenty pages long) and
should accurately reflect the central ideas of the article in as few words
as possible. Try not to intrude your own opinions or critical evalua-
tions into the summary. Besides requiring you to read the original
piece more closely, summaries are necessary first steps in developing
papers that synthesize materials from different sources. The test for a
good summary, of course, is whether a person reading it without having read the original article would get an accurate, balanced, and complete account of the original material.

Writing an effective summary is easier if you first compose a rough summary, using no more than two complete sentences to summarize each of the paragraphs or group of paragraphs in the original article. A student's rough summary of Hall's essay might appear as follows. Numbers show which paragraphs are summarized from the article.

1–3 Hall describes how a seemingly inexplicable event that occurred while he was staying in a Tokyo hotel, frequented mostly by Japanese, led him to understand that the same action can have a completely different significance from another culture's perspective. Without telling him, the hotel management had moved his personal belongings to a new room and had given his room to another guest.

4 Three days later when Hall is again moved without warning, he is less startled but begins to wonder why this had never happened during his stay at Frank Lloyd Wright's Imperial Hotel in Tokyo.

5 At another hotel in Hakone, Hall is given an *okata,* a kind of cotton robe, to wear instead of his clothes and is encouraged to greet other guests wearing the same *okata* when he sees them outside the hotel.

6–7 At a third hotel, a country inn near Kyoto, Hall discovers that he has been moved again, this time to an entirely different hotel in what he initially perceives to be a less desirable section of town. Hall interprets this as an insult and becomes angry that the Japanese see him as someone who can be moved around without asking his permission.

8 The neighborhood he had initially seen as less desirable turns out to be much more interesting and authentic than the environs of hotels where tourists usually stay.

9 Hall relates his feelings of being treated shabbily ("like a piece of derelict luggage") to the principle that in the United States, the degree of one's power and status is shown by how much control one has over personal space, whether in the Army or in corporations, where being moved to a smaller office means one is considered less valuable to the company.

10–11 Hall speculates that the equation of control over space with power may pertain only to the United States, since in England, members of Parliament have no formal offices, while their counterparts in the United States—congressmen and senators—attach great importance to the size of their offices. Hall begins to realize that he has been unconsciously applying an American cultural perspective to actions that can be explained only in the context of Japanese culture.

12 Hall postulates the existence of an instinctive "cultural logic" that varies from culture to culture, and he concludes that it is necessary to understand the cultural context in which an action takes place in order to interpret it as people would in that culture.

13–14 Once Hall suspends his own culturally based assumption that one's self-esteem depends on control over personal space, he learns from conversations with Japanese friends that in Japan one has an identity only as part of a group. Japanese workers are considered as family by the companies that hire them for life.

15 The emphasis Japanese society places on conforming to a group is evident in the behavior of Japanese tourists, who move as a coordinated group and closely follow their guide, while American tourists refuse to accept such discipline.

16 Hall realizes that wearing an *okata* and being moved to different rooms and to another, more authentic, hotel means that he is being treated in an informal manner reserved for family members. What Hall had misperceived as an insult—being moved without notice—was really intended as an honor signifying he had been accepted and was not being treated as a stranger.

Based on this list, a student's formulation of a thesis statement expressing the essential idea of Hall's essay appears this way:

> Every society has a hidden culture that governs behavior that might seem inexplicable to an outsider.

The final summary should contain both this thesis and your restatement of the author's main ideas without adding any comments that express personal feelings or responses to the ideas presented. Keep in mind that the purpose of a summary or concise restatement of the author's ideas in your own words is to test your understanding of the material. The summary would normally be introduced by mentioning the author as well as the title of the article:

> Edward T. Hall, writing in "Hidden Culture," believes every society has a hidden culture that governs behavior that might seem inexplicable to an outsider. In Japan, Hall's initial reactions of anger to being moved to another room in a hotel in Tokyo, having his clothes replaced by a cotton kimono or *okata* in Hakone, and being relocated to a different hotel in Kyoto led him to search for the reasons behind such seemingly bizarre events. Although control over space in America is related to status, Hall realizes that in other cultures, like England, where members of Parliament have no offices, this is not the case. Hall discovers that, rather than being an insult, being treated informally meant he was considered to be a member of the hotel "family."

Although some features of the original essay might have been mentioned, such as the significance of office size in corporations in the United States, the student's summary of Hall's essay is still an effective one. The summary accurately and fairly expresses the main ideas in the original.

USING YOUR READING JOURNAL TO GENERATE IDEAS FOR WRITING

You can use all the material in your reading journal (annotations converted to journal entries, reflections, observations, questions, rough and final summaries) to relate your own ideas to the ideas of the person who wrote the essay you are reading. Here are several different kinds of strategies you can use as you analyze an essay in order to generate material for your own:

1. What is missing in the essay? Information that is not mentioned is often just as significant as information the writer chose to include. First, you must have already summarized the main points in the article. Then, make up another list of points that are not discussed, that is, missing information that you would have expected an article of this kind to have covered or touched on. Write down the possible reasons why this missing material has been omitted, censored, or downplayed. What possible purpose could the author have had? Look for vested interests or biases that could explain why information of a certain kind is missing.

2. You might analyze an essay in terms of what you already know and what you didn't know about the issue. To do this, simply make a list of what concepts were already familiar to you and a second list of information or concepts that were new to you. Then write down three to five questions you would like answered about this new information and make a list of possible sources you might consult.

3. You might consider whether the author presents a solution to a problem. List the short-term and long-term effects or consequences of the action the writer recommends. You might wish to evaluate the solution to see whether positive short-term benefits are offset by possible negative long-term consequences not mentioned by the author. This might provide you with a starting point for your own essay.

4. After clearly stating what the author's position on an issue is, try to imagine other people in that society or culture who would view the same issue from a different perspective. How would the concerns of these people be different from those of the writer? Try to think of as many different people, representing as many different perspectives, as you can. Now, try to think of a solution that would satisfy both the author and at least one other person who holds a different viewpoint. Try to imagine that you are an arbitrator negotiating an agreement. How would your recommendation require both parties to compromise and reach an agreement?

Writing Your Essay

One of the basic writing forms you are expected to master in college is the analytical essay (often of approximately five pages) in which you argue for an interpretation. In it, you build on previously developed critical thinking and reading skills. When you write an analytical essay, you move beyond your personal reactions to what you have read, and evaluate some aspect of the article—the author's claims, use of evidence, chain of reasoning, organization, or style. You also need to recognize the author's values, beliefs, and purpose before writing your essay.

PREWRITING TECHNIQUES

Discovering how best to approach your topic is easier if you try one or several of the prewriting, or invention, strategies many writers have found helpful. Prewriting techniques allow you to explore ideas in an informal way before putting time and effort into writing a rough draft. The basic strategies we will discuss include freewriting, the five W's, and mapping (or clustering).

FREEWRITING

Freewriting is a technique for setting down whatever occurs to you on the topic within a few minutes. You will find you are more creative when you simply free-associate without stopping to censor, evaluate, or edit your ideas. Your goal is to get a clear perception of key aspects of the issue in order to discover how to focus your argument. At this point, you need not worry about spelling, punctuation, or grammar.

THE FIVE W'S

In this technique you write down your topic, and then ask yourself the questions that journalists often use to find out about a subject.

1. *Who* is involved?
2. *What* is at stake?
3. *Where* did it happen?
4. *When* did it happen?
5. *Why* is what happened important?

By answering some or all of these questions, you can get a clearer picture of the different aspects of the whole situation. You can then decide which of these elements to focus on to produce an effective essay.

MAPPING

This technique allows you to graphically plot the relationship between important ideas. Begin by writing down the word that contains a key idea or represents a starting point and draw a circle around it; when you think of related ideas, topics, or details that are connected to it, jot them down nearby and draw lines as a way of representing the connections between related ideas. When you group ideas in this way, you discover a map, or cluster, of ideas and patterns that will help you decide which ideas are central and which are subordinate. This strategy can help you narrow your topic and see details and examples that you can use to support your thesis. See page 18 for an example of mapping.

IDENTIFYING YOUR THESIS

As you explore and narrow your topic using the invention strategies mentioned above, try to identify an idea that expresses your opinion and contains a specific claim that your essay will explore and defend. Your thesis is a sentence or two that identifies the paper's topic and your opinion or the approach that you plan to take. The thesis or claim is an assertion that must be genuinely debatable; that is, there should be some alternative, or opposing, opinion. Because others might disagree with your assessment or interpretation, you must present evidence (most often, in the form of relevant quotations drawn from sources you use) and a chain of reasoning that explains your interpretation in a way that will persuade your readers. The thesis is a type of contract or promise; it tells readers what to expect.

For example, consider the following thesis that a student formulated based on her critical reading and annotation of Judith Ortiz Cofer's essay "The Myth of the Latin Woman" (reprinted in Chapter 3):

> In "The Myth of the Latin Woman," Judith Ortiz Cofer refutes the "Maria" stereotype by creating an impression of herself as an articulate, educated and accomplished Latina.

This example of a trial thesis (which may be revised as the paper takes shape) contains the title of the original essay, the author's name, and the student's primary assertion, stated as a single sentence. Considered as a contract, this thesis obligates the student to

1. Define the "Maria" stereotype and demonstrate that Cofer finds it demeaning
2. Show specifically how and where Cofer creates "an impression of herself as an articulate, educated and accomplished Latina"

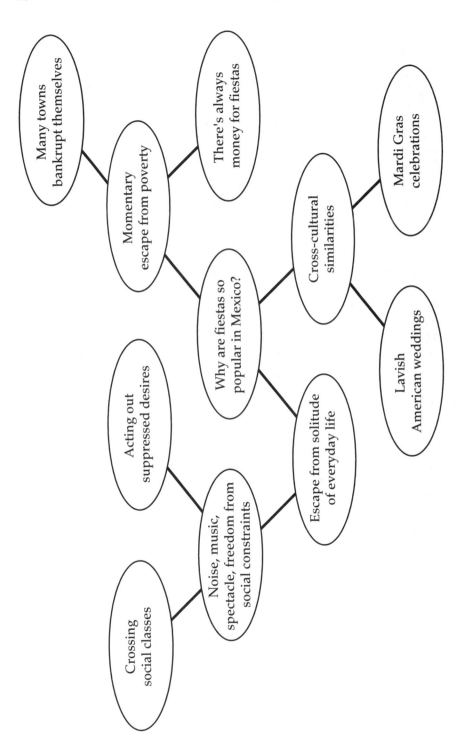

An example of mapping based on Octavio Paz's "Fiesta" (Chapter 8).

3. Analyze Cofer's use of rhetorical techniques to win her audience's sympathy

Each of these three ideas can then be developed in separate sections of the paper. You can also create an informal outline to explore the ideas and relationships in the thesis and test the kind of evidence that will best support these ideas. Remember your essay doesn't have to analyze every single aspect of the original. Discuss only those elements that support your thesis.

After formulating a thesis that expresses a claim, you need to start assembling evidence. You do this by summarizing (see pages 12–14), paraphrasing, and quoting particular passages that will illustrate and support your assertion. We will describe these techniques in the section "Providing Evidence from Sources" (page 23).

CREATING A ROUGH DRAFT

Creating a rough draft offers the best way in which to explore the ideas you developed during the prewriting stage and serves as a precursor to your final paper. A rough draft helps you see the relationships implicit in the materials you generated during your pre-writing activities, and in your reading journal (see page 11), annotations (see pages 11–12), and an informal outline, if you used one. Plan to write one section of the paper at a time.

WRITING THE INTRODUCTION

Some writers find it helpful to compose the introduction first, informing readers in a straightforward way of the issue, topic, or idea the essay will cover. At other times, the introduction is not sufficiently focused, so it is better to proceed to subsequent paragraphs and return to the introduction later when you have a clearer idea of the focus of the paper. Introductions should capture the readers' attention and can include one or more of the following:

- A provocative question that challenges readers to reexamine their beliefs on the subject
- A dramatic or amusing story or anecdote, or an attention-getting quotation
- A brief overview of the issue in its historical context
- A striking statistic
- A brief description of both sides of a debate
- A description of a central person, place, or event

Whichever of these you choose, be sure your introductory paragraph includes the idea your paper will develop and/or suggests the kind of analysis you intend to pursue in developing your thesis.

WRITING THE MIDDLE OF THE ESSAY

The choices open to you when you write the middle portion, or body, of your essay, depend on the best way to support your thesis. Each strategy or method of development is suited to a particular purpose. These organizational patterns (traditionally referred to as rhetorical modes) include:

illustration (or exemplification)

description

definition

classification/division

comparison and contrast

causal analysis

narration

To clarify and support a thesis, writers also use a wide variety of evidence—including examples drawn from personal experience, the testimony of experts, statistical data, and case histories (where the experiences of one person typify the experiences of many people in the same situation).

When you use *illustration* (or exemplification), you provide one or more examples that document or substantiate the idea you wish to clarify. In "Never Just Pictures" (Chapter 3), Susan Bordo cites tabloid cruelty toward a movie star who "appeared at the Academy Awards just a smidge more substantial than she had been in the movie" to support her claim that "our idolatry of the trim, tight body shows no signs of relinquishing its grip on our conceptions of beauty and normality."

Descriptions are powerful because they can evoke an image in readers' minds and create an emotional response. Effective descriptions use specific language, carefully chosen details, and an orderly sequence. For example, Gayatri Devi in "A Princess Remembers" (Chapter 1) conveys her amazement at the colorful chaos of train stations when as a child she traveled with her parents throughout India.

Definition is a useful method for specifying the basic nature of any phenomenon, idea, or condition. A definition can be a sentence that gives the exact meaning of a word or key term (to eliminate ambiguity), or it might extend several paragraphs or even become a complete essay. For example, the definition of the term *hijab* (meaning barrier or curtain) is central to Elizabeth W. Fernea and Robert A. Fernea's investigation "A Look Behind the Veil" (Chapter 3).

Writers use *classification* to sort or group ideas, issues, and topics, into categories based on one or more criteria. Temple Grandin in "Thinking in Pictures" (Chapter 7) uses this technique to help readers understand autistic people's visual style of thinking; first, she explains how they process different kinds of words (nouns, prepositions, and verbs) and then different kinds of texts.

Comparison and *contrast* are useful techniques for helping audiences understand basic differences and for pointing out unsuspected similarities between two or more subjects. In "One Man's Mutilation Is Another Man's Beautification" in Chapter 2, Germaine Greer compares and contrasts how Western and tribal cultures employ tattoos, piercings, and body adornments. Comparisons may be arranged either subject by subject (in which the writer discusses all the relevant features of one and then retraces the same points for the other) or point by point (which alternates between relevant features of the two subjects).

Causal analysis is a technique often used in persuasive essays. Its purpose is to determine whether a cause-and-effect relationship exists. For example, Nawal El-Saadawi in "Circumcision of Girls" (Chapter 3) works backward from an effect to seek the cause(s) that could have produced the observed effect: "In the final analysis we can safely say that female circumcision, the chastity belt, and other savage practices applied to women are basically the result of the economic interests that govern society." Writers can also explore potential effects from a known cause as Daniela Deane does in "The Little Emperors" (Chapter 1) when she forecasts dire social consequences from China's one-child policy. Causal analysis can go off track when a writer confuses sequence with causation (called the *post-hoc fallacy*) and assumes that because one event happens after another the early event must have caused the later one.

Narration is a recounting of events to entertain and to persuade. For example, Judith Ortiz Cofer relates various anecdotes in "The Myth of the Latin Woman" (Chapter 3) to illustrate the pervasiveness of the "Maria" stereotype. An entire essay can take the form of a narrative. In "Why I Quit the Company" (Chapter 4) Tomoyuki Iwashita recounts the history of his employment with a prestigious corporation as a framework for his readers to understand why he decided to quit.

WRITING THE CONCLUSION

The conclusion brings together the lines of reasoning developed in the body of the essay. Your readers should feel that you fulfilled the promise you made when you presented your thesis. You can achieve a sense of closure in several ways, including:

- Summarizing the points made in the paper as they relate to the thesis
- Referring to points presented in the opening paragraph or introduction
- Challenging the reader to think further about the issue

REVISING YOUR ESSAY

You will probably revise several times, and you may wish to read your paper aloud to discover errors in grammar, syntax, or style. Many campuses have writing centers or tutoring services that can help you.

First, examine your essay's overall structure. Is the introduction effective? Then, evaluate whether the sections follow each other in a logical manner. Are the issues raised in the best possible order? Let your thesis guide you as to the best sequence to follow. Do transitions help readers to perceive relationships between different sections of your paper? Check to see whether some of your assumptions need to be supported with more evidence.

Next, consider whether each paragraph has enough supporting evidence and is clearly related to your thesis. You can improve your style by recasting passive sentences into the active voice. You can also express your ideas more clearly by substituting single words for roundabout phrases (such as *because* for *due to the fact that*). Consider how you might improve your choice of words by eliminating confusing metaphors, jargon, and clichés. Lastly, rework your title to more accurately reflect your claim.

PROOFREADING AND FORMATTING

Proofreading means focusing on spelling, punctuation, repeated words, spacing, margins, and anything else that would mar the look of the final paper. Make a list of words that you consistently misspell and check it when you proofread.

If you use a computer, do not rely on your computer's spell-check program because it cannot tell you when you have typed the wrong word—for example, *too* for *two, piece* for *peace,* and *there* for *their.* Most English and Humanities instructors require papers to be formatted in Modern Language Association (MLA) style. Guidelines are available at http://www.mla.org. The latest edition of the published guidelines is *MLA Handbook for Writers of Research Papers,* sixth ed., by Joseph

Gibaldi (New York: MLA, 2003). Unless your instructor specifies otherwise, the following format is standard in MLA style:

- 1-inch margins on the top, bottom, and sides of each page
- Your last name and page number on each page, upper right corner
- ½-inch indentation of the first line of each paragraph
- Double-spaced text in the standard 12-point font
- Works Cited (or References) on a separate page at the end of the paper (following MLA citation guidelines)
- Your name, the name of the course, your professor, and the date in the upper left corner of the first page of the essay

PROVIDING EVIDENCE FROM SOURCES

After formulating a thesis, you must support it with reasons, arguments, and analyses, based on relevant passages in the text. For some papers, you may do additional research, using books and journals from your library, or information found on the Internet (we have provided Web sites for half the readings in the questions following the selections and key search terms for each selection at the back of the book). Whatever sources you use, whether print or electronic, you must evaluate the quality of the information and select material that genuinely illuminates your argument.

Paraphrases

A good portion of your analysis will rely on paraphrasing information from your sources. Paraphrasing is a restatement of an author's ideas in your own words. Unlike summaries (which compress entire articles down to several paragraphs), paraphrases aim to convey the complexity and richness of the original passage—the ideas, the tone, and the pattern of reasoning. Your paraphrase must be different enough from the original so that you do not commit plagiarism (using someone else's words as if they were your own).

QUOTATIONS

Quotations are an indispensable form of evidence to use to illustrate or support your assertions. Direct quotation requires you to copy the author's words exactly as they appear in the original. Direct quotations are preferable to paraphrases when the original passage is important or memorable. On the other hand, be sure that your paper is not a patchwork of stiched-together quotations.

Brief quotations (of fewer than four lines) are normally run into the text and enclosed in double quotation marks (" "). Include the author's name with the quotation either in the text or in a parenthetical reference and be sure to reproduce all punctuation and capitalization as it appears in the original. (See the MLA guidelines.)

Longer quotations (of more than four lines) are separated from the text, indented 1 inch from the left margin, double-spaced like the rest of the manuscript, and reproduced without quotation marks. These block quotations are introduced with a colon (:) if they follow a grammatically complete introductory clause. Parenthetical citation of page numbers follows the quotation's final punctuation. If you need to omit a part of the quotation in order to more easily integrate it into your own text, you must place ellipses or three spaced periods (. . .) where the omitted phrase occurred.

ELECTRONIC SOURCES

If you use sources from the Internet, you must be especially careful to assess their validity because anyone can create a Web page and post information. Ideally, information found on the Internet should be able to be corroborated by print sources such as books and journals.

When you begin the process of locating and evaluating information on the Internet, it is important that you focus the topic of your research as exactly as possible. Conduct your search using a sequence or string of search terms (we offer a list of these terms for each selection at the back of this book) that will narrow the list of Web pages to those that most closely match your inquiry. For example, if you want information about Octavio Paz's article on fiestas in Mexico ("Fiesta" in Chapter 8) the use of the keywords "Mexican fiestas" and "expenditures" will turn up only those sources that are appropriate to your research. When you find a Web site that you wish to quote, make a careful note of the specific address because you will need to acknowledge it within your paper and in the list of Works Cited (for information on documenting electronic sources, see the MLA Web site at http://www.mla.org or consult the sixth edition of their handbook). Web pages should be evaluated as to their timeliness, relevance, authoritativeness, and lack of bias. The most reliable Web pages have links that provide information about the creator or at least give the e-mail address of the creator or Web master.

WHAT KIND OF ARGUMENT ARE YOU MAKING?

The purpose of any argument is to persuade an audience to accept the validity (or at least the likelihood) of an idea, proposition, or claim. The claim is an assertion that would raise doubt if it were not supported with sound evidence and persuasive reasoning. Different kinds of arguments seek to accomplish different objectives or goals. Generally speaking, four kinds of goals can be identified (we have classified selections that are arguments according to type in the rhetorical table of contents).

1. People can disagree about the essential nature of the subject under discussion, what it is similar to or different from, or how it should be defined. These are called *arguments of fact.*
2. Even if people agree about the essential nature of X, they may disagree about what caused it or what effects it would cause, in turn. These are *arguments of causation.*
3. Even if all sides agree on what X is, what caused it, and what its effects may be, they may disagree over whether it is good or bad, or whether its effects are harmful or beneficial. These are *arguments about value.*
4. The most complex kind of argument—those that require not merely agreement, but action on the part of the audience—are known as *policy arguments.*

For convenience, we will discuss each of these four types separately, but it should be realized that real-world arguments frequently rely on more than just one type of claim.

- *Arguments of fact* define a key term or concept in a way that clearly distinguishes it from all other things with which it might be confused. An entire argument can often hinge on the definition of a key term or concept. For example, Judith Ortiz Cofer's essay "The Myth of the Latin Woman" (Chapter 3) turns on the question of how the Latina stereotype ought to be defined. She not only identifies its key features; she explains how it operates to allow people to rationalize their discrimination against Hispanic women.
- *Arguments of causation* try to answer the question, what caused X to be the way it is? or, what will happen as a result of X? Causal arguments also offer plausible explanations as to the cause(s) of a series of events, or a trend. For example, in "Want-Creation Fuels Americans' Addictiveness" (Chapter 6) Philip Slater argues that the "quick fix" mentality, or an "intolerance of any constraint or obstacle," is the cause of pervasive drug use (of heroin, cocaine, alcohol, speed, tranquilizers, and barbiturates) in American culture. This kind of claim obligates the writer to demonstrate the means by which the effect was produced.
- *Arguments about value* make claims about value that do not merely express personal likes or dislikes, but offer reasoned judgments based on identifiable standards (ethical, moral,

aesthetic, or utilitarian). They must demonstrate that the criterion applied is an appropriate one, and also consider the beliefs and attitudes the audience holds about the issue. Writers frequently use the rhetorical pattern of comparison and contrast to organize this kind of argument, as Stephen Chapman does in "The Prisoner's Dilemma" (Chapter 6). Chapman evaluates both Middle Eastern and Western methods of punishment to determine which is more barbaric. For him, the crux of the issue is: "Would you rather be subjected to a few minutes of intense pain and considerable public humiliation, or be locked away for two or three years in a prison cell crowded with ill-tempered sociopaths?"

- *Policy arguments* try to answer the question, What ought, should, or must we do about X. This type of argument first establishes that a serious problem exists, investigates the circumstances that created it, describes who suffers because of it, and weighs different solutions before selecting one that will be feasible, effective, and attractive to the audience to whom it is proposed. Martin Luther King Jr. in his speech "I Have a Dream" (Chapter 5) uses argumentation (and persuasion) to reaffirm minority rights as a way of renewing the aspirations put forward by America's founding fathers. The effectiveness of the speech depends in large part on the audience's sense of King as a man of high moral character. In arguments that appeal to the emotions as well as the intellect, the audience's favorable perception of the writer enhances his or her credibility.

A Final Word

The readings in this anthology present innovative ideas and require close and careful reading. Being a critical reader means taking an active role rather than passively absorbing information. Maintain an active, questioning perspective by carefully looking at the assumptions on which the author's argument rests. Evaluate the quality of the evidence presented and assess how it serves to support the author's case. Compare what one writer says with the observations and claims of other writers. Create a dialogue with the text as if you were talking to another person.

1

The Family in Different Cultures

As the family goes, so goes the nation and so goes the whole world in which we live.
—John Paul II [Karol Wojtyła] (1920–2005), Polish Ecclesiastic, Pope. Quoted in: *Observer* (London, 7 December 1986)

———————◆———————

The family has been the most enduring basis of culture throughout the world and has provided a stabilizing force in all societies. The complex network of dependencies, relationships, and obligations may extend outward from parents and children to include grandparents, cousins, aunts and uncles, and more distantly related relatives. In some cultures, the entire community or tribe is seen as an extended family. The unique relationships developed among members of a family provide a universal basis for common experiences, emotions, perceptions, and expectations. At the same time, each family is different, with its own unique characteristic relationships and bonds. Family relationships continue to exert a profound influence on one's life long after childhood. In the context of the family we first learn what it means to experience the emotions of love, hope, fear, anger, and contentment. The works in this chapter focus on parent-child relationships, explore the connections between grandparents and grandchildren, and depict the impact of the cultural values on these relationships.

The structure of the family is subject to a wide range of economic and social influences in virtually all cultures. For example, child rearing in China is a vastly different enterprise from what it is in America because of the enormous differences in economic circumstances and political systems. The variety of family structures depicted by writers of many different nationalities offers insight into how the concept of the family is modified according to the constraints, beliefs, and needs of particular societies.

For many, the family history is inseparable from the stories told about particular members, which define the character of the family and its relationship to the surrounding society. These stories can be told for entertainment or education and often explain old loyalties and antagonisms. Some are written and some are part of an oral history related by one generation to the next. The complex portraits of family life offered in this chapter allow us to share, sympathize, and identify with writers from diverse cultures and more completely understand your own family experiences in the light of theirs.

The African-American writer Gayle Pemberton, in "Antidisestablishmentarianism," describes how her independent grandmother taught her to think for herself. Amy Tan, in "The Language of Discretion," relates her own experiences to refute the misperception that Chinese people are "discreet" and modest. A father's boorish behavior undermines what was to have been a happy reunion between a son and his father in John Cheever's story "Reunion." Fritz Peters in "Boyhood with Gurdjieff" recalls an experience from his childhood in France when he learned compassion. Steve Sailer, in "The Cousin Marriage Conundrum," calls our attention to an important but neglected feature of Iraqi culture. The current Maharani of Jaipur, Gayatri Devi, recalls the opulent splendor of her childhood home in "A Princess Remembers." Last, Daniela Deane reports on the unanticipated results of China's one-child policy in "The Little Emperors."

Gayle Pemberton

Antidisestablishmentarianism

———————◆———————

*Gayle Pemberton (b. 1948) is the William R. Kenan Professor of the Hu-
manities at Wesleyan University and chair of the African-American
Studies Department. She was raised in Chicago and Ohio, received a
Ph.D. in English and American literature at Harvard University, and
has served as the associate director of African-American Studies at
Princeton University. Pemberton has taught at Smith, Reed, and Bow-
doin Colleges. The following chapter, drawn from her memoir* The
Hottest Water in Chicago *(1992), recounts the influential role her
grandmother played in her life.*

Before You Read

As you read this memoir, consider how the attitude of Pemberton's grandmother offers insight into the social forces that shaped the responses of
blacks during that era.

———————◆———————

1   Okay, so where's Gloria Lockerman? I want to know. Gloria Lockerman was partially responsible for ruining my life. I might never have
ended up teaching literature if it had not been for her. I don't want to
"call her out." I just want to know how things are, what she's doing.
Have things gone well, Gloria? How's the family? What's up?

2   Gloria Lockerman, in case you don't recall, won scads of money on
"The $64,000 Question." Gloria Lockerman was a young black child,
like me, but she could spell anything. Gloria Lockerman became my
nemesis with her ability, her a-n-t-i-d-i-s-e-s-t-a-b-l-i-s-h-m-e-n-t-a-r-i-
a-n-i-s-m.

3   My parents, my sister, and I shared a house in Dayton, Ohio, with
my father's mother and her husband, my stepgrandfather, during the
middle fifties. Sharing is an overstatement. It was my grandmother's
house. Our nuclear group ate in a makeshift kitchen in the basement;
my sister and I shared a dormer bedroom, and my parents actually had
a room on the main floor of the house—several parts of which were off-
limits. These were the entire living room, anywhere within three feet of
Grandma's African violets, the windows and venetian blinds, anything
with a doily on it, the refrigerator, and the irises in the backyard.

4   It was an arrangement out of necessity, given the unimpressive state of our combined fortunes, and it did not meet with any one's satisfaction. To make matters worse, we had blockbusted a neighborhood. So, for the first year, I integrated the local elementary school—a thankless and relatively inhuman experience. I remember one day taking the Sunday paper route for a boy up the block who was sick. It was a beautiful spring day, dewy, warm. I walked up the three steps to a particular house and placed the paper on the stoop. Suddenly, a full-grown man, perhaps sixty or so, appeared with a shotgun aimed at me and said that if he ever saw my nigger ass on his porch again he'd blow my head off. I know—typical American grandfather.

5   Grandma liked spirituals, preferably those sung by Mahalia Jackson. She was not a fan of gospel and I can only imagine what she'd say if she were around to hear what's passing for inspirational music these days. She also was fond of country singers, and any of the members of "The Lawrence Welk Show." ("That Jimmy. Oh, I love the way he sings. He's from Iowa.") She was from Iowa, Jimmy was from Iowa, my father was from Iowa. She was crazy about Jimmy Dean too, and Tennessee Ernie Ford, and "Gunsmoke." She could cook with the finest of them and I wish I could somehow recreate her Parkerhouse rolls, but I lack bread karma. Grandma liked flowers (she could make anything bloom) and she loved her son.

6   She disliked white people, black people in the aggregate and pretty much individually too, children—particularly female children— her daughter, her husband, my mother, Episcopalianism, Catholicism, Judaism, and Dinah Shore. She had a hot temper and a mean streak. She also suffered from several nagging ailments: high blood pressure, ulcers, an enlarged heart, ill-fitting dentures, arteriosclerosis, and arthritis—enough to make anyone hot tempered and mean, I'm sure. But to a third grader, such justifications and their subtleties were ultimately beyond me and insufficient, even though I believe I understood in part the relationship between pain and personality. Grandma scared the daylights out of me. I learned to control my nervous stomach enough to keep from getting sick daily. So Grandma plus school plus other family woes and my sister still predicting the end of the world every time the sirens went off—Grandma threatened to send her to a convent—made the experience as a whole something I'd rather forget, but because of the mythic proportions of family, can't.

7   I often think that it might have been better had I been older, perhaps twenty years older, when I knew Grandma. But I realize that she would have found much more wrong with me nearing thirty than she did when I was eight or nine. When I was a child, she could blame most of my faults on my mother. Grown, she would have had no recourse but to damn me to hell.

8   Ah, but she is on the gene. Grandma did everything fast. She cooked, washed, cleaned, moved—everything was at lightning speed. She passed this handicap on to me, and I have numerous bruises, cuts, and burns to show for it. Watching me throw pots and pans around in the creation of a meal, my mother occasionally calls me by my grandmother's first name. I smile back, click my teeth to imitate a slipping upper, and say something unpleasant about someone.

9   Tuesday nights were "The $64,000 Question" nights, just as Sundays we watched Ed Sullivan and Saturdays were reserved for Lawrence Welk and "Gunsmoke." We would all gather around the television in what was a small, informal family section between the verboten real living room and the mahogany dining table and chairs, used only three or four times a year. I don't remember where I sat, but it wasn't on the floor since that wasn't allowed either.

10   As we watched these television programs, once or twice I sat briefly on Grandma's lap. She was the world's toughest critic. No one was considered worthy, apart from the above-mentioned. To her, So-and-So or Whosits could not sing, dance, tell a joke, read a line—nothing. In her hands "Ted Mack's Amateur Hour" would have lasted three minutes. She was willing to forgive only very rarely—usually when someone she liked gave a mediocre performance on one of her favorite shows.

11   I must admit that Grandma's style of teaching critical thinking worked as well as some others I've encountered. My father had a different approach. Throughout my youth he would play the music of the thirties and forties. His passion was for Billie Holiday, with Ella Fitzgerald, Peggy Lee, Sarah Vaughan, and a few others thrown in for a touch of variety. He enjoyed music, and when he wanted to get some musical point across, he would talk about some nuance of style that revealed the distinction between what he called "really singing" and a failure. He would say, "Now, listen to that there. Did you catch it? Hear what she did with that note?" With Grandma it was more likely to be:

12   "Did you hear that?"

13   "What?" I might ask.

14   "That. What she just sang."

15   "Yes."

16   "Well, what do you think of it?"

17   "It's okay, I guess."

18   "Well, that was garbage. She can't sing a note. That stinks. She's a fool."

19   Message across. We all choose our own pedagogical techniques.

20   Game shows are, well, game shows. I turned on my television the other day, and as I clicked through channels looking for something to watch I stopped long enough to hear an announcer say that the guest

contestant was going to do something or other in 1981. Reruns of game shows? Well, why not? What difference does it make if the whole point is to watch people squirm, twist, sweat, blare, weep, convulse to get their hands on money and gifts, even if they end up being just "parting gifts"? (I won some of them myself once: a bottle of liquid Johnson's Wax, a box of Chunkies, a beach towel with the name of a diet soda on it, plus a coupon for a case of the stuff, and several boxes of Sugar Blobs—honey-coated peanut butter, marshmallow, and chocolate flavored crispies, dipped in strawberry flavoring for that special morning taste treat!)

21   Game shows in the fifties were different, more exciting. I thought the studio sets primitive even when I was watching them then. The clock on "Beat the Clock," the coat and crown on "Queen for a Day"—nothing like that mink on "The Big Payoff" that Bess Meyerson modeled—and that wire card flipper on "What's My Line" that John Charles Daly used—my, was it flimsy looking. The finest set of all, though, was on "The $64,000 Question." Hal March would stand outside the isolation booth, the door closing on the likes of Joyce Brothers, Catherine Kreitzer, and Gloria Lockerman, the music would play, and the clock would begin ticking down, like all game show clocks: *TOOT-toot-TOOT-toot-TOOT-toot-BUZZZZZZ.*

22   There were few opportunities to see black people on television in those days. I had watched "Amos 'n' Andy" when we lived in Chicago. But that show was a variation on a theme. Natives running around or jumping up and down or looking menacing in African adventure movies; shuffling, subservient, and clowning servants in local color movies (or any other sort); and "Amos 'n' Andy" were all the same thing: the perpetuation of a compelling, deadly, darkly humorous, and occasionally laughable idea. Nonfictional blacks on television were limited to Sammy Davis, Jr., as part of the Will Mastin Trio and afterward, or Peg Leg Bates on "The Ed Sullivan Show" on Sunday, or the entertainers who might show up on other variety shows, or Nat King Cole during his fifteen-minute program. Naturally, the appearance of Gloria Lockerman caused a mild sensation as we watched "The $64,000 Question," all assembled.

23   "Look at her," Grandma said.

24   I braced myself for the torrent of abuse that was about to be leveled at the poor girl.

25   "You ought to try to be like that," Grandma said.

26   "Huh?" I said.

27   "What did you say?"

28   "Yes, ma'am."

29   I was shocked, thrown into despair. I had done well in school, as well as could be hoped. I was modestly proud of my accomplishments, and given the price I was paying every day—and paying in silence, for

I never brought my agonies at school home with me—I didn't need Gloria Lockerman thrown in my face. Gloria Lockerman, like me, on television, spelling. I was perennially an early-round knockout in spelling bees.

30   My sister understands all of this. Her own story is slightly different and she says she'll tell it all one day herself. She is a very good singer and has a superb ear; with our critical training, what more would she need? Given other circumstances, she might have become a performer herself. When she was about eleven Leslie Uggams was on Arthur Godfrey's "Talent Scouts" and was soon to be tearing down the "Name That Tune" runway, ringing the bell and becoming moderately famous. No one ever held Leslie Uggams up to my sister for image consciousness-raising. But my sister suffered nevertheless. She could out-sing Leslie Uggams and probably run as fast; she knew the songs and didn't have nearly so strange a last name. But, there she was, going nowhere in the Middle West, and there was Leslie Uggams on her way to "Sing Along With Mitch." To this day, my sister mumbles if she happens to see Leslie Uggams on television—before she can get up to change the channel—or hears someone mention her name. I told her I saw Leslie Uggams in the flesh at a club in New York. She was sitting at a table, just like the rest of us, listening with pleasure to Barbara Cook. My sister swore at me.

31   Grandma called her husband "Half-Wit." He was a thin, small-boned man who looked to me far more like an Indian chief than like a black man. He was from Iowa too, but that obviously did not account for enough in Grandma's eyes. He had a cracking tenor voice, a head full of dead straight black hair, reddish, dull brown skin, and large sad, dark brown eyes. His craggy face also reminded me of pictures I'd seen of Abraham Lincoln—but, like all political figures and American forefathers, Lincoln, to my family, was fair game for wisecracks, so that resemblance did Grandpa no good either. And for reasons that have gone to the grave with both of them, he was the most thoroughly henpecked man I have ever heard of, not to mention seen.

32   Hence, domestic scenes had a quality of pathos and high humor as far as I was concerned. My sister and I called Grandpa "Half-Wit" when we were alone together, but that seemed to have only a slight effect on our relations with him and our willingness to obey him—though I cannot recall any occasions calling for his authority. Grandma was Grandma, Half-Wit was Half-Wit—and we lived with the two of them. I have one particularly vivid memory of Grandma, an aficionada of the iron skillet, chasing him through the house waving it in the air, her narrow, arthritis-swollen wrist and twisted knuckles turning the heavy pan as if it were a lariat. He didn't get hurt; he was fleet of foot and made it out the back door before she caught him. My father's real father had been dead since the thirties and divorced from Grandma

since the teens—so Half-Wit had been in place for quite some years and was still around to tell the story, if he had the nerve.

33   Grandma had a glass menagerie, the only one I've seen apart from performances of the Williams play. I don't think she had a unicorn, but she did have quite a few pieces. From a distance of no less than five feet I used to squint at the glass forms, wondering what they meant to Grandma, who was herself delicate of form but a powerhouse of strength, speed, and temper. I also wondered how long it would take me to die if the glass met with some unintended accident caused by me. Real or imagined unpleasantries, both in the home and outside of it, helped develop in me a somewhat melancholic nature. And even before we had moved to Ohio I found myself laughing and crying at the same time.

34   In the earlier fifties, in Chicago, I was allowed to watch such programs as "The Ernie Kovacs Show," "Your Show of Shows," "The Jackie Gleason Show," "The Red Skelton Show," and, naturally, "I Love Lucy." I was continually dazzled by the skits and broad humor, but I was particularly taken with the silent sketches, my favorite comedians as mime artists: Skelton as Freddy the Freeloader, Caesar and Coca in a number of roles, thoroughly outrageous Kovacs acts backed by Gershwin's "Rialto Ripples." My father was a very funny man and a skillful mime. I could tell when he watched Gleason's Poor Soul that he identified mightily with what was on the screen. It had nothing to do with self-pity. My father had far less of it than other men I've met with high intelligence, financial and professional stress, and black faces in a white world. No, my father would even say that we were all poor souls; it was the human condition. His mimicking of the Gleason character—head down, shoulders tucked, stomach sagging, feet splayed—served as some kind of release. I would laugh and cry watching either of them.

35   But my absolute favorite was Martha Raye, who had a way of milking the fine line between tragedy and comedy better than most. I thought her eyes showed a combination of riotous humor and terror. Her large mouth contorted in ways that seemed to express the same two emotions. Her face was a mask of profound sadness. She did for me what Sylvia Sidney did for James Baldwin. In *The Devil Finds Work*, Baldwin says, "Sylvia Sidney was the only American film actress who reminded me of a colored girl, or woman—which is to say that she was the only American film actress who reminded me of reality." The reality Raye conveyed to me was of how dreams could turn sour in split-seconds, and how underdogs, even when winning, often had to pay abominable prices. She also could sing a jazz song well, with her husky scat phrasing, in ways that were slightly different from those of my favorite singers, and almost as enjoyable.

36   There were no comedic or dramatic images of black women on the screen—that is, apart from Sapphire and her mother on "Amos 'n'

Andy." And knowing Grandma and Grandpa taught me, if nothing else suggested it, that what I saw of black life on television was a gross burlesque—played to the hilt with skill by black actors, but still lacking reality.

37   Black female singers who appeared on television were, like their music, sacrosanct, and I learned from their styles, lyrics, and improvisations, lessons about life that mime routines did not reveal. Still, it was Martha Raye, and occasionally Lucille Ball and Imogene Coca at their most absurd, that aligned me with my father and his Poor Soul, and primed me to both love and despise Grandma and to see that in life most expressions, thoughts, acts, and intentions reveal their opposite polarities simultaneously.

38   Grandma died in 1965. I was away, out of the country, and I missed her funeral—which was probably a good idea since I might have been tempted to strangle some close family friend who probably would have launched into a "tsk, tsk, tsk" monologue about long-suffering grandmothers and impudent children. But, in another way, I'm sorry I didn't make it. Her funeral might have provided some proper closure for me, might have prompted me to organize her effect on my life sooner than I did, reconciling the grandmother who so hoped I would be a boy that she was willing to catch a Constellation or a DC-3 to witness my first few hours, but instead opted to take the bus when she heard the sad news, with the grandmother who called me "Sally Slapcabbage" and wrote to me and my sister regularly, sending us the odd dollar or two, until her death.

39   I remember coming home from school, getting my jelly sandwich and wolfing it down, and watching "The Mickey Mouse Club," my favorite afternoon show, since there was no afternoon movie. I had noticed and had been offended by the lack of black children in the "Club," but the cartoons, particularly those with Donald Duck, were worth watching. On this particular episode—one of the regular guest act days—a group of young black children, perhaps nine or ten of them, came on and sang, with a touch of dancing, "Old MacDonald Had a Farm," in an up-tempo, jazzy version. In spite of the fact that usually these guest days produced some interesting child acts, I became angry with what I saw. I felt patronized, for myself and for them. Clearly a couple of them could out-sing and out-dance any Mouseketeer—something that wasn't worth giving a thought to—but this performance was gratuitous, asymmetrical, a nonsequitur, like Harpo Marx marching through the Negro section in *A Day at the Races*, blowing an imaginary horn and exciting the locals to much singing, swinging, and dancing to a charming ditty called "Who Dat Man?"

40   I must have mumbled something as I watched the group singing "Old MacDonald." Grandma, passing through, took a look at what was on the screen, and at me, turned off the television, took my hand,

led me to her kitchen, and sat me down at the table where she and Half-Wit ate, poured me some milk, and without so much as a blink of her eye, said, "Pay no attention to that shit."

✧ *Evaluating the Text*

1. What impression do you get of the circumstances surrounding Pemberton's early life? How do they help explain why her grandmother was so influential in shaping her outlook on life?

2. How would you characterize the voice that you hear in Pemberton's essay? What personality traits does she possess as a writer? Why is it important to know that the narrator's family was the only black family in that neighborhood? What can you infer about her experiences at school?

3. In what ways was the media's presentation of African Americans in the 1950s stereotyped? How does this help explain Pemberton's grandmother's reaction to Gloria Lockerman?

✧ *Exploring Different Perspectives*

1. Compare the role extended families play in the account by Pemberton and Steve Sailer's "The Cousin Marriage Conundrum."

2. Compare the role that Pemberton's grandmother played in her life with that of Amy Tan's mother in "Language of Discretion."

✧ *Extending Viewpoints through Writing and Research*

1. To what extent did one of your grandparents or relatives exert a shaping influence on your outlook, personality, and expectations? Describe one or two key incidents that illustrate this.

2. In your view, what television shows either reflect or fail to reflect African-American life in the United States today?

Amy Tan

The Language of Discretion

———◆———

Amy Tan was born in Oakland, California, in 1952. She studied linguistics and worked with disabled children. Tan's first novel, The Joy Luck Club *(1989), was widely praised for its depiction of the relationship between Chinese mothers and their American-born daughters. Tan has also written* The Kitchen God's Wife *(1991),* The Hundred Secret Senses *(1995), and* The Opposite of Fate: A Book of Musings *(2003). "The Language of Discretion" was published in 1990.*

Before You Read

Consider how knowing two languages could prove distracting in terms of which one to talk in, think in, or dream in.

———◆———

1   At a recent family dinner in San Francisco, my mother whispered to me: "Sau-sau [Brother's Wife] pretends too hard to be polite! Why bother? In the end, she always takes everything."

2   My mother thinks like a *waixiao*, an expatriate, temporarily away from China since 1949, no longer patient with ritual courtesies. As if to prove her point, she reached across the table to offer my elderly aunt from Beijing the last scallop from the Happy Family seafood dish.

3   Sau-sau scowled. "*B'yao, zhen b'yao!*" (I don't want it, really I don't!) she cried, patting her plump stomach.

4   "Take it! Take it!" scolded my mother in Chinese.

5   "Full, I'm already full," Sau-sau protested weakly, eyeing the beloved scallop.

6   "Ai!" exclaimed my mother, completely exasperated. "Nobody else wants it. If you don't take it, it will only rot!"

7   At this point, Sau-sau sighed, acting as if she were doing my mother a big favor by taking the wretched scrap off her hands.

8   My mother turned to her brother, a high-ranking communist official who was visiting her in California for the first time: "In America a Chinese person could starve to death. If you say you don't want it, they won't ask you again forever."

9   My uncle nodded and said he understood fully: Americans take things quickly because they have no time to be polite.

10   I thought about this misunderstanding again—of social contexts failing in translation—when a friend sent me an article from the *New York Times Magazine* (24 April 1988). The article, on changes in New York's Chinatown, made passing reference to the inherent ambivalence of the Chinese language.

11   Chinese people are so "discreet and modest," the article stated, there aren't even words for "yes" and "no."

12   That's not true, I thought, although I can see why an outsider might think that. I continued reading.

13   If one is Chinese, the article went on to say, "One compromises, one doesn't hazard a loss of face by an overemphatic response."

14   My throat seized. Why do people keep saying these things? As if we truly were those little dolls sold in Chinatown tourist shops, heads bobbing up and down in complacent agreement to anything said!

15   I worry about the effect of one-dimensional statements on the unwary and guileless. When they read about this so-called vocabulary deficit, do they also conclude that Chinese people evolved into a mild-mannered lot because the language only allowed them to hobble forth with minced words?

16   Something enormous is always lost in translation. Something insidious seeps into the gaps, especially when amateur linguists continue to compare, one-for-one, language differences and then put forth notions wide open to misinterpretation: that Chinese people have no direct linguistic means to make decisions, assert or deny, affirm or negate, just say no to drug dealers, or behave properly on the witness stand when told, "Please answer yes or no."

17   Yet one can argue, with the help of renowned linguists, that the Chinese are indeed up a creek without "yes" and "no." Take any number of variations on the old language-and-reality theory stated years ago by Edward Sapir: "Human beings . . . are very much at the mercy of the particular language which has become the medium for their society. . . . The fact of the matter is that the 'real world' is to a large extent built up on the language habits of the group."[1]

18   This notion was further bolstered by the famous Sapir-Whorf hypothesis, which roughly states that one's perception of the world and how one functions in it depends a great deal on the language used. As Sapir, Whorf, and new carriers of the banner would have us believe, language shapes our thinking, channels us along certain patterns embedded in words, syntactic structures, and intonation patterns. Language has become the peg and the shelf that enables us to sort out and categorize the world. In English, we see "cats" and "dogs"; what if the language had also specified *glatz*, meaning "animals that leave fur on the sofa," and *glotz*, meaning "animals that leave fur and drool on the

[1]Edward Sapir, *Selected Writings*, ed. D. G. Mandelbaum (Berkeley and Los Angeles, 1949).

sofa"? How would language, the enabler, have changed our perceptions with slight vocabulary variations?

19   And if this were the case—of language being the master of destined thought—think of the opportunities lost from failure to evolve two little words, *yes* and *no,* the simplest of opposites! Ghenghis Khan could have been sent back to Mongolia. Opium wars might have been averted. The Cultural Revolution could have been sidestepped.

20   There are still many, from serious linguists to pop psychology cultists, who view language and reality as inextricably tied, one being the consequence of the other. We have traversed the range from the Sapir-Whorf hypothesis to est and neurolinguistic programming, which tell us "you are what you say."

21   I too have been intrigued by the theories. I can summarize, albeit badly, ages-old empirical evidence: of Eskimos and their infinite ways to say "snow," their ability to *see* the differences in snowflake configurations, thanks to the richness of their vocabulary, while non-Eskimo speakers like myself founder in "snow," "more snow," and "lots more where that came from."

22   I too have experienced dramatic cognitive awakenings via the word. Once I added "mauve" to my vocabulary I began to see it everywhere. When I learned how to pronounce *prix fixe,* I ate French food at prices better than the easier-to-say *á la carte* choices.

23   But just how seriously are we supposed to take this?

24   Sapir said something else about language and reality. It is the part that often gets left behind in the dot-dot-dots of quotes: ". . . No two languages are ever sufficiently similar to be considered as representing the same social reality. The worlds in which different societies live are distinct worlds, not merely the same world with different labels attached."

25   When I first read this, I thought, Here at last is validity for the dilemmas I felt growing up in a bicultural, bilingual family! As any child of immigrant parents knows, there's a special kind of double bind attached to knowing two languages. My parents, for example, spoke to me in both Chinese and English; I spoke back to them in English.

26   "Amy-ah!" they'd call to me.

27   "What?" I'd mumble back.

28   "Do not question us when we call," they scolded me in Chinese. "It is not respectful."

29   "What do you mean?"

30   "Ai! Didn't we just tell you not to question?"

31   To this day, I wonder which parts of my behavior were shaped by Chinese, which by English. I am tempted to think, for example, that if I am of two minds on some matter it is due to the richness of my linguistic experiences, not to any personal tendencies toward wishy-washiness. But which mind says what?

32   Was it perhaps patience—developed through years of deciphering my mother's fractured English—that had me listening politely while a woman announced over the phone that I had won one of five valuable prizes? Was it respect—pounded in by the Chinese imperative to accept convoluted explanations—that had me agreeing that I might find it worth-while to drive seventy-five miles to view a time-share resort? Could I have been at a loss for words when asked, "Wouldn't you like to win a Hawaiian cruise or perhaps a fabulous Star of India designed exclusively by Carter and Van Arpels?"

33   And when this same woman called back a week later, this time complaining that I had missed my appointment, obviously it was my type A language that kicked into gear and interrupted her. Certainly, my blunt denial—"Frankly I'm not interested"—was as American as apple pie. And when she said, "But it's in Morgan Hill," and I shouted, "Read my lips. I don't care if it's Timbuktu," you can be sure I said it with the precise intonation expressing both cynicism and disgust.

34   It's dangerous business, this sorting out of language and behavior. Which one is English? Which is Chinese? The categories manifest themselves: passive and aggressive, tentative and assertive, indirect and direct. And I realize they are just variations of the same theme: that Chinese people are discreet and modest.

35   Reject them all!

36   If my reaction is overly strident, it is because I cannot come across as too emphatic. I grew up listening to the same lines over and over again, like so many rote expressions repeated in an English phrasebook. And I too almost came to believe them.

37   Yet if I consider my upbringing more carefully, I find there was nothing discreet about the Chinese language I grew up with. My parents made everything abundantly clear. Nothing wishy-washy in their demands, no compromises accepted: "Of course you will become a famous neurosurgeon," they told me. "And yes, a concert pianist on the side."

38   In fact, now that I remember, it seems that the more emphatic outbursts always spilled over into Chinese: "Not that way! You must wash rice so not a single grain spills out."

39   I do not believe that my parents—both immigrants from mainland China—are an exception to the modest-and-discreet rule. I have only to look at the number of Chinese engineering students skewing minority ratios at Berkeley, MIT, and Yale. Certainly they were not raised by passive mothers and fathers who said, "It is up to you, my daughter. Writer, welfare recipient, masseuse, or molecular engineer—you decide."

40   And my American mind says, See, those engineering students weren't able to say no to their parents' demands. But then my Chinese mind remembers: Ah, but those parents all wanted their sons and daughters to be *pre-med*.

41   Having listened to both Chinese and English, I also tend to be suspicious of any comparisons between the two languages. Typically, one language—that of the person doing the comparing—is often used as the standard, the benchmark for a logical form of expression. And so the language being compared is always in danger of being judged deficient or superfluous, simplistic or unnecessarily complex, melodious or cacophonous. English speakers point out that Chinese is extremely difficult because it relies on variations in tone barely discernible to the human ear. By the same token, Chinese speakers tell me English is extremely difficult because it is inconsistent, a language of too many broken rules, of Mickey Mice and Donald Ducks.

42   Even more dangerous to my mind is the temptation to compare both language and behavior *in translation*. To listen to my mother speak English, one might think she has no concept of past or future tense, that she doesn't see the difference between singular and plural, that she is gender blind because she calls my husband "she." If one were not careful, one might also generalize that, based on the way my mother talks, all Chinese people take a circumlocutory route to get to the point. It is, in fact, my mother's idiosyncratic behavior to ramble a bit.

43   Sapir was right about differences between two languages and their realities. I can illustrate why word-for-word translation is not enough to translate meaning and intent. I once received a letter from China which I read to non-Chinese speaking friends. The letter, originally written in Chinese, had been translated by my brother-in law in Beijing. One portion described the time when my uncle at age ten discovered his widowed mother (my grandmother) had remarried—as a number three concubine, the ultimate disgrace for an honorable family. The translated version of my uncle's letter read in part:

> In 1925, I met my mother in Shanghai. When she came to me, I didn't have greeting to her as if seeing nothing. She pull me to a corner secretly and asked me why didn't have greeting to her. I couldn't control myself and cried, "Ma! Why did you leave us? People told me: one day you ate a beancake yourself. Your sister in-law found it and sweared at you, called your names. So . . . is it true?" She clasped my hand and answered immediately, "It's not true, don't say what like this." After this time, there was a few chance to meet her.

44   "What!" cried my friends. "Was eating a beancake so terrible?"

45   Of course not. The beancake was simply a euphemism; a ten-year-old boy did not dare question his mother on something as shocking as concubinage. Eating a beancake was his equivalent for committing this selfish act, something inconsiderate of all family members, hence, my grandmother's despairing response to what seemed like a ludicrous

charge of gluttony. And sure enough, she was banished from the family, and my uncle saw her only a few times before her death.

46   While the above may fuel people's argument that Chinese is indeed a language of extreme discretion, it does not mean that Chinese people speak in secrets and riddles. The contexts are fully understood. It is only to those on the *outside* that the language seems cryptic, the behavior inscrutable.

47   I am, evidently, one of the outsiders. My nephew in Shanghai, who recently started taking English lessons, has been writing me letters in English. I had told him I was a fiction writer, and so in one letter he wrote, "Congratulate to you on your writing. Perhaps one day I should like to read it." I took it in the same vein as "Perhaps one day we can get together for lunch." I sent back a cheery note. A month went by and another letter arrived from Shanghai. "Last one perhaps I hadn't writing distinctly," he said. "In the future, you'll send a copy of your works for me."

48   I try to explain to my English-speaking friends that Chinese language use is more *strategic* in manner, whereas English tends to be more direct; an American business executive may say, "Let's make a deal," and the Chinese manager may reply, "Is your son interested in learning about your widget business?" Each to his or her own purpose, each with his or her own linguistic path. But I hesitate to add more to the pile of generalizations, because no matter how many examples I provide and explain, I fear that it appears defensive and only reinforces the image: that Chinese people are "discreet and modest"—and it takes an American to explain what they really mean.

49   Why am I complaining? The description seems harmless enough (after all, the *New York Times Magazine* writer did not say "slippery and evasive"). It is precisely the bland, easy acceptability of the phrase that worries me.

50   I worry that the dominant society may see Chinese people from a limited—and limiting—perspective. I worry that seemingly benign stereotypes may be part of the reason there are few Chinese in top management positions, in mainstream political roles. I worry about the power of language: that if one says anything enough times—in *any* language—it might become true.

51   Could this be why Chinese friends of my parents' generation are willing to accept the generalization?

52   "Why are you complaining?" one of them said to me. "If people think we are modest and polite, let them think that. Wouldn't Americans be pleased to admit they are thought of as polite?"

53   And I do believe anyone would take the description as a compliment—at first. But after a while, it annoys, as if the only things that people heard one say were phatic remarks: "I'm so pleased to meet

you. I've heard many wonderful things about you. For me? You shouldn't have!"

54   These remarks are not representative of new ideas, honest emotions, or considered thought. They are what is said from the polite distance of social contexts: of greetings, farewells, wedding thank-you notes, convenient excuses, and the like.

55   It makes me wonder though. How many anthropologists, how many sociologists, how many travel journalists have documented so-called "natural interactions" in foreign lands, all observed with spiral notebook in hand? How many other cases are there of the long-lost primitive tribe, people who turned out to be sophisticated enough to put on the stone-age show that ethnologists had come to see?

56   And how many tourists fresh off the bus have wandered into Chinatown expecting the self-effacing shopkeeper to admit under duress that the goods are not worth the price asked? I have witnessed it.

57   "I don't know," the tourist said to the shopkeeper, a Cantonese woman in her fifties. "It doesn't look genuine to me. I'll give you three dollars."

58   "You don't like my price, go somewhere else," said the shopkeeper.

59   "You are not a nice person," cried the shocked tourist, "not a nice person at all!"

60   "Who say I have to be nice," snapped the shopkeeper.

61   "So how does one say 'yes' and 'no' in Chinese?" ask my friends a bit warily.

62   And here I do agree in part with the *New York Times Magazine* article. There is no one word for "yes" or "no"—but not out of necessity to be discreet. If anything, I would say the Chinese equivalent of answering "yes" or "no" is dis*crete,* that is, specific to what is asked.

63   Ask a Chinese person if he or she has eaten, and he or she might say *chrle* (eaten already) or perhaps *meiyou* (have not).

64   Ask, "So you had insurance at the time of the accident?" and the response would be *dwei* (correct) or *meiyou* (did not have).

65   Ask, "Have you stopped beating your wife?" and the answer refers directly to the proposition being asserted or denied: stopped already, still have not, never beat, have no wife.

66   What could be clearer?

67   As for those who are still wondering how to translate the language of discretion, I offer this personal example.

68   My aunt and uncle were about to return to Beijing after a three-month visit to the United States. On their last night I announced I wanted to take them out to dinner.

69   "Are you hungry?" I asked in Chinese.

70   "Not hungry," said my uncle promptly, the same response he once gave me ten minutes before he suffered a low-blood-sugar attack.

71   "Not too hungry," said my aunt. "Perhaps you're hungry?"

72   "A little," I admitted.

73   "We can eat, we can eat," they both consented.

74   "What kind of food?" I asked.

75   "Oh, doesn't matter. Anything will do. Nothing fancy, just some simple food is fine."

76   "Do you like Japanese food? We haven't had that yet," I suggested.

77   They looked at each other.

78   "We can eat it," said my uncle bravely, this survivor of the Long March.

79   "We have eaten it before," added my aunt. "Raw fish."

80   "Oh, you don't like it?" I said. "Don't be polite. We can go somewhere else."

81   "We are not being polite. We can eat it," my aunt insisted.

82   So I drove them to Japantown and we walked past several restaurants featuring colorful plastic displays of sushi.

83   "Not this one, not this one either," I continued to say, as if searching for a Japanese restaurant similar to the last. "Here it is," I finally said, turning into a restaurant famous for its Chinese fish dishes from Shandong.

84   "Oh, Chinese food!" cried my aunt, obviously relieved.

85   My uncle patted my arm. "You think Chinese."

86   "It's your last night here in America," I said. "So don't be polite. Act like an American."

87   And that night we ate a banquet.

✦ Evaluating the Text

1. How does the opening episode illustrate Tan's observation that Americans do not practice the same ritual courtesies as the Chinese? How did the common stereotype that paints the Chinese as unwilling to be confrontational arise?

2. What is the Sapir-Whorf hypothesis and how do Tan's experiences lead her to accept or reject this concept? For example, does she believe that speakers of different languages possess different views of the world?

3. Why is the distinction between "discreet" and "discrete" an important one in the development of Tan's essay?

✦ Exploring Different Perspectives

1. How might the narrator's father in John Cheever's "Reunion" benefit from the kind of restraint discussed by Tan?

2. Are the expectations in Tan's Chinese-American family radically different from those described in Daniela Deane's "The Little Emperors"? Why or why not and if so, how?

✧ *Extending Viewpoints through Writing and Research*

1. How strongly do you believe that the language we speak influences our view of the world and influences our behavior?

2. Have you ever been the object of a cross-cultural misperception based on your use of language? What cues, behaviors, or customs did others misperceive and what steps did you take to correct this misperception?

3. For further research on topics and themes in Tan's writings, consult http://www.luminarium.org/contemporary/amytan/.

John Cheever

Reunion

◆

John Cheever (1912–1982) was born in Quincy, Massachusetts. His parents had planned for him to attend Harvard, but he was expelled at seventeen from the Thayer Academy for smoking, which marked the end of his formal education. Although he wrote five novels, he is best known for his deftly constructed short stories of suburban affluent America that frequently appeared in The New Yorker. *Collections of his work include* The Enormous Radio *(1953),* The House Breaker of Shady Hill *(1958),* The Brigadier and the Golf Widow *(1964), and* The Stories of John Cheever *(1978), which won a Pulitzer Prize, and from which "Reunion" is reprinted.*

Before You Read

Consider whether you have ever become disillusioned with an older relative.

◆

1   The last time I saw my father was in Grand Central Station. I was going from my grandmother's in the Adirondacks to a cottage on the Cape that my mother had rented, and I wrote my father that I would be in New York between trains for an hour and a half and asked if we could have lunch together. His secretary wrote to say that he would meet me at the information booth at noon, and at twelve o'clock sharp I saw him coming through the crowd. He was a stranger to me—my mother divorced him three years ago, and I hadn't been with him since—but as soon as I saw him I felt that he was my father, my flesh and blood, my future and my doom. I knew that when I was grown I would be something like him; I would have to plan my campaigns within his limitations. He was a big, good-looking man, and I was terribly happy to see him again. He struck me on the back and shook my hand. "Hi, Charlie," he said. "Hi, boy. I'd like to take you up to my club, but it's in the Sixties, and if you have to catch an early train I guess we'd better get something to eat around here." He put his arm around me, and I smelled my father the way my mother sniffs a rose. It was a rich compound of whiskey, aftershave lotion, shoe polish, woolens, and the rankness of a mature male. I hoped that someone would see us together. I wished that we could be photographed. I wanted some record of our having been together.

2   We went out of the station and up a side street to a restaurant. It was still early, and the place was empty. The bartender was quarreling with a delivery boy, and there was one very old waiter in a red coat down by the kitchen door. We sat down, and my father hailed the waiter in a loud voice. *"Kellner!"* he shouted. *"Garçon! Cameriere! You!"* His boisterousness in the empty restaurant seemed out of place. "Could we have a little service here!" he shouted. "Chop-chop." Then he clapped his hands. This caught the waiter's attention, and he shuffled over to our table.

3   "Were you clapping your hands at me?" he asked.

4   "Calm down, calm down, *sommelier,*" my father said. "If it isn't too much to ask of you—if it wouldn't be too much above and beyond the call of duty, we would like a couple of Beefeater Gibsons."

5   "I don't like to be clapped at," the waiter said.

6   "I should have brought my whistle," my father said. "I have a whistle that is audible only to the ears of old waiters. Now, take out your little pad and your little pencil and see if you can get this straight: two Beefeater Gibsons. Repeat after me: two Beefeater Gibsons."

7   "I think you'd better go somewhere else," the waiter said quietly.

8   "That," said my father, "is one of the most brilliant suggestions I have ever heard. Come on, Charlie, let's get the hell out of here."

9   I followed my father out of that restaurant into another. He was not so boisterous this time. Our drinks came, and he cross-questioned me about the baseball season. He then struck the edge of his empty glass with his knife and began shouting again. *"Garçon! Kellner! You!* Could we trouble you to bring us two more of the same."

10   "How old is the boy?" the waiter asked.

11   "That," my father said, "is none of your goddamned business."

12   "I'm sorry, sir," the waiter said, "but I won't serve the boy another drink."

13   "Well, I have some news for you," my father said. "I have some very interesting news for you. This doesn't happen to be the only restaurant in New York. They've opened another on the corner. Come on, Charlie."

14   He paid the bill, and I followed him out of that restaurant into another. Here the waiters wore pink jackets like hunting coats, and there was a lot of horse tack on the walls. We sat down, and my father began to shout again. "Master of the hounds! Tallyhoo and all that sort of thing. We'd like a little something in the way of a stirrup cup. Namely, two Bibson Geefeaters."

15   "Two Bibson Geefeaters?" the waiter asked, smiling.

16   "You know damned well what I want," my father said angrily. "I want two Beefeater Gibsons, and make it snappy. Things have changed in jolly old England. So my friend the duke tells me. Let's see what England can produce in the way of a cocktail."

17   "This isn't England," the waiter said.

18   "Don't argue with me," my father said. "Just do as you're told."

19   "I just thought you might like to know where you are," the waiter said.

20   "If there is one thing I cannot tolerate," my father said, "it is an impudent domestic. Come on, Charlie."

21   The fourth place we went to was Italian. "*Buon giorno,*" my father said. "*Per favore, possiamo avere due cocktail americani, forti, forti. Molto gin, poco vermut.*"

22   "I don't understand Italian," the waiter said.

23   "Oh, come off it," my father said. "You understand Italian, and you know damned well you do. *Vogliamo due cocktail americani. Subito.*"

24   The waiter left us and spoke with the captain, who came over to our table and said, "I'm sorry, sir, but this table is reserved."

25   "All right," my father said. "Get us another table."

26   "All the tables are reserved," the captain said.

27   "I get it," my father said. "You don't desire our patronage. Is that it? Well, the hell with you. *Vada all' inferno.* Let's go, Charlie."

28   "I have to get my train," I said.

29   "I'm sorry, sonny," my father said. "I'm terribly sorry." He put his arm around me and pressed me against him. "I'll walk you back to the station. If there had only been time to go up to my club."

30   "That's all right, Daddy," I said.

31   "I'll get you a paper," he said. "I'll get you a paper to read on the train."

32   Then he went up to a newsstand and said, "Kind sir, will you be good enough to favor me with one of your goddamned, no-good, ten-cent afternoon papers?" The clerk turned away from him and stared at a magazine cover. "Is it asking too much, kind sir," my father said, "is it asking too much for you to sell me one of your disgusting specimens of yellow journalism?"

33   "I have to go, Daddy," I said. "It's late."

34   "Now, just wait a second, sonny," he said. "Just wait a second. I want to get a rise out of this chap."

35   "Goodbye, Daddy," I said, and I went down the stairs and got my train, and that was the last time I saw my father.

✧ Evaluating the Text

1. What clues tell the reader how much the anticipated meeting with his father means to the boy in the story?

2. How would you characterize the father's attitude toward those of other nationalities and lower social classes?

3. How does the sequence of episodes that takes place in the story make clear why the boy would wish never to see his father again?

✧ Exploring Different Perspectives

1. How does Cheever's story shed light on the conditions in which the narrator's father becomes as spoiled as the "little emperors" are in Daniela Deane's analysis?

2. How does the theme of racism and stereotyping of minorities enter into Cheever's story and Gayle Pemberton's account "Antidisestablishmentaranism"?

✧ Extending Viewpoints through Writing and Research

1. Has the behavior of a relative or friend toward people of other nationalities or social classes ever caused you to feel shame or embarrassment as the boy does in Cheever's story? Describe the circumstances.

2. In your view, what significant role does alcoholism play in causing rifts between parents and children?

Fritz Peters

Boyhood with Gurdjieff

◆

Fritz Peters's (1916–1979) association with the philosopher and mystic George Gurdjieff began when Peters attended a school founded by Gurdjieff in Fontainebleau, France, where he spent four and a half years between 1924 and 1929. His experiences with Gurdjieff were always unpredictable and often enigmatic and rewarding. Peters wrote two books about his experiences, Boyhood with Gurdjieff *(1964) and* Gurdjieff Remembered *(1965). In the following essay, Peters reveals the highly unconventional methods Gurdjieff used to compel his protégé to develop compassion.*

Before You Read
Who in your life, other than a relative, has taught you great life lessons?

◆

1   The Saturday evening after Gurdjieff's return from America, which had been in the middle of the week, was the first general "assembly" of everyone at the Prieuré,[1] in the study-house. The study-house was a separate building, originally an airplane hangar. There was a linoleum-covered raised stage at one end. Directly in front of the stage there was a small, hexagonal fountain, equipped electrically so that various coloured lights played on the water. The fountain was generally used only during the playing of music on the piano which was to the left of the stage as one faced it.

2   The main part of the building, from the stage to the entrance at the opposite end, was carpeted with oriental rugs of various sizes, surrounded by a small fence which made a large, rectangular open space. Cushions, covered by fur rugs, surrounded the sides of this rectangle in front of the fence, and it was here that most of the students would normally sit. Behind the fence, at a higher level, were built-up benches, also covered with Oriental rugs, for spectators. Near the entrance of the building there was a small cubicle, raised a few feet from the floor, in which Gurdjieff habitually sat, and above this there was a balcony which was rarely used and then only for "important" guests. The cross-wise beams of the ceiling had painted material nailed to them,

---

[1] *Prieuré:* a priory; a large chateau in Fountainebleau, France, where G. I. Gurdjieff conducted his school.

and the material hung down in billows, creating a cloud-like effect. It was an impressive interior—with a church-like feeling about it. One had the impression that it would be improper, even when it was empty, to speak above a whisper inside the building.

3   On that particular Saturday evening, Gurdjieff sat in his accustomed cubicle, Miss Madison sat near him on the floor with her little black book on her lap, and most of the students sat around, inside the fence, on the fur rugs. New arrivals and "spectators" or guests were on the higher benches behind the fence. Mr. Gurdjieff announced that Miss Madison would go over all the "offences" of all the students and that proper "punishments" would be meted out to the offenders. All of the children, and perhaps I, especially, waited with bated breath as Miss Madison read from her book, which seemed to have been arranged, not alphabetically, but according to the number of offences committed. As Miss Madison had warned me, I led the list, and the recitation of my crimes and offences was a lengthy one.

4   Gurdjieff listened impassively, occasionally glancing at one or another of the offenders, sometimes smiling at the recital of a particular misdemeanour, and interrupting Miss Madison only to take down, personally, the actual number of individual black marks. When she had completed her reading, there was a solemn, breathless silence in the room and Gurdjieff said, with a heavy sigh, that we had all created a great burden for him. He said then that he would give out punishments according to the number of offences committed. Naturally, I was the first one to be called. He motioned to me to sit on the floor before him and then had Miss Madison re-read my offences in detail. When she had finished, he asked me if I admitted all of them. I was tempted to refute some of them, at least in part, and to argue extenuating circumstances, but the solemnity of the proceedings and the silence in the room prevented me from doing so. Every word that had been uttered had dropped on the assemblage with the clarity of a bell. I did not have the courage to voice any weak defence that might have come to my mind, and I admitted that the list was accurate.

5   With another sigh, and shaking his head at me as if he was very much put upon, he reached into his pocket and pulled out an enormous roll of bills. Once again, he enumerated the number of my crimes, and then laboriously peeled off an equal number of notes. I do not remember exactly how much he gave me—I think it was ten francs for each offence—but when he had finished counting, he handed me a sizeable roll of francs. During this process, the entire room practically screamed with silence. There was not a murmur from anyone in the entire group, and I did not even dare to glance in Miss Madison's direction.

6   When my money had been handed to me, he dismissed me and called up the next offender and went through the same process. As there were a great many of us, and there was not one individual who

had not done something, violated some rule during his absence, the process took a long time. When he had gone through the list, he turned to Miss Madison and handed her some small sum—perhaps ten francs, or the equivalent of one "crime" payment—for her, as he put it, "conscientious fulfilment of her obligations as director of the Prieuré."

7   We were all aghast; we had been taken completely by surprise, of course. But the main thing we all felt was a tremendous compassion for Miss Madison. It seemed to me a senselessly cruel, heartless act against her. I have never known Miss Madison's feelings about this performance; except for blushing furiously when I was paid, she showed no obvious reaction to anything at all, and even thanked him for the pittance he had given her.

8   The money that I had received amazed me. It was, literally, more money than I had ever had at one time in my life. But it also repelled me. I could not bring myself to do anything with it. It was not until a few days later, one evening when I had been summoned to bring coffee to Gurdjieff's room, that the subject came up again. I had had no private, personal contact with him—in the sense of actually talking to him, for instance—since his return. That evening—he was alone—when I had served him his coffee, he asked me how I was getting along; how I felt. I blurted out my feelings about Miss Madison and about the money that I felt unable to spend.

9   He laughed at me and said cheerfully that there was no reason why I should not spend the money any way I chose. It was my money, and it was a reward for my activity of the past winter. I said I could not understand why I should have been rewarded for having been dilatory about my jobs and having created only trouble.

10   Gurdjieff laughed again and told me that I had much to learn.

11   "What you not understand," he said, "is that not everyone can be trouble-maker, like you. This important in life—is ingredient, like yeast for making bread. Without trouble, conflict, life become dead. People live in status-quo, live only by habit, automatically, and without conscience. You good for Miss Madison. You irritate Miss Madison all time—more than anyone else, which is why you get most reward. Without you, possibility for Miss Madison's conscience fall asleep. This money should really be reward from Miss Madison, not from me. You help keep Miss Madison alive."

12   I understood the actual, serious sense in which he meant what he was saying, but I said that I felt sorry for Miss Madison, that it must have been a terrible experience for her when she saw us all receiving those rewards.

13   He shook his head at me, still laughing. "You not see or understand important thing that happen to Miss Madison when give money.

How you feel at time? You feel pity for Miss Madison, no? All other people also feel pity for Miss Madison, too."

14   I agreed that this was so.

15   "People not understand about learning," he went on. "Think necessary talk all time, that learn through mind, through words. Not so. Many things can only learn with feeling, even from sensation. But because man talk all time—use only formulatory centre—people not understand this. What you not see other night in studyhouse is that Miss Madison have new experience for her. Is poor woman, people not like, people think she funny—they laugh at. But other night, people not laugh. True, Miss Madison feel uncomfortable, feel embarrassed when I give money, feel shame perhaps. But when many people also feel for her sympathy, pity, compassion, even love, she understand this but not right away with mind. She feel, for first time in life, sympathy from many people. She not even know then that she feel this, but her life change; with you, I use you like example, last summer you hate Miss Madison. Now you not hate, you not think funny, you feel sorry. You even like Miss Madison. This good for her even if she not know right away—you will show; you cannot hide this from her, even if wish, cannot hide. So she now have friend, when used to be enemy. This good thing which I do for Miss Madison. I not concerned she understand this now—someday she understand and make her feel warm in heart. This unusual experience—this warm feeling—for such personality as Miss Madison who not have charm, who not friendly in self. Someday, perhaps even soon, she have good feeling because many people feel sorry, feel compassion for her. Someday she even understand what I do and even like me for this. But this kind learning take long time."

16   I understood him completely and was very moved by his words. But he had not finished.

17   "Also good thing for you in this," he said. "You young, only boy still, you not care about other people, care for self. I do this to Miss Madison and you think I do bad thing. You feel sorry, you not forget, you think I do bad thing to her. But now you understand not so. Also, good for you, because you feel about other person—you identify with Miss Madison, put self in her place, also regret what you do. Is necessary put self in place of other person if wish understand and help. This good for your conscience, this way is possibility for you learn not hate Miss Madison. All people same—stupid, blind, human. If I do bad thing, this make you learn love other people, not just self."

✦ Evaluating the Text

1. How did Gurdjieff's seemingly arbitrary allotment of rewards violate conventional expectations?

2. What consequences did this have in changing Peters's view of Miss Madison?

3. How does Peters's description of the elaborate ritual Gurdjieff follows in doling out rewards and punishments add to the suspense of his narrative?

✧ Exploring Different Perspectives

1. How do both Gurdjieff in Peters's essay and Gayle Pemberton's grandmother (see "Antidisestablishmentarianism") help the narrators learn something important about themselves?

2. How is public humiliation used by both Peters (of Miss Madison) and John Cheever (of the service people his father abuses) in "Reunion" to explain the changes in the narrator's attitudes?

✧ Extending Viewpoints through Writing and Research

1. What personal experiences have you had that forced you to completely reevaluate your attitude toward another person or group?

2. For more information about G. I. Gurdjieff, you might read *Meetings with Remarkable Men* (1963) and compare the way Gurdjieff presents himself in this book with the way Fritz Peters describes him.

Steve Sailer

The Cousin Marriage Conundrum

◆

Steve Sailer has contributed to National Interest, National Review, *and* National Post of Toronto *and is also a film critic for the* American Conservative *and the Monday columnist for* VDARE.com. *He is the founder of the Human Biodiversity Institute, a forum that hosts discussions by leading scientists and intellectuals. "The Cousin Marriage Conundrum" first appeared in* The American Conservative *(2003) and offers a provocative hypothesis that challenges the assumption that democracy can take root in Iraq and other countries in the Middle East.*

Before You Read

Consider why cousin marriages are generally not acceptable in American culture.

◆

1   Many prominent neoconservatives are calling on America not only to conquer Iraq (and perhaps more Muslim nations after that), but also to rebuild Iraqi society in order to jumpstart the democratization of the Middle East. Yet, Americans know so little about the Middle East that few of us are even aware of one of the building blocks of Arab Muslim cultures—cousin marriage. Not surprisingly, we are almost utterly innocent of any understanding of how much the high degree of inbreeding in Iraq could interfere with our nation building ambitions.

2   In Iraq, as in much of the region, nearly half of all married couples are first or second cousins to each other. A 1986 study of 4,500 married hospital patients and staff in Baghdad found that 46 percent were wed to a first or second cousin, while a smaller 1989 survey found 53 percent were "consanguineously" married. The most prominent example of an Iraqi first cousin marriage is that of Saddam Hussein and his first wife Sajida.

3   By fostering intense family loyalties and strong nepotistic urges, inbreeding makes the development of civil society more difficult. Many Americans have heard by now that Iraq is composed of three ethnic groups—the Kurds of the north, the Sunnis of the center, and the Shi'ites of the south. Clearly, these ethnic rivalries would complicate

the task of ruling or reforming Iraq. But that's just a top-down summary of Iraq's ethnic makeup. Each of those three ethnic groups is divisible into smaller and smaller tribes, clans, and inbred extended families—each with their own alliances, rivals, and feuds. And the engine at the bottom of these bedeviling social divisions is the oft-ignored institution of cousin marriage.

4   The fractiousness and tribalism of Middle Eastern countries have frequently been remarked. In 1931, King Feisal of Iraq described his subjects as "devoid of any patriotic idea, . . . connected by no common tie, giving ear to evil; prone to anarchy, and perpetually ready to rise against any government whatever." The clannishness, corruption, and coups frequently observed in countries such as Iraq appear to be tied to the high rates of inbreeding.

5   Muslim countries are usually known for warm, devoted extended family relationships, but also for weak patriotism. In the United States, where individualism is so strong, many assume that "family values" and civic virtues such as sacrificing for the good of society always go together. But, in Islamic countries, family loyalty is often at war with national loyalty. Civic virtues, military effectiveness, and economic performance all suffer.

6   Commentator Randall Parker wrote:

> Consanguinity [cousin marriage] is the biggest underappreciated factor in Western analyses of Middle Eastern politics. Most Western political theorists seem blind to the importance of pre-ideological kinship-based political bonds in large part because those bonds are not derived from abstract Western ideological models of how societies and political systems should be organized. . . . Extended families that are incredibly tightly bound are really the enemy of civil society because the alliances of family override any consideration of fairness to people in the larger society. Yet, this obvious fact is missing from 99 percent of the discussions about what is wrong with the Middle East. How can we transform Iraq into a modern liberal democracy if every government worker sees a government job as a route to helping out his clan at the expense of other clans?

7   Retired U.S. Army colonel Norvell De Atkine spent years trying to train America's Arab allies in modern combat techniques. In an article in *American Diplomacy* entitled, "Why Arabs Lose Wars," a frustrated De Atkine explained,

> First, the well-known lack of trust among Arabs for anyone outside their own family adversely affects offensive operations. In a culture in which almost every sphere of human endeavor, including business and social relationships, is based on a family struc-

ture, this basic mistrust of others is particularly costly in the stress of battle. Offensive action, at base, consists of fire and maneuver. The maneuver element must be confident that supporting units or arms are providing covering fire. If there is a lack of trust in that support, getting troops moving forward against dug-in defenders is possible only by officers getting out front and leading, something that has not been a characteristic of Arab leadership.

8   Similarly, as Francis Fukuyama described in his 1995 book *Trust: The Social Virtues and the Creation of Prosperity,* countries such as Italy with highly loyal extended families can generate dynamic family firms. Yet, their larger corporations tend to be rife with goldbricking, corruption, and nepotism, all because their employees don't trust each other to show their highest loyalty to the firm rather than their own extended families. Arab cultures are more family-focused than even Sicily, and thus their larger economic enterprises suffer even more.

9   American society is so biased against inbreeding that many Americans have a hard time even conceiving of marrying a cousin. Yet, arranged matches between first cousins (especially between the children of brothers) are considered the ideal throughout much of a broad expanse from North Africa through West Asia and into Pakistan and India.

10   In contrast, Americans probably disapprove of what scientists call "consanguineous" mating more than any other nationality. Three huge studies in the United States between 1941 and 1981 found that no more than 0.2 percent of all American marriages were between first cousins or second cousins.

11   Americans have long dismissed cousin marriage as something practiced only among hillbillies. That old stereotype of inbred mountaineers waging decades-long blood feuds had some truth to it. One study of 107 marriages in Beech Creek, Kentucky, in 1942 found 19 percent were consanguineous, although the Kentuckians were more inclined toward second-cousin marriages, while first-cousin couples are more common than second-cousin pairings in the Islamic lands.

12   Cousin marriage averages not much more than 1 percent in most European countries, and under 10 percent in the rest of the world outside that Morocco-to-southern-India corridor.

13   Muslim immigration, however, has been boosting Europe's low level of consanguinity. According to the leading authority on inbreeding, geneticist Alan H. Bittles of Edith Cowan University in Perth, Australia, "In the resident Pakistani community of some 0.5 million [in Britain] an estimated 50 percent to 60-plus percent of marriages are consanguineous, with evidence that their prevalence is increasing." (Bittles's Web site, www.consang.net, presents the results of several hundred studies of the prevalence of inbreeding around the world.)

14   European nations have recently become increasingly hostile toward the common practice among their Muslim immigrants of arranging marriages between their children and citizens of their home
country, frequently their relatives. One study of Turkish guest workers
in the Danish city of Ishøj found that 98 percent—first, second, and
third generation—married a spouse from Turkey who then came and
lived in Denmark. (Turks, however, are quite a bit less enthusiastic
about cousin marriage than are Arabs or Pakistanis, which correlates
with the much stronger degree of patriotism found in Turkey.)

15   European "family reunification" laws present an immigrant with
the opportunity to bring in his nephew by marrying his daughter to
him. Not surprisingly, "family reunification" almost always works just
in one direction—with the new husband moving from the poor Muslim country to the rich European country.

16   If a European-born daughter refused to marry her cousin from the
old country just because she doesn't love him, that would deprive her
extended family of the boon of an immigration visa. So, intense family
pressure can fall on the daughter to do as she is told.

17   The new Danish right-wing government has introduced legislation
to crack down on these kinds of marriages arranged to generate visas.
British Home Secretary David Blunkett has called for immigrants to
arrange more marriages within Britain.

18   Unlike the Middle East, Europe underwent what Samuel P. Hunt-
ington calls the "Romeo and Juliet revolution." Europeans became increasingly sympathetic toward the right of a young woman to marry
the man she loves. Setting the stage for this was the Catholic Church's
long war against cousin marriage, even out to fourth cousins or higher.
This weakened the extended family in Europe, thus lessening the advantages of arranged marriages. It also strengthened the nuclear family as well as broader institutions like the Church and the nation-state.

19   Islam itself may not be responsible for the high rates of inbreeding
in Muslim countries. (Similarly high levels of consanguinity are found
among Hindus in southern India, although there, uncle-niece marriages are socially preferred, even though their degree of genetic similarity is twice that of cousin marriages, with worse health consequences
for offspring.)

20   Rafat Hussain, a Pakistani-born senior lecturer at the University of
New England in Australia, told me, "Islam does not specifically en-
courage cousin marriages and, in fact, in the early days of the spread of
Islam, marriages outside the clan were highly desirable to increase cul-
tural and religious influence." She adds, "The practice has little do with
Islam (or in fact any religion) and had been a prevalent cultural norm
before Islam." Inbreeding (or "endogamy") is also common among
Christians in the Middle East, although less so than among Muslims.

21   The Muslim practice is similar to older Middle Eastern norms,
such as those outlined in Leviticus in the Old Testament. The lineage

of the Hebrew patriarchs who founded the Jewish people was highly inbred. Abraham said his wife Sarah was also his half-sister. His son Isaac married Rebekah, a cousin once removed. And Isaac's son Jacob wed his two first cousins, Leah and Rachel.

22   Jacob's dozen sons were the famous progenitors of the Twelve Tribes of Israel. Due to inbreeding, Jacob's eight legitimate sons had only six unique great-grandparents instead of the usual eight. That's because the inbred are related to their relatives through multiple paths.

23   Why do so many people around the world prefer to keep marriage in the family? Hussain noted, "In patriarchal societies where parents exert considerable influence and gender segregation is followed more strictly, marriage choice is limited to whom you know. While there is some pride in staying within the inner bounds of family for social or economic reasons, the more important issue is: Where will parents find a good match? Often, it boils down to whom you know and can trust."

24   Another important motivation—one that is particularly important in many herding cultures, such as the ancient ones from which the Jews and Muslims emerged—is to prevent inheritable wealth from being split among too many descendants. This can be especially important when there are economies of scale in the family business.

25   Just as the inbred have fewer unique ancestors than the outbred, they also have fewer unique heirs, helping keep both the inheritance and the brothers together. When a herd-owning patriarch marries his son off to his younger brother's daughter, he insures that his grandson and his grandnephew will be the same person. Likewise, the younger brother benefits from knowing that his grandson will also be the patriarch's grandson and heir. Thus, by making sibling rivalry over inheritance less relevant, cousin marriage emotionally unites families.

26   The anthropologist Carleton Coon also pointed out that by minimizing the number of relatives a Bedouin Arab nomad has, this system of inbreeding "does not overextend the number of persons whose deaths an honorable man must avenge."

27   Of course, there are also disadvantages to inbreeding. The best known is medical. Being inbred increases the chance of inheriting genetic syndromes caused by malign recessive genes. Bittles found that, after controlling for socioeconomic factors, the babies of first cousins had about a 30 percent higher chance of dying before their first birthdays.

28   The biggest disadvantage, however, may be political.

29   Are Muslims, especially Arabs, so much more loyal to their families than to their nations because, due to countless generations of cousin marriages, they are so much more genealogically related to their families than Westerners are related to theirs? Frank Salter, a political scientist at the Max Planck Institute in Germany whose new book *Risky Transactions: Trust, Kinship, and Ethnicity* takes a sociobiological look at the reason why Mafia families are indeed families, told me, "That's my hunch; at least it's bound to be a factor."

30   One of the basic laws of modern evolutionary science, quantified by the great Oxford biologist William D. Hamilton in 1964 under the name "kin selection," is that the more close the genetic relationship between two people, the more likely they are to feel loyalty and altruism toward each other. Natural selection has molded us not just to try to propagate our own genes, but to help our relatives, who possess copies of some of our specific genes, to propagate their own.

31   Nepotism is thus biologically inspired. Hamilton explained that the level of nepotistic feeling generally depends upon degree of genetic similarity. You share half your personally variable genes with your children and siblings, but one quarter with your nephews/nieces and grandchildren, so your nepotistic urges will tend to be somewhat less toward them. You share one eighth of your genes with your first cousins, and one thirty-second with your second cousin, so your feelings of family loyalty tend to fall off quickly.

32   But not as quickly if you and your relatives are inbred. Then, you'll be genealogically related to your kin via multiple pathways. You will all be genetically more similar, so your normal family feelings will be multiplied. For example, your son-in-law might also be the nephew you've cherished since his childhood, so you can lavish all the nepotistic altruism on him that in outbred Western societies would be split between your son-in-law and your nephew.

33   Unfortunately, nepotism is usually a zero-sum game, so the flip side of being materially nicer toward your relatives would be that you'd have less resources left with which to be civil, or even just fair, toward non-kin. So, nepotistic corruption is rampant in countries such as Iraq, where Saddam has appointed members of his extended family from his hometown of Tikrit to many key positions in the national government.

34   Similarly, a tendency toward inbreeding can turn an extended family into a miniature racial group with its own partially isolated gene pool. (Dog breeders use extreme forms of inbreeding to quickly create new breeds in a handful of generations.) The ancient Hebrews provide a vivid example of a partly inbred extended family (that of Abraham and his brothers) that evolved into its own ethnic group. This process has been going on for thousands of years in the Middle East, which is why not just the Jews but also tiny, ancient inbreeding groups such as the Samaritans and the John the Baptist–worshiping Sabeans still survive.

35   In summary, although neoconservatives constantly point to America's success at reforming Germany and Japan after World War II as evidence that it would be easy to do the same in the Middle East, the deep social structure of Iraq is the complete opposite of those two true nation-states, with their highly patriotic, cooperative, and (not surprisingly) outbred peoples. The Iraqis, in contrast, more closely resemble the Hatfields and the McCoys.

✦ *Evaluating the Text*

1. According to Sailer, what hitherto overlooked social practice may undermine attempts to democratize Iraq?

2. Why is this practice so foreign to American culture and so prevalent in Middle Eastern countries?

✦ *Exploring Different Perspectives*

1. How do both Sailer and Daniela Deane in "The Little Emperors" explore the interaction between political edicts and traditional custom?

2. What role do financial pressures play in the accounts by Sailer (in Iraq) and Gayatri Devi (in India) in "A Princess Remembers"?

✦ *Extending Viewpoints through Writing and Research*

1. How persuasive do you find the evidence and reasoning Sailer presents to support his thesis?

2. Would cousin marriage be a viable option for you? Why or why not?

3. Information about kinship, marriage systems, and cousin marriages is available at http://www.zaxistv.com/sociology/values/iraqmarriage.htm and http://www.parapundit.com/archives/001667.html.

How does this cartoon satirize a current political agenda for Iraq?

Gayatri Devi, with Santha Rama Rau

A Princess Remembers

---◆---

Gayatri Devi was born in 1919 in London and raised in West Bengal, India, as the daughter of the Maharajah of Cooch Behar and the Princess of Baroda. She married the Maharajah of Jaipur in 1940 and has had a distinguished career as a member of the Indian Parliament from 1962 to 1977. As the Maharani of Jaipur, she is the founder of the Gayatri Devi Girl's Public School in Rajasthan. The following chapter is drawn from her autobiography A Princess Remembers: The Memoirs of the Maharani of Jaipur *(1976), written with Santha Rama Rau, who is herself the author of eleven books, including* Home to India *(1945), and numerous magazine articles that have appeared in the* New Yorker, *the* New York Times Sunday Magazine, *and* Reader's Digest. *In this account, Devi recreates the palatial splendor of her childhood home and reveals the close ties she had with her mother.*

Before You Read

As you read, notice how Devi uses her personal experiences to raise the broader theme of the responsibilities that members of royalty had in traditional Indian society.

---◆---

1   During our childhood, our family often journeyed the two thousand miles from our home, the palace in Cooch Behar State, tucked into the north-east corner of India, right across the country to my grandparents' palace in the state of Baroda, on the shores of the Arabian Sea. All five of us children had watched with excited anticipation the packing of mountains of luggage. We seemed to be preparing for the most unlikely extremes of heat and cold, not to mention more predictable occasions such as a state visit or a horse show. On the day of our departure the station was a bedlam, what with all the luggage and staff that accompanied us wherever we went. But by the time we arrived everything was checked and on board, thanks to the efforts of our well-trained staff.

2   Nonetheless, my mother invariably had a deluge of instructions and questions as soon as we arrived. Where was the dressing-case that she wanted in her compartment? she would ask, in her slightly husky, appealing voice. Well, then, unload the baggage and find it. What about

her *puja* box, which contained the incenses and powders necessary for the performance of her morning prayers? Ah, there it was. Fortunately, that meant that no one need hurry back to the palace to fetch it.

3   When she did actually leave, telegrams were sent in all directions: PLEASE SEND MY GOLD TONGUE-SCRAPER, or, HAVE LEFT MY SPOON AND LITTLE ONYX BELL BEHIND, or, IN THE LEFT-HAND CUPBOARD IN THE THIRD DRAWER DOWN YOU'LL FIND MY GREEN SILK DRESSING-GOWN. Then came the supplementaries: NOT THE DARK GREEN, THE LIGHT GREEN, or, IN THAT CASE LOOK IN THE DRESSING-ROOM.

4   Anyway, once we got started, those week-long journeys were among the most cherished memories of my childhood. As a child it seemed to me that we occupied the whole train. We had at least three four-berth first-class compartments. My mother, elder sister, and a friend or relation occupied one; my younger sister, a governess, and myself were in another; my two brothers and their companion with an aide in another. Then the aides and secretaries would have a couple of second-class compartments, while the maids, valets, and butlers travelled third class.

5   In the twenties, a train trip by even the most plain-living Indian was reminiscent of a Bedouin migration, for everything in the way of bedding, food, and eating utensils had to be taken along. In those days most Indian trains had no dining-cars and did not provide sheets, blankets, pillows, or towels, although there were proper bathrooms where you could take a shower. We always travelled with our personal servants to cope with the daily necessities of living on the long journey to Baroda.

6   First there was the overnight trip from Cooch Behar to Calcutta, and we broke our journey for a couple of days in our house there. Then we set off again for the longest part of the trip. The cooks prepared "tiffin-carriers," a number of pans, each holding different curries, rice, lentils, curds, and sweets. The pans fitted into each other, and a metal brace held them all together so that you could carry in one hand a metal tower filled with food. But those tiffin-carriers were intended to supply us with only our first meal on the train. From then on we were in the hands of a chain of railway caterers. You could give your order to the railway man at one stop and know that instructions would be wired ahead to the next stop and that your meal would be served, on the thick railway crockery, as soon as the train came into the station. More often than not we hadn't finished before the train left the station—but that didn't matter. Another waiter would be ready to pick up empty containers, glasses, cutlery, and plates at any further stop that the train made.

7   For us children the excitement of travelling across India by train was not so much in the ingenious arrangements for meals and service

as in the atmosphere of the station platforms themselves. As soon as the train pulled in to any station, our carriage windows were immediately besieged by vendors of sweets, fruit, hot tea, and—my favourites—by men selling the charming, funny, painted wooden toys that I have seen nowhere except on Indian station platforms: elephants with their trunks raised to trumpet, lacquered in grey and scarlet, caparisoned in gold with floral designs picked out in contrasting colours; horses decked out as though for a bridegroom; camels, cheetahs, tigers, and dozens of others, all stiff and delightful, with wide, painted eyes and endearing, coquettish smiles. I wanted them all, but my mother said, "Nonsense, nonsense! You children have too many toys as it is." But she could never resist bargaining, so she had a lovely time with the fruit-, flower-, and sweets-vendors, and afterwards our compartment was filled with clinging tropical scents from all her purchases. I don't really know whether she was as good a bargainer as she thought—she was, by nature, very generous—and the vendors always went away looking appropriately bereaved, although with a secret air of satisfaction.

8   In any case, it didn't matter. All of us had the fun of chasing each other about the platforms, and when the train stayed in a station for an hour or more, we ate in the railway dining-room, ordering what we used to call "railway curry," designed to offend no palate—no beef, forbidden to Hindus; no pork, forbidden to Muslims; so, inevitably, lamb or chicken curries and vegetables. Railway curry therefore pleased nobody. Long before the train was due to leave we were summoned by our aides or governess or tutor, telling us to hurry, not to dawdle over our meal in the station restaurant; the train was leaving in five minutes. Of course it didn't, and we soon learned to trust the railway personnel, who let us loiter till the last possible moment before bustling us back to our compartments.

9   Finally we would arrive in Baroda to be met at the station by a fleet of Baroda State cars and driven to Laxmi Vilas, the Baroda Palace and my mother's girlhood home. It is an enormous building, the work of the same architect who built our own palace in Cooch Behar in the mid-nineteenth century. In Baroda, he had adopted what I believe architects describe as the "Indo-Saracenic" style. Whatever one calls it, it is certainly imposing. Marble verandas with scalloped arches supported by groups of slender pillars bordered the building. Impressive façades were topped by onion-shaped domes. Outside the main entrance were palm trees standing like sentries along the edges of perfectly kept lawns that were watered daily. Tall and rather municipal-looking street lights with spherical bulbs illuminated the grand approach. And always on duty were the splendid household guards, dressed in white breeches with dark blue jackets and black top-boots. Because we were the grandchildren of the Maharaja, the ruler of the state, every time we went in or out of the front gate they played the Baroda anthem.

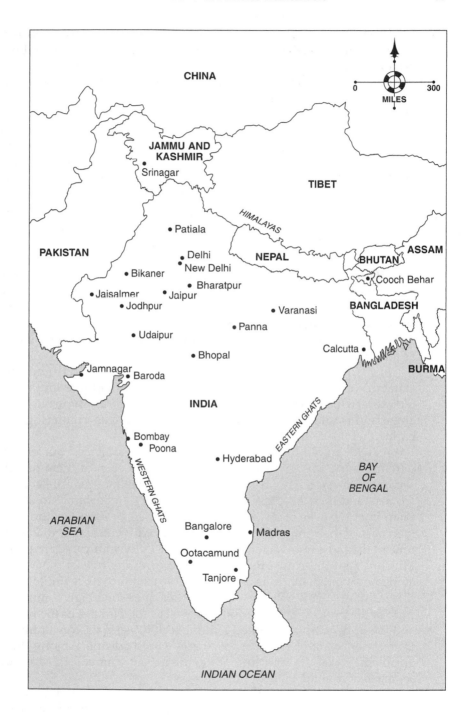

10   Inside, the palace was a strange blend of styles, partly Victorian, partly traditional Indian, with here and there a touch of antique English or French. There were courtyards with little pools surrounded by ferns and palms. Persian carpets flowed down interminable corridors. The halls were filled with displays of shields, swords, and armouries of spears. The sitting-rooms overflowed with French furniture, with photographs in silver frames, with ornaments and knickknacks on occasional tables. The palace also contained a gymnasium and a dispensary. Two doctors were permanently in residence, and one of them used to travel with my grandfather wherever he went.

11   Throughout the palace silent formality reigned, and there always seemed to be a number of anonymous, mysterious figures around— two or three sitting in every room. They must have had some proper place in the design of things, but we children never found out who they were or what they were doing. Waiting for an audience with our grandfather? Visiting from some other princely state? Guarding the many precious objects that were scattered throughout the palace? True to our training, we knew that we must pay our respects to our elders, so we may well have folded our hands in a *namaskar,* the traditional Indian greeting, or obeisance, to maidservants and companions as well as to distinguished guests.

12   In sharp contrast to our own decorous behaviour and the general standard of proper courtesy in the palace were the huge longtailed monkeys which roamed everywhere. They were easily aroused to anger and would often follow us down the passages, chattering and baring their teeth in a most terrifying manner.

13   As with all old Indian palaces and family residences, our grandparents' home was divided into two parts, and each of them had its separate entrance. This tradition of special zenana quarters for the women, and their keeping of purdah, literally "a curtain," to shield them from the eyes of any men other than their husband or the male members of their immediate family, was introduced into India at the time of the Muslim invasions during the twelfth century. At first only Muslims kept these customs, but later, during the rule of the Mogul emperors of India, which lasted from the sixteenth century until the Indian Mutiny of 1857 when the British took over sovereign command, most of the princely states of India as well as the families of the nobles and the upper classes adopted a number of Muslim customs ranging from styles of architecture to a rich and varied cuisine. Among these borrowings was the tradition of keeping their womenfolk carefully segregated from the view of outside eyes.

14   In Baroda the full tradition of purdah no longer existed; both my grandparents were too liberal to allow it. Strict purdah would have required the women to stay entirely within the zenana quarters and, if they had any occasion to venture outside, to travel well chaperoned,

only in curtained or shaded vehicles. But my grandparents treated the custom relatively loosely—women could go about fairly freely as long as they were chaperoned and had nothing to do with men outside their family circle. If, for instance, there was a cheetah hunt or a polo match, the ladies would all go together, separately from the men. They didn't have to be veiled; they just stayed on their side of the grounds and the men stayed on the opposite side. For us children, there were no restrictions at all. We wandered freely all over the palace, even to the billiard-room, which in Edwardian days was considered forbidden territory to any female.

15   My grandmother, a formidable lady, had grown up totally accepting the idea of purdah. Following the custom of her time and the tradition of her family, she had, through her early years, observed the strictest purdah, never appearing in public, and in private only before women, close male relatives, and her husband. When she was only fourteen, a marriage was arranged for her to the ruler of Baroda. Her family, like his, was Maratha, members of the Kshatriya caste, which included many warriors and rulers. Like other Indian communities, Marathas traditionally married among themselves. She was, besides, of the right noble background, and he, after the untimely death of his first wife, the Princess of Tanjore, wanted to marry again.

16   My grandfather, well ahead of his time in many of his attitudes and actions, hired tutors for my grandmother, first to teach her to read and write (she was illiterate when she was married), then to expand her education. Later still, he encouraged her to free herself from suffocating Indian traditions and to pursue a role in public life. It was owing to his liberal views that my grandmother emerged as an important leader in the women's movement in India. She became the president of the All-India Women's Conference, the largest women's organization in the world and one which concerns itself with women's rights as well as with the spread of education and the loosening of the constricting ties of orthodox Indian society on its women. She was not just a figure-head in this important office but a very effective spokeswoman for the emancipation of Indian women. Eventually she even wrote a book, now a standard reference work, on the position of Indian women in their society. After all, she could draw amply on her own experience, first as a sheltered, obedient daughter of a conservative family and later as a free and progressive wife.

17   But it wasn't for her—or for any of us, her three granddaughters or our mother—a total transformation. Within the family in the Baroda Palace she still retained much of the conventional manners and the severe sense of propriety of all upper-class Indian households. All of us always touched her feet as a sign of respect when we first arrived in Baroda, again before we left, and also on all ceremonial occasions. (This custom, still observed in most Hindu families, applied not only to our

grandmother but to all close relatives who were our seniors, even brothers, sisters, and cousins who might be just a few months older.)

18   It was at public functions that my grandparents made it most clear that they had more or less dispensed with the rules of purdah, for they always appeared together. Although they still maintained separate kitchens and separate household staffs, my grandfather came to take his meals with the rest of us, and with whatever visitors happened to be staying in Baroda, in my grandmother's dining-room. There she served the most marvellous food in the Indian way, on *thals*, round silver trays loaded with small matching silver bowls containing quantities of rice pilau, meat, fish and vegetable curries, lentils, pickles, chutneys, and sweets. She was a great gourmet and the food from her kitchen was delicious, whether it was the Indian chef who was presiding or, when she was unsure of the tastes of foreign visitors, the cook for English food who was in charge. She spent endless time and trouble consulting with her cooks, planning menus to suit the different guests she invited. It was dangerous to be even faintly appreciative of any dish, for if you took a second helping, she noticed and thrust a third and a fourth upon you, saying, "Come on, come on, you know you like this." Her kitchen was particularly well known for the marvellous pickles it produced and for the huge, succulent prawns from the estuary. Only when there were a large number of outside guests, and on ceremonial occasions like my grandfather's Diamond Jubilee, were meals served from his kitchen and in the banqueting hall on his side of the palace.

19   On religious and ceremonial occasions, durbars were held in his great audience hall. These were very elaborate affairs, something like holding court. The nobility and other important families came formally to offer their allegiance to their rulers—usually a token of a single gold coin.

20   Often we went duck shooting, sometimes we watched the falconing, and then there were the special thrills of elephant fights and, better yet, the tense and gripping cheetah hunts, a speciality of Baroda,when carefully trained cheetahs, hooded and chained, were taken out to the scrub land in shooting-brakes. There they were unhooded and let loose into a herd of black buck. With foot full down on the accelerator, one could just manage to keep pace with the astonishing speed of the animals during the chase.

21   My own favourite entertainment as a child came from the relatively tame performances of my grandfather's trained parrots. They used to ride tiny silver bicycles, drive little silver cars, walk tightropes, and enact a variety of dramatic scenes. I remember one in particular in which a parrot was run over by a car, examined by a parrot doctor, and finally carried off on a stretcher by parrot bearers. The grand climax of their performance was always a salute fired on a tiny silver cannon. It

made the most amazing noise for a miniature weapon, and the parrots were the only ones to remain unperturbed.

22   While my grandmother approved of all these innocent diversions for the children, she wanted us to retain the traditional skills of Indian girls. She wanted us, for instance, to learn how to cook proper Maratha food. My sisters, Ila and Menaka, showed talent and profited by the lessons, while I never seemed able to grasp even the rudiments of cooking.

23   Because almost every princely Indian family put strong emphasis on sports—and also because we ourselves were sports-mad—we used to get up at daybreak and go riding. By the time we returned, my grandmother's side of the palace was already bustling with activity, with maids preparing for the day, women waiting for an audience, and countless arrangements being made. We used to go in to say our required "Good morning" to her before we went to our rooms to settle down to lessons with our tutors. The floors of her apartments were covered, in the traditional Indian fashion, with vast white cloths. We had to take off our shoes before entering, and everyone except my grandmother sat on the floor.

24   I remember her from those days as an admirable, remarkable, and somewhat terrifying woman. She must have been beautiful when she was young. Even to my childish eyes, at that time, she was still handsome and immensely dignified. She wasn't tall, though she gave the impression of height partly because her manner was so very regal. But she had a sour sense of humour.

25   My grandfather was an impressive though kindly figure in our lives, and I remember how his eyes were always laughing. We often took our morning ride with him on the four-mile bridle-path around the Baroda Palace grounds. It was difficult to keep up with him because he liked strenuous exercise and had his favourite horse specially trained to trot very fast.

26   When we returned to the palace he would leave us and spend the rest of the morning dealing with work that he lumped under the comprehensive heading of "matters of state." Though I didn't know the details at the time, the ruler of an Indian princely state had important functions to fulfil and was a real sovereign to his people. The British, as they gradually took over the major role in India during the nineteenth century, made varying agreements with the different princes defining the division of responsibilities, although much was also left to evolving custom. One major point of all the agreements was that the princes could have relations with foreign powers only through the British. Each of the more important states—and Baroda was one of the most important—had a British Resident who was the voice of the British Government of India. But the states had their own laws, their

own courts of justice, their own taxes, and in many cases their own military forces, so that the people of each state looked towards the prince, and not towards anyone else, as the real governmental authority in their lives. My grandfather had, therefore, to confer with his ministers (who were responsible only to him) and to decide many things that affected the lives of millions of people.

27   I knew him, however, not as a statesman but as a man and a grandfather. One conversation with him lives clearly in my memory. I had gone to say good night to him. He was, as always at that time of day, at the billiard table. He stopped his game and said, in a friendly way, "Ah, I see you're off to bed. I hope you have a good sleep."

28   I explained to him that there was no question of sleep for some time to come as I had to think about all that had happened during the day.

29   "No, no," he said, gently but emphatically. "If you go to bed, you should sleep. If you are reading, you should read. If you are eating, you should eat. And if you are thinking, then you should think. Never mix the different activities. No good ever comes of it, and what's more, you can't enjoy—neither can you profit from—any of them."

30   Then, because he was playing billiards, he turned back to the table and gave the game his undivided attention once more. He lived by the clock all his life and did everything in strict order: up at sunrise, walk or ride, work until lunch, brief rest, work until tea, recreation, evening work, supper, reading. It had been the same for fifty years.

31   My grandfather was known as the Gaekwar of Baroda, Gaekwar being both a family name and a title. Most of the Indian princes had the hereditary titles of Maharaja ("Great King") or Raja (simply, "Ruler," or "King"), depending on the size, importance, and history of their states. I always knew that my grandfather was a special person but it was only years later, when I knew the full range of his background and accomplishments, that I realized what an extraordinary man he was.

32   He had spent the first twelve years of his life in a village about two hundred miles south of Baroda City. His father, a distant relative of the ruling family, was village headman and earned only a modest living from farming. However, when the previous ruler of Baroda was deposed by the British for misrule, someone from the family had to be chosen as a successor. My grandfather, along with one of his brothers and a cousin, was brought to the capital of the state and presented to the Dowager Maharani of Baroda, the widow of the deposed ruler's father. She was asked by the British to select one of the boys to be the new ruler, and her choice fell upon my grandfather.

33   Since he had been brought up in a village where a sound practical grasp of farming was considered the only necessary knowledge, he could neither read nor write, so the six years following his arrival at the palace were devoted exclusively to his education, and habits were instilled that lasted all his life. He always rose at six o'clock and went

to bed at ten, and with the exception of two hours' riding (considered an essential princely skill), one hour of games of various kinds suitable to his rank, and breaks for meals, the entire day was devoted to work. He learned to read and write in four languages: Marathi, the language of his princely ancestors; Gujarati, the language of the bulk of the population in Baroda; Urdu, the language of his Muslim subjects, employing the Arabic script; and, of course, English. India was still the "brightest jewel" in the British imperial crown, so he had to study English history as well as Indian; beyond that, he received intensive tuition in arithmetic, geography, chemistry, political economy, philosophy, Sanskrit, and something that his tutor called "conversations on given subjects," which was, I suppose, designed to fill any gaps in the small-talk of royal social life.

34   It is astonishing, when I think back on it, that these two people, brought up in such a tradition-ridden atmosphere, married in the customary way by an arrangement between their elders, should have become leaders of change and reform, encouraging new and more liberal ideas in an orthodox society. My grandfather devoted his life to modernizing the state of Baroda, building schools, colleges, libraries, and an outstanding museum and providing an admirable and just administration. He took an enthusiastic interest in everything from commissioning a special translation of *Alice in Wonderland* into Marathi to working for Hindu women's emancipation, even to the point of introducing the revolutionary concept of divorce in Baroda. (My mother used to tease my grandmother, undaunted by her rectitude, about having a husband who was so warm an advocate of divorce. My grandmother tried to be dignified and huffy but was soon overcome by that wonderful silent laugh of hers, her face contorted, her body shaking like a jelly, and not a sound out of her mouth.)

35   My grandfather felt particularly strongly about the inequalities and abuses that had evolved in Indian society and were protected by the caste system. Hindus are born into one of four castes, which are, in descending order, the Brahmins (originally the scholars and priests), the Kshatriyas (warriors and often, as a result of skill in conquest or a reward for success, rulers and large landowners), Vaisyas (usually businessmen, traders, artisans), and Sudras (usually the peasants, though all peasants are not Sudras). In a separate group were those Hindus who were excluded from the ordinary social and religious privileges of Hinduism and were known as Untouchables. They performed the most menial tasks—sweeping streets, cleaning latrines—and thus were thought to carry pollution to caste Hindus.

36   Mahatma Gandhi, in the emotional battle for the acceptance of the Untouchables by Hindu society, acted as their champion, changing their name to Harijans (Loved Ones of God) and insisting that they be allowed access to temples from which they had always been excluded.

Their legal battles were fought for them by one of the most brilliant men in Indian politics, Dr. Bhimrao Ramji Ambedkar, himself a Harijan. Dr. Ambedkar was one of my grandfather's special protégés, encouraged and educated by him when he was a penniless boy. After his long crusade for the advancement of his community, Dr. Ambedkar was appointed chairman of the committee that drafted the Constitution of free India.

37   My grandmother played a strong though less conspicuous part in the life of Baroda State. I can see her so plainly in the mornings, coping with her personal affairs—choosing saris, making up her mind about lengths of silk or cloth of gold that her maids held up, listening attentively to the cooks with menus for the day, giving orders to the tailor, asking about domestic details; in short, supervising the running of an enormous household—and still giving her alert attention to the grievances and complaints of any of her women subjects, whether it was the illness of a child or a dispute in a family about the inheritance of land.

38   This was all part of a maharani's duty, and so were the more ceremonial occasions, as when she presided over formal durbars in the women's apartments of the Baroda Palace. I especially remember the first one I saw, her birthday durbar. All the wives and womenfolk of the nobility and the great landowners were assembled in their richest clothes and jewellery to pay homage to my grandmother. She was seated on a *gaddi,* a cushioned throne, and wore a sari made of rose-pink cloth of gold, draped in the Maratha way with a pleated train between the legs.

39   Along with her dazzling sari, my grandmother wore all the traditional jewellery for this occasion, including heavy diamond anklets and a wealth of diamond rings on her fingers and toes. The noble ladies paid their respects to her with a formal folding of hands in a *namaskar* and offered her the traditional gold coin to signify their allegiance. At the end of the hall was a troupe of musicians and dancers from Tanjore in south India. Like many Indian princes, my grandfather maintained the troupe as palace retainers, and they always gave a performance of the classical south Indian dancing called *bharata natyam* at any important palace occasion. At such festive times, the family all ate off gold *thals,* while everyone else ate off silver. (This distinction always used to embarrass me.)

40   My mother, Princess Indira Gaekwar of Baroda, was the only daughter of these two extraordinary people. Because of their advanced views on education, she was one of the first Indian princesses to go to school and to graduate from Baroda College. She also accompanied her parents on their trips to England. One of the earliest stories I know about her tells how she and her four brothers, all quite small and dressed identically in white pyjama trousers and brocade jackets, with

gold-embroidered caps, were taken to Buckingham Palace to be presented to Queen Victoria. As they stood before her, the elderly Queen-Empress asked which one was the little girl. Five pairs of dark brown eyes stared back at her, and then, because they all enjoyed fooling grown-ups, one of the boys stepped forward. But they underestimated Queen Victoria, who, sensing that something was wrong, walked around to the back of the row of solemn children, and there a long black pigtail betrayed my mother.

41   It is difficult to describe my mother without slipping into unconvincing superlatives. She was, quite simply, the most beautiful and exciting woman any of us knew. Even now, when I have travelled widely and have met many famous beauties from all levels of society, she remains in my memory as an unparalleled combination of wit, warmth, and exquisite looks. She was photographed and painted many times, but while those pictures show the physical charm—the enormous eyes, the lovely modelling of her face, the slightly drooping mouth that made you want to make her smile, the tiny fragile figure—none of them captures the electric vitality that made her the focus of attention wherever she went. Her own passionate interest and concern for others made her both special and accessible to anybody. She was always called "Ma," not only by us but by friends and even by the peasants of Cooch Behar. As a child I was fascinated by her—what she said, what she did, what she wore. With her, nothing was ever dull and one felt that at any moment anything might happen.

42   She herself was oddly unaware of the impression she created, and this, I suppose, was due to her mother's fear, during her childhood, that she might become spoiled—an only daughter, adored by her father, loved and cherished by her brothers. If anyone commented favourably on my mother's looks, my grandmother would immediately counter the admiration with some deprecating comment like, "Her nose is too lumpy at the end—just look," or, "Her hair hasn't a trace of a curl to it."

43   My mother once told me that she had no idea that she was even passably good-looking until one day when her brothers were discussing some attractive girl they had met. Seeing their sister looking a bit dejected, one of them said, with true brotherly enthusiasm, "You know, you're not all that bad yourself."

44   For the first time she really *looked* at herself in the mirror and thought, Well, he may be right. I'm *not* all that bad.

✧ Evaluating the Text

1. What features of Devi's account give you the clearest idea of what her life was like in the privileged surroundings in which she was raised? What role do the different cultural customs reflected in her account play in Devi's life at the palace?

2. What kinds of things provided her with the most enjoyment? How was she educated and how was she made aware of the special responsibilities that she would have to assume as a member of royalty?

3. What impressions do you get of her grandparents and mother and their influence on her life?

✦ Exploring Different Perspectives

1. In what respects is Devi's childhood similar to and different from that of "the little emperors" in Daniela Deane's account?

2. In what way was Devi's mother as influential as Gayle Pemberton's grandmother was for her (see "Antidisestablishmentarianism")?

✦ Extending Viewpoints through Writing and Research

1. Contained in the panoramic sweep of Devi's description are innumerable fascinating aspects of her everyday life that she touches on but does not explore in depth. Choose one of these and, after doing some research, write a short essay that explains its function in Indian culture.

2. What is the most exotic place you have ever visited? Describe the architecture, everyday rituals, and customs that will bring your reader into this world.

Daniela Deane

The Little Emperors

—————◆—————

Daniela Deane is a staff writer who specializes in real estate for the Washington Post. *"The Little Emperors," which first appeared in the* Los Angeles Times Magazine, *July 26, 1992, describes the consequences of China's population management program that encourages couples to marry late and have only one child. Faced with a staggering doubling of the population during Mao Zedong's (Tse-tung's) rule, China, the world's most populous country, with 1.16 billion people, has for the most part adhered to this one-child policy for urban dwellers while allowing rural couples two children.*

Before You Read

As you read this article, underline what you consider to be the key points in Deane's analysis. In the margins, note your responses to what she says, including examples that illustrate or contradict her position.

—————◆—————

1   Xu Ming sits on the worn sofa with his short, chubby arms and legs splayed, forced open by fat and the layers of padded clothing worn in northern China to ward off the relentless chill. To reach the floor, the tubby 8-year-old rocks back and forth on his big bottom, inching forward slowly, eventually ending upright. Xu Ming finds it hard to move.

2   "He got fat when he was about 3," says his father, Xu Jianguo, holding the boy's bloated, dimpled hand. "We were living with my parents and they were very good to him. He's the only grandson. It's a tradition in China that boys are very loved. They love him very much, and so they feed him a lot. They give him everything he wants."

3   Xu Ming weighs 135 pounds, about twice what he should at his age. He's one of hundreds of children who have sought help in the past few years at the Beijing Children's Hospital, which recently began the first American-style fat farm for obese children in what was once the land of skin and bones.

4   "We used to get a lot of cases of malnutrition," says Dr. Ni Guichen, director of endocrinology at the hospital and founder of the weight reduction classes. "But in the last 10 years, the problem has become obese children. The number of fat children in China is growing

very fast. The main reason is the one-child policy," she says, speaking in a drab waiting room. "Because parents can only have one child, the families take extra good care of that one child, which means feeding him too much."

5   Bulging waistlines are one result of China's tough campaign to curb its population. The one-child campaign, a strict national directive that seeks to limit each Chinese couple to a single son or daughter, has other dramatic consequences: millions of abortions, fewer girls and a generation of spoiled children.

6   The 10-day weight-reduction sessions—a combination of exercise, nutritional guidance and psychological counseling—are very popular. Hundreds of children—some so fat they can hardly walk—are turned away for each class.

7   According to Ni, about 5% of children in China's cities are obese, with two obese boys for every overweight girl, the traditional preference toward boys being reflected in the amount of attention lavished on the child. "Part of the course is also centered on the parents. We try to teach them how to bring their children up properly, not just by spoiling them," Ni says.

8   Ming's father is proud that his son, after two sessions at the fat farm, has managed to halve his intake of *jiaozi*, the stodgy meat-filled dumplings that are Ming's particular weakness, from 30 to 15 at a sitting. "Even if he's not full, that's all he gets," he says. "In the beginning, it was very difficult. He would put his arms around our necks and beg us for more food. We couldn't bear it, so we'd give him a little more."

9   Ming lost a few pounds but hasn't been able to keep the weight off. He's a bit slimmer now, but only because he's taller. "I want to lose weight," says Ming, who spends his afternoons snacking at his grandparents' house and his evenings plopped in front of the television set at home. "The kids make fun of me, they call me a fat pig. I hate the nicknames. In sports class, I can't do what the teacher says. I can run a little bit, but after a while I have to sit down. The teacher puts me at the front of the class where all the other kids can see me. They all laugh and make fun of me."

10   The many fat children visible on China's city streets are just the most obvious example of 13 years of the country's one-child policy. In the vast countryside, the policy has meant shadowy lives as second-class citizens for thousands of girls, or, worse, death. It has made abortion a way of life and a couple's sexual intimacy the government's concern. Even women's menstrual cycles are monitored. Under the directive, couples literally have to line up for permission to procreate. Second children are sometimes possible, but only on payment of a heavy fine.

11   The policy is an unparalleled intrusion into the private lives of a nation's citizens, an experiment on a scale never attempted elsewhere

in the world. But no expert will argue that China—by far the world's most populous country with 1.16 billion people—could continue without strict curbs on its population.

12   China's communist government adopted the one-child policy in 1979 in response to the staggering doubling of the country's population during Mao Tse-tung's rule. Mao, who died in 1976, was convinced that the country's masses were a strategic asset and vigorously encouraged the Chinese to produce even-larger families.

13   But large families are now out for the Chinese—20% of the world's population living on just 7% of the arable land. "China has to have a population policy," says Huang Baoshan, deputy director of the State Family Planning Commission. With the numbers ever growing, "how can we feed them, house them?"

14   Dinner time for one 5-year-old girl consists of granddad chasing her through the house, bowl and spoon in hand, barking like a dog or mewing like a cat. If he performs authentically enough, she rewards him by accepting a mouthful of food. No problem, insists granddad, "it's good exercise for her."

15   An 11-year-old boy never gets up to go to the toilet during the night. That's because his mother, summoned by a shout, gets up instead and positions a bottle under the covers for him. "We wouldn't want him to have to get up in the night," his mother says.

16   Another mother wanted her 16-year-old to eat some fruit, but the teen-ager was engrossed in a video game. Not wanting him to get his fingers sticky or daring to interrupt, she peeled several grapes and popped one after another into his mouth. "Not so fast," he snapped. "Can't you see I have to spit out the seeds?"

17   Stories like these are routinely published in China's newspapers, evidence that the government-imposed birth-control policy has produced an emerging generation of spoiled, lazy, selfish, self-centered and overweight children. There are about 40 million only children in China. Dubbed the country's "Little Emperors," their behavior toward their elders is likened to that of the young emperor Pu Yi, who heaped indignities on his eunuch servants while making them cater to his whims, as chronicled in Bernardo Bertolucci's film *The Last Emperor.*

18   Many studies on China's only children have been done. One such study confirmed that only children generally are not well liked. The study, conducted by a team of Chinese psychologists, asked a group of 360 Chinese children, half who have siblings and half who don't, to rate each other's behavior. The only children were, without fail, the least popular, regardless of age or social background. Peers rated them more uncooperative and selfish than children with brothers and sisters. They bragged more, were less helpful in group activities and more apt to follow their own selfish interests. And they wouldn't share their toys.

19   The Chinese lay a lot of blame on what they call the "4-2-1" syndrome—four doting grandparents, two overindulgent parents, all pinning their hopes and ambitions on one child.

20   Besides stuffing them with food, Chinese parents have very high expectations of their one *bao bei,* or treasured object. Some have their still-in-strollers babies tested for IQ levels. Others try to teach toddlers Tang Dynasty poetry. Many shell out months of their hard-earned salaries for music lessons and instruments for children who have no talent or interest in playing. They fill their kids' lives with lessons in piano, English, gymnastics and typing.

21   The one-child parents, most of them from traditionally large Chinese families, grew up during the chaotic, 10-year Cultural Revolution, when many of the country's cultural treasures were destroyed and schools were closed for long periods of time. Because many of that generation spent years toiling in the fields rather than studying, they demand—and put all their hopes into—academic achievement for their children.

22   "We've already invested a lot of money in his intellectual development," Wang Zhouzhi told me in her Spartan home in a tiny village of Changping country outside Beijing, discussing her son, Chenqian, an only child. "I don't care how much money we spend on him. We've bought him an organ and we push him hard. Unfortunately, he's only a mediocre student," she says, looking toward the 10-year-old boy. Chenqian, dressed in a child-sized Chinese army uniform, ate 10 pieces of candy during the half-hour interview and repeatedly fired off his toy pistol, all without a word of reproach from his mother.

23   Would Chenqian have liked a sibling to play with? "No," he answers loudly, firing a rapid, jarring succession of shots. His mother breaks in: "If he had a little brother or sister, he wouldn't get everything he wants. Of course he doesn't want one. With only one child, I give my full care and concern to him."

24   But how will these children, now entering their teen-age years and moving quickly toward adulthood, become the collectivist-minded citizens China's hard-line communist leadership demands? Some think they never will. Ironically, it may be just these overindulged children who will change Chinese society. After growing up doing as they wished, ruling their immediate families, they're not likely to obey a central government that tells them to fall in line. This new generation of egotists, who haven't been taught to take even their parents into consideration, simply may not be able to think of the society as a whole— the basic principle of communism.

25   The need for family planning is obvious in the cities, where living space is limited and the one-child policy is strictly enforced and largely successful. City dwellers are slowly beginning to accept the notion that

smaller families are better for the country, although most would certainly want two children if they could have them. However, in the countryside, where three of every four Chinese live—nearly 900 million people—the goal of limiting each couple to only one child has proved largely elusive.

26   In the hinterlands, the policy has become a confusing patchwork of special cases and exceptions. Provincial authorities can decide which couples can have a second child. In the southern province of Guangdong, China's richest, two children are allowed and many couples can afford to pay the fine to have even a third or fourth child. The amounts of the fines vary across the country, the highest in populous Sichuan province, where the fine for a second child can be as much as 25% of a family's income over four years. Special treatment has been given to China's cultural minorities such as the Mongolians and the Tibetans because of their low numbers. Many of them are permitted three or four children without penalty, although some Chinese social scientists have begun to question the privilege.

27   "It's really become a two-child policy in the countryside," says a Western diplomat. "Because of the traditional views on labor supply, the traditional bias toward the male child, it's been impossible for them to enforce a one-child policy outside the cities. In the countryside, they're really trying to stop that third child."

28   Thirteen years of strict family planning have created one of the great mysteries of the vast and remote Chinese countryside: Where have all the little girls gone? A Swedish study of sex ratios in China, published in 1990, and based on China's own census data, concluded that several million little girls are "missing"—up to half a million a year in the years 1985 to 1987—since the policy was introduced in late 1979.

29   In the study, and in demographic research worldwide, sex ratio at birth in humans is shown to be very stable, between 105 and 106 boys for every 100 girls. The imbalance is thought to be nature's way of compensating for the higher rates of miscarriage, stillbirth and infant mortality among boys.

30   In China, the ratio climbed consistently during the 1980s, and it now rests at more than 110 boys to 100 girls. "The imbalance is evident in some areas of the country," says Stirling Scruggs, director of the United Nations Population Fund in China. "I don't think the reason is widespread infanticide. They're adopting out girls to try for a boy, they're hiding their girls, they're not registering them. Throughout Chinese history, in times of famine, and now as well, people have been forced to make choices between boys and girls, and for many reasons, boys always win out."

31   With the dismantling of collectives, families must, once again, farm their own small plots and sons are considered necessary to do the work. Additionally, girls traditionally "marry out" of their families,

transferring their filial responsibilities to their in-laws. Boys carry on the family name and are entrusted with the care of their parents as they age. In the absence of a social security system, having a son is the difference between starving and eating when one is old. To combat the problem, some innovative villages have begun issuing so-called girl insurance, an old-age insurance policy for couples who have given birth to a daughter and are prepared to stop at that.

32   "People are scared to death to be childless and penniless in their old age," says William Hinton, an American author of seven books chronicling modern China. "So if they don't have a son, they immediately try for another. When the woman is pregnant, they'll have a sex test to see if it's a boy or a girl. They'll abort a girl, or go in hiding with the girl, or pay the fine, or bribe the official or leave home. Anything. It's a game of wits."

33   Shen Shufen, a sturdy, round-faced peasant woman of 33, has two children—an 8-year-old girl and a 3-year-old boy—and lives in Sihe, a dusty, one-road, mud-brick village in the countryside outside Beijing. Her husband is a truck driver. "When we had our girl, we knew we had to have another child somehow. We saved for years to pay the fine. It was hard giving them that money, 3,000 yuan ($550 in U.S. dollars), in one night. That's what my husband makes in three years. I was so happy when our second child was a boy."

34   The government seems aware of the pressure its policies put on expectant parents, and the painful results, but has not shown any flexibility. For instance, Beijing in 1990 passed a law forbidding doctors to tell a couple the results of ultrasound tests that disclose the sex of their unborn child. The reason: Too many female embryos were being aborted.

35   And meanwhile, several hundred thousand women—called "guerrilla moms"—go into hiding every year to have their babies. They become part of China's 40-million-strong floating population that wanders the country, mostly in search of work, sleeping under bridges and in front of railway stations. Tens of thousands of female children are simply abandoned in rural hospitals.

36   And although most experts say female infanticide is not widespread, it does exist. "I found a dead baby girl," says Hinton. "We stopped for lunch at this mountain ravine in Shaanxi province. We saw her lying there, at the bottom of the creek bed. She was all bundled up, with one arm sticking out. She had been there a while, you could tell, because she had a little line of mold growing across her mouth and nostrils."

37   Death comes in another form, too: neglect. "It's female neglect, more than female infanticide, neglect to the point of death for little girls," says Scruggs of the U.N. Population Fund. "If you have a sick child, and it's a girl," he says, "you might buy only half the dose of medicine she needs to get better."

38   Hundreds of thousands of unregistered little girls—called "black children"—live on the edge of the law, unable to get food rations, immunizations or places in school. Many reports are grim. The government-run China News Service reported last year that the drowning of baby girls had revived to such an extent in Guangxi province that at least 1 million boys will be unable to find wives in 20 years. And partly because of the gender imbalance, the feudalistic practice of selling women has been revived.

39   The alarming growth of the flesh trade prompted authorities to enact a law in January that imposes jail sentences of up to 10 years and heavy fines for people caught trafficking. The government also recently began broadcasting a television dramatization to warn women against the practice. The public-service message shows two women, told that they would be given high-paying jobs, being lured to a suburban home. Instead, they are locked in a small, dark room, and soon realize that they have been sold.

40   Li Wangping is nervous. She keeps looking at the air vents at the bottom of the office door, to see if anyone is walking by or, worse still, standing there listening. She rubs her hands together over and over. She speaks in a whisper. "I'm afraid to get into trouble talking to you," Li confides. She says nothing for a few minutes.

41   "After my son was born, I desperately wanted another baby," the 42-year-old woman finally begins. "I just wanted to have more children, you understand? Anyway, I got pregnant three times, because I wasn't using any birth control. I didn't want to use any. So, I had to have three abortions, one right after the other. I didn't want to at all. It was terrible killing the babies I wanted so much. But I had to."

42   By Chinese standards, Li (not her real name) has a lot to lose if she chooses to follow her maternal yearnings. As an office worker at government-owned CITIC, a successful and dynamic conglomerate, she has one of the best jobs in Beijing. Just being a city dweller already puts her ahead of most of the population.

43   "One of my colleagues had just gotten fired for having a second child. I couldn't afford to be fired," continues Li, speaking in a meeting room at CITIC headquarters. "I had to keep everything secret from the family-planning official at CITIC, from everyone at the office. Of course, I'm supposed to be using birth control. I had to lie. It was hard lying, because I felt so bad about everything."

44   She rubs her hands furiously and moves toward the door, staring continuously at the air slats. "I have to go now. There's more to say, but I'm afraid to tell you. They could find me."

45   China's family-planning officials wield awesome powers, enforcing the policy through a combination of incentives and deterrents. For those who comply, there are job promotions and small cash awards.

For those who resist, they suffer stiff fines and loss of job and status within the country's tightly knit and heavily regulated communities. The State Family Planning Commission is the government ministry entrusted with the tough task of curbing the growth of the world's most populous country, where 28 children are born every minute. It employs about 200,000 full-time officials and uses more than a million volunteers to check the fertility of hundreds of millions of Chinese women.

46   "Every village or enterprise has at least one family-planning official," says Zhang Xizhi, a birth-control official in Changping county outside Beijing. "Our main job is propaganda work to raise people's consciousness. We educate people and tell them their options for birth control. We go down to every household to talk to people. We encourage them to have only one child, to marry late, to have their child later."

47   Population police frequently keep records of the menstrual cycles of women of childbearing age, on the type of birth control they use and the pending applications to have children. If they slip up, street committees—half-governmental, half-civilian organizations that have sprung up since the 1949 communist takeover—take up the slack. The street committees, made up mostly of retired volunteers, act as the central government's ear to the ground, snooping, spying and reporting on citizens to the authorities.

48   When a couple wants to have a child—even their first, allotted one—they must apply to the family-planning office in their township or workplace, literally lining up to procreate. "If a woman gets pregnant without permission, she and her husband will get fined, even if it's their first," Zhang says. "It is fair to fine her, because she creates a burden on the whole society by jumping her place in line."

49   If a woman in Nanshao township, where Zhang works, becomes pregnant with a second child, she must terminate her pregnancy unless she or her husband or their first child is disabled or if both parents are only children. Her local family-planning official will repeatedly visit her at home to pressure her to comply. "Sometimes I have to go to people's homes five or six times to explain everything to them over and over to get them to have an abortion," says Zhang Cuiqing, the family-planning official for Sihe village, where there are 2,900 married women of childbearing age, of which 2,700 use some sort of birth control. Of those, 570 are sterilized and 1,100 have IUDs. Zhang recites the figures proudly, adding, "If they refuse, they will be fined between 20,000 and 50,000 yuan (U.S. $3,700 to $9,500)." The average yearly wage in Sihe is 1,500 yuan ($285).

50   The lack of early sexual education and unreliable IUDs are combining to make abortion—which is free, as are condoms and IUDs—a cornerstone of the one-child policy. Local officials are told not to use force, but rather education and persuasion, to meet their targets. However,

the desire to fulfill their quotas, coupled with pressure from their bosses in Beijing, can lead to abuses by overzealous officials.

51   "Some local family-planning officials are running amok, because of the targets they have to reach," a Western health specialist says, "and there are a bunch of people willing to turn a blind eye to abuses because the target is so important."

50   The official *Shanghai Legal Daily* last year reported on a family-planning committee in central Sichuan province that ordered the flogging of the husbands of 10 pregnant women who refused to have abortions. According to the newspaper, the family-planning workers marched the husbands one by one into an empty room, ordered them to strip and lie on the floor and then beat them with a stick, once for every day their wives were pregnant.

53   "In some places, yes, things do happen," concedes Huang of the State Family Planning Commission. "Sometimes, family-planning officials do carry it too far."

54   The young woman lies still on the narrow table with her eyes shut and her legs spread while the doctor quickly performs a suction abortion. A few moments, and the fetus is removed. The woman lets out a short, sharp yell. "OK, next," the doctor says.

55   She gets off the table and, holding a piece of cloth between her legs to catch the blood and clutching her swollen womb, hobbles over to a bed and collapses. The next patient gets up and walks toward the abortion table. No one notices a visitor watching. "It's very quick, it only takes about five minutes per abortion," says Dr. Huang Xiaomiao, chief physician at Beijing's Maternity Hospital. "No anesthetic. We don't use anesthetic for abortions or births here. Only for Cesarean sections, we use acupuncture."

56   Down the hall, 32-year-old Wu Guobin waits to be taken into the operating room to have her Fallopian tubes untied—a reversal of an earlier sterilization. "After my son was killed in an accident last year, the authorities in my province said I could try for another." In the bed next to Wu's, a dour-faced woman looks ready to cry. "She's getting sterilized," the nurse explains. "Her husband doesn't want her to, but her first child has mental problems."

57   Although it's a maternity hospital, the Family Planning Unit— where abortions, sterilizations, IUD insertions and the like are carried out—is the busiest department. "We do more abortions than births," says Dr. Fan Huimin, head of the unit. "Between 10 and 20 a day."

58   Abortions are a way of life in China, where about 10.5 million pregnancies are terminated each year. (In the United States, 1.6 million abortions are performed a year, but China's population is four to five times greater than the United States'.) One fetus is aborted for about

every two children born and Chinese women often have several abortions. Usually, abortions are performed during the first trimester. But because some women resist, only to cave in under mental bullying further into their terms, abortions are also done in the later months of pregnancy, sometimes up till the eighth month.

59   Because of their population problem, the Chinese have become pioneers in contraceptive research. China will soon launch its own version of the controversial French abortion pill RU-486, which induces a miscarriage. They have perfected a non-scalpel procedure for male sterilization, with no suture required, allowing the man to "ride his bicycle home within five minutes." This year, the government plans to spend more than the $34 million it spent last year on contraception. The state will also buy some 961 million condoms to be distributed throughout the country, 11% more than in 1991.

60   But even with a family-planning policy that sends a chill down a Westerner's spine and touches every Chinese citizen's life, 64,000 babies are born every day in China and overpopulation continues to be a paramount national problem. Officials have warned that 24 million children will be born in 1992—a number just slightly less than the population of Canada. "The numbers are staggering," says Scruggs, the U.N. Population Fund official, noting that "170 million people will be added in the 1990s, which is the current population of England, France and Italy combined. There are places in China where the land can't feed that many more people as it is."

61   China estimates that it has prevented 200 million births since the one-child policy was introduced. Women now are having an average of 2.4 children as compared to six in the late '60s. But the individual sacrifice demanded from every Chinese is immense.

62   Large billboards bombard the population with images of happy families with only one child. The government is desperately trying to convince the masses that producing only one child leads to a wealthier, healthier and happier life. But foreigners in China tell a different story, that the people aren't convinced. They tell of being routinely approached—on the markets, on the streets, on the railway and asked about the contraceptive policies of their countries. Expatriate women in Beijing all tell stories of Chinese women enviously asking them how many sons they have and how many children they plan to have. They explain that they only have one child because the government allows them only one.

63   "When I'm out with my three children on the weekend," says a young American father who lives in Beijing, "people are always asking me why am I allowed to have three children. You can feel when they ask you that there is envy there. There's a natural disappointment among the people. They just want to have more children. But there's a resigned understanding, an acceptance that they just can't."

✧ Evaluating the Text

1. How has the one-child policy affected the ratio of the sexes of children? What Chinese cultural values and economic forces are responsible for the preference for boys?

2. How do the experiences of the parents help explain the kinds of expectations and hopes they have attached to their "little emperors"?

3. In your view, what will be the effects on Chinese society when this new generation of "little emperors" becomes adult? How does the way in which they have been raised create a potential conflict with the collectivist value system underlying Chinese society?

✧ Exploring Different Perspectives

1. Compare and contrast the effects on children in indulgent environments such as those described by Deane and by Gayatri Devi in "A Princess Remembers."

2. How do the issues of who one marries (or doesn't) result from the different political environments in Deane's account of contemporary China and in Steve Sailer's analysis of modern-day Iraq in "The Cousin Marriage Conundrum"?

✧ Extending Viewpoints through Writing and Research

1. What picture do you get of the extent to which the government in China intrudes into the everyday life of the Chinese citizen?

2. If you are an only child, to what extent have you been treated similarly to the only children in China? Have you wished that you had brothers and/or sisters? Why or why not? If you have siblings, would you have preferred to be an only child? Explain your reactions.

3. The current results of the one-child policy in China are analyzed at http://www.researchmatters.harvard.edu/story.php?article_id =767 and http://www.theglitteringeye.com/archives/000939.html.

Connecting Cultures

———◆———

Gayle Pemberton, "Antidisestablishmentarianism"

In what ways do the grandmothers of Pemberton and Mary Crow Dog (see "Civilize Them with a Stick," in Chapter 5) offer advice and a historical perspective on racism in American culture?

Amy Tan, "The Language of Discretion"

What insights do Tan and Kyoko Mori in "Polite Lies" (Chapter 7) give into the role that unspoken rules play in conversation in Asian cultures?

John Cheever, "Reunion"

Compare the reasons why the son in Cheever's story and the daughter in Hanan Al-Shaykh's "The Persian Carpet" (Chapter 2) are estranged from a parent.

Fritz Peters, "Boyhood with Gurdjieff"

What insights that involve money do Peters's essay and Helena Norberg-Hodge's "Learning from Ladakh" in Chapter 4 offer?

Steve Sailer, "The Cousin Marriage Conundrum"

How are the principles governing marriage in Iraq, according to Sailer, very different from those in Japan (see Nicholas Bornoff's "The Marriage Go-Round" in Chapter 3)?

Gayatri Devi, "A Princess Remembers"

Contrast the very different life experiences and social perspectives in India offered by Devi and Viramma in "A Pariah's Life" (Chapter 5).

Daniela Deane, "The Little Emperors"

What unexpected similarities can you find in child-centered societies described by Deane and by Eric Schlosser in "Kid Kustomers" (Chapter 6)?

2
Turning Points

*The old believe everything. The middle-aged suspect everything.
The young know everything.*
> —Oscar Wilde (1854–1900), *The Picture
> of Dorian Gray* (1891)

———————————◆———————————

In virtually every society, certain rites or ceremonies are used to signal adulthood. Although many of these occasions are informal, some are quite elaborate and dramatic. This chapter offers a range of perspectives that illustrate how such turning points are marked by informal and formal rituals across a broad spectrum of cultures. These moments within insight may be private psychological turning points of ceremonies that initiate the individual into adulthood within a community. These crucial moments, in which individuals move from childhood innocence to adult awareness, often involve learning a particular society's rules governing what should or should not be done under different circumstances—as well as values, knowledge, and expectations as to how one should present oneself in a wide variety of situations.

These turning points often occur during adolescence, when we explore the limits of what society will and will not allow us to do. This is the time in which rebellion and defiance against society's rules take place. We acquire societal norms through imitation and instruction into what behavior patterns our society deems acceptable or unacceptable. From internalizing these values we get a sense of personal and social identity. This is often the time when we form our first voluntary associations or friendships and discover our capacity to trust and develop relationships, both strong or fragile, that can lead to reward or disappointment.

In some cases, belonging to a group, association, fraternity, or sorority involves passing some initiation or test to gain acceptance. Because this chapter is rich in a wide variety of perspectives, it invites you to make discoveries about the turning points in your own life.

The essays and short work of fiction in this chapter focus on the psychological and cultural forces that shape the identity of those who are about to be initiated into their respective communities. The Chinese-American writer Sucheng Chan describes with honesty and humor her struggle to confront her disabilities, in "You're Short, Besides!" From Ireland, we read the moving narrative of Christy Brown, who, in "The Letter 'A'," describes his struggle to communicate signs of intelligence by drawing the letter 'A' with his left foot after having been diagnosed as hopelessly retarded by cerebral palsy. The Lebanese writer, Hanan Al-Shaykh, tells a story—"The Persian Carpet"—of a moment of discovery that permanently alters the relationship between a girl and her mother. The German writer Sabine Reichel, in her essay "Learning What Was Never Taught," tells of the difficulties she faced in finding out about the Holocaust from her teachers. The international French explorer, Douchan Gersi, offers a hair-raising account appropriately titled "Initiated into an Iban Tribe of Headhunters," a firsthand narrative based on his experiences in modern-day Borneo. In "Chopsticks" Guanlong Cao provides an appreciative analysis of the importance of hand-made chopsticks that could serve as a romantic gift. Germaine Greer, in "One Man's Mutilation Is Another Man's Beautification," addresses the issue of extreme body decoration in cultures around the world.

Sucheng Chan

You're Short, Besides!

————◆————

Sucheng Chan graduated from Swarthmore College in 1963 and received an M.A. from the University of Hawaii in 1965. In 1973 she earned a Ph.D. from the University of California at Berkeley, where she subsequently taught for a decade. She is currently professor of history and chair of Asian-American studies at the University of California at Santa Barbara. Her works include Quiet Odyssey: A Pioneer Korean Woman in America *(1990) and the award-winning* The Asian Americans: An Interpretive History *(1991). "You're Short, Besides!" first appeared in* Making Waves: An Anthology of Writing by and about Asian-American Women *(1989). In recent years, she has served as the editor of numerous collections, including* Remapping Asian American History *(2001). She is the author of* In Defense of Asian American Studies *(2005).*

Before You Read

Consider to what extent culture shapes concepts of normalcy and disability and the ways in which Asian cultures in Chan's view differ from Western ones.

————◆————

1 When asked to write about being a physically handicapped Asian American woman, I considered it an insult. After all, my accomplishments are many, yet I was not asked to write about any of them. Is being handicapped the most salient feature about me? The fact that it might be in the eyes of others made me decide to write the essay as requested. I realized that the way I think about myself may differ considerably from the way others perceive me. And maybe that's what being physically handicapped is all about.

2 I was stricken simultaneously with pneumonia and polio at the age of four. Uncertain whether I had polio of the lungs, seven of the eight doctors who attended me—all practitioners of Western medicine—told my parents they should not feel optimistic about my survival. A Chinese fortune teller my mother consulted also gave a grim prognosis, but for an entirely different reason: I had been stricken because my name was offensive to the gods. My grandmother had named me "grandchild of wisdom," a name that the fortune teller said was too presumptuous for a girl. So he advised my parents to change

my name to "chaste virgin." All these pessimistic predictions notwith-standing, I hung onto life, if only by a thread. For three years, my body was periodically pierced with electric shocks as the muscles of my legs atrophied. Before my illness, I had been an active, rambunctious, pre-cocious, and very curious child. Being confined to bed was thus a men-tal agony as great as my physical pain. Living in war-torn China, I received little medical attention; physical therapy was unheard of. But I was determined to walk. So one day, when I was six or seven, I in-structed my mother to set up two rows of chairs to face each other so that I could use them as I would parallel bars. I attempted to walk by holding my body up and moving it forward with my arms while drag-ging my legs along behind. Each time I fell, my mother gasped, but I badgered her until she let me try again. After four nonambulatory years, I finally walked once more by pressing my hands against my thighs so my knees wouldn't buckle.

3   My father had been away from home during most of those years because of the war. When he returned, I had to confront the guilt he felt about my condition. In many East Asian cultures, there is a strong folk belief that a person's physical state in this life is a reflection of how morally or sinfully he or she lived in previous lives. Furthermore, be-cause of the tendency to view the family as a single unit, it is believed that the fate of one member can be caused by the behavior of another. Some of my father's relatives told him that my illness had doubtless been caused by the wild carousing he did in his youth. A well-meaning but somewhat simple man, my father believed them.

4   Throughout my childhood, he sometimes apologized to me for having to suffer retribution for his former bad behavior. This upset me; it was bad enough that I had to deal with the anguish of not being able to walk, but to have to assuage his guilt as well was a real burden! In other ways, my father was very good to me. He took me out often, car-rying me on his shoulders or back, to give me fresh air and sunshine. He did this until I was too large and heavy for him to carry. And ever since I can remember, he has told me that I am pretty.

5   After getting over her anxieties about my constant falls, my mother decided to send me to school. I had already learned to read some words of Chinese at the age of three by asking my parents to teach me the sounds and meaning of various characters in the daily newspaper. But between the ages of four and eight, I received no edu-cation since just staying alive was a full-time job. Much to her chagrin, my mother found no school in Shanghai, where we lived at the time, which would accept me as a student. Finally, as a last resort, she ap-proached the American School, which agreed to enroll me only if my family kept an *amah* (a servant who takes care of children) by my side at all times. The tuition at the school was twenty U.S. dollars per month—a huge sum of money during those years of runaway inflation

in China—and payable only in U.S. dollars. My family afforded the high cost of tuition and the expense of employing a full-time *amah* for less than a year.

6   We left China as the Communist forces swept across the country in victory. We found an apartment in Hong Kong across the street from a school run by Seventh-Day Adventists. By that time I could walk a little, so the principal was persuaded to accept me. An *amah* now had to take care of me only during recess when my classmates might easily knock me over as they ran about the playground.

7   After a year and a half in Hong Kong, we moved to Malaysia, where my father's family had lived for four generations. There I learned to swim in the lovely warm waters of the tropics and fell in love with the sea. On land I was a cripple; in the ocean I could move with the grace of a fish. I liked the freedom of being in the water so much that many years later, when I was a graduate student in Hawaii, I became greatly enamored with a man just because he called me a "Polynesian water nymph."

8   As my overall health improved, my mother became less anxious about all aspects of my life. She did everything possible to enable me to lead as normal a life as possible. I remember how once some of her colleagues in the high school where she taught criticized her for letting me wear short skirts. They felt my legs should not be exposed to public view. My mother's response was, "All girls her age wear short skirts, so why shouldn't she?"

9   The years in Malaysia were the happiest of my childhood, even though I was constantly fending off children who ran after me calling, *"Baikah! Baikah!"* ("Cripple! Cripple!" in the Hokkien dialect commonly spoken in Malaysia). The taunts of children mattered little because I was a star pupil. I won one award after another for general scholarship as well as for art and public speaking. Whenever the school had important visitors my teacher always called on me to recite in front of the class.

10   A significant event that marked me indelibly occurred when I was twelve. That year my school held a music recital and I was one of the students chosen to play the piano. I managed to get up the steps to the stage without any problem, but as I walked across the stage, I fell. Out of the audience, a voice said loudly and clearly, "Ayah! A *baikah* shouldn't be allowed to perform in public." I got up before anyone could get on stage to help me and, with tears streaming uncontrollably down my face, I rushed to the piano and began to play. Beethoven's "Für Elise" had never been played so fiendishly fast before or since, but I managed to finish the whole piece. That I managed to do so made me feel really strong. I never again feared ridicule.

11   In later years I was reminded of this experience from time to time. During my fourth year as an assistant professor at the University of

California at Berkeley, I won a distinguished teaching award. Some weeks later I ran into a former professor who congratulated me enthusiastically. But I said to him, "You know what? I became a distinguished teacher by *limping* across the stage of Dwinelle 155!" (Dwinelle 155 is a large, cold, classroom that most colleagues of mine hate to teach in.) I was rude not because I lacked graciousness but because this man, who had told me that my dissertation was the finest piece of work he had read in fifteen years, had nevertheless advised me to eschew a teaching career.

12   "Why?" I asked.

13   "Your leg . . ." he responded.

14   "What about my leg?" I said, puzzled.

15   "Well, how would you feel standing in front of a large lecture class?"

16   "If it makes any difference, I want you to know I've won a number of speech contests in my life, and I am not the least bit self-conscious about speaking in front of large audiences. . . . Look, why don't you write me a letter of recommendation to tell people how brilliant I am, and let *me* worry about my leg!"

17   This incident is worth recounting only because it illustrates a dilemma that handicapped persons face frequently: those who care about us sometimes get so protective that they unwittingly limit our growth. This former professor of mine had been one of my greatest supporters for two decades. Time after time, he had written glowing letters of recommendation on my behalf. He had spoken as he did because he thought he had my best interest at heart; he thought that if I got a desk job rather than one that required me to be a visible, public person, I would be spared the misery of being stared at.

18   Americans, for the most part, do not believe as Asians do that physically handicapped persons are morally flawed. But they are equally inept at interacting with those of us who are not able-bodied. Cultural differences in the perception and treatment of handicapped people are most clearly expressed by adults. Children, regardless of where they are, tend to be openly curious about people who do not look "normal." Adults in Asia have no hesitation in asking visibly handicapped people what is wrong with them, often expressing their sympathy with looks of pity, whereas adults in the United States try desperately to be polite by pretending not to notice.

19   One interesting response I often elicited from people in Asia but have never encountered in America is the attempt to link my physical condition to the state of my soul. Many a time while living and traveling in Asia people would ask me what religion I belonged to. I would tell them that my mother is a devout Buddhist, that my father was baptized a Catholic but has never practiced Catholicism, and that I am an agnostic. Upon hearing this, people would try strenuously to convert

me to their religion so that whichever God they believed in could bless me. If I would only attend this church or that temple regularly, they urged, I would surely get cured. Catholics and Buddhists alike have pressed religious medallions into my palm, telling me if I would wear these, the relevant deity or saint would make me well. Once while visiting the tomb of Muhammad Ali Jinnah in Karachi, Pakistan, an old Muslim, after finishing his evening prayers, spotted me, gestured toward my legs, raised his arms heavenward, and began a new round of prayers, apparently on my behalf.

20   In the United States adults who try to act "civilized" toward handicapped people by pretending they don't notice anything unusual sometimes end up ignoring handicapped people completely. In the first few months I lived in this country, I was struck by the fact that whenever children asked me what was the matter with my leg, their adult companions would hurriedly shush them up, furtively look at me, mumble apologies, and rush their children away. After a few months of such encounters, I decided it was my responsibility to educate these people. So I would say to the flustered adults, "It's okay, let the kid ask." Turning to the child, I would say, "When I was a little girl, no bigger than you are, I became sick with something called polio. The muscles of my leg shrank up and I couldn't walk very well. You're much luckier than I am because now you can get a vaccine to make sure you never get my disease. So don't cry when your mommy takes you to get a polio vaccine, okay?" Some adults and their little companions I talked to this way were glad to be rescued from embarrassment; others thought I was strange.

21   Americans have another way of covering up their uneasiness: they become jovially patronizing. Sometimes when people spot my crutch, they ask if I've had a skiing accident. When I answer that unfortunately it is something less glamorous than that they say, "I bet you *could* ski if you put your mind to it!" Alternately, at parties where people dance, men who ask me to dance with them get almost belligerent when I decline their invitation. They say, "Of course you can dance if you *want* to!" Some have given me pep talks about how if I would only develop the right mental attitude, I would have more fun in life.

22   Different cultural attitudes toward handicapped persons came out clearly during my wedding. My father-in-law, as solid a representative of middle America as could be found, had no qualms about objecting to the marriage on racial grounds, but he could bring himself to comment on my handicap only indirectly. He wondered why his son, who had dated numerous high school and college beauty queens, couldn't marry one of them instead of me. My mother-in-law, a devout Christian, did not share her husband's prejudices, but she worried aloud about whether I could have children. Some Chinese friends of my parents, on the other hand, said that I was lucky to have found such a

noble man, one who would marry me despite my handicap. I, for my part, appeared in church in a white lace wedding dress I had designed and made myself—a miniskirt!

23   How Asian Americans treat me with respect to my handicap tells me a great deal about their degree of acculturation. Recent immigrants behave just like Asians in Asia; those who have been here longer or who grew up in the United States behave more like their white counterparts. I have not encountered any distinctly Asian American pattern of response. What makes the experience of Asian American handicapped people unique is the duality of responses we elicit.

24   Regardless of racial or cultural background, most handicapped people have to learn to find a balance between the desire to attain physical independence and the need to take care of ourselves by not overtaxing our bodies. In my case, I've had to learn to accept the fact that leading an active life has its price. Between the ages of eight and eighteen, I walked without using crutches or braces but the effort caused my right leg to become badly misaligned. Soon after I came to the United States, I had a series of operations to straighten out the bones of my right leg; afterwards though my leg looked straighter and presumably better, I could no longer walk on my own. Initially my doctors fitted me with a brace, but I found wearing one cumbersome and soon gave it up. I could move around much more easily—and more important, faster—by using one crutch. One orthopedist after another warned me that using a single crutch was a bad practice. They were right. Over the years my spine developed a double-S curve and for the last twenty years I have suffered from severe, chronic back pains, which neither conventional physical therapy nor a lighter work load can eliminate.

25   The only thing that helps my backaches is a good massage, but the soothing effect lasts no more than a day or two. Massages are expensive, especially when one needs them three times a week. So I found a job that pays better, but at which I have to work longer hours, consequently increasing the physical strain on my body—a sort of vicious circle. When I was in my thirties, my doctors told me that if I kept leading the strenuous life I did, I would be in a wheelchair by the time I was forty. They were right on target; I bought myself a wheelchair when I was forty-one. But being the incorrigible character that I am, I use it only when I am *not* in a hurry!

26   It is a good thing, however, that I am too busy to think much about my handicap or my backaches because pain can physically debilitate as well as cause depression. And there are days when my spirits get rather low. What has helped me is realizing that being handicapped is akin to growing old at an accelerated rate. The contradiction I experience is that often my mind races along as though I'm only twenty while my body feels about sixty. But fifteen or twenty years hence,

unlike my peers who will have to cope with aging for the first time, I shall be full of cheer because I will have already fought, and I hope won, that battle long ago.

27 Beyond learning how to be physically independent and, for some of us, living with chronic pain or other kinds of discomfort, the most difficult thing a handicapped person has to deal with, especially during puberty and early adulthood, is relating to potential sexual partners. Because American culture places so much emphasis on physical attractiveness, a person with a shriveled limb, or a tilt to the head, or the inability to speak clearly, experiences great uncertainty—indeed trauma—when interacting with someone to whom he or she is attracted. My problem was that I was not only physically handicapped, small, and short, but worse, I also wore glasses and was smarter than all the boys I knew! Alas, an insurmountable combination. Yet somehow I have managed to have intimate relationships, all of them with extraordinary men. Not surprisingly, there have also been countless men who broke my heart—men who enjoyed my company "as a friend," but who never found the courage to date or make love with me, although I am sure my experience in this regard is no different from that of many able-bodied persons.

28 The day came when my backaches got in the way of having an active sex life. Surprisingly that development was liberating because I stopped worrying about being attractive to men. No matter how headstrong I had been, I, like most women of my generation, had had the desire to be alluring to men ingrained into me. And that longing had always worked like a brake on my behavior. When what men think of me ceased to be compelling, I gained greater freedom to be myself.

29 I've often wondered if I would have been a different person had I not been physically handicapped. I really don't know, though there is no question that being handicapped has marked me. But at the same time I usually do not *feel* handicapped—and consequently, I do not act handicapped. People are therefore less likely to treat me as a handicapped person. There is no doubt, however, that the lives of my parents, sister, husband, other family members, and some close friends have been affected by my physical condition. They have had to learn not to hide me away at home, not to feel embarrassed by how I look or react to people who say silly things to me, and not to resent me for the extra demands my condition makes on them. Perhaps the hardest thing for those who live with handicapped people is to know when and how to offer help. There are no guidelines applicable to all situations. My advice is, when in doubt, ask, but ask in a way that does not smack of pity or embarrassment. Most important, please don't talk to us as though we are children.

30 So, has being physically handicapped been a handicap? It all depends on one's attitude. Some years ago, I told a friend that I had once

said to an affirmative action compliance officer (somewhat sardon-
ically since I do not believe in the head count approach to affirmative
action) that the institution which employs me is triply lucky because it
can count me as non-white, female and handicapped. He responded,
"Why don't you tell them to count you four times? . . . Remember,
you're short, besides!"

✧ Evaluating the Text

1. What insight into cross-cultural perceptions of disabilities do you
   get from Chan's account? Specifically, how do Asian perceptions
   of disabilities differ from those in America?

2. To what extent did Chan have to overcome the well-meaning advice of family and friends and discount their perception of her diminished potential?

3. Chan has very strongly developed views; that is, she is an agnostic, doesn't believe in affirmative action, is uninhibited about sex,
   and has an unusual attitude toward the debilitating nature of her
   handicap. Which of her responses toward events made you aware
   of her unique personality?

✧ Exploring Different Perspectives

1. What personal attributes link Chan with Christy Brown in confronting disabilities in "The Letter 'A'"?

2. Discuss the overlapping perspectives on Chinese culture that
   emerge from the accounts by Chan and Guanlong Cao in
   "Chopsticks."

✧ Extending Viewpoints through Writing and Research

1. To what extent are attitudes toward disability conditioned by cultural forces?

2. Do you know anyone who has a sense of irony and detachment
   similar to Chan's toward a disability or ailment? Write a short account of how this attitude enables him or her to cope with circumstances that might devastate another person.

3. How disability is viewed in Chinese culture can be found at
   http://cirrie.buffalo.edu/china.html.

Christy Brown

The Letter "A"

— ◆ —

Christy Brown (1932–1981) was born in Dublin, the tenth child in a family of twenty-two. Brown was diagnosed as having cerebral palsy and being hopelessly retarded. An intense personal struggle and the loving attention and faith of his mother resulted in a surprising degree of rehabilitation. Brown's autobiography, My Left Foot *(1954), describing his struggle to overcome his massive handicap, was the basis for the 1989 Academy Award–winning film. Brown is also the author of an internationally acclaimed novel,* Down All the Days *(1970). "The Letter 'A,'" from his autobiography, describes the crucial moment when he first communicated signs of awareness and intelligence.*

Before You Read

Notice how Brown draws on his own experiences to raise the larger issue of how children with disabilities should be treated.

— ◆ —

1   I was born in the Rotunda Hospital,[1] on June 5th, 1932. There were nine children before me and twelve after me, so I myself belong to the middle group. Out of this total of twenty-two, seventeen lived, but four died in infancy, leaving thirteen still to hold the family fort.

2   Mine was a difficult birth, I am told. Both mother and son almost died. A whole army of relations queued up outside the hospital until the small hours of the morning, waiting for news and praying furiously that it would be good.

3   After my birth Mother was sent to recuperate for some weeks and I was kept in the hospital while she was away. I remained there for some time, without name, for I wasn't baptized until my mother was well enough to bring me to church.

4   It was Mother who first saw that there was something wrong with me. I was about four months old at the time. She noticed that my head had a habit of falling backward whenever she tried to feed me. She attempted to correct this by placing her hand on the back of my neck to keep it steady. But when she took it away, back it would drop again. That was the first warning sign. Then she became aware of other defects as I got older. She saw that my hands were clenched nearly all of

[1]Rotunda Hospital, a hospital in Dublin, Ireland.

the time and were inclined to twine behind my back; my mouth couldn't grasp the teat of the bottle because even at that early age my jaws would either lock together tightly, so that it was impossible for her to open them, or they would suddenly become limp and fall loose, dragging my whole mouth to one side. At six months I could not sit up without having a mountain of pillows around me. At twelve months it was the same.

5 Very worried by this, Mother told my father her fears, and they decided to seek medical advice without any further delay. I was a little over a year old when they began to take me to hospitals and clinics, convinced that there was something definitely wrong with me, something which they could not understand or name, but which was very real and disturbing.

6 Almost every doctor who saw and examined me labeled me a very interesting but also a hopeless case. Many told Mother very gently that I was mentally defective and would remain so. That was a hard blow to a young mother who had already reared five healthy children. The doctors were so very sure of themselves that Mother's faith in me seemed almost an impertinence. They assured her that nothing could be done for me.

7 She refused to accept this truth, the inevitable truth—as it then seemed—that I was beyond cure, beyond saving, even beyond hope. She could not and would not believe that I was an imbecile, as the doctors told her. She had nothing in the world to go by, not a scrap of evidence to support her conviction that, though my body was crippled, my mind was not. In spite of all the doctors and specialists told her, she would not agree. I don't believe she knew why—she just knew, without feeling the smallest shade of doubt.

8 Finding that the doctors could not help in any way beyond telling her not to place her trust in me, or, in other words, to forget I was a human creature, rather to regard me as just something to be fed and washed and then put away again, Mother decided there and then to take matters into her own hands. I was *her* child, and therefore part of the family. No matter how dull and incapable I might grow up to be, she was determined to treat me on the same plane as the others, and not as the "queer one" in the back room who was never spoken of when there were visitors present.

9 That was a momentous decision as far as my future life was concerned. It meant that I would always have my mother on my side to help me fight all the battles that were to come, and to inspire me with new strength when I was almost beaten. But it wasn't easy for her because now the relatives and friends had decided otherwise. They contended that I should be taken kindly, sympathetically, but not seriously. That would be a mistake. "For your own sake," they told her, "don't look to this boy as you would to the others; it would only break

your heart in the end." Luckily for me, Mother and Father held out against the lot of them. But Mother wasn't content just to say that I was not an idiot: she set out to prove it, not because of any rigid sense of duty, but out of love. That is why she was so successful.

10   At this time she had the five other children to look after besides the "difficult one," though as yet it was not by any means a full house. They were my brothers, Jim, Tony, and Paddy, and my two sisters, Lily and Mona, all of them very young, just a year or so between each of them, so that they were almost exactly like steps of stairs.

11   Four years rolled by and I was now five, and still as helpless as a newly born baby. While my father was out at bricklaying, earning our bread and butter for us, Mother was slowly, patiently pulling down the wall, brick by brick, that seemed to thrust itself between me and the other children, slowly, patiently penetrating beyond the thick curtain that hung over my mind, separating it from theirs. It was hard, heart-breaking work, for often all she got from me in return was a vague smile and perhaps a faint gurgle. I could not speak or even mumble, nor could I sit up without support on my own, let alone take steps. But I wasn't inert or motionless. I seemed, indeed, to be convulsed with movement, wild, stiff, snakelike movement that never left me, except in sleep. My fingers twisted and twitched continually, my arms twined backwards and would often shoot out suddenly this way and that, and my head lolled and sagged sideways. I was a queer, crooked little fellow.

12   Mother tells me how one day she had been sitting with me for hours in an upstairs bedroom, showing me pictures out of a great big storybook that I had got from Santa Claus last Christmas and telling me the names of the different animals and flowers that were in them, trying without success to get me to repeat them. This had gone on for hours while she talked and laughed with me. Then at the end of it she leaned over me and said gently into my ear:

13   "Did you like it, Chris? Did you like the bears and the monkeys and all the lovely flowers? Nod your head for yes, like a good boy."

14   But I could make no sign that I had understood her. Her face was bent over mine hopefully. Suddenly, involuntarily, my queer hand reached up and grasped one of the dark curls that fell in a thick cluster about her neck. Gently she loosened the clenched fingers, though some dark strands were still clutched between them.

15   Then she turned away from my curious stare and left the room, crying. The door closed behind her. It all seemed hopeless. It looked as though there was some justification for my relatives' contention that I was an idiot and beyond help.

16   They now spoke of an institution.

17   "Never!" said my mother almost fiercely, when this was suggested to her. "I know my boy is not an idiot; it is his body that is shattered, not his mind. I'm sure of that."

18   Sure? Yet inwardly, she prayed God would give her some proof of
her faith. She knew it was one thing to believe but quite another thing
to prove.

19   I was now five, and still I showed no real sign of intelligence. I
showed no apparent interest in things except with my toes—more especially those of my left foot. Although my natural habits were clean, I
could not aid myself, but in this respect my father took care of me. I
used to lie on my back all the time in the kitchen or, on bright warm
days, out in the garden, a little bundle of crooked muscles and twisted
nerves, surrounded by a family that loved me and hoped for me and
that made me part of their own warmth and humanity. I was lonely,
imprisoned in a world of my own, unable to communicate with others,
cut off, separated from them as though a glass wall stood between my
existence and theirs, thrusting me beyond the sphere of their lives and
activities. I longed to run about and play with the rest, but I was unable to break loose from my bondage.

20   Then, suddenly, it happened! In a moment everything was
changed, my future life molded into a definite shape, my mother's
faith in me rewarded, and her secret fear changed into open triumph.

21   It happened so quickly, so simply after all the years of waiting and
uncertainty, that I can see and feel the whole scene as if it had happened last week. It was the afternoon of a cold, gray December day.
The streets outside glistened with snow, the white sparkling flakes
stuck and melted on the windowpanes and hung on the boughs of the
trees like molten silver. The wind howled dismally, whipping up little
whirling columns of snow that rose and fell at every fresh gust. And
over all, the dull, murky sky stretched like a dark canopy, a vast infin-
ity of grayness.

22   Inside, all the family were gathered round the big kitchen fire that
lit up the little room with a warm glow and made giant shadows dance
on the walls and ceiling.

23   In a corner Mona and Paddy were sitting, huddled together, a few
torn school primers before them. They were writing down little sums
onto an old chipped slate, using a bright piece of yellow chalk. I was
close to them, propped up by a few pillows against the wall, watching.

24   It was the chalk that attracted me so much. It was a long, slender
stick of vivid yellow. I had never seen anything like it before, and it
showed up so well against the black surface of the slate that I was fascinated by it as much as if it had been a stick of gold.

25   Suddenly, I wanted desperately to do what my sister was doing.
Then—without thinking or knowing exactly what I was doing, I
reached out and took the stick of chalk out of my sister's hand—with
my left foot.

26   I do not know why I used my left foot to do this. It is a puzzle to
many people as well as to myself, for, although I had displayed a curi-

ous interest in my toes at an early age, I had never attempted before this to use either of my feet in any way. They could have been as useless to me as were my hands. That day, however, my left foot, apparently by its own volition, reached out and very impolitely took the chalk out of my sister's hand.

27   I held it tightly between my toes, and, acting on an impulse, made a wild sort of scribble with it on the slate. Next moment I stopped, a bit dazed, surprised, looking down at the stick of yellow chalk stuck between my toes, not knowing what to do with it next, hardly knowing how it got there. Then I looked up and became aware that everyone had stopped talking and was staring at me silently. Nobody stirred. Mona, her black curls framing her chubby little face, stared at me with great big eyes and open mouth. Across the open hearth, his face lit by flames, sat my father, leaning forward, hands outspread on his knees, his shoulders tense. I felt the sweat break out on my forehead.

28   My mother came in from the pantry with a steaming pot in her hand. She stopped midway between the table and the fire, feeling the tension flowing through the room. She followed their stare and saw me in the corner. Her eyes looked from my face down to my foot, with the chalk gripped between my toes. She put down the pot.

29   Then she crossed over to me and knelt down beside me, as she had done so many times before.

30   "I'll show you what to do with it, Chris," she said, very slowly and in a queer, choked way, her face flushed as if with some inner excitement.

31   Taking another piece of chalk from Mona, she hesitated, then very deliberately drew, on the floor in front of me, *the single letter "A."*

32   "Copy that," she said, looking steadily at me. "Copy it, Christy."

33   I couldn't.

34   I looked about me, looked around at the faces that were turned towards me, tense, excited faces that were at that moment frozen, immobile, eager, waiting for a miracle in their midst.

35   The stillness was profound. The room was full of flame and shadow that danced before my eyes and lulled my taut nerves into a sort of waking sleep. I could hear the sound of the water tap dripping in the pantry, the loud ticking of the clock on the mantel shelf, and the soft hiss and crackle of the logs on the open hearth.

36   I tried again. I put out my foot and made a wild jerking stab with the chalk which produced a very crooked line and nothing more. Mother held the slate steady for me.

37   "Try again, Chris," she whispered in my ear. "Again."

38   I did. I stiffened my body and put my left foot out again, for the third time. I drew one side of the letter. I drew half the other side. Then the stick of chalk broke and I was left with a stump. I wanted to fling it away and give up. Then I felt my mother's hand on my shoulder. I tried once more. Out went my foot. I shook, I sweated and strained every

muscle. My hands were so tightly clenched that my fingernails bit into the flesh. I set my teeth so hard that I nearly pierced my lower lip. Everything in the room swam till the faces around me were mere patches of white. But—I drew it—*the letter "A."* There it was on the floor before me. Shaky, with awkward, wobbly sides and a very uneven center line. But it *was* the letter "A." I looked up. I saw my mother's face for a moment, tears on her cheeks. Then my father stooped and hoisted me onto his shoulder.

39　　I had done it! It had started—the thing that was to give my mind its chance of expressing itself. True, I couldn't speak with my lips. But now I would speak through something more lasting than spoken words—written words.

40　　That one letter, scrawled on the floor with a broken bit of yellow chalk gripped between my toes, was my road to a new world, my key to mental freedom. It was to provide a source of relaxation to the tense, taut thing that was I, which panted for expression behind a twisted mouth.

✧ *Evaluating the Text*

1. What unusual signs alerted Christy's mother that he might be physically impaired? What did her response to the doctors' diagnosis reveal about her as a person and her attitude toward Christy?

2. What did Christy's mother hope to achieve by showing him pictures of animals and flowers? How did her friends and relatives react to her decision to treat Christy as if he were capable of mental development? How would Christy's day-to-day treatment have differed if his mother had not treated him as a member of the family?

3. Why does the narrative shift from Christy's mother's perspective to Christy's recollection of the day he was able to form the letter *A* with his left foot?

4. From the point of view of Christy's mother, father, and siblings, how did they know that his forming the letter *A* was a sign of intelligence and not merely an imitative gesture? How does the conclusion of this account suggest that this moment had deeper meaning for Christy than it did even for his family? What did this mean to him?

✧ *Exploring Different Perspectives*

1. Discuss the contrasting purpose of Brown's attempt to communicate his normalcy with those Germaine Greer describes in "One Man's Mutilation Is Another Man's Beautification."

2. What cultural prejudices toward disability can be seen in Ireland according to Brown and in China as described by Sucheng Chan?

✧ *Extending Viewpoints through Writing and Research*

1. On any given day, how do you think Christy would have been treated if his mother had not made the decision to treat him as a member of the family? Write a brief account analyzing why over a period of time the difference in the way he was treated might have been capable of producing the unexpected development Christy describes. Include in your account such everyday events as meals and visits from friends.

2. Rent a copy of the 1989 Academy Award–winning film *My Left Foot,* based on Christy Brown's autobiography of the same name, and discuss which treatment, film or written word, more effectively dramatized the issues at stake and the feelings of Christy and his family at the moment when he drew the letter *A.*

3. If you have ever been temporarily physically incapacitated or have a disability, write an essay that will help your audience understand your plight and the visible and subtle psychological aspects of discrimination that the disabled must endure every day.

Hanan Al-Shaykh

The Persian Carpet

◆

Hanan al-Shaykh was born in 1945 in Lebanon and was raised in a tradi-
tional Shiite Muslim family. She began her studies at the American Col-
lege for Girls in Cairo in 1963 and four years later returned to Beirut
where she worked as a journalist and began writing short stories and nov-
els. Originally written in Arabic, al-Shaykh's works have been published
in Lebanon and have been acclaimed for her capacity to realistically create
situations in which her protagonists, often women, gain a new perspec-
tive despite the cultural pressures forced upon them. Two of her novels,
The Story of Zahra *(1986) and* Women of Sand and Myrrh *(1989),*
have been translated into English. "The Persian Carpet," translated by
Denys Johnson-Davies (1983) from Arabic Short Stories, *closely ob-*
serves the behavior and emotions of a girl who is forced to realize that the
circumstances that led to her parents getting divorced were very different
from what she had believed as a child. Her latest works are Beirut Blues
(1996) and Only in London *(2001).*

Before You Read

As you read, evaluate whether you would consider the narrator/protago-
nist to be reliable or unreliable. In what way do the mother's actions trans-
gress the cultural values of this Muslim society?

◆

1   When Maryam had finished plaiting my hair into two pigtails, she
put her finger to her mouth and licked it, then passed it over my eyebrows, moaning: "Ah, what eyebrows you have—they're all over the
place!" She turned quickly to my sister and said: "Go and see if your
father's still praying." Before I knew it my sister had returned and was
whispering "He's still at it," and she stretched out her hands and
raised them skywards in imitation of him. I didn't laugh as usual, nor
did Maryam; instead, she took up the scarf from the chair, put it over
her hair and tied it hurriedly at the neck. Then, opening the wardrobe
carefully, she took out her handbag, placed it under her arm and
stretched out her hands to us. I grasped one and my sister the other.
We understood that we should, like her, proceed on tiptoe, holding our
breath as we made our way out through the open front door. As we
went down the steps, we turned back towards the door, then towards

the window. Reaching the last step, we began to run, only stopping when the lane had disappeared out of sight and we had crossed the road and Maryam had stopped a taxi.

2   Our behaviour was induced by fear, for today we would be seeing my mother for the first time since her separation by divorce from my father. He had sworn he would not let her see us, for, only hours after the divorce, the news had spread that she was going to marry a man she had been in love with before her family had forced her into marrying my father.

3   My heart was pounding. This was not from fear or from running but was due to anxiety and a feeling of embarrassment about the meeting that lay ahead. Though in control of myself and my shyness, I knew that I would be incapable—however much I tried—of showing my emotions, even to my mother; I would be unable to throw myself into her arms and smother her with kisses and clasp her head as my sister would do with such spontaneity. I had thought long and hard about this ever since Maryam had whispered in my ear—and in my sister's—that my mother had come from the south and that we were to visit her secretly the following day. I began to imagine that I would make myself act exactly as my sister did, that I would stand behind her and imitate her blindly. Yet I know myself: I have committed myself to myself by heart. However much I tried to force myself, however much I thought in advance about what I should and shouldn't do, once I was actually faced by the situation and was standing looking down at the floor, my forehead puckered into an even deeper frown, I would find I had forgotten what I had to resolved to do. Even then, though I would not give up hope but would implore my mouth to break into a smile; it would none the less be to no avail.

4   When the taxi came to a stop at the entrance to a house, where two lions stood on columns of red sandstone, I was filled with delight and immediately forgot my apprehension. I was overcome with happiness at the thought that my mother was living in a house where two lions stood at the entrance. I heard my sister imitate the roar of a lion and I turned to her in envy. I saw her stretching up her hands in an attempt to clutch the lions. I thought to myself: She's always uncomplicated and jolly, her gaiety never leaves her, even at the most critical moments—and here she was, not a bit worried about this meeting.

5   But when my mother opened the door and I saw her, I found myself unable to wait and rushed forward in front of my sister and threw myself into her arms. I had closed my eyes and all the joints of my body had grown numb after having been unable to be at rest for so long. I took in the unchanged smell of her hair, and I discovered for the first time how much I had missed her and wished that she would come back and live with us, despite the tender care shown to us by my father

and Maryam. I couldn't rid my mind of that smile of hers when my father agreed to divorce her, after the religious sheikh had intervened
following her threats to pour kerosene over her body and set fire to
herself if my father wouldn't divorce her. All my senses were numbed
by that smell of her, so well perserved in my memory. I realized how
much I had missed her, despite the fact that after she'd hurried off behind her brother to get into the car, having kissed us and started to cry,
we had continued with the games we were playing in the lane outside
our house. As night came, and for the first time in a long while we did
not hear her squabbling with my father, peace and quiet descended
upon the house—except that is for the weeping of Maryam, who was
related to my father and had been living with us in the house ever
since I was born.

6   Smiling, my mother moved me away from her so that she could
hug and kiss my sister, and hug Maryam again, who had begun to cry.
I heard my mother, who was in tears, say to her "Thank you," and she
wiped her tears with her sleeve and looked me and my sister up and
down, saying: "God keep them safe, how they've sprung up!" She put
both arms round me, while my sister buried her head in my mother's
waist, and we all began to laugh when we found that it was difficult
for us to walk like that. Reaching the inner room, I was convinced her
new husband was inside because my mother said, sniffing: "Mahmoud loves you very much and he would like it if your father would
give you to me so that you can live with us and become his children
too." My sister laughed and answered: "Like that we'd have two fathers." I was still in a benumbed state, my hand placed over my
mother's arm, proud at the way I was behaving, at having been able
without any effort to be liberated from myself, from my shackled
hands, from the prison of my shyness, as I recalled to mind the picture
of my meeting with my mother, how I had spontaneously thrown myself at her, something I had thought wholly impossible, and my kissing
her so hard I had closed my eyes.

7   Her husband was not there. As I stared down at the floor I froze.
In confusion I looked at the Persian carpet spread out on the floor, then
gave my mother a long look. Not understanding the significance of my
look, she turned and opened a cupboard from which she threw me an
embroidered blouse, and moving across to a drawer in the dressing-
table, she took out an ivory comb with red hearts painted on it and
gave it to my sister. I stared down at the Persian carpet, trembling with
burning rage. Again I looked at my mother and she interpreted my
gaze as being one of tender longing, so she put her arms round me,
saying: "You must come every other day, you must spend the whole
of Friday at my place." I remained motionless, wishing that I could
remove her arms from around me and sink my teeth into that white
forearm. I wished that the moment of meeting could be undone and

re-enacted, that she could again open the door and I could stand there—as I should have done—with my eyes staring down at the floor and my forehead in a frown.

8 The lines and colours of the Persian carpet were imprinted on my memory. I used to lie on it as I did my lessons; I'd be so close to it that I'd gaze at its pattern and find it looking like slices of red water-melon repeated over and over again. But when I sat down on the couch, I would see that each slice of melon had changed into a comb with thin teeth. The cluster of flowers surrounding its four sides were purple-coloured. At the beginning of summer my mother would put moth-balls on it and on the other ordinary carpets and would roll them up and place them on top of the cupboard. The room would look stark and depressing until autumn came, when she would take them up to the roof and spread them out. She would gather up the mothballs, most of which had dissolved from the summer's heat and humidity, then, having brushed them with a small broom, she'd leave them there. In the evening she'd bring them down and lay them out where they belonged. I would be filled with happiness as their bright colours once again brought the room back to life. This particular carpet, though, had disappeared several months before my mother was divorced. It had been spread out on the roof in the sun and in the afternoon my mother had gone up to get it and hadn't found it. She had called my father and for the first time I had seen his face flushed with anger. When they came down from the roof, my mother was in a state of fury and bewilderment. She got in touch with the neighbors, all of whom swore they hadn't seen it. Suddenly my mother exclaimed: "Ilya!" Everyone stood speechless: not a word from my father or from my sister or from our neighbours Umm Fouad and Abu Salman. I found myself crying out: "Ilya? Don't say such a thing, it's not possible."

9 Ilya was an almost blind man who used to go round the houses of the quarter repairing cane chairs. When it came to our turn, I would see him, on my arrival back from school, seated on the stone bench outside the house with piles of straw in front of him and his red hair glinting in the sunlight. He would deftly take up the strands of straw and, like fishes, they'd slip through the mesh. I would watch him as he coiled them round with great dexterity, then bring them out again until he had formed a circle of straw for the seat of the chair, just like the one that had been there before. Everything was so even and precise: it was as though his hands were a machine and I would be amazed at the speed and nimbleness of his fingers. Sitting as he did with his head lowered, it looked as though he were using his eyes. I once doubted that he could see more than vague shapes in front of him, so I squatted down and looked into his rosy-red face and was able to see his half-closed eyes behind his glasses. They had in them a white line that pricked at my heart and sent me hurrying off to the kitchen, where I

found a bag of dates on the table, and I heaped some on a plate and
gave them to Ilya.

10   I continued to stare at the carpet as the picture of Ilya, red of face
and hair, appeared to me. I was made aware of his hand as he walked
up the stairs on his own; of him sitting on his chair, of his bargaining
over the price for his work, of how he ate and knew that he had finished everything on the plate, of his drinking from the pitcher, with the
water flowing easily down his throat. Once at midday, having been
taught by my father that before entering a Muslim house he should say
"Allah" before knocking at the door and entering, as a warning to my
mother in case she were unveiled, my mother rushed at him and asked
him about the carpet. He made no reply, merely making a sort of sobbing noise. As he walked off, he almost bumped into the table and, for
the first time, tripped. I went up to him and took him by the hand. He
knew me by the touch of my hand, because he said to me in a half-
whisper: "Never mind, child." Then he turned round to leave. As he
bent over to put on his shoes, I thought I saw tears on his cheeks. My
father didn't let him leave before saying to him: "Ilya, God will forgive
you if you tell him the truth." But Ilya walked off, steadying himself
against the railings. He took an unusually long time as he felt his way
down the stairs. Then he disappeared from sight and we never saw
him again.

✧ Evaluating the Text

1. What circumstances have made it necessary for the protagonist
   and her sister to visit their mother in secret?

2. What details suggest how much it means to her to see her mother
   again? Why is her reaction on first seeing her mother especially
   poignant and ironic in view of what she discovers subsequently?

3. Why does seeing the Persian carpet cause the young girl to experience such a dramatic change in attitude toward her mother? How
   does seeing what Ilya, the blind man, meant to her enable the
   reader to understand her feelings of anger?

✧ Exploring Different Perspectives

1. Contrast the relationship Christy Brown has with his mother with
   that of the young girl and her mother in Hanan Al-Shaykh's story,
   "The Persian Carpet."

2. What explains the ultimate disillusionment of the narrator in Al-
   Shaykh's story and of Douchan Gersi in "Initiated into an Iban
   Tribe of Headhunters"?

✧ Extending Viewpoints through Writing and Research

1. Did you ever experience a moment of disillusionment with an adult member of your family that represented a turning point in your relationship? Describe your experience.

2. Write about one of your grandparents or parents through an object you connect with him or her. Under what circumstances did you first come across this object? What associations connect this object with your parent or grandparent?

3. Discuss a belief you once held that you no longer hold. What evidence led you to hold that original belief? Was it something you were told, read, or personally experienced? What new experiences raised doubts about this belief? How did you change your attitude in response to these new experiences? What actions have you taken that you would not have taken previously that reflect this changed attitude or revised belief?

Sabine Reichel

Learning What Was Never Taught

◆

Sabine Reichel was born in Hamburg, Germany, in 1946. She has had a varied career as a social worker, filmmaker, and freelance journalist. Dissatisfied with the silence she and others of her generation encountered concerning the Holocaust, she spent six months interviewing soldiers and teachers. The results were published in her book What Did You Do in the War, Daddy? *(1989), in which the following essay first appeared. The acclaimed 1990 film* The Nasty Girl *is based on her account.*

Before You Read

Consider how disturbing it would be if accounts in history books did not correspond to what you knew to be true.

◆

1   I remember Herr Stock and Fräulein Lange without much affection. Partly because they weren't extraordinary people, partly because they failed their profession. They were my history teachers, ordinary civil servants, singled out to bring the tumultuous events of European history into perspective for a classroom of bored German schoolkids.

2   As it happened, Hitler and the Third Reich were the subjects under discussion when we were about fourteen years old, which is not to say that we discussed anything at all. I always thought that the decision to study the subject then was the result of a carefully calculated estimate by the school officials—as if German students were emotionally and intellectually ready to comprehend and digest the facts about Nazi Germany at exactly the age of 14.3. I learned much later that it had nothing to do with calculation; it was a matter of sequence. German history is taught chronologically, and Hitler was there when we were fourteen, whether we were ready or not.

3   Teaching this particular period was a thankless, though unavoidable, task. It was accompanied by sudden speech impediments, hoarse voices, uncontrollable coughs, and sweaty upper lips. A shift of mood would creep into the expansive lectures about kings and conquerors from the old ages, and once the Weimar Republic came to an end our teachers lost their proud diction.

4   We knew what it meant. We could feel the impending disaster. Only a few more pages in the history book, one last nervous swallowing, and then in a casual but controlled voice, maybe a touch too loud, Fräulein Lange would ask, "We are now getting to a dark chapter in German history. I'm sure you all know what I mean?"

5   We did, because each of us had already skimmed through the whole book countless times in search of exotic material and, naturally, had come across the man with the mustache. We knew that she was referring to the terrible time between 1933 and 1945 when Germany fell prey to a devil in brown disguise. There were fifteen pages devoted to the Third Reich, and they were filled with incredible stories about a mass movement called National Socialism which started out splendidly and ended in a catastrophe for the whole world.

6   And then there was an extra chapter, about three-quarters of a page long. It was titled "The Extermination of the Jews," and I had read it in my room at home many times. I always locked the door because I didn't want anybody to know what I was reading. Six million Jews were killed in concentration camps, and as I read about Auschwitz and the gas chambers a wave of feelings—fearful fascination mingled with disgust—rushed over me. But I kept quiet. What monsters must have existed then. I was glad it had all happened in the past and that the cruel Germans were gone, because, as the book pointed out, the ones responsible were punished. I couldn't help feeling alarmed by something I couldn't put my finger on. How could so many innocent people be murdered?

7   There was no explanation for my unspoken questions, no answers in Fräulein Lange's helpless face. She seemed embarrassed and distraught, biting her lip and looking down at her orthopedic shoes while trying to summarize the Third Reich in fifty minutes. That worked out to one minute for every one million people killed in World War II . . . and twenty-six lines for six million Jews, printed on cheap, yellowish paper in a German history book published in 1960. An efficient time-saver, the German way.

8   We never read that particular chapter aloud with our teacher as we did with so many other ones. It was the untouchable subject, isolated and open to everyone's personal interpretation. There was a subtle, unspoken agreement between teacher and student not to dig into something that would cause discomfort on all sides. Besides, wanting to have known more about concentration camps as a student would have been looked upon as sick.

9   All things must come to an end, however, and once the Third Reich crumbled in our classroom to the sound of hastily turning pages, the suffocating silence was lifted. Everybody seemed relieved, especially Fräulein Lange, who became her jolly old self again. She had

survived two world wars, she would survive a bunch of unapprecia-
tive teenagers.

10   In her late fifties in 1960, Fräulein Lange was a tiny, wrinkled
woman who matched my idea of the institutional matron right down
to her baggy skirt, steel-gray bun at the nape of her neck, and seamed
stockings. She also had a trying predilection for Gutenberg, the inven-
ter of movable type, whom we got to know more intimately than
Hitler. But she did her duty, more or less. German teachers had to teach
history whether they liked it or not.

11   The teachers of my time had all been citizens of the Third Reich
and therefore participants in an epoch that only a few years after its
bitter collapse had to be discussed in a neutral fashion. But what could
they possibly have said about this undigested, shameful subject to a
partly shocked, partly bored class of adolescents? They had to preserve
their authority in order to appear credible as teachers. Yet they were
never put to the test. A critical imagination and unreasonable curiosity
were unwelcome traits in all the classrooms of my twelve years in
school. There was no danger that a precocious student would ever corner a teacher and demand more facts about the Nazis; they could walk
away unscathed. We didn't ask our parents at home about the Nazis;
nor did we behave differently in school.

12   The truth was that teachers were not allowed to indulge in private
views of the Nazi past. There were nationwide guidelines for handling
this topic, including one basic rule: The Third Reich and Adolf Hitler
should be condemned unequivocally, without any specific criticism or
praise. In reality, however, there were basically three ways to deal with
the German past: (1) to go through the chapter as fast as possible,
thereby avoiding any questions and answers; (2) to condemn the past
passionately in order to deflate any suspicion about personal involvement; (3) to subtly legitimate the Third Reich by pointing out that it
wasn't really as bad as it seemed; after all, there were the *Autobahnen*.[1]

13   But no matter what the style of prevarication, the German past was
always presented as an isolated, fatal accident, and so the possibility of
investigating the cause of such a disaster was, of course, eliminated.
Investigating crimes reinforces guilt. If something is programmatically
depicted as black and bad, one doesn't look for different shades and
angles. The Third Reich was out of reach for us; it couldn't be cut down
to size.

14   I wonder now what could have been accomplished by a teacher
who had taken part in the war—as a soldier, or a Nazi, or an anti-
Nazi—and who talked candidly about his personal experience. But
that never happened. Instead we were showered with numbers and

---

[1]*Autobahnen:* an extensive network of freeways without mandatory speed limits,
constructed during the Third Reich.

dates. A few million dead bodies are impossible to relate to; raw numbers don't evoke emotions. Understanding is always personal. Only stories that humanized the numbers might have reached us. Had we been allowed to draw a connection between ourselves and the lives of other people, we might have been able to identify and feel compassion. But we were not aware of how blatantly insufficiently the past was handled in school because we resented the subject as much as the teacher who was somewhat entangled in it. Teenagers generally have little interest in history lessons; we learned facts and dates in order to pass a test or get a good grade and weren't convinced that comprehension of the warp and woof of historical events made any difference to the world or anybody in particular.

15   Another history teacher in a new school I attended in 1962 took an activist approach, mixing pathos and drama into a highly entertaining theatrical performance. To introduce highlights of the Third Reich there was no finer actor than Herr Stock. His voice was angry, his brows furrowed, and his fist was raised when he talked about the Führer's ferocious reign. Some of the more outgoing male teachers might even mimic parts of a Hitler speech. Yet when it came time to discuss the war itself, everything went downhill. His hands stopped moving, his voice became reproachful—no more victories to report. His saddest expression was reserved for the tragic end of "Germany under National Socialist dictatorship." It was time for the untouchable chapter again, the chapter that made Herr Stock nervously run his hands over his bald head, clear his throat, and mumble something about "six million Jews." It was the chapter that made him close the book with a clap, turn his back to the class, and announce with a palpable sigh of relief, "Recess."

16   In our next history lesson that chapter was usually forgotten, nd nobody followed up with any questions. Happy to have escaped interrogation, Herr Stock turned the pages quickly, ignoring "unpleasantries" like capitulation, denazification, and the humiliating aftermath of a defeated nation. The dark clouds were gone, the past had been left behind, and he turned jocular and voluble again.

17   But Herr Stock wasn't really talking to us, he was rather trying to convince us of something, assuming the stance of a prosecutor. For him, the scandal wasn't the casualties of World War II, but the resulting partition of Germany and the malevolence of the Russians. Rage, anger, and disappointment over the lost war, always repressed or directed at others, could be openly displayed now, disguised as righteousness. "They" had stolen parts of Germany—no word of what we stole from other countries. The Russians were war criminals; the Germans were victims.

18   If I had been unexpectedly curious about Nazi Germany, I would have received little help from my history books. The conclusions to be

drawn from a twelve-year catastrophe packed with enough dramatic material to fill a library were reduced to a few cryptic phrases: "The Germans showed very little insight" and "No real feelings of contrition were expressed." Teachers and history books were their own best examples of how to eviscerate the Nazi terror without ever really trying to come to terms with it.

19   But a new chapter, a new era, and a magic word—*Wirtschafts-wunder*[2]—soon revived our classroom and inspired another patriotic performance by Herr Stock. The undisputed star of German history education in the sixties was the remarkable reconstruction of postwar Germany. Now here was something an old schoolteacher could sink his teeth into. Gone were stutters and coughs. A nation of survivors had rolled up its sleeves, and Herr Stock had certainly been one of them. Here was a chance to rehabilitate Germany and put some gloss over its rotten core. Postwar Germany was a genuine communal construction, a well-made product, mass-manufactured by and for the tastes of the former citizens of the Reich. Every German with two functioning hands had taken part in rebuilding Germany, and history teachers all over the country waxed nostalgic about the united strength, the grim determination, and the close camaraderie that had helped build up Germany brick by brick.

20   We school children couldn't have cared less about these achievements. We were all born under occupation; the postwar years were ours too and the memories of ruins and poverty were just as indelible—if not as traumatic—as they had been for our parents. But in his enthusiasm he overlooked the fact that his words were falling on deaf ears: we didn't like Herr Stock; nor did we trust or admire him. In all this excitement about the "economic miracle," another, even greater miracle was conveniently left unexplained. On page 219 of my history book, Germany was described as a nation living happily under National Socialism and a seemingly accepted Führer without any visible crisis of conscience. Yet only fourteen pages later the same *Volk*[3] is depicted in the midst of an entirely different world, miraculously denazified and retrained, its murderous past neatly tucked away behind a tattered but nevertheless impenetrable veil of forgetfulness.

21   How did they do it? The existing Federal Republic of Germany is only one state away from the Nazi Reich. Where did they unload the brown ballast? The role change from obedient Nazi citizen to obedient *Bundes*[4] citizen went too smoothly from *"Sieg Hail!"* to democracy, and from marching brown uniforms to marching gray flannel suits. Where

---

[2]*Wirtschaftswunder:* "wonder of economics," the name given to the phenomenal recovery of the German economy after World War II.
[3]*Volk:* "people" or "folk," as in Volkswagen (literally, "people's car").
[4]*Bundes:* "federal," an adjective.

was the genuine substance which had initially constituted the basic foundation and ideology of the Third Reich? Could it still be there, hidden, repressed, put on ice?

22   Such questions were never asked, or encouraged. The schoolteachers that I encountered were a uniformly intimidating group of people (with one glorious exception): older men and women who demanded respect, order, and obedience. They were always curbing my curiosity with the clobbering logic of people who get paid for controlling outbursts of independent thinking. Their assessment of my character in report cards read: "She talks too much and could accomplish more if she would be more diligent."

23   Even though prohibited when I went to school, corporal punishment in many forms was still practiced with parental support, and my own classroom recollections are thick with thin-lipped, hawk-eyed, bespectacled men and women with mercilessly firm hands ready to take up the switch.

24   I always felt powerless toward teachers, and all of these emotions crystallized in 1983, when I was preparing to interview one of them. I couldn't help feeling a little triumphant. I was asking the questions now because I had discovered a slight spot on their white vests, something I couldn't see clearly when I was young and under their control. Now I had the power to make them nervous. My victory over German authority seemed complete. A schoolgirl's revenge?

25   But that wasn't all. I had a genuine interest in finding out how teachers in Germany feel today about their past failures. Had they found new ways to justify their damaging elisions, euphemisms, and omissions? More than any other age group, my generation was in desperate need not only of historical education but also of some form of emotional assistance from the adults who were linked to that not so distant yet unspeakable past.

26   In a way, I was looking for Herr Stock. But teachers as mediocre as he and Fräulein Lange had little to contribute to the kind of discussion I had in mind. I wanted the perspective of a teacher who had at least attempted to come to grips with his past. I was lucky to find one in Cäsar Hagener, a seventy-six-year-old former teacher and history professor. Hagener lives with his wife in a cozy, old-fashioned house with a garden in a suburb of Hamburg, in a quiet, safe neighborhood with lots of trees, many dachshunds, and little activity. He owns the type of one-family house, surrounded by a fence, that was commonly built in the thirties. A German house must have a fence. A house without a fence is disorderly, like a coat with a missing button.

27   Cäsar Hagener exuded integrity and an appealing friendliness— yet I found it impossible to forget that he had also been a teacher in the Third Reich. Hitler had envisioned a training program that would make every German youth "resilient as leather, fast as a weasel, and

hard as Krupp steel." He believed that "too much education spoils the youth." (Not surprisingly, after a few years of dictatorship 30 percent of the university professors, including Jews, had left the country.)

28   In 1933, Cäsar Hagener was a teacher of pedagogy and history at a liberal school in Hamburg, and when he heard that Hitler was appointed Reichs Chancellor he happened to be studying *Das Kapital*[5] together with some left-wing colleagues. "My friend said to me, 'It'll be over in no time. When you and I write a history book in twenty years, the Nazis will only be a footnote.'"

29   Even a skillful dictator like Hitler couldn't turn a country upside down overnight, and school life changed slowly under the Nazis. "But after 1934, the Nazis began to investigate the teachers' adaptation to the new order. Some were fired, and some were retrained in special camps. We had, of course, some 'overnight' Nazis who were strutting around in uniform, which didn't impress the students, who were quite critical. Later, in 1937, the young teachers were told to join the Nazi Party or else, so I joined the Party. Still, the first years of National Socialism were almost bearable."

30   However, at least once a week, teachers and students had to muster for the raising of the swastika flag and the singing of the "Horst-Wessel-Lied" or other Nazi songs. The Führer's speeches were required listening on the popular *Volksempfänger* for teachers and older students, while the nazified text in the new schoolbooks read like this: "If a mental patient costs 4 Reichsmarks a day in maintenance, a cripple 5.50, and a criminal 3.50, and about 50,000 of these people are in our institutions, how much does it cost our state at a daily rate of 4 Reichsmarks—and how many marriage loans of 1,000 Reichsmarks per couple could have been given out instead?"

31   The new features of Nazi education like race hygierie and heredity theory were given different degrees of importance in different schools. Hagener prepared himself: "I made sure to get a class with school beginners because children of that age weren't taught history or any of that Nazi nonsense. Besides, as a teacher, you were pretty much independent in your classroom and could make your own decision about what to say and what to skip. There were ways of getting around the obnoxious Nazi ideology."

32   The first public action by the Nazis right after January 1933 was to purge public and school libraries of "Jewish and un-German elements," leaving empty spaces on the shelves, since new "literature" wasn't written yet and new schoolbooks, adapted to the Nazis' standards, weren't printed until 1936. That same year they initiated compulsory membership in the Hitler Youth, starting at the age of ten with boys

[5]*Das Kapital:* the classic text by Karl Marx (1867) published in English in 1887 and edited by Frederick Engels.

organized into Jungvolk and Hitler Jungen and girls and young women into the Bund Deutscher Mädel (League of German Girls). What the Reich of the future needed were fearless, proud men of steel and yielding, fertile women—preferably blond—not effete intellectuals.

33   "The children can't be blamed for having been enthusiastic members of the Hitler Youth," Cäsar Hagener points out. "They grew up with that ideology and couldn't be expected to protect themselves from National Socialism; to do so, children would have had to be unaffected by all outside influences. It was their world, and the Hitler Youth programs were very attractive, with sports, contests, and decorations. It was possible for the son of a Communist or a Social Democrat to become a highly decorated Hitler Youth leader. I accuse the teachers who didn't perceive what was going on, and who taught Nazi ideology and glorified war, of having failed their profession."

34   In the last years of the war there was not much academic activity in Germany. The Nazi state was concerned with other problems besides education. Many schools were destroyed by bombs and virtually all Germans between fifteen and sixty years of age—Cäsar Hagener was drafted in 1940—were mobilized for the *Endkampf* (the final struggle) by the end of 1944. Hunger, death, and the will to survive prevailed over culture and education. Who needs to know algebra when the world is falling apart?

35   In 1945 denazification fever broke out in the defeated nation and reversed the roles of master and servant. For over a decade the country had been straining to purge itself of "un-German elements," and now the occupying powers were trying to purge it of all Nazi elements. Yet their efforts only exposed the unfeasibility of such a gargantuan task, since it involved much more than just the Nazi Party and the SS. Twelve years under the swastika had produced all kinds of "literature," art, music, film—indeed, a whole society had to be taken apart and its guiding principles destroyed. Naturally, reforming the educational system was a high priority, and millions of schoolbooks were thrown out, but some had to be preserved. The specially assigned Allied education officers decided which schoolbooks could still be used (after tearing out a Nazi-contaminated page or censoring a suspicious chapter or two). The approved books were stamped, and were circulated until new ones could be printed, which wasn't until the early fifties.

36   "The British, our occupiers, did everything wrong, because nothing could be worked out intellectually. They came over here with certain expectations and this incredibly bad image of the enemy, and they were very surprised to find their task not as easy as they had thought. They tried to control the situation by being very strict."

37   Reforming the faculty was even more problematic, since many teachers had been forced to join the Nazi Party and it wasn't always easy to tell who was a "real" Nazi and who wasn't. As a rule of thumb,

those who appeared to have cooperated unwillingly were permitted to continue teaching, younger teachers who had been educated under the Nazi regime were retrained in special seminars, while those who had been active supporters were barred from teaching for as long as two years.

38   Cäsar Hagener still gets angry over how easily former colleagues were rehired. "After 1945, nobody seemed to remember what a Nazi was, and people who I knew were definitely Nazis by nature landed on top again. I was one of a group of young teachers who protested violently against this tendency—and I felt like a McCarthy witch-hunter. I saw these people as criminals who did a lot of harm to us teachers."

39   Still, the main consideration was that teachers were badly needed. The war had wiped out a whole generation of young men, and keeping professionals from their profession in Germany after 1945 was as uneconomical as it was impractical: what was left was what Germany's children got. It's safe to say that by 1950 almost all teachers were back in schools and universities regardless of their past.

40   In the years immediately following the war, the few schools that were not badly damaged were overcrowded with children of all ages and several grades gathered together in one room. There was cardboard in place of windows, and opening umbrellas inside the school on rainy days was as natural as being sent home for a "cold-weather holiday" because there was no heat. The teacher had to be a good-humored ringmaster, innovative and full of stories; because of the book shortage, he had to know his lessons by heart. The students also needed good memories, because there wasn't any paper. Arithmetic and grammar assignments were often written down on the margins of newspapers.

41   It might have been the only time in Germany when school lessons were extemporaneous, personal, and an accurate reflection of real life. School was suddenly a popular place where humanity prevailed over theory. Teachers were not merely authority figures but people who had been harmed by the war just like the students and their families, and much of the time was spent discussing how to steal potatoes and coal and other survival tactics, which were more pressing than Pythagoras.

42   How did a teacher in those years explain history while it was happening? The change from "Nazis are good" to "Nazis are bad" must have been a confusing experience for the uprooted, disillusioned children of the Third Reich. Children weren't denazified. They had to adapt to "democracy" without shedding a brown skin. All the values they had learned to defend so passionately crumbled before their eyes and the reality they once trusted was rearranged silently, without their consent. The glorious, thunderous Third Reich was a gyp. The Jews weren't "*Volks* enemy number one" anymore. And as for the Führer, he wasn't a superhuman hero, but a vicious little coward, a maniac who

wanted to exterminate a whole people and almost succeeded. What irreparable mistrust must have become lodged in the minds of all these young Germans whose youth was trampled flat by goose-stepping jackboots.

43   But teachers didn't explain history at all. "I'm afraid to say that it didn't occur to the students to bring up Adolf in any form. We had all survived and dealt mostly with the effects of the war in a practical sense. I tried to do nice, positive things with the children, who had it bad enough as it was," Cäsar Hagener explains, and adds, almost surprised, "It is amazing how extremely apolitical we were. Any reflection was impossible under the circumstances, because everything was defined in terms of the struggle of daily life, which had a dynamic all by itself."

44   He also knows why the adolescents of the fifties and sixties were as uninquisitive as their teachers and parents were silent. "There was strong resentment toward the grown-ups. The teenagers had a fine sense for the things that didn't quite fit together with the Nazis. I didn't have any luck with my own three sons; they frustrated my desire to talk about the past by calling it lecturing, so I ended up talking about it mostly in foreign countries, where the people seemed to be more interested in it."

45   Things have changed radically during the last twenty years. There has been a small revolution in the German classroom. While teachers after the war were much younger and more outspoken than their predecessors, students became rebellious and undisciplined.

46   Cäsar Hagener remembers his school days. "My own generation and my students lived in a very strict and conformist structure which existed much earlier than 1933. Sure, there were provocative and rebellious personalities, but this phenomenon of developing an independent mind is new. Today it wouldn't be possible to stand in front of a class in uniform and in all seriousness talk about racial theory. The students would die laughing."

47   German students today often know more facts about the Third Reich than both their parents and the immediate postwar generation and are not afraid to ask questions. Yet their interest in Nazism is strictly intellectual, and they generally succeed in remaining emotionally detached. They don't know yet that they can't escape the past. Tragically, almost all of Cäsar Hagener's contemporaries have managed to escape their Nazi past. In his opinion: "You can't put a whole nation on the couch. I find my own contemporaries just plain terrible and I don't have much contact with many old friends anymore. In their eyes I'm too critical, a guy who fouls his own nest and who can't see the good sides of the Nazi era—which infuriates and bores me at the same time. They reject the radical examination of the past. But it's necessary, since we know better than most that terrible things can and did happen."

✧ *Evaluating the Text*

1. How did Reichel's search for a satisfactory explanation about the Holocaust change her relationship with her family and school authorities?

2. How did Reichel's interview with Herr Hagener provide insights into the pressures to which teachers were subjected and give her some of the answers she sought?

✧ *Exploring Different Perspectives*

1. Discuss how Reichel's account and Hanan Al-Shaykh's story "The Persian Carpet" provide insight into how children come to view adults more realistically.

2. In what ways do Reichel and Sucheng Chan ("You're Short, Besides!") have to overcome the challenge of being outside the mainstream of their societies?

✧ *Extending Viewpoints through Writing and Research*

1. To what extent does the public nature of the war in Iraq, seen on television 24/7, distinguish it from World War II in terms of people being able to deny knowledge of what is happening, as they did in Germany?

2. You might wish to rent the subtitled acclaimed German film, *The Nasty Girl* (1990), which is based on Reichel's account, and compare it with her essay.

Douchan Gersi

Initiated into an Iban Tribe of Headhunters

◆

Douchan Gersi was the producer of the National Geographic television series called Discovery. *He has traveled extensively throughout the Philippines, New Zealand, the Polynesian and Melanesian Islands, the Sahara Desert, Africa, New Guinea, and Peru. "Initiated into an Iban Tribe of Headhunters," from his book* Explorer *(1987), tells of the harrowing initiation process he underwent to become a member of the Iban Tribe in Borneo.*

The Iban are a friendly and hospitable people who are a majority of the Sarawak population of northwest Borneo. They are well known for their textile weaving, woodcarving, and weaving of intricate mats and baskets. An accomplished Iban man not only would be proficient in argument and courageous in hunting, but also would be skillful in woodcarving. The traditional Iban dwelling is the longhouse (which is nearly always built by the bank of a navigable river), a semipermanent structure housing twenty or more families in separate apartments. The longhouse is decorated with drums, gongs, weavings, and hanging skulls from days gone by. The area in which they live is also prized for its orangutan population, a protected species that has resulted in a burgeoning tourism trade. The Iban have many festivals through which they maintain their cultural identity and heritage. Superstitions abound and the carved wood charms (often symbolized by crocodile and python figures) play a crucial role in protecting families from malevolent spirits.

Before You Read

Consider the ways in which rites of passage provide a means by which cultures divide "us" from "them."

◆

The hopeful man sees success where others see shadows and storm.

—O. S. Marden.

1   Against Tawa's excellent advice I asked the chief if I could become a member of their clan. It took him a while before he could give me an answer, for he had to question the spirits of their ancestors and wait for

their reply to appear through different omens: the flight of a blackbird, the auguries of a chick they sacrificed. A few days after the question, the answer came:

2   "Yes . . . but!"

3   The "but" was that I would have to undergo their initiation. Without knowing exactly what physical ordeal was in store, I accepted. I knew I had been through worse and survived. It was to begin in one week.

4   Late at night I was awakened by a girl slipping into my bed. She was sweet and already had a great knowledge of man's morphology. Like all the others who came and "visited" me this way every night, she was highly skilled in the arts of love. Among the Iban, only unmarried women offer sexual hospitality, and no one obliged these women to offer me their favors. Sexual freedom ends at marriage. Unfaithfulness—except during yearly fertility celebrations when everything, even incest at times, is permitted—is punished as an offense against their matrimonial laws.

5   As a sign of respect to family and the elders, sexual hospitality is not openly practiced. The girls always came when my roommates were asleep and left before they awoke. They were free to return or give their place to their girlfriends.

6   The contrast between the violence of some Iban rituals and the beauty of their art, their sociability, their kindness, and their personal warmth has always fascinated me. I also witnessed that contrast among a tribe of Papuans (who, besides being headhunters, practice cannibalism) and among some African tribes. In fact, tribes devoted to cannibalism and other human sacrifices are often among the most sociable of people, and their art, industry, and trading systems are more advanced than other tribes that don't have these practices.

7   For my initiation, they had me lie down naked in a four-foot-deep pit filled with giant carnivorous ants. Nothing held me there. At any point I could easily have escaped, but the meaning of this rite of passage was not to kill me. The ritual was intended to test my courage and my will, to symbolically kill me by the pain in order for me to be reborn as a man of courage. I am not sure what their reactions would have been if I had tried to get out of the pit before their signal, but it occurred to me that although the ants might eat a little of my flesh, the Iban offered more dramatic potentials.

8   Since I wore, as Iban do, a long piece of cloth around my waist and nothing more, I had the ants running all over my body. They were everywhere. The pain of the ants' bites was intense, so I tried to relax to decrease the speed of my circulation and therefore the effects of the poison. But I couldn't help trying to get them away from my face where they were exploring every inch of my skin. I kept my eyes closed, inhaling through my almost closed lips and exhaling through my nose to chase them away from there.

9   I don't know how long I stayed in the pit, waiting with anguish for the signal which would end my ordeal. As I tried to concentrate on my relaxing, the sound of the beaten gongs and murmurs of the assistants watching me from all around the pit started to disappear into a chaos of pain and loud heartbeat.

10   Then suddenly I heard Tawa and the chief calling my name. I removed once more the ants wandering on my eyelids before opening my eyes and seeing my friends smiling to indicate that it was over. I got out of the pit on my own, but I needed help to rid myself of the ants, which were determined to eat all my skin. After the men washed my body, the shaman applied an herbal mixture to ease the pain and reduce the swellings. I would have quit and left the village then had I known that the "pit" experience was just the hors d'oeuvre.

11   The second part of the physical test started early the next morning. The chief explained the "game" to me. It was Hide and Go Seek Iban-style. I had to run without any supplies, weapons, or food, and for three days and three nights escape a group of young warriors who would leave the village a few hours after my departure and try to find me. If I were caught, my head would be used in a ceremony. The Iban would have done so without hate. It was simply the rule of their life. Birth and death. A death that always engenders new life.

12   When I asked, "What would happen if someone refused this part of the initiation?" the chief replied that such an idea wasn't possible. Once one had begun, there was no turning back. I knew the rules governing initiations among the cultures of tradition but never thought they would be applied to me. Whether or not I survived the initiation, I would be symbolically killed in order to be reborn among them. I had to die from my present time and identity into another life. I was aware that, among some cultures, initiatory ordeals are so arduous that young initiates sometimes really die. These are the risks if one wishes to enter into another world.

13   I was given time to get ready and the game began. I ran like hell without a plan or, it seemed to me, a prayer of surviving. Running along a path I had never taken, going I knew not where, I thought about every possible way I could escape from the young warriors. To hide somewhere. But where? Climb a tree and hide in it? Find a hole and squeeze in it? Bury myself under rocks and mud? But all of these seemed impossible. I had a presentiment they would find me anyway. So I ran straight ahead, my head going crazy by dint of searching for a way to safely survive the headhunters.

14   I would prefer staying longer with ants, I thought breathlessly. It was safer to stay among them for a whole day since they were just simple pain and fear compared to what I am about to undergo. I don't want to die.

15   For the first time I realized the real possibility of death—no longer in a romantic way, but rather at the hands of butchers.

16   Ten minutes after leaving the long house, I suddenly heard a call coming from somewhere around me. Still running, I looked all around trying to locate who was calling, and why. At the second call I stopped, cast my gaze about, and saw a woman's head peering out from the bushes. I recognized her as one of my pretty lovers. I hesitated, not knowing if she were part of the hunting party or a goddess come to save me. She called again. I thought, God, what to do? How will I escape from the warriors? As I stood there truly coming into contact with my impossible situation, I began to panic. She called again. With her fingers she showed me what the others would do if they caught me. Her forefinger traced an invisible line from one side of her throat to the other. If someone was going to kill me, why not her? I joined her and found out she was in a lair. I realized I had entered the place where the tribe's women go to hide during their menstruation. This area is taboo for men. Each woman was her own refuge. Some have shelters made of branches, others deep covered holes hidden behind bushes with enough space to eat and sleep and wait until their time is past.

17   She invited me to make myself comfortable. That was quite difficult since it was just large enough for one person. But I had no choice. And after all, it was a paradise compared to what I would have undergone had I not by luck crossed this special ground.

18   Nervously and physically exhausted by my run and fear and despair, I soon fell asleep. Around midnight I woke. She gave me rice and meat. We exchanged a few words. Then it was her turn to sleep.

19   The time I spent in the lair with my savior went fast. I tried to sleep all day long, an escape from the concerns of my having broken a taboo. And I wondered what would happen to me if the headhunters were to learn where I spent the time of my physical initiation.

20   Then, when it was safe, I snuck back to the village . . . in triumph. I arrived before the warriors, who congratulated and embraced me when they returned. I was a headhunter at last.

21   I spent the next two weeks quietly looking at the Iban through new eyes. But strangely enough, instead of the initiation putting me closer to them, it had the opposite effect. I watched them more and more from an anthropological distance: my Iban brothers became an interesting clan whose life I witnessed but did not really share. And then suddenly I was bored and yearned for my own tribe. When Tawa had to go to an outpost to exchange pepper grains for other goods, I took a place aboard his canoe. Two days later I was in a small taxi-boat heading toward Sibu, the first leg in civilization on my voyage home.

22   I think of them often. I wonder about the man I tried to cure. I think about Tawa and the girl who saved my life, and all the others sitting on the veranda. How long will my adopted village survive before being destroyed like all the others in the way of civilization? And what

has become of those who marked my flesh with the joy of their lives and offered me the best of their souls? If they are slowly vanishing from my memories, I know that I am part of the stories they tell. I know that my life among them will be perpetuated until the farthest tomorrow. Now I am a story caught in a living legend of a timeless people.

✧ *Evaluating the Text*

1. What do the unusual sexual customs of hospitality bestowed upon outsiders suggest about the different cultural values of the Iban? Do these customs suggest that the initiation would be harsher or milder than Gersi expected? Interpret this episode as it relates to the probable nature of Gersi's forthcoming initiation.

2. In a paragraph, explain the nature of the "hide and go seek" game that constituted the main test for a candidate. Explain why the use of the lighthearted term *game* is ironic in this context.

3. How does the reappearance of one of the girls who had earlier paid a nocturnal "visit" to Gersi result in his finding a safe hiding place? What does the nature of the hiding place reveal about the tribe's taboos?

4. Explain in what way the initiation resulted in Gersi feeling quite different than he had expected. That is, instead of feeling he was now part of the tribe, he actually felt more distant from them than he had felt before the initiation. To what factors do you attribute the unexpected sense of alienation? What did he discover about his own preconceptions during the initiation that stripped away certain romantic ideas he had about the Iban and the ability of any outsider to truly become a member of the tribe?

✧ *Exploring Different Perspectives*

1. What insights do Gersi and Germaine Greer offer into the importance of belonging in a tribal culture?

2. Compare the motivations of Gersi and those that Germaine Greer (in "One Man's Mutilation Is Another Man's Beautification") discusses in terms of volunteering for dangerous initiation rituals.

✧ *Extending Viewpoints through Writing and Research*

1. If you have ever been initiated into a fraternity or sorority or any other organization, compare the nature of Gersi's initiation with the one you experienced. In particular, try to identify particular

stages in these initiations that mark the "death" of the outsider and the "rebirth" of the initiated member.

2. Examine any religious ritual, such as confirmation in the Catholic Church, and analyze it in terms of an initiation rite. For example, the ceremony of the Catholic Church by which one is confirmed as an adult member follows this pattern. A period of preparation is spent the year before confirmation. The ceremony has several stages, including confession, communion, and subsequent confirmation. Candidates are routinely quizzed prior to communion about their knowledge of basic theology and must be sponsored by a member in good standing of the Catholic community. For example, what is the significance of the newly chosen confirmation name? What responsibilities and obligations do candidates incur who complete the confirmation ceremony?

3. What was your reaction to learning that the culture Gersi describes is one that exists today (in Borneo) two days away from taxi-boats and civilization? Would you ever consider undertaking a journey to such a place? Describe the most exotic place you want to visit, and explain why you would want to go there.

4. A recent visit by students to the Iban with accompanying pictures can be found at http://www.telangusan.com/studentsinborneo.htm.

Guanlong Cao

Chopsticks

◆

Guanlong Cao (Kuan-lung Ts'ao) was raised in Shanghai, China. Under communist rule, his family lost their possessions, and all six were forced to live in a small attic over a button factory. Cao describes his life from the 1950s through the 1970s in his award-winning book The Attic: Memoirs of a Chinese Landlord's Son, *translated by Cao and Nancy Moskin (1996); this selection is a chapter in that book. Cao emigrated to the United States in 1987 and, at forty-two, graduated from Middlebury College; he later received an M.A. in fine arts from Tufts University. His artwork includes sculpture, photographs, and paintings. In "Chopsticks," Cao describes the obsession of students at the automotive school he attended with making their own chopsticks from stolen bamboo. In a situation in which food was rationed, devoting so much time and care to making chopsticks had special significance.*

Before You Read
Consider how using chopsticks changes your relationship to the food.

◆

1   I always think chopsticks are an invention unique to Asian culture. Its historical and cognitive significance is no less than that of the Great Wall, the compass, gunpowder, and paper.

2   The greatest wisdom appears to be foolishness. Complexity ultimately ends in simplicity. Maybe it is because chopsticks are so simple that, just as air's weight was long ignored and white light was mislabeled as colorless, in thousands of years no one has ever scientifically or conscientiously researched them. A sensitive probe for examining the characteristics of Asian culture has been ignored. In my four years at the automotive school, I witnessed and experienced a splendid chopsticks civilization. I record it here for the benefit of future researchers.

3   In those days almost every male student carried an elongated pouch hanging from his belt. It was fashioned from canvas, leather, or leatherette. Like a warrior's dagger, it dangled all day from the student's waist.

4   Female students didn't wear belts, so the slim bags usually hung from a cord around their necks. Their materials were more delicate: nylon, silk, or linen. Embroidery was often added as an embellishment.

5   Within these bags were chopsticks.

6   Because the rationed food offered insufficient calories, oxygen-intensive activities were not encouraged. Chess, card games, and calligraphy were the officially recommended pastimes. But the most popular activity was making chopsticks.

7   The number of students at the school increased each year, and new dormitories were constantly being built. Owing to limited funds, the dormitory roofs were constructed out of tar paper, straw, and bamboo. That bamboo became the primary source of chopstick lumber.

8   The selection of material was critical. Segments close to the plant's roots were too short. The meat between the skin and hollow core of the segments close to the top was too thin. A bamboo tree about one inch thick provided only a few middle segments that could be used to make quality chopsticks.

9   The bamboo poles were covered with a tarp and stored on the construction site. In the evenings, taking advantage of the absence of the construction workers, we started looting.

10   If only a few trees were missing, nobody would have noticed. But when an idea becomes a fad, things can easily get out of hand. There were hundreds of students. A newly delivered pile of bamboo would be half gone the morning after an all-out moonlit operation.

11   The superintendent of the construction site was furious and demanded that the student dormitories be searched. We got scared and threw our booty out the windows. The superintendent called a meeting of the school leaders to deal with the problem. He arrived with both arms laden with cut segments of bamboo. With a crash, he slammed the sticks down on the meeting table. The leaders, gathered around the table, looked like diners at an exotic feast.

12   The next day, a large notice was posted listing the price of the transgression: one bamboo tree = one big demerit. But the punishment was never really put into effect. After the immediate storm passed, the bamboo continued to go missing, but not in the same flagrant quantities.

13   After a bamboo segment was split open, it had to be dried in the shade for about a week. Experienced students put their bamboo strips on the mosquito netting over their beds. Their rising body heat helped evaporate the moisture.

14   Although the bamboo's skin is hard, it must be stripped away. If left on, the different densities of the inner and outer materials cause the chopsticks to warp. The best part comes from the quarter inch of meat just inside the skin. There the texture is even and dense, and the split will go precisely where the knife directs it.

15   The student-made chopsticks usually had a round cross-section. Round chopsticks require little skill to make. Wrap sandpaper around the strip of bamboo and sand for an hour or two, and a round cross-section is the result.

16   Only experts dared to make square cross-sectioned chopsticks. To make the four sides straight and symmetrical from tail to tip required real expertise. Sandpaper could not be used, because it would wear away the sharp edges you were trying to create.

17   To begin the procedure, you have to soak a fine-grained brick in water for a couple of days, and then grind it flat on a concrete floor. Laying the roughed-out chopstick on the brick, with one finger applying pressure to the tail and another to the top, you slowly ground the stick on the brick. Water was dripped on the brick to ensure fine grinding. Only by this painstaking process could chopsticks be formed with clear edges and smooth surfaces.

18   A boy student unprecedently produced a pair of five-sided chopsticks, which created a sensation on campus. The boy dedicated his efforts to a girl on whom he had a crush. Unfortunately, his gift was spurned and, desolate, he broke the chopsticks in front of his peers. This became the classic tragedy of the school year.

19   In addition to varying cross-sections, the top two or three inches were another place to show off your skill. The usual decoration was a few carved lines with inlaid color. Some students borrowed techniques from seal carving and sculpted miniature cats, turtles, and dragons out of the upper portions of the sticks. One student, who was good at calligraphy, carved two lines of a Song dynasty poem on his chopsticks:

> "Vinegar fish from the West Lake," read one of them.
> "Cinnamon meat from East Hill," read the other.

20   He cherished the chopsticks as sacred objects, not intended for daily use. He employed them only on special occasions or festival days when excitement rippled through the student body:

> "Today we are going to eat meat!"

21   Only then would he take his chopsticks from his trunk. Applying a thin layer of beeswax, he would polish them for at least ten minutes with a piece of suede. Then they were ready to be brought into the dining room.

22   Following the epochal five-sided masterpiece, chopsticks became a popular gift for boys to give to girls. If the girl liked the boy, she would accept his present and later give a gift to her admirer—a sleeve for chopsticks. The pains-taking needlework expressed her sentimental attachment. We had never heard about Freud, but with our raw wisdom we subconsciously felt that there was some symbolic meaning, which could hardly be expressed in words, in this exchange, in the coming and going of the chopsticks and the sleeves. But school regulations clearly stated:

NO DATING ON CAMPUS

23   I think the regulation was well supported by science. Dating belonged to the category of oxygen-intensive activities. Before you could
open your mouth, your heart started jumping and your cheeks were
burning, clearly indicating a rapid consumption of valuable calories.

✧ Evaluating the Text

1. Cao mentions that food at the automotive school was not plentiful
   and having meat was a special event. What is the relationship between the scarcity of food and the fact that the students spent so
   much time and effort making their own chopsticks?

2. What picture do you get of the relationship between the students
   and the authorities? What is Cao's attitude toward the authorities?
   How does Cao's use of irony and language convey his feelings
   about these experiences?

3. Cao describes how the chopstick-making enterprise took over student life at the school. What did it mean to them individually and
   as a group? What campuswide activities or projects have galva-
   nized the student population at your school?

✧ Exploring Different Perspectives

1. In what way is the making of the chopsticks a ritual intended to
   bind one to a group, as Cao describes it, similar to that of Douchan
   Gersi in "Initiated into an Iban Tribe of Headhunters"?

2. In what way are personal relationships and romance primary objectives in accounts by Cao and Sucheng Chan in "You're Short,
   Besides!"?

✧ Extending Viewpoints through Writing and Research

1. What are some of the differences between eating in a Chinese
   restaurant and a more traditional American restaurant? Research
   some of the ways in which authentic Chinese meals (as opposed to
   Americanized Chinese meals) differ from Western meals. Write a
   short essay exploring the cultural implications of the different
   table manners and social relationships among the diners in the
   two settings.

2. Cutting up food so that it can be cooked quickly (and eaten with
   chopsticks) is much more fuel efficient than is the Western custom
   of roasting or broiling large slabs of meat or boiling vegetables for
   long periods of time. Discuss these contrasts in food preparation
   in terms of the utensils employed and the attitudes toward food
   that are implicit to them.

Whose experience in using chopsticks more closely matches your own?

Germaine Greer

One Man's Mutilation Is Another Man's Beautification

——————◆——————

Germaine Greer (b. 1939), an Australian academic, writer and broadcaster, was educated at the University of Sydney (M.A., 1963) and at the University of Cambridge (Ph.D. 1968). Greer is widely regarded as one of the most significant feminist voices of the twentieth century whose unique perspective is embodied in such works as her ground-breaking The Female Eunuch *(1971),* Slip-shod Sibyls *(1995),* The Whole Woman *(1999),* The Beautiful Boy *(2003), and most recently* Beautiful and Whitefella Jump Up: The Shortest Way to Nationhood *(2004). In the following essay drawn from* The Madwoman's Underclothes *(1986), Greer explores the cultural significance of ways of embellishing—and even mutilating—the human body.*

Before You Read

Evaluate your attitude toward various forms of body modification such as piercing and tatoos.

——————◆——————

1   Humans are the only animals which can consciously and deliberately change their appearance according to their own whims. Most animals groom themselves, but humans are tempted to manipulate their appearance in ways much more radical than those open to other animals, not simply because they are able to use tools upon themselves, but also because of some peculiarities in the way in which humans are made. The human body is a curiously ambiguous structure, partaking of almost contradictory attributes. For example, humans are neither furry nor hairless, but variously naked, slightly hairy, and very hirsute. All these variations may be found on the body of a single individual at the same time. Humans are then confronted with a series of managerial problems: among the ways in which they express their cultural identities are the contrasting ways in which they handle these problems.

2   The Australian Aborigines used to conserve hair; not only did they not eliminate whatever hair was growing on their bodies, they collected extra human hair to work into a thick girdle for men to wear about their hips. We would look askance at anyone who could not bear

to discard fallen hair, now that hair shirts are out of fashion, but sophisticated Western people often wear the hair of others as a postiche or toupee. Where the scalp-hunter once sought to augment his physical or psychic power by acquiring the hair of others, the literate people of the twentieth century feel that they will acquire youth and beauty through bought hair. They will even pay to have hair stitched into their scalps in a very costly and laborious development of the ancient practice of needle-working living flesh.

3   Some people identify themselves partly by their refusal to cut hair, as do the Sikhs, who twist the long silky hair of their beards together with what grows on their heads, tie the whole lot up in a chignon, and cover it with a turban. Others insist on the removal of any hair, wherever it is, and they too may choose a turban, this time to hide a bald head. Western conventions of hair management often appeal to younger or recalcitrant members of societies with strict rules for hair management because they find them more convenient; in fact, they are very subtle and difficult, requiring minute calculations of the degree of shagginess which is appropriate to age, and economic and social status. The rejection of traditional modes of hair management has less to do with convenience and common sense than with the desire to break out of the confinement of the group. A shaven Sikh might object that he is as much Sikh as ever; he may claim that his elimination of his identifying marks was simply to pour out the bath water while retaining the baby, but in fact he has summarily loosened his ties with his religious group in order to be accepted into another group. If he keeps his steel bracelet, which will be recognized by other Sikhs, it is because he does not wish to lose all the advantages connected with belonging to that group. When a Sikh takes his employer to court for refusing to allow him to wear his turban at work, it is not a mere formality. He is making a serious bid to limit his employer's power over his life.

4   The impact of technological culture can be measured by the degree of acceptance of Western conventions of body management throughout the world. Fashion, because it is beyond logic, is deeply revealing. Women all over the world have adopted, often in addition to their traditional accoutrements, four Western conventions: high-heeled shoes, lipstick, nail varnish, and the brassiere. The success of all of these fashions, which are not even remotely connected with comfort or common sense, is an indication of the worldwide acceptance of the Western notion that the principal duties of women are sexual attraction and vicarious leisure. The women who have accepted these fashions will justify their decision by saying that all four are more attractive than the alternatives. All that they are really saying is that they themselves were more attracted to alien styles than they were to the styles adopted by their mothers and grandmothers. To give the full answer would be to

expose the tensions which are destroying traditional lifestyles all over the world. There is a slight traffic in the opposite direction. Distinguished lady professors of economics may reject high heels, lipstick, nail varnish, and brassiere, and adopt the dress of a Punjabi peasant laborer; Iranian girls may resume the chador. In each case the motive for the change is clearly political; what is not so often realized is that it is equally political when it happens the other way around.

5   Because what we do with our bodies is so revealing we try to insist that it has no meaning at all. A man whose hair is cut regularly and at great expense, who shaves his face in a careful pattern, will say that he is not concerned with his appearance, while a man with a beard will maintain that he simply cannot be bothered shaving, but the truth is that both have selected an image which they feel best expresses their characters and chosen social roles. The man with a beard probably shaves some part of his face and neck quite regularly, and definitely trims the beard itself. He may frequently be seen grooming it with his hands, patting and stroking it into his preferred shape. Between the shaggy bearded man and the smooth clean-shaven man there lies a vast range of tonsorial modes, all of which have meanings relative to each other. The man who grows his sideburns long is expressing something about his class and his age group. The man who lets his cheek whiskers grow in tufts or shaves his sideburns off is also projecting some part of a chosen self-image. All kinds of curious facial topiary are accepted provided that they have some pedigree within our cultural tradition. The association of such variations as curled and waxed mustaches, Mexican revolutionary mustaches, pencil mustaches, and toothbrush mustaches are endlessly subtle and constantly being remade.

6   In the recent past we came to accept long flowing hair as a possible masculine alternative; with the passing of time our initial reactions of outrage have softened into acceptance. Men's long curls are now a sign of nostalgia for the sixties, the last quiver of hippie energy, which was never anything to be feared. By contrast, the man who completely shaves his head still shocks us. It is as if he is flaunting a violence that he has done to himself. Other men, hairless through no choice of their own, may have wigs on the National Health to hide their embarrassing nakedness. Western youths whose heads are shaven in accordance with the practice of oriental monastics will wear wigs when they go to badger people in airports because shaven heads are so alienating to our sensibilities. The man who shaves his head and does not cover it is indulging in a form of indecent exposure, the purpose of which, as usual, is intimidation.

7   The shaving of women's heads is considered so disfiguring that it seemed adequate punishment for women who collaborated with the Nazis in the Second World War, and yet there are many cultures whose women shave all or part of their heads and would feel dirty or un-

kempt if they did not. Girls who shave off all the hair except what grows on the crown of their heads are doing no more than the Turkana women of Kenya have always done, but by doing it in a society where such styles have never been seen, they defy the accepted norms and court rejection. The coxcomb and its variants, sometimes called the Mohawk or Mohican hairstyle, imitate the intimidating shapes of the advanced crests of fighting birds. A less daring version, for it can be tamed into smoothness when the wearer is in the haunts of the smooth, is the teased mop. The ferocity mimicked by the hairstyle is further expressed in the studded belts and armlets and earrings in the shape of a skull, but it is clearly a mere affectation. The camp aggressiveness of the display stands in inverse ratio to the social power wielded by the group. Their cultural uniformity is actually competitiveness and does not lead to solidarity.

8   In most societies which modify the body, the visible changes are outward signs of the fulfillment of the rites of passage. The acceptance of the newborn into the community at a naming ceremony or its equivalent may be marked by a ritual haircut, the shape of which may indicate his or her clan or totem. The approach of puberty may be signaled by circumcision or scarification or the adoption of a new hairstyle. The prelude to marriage may require further scarification or tattooing or fattening or a period of special body painting, while marriage itself may be signified by drastic changes in appearance, especially for women. The birth of children, achievement of elder status, or the death of a spouse bring the last changes. In classless societies where property is either held in common or kept to a minimum, all changes in status must involve changes in physical appearance. Where no one carries an identity card which will, say, permit him to drink in the company of adults, everyone who may must be distinguished by a sign. The achievement of these signs is one of the most important satisfactions of such societies. Before imperialists brought mirrors, such people could not confer the signs upon themselves: The recognition of a transition was given dramatic form by the ceremony of the conferring of signs in which the interested parties all acted as a group.

9   In Western society the outward signs of social status have withered into mere vestiges. Pubescent boys may live through intense dramas of hair cultivation, struggling for a mustache or bushy sideburns or simply longing to shave every day. Little girls may covet high heels and brassieres and long for the day that they can wear make-up, but the menarche will not be marked in any way: Marriageability will be signified only by the absence of an inconspicuous ring on the fourth finger of the left hand. In Jewish society, circumcision is still a rite of passage, but once the bar mitzvah is over, the initiate cannot be recognized by any other outward sign. Married women used to be expected to dress differently from girls: a pale echo of the sixteenth-century custom

which required married women to wear closed bodices and hide their hair under a cap. This persisted into the twentieth century when married women were expected to wear hats on social occasions, but has now died out.

10   The disappearance of distinguishing marks of social status in industrial societies is not meaningless, nor can it be construed to mean that human beings have outgrown such childish things. It is an accurate reflection of the fact that social relationships, particularly kinship relations, have been and are under intense pressure from economic relationships. The one insignia that is worn, in the United States more than in Europe but the strengthening of the trend is apparent, is the insignia of the employer. The family is no longer the dominant group and human beings are no longer differentiated on the grounds of their status within it. Instead they are differentiated by their consumer behavior, employment status, income, and possessions: The contrasts are so striking that it is considered indiscreet and tasteless to flaunt them by display of wealth. Instead the degrees of difference are signaled, more or less subtly, by grooming and by some carefully chosen attributes; hints to those who know how to take them are conveyed by the watch, the pen, the attaché case, the note case, the cuff links. Along with the indications of success are clues to other allegiances, the college ring, the lodge pin, the old school tie. Democracy and uniformity in outward appearance are necessitated by the extreme differentiation in economic circumstances, which might otherwise become a source of tension.

11   In tribal societies, where economic activity is static, limited as it is to the repetitive daily functions of survival, there is time to elaborate the paraphernalia of status considered in all but economic terms and immense satisfaction connected with doing so. The individual who proceeds through the stages all duly solemnized has conferred an elegance and order upon the struggle, and within that wider function there is scope for individual expression and aesthetic concerns.

12   The motives for Western beautification are very different. . . . People who are excluded from economic activity . . . cannot compensate by celebrating other forms of status for these have been eliminated. Unhappily, as the social roles which evolve out of family relationships ceased to command respect, the number of older people condemned to live for many years outside the sphere of economic activity in conditions of mere survival increased and will go on increasing. Among the displacement activities which this group must now concentrate on in order to beguile the time between retirement and the grave, there are a number connected with futile imitation of the group from which they have been excluded. As there is no prestige or power connected with being old, it is important to deny the aging process itself. Where once humans celebrated the achievement of seniority and longevity, they now invest as much energy or more in trying to resist the in-

evitable. Where hair coloring used to be done for fun, it is now done for camouflage.

13   A full head of strawberry blonde curls is only acquired by a sixty-year-old after regular orgies of dying, setting, and backcombing, all of which actually speed the degeneration of the scalp and the hair shaft. There is a good deal of pain involved as the dyes bite into sensitive old skin and the hot dryers tighten the hair, driving the pins still further into the old scalp. The ordeal is worth it if the sufferer sees herself rejuvenated by it; the suffering is an essential part of the prophylaxis, but it must be accompanied by words of tenderness and filial care from the torturers. We are not surprised to see the hairdresser as a shaman, hung about with amulets, his face suffused with long-suffering compassion. The payment of money for his services guarantees that the job has been well done; an old lady with a fifty-dollar hairstyle is still a person to be reckoned with. . . .

14   . . . We are in the midst of a cultural upheaval in which the body, which for aeons was a holy thing, its excretions and its orifices feared and revered, is becoming reified. It is becoming a toy, an asset, a commodity, an instrumentality for human will, and the pace of the change is much too fast. The intolerability of pictures of stainless steel meticulously carving out faces and breasts, isolating the unwanted and throwing it in the trash, tells us that we are still superstitious. We still suspect that the fantasy which is being imposed upon the body is less potent and less various than the body itself. Yet we cannot ease our anxiety by sneering, for we know the callousness which characterizes our treatment of the old and obese. We can understand why people who have the money will endure pain and risk death rather than go on living inside the bodies which bear the marks of their own history. Cosmetic surgery is the secular version of confession and absolution. It has taken the place of all our lost ceremonies of death and rebirth. It is reincarnation.

15   Most societies reject the grossly deformed. All societies have notions of beauty and fitness to which they aspire: relatively non-neurotic societies tend to admire characteristics which are well-distributed among their people, because distance from the culturally recognized norm causes suffering. We are affected by our bodies just as our behavior marks them. Peculiar looking people tend to behave peculiarly. Criminologists have known for many years that cosmetic surgery may do more for a social delinquent than years of custody and psychiatric care, when it comes to rehabilitation.

16   Once we begin to sculpt the body to our own aesthetic requirements we enter a realm of shifting values to which there is no guide. In essence, beautification and mutilation are the same activity. The African women who practice genital mutilation do so primarily because they think the result is more attractive; the unreconstructed genitalia are disgusting

to them. Very few Westerners really find the female genitalia beautiful, but most of them would be horrified, even nauseated, by the sight of an infibulated vagina. None of them, by contrast, would cry out in disgust at the sight of a mutilated penis, stripped of its foreskin; all of them would be unpleasantly affected by the sight of a subincised penis.

17   Some mutilations have an ulterior purpose; the biting off of little finger joints of the newborn by Aboriginal mothers may be a way of deflecting the attention of evil spirits who would covet a perfect child. The custom of branding sickly infants in India may incidentally eliminate the feebler ones before too much energy has been invested in their care, and even, perhaps activate sluggish resistance to the pathogens in the environment. In any event, the brands are carefully placed. The endurance of pain, especially in poor communities where pain and discomfort are daily realities, is another important aspect of beautification/mutilation. Scarification is valued not only because it is symmetrically placed about the body and not only because it implies the achievement of new status, but because it hurts. Where survival is only achieved by constant effort, stoicism and willpower are immensely important. The young woman who lies unflinching while the circumciser grinds her clitoris off between two stones is proving that she will make a good wife, equal to all the anguish of child-bearing and daily toil, not only to the witnesses of her bravery, but more importantly, to herself.

18   Industrialized society is the first in which endurance of physical pain is not a condition of survival. We have identified pain as our enemy and have done our best to eradicate even its most manageable manifestations. Scars have no value for us and their aesthetic appeal has perished alongside their moral value. A few women might confess that they feel strangely drawn to men with scarred faces (or eye-patches or limps) but it is generally considered to be an aberrant taste. Yet, augmentation mammoplasty is no more after all than a raised scar. The great difference between ancient and modern beautification/mutilation procedures is that nowadays we must conceal the fact of the procedure itself. The association of sculpted breasts with pain is anaphrodisiac, so much so, that a man who guesses that what he is admiring was produced by a knife, may lose all interest. Some women may boast of their cosmetic operations, but this is a safety valve against the possibility that they will be found out.

19   Most mutilations which have been accepted as beautiful are so by consensus; historically the most astonishing distortions have been admired, necks so elongated that they could not hold up the head unless supported by brass rings, teeth filed and knocked out, lips stretched to accommodate large discs, earlobes stretched until they hung down in large loops. However outré the punks may appear they are the merest beginners in the arts of mutilation. The admiration of certain disfigurements is an important part of the process of self-definition: Contempt

for the same practices is one of the ways in which other groups insist upon their separateness. We are not surprised to find the greatest contrasts in groups living side by side. When genetic equipment and economic status are both very similar, contrasting cultural practices become immensely important; they become the expression of the group's introverted altruism. In most tribal societies the attitude is more or less pluralistic; a group of labret wearers, for example, will simply define themselves as labret wearers, without making any attempt to impose labrets on others or to deride them for being without them. Western industrial society, deluded perhaps by its own vastness and uniformity, is not pluralistic, but utterly convinced that its own practices are the product of enlightenment and ought to be followed by all progressive peoples. Thus Western women, fully accoutred with nail polish (which is incompatible with manual work), high-heeled shoes (disastrous for the posture and hence the back, and quite unsuitable for walking long distances over bad roads), and brassieres (which imitate the shape of a pubescent non-lactating breast rather than the useful organs to be found in most of the world) denounce female circumcision, without the shadow of a suspicion that their behavior is absurd.

20   Yet within this bland but crushing orthodoxy there are spores of something different. Our unemployed young have reverted to tribal practices. They indulge in flamboyant mutilation/beautification which is not understood, let alone appreciated in our common judgment. Teenage daughters come to their parents' dinner parties covered with blue spots, with blue hair standing on end. Deviant groups cemented by shared ritual intoxication or guilt or ordeal or all of these are budding in our rotting inner cities, terrorizing us with raucous music and insulting doggerel. If they had the power to grow like a malignant organism and invade the whole of the body politic we might have reason to be afraid. Like millions of generations of body decorators before them, they have no economic activity beyond survival; they could be toughened by the necessity of existing on the little that society will mete out to them so that they accumulate the collective power to strike at its unprotected underbelly. Or they could fritter away their spare energy in intercommunal war, as gangs have always done. The body art of the urban deviant is unlike any which has appeared on earth before in that it has no socially constructed significance. There is . . . [no] . . . mutual decoration; no young warriors apply magical designs to each other's backs. No priests and witches or mothers and aunts confer new powers upon an initiate. The only human interactions we see are commercial. The manicurists, the cosmetologists, the surgeons, the hairdressers, the tattooists are all professionals. Between the dancer and the dance has been interposed the mirror; the clients have come to the professionals after long and lonely contemplation of the self which dissatisfies them. Individuals do not modify their bodies to please

others or to clarify their relationship to others. Rather they inflict changes upon themselves in order to approximate to narcissistic needs which may have been projected on to putative others.

21   Inside the bodies they have reconstructed, the body builders live incommunicado. The illustrated men disappear behind designs imported from a highly structured alien culture into which they themselves could never be accepted. The body building, the tattooing, the cultivation of cockscombs, the driving of rings, bolts, barbs, and studs through labia, lobes, cartilage, nipples, foreskin are all displacement activities. A caged bird suffering from loneliness and sensory deprivation will turn upon itself and pluck out all its feathers or peck off its own leg. Middle-aged women rejected by their children will turn to surgery, restlessly beautifying/mutilating to no purpose, and a good deal of their activity will be directed against their sexuality. The body builders will proceed until they have become epicene monsters, all body hair shaved off so that the light can catch the slick greased muscles. . . . One of the most potent symbols among all natural symbols is the breast, not only the female breast but by extension the male simulacrum. Only groups doomed to extinction have ever attacked the nipples; cutting, piercing, and distorting them . . . is something hideously strange. . . . Attacks upon the genitalia and the secondary sexual characteristics are attacks upon the continuity of the species; they are only conceivable in lives which are confined to their own duration, on bodies which must be their own gratification, among human contacts which are fleeting and self-centered. . . .

22   The right to economic activity is no longer a right which our society can guarantee to everyone. We are on the brink of an era in which most people will be condemned to a life of enforced leisure and mere subsistence. It may very well be that these displacement activities will have to evolve into legitimate art forms involving a strong and healthy body decorated with skill, sophistication, and meaning. Perhaps human worker bees will some day be delighted by the displays of squads of human butterflies bred and trained to dance the drab streets as living works of art. It would be a great pity if the dazzling tradition of human body art were to perish in a waste of dreary conformity on the one hand and neurotic self-distortion on the other.

✧ Evaluating the Text

   1. In what ways do the motives for body modification in tribal cultures differ from those in Western societies? Which examples in Greer's essay best illustrate the cultural forces that underlie the desire to decorate, modify, and even mutilate oneself?

2. Greer devotes a considerable portion of her essay to the body modification practices of women. Which features of her essay reveal an awareness of the unique pressures to which females are subjected in contemporary society?

3. How would you characterize Greer's attitude toward the customs she describes? How persuasive do you find her analysis? Do you disagree with her on some points—for example, her explanations for body piercing in Western cultures? Explain your reactions.

✧ *Exploring Different Perspectives*

1. What factors might explain the difference in tone in Greer's attitude toward the customs she describes and Guanlong Cao's about making chopsticks?

2. How do the designs in the Persian carpet in Hanan Al-Shaykh's story function as a symbol in the same way as the markings described by Greer in terms of what they say about the owners?

✧ *Extending Viewpoints through Writing and Research*

1. What body modifications have you undergone or considered making? In what way would these changes either bring you into conformity with accepted norms or define you in opposition to those norms? Were any of the modifications associated with a rite of passage, that is, with the beginning of a new phase of your life? Describe your experiences and analyze their cultural meanings. In your opinion, why does Western society generally approve of ear piercing while disapproving to various degrees of other forms of body piercing (nose piercing, naval piercing, nipple piercing, genital piercing, or tongue piercing)?

2. Greer's tone in this piece is sharp and questioning. How does her style differ from that of a typical fashion magazine, such as *Vogue, Glamour,* or *Esquire,* when she analyzes a feature of Western fashion? Greer treats the familiar and commonplace as if it were unfamiliar. Does this make her essay more or less effective? Why?

3. For an online exhibition of body art see http://www.bodyart .com/bodyart/.

To what extent does this picture illustrate Greer's thesis about rebellion?

Connecting Cultures

◆

Sucheng Chan, "You're Short, Besides!"

What ironic paradox emerges from Valerie Steele and John S. Majors's discussion (see "China Chic: East Meets West" in Chapter 8) of foot binding and Chinese attitudes toward disability in Chan's narrative?

Christy Brown, "The Letter 'A'"

Compare and contrast the attitudes of the parents toward their children in Brown's account and in Mahdokht Kashkuli's story "The Button" in Chapter 5.

Hanan Al-Shaykh, "The Persian Carpet"

Compare the issue of betrayal in Al-Shaykh's story and in Nawal El-Saadawi's "Circumcision of Girls" in Chapter 3.

Sabine Reichel, "Learning What Was Never Taught"

Compare accounts by Reichel with Rae Yang's "At the Center of the Storm" (Chapter 6) in terms of students trying to understand their culture's past wars and revolutions.

Douchan Gersi, "Initiated into an Iban Tribe of Headhunters"

Compare the courage shown to gain acceptance by Gersi and by Victor Villaseñor's father in "Rain of Gold" (Chapter 4).

Guanlong Cao, "Chopsticks"

What do we learn about the role of artifacts in different cultural settings from Cao's account and Harold Miner's "Body Ritual Among the Nacirema" (Chapter 8)?

Germaine Greer, "One Man's Mutilation Is Another Man's Beautification"

Compare the motives underlying body modification in Greer's account with the role of foot binding in China described by Valerie Steele and John S. Majors in "China Chic: East Meets West" in Chapter 8.

3

How Culture Shapes Gender Roles

*Because of our social circumstances, male and female are really
two cultures and their life experiences are utterly different.*
—Kate Millett (b. 1934, U.S. feminist writer),
Sexual Politics (1969)

◆

Culture plays an enormous part in shaping the expectations we attach
to sex roles. This process, sometimes called *socialization*, determines
how each of us assimilates our culture's ideas of what it means to act as
a male or female. We tend to acquire a sense of our own sexual identity
in conjunction with societal expectations. Yet, these expectations differ
strikingly from culture to culture. For example, in male-dominated
Islamic Middle Eastern societies, the gender roles and relationships
between men and women are very different from those in modern
Western industrial societies.

The characteristics that define gender roles have varied widely
throughout history in cultures as diverse as those in Europe, Asia, the
Middle East, and the Americas. The responsibilities and obligations
that collectively define what it means to be a woman or a man in different societies have changed dramatically in those societies, which
have themselves changed in recent times. The movement toward
equality between the sexes—a transformation that has been only partially realized—has allowed women to assume positions of leadership
and perform tasks in the workplace, in the professions, and in society
that were traditionally reserved for men. The works in this chapter address the changing cultural expectations attached to being a man or a
woman as well as the psychological and social stresses produced by
these changes in redrawing the boundaries of gender roles, marriage,
and parenthood.

How you see yourself is determined in large part by the social
meanings attached to specific behavior for men and women in your

culture—beginning with the fairy tales told to children, extending through the conceptions of masculinity and femininity promulgated by the media, and including opportunities available in the workplace.

The authors in this chapter provide insight into the way in which we acquire specific sexual identities, because of the cultural expectations, pressures, and values that shape the choices we make. How we feel about ourselves and our life experiences reveals the powerful role played by gender stereotypes in shaping our personal development. Some writers in this chapter speak out against the constricting effects of these rigid cultural expectations that enforce inflexible images of masculine and feminine behavior. These restrictive stereotypes legitimize and perpetuate gender inequality.

Susan Bordo, in "Never Just Pictures," perceptively analyzes the cultural pressures that compel women to starve themselves to be thin. Barbara Kantrowitz, in "The New Face of Marriage," discusses the issue of same-sex marriage as it exists in many countries around the world. Judith Ortiz Cofer, in "The Myth of the Latin Woman," describes how different cultural expectations in her native Puerto Rico and the United States resulted in her being stereotyped as a "hot-blooded Latina." An Egyptian physician and feminist, Nawal El Saadawi, in "Circumcision of Girls," analyzes the cultural prejudices that still encourage the practice of female circumcision in many Middle Eastern countries.

The Lebanese writer Shirley Saad, in "Amina," tells the story of a woman who has given birth to only girls and fears that her husband will take another wife in order to have a son. Elizabeth W. Fernea and Robert A. Fernea, in "A Look Behind the Veil," investigate the practice of *purdah* and its role in preserving Islamic values in a patriarchal culture. Serena Nanda, in "Arranging a Marriage in India," describes her participation in the lengthy process of getting her friend's son married. Nicholas Bornoff, in "The Marriage Go-Round," analyzes how social expectations control courtship and marriage in modern-day Japan.

Susan Bordo

Never Just Pictures

◆

Susan Bordo is a professor of English and women's studies at the University of Kentucky and was awarded the Singletary Chair of Humanities. Bordo's book Unbearable Weight: Feminism, Western Culture and the Body *(1993) examines the myths, ideologies, and pathologies of the modern female body. She is also the author of* The Male Body: A New Look at Men in Public and Private *(1999). "Never Just Pictures" first appeared in* Twilight Zones: The Hidden Life of Cultural Images from Plato to O.J. *(1997).*

Before You Read

Before you read Bordo's essay, which raises questions about the images of women presented in advertising, think about some current ads for women's products. Do the ads encourage women to be dissatisfied with the way they look? Whether you are male or female, what part, if any, do the media play in your concept of how you should look?

◆

Bodies and Fantasies

1   When Alicia Silverstone, the svelte nineteen-year-old star of *Clueless,* appeared at the Academy Awards just a smidge more substantial than she had been in the movie, the tabloids ribbed her cruelly, calling her "fatgirl" and "buttgirl" (her next movie role is Batgirl) and "more *Babe* than babe."[1] Our idolatry of the trim, tight body shows no signs of relinquishing its grip on our conceptions of beauty and normality. Since I began exploring this obsession it seems to have gathered momentum, like a spreading mass hysteria. Fat is the devil, and we are continually beating him—"eliminating" our stomachs, "busting" our thighs, "taming" our tummies—pummeling and purging our bodies, attempting to make them into something other than flesh. On television, infomercials hawking miracle diet pills and videos promising to turn our body parts into steel have become as commonplace as aspirin ads. There hasn't been a tabloid cover in the past few years that didn't boast of an inside scoop on some star's diet regime, a "fabulous" success story of weight loss, or a tragic relapse. (When they can't come up with a current one, they scrounge up an old one; a few weeks ago the *National Inquirer* ran a story on Joan Lunden's fifty-pound weight loss

fifteen years ago!) Children in this culture grow up knowing that you can never be thin enough and that being fat is one of the worst things one can be. One study asked ten- and eleven-year-old boys and girls to rank drawings of children with various physical handicaps; drawings of fat children elicited the greatest disapproval and discomfort, over pictures of kids with facial disfigurements and missing hands.

2   Psychologists commonly believe that girls with eating disorders suffer from "body image disturbance syndrome": they are unable to see themselves as anything but fat, no matter how thin they become. If this is a disorder, it is one that has become a norm of cultural perception. Our ideas about what constitutes a body in need of a diet have become more and more pathologically trained on the slightest hint of excess. This ideal of the body beautiful has largely come from fashion designers and models. (Movie stars, who often used to embody a more voluptuous ideal, are now modeling themselves after the models.) They have taught us "to love a woman's pelvis, her hipbones jutting out through a bias-cut gown . . . the clavicle in its role as a coat hanger from which clothes are suspended."[2] (An old fashion industry justification for skinniness in models was that clothes just don't "hang right" on heftier types.) The fashion industry has taught us to regard a perfect healthy, nonobese body . . . as an unsightly "before" ("Before CitraLean, no wonder they wore swimsuits like that"). In fact, those in the business have admitted that models have been getting thinner since 1993, when Kate Moss first repopularized the waif look. British models Trish Goff and Annie Morton make Moss look well fed by comparison,[3] and recent ad campaigns for Jil Sander go way beyond the thin-body-as-coat-hanger paradigm to a blatant glamorization of the cadaverous, starved look itself. . . . More and more ads featuring anorexic-looking young men are appearing too.

3   The main challenge to such images is a muscular aesthetic that *looks* more life-affirming but is no less punishing and compulsion-inducing in its demands on ordinary bodies. During the 1996 Summer Olympics—which were reported with unprecedented focus and hype on the fat-free beauty of muscular bodies—commentators celebrated the "health" of this aesthetic over anorexic glamour. But there is growing evidence of rampant eating disorders among female athletes, and it's hard to imagine that those taut and tiny Olympic gymnasts—the idols of preadolescents across the country—are having regular menstrual cycles. Their skimpy level of body fat just won't support it. During the Olympics I heard a commentator gushing about how great it was that the 1996 team was composed of eighteen- and nineteen-year-old women rather than little girls. To me it is far more disturbing that these nineteen-year-olds still *look* (and talk) like little girls. As I watched them vault and leap, my admiration for their tremendous

skill and spirit was shadowed by thoughts of what was going on *inside* their body—the hormones unreleased because of insufficient body fat, the organ development delayed, perhaps halted.

4   Is it any wonder that despite media attention to the dangers of starvation dieting and habitual vomiting, eating disorders have spread throughout the culture?[4] In 1993 in *Unbearable Weight* I argued that the old clinical generalizations positing distinctive class, race, family, and "personality" profiles for the women most likely to develop an eating disorder were being blasted apart by the normalizing power of mass imagery. Some feminists complained that I had not sufficiently attended to racial and ethnic "difference" and was assuming the white, middle-class experience as the norm. Since then it has been widely acknowledged among medical professionals that the incidence of eating and body-image problems among African American, Hispanic, and Native American women has been grossly underestimated and is on the increase.[5] Even the gender gap is being narrowed, as more and more men are developing eating disorders and exercise compulsions too. (In the mid-eighties the men in my classes used to yawn and pass notes when we discussed the pressure to diet; in 1996 they are more apt to protest if the women in the class talk as though it's their problem alone.)

5   The spread of eating disorders, of course, is not just about images. The emergence of eating disorders is a complex, multilayered cultural "symptom," reflecting problems that are historical as well as contemporary, arising in our time because of the confluence of a number of factors.[6] Eating disorders are overdetermined in this culture. They have to do not only with new social expectations of women and ambivalence toward their bodies but also with more general anxieties about the body as the source of hungers, needs, and physical vulnerabilities not within our control. These anxieties are deep and longstanding in Western philosophy and religion, and they are especially acute in our own time. Eating disorders are also linked to the contradictions of consumer culture, which is continually encouraging us to binge on our desires at the same time as it glamorizes self-discipline and scorns fat as a symbol of laziness and lack of willpower. And these disorders reflect, too, our increasing fascination with the possibilities of reshaping our bodies and selves in radical ways, creating new bodies according to our mind's design.

6   The relationship between problems such as these and cultural images is complex. On the one hand, the idealization of certain kinds of bodies foments and perpetuates our anxieties and insecurities, that's clear. Glamorous images of hyperthin models certainly don't encourage a more relaxed or accepting attitude toward the body, particularly among those whose own bodies are far from that ideal. But, on the other hand, such images carry fantasized solutions *to* our anxieties and insecurities, and that's part of the reason why they are powerful. They

speak to us not just about how to be beautiful or desirable but about how to get control of our lives, get safe, be cool, avoid hurt. When I look at the picture of a skeletal and seemingly barely breathing young woman . . . , for example, I do not see a vacuous fashion ideal. I see a visual embodiment of what novelist and ex-anorexic Stephanie Grant means when she says in her autobiographical novel, *The Passion of Alice*, "If I had to say my anorexia was about any single thing, I would have said it was about living without desire. Without longing of any kind."[7]

7   Now, this may not seem like a particularly attractive philosophy of life (or a particularly attractive body, for that matter). Why would anyone want to look like death, you might be asking. Why would anyone want to live without desire? But recent articles in both the *New Yorker* and the *New York Times* have noted a new aesthetic in contemporary ads, in which the models appear dislocated and withdrawn, with chipped black nail polish and greasy hair, staring out at the viewer in a deathlike trance, seeming to be "barely a person." Some have called this wasted look "heroin chic": ex-model Zoe Fleischauer recalls that "they wanted models that looked like junkies. The more skinny and fucked-up you look, the more everybody thinks you're fabulous."[8]

8   Hilton Als, in the *New Yorker*, interprets this trend as making the statement that fashion is dead and beauty is "trivial in relation to depression."[9] I read these ads very differently. Although the photographers may see themselves as ironically "deconstructing" fashion, the reality is that no fashion advertisement can declare fashion to be dead—it's virtually a grammatical impossibility. Put that frame around the image, whatever the content, and we are instructed to find it glamorous. These ads are not telling us that beauty is trivial in relation to depression, they are telling us that depression is beautiful, that being wasted is *cool*. . . . The question then becomes not "Is fashion dead?" but "Why has death become glamorous?"

9   Freud tells us that in the psyche death represents not the destruction of the self but its return to a state prior to need, thus freedom from unfulfilled longing, from anxiety over not having one's needs met. Following Freud, I would argue that ghostly pallor and bodily disrepair, in "heroin chic" images, are about the allure, the safety, of being beyond needing, beyond caring, beyond desire. Should we be surprised at the appeal of being without desire in a culture that has invested our needs with anxiety, stress, and danger, that has made us craving and hungering machines, creatures of desire, and then repaid us with addictions, AIDS, shallow and unstable relationships, and cutthroat competition for jobs and mates? To have given up the quest for fulfillment, to be unconcerned with the body or its needs—or its vulnerability—is much wiser than to care.

10   So, yes, the causes of eating disorders are "deeper" than just obedience to images. But cultural images themselves *are* deep. And the

way they become imbued and animated with such power is hardly mysterious. Far from being the purely aesthetic inventions that designers and photographers would like to have us believe they are—"It's just fashion, darling, nothing to get all politically steamed up about"— they reflect the designers' cultural savvy, their ability to sense and give form to flutters and quakes in the cultural psyche. These folks have a strong and simple motivation to hone their skills as cultural Geiger counters. It's called the profit motive. They want their images and the products associated with them to sell.

11   The profit motive can sometimes produce seemingly "transgressive" wrinkles in current norms. Recently designers such as Calvin Klein and Jil Sander have begun to use rather plain, ordinary-looking, unmadeup faces in their ad campaigns. Unlike the models in "heroin chic" ads, these men and women do not appear wasted so much as unadorned, unpolished, stripped of the glamorous veneer we have come to expect of fashion spreads. While many of them have interesting faces, few of them qualify as beautiful by any prevailing standards. They have rampant freckles, moles in unbeautiful places, oddly proportioned heads. Noticing these ads, I at first wondered whether we really were shifting into a new gear, more genuinely accepting of diversity and "flaws" in appearance. Then it suddenly hit me that these imperfect faces were showing up in clothing and perfume ads only and the *bodies* in these ads were as relentlessly normalizing as ever— not one plump body to complement the facial "diversity."

12   I now believe that what we are witnessing here is a commercial war. Clothing manufacturers, realizing that many people—particularly young people, at whom most of these ads are aimed—have limited resources and that encouraging them to spend all their money fixing up their faces rather than buying clothes is not in their best interests, are reasserting the importance of body over face as the "site" of our fantasies. In the new codes of these ads a too madeup look signifies a lack of cool, too much investment in how one looks. "Just Be," Calvin Klein tells us in a recent CK One ad. But looks—a lean body—still matter enormously in these ads, and we are still being told *how* to be—in the mode which best serves Calvin Klein. And all the while, of course, makeup and hair products continue to promote their own self-serving aesthetics of facial perfection.

NOTES

1. I give great credit to Alicia Silverstone for her response to these taunts. In *Vanity Fair* she says, "I do my best. But it's much more important to me that my brain be working in the morning than getting up early and doing exercise. . . . The most important thing for me is that I eat and that I sleep and that I get the work done, but unfortunately . . . it's the perception that women in film should look a certain way" ("Hollywood Princess," September 1996, pp. 292–294). One wonders how long she will manage to retain such a sane attitude!

2. Holly Brubach, "The Athletic Aesthetic," *The New York Times Magazine*, June 23, 1996, p. 51.

3. In early 1996 the Swiss watch manufacturer Omega threatened to stop advertising in British *Vogue* because of *Vogue*'s use of such hyperthin models, but it later reversed this decision. The furor was reminiscent of boycotts that were threatened in 1994 when Calvin Klein and Coca-Cola first began to use photos of Kate Moss in their ads. In neither case has the fashion industry acknowledged any validity to the charge that their imagery encourages eating disorders. Instead, they have responded with defensive "rebuttals."

4. Despite media attention to eating disorders, an air of scornful impatience with "victim feminism" has infected attitudes toward women's body issues. Christina Hoff-Sommers charges Naomi Wolf (*The Beauty Myth*) with grossly inflating statistics on eating disorders and she poo-poos the notion that women are dying from dieting. Even if some particular set of statistics is inaccurate, why would Sommers want to deny the reality of the problem, which as a teacher she can surely see right before her eyes?

5. For the spread of eating disorders in minority groups, see, for example, "The Art of Integrating Diversity: Addressing Treatment Issues of Minority Women in the 90's," in *The Renfrew Perspective*, Winter 1994; see also Becky Thompson, *A Hunger So Wide and So Deep* (Minneapolis: University of Minnesota Press, 1994).

6. See my *Unbearable Weight* (Berkeley: University of California Press, 1993).

7. Stephanie Grant, *The Passion of Alice* (New York: Houghton Mifflin, 1995), 58.

8. Zoe Fleischauer quoted in "Rockers, Models, and the New Allure of Heroin," *Newsweek*, August 26, 1996.

9. Hilton Als, "Buying the Fantasy," *The New Yorker*, October 10, 1996, p. 70.

✧ Evaluating the Text

1. How do the pervasive eating disorders so common in U.S. culture suggest an underlying confusion in values associated with being fat?

   Since this was written in 1997 we have seen more and more ads with fleshier models and some campaigns actually flaunt the big-girl look. In your opinion, will this help girls to stop harming themselves to be thin?

2. What relationships between social classes, men and women, and ethnic minorities and mainstream society, underlie Bordo's thesis? What role do the media and advertising play in urging women to reshape their bodies to fit cultural stereotypes?

✧ Exploring Different Perspectives

1. How do Bordo and Judith Ortiz Cofer in "The Myth of the Latin Woman" deal with the psychological effects of stereotyping based on appearance?

2. Compare and contrast the cultural pressures on women in America, according to Bordo, and those in Middle Eastern countries as discussed by Nawal El Saadawi in "Circumcision of Girls."

❖ *Extending Viewpoints through Writing and Research*

1. Our attitudes toward food are invariably connected with cultural messages about losing weight and being thin. Analyze the promotional claims for any weight loss program, diet, or exercise video, and in a short essay, discuss how cultural values are interwoven with the message.

2. You might rent the 2002 film, *Shallow Hal,* and in a few paragraphs, discuss what the movie says about American values regarding weight and appearance. To what extent has your own self-image been determined by prevailing cultural expectations of the kind described by Bordo? What parts of your body or aspects of your appearance would you change and why?

" I WANT TO BE THIN LIKE ALLY M⊂BEAL, STACKED LIKE BARBIE and ETERNALLY YOUNG LIKE A SUPERMODEL....
NOW IF YOU'LL EXCUSE ME, I HAVE TO GO VOMIT MY HAPPY MEAL. "

Is this cartoon realistic or exaggerated?

Barbara Kantrowitz

The New Face of Marriage

◆

Barbara Kantrowitz, the lead editor[1] for this article, which appeared in the March 1, 2004, issue of Newsweek International, *has been an editor and writer at* Newsweek *since 1985. She has written many cover stories on education and family issues and has won numerous awards. Kantrowitz, who is a graduate of Cornell University and the Columbia University Graduate School of Journalism, is also a published fiction writer. The debate over same-sex marriage and the proposed constitutional amendment to prohibit it is a signal that the institution of marriage is undergoing a radical transformation both here and abroad.*

Before You Read

Consider whether the government should have a say in same-sex marriages.

◆

1   Los Angeles actresses Alice Dodd and Jillian Armenante got married four years ago at a raucous wedding in New Jersey before 250 friends and family members. Even so, when San Francisco Mayor Gavin Newsom began issuing same-sex marriage licenses in mid-February—in open defiance of California law—the couple drove 650 kilometers north and waited in line for seven hours at city hall to tie the knot again. "Uncle Sam couldn't make it to our first wedding," says Armenante. "We thought it would be nice if he came to our second." They were among the more than 3,000 gay and lesbian couples that had exchanged vows by the end of last week, even though it's still not clear whether their marriages will stand up in court.

2   To supporters of gay rights, the scene was deeply moving: elderly men and women who had spent a lifetime waiting to make their unions legal, parents with infants in their arms, middle-aged lawyers and doctors. But to opponents, the peaceful scene was a provocative call to arms. American conservatives say San Francisco is proof of the anarchy they've predicted if officials act on their own before the legal

[1]With Brad Stone, Pat Wingert, Karen Springen, Julie Scelfo, Barry Brown, Liat Radcliffe, Stefan Theil, Melissa Roberts, Kay Itoi, Mac Margolis, Peter Hudson, and bureau reports.

153

debate over gay marriage is settled. "There are millions of Americans angry and disgusted by what they see on the TV—two brides, two grooms, but not a man and a woman," says Randy Thomasson, executive director of the Campaign for California Families, which is fighting the San Francisco marriages in court. "This is the new civil war in America."

3   The issue threatens to be a defining one in the current U.S. presidential election. Under pressure from his evangelical Christian supporters, President George W. Bush has been dancing around it for months. Although he keeps reiterating his view that marriage should be limited to the union of a man and a woman, he has stopped short of a full public endorsement of a constitutional amendment that would ban same-sex weddings. His most likely Democratic opponent, Massachusetts Sen. John Kerry, has said he opposes gay marriage but thinks the issue is up to each state to decide.

4   The debate is gaining momentum. Civil unions between same-sex couples are currently legal in only one state—Vermont—but at the end of last week officials in New Mexico's Sandoval County began issuing licenses to gays before being shut down by the state's attorney general. The next move will most likely be in court, not only in California, but also in Massachusetts, where the state's Supreme Judicial Court essentially legalized gay marriage in November. State officials have until mid-May to say how they will comply.

5   Much of the rest of the world is watching America's struggle with curiosity. In many places, same-sex marriage is simply a ho-hum issue. Last week even the 81-year-old king of Cambodia, Norodom Sihanouk, said that as a "liberal democracy," his country should allow gays and lesbians to marry. The Netherlands became the first country to legalize same-sex marriages, in 2001; Belgium followed earlier last year, as did two Canadian provinces, Ontario and British Columbia. In Brazil, stable gay and lesbian couples can inherit from each other and claim one another as dependents in tax returns. In the Argentine province Rio Negro and the capital of Buenos Aires, new laws allow registered gay couples to qualify for family welfare payments. While critics contend that same-sex weddings will destroy the "sanctity" of traditional unions, many scholars say that it's actually heterosexual couples who are radically redefining marriage. Many countries, including Norway, Sweden, Denmark and its province Greenland, have registered partnership laws that extend some benefits of marriage to unmarried couples, both gay and straight. Germany has quietly expanded rights for cohabitating couples, while in 1998, France approved the Pacte Civil de Solidarite—a kind of intermediate step between casual cohabitation and formal marriage that provides tax and health benefits. "There is no way to turn back the wheel," says sociologist Dieter Bruhl of Germany's University of Oldenburg. "Today mar-

riage is an institution at the free disposal of individualized members of a highly differentiated society."

6   Across the world, the old model—marriage and then kids—has given way to a dizzying array of family arrangements that reflect more lenient attitudes about cohabitation, divorce and illegitimate births. University of Chicago sociologist Linda Waite, author of *The Case for Marriage,* says that gay couples are "really swimming against the tide. What they want is something that maybe heterosexual couples take for granted: the social, religious and legal recognition of a union."

7   On the other hand, this increasingly diverse family album could be one reason why the push for gay marriage has struck a nerve among some social conservatives. The institution of marriage is so battered that many consider gay unions the last straw, says Princeton historian Hendrik Hartog, author of *Man and Wife in America.* "They see gay marriage as a boundary case," he says—in other words, a step too far.

8   Marriage rates are tumbling virtually everywhere. In 1990, eight out of every 1,000 Brazilians got married; a decade later that number had dropped to 5.7. In Europe as well, marriage rates are plummeting and illegitimate births are increasingly common. Divorce rates are rising; Germany's divorce rate reached a record high last year—and new marriages approached a record low. "We've moved from de jure to de facto marriage," says Kathleen Kiernan of the London School of Economics. She estimates that 50 percent of 25- to 34-year-olds in Europe are cohabiting. The numbers are highest, perhaps 70 percent, in Scandinavia, especially Sweden. The Swedes have even created their own term for someone who cohabits: "sambo," or "living together": a word that appears on official forms besides the options "married" and "single." Another new word, "sarbo," refers to people who consider themselves a couple but live apart.

9   In many countries, women see little reason to forgo their newly won independence. The number of thirtysomething single women in Japan has increased drastically in recent years. "They don't have a good reason to get married or, rather, a good reason to put a stop to their single lives," says Keiko Oshima, chief planner at Gauss Life Psychology Institute, a marketing agency in Tokyo. A Yomiuri Shimbun survey conducted in August found that 52 percent of people believed that a woman could be happy without marriage. The same poll found that only 45 percent thought that a man became a "real man" when he had his own family. Nearly one in three Tokyo women in their 30s is unmarried, in a culture where getting married at 25 was once the norm.

10   Establishing a family used to involve four steps: a marital ceremony, moving in together, beginning a sex life and finally having children. Today couples pick and choose not only the steps but also which will come first. Thirty years ago, says Kiernan, only five of 19 European countries reported 10 percent or more of children born out of

wedlock. Today only Greece remains below that threshold, and the European average has jumped to 30 percent.

11   Those figures are of great concern to researchers, who say that children suffer without the emotional and economic support of two parents—and thrive when reared in stable two-parent families. Married
couples tend to have more assets, live longer and are better adjusted
emotionally than their single counterparts. Fewer money worries may
contribute to that well-being, but having someone around to watch out
for you also helps, says Evelyn Lehrer, a professor of economics at the
University of Illinois.

12   While the decline of marriage may seem to portend some kind of
social cataclysm, scholars say the institution has always been in flux,
responding to the particular needs of different eras. "Throughout
much of history, if you acted like you were married, then you were
treated like you were married," says marriage historian Stephanie
Coontz of Evergreen State University in Washington. Religion, a major
part of the current defense of "traditional" marriage, didn't even enter
the picture, Coontz says, until the ninth century, and then only to prevent European aristocrats from marrying close relatives. The goal was
to make sure noble families didn't consolidate too much power. (Com-
moners could still hook up with anyone they fancied.)

13   Even in modern times, traditional marriage has never been a universal institution. Carlos Eroles, a lecturer in social work at the University of Buenos Aires, says that throughout Argentina's history, the
lower classes and especially farm laborers tended to cohabit, while the
upper classes married. Marriage became more widespread after the influx of millions of immigrants from Spain and Italy, both conservative
Roman Catholic countries, during the nineteenth and early twentieth
centuries.

14   What's most amazing, perhaps, is that the ideal of marriage has
such staying power. The push by gay activists to gain equal rights in
marriage was initially motivated by the desire to obtain the legal benefits of being a spouse, such as health insurance and inheritance rights.
But many say that it's equally important to make a public statement of
affection and commitment—a view of marriage that crosses political
and social boundaries. In 1998, Australian Jackie Stricker married Dr.
Kerryn Phelps under a chuppah (the Jewish marriage canopy) in a Park
Avenue apartment. "The rabbi read verses from the Book of Ruth:
'Where you go, I will go'," Stricker recalls. "It was incredibly romantic."
The two women are now back in Australia, where gay couples have
some limited rights but can't legally marry. "No group in any society
should be grateful for crumbs from the table masquerading as grand
gestures," says Phelps. "I feel robbed of the language of being married,
of being the daughter-in-law, the wife, the aunt, the stepmother." And
when the law says "You can't," the sweetest words are "I do."

✧ *Evaluating the Text*

1. What are the pros and cons of legalizing same-sex marriage, according to the author?

2. How does the author provide a context for this discussion by citing a wide range of statistics and customs regarding the institution of marriage worldwide?

3. To what extent have other countries moved in the direction of allowing same-sex marriages that the United States is just starting to consider?

✧ *Exploring Different Perspectives*

1. What are the different objectives marriage is supposed to achieve (for same-sex couples), according to Kantrowitz, and in Lebanon, according to Shirley Saad, in "Amina"?

2. Compare the changing picture of marriage in Kantrowitz's article with the constraints governing marriage in India as described by Serena Nanda in "Arranging a Marriage in India."

✧ *Extending Viewpoints through Writing and Research*

1. Do some research to discover how this issue influenced the outcome of the 2004 presidential election.

2. In your opinion, to what extent are gender roles culturally produced rather than biologically determined?

3. A current debate on same-sex marriage can be found at http://en.wikipedia.org/wiki/same-sex_marriage.

Judith Ortiz Cofer

The Myth of the Latin Woman

◆

Judith Ortiz Cofer, a poet and novelist, was born in 1952 in Hormigueros, Puerto Rico. After her father, a career navy officer, retired, the family set- tled in Georgia where Cofer attended Augusta College. During college she married and, with her husband and daughter, moved to Florida where she finished a master's degree in English at Florida Atlantic University. A fellowship allowed her to pursue graduate work at Oxford University, af- ter which she returned to Florida and began teaching English and writing poetry. Her first volume of poetry, Peregrina *(1985), won the Riverstone International Poetry Competition and was followed by two more poetry collections,* Reaching for the Mainland *(1987) and* Terms of Survival *(1988). Her first novel,* The Line of the Sun *(1989), was listed as one of 1989's "twenty-five books to remember" by the New York City Public Library System. Her recent works include a collection of short stories,* An Island Like You: Stories of the Barrio *(1995), and* The Year of Our Revolution *(1998). Cofer is a Professor of English and Creative Writing at the University of Georgia. In the following essay, drawn from her col- lection* The Latin Deli: Prose and Poetry *(1993), Cofer explores the destructive effects of the Latina stereotype. Most recently, she has written* Call Me Maria: A Novel *(2004).*

Before You Read

As you read, notice how Cofer's desire to succeed as a writer is a reaction to the repeated instances in which she is misperceived because of her ethnicity.

◆

1   On a bus trip to London from Oxford University where I was earn- ing some graduate credits one summer, a young man, obviously fresh from a pub, spotted me and as if struck by inspiration went down on his knees in the aisle. With both hands over his heart he broke into an Irish tenor's rendition of "Maria" from *West Side Story*. My politely amused fellow passengers gave his lovely voice the round of gentle ap- plause it deserved. Though I was not quite as amused, I managed my version of an English smile: no show of teeth, no extreme contortions of the facial muscles—I was at this time of my life practicing reserve and cool. Oh, that British control, how I coveted it. But "Maria" had

followed me to London, reminding me of a prime fact of my life: you can leave the island, master the English language, and travel as far as you can, but if you are a Latina, especially one like me who so obviously belongs to Rita Moreno's gene pool, the island travels with you.

2   This is sometimes a very good thing—it may win you that extra minute of someone's attention. But with some people, the same things can make *you* an island—not a tropical paradise but an Alcatraz, a place nobody wants to visit. As a Puerto Rican girl living in the United States and wanting like most children to "belong," I resented the stereotype that my Hispanic appearance called forth from many people I met.

3   Growing up in a large urban center in New Jersey during the 1960s, I suffered from what I think of as "cultural schizophrenia." Our life was designed by my parents as a microcosm of their *casas* on the island. We spoke in Spanish, ate Puerto Rican food bought at the *bodega*, and practiced strict Catholicism at a church that allotted us a one-hour slot each week for mass, performed in Spanish by a Chinese priest trained as a missionary for Latin America.

4   As a girl I was kept under strict surveillance by my parents, since my virtue and modesty were, by their cultural equation, the same as their honor. As a teenager I was lectured constantly on how to behave as a proper *senorita*. But it was a conflicting message I received, since the Puerto Rican mothers also encouraged their daughters to look and act like women and to dress in clothes our Anglo friends and their mothers found too "mature" and flashy. The difference was, and is, cultural; yet I often felt humiliated when I appeared at an American friend's party wearing a dress more suitable to a semi-formal than to a playroom birthday celebration. At Puerto Rican festivities, neither the music nor the colors we wore could be too loud.

5   I remember Career Day in our high school, when teachers told us to come dressed as if for a job interview. It quickly became obvious that to the Puerto Rican girls "dressing up" meant wearing their mothers' ornate jewelry and clothing, more appropriate (by mainstream standards) for the company Christmas party than as daily office attire. That morning I had agonized in front of my closet, trying to figure out what a "career girl" would wear. I knew how to dress for school (at the Catholic school I attended, we all wore uniforms), I knew how to dress for Sunday mass, and I knew what dresses to wear for parties at my relatives' homes. Though I do not recall the precise details of my Career Day outfit, it must have been a composite of these choices. But I remember a comment my friend (an Italian American) made in later years that coalesced my impressions of that day. She said that at the business school she was attending, the Puerto Rican girls always stood out for wearing "everything at once." She meant, of course, too much

jewelry, too many accessories. On that day at school we were simply made the negative models by the nuns, who were themselves not credible fashion experts to any of us. But it was painfully obvious to me that to the others, in their tailored skirts and silk blouses, we must have seemed "hopeless" and "vulgar." Though I now know that most adolescents feel out of step much of the time, I also know that for the Puerto Rican girls of my generation that sense was intensified. The way our teachers and classmates looked at us that day in school was just a taste of the cultural clash that awaited us in the real world, where prospective employers and men on the street would often misinterpret our tight skirts and jingling bracelets as a "come-on."

6   Mixed cultural signals have perpetuated certain stereotypes—for example, that of the Hispanic woman as the "hot tamale" or sexual firebrand. It is a one-dimensional view that the media have found easy to promote. In their special vocabulary, advertisers have designated "sizzling" and "smoldering" as the adjectives of choice for describing not only the foods but also the women of Latin America. From conversations in my house I recall hearing about the harassment that Puerto Rican women endured in factories where the "boss-men" talked to them as if sexual innuendo was all they understood, and worse, often gave them the choice of submitting to their advances or being fired.

7   It is custom, however, not chromosomes, that leads us to choose scarlet over pale pink. As young girls, it was our mothers who influenced our decisions about clothes and colors—mothers who had grown up on a tropical island where the natural environment was a riot of primary colors, where showing your skin was one way to keep cool as well as to look sexy. Most important of all, on the island, women perhaps felt freer to dress and move more provocatively since, in most cases, they were protected by the traditions, mores, and laws of a Spanish/Catholic system of morality and machismo whose main rule was: *You may look at my sister, but if you touch her I will kill you.* The extended family and church structure could provide a young woman with a circle of safety in her small pueblo on the island; if a man "wronged" a girl, everyone would close in to save her family honor.

8   My mother has told me about dressing in her best party clothes on Saturday nights and going to the town's plaza to promenade with her girlfriends in front of the boys they liked. The males were thus given an opportunity to admire the women and to express their admiration in the form of *piropos:* erotically charged street poems they composed on the spot. (I have myself been subjected to a few *piropos* while visiting the island, and they can be outrageous, although custom dictates that they must never cross into obscenity.) This ritual, as I understand it, also entails a show of studied indifference on the woman's part; if she is "decent," she must not acknowledge the man's impassioned words. So I do understand how things can be lost in translation. When

a Puerto Rican girl dressed in her idea of what is attractive meets a man from the mainstream culture who has been trained to react to certain types of clothing as a sexual signal, a clash is likely to take place. I remember the boy who took me to my first formal dance leaning over to plant a sloppy, over-eager kiss painfully on my mouth; when I didn't respond with sufficient passion, he remarked resentfully: "I thought you Latin girls were supposed to mature early," as if I were expected to *ripen* like a fruit or vegetable, not just grow into womanhood like other girls.

9   It is surprising to my professional friends that even today some people, including those who should know better, still put others "in their place." It happened to me most recently during a stay at a classy metropolitan hotel favored by young professional couples for weddings. Late one evening after the theater, as I walked toward my room with a colleague (a woman with whom I was coordinating an arts program), a middle-aged man in a tuxedo, with a young girl in satin and lace on his arm, stepped directly into our path. With his champagne glass extended toward me, he exclaimed "Evita!"[1]

10   Our way blocked, my companion and I listened as the man half-recited, half-bellowed "Don't Cry for Me, Argentina." When he finished, the young girl said: "How about a round of applause for my daddy?" We complied, hoping this would bring the silly spectacle to a close. I was becoming aware that our little group was attracting the attention of the other guests. "Daddy" must have perceived this too, and he once more barred the way as we tried to walk past him. He began to shout-sing a ditty to the tune of "La Bamba"—except the lyrics were about a girl named Maria whose exploits rhymed with her name and gonorrhea. The girl kept saying "Oh, Daddy" and looking at me with pleading eyes. She wanted me to laugh along with the others. My companion and I stood silently waiting for the man to end his offensive song. When he finished, I looked not at him but at his daughter. I advised her calmly never to ask her father what he had done in the army. Then I walked between them and to my room. My friend complimented me on my cool handling of the situation, but I confessed that I had really wanted to push the jerk into the swimming pool. This same man—probably a corporate executive, well-educated, even worldly by most standards—would not have been likely to regale an Anglo woman with a dirty song in public. He might have checked his impulse by assuming that she could be somebody's wife or mother, or at least *somebody* who might take offense. But, to him, I was just an Evita or a Maria: merely a character in his cartoon-populated universe.

11   Another facet of the myth of the Latin woman in the United States is the menial, the domestic—Maria the housemaid or countergirl. It's

[1]A musical about Eva Duarte de Peron, the former first lady of Argentina.

true that work as domestics, as waitresses, and in factories is all that's available to women with little English and few skills. But the myth of the Hispanic menial—the funny maid, mispronouncing words and cooking up a spicy storm in a shiny California kitchen—has been perpetuated by the media in the same way that "Mammy" from *Gone with the Wind* became America's idea of the black woman for generations. Since I do not wear my diplomas around my neck for all to see, I have on occasion been sent to that "kitchen" where some think I obviously belong.

12   One incident has stayed with me, though I recognize it as a minor offense. My first public poetry reading took place in Miami, at a restaurant where a luncheon was being held before the event. I was nervous and excited as I walked in with notebook in hand. An older woman motioned me to her table, and thinking (foolish me) that she wanted me to autograph a copy of my newly published slender volume of verse, I went over. She ordered a cup of coffee from me, assuming that I was the waitress. (Easy enough to mistake my poems for menus, I suppose.) I know it wasn't an intentional act of cruelty. Yet of all the good things that happened later, I remember that scene most clearly, because it reminded me of what I had to overcome before anyone would take me seriously. In retrospect I understand that my anger gave my reading fire. In fact, I have almost always taken any doubt in my abilities as a challenge, the result most often being the satisfaction of winning a convert, of seeing the cold, appraising eyes warm to my words, the body language change, the smile that indicates I have opened some avenue for communication. So that day as I read, I looked directly at that woman. Her lowered eyes told me she was embarrassed at her faux pas, and when I willed her to look up at me, she graciously allowed me to punish her with my full attention. We shook hands at the end of the reading and I never saw her again. She has probably forgotten the entire incident, but maybe not.

13   Yet I am one of the lucky ones. There are thousands of Latinas without the privilege of an education or the entrees into society that I have. For them life is a constant struggle against the misconceptions perpetuated by the myth of the Latina. My goal is to try to replace the old stereotypes with a much more interesting set of realities. Every time I give a reading, I hope the stories I tell, the dreams and fears I examine in my work, can achieve some universal truth that will get my audience past the particulars of my skin color, my accent, or my clothes.

14   I once wrote a poem in which I called all Latinas "God's brown daughters." This poem is really a prayer of sorts, offered upward, but also, through the human-to-human channel of art, outward. It is a prayer for communication and for respect. In it, Latin women pray "in Spanish to an Anglo God/ with a Jewish heritage," and they are "fervently hoping/ that if not omnipotent,/ at least He be bilingual."

✧ Evaluating the Text

1. What characteristics define, from Cofer's perspective, the "Maria" stereotype in terms of style, clothes, and behavior? How has this stereotype been a source of harassment for Cofer?

2. How has the desire to destroy this stereotype and its underlying attitudes motivated Cofer to write the kinds of works she has?

3. How does Cofer use her personal experiences as a springboard to understanding sexual stereotyping of Latinas?

✧ Exploring Different Perspectives

1. What constraints operate in Puerto Rican culture, according to Cofer, to guard the modesty of women as compared to those in Middle Eastern societies that practice *purdah,* as described by Elizabeth W. Fernea and Robert A. Fernea in "A Look Behind the Veil"?

2. How do both Cofer and Kantrowitz in "The New Face of Marriage" seek to replace sexual stereotypes with realistic portraits?

✧ Extending Viewpoints through Writing and Research

1. Have you ever been in a situation where someone who is unaware of your ethnic, racial, or religious background disparaged the group to which you belong? What did you do?

2. Create a character sketch of a male chauvinist.

Nawal El Saadawi

Circumcision of Girls

◆

Nawal El Saadawi is an Egyptian physician and feminist writer whose work publicizing the injustices and brutalities to which Arab women are subject is well known throughout the world. Born in the village of Kafr-tahla on the banks of the Nile, in 1931, she began her medical practice in rural areas, then in Cairo, and became Egypt's Director of Public Health. The publication of her first nonfiction book, Women and Sex *(1972), re-sulted in her dismissal from her post by Anwar Sadat, imprisonment, and censorship of her books on the status, psychology, and sexuality of women. Her works are now banned in Egypt, Saudi Arabia, and Libya. The fol-lowing chapter, "Circumcision of Girls," is from* The Hidden Face of Eve: Women in the Arab World *(1980, translated and edited by Saadawi's husband, Dr. Sherif Hetata), a work depicting the hitherto un-publicized but culturally accepted procedure of female circumcision, a practice to which she herself was subjected at the age of eight.* A Daugh-ter of Isis: The Autobiography of Nawal El Saadawi *was translated into English from the Arabic in 1999. Her most recent work is* The Fall of the Imam *(2002).*

Before You Read

Consider how El Saadawi is careful to present herself as a physician ar-ticulating and supporting a claim, and not as someone who is simply a victim.

◆

1   The practice of circumcising girls is still a common procedure in a number of Arab countries such as Egypt, the Sudan, Yemen and some of the Gulf states.

2   The importance given to virginity and an intact hymen in these so-cieties is the reason why female circumcision still remains a very wide-spread practice despite a growing tendency, especially in urban Egypt, to do away with it as something outdated and harmful. Behind circum-cision lies the belief that, by removing parts of girls' external genital or-gans, sexual desire is minimized. This permits a female who has reached the 'dangerous age' of puberty and adolescence to protect her virginity, and therefore her honour, with greater ease. Chastity was im-posed on male attendants in the female harem by castration which turned them into inoffensive eunuchs. Similarly female circumcision is

meant to preserve the chastity of young girls by reducing their desire for sexual intercourse.

3   Circumcision is most often performed on female children at the age of seven or eight (before the girl begins to get menstrual periods). On the scene appears the *daya* or local midwife. Two women members of the family grasp the child's thighs on either side and pull them apart to expose the external genital organs and to prevent her from struggling—like trussing a chicken before it is slain. A sharp razor in the hand of the *daya* cuts off the clitoris.

4   During my period of service as a rural physician, I was called upon many times to treat complications arising from this primitive operation, which very often jeopardized the life of young girls. The ignorant *daya* believed that effective circumcision necessitated a deep cut with the razor to ensure radical amputation of the clitoris, so that no part of the sexually sensitive organ would remain. Severe hemorrhage was therefore a common occurrence and sometimes led to loss of life. The *dayas* had not the slightest notion of asepsis, and inflammatory conditions as a result of the operation were common. Above all, the lifelong psychological shock of this cruel procedure left its imprint on the personality of the child and accompanied her into adolescence, youth and maturity. Sexual frigidity is one of the after-effects which is accentuated by other social and psychological factors that influence the personality and mental make-up of females in Arab societies. Girls are therefore exposed to a whole series of misfortunes as a result of outdated notions and values related to virginity, which still remains the fundamental criterion of a girl's honour. In recent years, however, educated families have begun to realize the harm that is done by the practice of female circumcision.

5   Nevertheless a majority of families still impose on young female children the barbaric and cruel operation of circumcision. The research that I carried out on a sample of 160 Egyptian girls and women showed the 97.5% of uneducated families still insisted on maintaining the custom, but this percentage dropped to 66.2% among educated families.[1]

6   When I discussed the matter with these girls and women it transpired that most of them had no idea of the harm done by circumcision, and some of them even thought that it was good for one's health and conducive to cleanliness and 'purity.' (The operation in the common language of the people is in fact called the cleansing or purifying operation.) Despite the fact that the percentage of educated women who have undergone circumcision is only 66.2%, as compared with 97.5% among uneducated women, even the former did not realize the effect that this amputation of the clitoris could have on their psychological and sexual health. The dialogue that occurred between these women and myself would run more or less as follows:

7   'Have you undergone circumcision?'

8   'Yes.'

9   'How old were you at the time?'

10   'I was a child, about seven or eight years old.'

11   'Do you remember the details of the operation?'

12   'Of course. How could I possibly forget?'

13   'Were you afraid?'

14   'Very afraid. I hid on top of the cupboard [in other cases she would say under the bed, or in the neighbour's house], but they caught hold of me, and I felt my body tremble in their hands.'

15   'Did you feel any pain?'

16   'Very much so. It was like a burning flame and I screamed. My mother held my head so that I could not move it, my aunt caught hold of my right arm and my grandmother took charge of my left. Two strange women whom I had not seen before tried to keep me from moving my thighs by pushing them as far apart as possible. The *daya* sat between these two women, holding a sharp razor in her hand which she used to cut off the clitoris. I was scared and suffered such great pain that I lost consciousness at the flame that seemed to sear me through and through.'

17   'What happened after the operation?'

18   'I had severe bodily pains, and remained in bed for several days, unable to move. The pain in my external genital organs led to retention of urine. Every time I wanted to urinate the burning sensation was so unbearable that I could not bring myself to pass water. The wound continued to bleed for some time, and my mother used to change the dressing for me twice a day.'

19   'What did you feel on discovering that a small organ in your body had been removed?'

20   'I did not know anything about the operation at the time, except that it was very simple, and that it was done to all girls for purposes of cleanliness, purity and the preservation of a good reputation. It was said that a girl who did not undergo this operation was liable to be talked about by people, her behaviour would become bad, and she would start running after men, with the result that no one would agree to marry her when the time for marriage came. My grandmother told me that the operation had only consisted in the removal of a very small piece of flesh from between my thighs, and that the continued existence of this small piece of flesh in its place would have made me unclean and impure, and would have caused the man whom I would marry to be repelled by me.'

21   'Did you believe what was said to you?'

22   'Of course I did. I was happy the day I recovered from the effects of the operation, and felt as though I was rid of something which had to be removed, and so had become clean and pure.'

23   Those were more or less the answers that I obtained from all those interviewed, whether educated or uneducated. One of them was a medical student from Ein Shams School of Medicine. She was preparing for her final examinations and I expected her answers to be different but in fact they were almost identical to the others. We had quite a long discussion which I reproduce here as I remember it.

24   'You are going to be a medical doctor after a few weeks, so how can you believe that cutting off the clitoris from the body of a girl is a healthy procedure, or at least not harmful?'

25   'This is what I was told by everybody. All the girls in my family have been circumcised. I have studied anatomy and medicine, yet I have never heard any of the professors who taught us explain that the clitoris had any function to fulfill in the body of a woman, neither have I read anything of the kind in the books which deal with the medical subjects I am studying.'

26   'That is true. To this day medical books do not consider the science of sex as a subject which they should deal with. The organs of a woman worthy of attention are considered to be only those directly related to reproduction, namely the vagina, the uterus and the ovaries. The clitoris, however, is an organ neglected by medicine, just as it is ignored and disdained by society.'

27   'I remember a student asking the professor one day about the clitoris. The professor went red in the face and answered him curtly, saying that no one was going to ask him about this part of the female body during examinations, since it was of no importance.'

28   My studies led me to try and find out the effect of circumcision on the girls and women who had been made to undergo it, and to understand what results it had on the psychological and sexual life. The majority of the normal cases I interviewed answered that the operation had no effect on them. To me it was clear that in the face of such questions they were much more ashamed and intimidated than the neurotic cases were. But I did not allow myself to be satisfied with these answers, and would go on to question them closely about their sexual life both before and after the circumcision was done. Once again I will try to reproduce the dialogue that usually occurred.

29   'Did you experience any change of feeling or of sexual desire after the operation?'

30   'I was a child and therefore did not feel anything.'

31   'Did you not experience any sexual desire when you were a child?'

32   'No, never. Do children experience sexual desire?'

33   'Children feel pleasure when they touch their sexual organs, and some form of sexual play occurs between them, for example, during the game of bride and bridegroom usually practised under the bed. Have you never played this game with your friends when still a child?'

34   At these words the young girl or woman would blush, and her eyes would probably refuse to meet mine, in an attempt to hide her confusion. But after the conversation had gone on for some time, and an atmosphere of mutual confidence and understanding had been established, she would begin to recount her childhood memories. She would often refer to the pleasure she had felt when a man of the family permitted himself certain sexual caresses. Sometimes these caresses would be proffered by the domestic servant, the house porter, the private teacher or the neighbour's son. A college student told me that her brother had been wont to caress her sexual organs and that she used to experience acute enjoyment. However after undergoing circumcision she no longer had the same sensation of pleasure. A married woman admitted that during intercourse with her husband she had never experienced the slightest sexual enjoyment, and that her last memories of any form of pleasurable sensation went back twenty years, to the age of six, before she had undergone circumcision. A young girl told me that she had been accustomed to practise masturbation, but had given it up completely after removal of the clitoris at the age of ten.

35   The further our conversations went, and the more I delved into their lives, the more readily they opened themselves up to me and uncovered the secrets of childhood and adolescence, perhaps almost forgotten by them or only vaguely realized.

36   Being both a woman and a medical doctor I was able to obtain confessions from these women and girls which it would be almost impossible, except in very rare cases, for a man to obtain. For the Egyptian woman, accustomed as she is to a very rigid and severe upbringing built on a complete denial of any sexual life before marriage, adamantly refuses to admit that she has even known, or experienced, anything related to sex before the first touches of her husband. She is therefore ashamed to speak about such things with any man, even the doctor who is treating her.

37   My discussions with some of the psychiatrists who had treated a number of the young girls and women in my sample, led me to conclude that there were many aspects of the life of these neurotic patients that remained unknown to them. This was due either to the fact that the psychiatrist himself had not made the necessary effort to penetrate deeply into the life of the woman he was treating, or to the tendency of the patient herself not to divulge those things which her upbringing made her consider matters not to be discussed freely, especially with a man.

38   In fact the long and varied interchanges I had over the years with the majority of practising psychiatrists in Egypt, my close association with a large number of my medical colleagues during the long periods I spent working in health centres and general or specialized hospitals and, finally, the four years I spent as a member of the National Board of

the Syndicate of Medical Professions, have all led me to the firm conclusion that the medical profession in our society is still incapable of understanding the fundamental problems with which sick people are burdened, whether they be men or women, but especially if they are women. For the medical profession, like any other profession in society, is governed by the political, social and moral values which predominate, and like other professions is one of the institutions which is utilized more often than not to protect these values and perpetuate them.

39   Men represent the vast majority in the medical profession, as in most professions. But apart from this, the mentality of women doctors differs little, if at all, from that of the men, and I have known quite a number of them who were even more rigid and backward in outlook than their male colleagues.

40   A rigid and backward attitude towards most problems, and in particular towards women and sex, predominates in the medical profession, and particularly within the precincts of the medical colleges in the Universities.

41   Before undertaking my research study on 'Women and Neurosis' at Ein Shams University, I had made a previous attempt to start it at the Kasr El Eini Medical College in the University of Cairo, but had been obliged to give up as a result of the numerous problems I was made to confront. The most important obstacle of all was the overpowering traditionalist mentality that characterized the professors responsible for my research work, and to whom the word 'sex' could only be equated to the word 'shame.' 'Respectable research' therefore could not possibly have sex as its subject, and should under no circumstances think of penetrating into areas even remotely related to it. One of my medical colleagues in the Research Committee advised me not to refer at all to the question of sex in the title of my research paper, when I found myself obliged to shift to Ein Shams University. He warned me that any such reference would most probably lead to fundamental objections which would jeopardize my chances of going ahead with it. I had initially chosen to define my subject as 'Problems that confront the sexual life of modern Egyptian women,' but after prolonged negotiations I was prevailed to delete the word 'sexual' and replace it by 'psychological.' Only thus was it possible to circumvent the sensitivities of the professors at the Ein Shams Medical School and obtain their consent to go ahead with the research.

42   After I observed the very high percentages of women and girls who had been obliged to undergo circumcision, or who had been exposed to different forms of sexual violation or assault in their childhood, I started to look for research undertaken in these two areas, either in the medical colleges or in research institutes, but in vain. Hardly a single medical doctor or researcher had ventured to do any work on these subjects, in view of the sensitive nature of the issues

involved. This can also be explained by the fact that most of the research carried out in such institutions is of a formal and superficial nature, since its sole aim is to obtain a degree or promotion. The path of safety is therefore the one to choose, and safety means to avoid carefully all subjects of controversy. No one is therefore prepared to face difficulties with the responsible academic and scientific authorities, or to engage in any form of struggle against them, or their ideas. Nor is anyone prepared to face up to those who lay down the norms of virtue, morals and religious behaviour in society. All the established leaderships in the area related to such matters suffer from a pronounced allergy to the word 'sex,' and any of its implications, especially if it happens to be linked to the word 'woman.'

43   Nevertheless I was fortunate enough to discover a small number of medical doctors who had the courage to be different, and therefore to examine some of the problems related to the sexual life of women. I would like to cite, as one of the rare examples, the only research study carried out on the question of female circumcision in Egypt and its harmful effects. This was the joint effort of Dr. Mahmoud Koraim and Dr. Rushdi Ammar, both from Ein Shams Medical College, and which was published in 1965. It is composed of two parts, the first of which was printed under the title *Female Circumcision and Sexual Desire*,[2] and the second, under the title *Complications of Female Circumcision*.[3] The conclusions arrived at as a result of this research study, which covered 651 women circumcised during childhood, may be summarized as follows:

44   1. Circumcision is an operation with harmful effects on the health of women, and is the cause of sexual shock to young girls. It reduces the capacity of a woman to reach the peak of her sexual pleasure (i.e., orgasm) and has a definite though lesser effect in reducing sexual desire.

45   2. Education helps to limit the extent to which female circumcision is practised, since educated parents have an increasing tendency to refuse the operation for their daughters. On the other hand, uneducated families still go in for female circumcision in submission to prevailing traditions, or in the belief that removal of the clitoris reduces the sexual desire of the girl, and therefore helps to preserve her virginity and chastity after marriage.

46   3. There is no truth whatsoever in the idea that female circumcision helps in reducing the incidence of cancerous disease of the external genital organs.

47   4. Female circumcision in all its forms and degrees, and in particular the fourth degree known as Pharaonic or Sudanese excision, is

accompanied by immediate or delayed complications such as inflammations, haemorrhage, disturbances in the urinary passages, cysts or swellings that can obstruct the urinary flow or the vaginal opening.

48   5. Masturbation in circumcised girls is less frequent than was observed by Kinsey in girls who have not undergone this operation.

49   I was able to exchange views with Dr. Mahmoud Koraim during several meetings in Cairo. I learnt from him that he had faced numerous difficulties while undertaking his research, and was the target of bitter criticism from some of his colleagues and from religious leaders who considered themselves the divinely appointed protectors of morality, and therefore required to shield society from such impious undertakings, which constituted a threat to established values and moral codes.

50   The findings of my research study coincide with some of the conclusions arrived at by my two colleagues on a number of points. There is no longer any doubt that circumcision is the source of sexual and psychological shock in the life of the girl, and leads to a varying degree of sexual frigidity according to the woman and her circumstances. Education helps parents realize that this operation is not beneficial, and should be avoided, but I have found that the traditional education given in our schools and universities, whose aim is simply some certificate, or degree, rather than instilling useful knowledge and culture, is not very effective in combating the long-standing, and established traditions that govern Egyptian society, and in particular those related to sex, virginity in girls, and chastity in women. These areas are strongly linked to moral and religious values that have dominated and operated in our society for hundreds of years.

51   Since circumcision of females aims primarily at ensuring virginity before marriage, and chastity throughout, it is not to be expected that its practice will disappear easily from Egyptian society or within a short period of time. A growing number of educated families are, however, beginning to realize the harm that is done to females by this custom, and are therefore seeking to protect their daughters from being among its victims. Parallel to these changes, the operation itself is no longer performed in the old primitive way, and the more radical degrees approaching, or involving, excision are dying out more rapidly. Nowadays, even in upper Egypt and the Sudan, the operation is limited to the total, or more commonly the partial, amputation of the clitoris. Nevertheless, while undertaking my research, I was surprised to discover, contrary to what I had previously thought, that even in educated urban families over 50% still consider circumcision as essential to ensure female virginity and chastity.

52   Many people think that female circumcision only started with the advent of Islam. But as a matter of fact it was well known and widespread in some areas of the world before the Islamic era, including in the Arab peninsula. Mahomet the Prophet tried to oppose this custom since he considered it harmful to the sexual health of the woman. In one of his sayings the advice reported as having been given by him to Om Attiah, a woman who did tattooings and circumcision, runs as follows: 'If you circumcise, take only a small part and refrain from cutting most of the clitoris off . . . The woman will have a bright and happy face, and is more welcome to her husband, if her pleasure is complete.'[4]

53   This means that the circumcision of girls was not originally an Islamic custom, and was not related to monotheistic religions, but was practised in societies with widely varying religious backgrounds, in countries of the East and the West, and among peoples who believed in Christianity, or in Islam, or were atheistic . . . Circumcision was known in Europe as late as the 19th century, as well as in countries like Egypt, the Sudan, Somaliland, Ethiopia, Kenya, Tanzania, Ghana, Guinea and Nigeria. It was also practised in many Asian countries such as Sri Lanka and Indonesia, and in parts of Latin America. It is recorded as going back far into the past under the Pharaonic Kingdoms of Ancient Egypt, and Herodotus mentioned the existence of female circumcision seven hundred years before Christ was born. This is why the operation as practised in the Sudan is called 'Pharaonic excision.'

54   For many years I tried in vain to find relevant sociological or anthropological studies that would throw some light on the reasons why such a brutal operation is practised on females. However I did discover other practices related to girls and female children which were even more savage. One of them was burying female children alive almost immediately after they were born, or even at a later stage. Other examples are the chastity belt, or closing the aperture of the external genital organs with steel pins and a special iron lock.[5] This last procedure is extremely primitive and very much akin to Sudanese circumcision where the clitoris, external lips and internal lips are completely excised, and the orifice of the genital organs closed with a flap of sheep's intestines leaving only a very small opening barely sufficient to let the tip of the finger in, so that the menstrual and urinary flows are not held back. This opening is slit at the time of marriage and widened to allow penetration of the male sexual organ. It is widened again when a child is born and then narrowed down once more. Complete closure of the aperture is also done on a woman who is divorced, so that she literally becomes a virgin once more and can have no sexual intercourse except in the eventuality of marriage, in which case the opening is restored.

55   In the face of all these strange and complicated procedures aimed at preventing sexual intercourse in women except if controlled by the husband, it is natural that we should ask ourselves why women, in

particular, were subjected to such torture and cruel suppression. There seems to be no doubt that society, as represented by its dominant classes and male structure, realized at a very early stage that sexual desire in the female is very powerful, and that women, unless controlled and subjugated by all sorts of measures, will not submit themselves to the moral, social, legal and religious constraints with which they have been surrounded, and in particular the constraints related to monogamy. The patriarchal system, which came into being when society had reached a certain stage of development and which necessitated the imposition of one husband on the woman whereas a man was left free to have several wives, would never have been possible, or have been maintained to this day, without the whole range of cruel and ingenious devices that were used to keep her sexuality in check and limit her sexual relations to only one man, who had to be her husband. This is the reason for the implacable enmity shown by society towards female sexuality, and the weapons used to resist and subjugate the turbulent force inherent in it. The slightest leniency in facing this 'potential danger' meant that woman would break out of the prison bars to which marriage had confined her, and step over the steely limits of a monogamous relationship to a forbidden intimacy with another man, which would inevitably lead to confusion in succession and inheritance, since there was no guarantee that a strange man's child would not step into the waiting line of descendants. Confusion between the children of the legitimate husband and the outside lover would mean the unavoidable collapse of the patriarchal family built around the name of the father alone.

56   History shows us clearly that the father was keen on knowing who his real children were, solely for the purpose of handing down his landed property to them. The patriarchal family, therefore, came into existence mainly for economic reasons. It was necessary for society simultaneously to build up a system of moral and religious values, as well as a legal system capable of protecting and maintaining these economic interests. In the final analysis we can safely say that female circumcision, the chastity belt and other savage practices applied to women are basically the result of the economic interests that govern society. The continued existence of such practices in our society today signifies that these economic interests are still operative. The thousands of *dayas*, nurses, paramedical staff and doctors, who make money out of female circumcision, naturally resist any change in these values and practices which are a source of gain to them. In the Sudan there is a veritable army of *dayas* who earn a livelihood out of the series of operations performed on women, either to excise their external genital organs, or to alternately narrow and widen the outer aperture according to whether the woman is marrying, divorcing, remarrying, having a child or recovering from labour.[6]

57   Economic factors and, concomitantly, political factors are the basis upon which such customs as female circumcision have grown up. It is important to understand the facts as they really are, the reasons that lie behind them. Many are the people who are not able to distinguish between political and religious factors, or who conceal economic and political motives behind religious arguments in an attempt to hide the real forces that lie at the basis of what happens in society and in history. It has very often been proclaimed that Islam is at the root of female circumcision, and is also responsible for the under-privileged and backward situation of women in Egypt and the Arab countries. Such a contention is not true. If we study Christianity it is easy to see that this religion is much more rigid and orthodox where women are concerned than Islam. Nevertheless, many countries were able to progress rapidly despite the preponderance of Christianity as a religion. This progress was social, economic, scientific and also affected the life and position of women in society.

58   That is why I firmly believe that the reasons for the lower status of women in our societies, and the lack of opportunities for progress afforded to them, are not due to Islam, but rather to certain economic and political forces, namely those of foreign imperialism operating mainly from the outside, and of the reactionary classes operating from the inside. These two forces cooperate closely and are making a concerted attempt to misinterpret religion and to utilize it as an instrument of fear, oppression and exploitation.

59   Religion, if authentic in the principles it stands for, aims at truth, equality, justice, love and a healthy wholesome life for all people, whether men or women. There can be no true religion that aims at disease, mutilation of the bodies of female children, and amputation of an essential part of their reproductive organs.

60   If religion comes from God, how can it order man to cut off an organ created by Him as long as that organ is not diseased or deformed? God does not create the organs of the body haphazardly without a plan. It is not possible that He should have created the clitoris in woman's body only in order that it be cut off at an early stage in life. This is a contradiction into which neither true religion nor the Creator could possibly fall. If God has created the clitoris as a sexually sensitive organ, whose sole function seems to be the procurement of sexual pleasure for women, it follows that He also considers such pleasure for women as normal and legitimate, and therefore as an integral part of mental health. The psychic and mental health of women cannot be complete if they do not experience sexual pleasure.

61   There are still a large number of fathers and mothers who are afraid of leaving the clitoris intact in the bodies of their daughters. Many a time they have said to me that circumcision is a safeguard against the mistakes and deviations into which a girl may be led. This

way of thinking is wrong and even dangerous because what protects a boy or a girl from making mistakes is not the removal of a small piece of flesh from the body, but consciousness and understanding of the problems we face, and a worthwhile aim in life, an aim which gives it meaning and for whose attainment we exert our mind and energies. The higher the level of consciousness to which we attain, the closer our aims draw to human motives and values, and the greater our desire to improve life and its quality, rather than to indulge ourselves in the mere satisfaction of our senses and the experience of pleasure, even though these are an essential part of existence. The most liberated and free of girls, in the true sense of liberation, are the least preoccupied with sexual questions, since these no longer represent a problem. On the contrary, a free mind finds room for numerous interests and the many rich experiences of a cultured life. Girls that suffer sexual suppression, however, are greatly preoccupied with men and sex. And it is a common observation that an intelligent and cultured woman is much less engrossed in matters related to sex and to men than is the case with ordinary women, who have not got much with which to fill their lives. Yet at the same time such a woman takes much more initiative to ensure that she will enjoy sex and experience pleasure, and acts with a greater degree of boldness than others. Once sexual satisfaction is attained, she is able to turn herself fully to other important aspects of life.

62   In the life of liberated and intelligent women, sex does not occupy a disproportionate position, but rather tends to maintain itself within normal limits. In contrast, ignorance, suppression, fear and all sorts of limitations exaggerate the role of sex in the life of girls and women, and cause it to swell out of all proportion and to end up by occupying the whole, or almost the whole, of their lives.

REFERENCES

1. This research study was carried out in the years 1973 and 1974 in the School of Medicine, Ein Shams University, under the title: *Women and Neurosis.*
2. *Female Circumcision and Sexual Desire,* Mahmoud Koraim and Rushdi Ammar (Ein Shams University Press, Cairo, 1965).
3. *Complications of Female Circumcision,* the same authors (Cairo, 1965).
4. See *Dawlat El Nissa'a,* Abdel Rahman El Barkouky, first edition (Renaissance Bookshop, Cairo, 1945).
5. Desmond Morris, *The Naked Ape* (Corgi, 1967), p. 76.
6. Rose Oldfield, 'Female genital mutilation, fertility control, women's roles, and patrilineage in modern Sudan,' *American Ethnologist,* Vol. II, No. 4, November 1975.

✧ *Evaluating the Text*

1. How does the fact that El Saadawi herself is a physician who has treated girls suffering the medical complications of circumcision enhance the credibility of her analysis?

2. Why does El Saadawi find it so distressing that, even among the educated (of whom two-thirds have undergone the operation), few women have given up the cultural programming that female circumcision is a purifying or cleansing procedure?

3. What are the psychological and economic objectives of female circumcision? How, in El Saadawi's view, does it function as one of the main methods by which the countries of Sudan, Yemen, Saudi Arabia, and Libya keep their social structure intact and ensure the transmission of property from one generation to the next?

4. Do you believe that the 160 interviews she conducted would be a sample sufficiently large to form the basis for generalizations? Why was the interview with the medical student particularly significant? What harmful psychological effects of female circumcision did El Saadawi discover from the interviews she conducted?

5. What prevailing beliefs did Koraim and Ammar's study about the supposed medical efficacy of circumcision disclose to be baseless? How does El Saadawi use the results of their study in her analysis?

6. How does El Saadawi's reference to Mahomet's comment support her claim that female circumcision was not originally an Islamic custom? How is this phase of her argument intended to undercut claims by religious leaders that they are simply upholding Islamic religious values?

✧ Exploring Different Perspectives

1. To what extent is female circumcision as portrayed by El Saadawi part of the same restricting value system as *purdah* as described by Elizabeth W. Fernea and Robert A. Fernea in "A Look Behind the Veil"?

2. Are the cultural pressures on women caused by pervasive advertising in America, as discussed by Susan Bordo in "Never Just Pictures," as damaging psychologically as female circumcision is in Middle Eastern countries?

✧ Extending Viewpoints through Writing and Research

1. Compare and contrast the value placed on female virginity in the cultures El Saadawi is describing with contemporary American society. What factors do you think explain the differences, and how do these differences reflect the different ways women are viewed in these two cultures?

2. Is there any outdated custom or practice that you would like to eliminate in contemporary society? Formulate your response as an

argument, making sure that you cite evidence and give cogent reasons to support your views. You should also attempt to anticipate the objections opponents to your views might raise and think of responses to each of these possible objections.

3. Drawing on El Saadawi's essay, explore the relationship between law and custom and women's freedom of choice. How is the societal practice of female circumcision intended to take the power of choice out of the woman's hands as to what she will do with her body? Discuss possible similarities between this practice and issues arising from the continuing abortion debate in America.

4. For research on female genital mutilation (FGM), consult http://en.wikipedia.org/wiki/Female_circumcision.

Shirley Saad

Amina

◆

Shirley Saad was born in Cairo in 1947 to a Lebanese father and a Polish-Romanian mother. Saad was educated at St. Clare's College by Irish nuns and spoke English, French, and Italian until the 1952 revolution in which Gamal Abdel Nasser gained power, after which the study of Arabic became mandatory in the schools. In 1961 her family moved to Lebanon. Largely self-taught, Saad was influenced by reading the novels of Hanan al-Shaykh and, while she lived in Abu Dhabi, started writing stories about restrictions imposed on women in the Arabic world. "Amina" sympathizes with the plight of a woman who has just given birth to a child and is apprehensive that her husband will take another wife if the child is not a son.

Before You Read

Consider whether, as a parent, having a boy or girl would be more important to you and why.

◆

1   Amina opened her eyes and for a moment wondered where she was. Then she remembered and a moan escaped her lips. The English nurse hurried over and bent down, "Don't you worry now," she said. "You'll be fine and the baby is all right."

2   Amina asked, not daring to hope, "Is it a boy or a girl?"

3   "A girl," replied the nurse cheerfully. "A beautiful, bouncing, four kilograms girl. *Mabruk*, congratulations."

4   "*Allah yi barek fi omrek*," murmured Amina as she sank back on her pillows. Another girl!

5   What a catastrophe. What would happen to her now? She had brought four girls into the world, four girls in six years of marriage. She felt tears running down her cheeks, and remembered how happy and proud she had been when her mother told her that she was engaged to be married.

6   She had seen Hamid twice, once at her cousin's house when he arrived unexpectedly. The girls all scattered to their quarters to put on their masks and veils. The next time, he came with his father to ask for her hand in marriage. The houseboy serving the coffee told the Indian housegirl who in turn, ran and told her mistress. So, she had gone to

peek through the partition between the men's and women's *majlis*. She saw Hamid and his father sipping coffee and being congratulated by all the men in the family. They embraced and rubbed noses, big smiles on everyone's faces.

7   Amina remembered her wedding, the noise and the bustle, her hennaed hands and feet, the whispers among the older women which frightened her and the anticipation. Finally, she found herself alone with this stranger, who had turned out to be very kind and gentle and considerate.

8   Well, there would be no henna and celebration for this girl. God, why couldn't she have a boy? Just one, that's all she wanted, just one little baby boy.

9   She wished the midwife hadn't told her when she had that miscarriage that it had been a boy. The only one in six years, and she had to go and lose it. It was her fault too. She had no business climbing a ladder at five months. She slipped and fell and the doctors kept her in the hospital for a week, then told her she was all right and could go home. But there was no movement, no life, so she went back to the hospital and after two weeks of tests and X-rays and hope and despair, they finally decided the baby was dead.

10   After that, she had two more girls, and now the fourth.

11   Would Hamid divorce her? Would he take a second wife? His older brother had been pressing for two years now, urging him to take a second wife. Hamid loved Amina and his daughters, but he was human. He did have all that money and the social and political position and no boy to leave it to.

12   Her mother came in, then her sister-in-law. Each one kissed her and said "*Mabruk*," but she could tell they were not really happy. Her mother was especially fearful for her daughter's future and felt that some of the disgrace fell on her and the family too. The sisters-in-law were secretly jubilant, because they had boys. Hamid's social status and half his fortune would revert to their own sons if he never had any boys of his own. Of course, he was still young and he and Amina might try again. But for the moment the in-laws left reassured and falsely commiserated with Amina on her bad luck.

13   "It is God's will," they murmured, smiling under their masks. Their mouths were sad, but Amina could see the twinkle in their eyes. "God's will be done."

14   Friends started coming into the room. They kissed Amina and said "*Mabruk*," then sat on the floor, cross-legged. Arranging their robes around them, they sipped coffee from little thimble cups, eating fruits and sweets.

15   Her cousin Huda came too. She wore a long, velvet dress, embroidered on the sides and bodice, loose and flowing, to conceal her belly.

She was in her sixth month and looked radiantly serene. She sat on the carpet and sipped her coffee.

16   Amina thought bitterly, "She already has two daughters and three sons. What does she need another baby for? She's not so young any more."

17   As if she had read her thoughts, Huda said, "This is my last baby. It will be the baby for my old age. The others are married or away at school all day. An empty house is a sad house. You need many sons and daughters to keep your husband happy. You are still young, Amina. God has given you four daughters, maybe the next four will be boys. God's will be done."

18   "As God wills it, so be it," murmured the other ladies smugly.

19   Hamid came in and the ladies all stood up, saluted him deferentially, and hastily went into the next room. The maid served them more coffee. Hamid looked at his wife, tried to smile and searched for something nice to say. He thought she must be tired, disappointed, ashamed of having failed him one more time and afraid of being repudiated.

20   He sat down near the bed and said, "Well, mother of my children, we will just have to try again, won't we?"

21   Amina burst into tears of sorrow, shame and relief.

22   "Don't cry," he said, distressed. "The important thing is that you and the girls are in good health," smiling. "As long as we are young, we will try again, eh?"

23   Amina blushed under her mask and pulled her veil around her face. He patted her hand, got up, and left the room.

24   The ladies came rushing back in, like a flock of crows, eager for the news, good or bad.

25   Amina's mother said solicitously, "What did he say, my daughter?"

26   "He said better luck next time, Mother!"

27   The mother let out a sigh of relief. They had another year's reprieve. The women congratulated Amina and left to spread the news.

28   Amina sank back on to her pillows and drifted off to sleep.

✧ Evaluating the Text

1. What insight do you gain into the kind of societal and personal pressures Amina is under from the reactions of her mother and in-laws?

2. How is the story shaped to build up suspense first as to the sex of the child and, second, as to how her husband will react to this news?

3. What does Amina's husband's reaction reveal about him and his feelings for her?

4. How would you characterize the author's attitude toward the events she describes?

✧ Exploring Different Perspectives

1. How are the expectations for women in Lebanon in "Amina" different from those for young women in Japan as described by Nicholas Bornoff in "The Marriage Go-Round"?

2. Compare the social pressures on women in Saad's story to Susan Bordo's analysis in "Never Just Pictures."

✧ Extending Viewpoints through Writing and Research

1. How does the conflict between private affection and public obligations reveal the values that govern women's lives in Middle Eastern society?

2. What recent developments (e.g., ultrasound clinics in India and genetic screening in the United States) illustrate the pressure on women to produce sons? How has the one-child policy in China and accompanying female infanticide resulted in an imbalance of 70 million more males? What are the social consequences of this policy?

3. Do you consider having children important to your future? Why or why not? What do you think having a family will mean in the future?

What advances in science have made this scenario feasible?

Elizabeth W. Fernea and Robert A. Fernea

A Look Behind the Veil

◆

One of the most interesting examples of how clothes reflect cultural be-liefs can be seen in the Middle Eastern custom of veiling women. Eliza-beth W. Fernea and Robert A. Fernea have done extensive research in Iraq, Morocco, Egypt, and Afghanistan and are the authors of a number of books, including the award-winning The Arab World: Personal En-counters *(1987) and its sequel,* The Arab World: Forty Years of Change *(1997). Elizabeth W. Fernea has also written* In Search of Is-lamic Feminism: One Woman's Global Journey *(1998). Her most re-cent work is* Remembering Childhood in the Middle East Memoirs from a Century of Changes *(2002). She is currently professor of Mid-dle Eastern studies at the University of Texas at Austin.*

Before You Read

As you read, consider the ways in which *purdah* defines how a woman must present herself in Middle Eastern cultures.

◆

1   What objects do we notice in societies other than our own? Ishi, the last of a "lost" tribe of North American Indians who stumbled into 20th Century California in 1911, is reported to have said that the truly interesting objects in the white man's culture were pockets and matches. Rifa'ah Tahtawi, one of the first young Egyptians to be sent to Europe to study in 1826, wrote an account of French society in which he noted that Parisians used many unusual articles of dress, among them something called a belt. Women wore belts, he said, apparently to keep their bosoms erect, and to show off the slimness of their waists and the fullness of their hips. Europeans are still fascinated by the Stet-son hats worn by American cowboys; an elderly Dutch lady of our ac-quaintance recently carried six enormous Stetsons back to The Hague as presents for the male members of her family.

2   Many objects signify values in society and become charged with meaning, a meaning that may be different for members of the society and for observers of that society. The veil is one object used in Middle Eastern societies that stirs strong emotions in the West. "The feminine

veil has become a symbol: that of the slavery of one portion of humanity," wrote French ethnologist Germaine Tillion in 1966. A hundred years earlier, Sir Richard Burton, British traveler, explorer, and translator of the *Arabian Nights,* recorded a different view. "Europeans inveigh against this article [the face veil] . . . for its hideousness and jealous concealment of charms made to be admired," he wrote in 1855. "It is, on the contrary, the most coquettish article of woman's attire . . . it conceals coarse skins, fleshy noses, wide mouths and vanishing chins, whilst it sets off to best advantage what in these lands is most lustrous and liquid—the eye. Who has not remarked this at a masquerade ball?"

3   In the present generation, the veil and purdah, or seclusion, have become a focus of attention for Western writers, both popular and academic, who take a measure of Burton's irony and Tillion's anger to equate modernization of the Middle East with the discarding of the veil. "Iranian women return to veil in a resurgence of spirituality," headlines one newspaper; another writes, "Iran's 16 million women have come a long way since their floor-length cotton veil officially was abolished in 1935." The thousands of words written about the appearance and disappearance of the veil and of purdah do little to help us understand the Middle East or the cultures that grew out of the same Judeo-Christian roots as our own. The veil and the all-enveloping garments that inevitably accompany it (the *milayah* in Egypt, the *abbayah* in Iraq, the *chadoor* in Iran, the *yashmak* in Turkey, the *burqa* in Afghanistan, and the *djellabah* and the *haik* in North Africa) are only the outward manifestations of a cultural pattern and idea that is rooted deep in Mediterranean society.

4   "Purdah" is a Persian word meaning curtain or barrier. The Arabic word for veiling and secluding comes from the root *hajaba.* A *hijab* is an amulet worn to keep away the evil eye; it also means a diaphragm used to prevent conception. The gatekeeper or doorkeeper who guards the entrance to a government minister's office is a *hijab,* and in casual conversation a person might say, "I want to be more informal with my friend so-and-so, but she always puts a *hijab* (barrier) between us."

5   In Islam, the Koranic verse that sanctions the barrier between men and women is called the Sura of the *hijab* (curtain): "Prophet, enjoin your wives, your daughters and the wives of true believers to draw their veils close round them. That is more proper, so that they may be recognized and not molested. Allah is forgiving and merciful."

6   Certainly seclusion and some forms of veiling had been practiced before the time of Muhammad, at least among the upper classes, but it was his followers who apparently felt that his women should be placed in a special category. According to history, the *hijab* was established after a number of occasions on which Muhammad's wives were insulted by people who were coming to the mosque in search of the prophet. When chided for their behavior, they said they had mistaken

Muhammad's wives for slaves. The *hijab* was established, and in the words of the historian Nabia Abbott, "Muhammad's women found themselves, on the one hand, deprived of personal liberty, and on the other hand, raised to a position of honor and dignity."

7   The veil bears many messages and tells us many things about men and women in Middle East society; but as an object in and of itself it is far less important to members of the society than the values it represents. Nouha al Hejailan, wife of the Saudi Arabian ambassador to London, told Sally Quinn of *The Washington Post*, "If I wanted to take it all off (her *abbayah* and veil), I would have long ago. It wouldn't mean as much to me as it does to you." Early Middle Eastern feminists felt differently. Huda Sh'arawi, an early Egyptian activist who formed the first Women's Union, made a dramatic gesture of removing her veil in public to demonstrate her dislike of society's attitudes toward women and her defiance of the system. But Basima Bezirgan, a contemporary Iraqui feminist, says, "Compared to the real issues that are involved between men and women in the Middle East today, the veil is unimportant." A Moroccan linguist who buys her clothes in Paris laughs when asked about the veil. "My mother wears a *djellabah* and a veil. I have never worn them. But so what? I still cannot get divorced as easily as a man, and I am still a member of my family group and responsible to them for everything I do. What is the veil? A piece of cloth."

8   "The seclusion of women has many purposes," states Egyptian anthropologist Nadia Abu Zahra. "It expresses men's status, power, wealth, and manliness. It also helps preserve men's image of virility and masculinity, but men do not admit this; on the contrary they claim that one of the purposes of the veil is to guard women's honor." The veil and purdah are symbols of restriction, to men as well as to women. A respectable woman wearing a veil on a public street is signaling, "Hands off. Don't touch me or you'll be sorry." Cowboy Jim Sayre of Deadwood, South Dakota, says, "If you deform a cowboy's hat, he'll likely deform you." In the same way, a man who approaches a veiled woman is asking for trouble; not only the woman but also her family is shamed, and serious problems may result. "It is clear," says Egyptian anthropologist Ahmed Abou Zeid, "that honor and shame which are usually attributed to a certain individual or a certain kinship group have in fact a bearing on the total social structure, since most acts involving honor or shame are likely to affect the existing social equilibrium."

9   Veiling and seclusion almost always can be related to the maintenance of social status. Historically, only the very rich could afford to seclude their women, and the extreme example of this practice was found among the sultans of prerevolutionary Turkey. Stories of these secluded women, kept in harems and guarded by eunuchs, formed the basis for much of the Western folklore concerning the nature of male-female relationships in Middle East society. The stereotype is of course

contradictory; Western writers have never found it necessary to reconcile the erotic fantasies of the seraglio with the sexual puritanism attributed to the same society.

10   Poor men could not always afford to seclude or veil their women, because the women were needed as productive members of the family economic unit, to work in the fields and in cottage industries. Delta village women in Egypt have never been veiled, nor have the Berber women of North Africa. But this lack of veiling placed poor women in ambiguous situations in relation to strange men.

11   "In the village, no one veils, because everyone is considered a member of the same large family," explained Aisha bint Mohammed, a working-class wife of Marrakech. "But in the city, veiling is *sunnah*, required by our religion." Veiling is generally found in towns and cities, among all classes, where families feel that it is necessary to distinguish themselves from other strangers in the city.

12   Veiling and purdah not only indicate status and wealth, they also have some religious sanction and protect women from the world outside the home. Purdah delineates private space, distinguishes between the public and private sectors of society, as does the traditional architecture of the area. Older Middle Eastern houses do not have picture windows facing the street, nor walks leading invitingly to front doors. Family life is hidden from strangers; behind blank walls may lie courtyards and gardens, refuges from the heat, the cold, the bustle of the outside world, the world of non-kin that is not to be trusted. Outsiders are pointedly excluded.

13   Even within the household, among her close relatives, a traditional Muslim woman veils before those kinsmen whom she could legally marry. If her maternal or paternal male cousins, her brothers-in-law, or sons-in-law come to call, she covers her head, or perhaps her whole face. To do otherwise would be shameless.

14   The veil does more than protect its wearers from known and unknown intruders; it can also be used to conceal identity. Behind the anonymity of the veil, women can go about a city unrecognized and uncriticized. Nadia Abu Zahra reports anecdotes of men donning women's veils in order to visit their lovers undetected; women may do the same. The veil is such an effective disguise that Nouri Al-Said, the late prime minister of Iraq, attempted to escape death by wearing the *abbayah* and veil of a woman; only his shoes gave him away.

15   Political dissidents in many countries have used the veil for their own ends. The women who marched, veiled, through Cairo during the Nationalist demonstrations against the British after World War I were counting on the strength of Western respect for the veil to protect them against British gunfire. At first they were right. Algerian women also used the protection of the veil to carry bombs through French army checkpoints during the Algerian revolution. But when the French dis-

covered the ruse, Algerian women discarded the veil and dressed like Europeans to move about freely.

16   The multiple meanings and uses of purdah and the veil do not explain how the pattern came to be so deeply embedded in Mediterranean society. Its origins lie somewhere in the basic Muslim attitudes about men's roles and women's roles. Women, according to Fatima Mernissi, a Moroccan sociologist, are seen by men in Islamic societies as in need of protection because they are unable to control their sexuality, are tempting to men, and hence are a danger to the social order. In order words, they need to be restrained and controlled so that society may function in an orderly way.

17   The notion that women present a danger to the social order is scarcely limited to Muslim society. Anthropologist Julian Pitt-Rivers has pointed out that the supervision and seclusion of women is also to be found in Christian Europe, even though veiling was not usually practiced there. "The idea that women not subjected to male authority are a danger is a fundamental one in the writings of the moralists from the Archpriest of Talavera to Padre Haro, and it is echoed in the modern Andalusian *pueblo*. It is bound up with the fear of ungoverned female sexuality which had been an integral element of European folklore ever since prudent Odysseus lashed himself to the mast to escape the sirens."

18   Pitt-Rivers is writing about Mediterranean society, which, like all Middle Eastern societies, is greatly concerned with honor and shame rather than with individual guilt. The honor of the Middle Eastern extended family, its ancestors and its descendants, is the highest social value. The misdeeds of the grandparents are indeed visited on the children. Men and women always remain members of their natal families. Marriage is a legal contract but a fragile one that is often broken; the ties between brother and sister, mother and child, father and child are lifelong and enduring. The larger family is the group to which the individual belongs and to which the individual owes responsibility in exchange for the social and economic security that the family group provides. It is the group, not the individual, that is socially shamed or socially honored.

19   Male honor and female honor are both involved in the honor of the family, but each is expressed differently. The honor of a man, *sharaf*, is a public matter, involving bravery, hospitality, piety. It may be lost, but it may also be regained. The honor of a woman, *'ard*, is a private matter involving only one thing, her sexual chastity. Once lost, it cannot be regained. If the loss of female honor remains only privately known, a rebuke—and perhaps a reveiling—may be all that takes place. But if the loss of female honor becomes public knowledge, the other members of the family may feel bound to cleanse the family name. In extreme cases, the cleansing may require the death of the offending

female member. Although such killings are now criminal offenses in the Middle East, suspended sentences are often given, and the newspapers in Cairo and Baghdad frequently carry sad stories of runaway sisters "gone bad" in the city and revenge taken upon them in the name of family honor by their brothers or cousins.

20   This emphasis on female chastity, many say, originated in the patrilineal society's concern with the paternity of the child and the inheritance that follows the male line. How does a man know that the child in his wife's womb is his own, and not that of another man? Obviously he cannot know unless his wife is a virgin at marriage. From this consideration may have developed the protective institutions called variously purdah, seclusion, or veiling.

21   Middle Eastern women also look upon seclusion as practical protection. In the Iraqi village where we lived from 1956 to 1958, one of us (Elizabeth) wore the *abbayah* and found that it provided a great sense of protection from prying eyes, dust, heat, flies. Parisian ladies visiting Istanbul in the 16th Century were so impressed by the ability of the all-enveloping garment to keep dresses clean of mud and manure and to keep women from being attacked by importuning men that they tried to introduce it into French fashion.

22   Perhaps of greater importance for many women reared in traditional cultures is the degree to which their sense of personal identity is tied to the use of the veil. Many women have told us that they felt self-conscious, vulnerable, and even naked when they first walked on a public street without the veil and *abbayah*—as if they were making a display of themselves.

23   The resurgence of the veil in countries like Morocco, Libya, and Algeria, which have recently established their independence from colonial dominance, is seen by some Middle Eastern and Western scholars as an attempt by men to reassert their Muslim identity and to reestablish their roles as heads of families. The presence of the veil is a sign that the males of the household are once more able to assume the responsibilities that were disturbed or usurped by foreign colonial powers.

24   But a veiled woman is seldom seen in Egypt or in many parts of Lebanon, Syria, Iran, Tunisia, Turkey, or the Sudan. And as respectable housewives have abandoned the veil, in some of these Middle Eastern countries prostitutes have put it on. They indicate their availability by manipulating the veil in flirtatious ways, but as Burton pointed out more than a century ago, prostitutes are not the first to discover the veil's seductiveness. Like women's garments in the West, the veil can be sturdy, utilitarian, and forbidding—or it can be filmy and decorative, hinting at the charms beneath it.

25   The veil is the outward sign of a complex reality. Observers are often deceived by the absence of that sign, and fail to see that in most

Middle Eastern societies (and in many parts of Europe) basic attitudes are unchanged. Women who have taken off the veil continue to play the old roles within the family, and their chastity remains crucial. A woman's behavior is still the key to the honor and the reputation of her family.

26   In Middle Eastern societies, feminine and masculine continue to be strong polarities of identification. This is marked contrast to Western society, where for more than a generation social critics have been striving to blur distinctions in dress, in status, and in type of labor. Almost all Middle Eastern reformers (most of whom are middle and upper class) are still arguing from the assumption of a fundamental difference between men and women. They do not demand an end to the veil (which is passing out of use anyway) but an end to the old principles, which the veil symbolizes, that govern patrilineal society. Middle Eastern reformers are calling for equal access to divorce, child custody, and inheritance; equal opportunities for education and employment; abolition of female circumcision and "crimes of honor"; and a law regulating the age of marriage.

27   An English woman film director, after several months in Morocco, said in an interview, "This business about the veil is nonsense. We all have our veils, between ourselves and other people. That's not what the Middle East is about. The question is what veils are used for, and by whom." The veil triggers Western reactions simply because it is the dramatic, visible sign of vexing questions, questions that are still being debated, problems that have still not been solved, in the Middle East or in Western societies.

28   Given the biological differences between men and women, how are the sexes to be treated equitably? Men and women are supposed to share the labor of society and yet provide for the reproduction and nurture of the next generation. If male fear and awe of women's sexuality provokes them to control and seclude women, can they be assuaged? Rebecca West said long ago that "the difference between men and women is the rock on which civilization will split before it can reach any goal that could justify its expenditure of effort." Until human beings come to terms with this basic issue, purdah and the veil, in some form, will continue to exist in both the East and the West.

REFERENCES

Abou-Zeid, Ahmed, "Honor and Shame among the Bedouins of Egypt," *Honor and Shame: The Values of Mediterranean Society,* ed. by J. G. Peristiany, University of Chicago Press, 1966.

Fernea, Elizabeth Warnock, *Guests of the Sheik: An Ethnology of an Iraqi Village,* Doubleday/Anchor, 1969.

Fernea, Elizabeth Warnock, and Basima Qattan Bezirgan, eds., *Middle Eastern Muslim Women Speak,* University of Texas Press, 1977.

Levy, Reuben, *The Social Structure of Islam,* Cambridge University Press, 1965.
Mernissi, Fatima, *Beyond the Veil: Male-Female Dynamics in a Modern Muslim Society,* Schenkman Publishing Company, 1975.
Pitt-Rivers, Julian, *The Fate of Schechem: or The Politics of Sex,* Cambridge University Press, 1977.

✧ *Evaluating the Text*

1. Why, according to the authors, is the practice of veiling women in Middle Eastern countries most frequently encountered in affluent, male-dominated extended families? What attitudes toward female sexuality help explain the veiling of women and the practice of *purdah*?

2. The authors use interviews and the testimony of experts to support their analysis as to why veiling and *purdah* continue to exist in Middle Eastern societies. Do you detect a bias on the authors' part either for or against this practice? Explain your answer.

3. How is the practice of veiling tied in with other important cultural values and institutions in Middle Eastern societies?

✧ *Exploring Different Perspectives*

1. Compare the safeguards within Puerto Rican culture, as described by Judith Ortiz Cofer in "Myth of the Latin Woman" that protect women's modesty with the very different constraints in Middle Eastern societies that practice *purdah*.

2. How does the practice of veiling as depicted by Elizabeth W. Fernea and Robert A. Fernea contrast with Susan Bordo's analysis of what makes a woman desirable in American culture?

✧ *Extending Viewpoints through Writing and Research*

1. Select one of the following, and write an essay in response. Create a dialogue between someone who is in favor of the practice of veiling and someone who is very much against it. If you were a woman living in a society where wearing the chador was a matter of personal choice, would you choose to do so or not? Explain your answer. If you were a man in that society, would you prefer to see women completely veiled? Why or why not?

2. To what extent have traditional cultural values changed since the Ferneas did their groundbreaking study in 1979?

3. For current views on veiling (*hijab*) consult http://www.brandeis.edu/projects/fse/pages/veiling.html.

What do the facial expressions and body language of these Moroccan women communicate? Would you have guessed that right after this photo was taken they dropped their veils in protest?

Serena Nanda

Arranging a Marriage in India

◆

Serena Nanda is professor of anthropology at John Jay College of Criminal Justice, City University of New York. Her fields of interest are visual anthropology, gender, and culture and law. She has carried out field studies in India, in tribal development, and on the social lives of women in urban India. Her published works include Cultural Anthropology, *third edition (1987),* American Cultural Pluralism and Law *(1990), and* Neither Man nor Woman: The Hijras of India *(1990), which won the Ruth Benedict Prize. In the following selection, which first appeared in* The Naked Anthropologist: Tales from Around the World, *edited by Philip R. DeVita (1992). Her most recent work (with Richard L. Warms) is* Cultural Anthropology, *eighth edition (2004). Nanda looks at the cultural forces that have resulted in the practice of arranged marriages in Indian society.*

Before You Read

Note the kinds of considerations that are important in arranging a marriage in India and how these reflect important cultural values.

◆

Sister and doctor brother-in-law invite correspondence from North Indian professionals only, for a beautiful, talented, sophisticated, intelligent sister, 5'3", slim, M.A. in textile design, father a senior civil officer. Would prefer immigrant doctors, between 26–29 years. Reply with full details and returnable photo.

A well-settled uncle invites matrimonial correspondence from slim, fair, educated South Indian girl, for his nephew, 25 years, smart, M.B.A., green card holder, 5'6". Full particulars with returnable photo appreciated.
> —Matrimonial Advertisements, *India Abroad*

1   In India, almost all marriages are arranged. Even among the educated middle classes in modern, urban India, marriage is as much a concern of the families as it is of the individuals. So customary is the practice of arranged marriage that there is a special name for a marriage which is not arranged: It is called a "love match."

2   On my first field trip to India, I met many young men and women whose parents were in the process of "getting them married." In many cases, the bride and groom would not meet each other before the marriage. At most they might meet for a brief conversation, and this meeting would take place only after their parents had decided that the match was suitable. Parents do not compel their children to marry a person who either marriage partner finds objectionable. But only after one match is refused will another be sought.

3   As a young American woman in India for the first time, I found this custom of arranged marriage oppressive. How could any intelligent young person agree to such a marriage without great reluctance? It was contrary to everything I believed about the importance of romantic love as the only basis of a happy marriage. It also clashed with my strongly held notions that the choice of such an intimate and permanent relationship could be made only by the individuals involved. Had anyone tried to arrange my marriage, I would have been defiant and rebellious!

4   At the first opportunity, I began, with more curiosity than tact, to question the young people I met on how they felt about this practice. Sita, one of my young informants, was a college graduate with a degree in political science. She had been waiting for over a year while her parents were arranging a match for her. I found it difficult to accept the docile manner in which this well-educated young woman awaited the outcome of a process that would result in her spending the rest of her life with a man she hardly knew, a virtual stranger, picked out by her parents.

5   "How can you go along with this?" I asked her, in frustration and distress. "Don't you care who you marry?"

6   "Of course I care," she answered. "This is why I must let my parents choose a boy for me. My marriage is too important to be arranged by such an inexperienced person as myself. In such matters, it is better to have my parents' guidance."

7   I had learned that young men and women in India do not date and have very little social life involving members of the opposite sex. Although I could not disagree with Sita's reasoning, I continued to pursue the subject.

8   "But how can you marry the first man you have ever met? Not only have you missed the fun of meeting a lot of different people, but you have not given yourself the chance to know who is the right man for you."

9   "Meeting with a lot of different people doesn't sound like any fun at all," Sita answered. "One hears that in America the girls are spending more time worrying about whether they will meet a man and get married. Here we have the chance to enjoy our life and let our parents do this work and worrying for us."

10   She had me there. The high anxiety of the competition to "be popular" with the opposite sex certainly was the most prominent feature of life as an American teenager in the late fifties. The endless worrying about the rules that governed our behavior and about our popularity ratings sapped both our self-esteem and our enjoyment of adolescence. I reflected that absence of this competition in India most certainly may have contributed to the self-confidence and natural charm of so many of the young women I met.

11   And yet, the idea of marrying a perfect stranger, whom one did not know and did not "love," so offended my American ideas of individualism and romanticism, that I persisted with my objections.

12   "I still can't imagine it," I said. "How can you agree to marry a man you hardly know?"

13   "But of course he will be known. My parents would never arrange a marriage for me without knowing all about the boy's family background. Naturally we will not rely only on what the family tells us. We will check the particulars out ourselves. No one will want their daughter to marry into a family that is not good. All these things we will know beforehand."

14   Impatiently, I responded, "Sita, I don't mean know the family, I mean, know the man. How can you marry someone you don't know personally and don't love? How can you think of spending your life with someone you may not even like?"

15   "If he is a good man, why should I not like him?" she said. "With you people, you know the boy so well before you marry, where will be the fun to get married? There will be no mystery and no romance. Here we have the whole of our married life to get to know and love our husband. This way is better, is it not?"

16   Her response made further sense, and I began to have second thoughts on the matter. Indeed, during months of meeting many intelligent young Indian people, both male and female, who had the same ideas as Sita, I saw arranged marriages in a different light. I also saw the importance of the family in Indian life and realized that a couple who took their marriage into their own hands was taking a big risk, particularly if their families were irreconcilably opposed to the match. In a country where every important resource in life—a job, a house, a social circle—is gained through family connections, it seemed foolhardy to cut oneself off from a supportive social network and depend solely on one person for happiness and success.

17   Six years later I returned to India to again do fieldwork, this time among the middle class in Bombay, a modern, sophisticated city. From the experience of my earlier visit, I decided to include a study of arranged marriages in my project. By this time I had met many Indian couples whose marriages had been arranged and who seemed very

happy. Particularly in contrast to the fate of many of my married friends in the United States who were already in the process of divorce, the positive aspects of arranged marriages appeared to me to outweigh the negatives. In fact, I thought I might even participate in arranging a marriage myself. I had been fairly successful in the United States in "fixing up" many of my friends, and I was confident that my match-making skills could be easily applied to this new situation, once I learned the basic rules. "After all," I thought, "how complicated can it be? People want pretty much the same things in a marriage whether it is in India or America."

18   An opportunity presented itself almost immediately. A friend from my previous Indian trip was in the process of arranging for the marriage of her eldest son. In India there is a perceived shortage of "good boys," and since my friend's family was eminently respectable and the boy himself personable, well educated, and nice looking, I was sure that by the end of my year's fieldwork, we would have found a match.

19   The basic rule seems to be that a family's reputation is most important. It is understood that matches would be arranged only within the same caste and general social class, although some crossing of sub-castes is permissible if the class positions of the bride's and groom's families are similar. Although dowry is now prohibited by law in India, extensive gift exchanges took place with every marriage. Even when the boy's family do not "make demands," every girl's family nevertheless feels the obligation to give the traditional gifts, to the girl, to the boy, and to the boy's family. Particularly when the couple would be living in the joint family—that is, with the boy's parents and his married brothers and their families, as well as with unmarried siblings—which is still very common even among the urban, upper-middle class in India, the girl's parents are anxious to establish smooth relations between their family and that of the boy. Offering the proper gifts, even when not called "dowry," is often an important factor in influencing the relationship between the bride's and groom's families and perhaps, also, the treatment of the bride in her new home.

20   In a society where divorce is still a scandal and where, in fact, the divorce rate is exceedingly low, an arranged marriage is the beginning of a lifetime relationship not just between the bride and groom but between their families as well. Thus, while a girl's looks are important, her character is even more so, for she is being judged as a prospective daughter-in-law as much as a prospective bride. Where she would be living in a joint family, as was the case with my friend, the girl's ability to get along harmoniously in a family is perhaps the single most important quality in assessing her suitability.

21   My friend is a highly esteemed wife, mother, and daughter-in-law. She is religious, soft-spoken, modest, and deferential. She rarely gossips and never quarrels, two qualities highly desirable in a woman. A

family that has the reputation for gossip and conflict among its womenfolk will not find it easy to get good wives for their sons. Parents will not want to send their daughter to a house in which there is conflict.

22   My friend's family were originally from North India. They had lived in Bombay, where her husband owned a business, for forty years. The family had delayed in seeking a match for their eldest son because he had been an Air Force pilot for several years, stationed in such remote places that it had seemed fruitless to try to find a girl who would be willing to accompany him. In their social class, a military career, despite its economic security, has little prestige and is considered a drawback in finding a suitable bride. Many families would not allow their daughters to marry a man in an occupation so potentially dangerous and which requires so much moving around.

23   The son had recently left the military and joined his father's business. Since he was a college graduate, modern, and well traveled, from such a good family, and, I thought, quite handsome, it seemed to me that he, or rather his family, was in a position to pick and choose. I said as much to my friend.

24   While she agreed that there were many advantages on their side, she also said, "We must keep in mind that my son is both short and dark; these are drawbacks in finding the right match." While the boy's height had not escaped my notice, "dark" seemed to me inaccurate; I would have called him "wheat" colored perhaps, and in any case, I did not realize that color would be a consideration. I discovered, however, that while a boy's skin color is a less important consideration than a girl's, it is still a factor.

25   An important source of contacts in trying to arrange her son's marriage was my friend's social club in Bombay. Many of the women had daughters of the right age, and some had already expressed an interest in my friend's son. I was most enthusiastic about the possibilities of one particular family who had five daughters, all of whom were pretty, demure, and well educated. Their mother had told my friend, "You can have your pick for your son, whichever one of my daughters appeals to you most."

26   I saw a match in sight. "Surely," I said to my friend, "we will find one there. Let's go visit and make our choice." But my friend held back; she did not seem to share my enthusiasm, for reasons I could not then fathom.

27   When I kept pressing for an explanation of her reluctance, she admitted, "See, Serena, here is the problem. The family has so many daughters, how will they be able to provide nicely for any of them? We are not making any demands, but still, with so many daughters to marry off, one wonders whether she will even be able to make a proper wedding. Since this is our eldest son, it's best if we marry him to a girl who is the only daughter, then the wedding will truly be a gala affair."

I argued that surely the quality of the girls themselves made up for any deficiency in the elaborateness of the wedding. My friend admitted this point but still seemed reluctant to proceed.

28   "Is there something else," I asked her, "some factor I have missed?" "Well," she finally said, "there is one other thing. They have one daughter already married and living in Bombay. The mother is always complaining to me that the girl's in-laws don't let her visit her own family often enough. So it makes me wonder, will she be that kind of mother who always wants her daughter at her own home? This will prevent the girl from adjusting to our house. It is not a good thing." And so, this family of five daughters was dropped as a possibility.

29   Somewhat disappointed, I nevertheless respected my friend's reasoning and geared up for the next prospect. This was also the daughter of a woman in my friend's social club. There was clear interest in this family and I could see why. The family's reputation was excellent; in fact, they came from a subcaste slightly higher than my friend's own. The girl, who was an only daughter, was pretty and well educated and had a brother studying in the United States. Yet, after expressing an interest to me in this family, all talk of them suddenly died down and the search began elsewhere.

30   "What happened to that girl as a prospect?" I asked one day. "You never mention her any more. She is so pretty and so educated, what did you find wrong?"

31   "She is too educated. We've decided against it. My husband's father saw the girl on the bus the other day and thought her forward. A girl who 'roams about' the city by herself is not the girl for our family." My disappointment this time was even greater, as I thought the son would have liked the girl very much. But then I thought, my friend is right, a girl who is going to live in a joint family cannot be too independent or she will make life miserable for everyone. I also learned that if the family of the girl has even a slightly higher social status than the family of the boy, the bride may think herself too good for them, and this too will cause problems. Later my friend admitted to me that this had been an important factor in her decision not to pursue the match.

32   The next candidate was the daughter of a client of my friend's husband. When the client learned that the family was looking for a match for their son, he said, "Look no further, we have a daughter." This man then invited my friends to dinner to see the girl. He had already seen their son at the office and decided that "he liked the boy." We all went together for tea, rather than dinner—it was less of a commitment—and while we were there, the girl's mother showed us around the house. The girl was studying for her exams and was briefly introduced to us.

33   After we left, I was anxious to hear my friend's opinion. While her husband liked the family very much and was impressed with his client's business accomplishments and reputation, the wife didn't like

the girl's looks. "She is short, no doubt, which is an important plus point, but she is also fat and wears glasses." My friend obviously thought she could do better for her son and asked her husband to make his excuses to his client by saying that they had decided to postpone the boy's marriage indefinitely.

34   By this time almost six months had passed and I was becoming impatient. What I had thought would be an easy matter to arrange was turning out to be quite complicated. I began to believe that between my friend's desire for a girl who was modest enough to fit into her joint family, yet attractive and educated enough to be an acceptable partner for her son, she would not find anyone suitable. My friend laughed at my impatience: "Don't be so much in a hurry," she said. "You Americans want everything done so quickly. You get married quickly and then just as quickly get divorced. Here we take marriage more seriously. We must take all the factors into account. It is not enough for us to learn by our mistakes. This is too serious a business. If a mistake is made we have not only ruined the life of our son or daughter, but we have spoiled the reputation of our family as well. And that will make it much harder for their brothers and sisters to get married. So we must be very careful."

35   What she said was true and I promised myself to be more patient, though it was not easy. I had really hoped and expected that the match would be made before my year in India was up. But it was not to be. When I left India my friend seemed no further along in finding a suitable match for her son than when I had arrived.

36   Two years later, I returned to India and still my friend had not found a girl for her son. By this time, he was close to thirty, and I think she was a little worried. Since she knew I had friends all over India, and I was going to be there for a year, she asked me to "help her in this work" and keep an eye out for someone suitable. I was flattered that my judgment was respected, but knowing now how complicated the process was, I had lost my earlier confidence as a matchmaker. Nevertheless, I promised that I would try.

37   It was almost at the end of my year's stay in India that I met a family with a marriageable daughter whom I felt might be a good possibility for my friend's son. The girl's father was related to a good friend of mine and by coincidence came from the same village as my friend's husband. This new family had a successful business in a medium-sized city in central India and were from the same subcaste as my friend. The daughter was pretty and chic; in fact, she had studied fashion design in college. Her parents would not allow her to go off by herself to any of the major cities in India where she could make a career, but they had compromised with her wish to work by allowing her to run a small dressmaking boutique from their home. In spite of her desire to have a career, the daughter was both modest and home-loving

and had had a traditional, sheltered upbringing. She had only one other sister, already married, and a brother who was in his father's business.

38 I mentioned the possibility of a match with my friend's son. The girl's parents were most interested. Although their daughter was not eager to marry just yet, the idea of living in Bombay—a sophisticated, extremely fashion-conscious city where she could continue her education in clothing design—was a great inducement. I gave the girl's father my friend's address and suggested that when they went to Bombay on some business or whatever, they look up the boy's family.

39 Returning to Bombay on my way to New York, I told my friend of this newly discovered possibility. She seemed to feel there was potential but, in spite of my urging, would not make any moves herself. She rather preferred to wait for the girl's family to call upon them. I hoped something would come of this introduction, though by now I had learned to rein in my optimism.

40 A year later I received a letter from my friend. The family had indeed come to visit Bombay, and their daughter and my friend's daughter, who were near in age, had become very good friends. During that year, the two girls had frequently visited each other. I thought things looked promising.

41 Last week I received an invitation to a wedding: My friend's son and the girl were getting married. Since I had found the match, my presence was particularly requested at the wedding. I was thrilled. Success at last! As I prepared to leave for India, I began thinking, "Now, my friend's younger son, who do I know who has a nice girl for him . . . ?"

Epilogue

This essay was written from the point of view of a family seeking a daughter-in-law. Arranged marriage looks somewhat different from the point of view of the bride and her family. Arranged marriage continues to be preferred, even among the more educated, westernized sections of the Indian population. Many young women from these families still go along, more or less willingly, with the practice and also with the specific choices of their families. Young women do get excited about the prospects of their marriage, but there is also ambivalence and increasing uncertainty as the bride contemplates leaving the comfort and familiarity of her own home where, as a "temporary guest," she had often been indulged, to live among strangers. Even in the best situation she will now come under the close scrutiny of her husband's family. How she dresses, how she behaves, how she gets along with others, where she goes, how she spends her time, her domestic abilities—all this and much more—will be observed and commented on by a whole new set of relations. Her interaction with her family of birth will be monitored and curtailed considerably. Not only will she leave their home, but with increasing geographic mobility she may also live very far from them, perhaps even on another continent. Too much expression of her fondness for her own family or her desire to visit them may be interpreted as an inability to adjust to her new family and may become a source of conflict. In an arranged marriage the burden of adjustment is clearly heavier for a woman than for a man. And this is in the best of situations.

In less happy circumstances, the bride may be a target of resentment and hostility from her husband's family, particularly her mother-in-law or her husband's unmarried sisters, for whom she is now a source of competition for the affection, loyalty, and economic resources of their son or brother. If she is psychologically or even physically abused, her options are limited, because returning to her parents' home or divorce is still very stigmatized. For most Indians, marriage and motherhood are still considered the only suitable roles for a woman, even for those who have careers, and few women can comfortably contemplate remaining unmarried. Most families still consider "marrying off" their daughter as a compelling religious duty and social necessity. This increases a bride's sense of obligation to make the marriage a success, at whatever cost to her own personal happiness.

The vulnerability of a new bride may also be intensified by the issue of dowry, which, although illegal, has become a more pressing issue in the consumer-conscious society of contemporary urban India. In many cases, if a groom's family is not satisfied with the amount of dowry that a bride brings to her marriage, the young bride will be constantly harassed to get her parents to give more. In extreme cases, the bride may even be murdered, and the murder disguised as an accident or suicide. This also offers the husband's family an opportunity to arrange another match for him, thus bringing in another dowry. This phenomenon, called dowry death, calls attention not just to the evils of dowry, but also to larger issues of the powerlessness of women.

✧ *Evaluating the Text*

1. From an Indian perspective, what are the advantages of an arranged marriage?

2. What considerations are taken into account in arranging a marriage in India?

3. What role does Nanda play in helping to find a suitable bride for her friend's son? How would you characterize Nanda's attitude toward arranged marriage and in what way does it change over the course of events?

✦ Exploring Different Perspectives

1. Contrast the protocols that govern arranged marriages, and the role of class and caste, in India, in Nanda's account, and in Japan, according to Nicholas Bornoff?

2. Discuss the expectations regarding the role of women by their families in India and in Lebanon as portrayed in Shirley Saad's story.

✦ Extending Viewpoints through Writing and Research

1. Would you ever consider allowing your parents to arrange a marriage for you? If so, why would this be more advantageous or disadvantageous than finding someone for yourself?

2. What circumstances led your parents to get married? What considerations, in your opinion, played the most important role?

3. What did this essay add to your understanding of the pressures couples experience when getting married in India? To what extent are these pressures similar to or different from those experienced by couples in the United States?

4. For research on arranged marriages throughout the world consult http://womensissues.about.com/cs/arrangedmarriage/.

Nicholas Bornoff

The Marriage Go-Round

◆

Born in London of Anglo–French parentage, Nicholas Bornoff attended school in both England and France. After a year of studying graphic design, he went to film school in Paris, where he lived for a decade. In 1979 his work as a European language translator prompted him to move to Tokyo, where he subsequently lived for eleven years. While in Japan, Bornoff worked as an advertising copywriter, was a film critic for the Japan Times *newspaper, and wrote many articles on Japanese society, culture, and business practices. A freelance journalist, Bornoff now lives in London with his Japanese wife. He has written* The National Geographic Traveler: Japan *(2000).* Pink Samurai: The Pursuit and Politics of Sex in Japan *(1991), from which the following selection is taken, provides an exhaustive travelog and scholarly history of Japanese attitudes toward sex, censorship, courtship, and marriage.*

Before You Read
Consider what kind of wedding you would want and how elaborate it would be.

◆

The Honorable Once-Over

> *The fact that two families generally lived in widely separated areas and had no knowledge of each other prompted the use of a go-between initiating the marriage. Needless to say, the marriage partners themselves had little or no previous acquaintance with one another until the day of the wedding.*
> *—Harumi Befu,* Japan
> An Anthropological Introduction *(1971)*

1   The son and heir of the prosperous owner of a large local supermarket, Hiroshi Murakami formally asked his prospective father-in-law for his daughter's hand only days ago. Although he may have lost some sleep over the prospect, there was little chance that Yamashita would refuse him. Such a proposal is nothing more than a ritual involving participants from families who have already agreed on the outcome. Besides, Mayumi had undergone *omiai* (honorable seeing-meetings) or arranged-marriage introductions no less than twenty-

three times, so that Shigeru—who likes Hiroshi anyway—was more than relieved at her choice.

2   Obasan's one and only *omiai* had been for the benefit of her parents and that was that. With her mother and grandmother, it had merely been a pact sealed between families; until fairly recently, that used to set the more educated families apart from the peasants and the poor, who rarely bothered with formal marriage at all. According to ancient custom, too, a family with no sons can "adopt" their daughter's husband. Assuming the role of first son and their family name, he becomes a *yooshi*—a substitute heir assuring the transmission of the patriarchal line. In effect, the formula has also frequently formed a basis for male *marriages de convenance*, since a husband of lower status can thus take a step up the social ladder or enter a lucrative business partnership.

3   *Omiai* still determines roughly half of all marriages today, although the outcome is generally up to the couple concerned. Rather than choosiness, Mayumi's spurning of scores of bachelors might have had more to do with a former sweetheart. That the Yamashitas and his parents did not see eye to eye eventually prompted her to end the affair, which had been permissible as long as all traces of sexuality were concealed and it showed no signs of becoming serious. Shigeru always prides himself on his open mind and progressive spirit. Mayumi, after all, has been an office employee since she left school. She earns her own income, drives her own car and after office hours her time has largely been her own. There was one point, however, about which both her parents had been quite adamant: Mayumi was to be home by ten. A young lady of twenty-five has no business being out too late after dark—the dire consequences of which are stressed in a great many frightening posters hanging outside the country's plentiful police boxes.

4   That the proliferation of love hotels might allow Mayumi to do what she cannot do at night during the day is neither here nor there to her parents. What really matters is to keep up appearances. Like everyone else in most other contexts too, provided she upholds her own and the family's *tatemae* (front) and keeps her *honne* (true situation) strictly to herself, Mayumi can reasonably do as she pleases. But when it comes to Father, he may well remain remote and aloof as a patriarchical figurehead but, when he puts in a word, reverence for filial piety commands obedience.

5   The defiance underlying the passionate and unconventionally feminist verses of the poet Akiko Yosano (1878–1942) was perhaps instigated by her own past. Infuriated that his firstborn was not a son, her father dumped her with an aunt, until her brilliance prompted him to take her back home. While she was made to manage the family shop when her mother died, at twenty she was expressly forbidden to walk abroad during the day and locked in her bedroom at night. Yosano's leaving home to marry a noted poet marked the beginning of a career;

notwithstanding ostensible servitude to a husband, many women see greater freedom in marriage than in protracted spinsterhood.

6   Even when they have passed *tekireiki*—marriageable age—many single women live at home and their parents' words are law. It is not unusual to see a spinster in her thirties hastening home to honor a curfew before the end of a dinner with friends. I recall a 25-year-old office employee living alone who, faced with opposition over a fiancé, found that a noted Tokyo bank had complied with her father's demand to block her account. A painter of the same age was ordered back to the country by her parents in a bid to end her liaison with a noted avant-garde artist. Since they wanted an adoptive *yooshi* to help out on the farm, in 1988 this university graduate did as she was bidden as dutifully as a Sicilian peasant daughter of thirty years ago.

7   When Mayumi was still unmarried at the advanced age of twenty-five, however, the family began to share her mounting anxieties. The successive meetings came to nothing, the round of eligible bachelors began to deplete itself; Mayumi lived in such a state of panic that the strain showed on her face, and she soon feared that the *omiai* photographs sent round to prospects were too flattering. *Omiai* portraiture is one of the mainstays of the photographer's studios found in all but the smallest villages. It keeps them especially busy on 15 January during *Seijin no hi* or Adults Day, a national holiday observed by all young people who have turned twenty during the preceding year. Often displayed in their shop windows, the portraits find the young ladies in traditional attire and the gentlemen in business suits, seated in a chair in the Louis XV style or posed rigidly against a cloudy sylvan backdrop. Nineteenth-century photography—albeit in color—is charmingly alive and well in Japan.

8   Relatives or trusted parental friends, who are generally female and can expect a cash contribution for their services, act as *nakodo* (go-between) and present subsequent prints of snapshot size to the prospective family. Informal snapshots are often offered too and, if the girl concerned should have hobbies such as ballet or jazz dancing, skating or aerobics, pictures in accordingly skimpy attire and showing her to her best advantage might work further in her favor. Beach photographs, however, particularly in this age of shrinking swimwear, are out.

9   If expressing interest, the parties will be brought together during an excruciating meeting process, which finds the two families lunching together in a restaurant in a climate of strained conviviality. Both in immaculate tailored suits, the young man and woman in question stare unwaveringly at the tablecloth, hardly daring to exchange a glance—let alone a word. The girl eats practically nothing. The parents talk over their heads. The boy's father reels off his son's academic achievements and his prospects; the girl's father will extol her virtuous nature, schooling, hobbies, housekeeping abilities and fondness for

children. At some point, the two will be expected to say something, generally a tremulous and extremely modest version of the already very reticent paternal summary.

10   During the following week, if he doesn't like her, the boy will back out with a range of polite excuses. If he does, he will wipe his sweating palms on the back of his trousers, find his voice and at last grab the telephone to ask her out on a date. If shyness is common among young men in similar circumstances everywhere, its prevalence in Japan is betrayed by the fact that *omiai,* a practice widespread among the rural and the diffident, would otherwise have died out long ago. If mutually impressed, the couple will go out on what might well be a rather painful first date. It may be on a Saturday evening but, where the notion of night holds improper connotations, it might more properly occur on a Sunday afternoon. The scope of activities is pretty much universal, with movies and perhaps amusement parks high on the list, but the culminating meal or cup of coffee is discernible as an *omiai* date at a glance. Facing each other across the table, they are only nominally more comfortable than with their parents the previous week. Their eyes remain glued to their banana sundaes to avoid contact; they are only animated by the sheer relief of a waiter arriving to break the spell. After about a quarter of an hour of awkward silence, one often sees the boy look up with a sudden flash of inspiration, which culminates in his rather overloudly blurting out something such as "Do you like tennis?"

11   If the girl stares with blank embarrassment and gently shakes her head, their future as a couple may well be uncertain. If she happens to like tennis and they warm to each other, they will go from date to date, from restaurant to disco and from hotel to the Shinto altar.

12   The pious might opt for the more austere and less popular Buddhist ceremony and, today, the Christian wedding sometimes offers an exotic and romantic alternative to non-Christians. The staggering proliferation of posters throughout Japan's trains and subways presents a wide range of alternative weddings, as do TV commercials and newspaper and magazine advertisements. Some might offer bizarre fantasies such as parading the couple around the wedding hall in a white and gold Venetian gondola on wheels amidst clouds of dry ice and whisking them off to their honeymoon aboard a helicopter. There are underwater weddings for diving enthusiasts and even schemes to have Christian weddings staged in small, mercenary-minded churches in Europe. The underlying message is clear: Thou Shalt Get Married. Being considered as "un-adult" at the very least, detractors are viewed with the gravest suspicion. An eccentric couple of my acquaintance, living in separate cities but regularly meeting at weekends and spending holidays together, felt that their life was fine just as it was. Both being thirty, however, and pressured by their families, they simply staged a grand wedding and carried on exactly as before.

13   With the pull to get married as strong as it is, marriage agencies are a lucrative business. A cheaper alternative for lonely hearts is even to be found in local government offices, in which matchmaking is conducted by civil servants entering the names and particulars of interested parties in ledgers for a nominal fee. Founded in 1967, the Beauty Life Association for one had some 6,000 hopefuls on its books by the mid-seventies, when there were nearly 300 other private agencies catering to all ages and persuasions in Tokyo alone, not a few of which specialize in companions for the widowed and divorced. One might be forgiven for assuming that those who drop out of the *omiai* routine in favor of agencies might be more romantically than practically inclined, but this is far from being the general rule. Well-advertised on posters throughout the Tokyo transport system is an agency aptly called the Magpie Association, which not untypically targets young ladies with an eye to the main chance: "You can trust us. We arrange introductions only to the elite: doctors, lawyers, dentists."

14   Fully computerized, today's thousands of marriage agencies boast of their ability to match data and preferences to come up with perfect partnerships. Prim middle-aged ladies in business suits aim video cameras at prospects, providing them with what is only just a more animated alternative to the *omiai* photograph. Individuals pay a flat fee of 150,000 yen to join, couples confront each other over a table on the premises and if the romance—or progenitive business partnership—doesn't work out, they shell out 10,000 yen for the next time. One Tokyo agency calling itself Rodin and unabashedly targeting the elite demands a ten million yen registration fee, degrees and moneyed backgrounds and stages matchmaking procedures including chaste separate-room weekends in plush resorts, culminating with a grand wedding in New York.

15   If some women still throw away their lives by respecting their parents' wishes rather than their own feelings, the majority of people welcome *omiai* as a means of meeting members of the opposite sex—whether the outcome is marriage or not. Nevertheless, a grimly humorous phrase for marriage, especially among women, is *jinsei no hakaba*—the cemetery of life. The alternative to an *omiai* wedding procedure is *renai kekkon*—a love marriage. If the new trend still tends to be more of an urban fantasy concocted by the media than a reality, the fact is that girls and boys are nevertheless going out more together and more freely; the *renai* pattern is becoming more common.

16   When Mayumi Yamashita started to pine away reading wedding-wear and honeymoon magazines among the serried ranks of fluffy animals festooning her room, her parents found it difficult to get her out of the house at all. On the rare occasions when she did go out, other than to go to work, she not infrequently drove to Shinto shrines and prayed to the deities most likely to augur a good matrimonial future.

Finally, Shigeru resorted to a truly desperate measure: he relaxed the 10 P.M. curfew.

17   So for the few months before Mayumi and Hiroshi were introduced, she went to discos in Nagoya on Saturday nights. She sometimes even came home at two or three in the morning, and, in the meantime, she saw a whole lot of boys. But since wherever she went she was invariably with the same three girlfriends, the operative word here is "saw." The four girls would dance together on the dance floor and giggle as they tippled discreetly in the decotech interiors of fashionable café-bars, taking turns in being the teetotal and driving fourth. In one disco, a couple of boys sauntered up to ask them to dance, which found them raising their hands in front of their faces and giggling all the more as they shook their heads. Crestfallen and sheepishly grinning, the boys soon went back to join their comrades at another table.

18   Mayumi's aunt Etsuko had acted as the *nakodo* or go-between in the *omiai* process; Hiroshi's aunt was one of her colleagues in the administrative office of a neighboring town hall. Before Hiroshi, there had been the son of that Nagoya hotelier whom Mayumi had thought too fat, the young chartered accountant who had talked only of cars and golf in a whiny voice and the boy from the electronics store who suffered from acne. There had been that Yamaguchi boy, too, the one who owned three beauty salons and drove a Porsche. The Yamashitas didn't like him; he had a hairstyle like a gangster and Mayumi's mother pointed out that the signs outside his salons were *purple*. The family hardly needed the sort of fellow who puts up purple signs.

19   In one way or another, everyone agreed. To use purple was presumptuous—for it had once been the color of the mighty Tokugawa shogunate; mauve is precious for having been the dominant color of the effete Heian age. Worse still, as a marriage between red and blue, the color is ambiguous, risqué and thus so very *mizu shobai*.

Tying the Knot

*Statistics weren't available on those who decided to remarry.
Could there really be people out there who would be willing to
go through it all again? Irish wakes are much more fun.*
—Gail Nakada, The Tokyo Journal (June 1984)

20   A legacy of rich merchant ostentatiousness from the late Edo period, weddings are elaborate and expensive. From the exchange of relatively inexpensive symbolic tokens of good luck, the bride's parents have become increasingly saddled with items such as ruinously expensive suites of furniture and a supply of kimonos considered proper (though seldom worn) for the married woman's wardrobe. Wedding

expenses thus cover far more than just the ceremony, the cost of which is shared with the groom's parents. In the Nagoya area, ever a bastion of conservatism, the parents of one couple of my acquaintance indulged in a curious and ruinous game of one-upmanship in which the bride's parents, although far less well-off than the groom's, felt obliged to go all-out to contribute as much as they could to the most ostentatious wedding either could afford. That all this is a venerable custom is widely believed, although even a cursory glance at history would prove the notion to be fallacious; the high cost of weddings is upheld by peer pressure buttressed by the sacrosanct commerce sector, in the form of companies specializing only in weddings, furniture stores, clothiers, and the hotel and catering trade.

21   As "tradition" dictates, Mayumi's and Hiroshi's wedding will be a grand affair. The Yamashitas are comfortably off, but far from wealthy; it will take ten million yen out of their savings, even if Hiroshi's parents make substantial contributions. That's life. Besides, all relatives and wedding guests will place a white envelope on a silver tray at the entrance to the wedding hall. Along with their wishes of goodwill, it will contain a minimum of 10,000 yen in cash for a more casual guest, and substantially more for members of the family. In many cases the roster of guests includes business associates; the cash contributions from those wishing to curry favor with the groom or his father will be commensurate with their involvement or expectations. As with wedding presents, the exact value of each contribution will be carefully toted up afterwards, not through stinginess, but to gauge the effusiveness of subsequent thanks, the degree of favors owed in return and the value of presents marking similar occasions later on.

22   Arriving in a black Nissan limousine of the genus "Cedric" hired for the day, Mayumi will be presented to the groom at a large local Shinto shrine. She will be wearing majestic bridal finery, which is so astronomically expensive today that all but the wealthiest brides hire it. Red and white or plain white and for rent at about 100,000 yen, a wedding kimono is intricately embroidered with floral and bird motifs enhanced with gold and silver thread. On her head, the bride wears a traditional wig made of real human hair spiked with decorative hairpins and combs. A large starched crown in a plain white fabric completes a picture that will have taken a professional dresser almost an hour to prepare. Although she will undoubtedly be lovely, the new wife, with her whitened face and tiny, beestung red lips, will look totally unlike Mayumi Yamashita and very like a standard Japanese bride. Decked out in a black formal kimono and wide *hakama* striped trousers, the groom will meanwhile be processed in only a few minutes.

23   Then there is the Shinto ceremony. As the priest officiates, a *miko* shrine maiden will guide the couple through the proceedings; there is no rehearsal. As a robed *gagaku* ensemble plays instruments imported

from China some twelve hundred years ago, the bride and groom ritually exchange cups of sake three times. The groom then reads a document aloud, the gist of which is that he expects his wife to honor and obey. He will complete this by announcing his full name, while his wife announces her forename only, for she has now been adopted by her husband's family.

24   After the ceremony, a photographer freezes the stiffly posing newlyweds in front of their families and principal guests on film for eternity, and then there will be a reception held in one of the capacious wedding halls of a large hotel. Guests will file in over a plush red and yellow carpet in the rococo style beneath a ceiling dripping with shimmering crystal chandeliers. Before entering, Mayumi will have changed into her second kimono (again unlikely to be her own) and enter the room with the groom to the strains of Mendelssohn's Wedding March piped out at deafening volume. Carefully placed around the banqueting hall according to their station, guests sit before round tables impeccably set with flower pieces and a dazzling array of beautifully presented cold delicacies. The bride and groom preside almost invisibly at one end behind a jungle of flowers. Staring rigidly ahead, they might just exchange a few words together out of the corners of their mouths. In the process of becoming bride and groom they relinquish their identities.

25   Guests and family members are specially allotted functional roles essential to the event: one or two masters or mistresses of ceremony and a best man, and many will take turns in playing musical instruments and/or singing songs. Nearly all will rise in turn to deliver lengthy speeches, some extolling the background of the bride and others the groom's. We know what schools they went to, what their work and hobbies are and the names of their best friends who, being present, will soon be delivering speeches of their own. Nothing said will come as any kind of surprise, for had everyone not known all there was to know about the newlyweds, they could hardly be assembled here. One also commonly hears someone reading out a farewell letter from the bride to her parents, thanking them poignantly and profusely for her happy childhood years. Some wedding concerns enhance this with a syrupy musical backing and even a retrospect slide-show; either way, there is hardly a dry eye in the hall.

26   Many wedding halls offer all-inclusive package deals. A newly built hotel in Okazaki, Aichi prefecture, for instance, typically owes its vastness less to its room capacity than to the fact that it caters overwhelmingly for weddings. The capacious third and fourth floors are devoted to the entire process, which is conducted with conveyor-belt efficiency. The betrothed are encouraged to make plans months beforehand. Some shops on the third floor deploy selections of appropriate gifts, others offering wedding attire for hire or purchase; another

handles all the announcements, invitations and banquet place cards and the honeymoon can be organized in an adjacent travel agency. On the day, the bride can be processed in an all-inclusive beauty parlor providing everything from a sauna, through facials and make-up to dressing; a barbershop offers similar facilities for the groom. On the fourth floor are dressing rooms for each, on either side of an antechamber in which the guests of both families sit facing each other before the ceremony, which is held in a specially consecrated Shinto shrine a few doors down the corridor. Then everyone troops into the elevators to go down to the capacious banquet halls. Coming as part of the package is a professional wedding supervisor, who steers the couple firmly through their duties like a strict nanny. As does the shrine maiden or priestess during the Shinto ceremony, she will instruct them on how and when to move or speak. Under her guidance, they will ritually hammer open a keg of sake, which is ladled out to guests.

27   Then the bride sometimes dons a third wedding dress. These days it would generally be lacy, expensive and of Western design. While she is away changing, the speeches drone on as the groom's male friends and relatives might treat him to a quick toast; to avoid offending anyone, he will refuse none of the proferred glasses. Although he might find himself downing quite a formidable amount of sake, beer and whisky, this will be one of the very rare occasions when he will be expected to keep his composure when tipsy.

28   During the course of the reception, the bride will have no time to eat; but the sight of one eating would be untoward anyway. A demure doll, she might poke daintily at the delicacies before her with her chopsticks, perhaps daring to nibble at a shrimp. She will anyway soon be grabbed by the wedding supervisor and posed alongside the groom to allow guests to take photographs. These days there will be much amusement when he is even entreated to kiss the bride. The entire event is formalized and rigorously timed to last some three hours, not one second of which will be left to spontaneity or allow anyone time to themselves. Where timing could have left a gap, it will be filled with *Candoru Sabisu* (Candle Service), a ritual which finds the room plunged in darkness and the newlyweds passing from table to table, lighting candles with a gas taper and bowing low to each guest to express their thanks. These days, urban couples might throw a more informal party for their friends later on, but the practice is rarer in the country.

29   The couple will finally change into street clothes which, befitting the occasion, should in the bride's case be of a recognizable and expensive designer brand. Guests start wending their way home bearing huge white carrier bags and silk *furoshiki* bundles full of presents offered by the bride's family. These presents are often fantastically expensive; at the recent wedding of a renowned kabuki actor, for

instance, some 2,000 guests were each presented with a pair of small gilt silver chalices, each set with a ruby and a diamond in the bottom.

30   Glad that the exalting if agonizing ceremony is over, the exhausted couple will finally sink into the back of the limousine which carries them symbolically off to their conjugal life. Next, they will board a train for the nearest airport and on to their honeymoon, which may well take the form of a five-day package tour shuttling dozens of bewildered newlyweds to overcrowded tourist hotels in Hawaii, Guam and—recently capping the list—Australia. In tune with the more intrepid new breed, however, Hiroshi and Mayumi will be going to Europe. She has always wanted to go to Paris, which has the Champs-Élysées, and to London, which has Harrods. Wherever they go, this will be the first and probably the last trip they will make abroad until future progeny, the first of which should ideally be born within the first year of their marriage, grows up.

31   That the bride's parents wave tearfully at the departing car is virtually a universal phenomenon. A cherished bird has flown from the nest, leaving the progenitors facing their declining years. In Japan, however, the wedding was once far more poignant—a girl given into marriage became the property of her husband and his family. A custom observed from early times allowed a pregnant wife to go back to her parents' home to give birth, but among the spartan samurai she often never saw her family again.

✧ Evaluating the Text

1. What cultural values and social pressures underlie the practice of arranged marriages in modern-day Japan? How do these practices create and reflect established expectations of how men and women should act?

2. Which case histories did you find the most interesting and effective in illustrating the role arranged marriages play in Japan?

3. What features define Japanese weddings in terms of the expenses incurred, gifts received, pageantry, trousseaus, religious ceremonies, wedding outfits, and so on?

4. What features of traditional Japanese culture are still part of the modern wedding ritual? What does the persistence of these features imply about Japanese society?

✧ Exploring Different Perspectives

1. Why is the pageantry of weddings described by Bornoff subordinate to the existence of the ceremony itself for same-sex couples as discussed by Kantrowitz?

2. How do the rituals and customs that precede an arranged marriage in Japan resemble or differ from those in India as described by Serena Nanda?

✧ *Extending Viewpoints through Writing and Research*

1. How do Japanese cultural practices resemble or differ from those with which you are familiar that govern under what circumstances the prospective bride and groom meet each other?

2. If you were ever on a blind date, describe your experiences.

3. Write a personal ad describing yourself as you would wish to appear to meet someone suitable.

4. For a full description of Japanese marriage rituals, with illustrations, consult http://www.japaneselifestyle.com.au/culture/marriage_modern.html.

Connecting Cultures

◆

Susan Bordo, "Never Just Pictures"

What insights do Bordo and Germaine Greer (see "One Man's Mutilation Is Another Man's Beautification" in Chapter 2) offer into the cultural pressures to reshape one's body?

Barbara Kantrowitz, "The New Face of Marriage"

In what way do homosexuals in today's society, according to Kantrowitz, occupy a place comparable to that of blacks in turn-of-the-century Louisiana (see Kate Chopin's "Désirée's Baby" in Chapter 5)?

Judith Ortiz Cofer, "The Myth of the Latin Woman"

Compare and contrast the stereotyping of Hispanics in Cofer's narrative and Victor Villaseñor's account, "Rain of Gold" in Chapter 4.

Nawal El Saadawi, "Circumcision of Girls"

To what extent is female circumcision in Middle Eastern countries as described by El Saadawi comparable to foot binding in China as described by Valerie Steele and John S. Major in "China Chic: East Meets West" (Chapter 8)?

Shirley Saad, "Amina"

What similarities in marital expectations for women can you discover in Saad's story and in Kyoko Mori's account, "Polite Lies" in Chapter 7?

Elizabeth W. Fernea and Robert A. Fernea, "A Look Behind the Veil"

How does *purdah* (unveiling), discussed by Fernea and Fernea, enhance the allure of the Bedouin girl in Nabil Gorgy's story, "Cairo Is a Small City" in Chapter 8?

Serena Nanda, "Arranging a Marriage in India"

Compare the protocol governing marriage in India described by Nanda with those in Iraq as described by Steve Sailer in "The Cousin Marriage Conundrum" in Chapter 1.

Nicholas Bornoff, "The Marriage Go-Round"

What symbolic significance does the kimono play (see Liza Dalby's "Kimono" in Chapter 8) in the elaborate weddings described by Bornoff?

4

Work and the Environment

It is too difficult to think nobly when one thinks only of earning a living.

—Jean-Jacques Rousseau (1712–1778)
Swiss-born French philosopher, political
theorist, *Confessions*, Book 2, Chapter 9
(written 1766–1770; published 1781–1788)

◆

The way we identify ourselves in terms of the work we do is far-reaching. Frequently, the first question we ask when we meet someone is, "What do you do?" Through work we define ourselves and others.

Cultural values also play a part in influencing how we feel about the work we do. In addition to providing a means to live, work has an important psychological meaning in our culture. Some societies value work more than leisure; in other cultures, the reverse is true and work is viewed as something you do just to provide the necessities of life. In the United States, the work you perform is intertwined with a sense of identity and self-esteem.

Work in most societies involves the exchange of goods and services. Economies may range from the barter system, where goods are traded, to more complex market economies based on the reciprocal exchange of goods and services for money. The transformation of resources is a key element in creating jobs and a stable economy.

The attitude people have toward the work they do varies within and between cultures. For example, think of the momentous change in attitude toward the work women do in terms of equal opportunity and equal pay. In "Ritual Fighting" Deborah Tannen explains why women in the workplace tend to take arguments personally that men take for granted. Barbara Ehrenreich describes how she went "undercover" in order to discover the reality of the lives of unskilled workers in "Nickel-and-Dimed." Gerald W. Haslam, in "The Water Game," describes the incredible transformation of California's agricultural economy because of the access to water. Victor Villaseñor, in "Rain of Gold," re-creates the moment when his father had to prove himself as a Mexican worker on his first day blasting rocks in a mine. Helena Norberg-Hodge, in "Learning from Ladakh," describes the catastrophic changes in the lives of this traditional community wrought by materialism. Tomoyuki Iwashita, in "Why I Quit the Company," explains how in Japan the seeming security of lifetime employment does not offset sacrificing one's life for the corporation. Lastly, Catherine Lim, in the short story "Paper," explores the tragic consequences of greed in this tale of a middle-class couple caught up in the frenzy of the Singapore stock exchange.

Deborah Tannen

Ritual Fighting

❖

Deborah Tannen is a professor of linguistics at Georgetown University. She is the author of many books, including You Just Don't Understand: Men and Women in Conversation, *1990, and* That's Not What I Meant!: How Conversational Style Makes or Breaks Relationships, *1992. This essay is drawn from* Talking from 9 to 5: How Women's and Men's Conversational Styles Affect Who Gets Heard and Who Gets Credit and What Gets Done at Work, *1994. A recent work is* You're Wearing That?: Understanding mothers and daughters in conversation *(2006).*

Before You Read

What degree of confrontation is appropriate in a work setting and how would you characterize your style—oppositional or placating?

❖

1   If these are some rituals common among women that are often taken literally by men when used in a work setting, what are some rituals common among men at work that are often taken literally by women? One is ritual opposition.

2   In his book *Fighting for Life: Contest, Consciousness and Sexuality,* cultural linguist Walter Ong (who happens to be a Jesuit priest) shows that males are more likely than females to use "agonism"—a warlike, oppositional format—to accomplish a range of interactional goals that have nothing literally to do with fighting. Public debate is a prime example: Each debater takes one side of the argument and tries to muster all the arguments he can think of for that side, while trying his damnedest to undercut and attack the arguments for the other side. This is done regardless of his personal convictions, and regardless of his ability to see the other's point of view, just as lawyers are supposed to make the best argument they can for their client and try to undercut the opponent's case by whatever means they can. From such ritual opposition is supposed to come truth, or, in the case of the legal system, justice. In such contests, the role of language is particularly powerful. As Gregory Matoesian puts it in a book about rape trials, "The legal system is not necessarily about truth and falsity, but winning and losing, and that, in turn, depends largely on which side can best manipulate language."

3   A woman told me she watched with distaste and distress as her office-mate heatedly argued with another colleague about whose division would suffer necessary cuts in funding; but she went into shock when, shortly after this altercation, the two men were as friendly as ever. "How can you pretend that fight never happened?" she asked the man who shared her office. He responded, "Who's pretending it never happened?," as puzzled by her question as she was by his behavior. "It happened," he said, "and it's over." She mistook their ritual fighting for real.

4   The level of expression of emotion that accompanies opposition is also culturally relative. The British think Americans are extremely excitable, which is just what Americans think of Mediterraneans. The other side of the coin is that Mediterraneans think Americans are cold, just as Americans tend to regard the British.

5   Among Americans, many people expect the discussion of ideas to be a ritual fight—that is, explored through verbal opposition. When presenting their own ideas, they state them in the most certain and absolute form they can and wait to see if they are challenged. Their thinking is that if there are weaknesses, someone will point them out, and by trying to argue against those objections, they will find out how their ideas hold up. In this spirit, literary theorist Stanley Fish, who as chair of an academic department instituted many controversial changes, explained in an interview, "I would announce changes and see if anyone said anything. No one ever did." He took their silence as a go-ahead. The question is, how many of the professors in his department felt that complaining after the fact was an option, and how many thought that a policy already announced was nonnegotiable?

6   Those who expect someone who disagrees to challenge them openly may also respond to a colleague's ideas by challenging—questioning, trying to poke holes and find weak links—as a way of helping the colleague see whether the proposal will pan out. Although cultural background is an important influence as well, fewer women than men engage in ritual opposition, and many women do not like it. Missing the ritual nature of verbal opposition, they are likely to take such challenges as personal attacks. Worse, they find it impossible to do their best in a contentious environment.

7   The logic behind ritual opposition is that knowing your ideas will be scrutinized by others should encourage you to think more rigorously in advance. When you are publicly challenged, you rise to the occasion: Adrenaline makes your mind grow sharper, and you get ideas and insights you would not have thought of without the spur of battle. But if you are not accustomed to ritual opposition, or simply do not thrive on it, you will have a very different response. Knowing you are likely to be attacked for what you say, you begin to hear criticism of your ideas as soon as they are formed. Rather than making you think

more clearly, it makes you doubt what you know. When you state your ideas, you hedge in order to fend off potential attacks, making your arguments appear weak. Ironically, this is more likely to invite attack from agonistic colleagues than to fend it off. When you feel attacked, emotion does not sharpen your wits, but rather clouds your mind and thickens your tongue, so you can't articulate the ideas that were crystal clear before. Speakers with this style find their creative juices flowing in an atmosphere of mutual support but stopped up in the face of ritual opposition. People like this (many of whom are women) are not able to do their best work in the very environment that is bringing out the best in many of their co-workers—those who not only thrive in an agonistic climate but are probably helping to create it.

8   Not all companies encourage a style of verbal opposition; each company has its own distinctive culture, developed over time. Different companies tend to encourage more or less verbal opposition and argument. But within each company, there are people who are more or less given to the oppositional style. And in any conversation, those who are comfortable with open opposition have an advantage over those who do not. Regardless of which style is rewarded in a given company, it will be hard for those whose styles are different to do their best work.

9   At work, women often take it personally when someone disagrees with them or openly argues. An engineer who was the only woman among four men in a small company found that she had to be willing to take her colleagues on in animated argument in order to be taken seriously. Once she had done that, they seemed to accept and respect her. A similar discovery was made by a physician attending a staff meeting at her hospital who became more and more angered by a male colleague arguing against a point of view she had put forth. Her better judgment told her to hold her tongue, to avoid making an enemy of this senior colleague. But finally her anger got the best of her, and she rose to her feet and delivered an impassioned attack on his position. She sat down in a panic, certain she had permanently damaged her relationship with this powerful colleague and probably alienated others allied with him. To her amazement, he came up to her after the meeting and said, "That was a great rebuttal. I'm really impressed. Let's go out for a beer after work and hash out our approaches to this problem."

10   These different ways of doing the same interactional work were dramatized for me by two different journalists who interviewed me.

11   A man interviewed me for a feature article in a newspaper. His questions were challenging to the point of belligerence. He brought up potential criticisms of my work with such eagerness that I was sure his article would make me look terrible. To my amazement, he wrote a very flattering portrait, with no hint of the belligerence he had used to get information from me. Rather than repeating the potential criticisms,

he used only my responses. By confronting me, he had been giving me an opportunity to present myself in a positive light.

12   On another occasion, I was interviewed by a woman who talked to me as if she were talking to a friend. She spent several hours in my home and revealed a lot of personal information about herself, which encouraged me to be similarly self-revealing. Nothing in her manner led me to suspect she would write anything but a favorable article, and I began to blather on, confident that I was on safe turf. The article that resulted from this interview surprised me as much as the other one, but in the opposite way. She used the information I had given her to write a piece that cast me in an unflattering light. Whereas I was pleasantly relieved to see that the first article was more favorable than I expected, I felt betrayed and tricked by the second. I thought the woman who wrote it had misled me, pretending to take the stance of a friend so I would reveal more vulnerable sides of myself. In retrospect, I could see that both journalists were using routine conversational formats to encourage self-revelation. He tried to provoke an uncensored response by challenging, she by establishing rapport. Both were ways of getting me to let down my guard—which is, after all, a journalist's job. Both spoke in ways designed to direct the conversation along ritualized lines.

13   I suspect it was not coincidental that it was a man who positioned himself as my opponent to get me to let down my hair, and a woman who positioned herself as my friend. Another woman journalist told me that the part of her job she dislikes most is having to ask confrontational questions in interviews, challenging people by repeating to them the worst things others have said about them. Yet a man she worked with told her that was the part of the job he enjoyed the most.

✧ Evaluating the Text

1. What, in Tannen's view, explains why women tend to take personally objections that men would perceive as intended to provoke a clearer understanding of the issue? How does this different focus on the message or the messenger explain why there is so much misunderstanding between men and women in the workplace?

2. How do Tannen's several examples, drawn from the experiences of others and from her own experiences, illustrate, clarify, or support her thesis, or claim?

✧ Exploring Different Perspectives

1. Are the interactions and conversational styles of men and women as discussed by Tannen also present in the working-class environment described by Barbara Ehrenreich in "Nickel-and-Dimed"?

2. In what ways can Victor Villaseñor's struggle for acceptance be seen as a more extreme form of the ritual opposition common among men at work that is described by Tannen?

✧ *Extending Viewpoints through Writing and Research*

1. In your opinion would the confrontational style of debate within a company be more comfortable for male employees than for women? Why or why not?

2. Do any of your recent interactions seem to confirm Tannen's observations? In which of these encounters can you most clearly see the difference in conversational styles described by Tannen?

Barbara Ehrenreich

Nickel-and-Dimed

On (Not) Getting by in America

◆

Barbara Ehrenreich is an investigative reporter who went undercover to discover the realities of the low-wage service worker. She was researching the consequences of the changes in the welfare system passed in 1995 that limited the length of time that single women with dependent children could receive benefits. The question she tried to answer was whether un- skilled workers could generate an income they could live on without help from the government. As her following report reveals, the answer is no. This piece was originally published in Harper's *magazine, 1999, and later was included in her book* Nickel-and-Dimed: On (Not) Getting by in America *(2001). Her most recent work is* Bait and Switch *(2005).*

Before You Read

Notice how Ehrenreich draws on her own experiences to raise the larger issue of how difficult it is for unskilled workers to survive on a minimum wage. To help you understand her rather complicated analysis, underline and annotate those parts of the selection in which she explores the eco- nomic day-to-day consequences of being a worker on the margins of our society.

◆

1   At the beginning of June 1998 I leave behind everything that nor- mally soothes the ego and sustains the body—home, career, compan- ion, reputation, ATM card—for a plunge into the low-wage workforce. There, I become another, occupationally much diminished "Barbara Ehrenreich"—depicted on job-application forms as a divorced home- maker whose sole work experience consists of housekeeping in a few private homes. I am terrified, at the beginning, of being unmasked for what I am: a middle-class journalist setting out to explore the world that welfare mothers are entering, at the rate of approximately 50,000 a month, as welfare reform kicks in. Happily, though, my fears turn out to be entirely unwarranted: during a month of poverty and toil, my name goes unnoticed and for the most part unuttered. In this par- allel universe where my father never got out of the mines and I never got through college, I am "baby," "honey," "blondie," and, most com- monly, "girl."

2   My first task is to find a place to live. I figure that if I can earn $7
an hour—which, from the want ads, seems doable—I can afford to
spent $500 on rent, or maybe, with severe economies, $600. In the Key
West area, where I live, this pretty much confines me to flophouses and
trailer homes—like the one, a pleasing fifteen-minute drive from town,
that has no air-conditioning, no screens, no fans, no television, and, by
way of diversion, only the challenge of evading the landlord's Dober-
man pinscher. The big problem with this place, though, is the rent,
which at $675 a month is well beyond my reach. All right, Key West is
expensive. But so is New York City, or the Bay Area, or Jackson Hole,
or Telluride, or Boston, or any other place where tourists and the
wealthy compete for living space with the people who clean their toilets and fry their hash browns.[1] Still, it is a shock to realize that "trailer
trash" has become, for me, a demographic category to aspire to.

3   So I decide to make the common trade-off between affordability
and convenience, and go for a $500-a-month efficiency thirty miles up
a two-lane highway from the employment opportunities of Key West,
meaning forty-five minutes if there's no road construction and I don't
get caught behind some sun-dazed Canadian tourists. I hate the drive,
along a roadside studded with white crosses commemorating the more
effective head-on collisions, but it's a sweet little place—a cabin, more
or less, set in the swampy back yard of the converted mobile home
where my landlord, an affable TV repairman, lives with his bartender
girlfriend. Anthropologically speaking, a bustling trailer park would
be preferable, but here I have a gleaming white floor and a firm mattress, and the few resident bugs are easily vanquished.

4   Besides, I am not doing this for the anthropology. My aim is nothing so mistily subjective as to "experience poverty" or find out how it
"really feels" to be a long-term low-wage worker. I've had enough un-
chosen encounters with poverty and the world of low-wage work to
know it's not a place you want to visit for touristic purposes; it just
smells too much like fear. And with all my real-life assets—bank account, IRA, health insurance, multiroom home—waiting indulgently
in the background, I am, of course, thoroughly insulated from the ter-
rors that afflict the genuinely poor.

5   No, this is a purely objective, scientific sort of mission. The humanitarian rationale for welfare reform—as opposed to the more punitive
and stingy impulses that may actually have motivated it—is that work
will lift poor women out of poverty while simultaneously inflating
their self-esteem and hence their future value in the labor market.
Thus, whatever the hassles involved in finding child care, transportation, etc., the transition from welfare to work will end happily, in
greater prosperity for all. Now there are many problems with this comforting prediction, such as the fact that the economy will inevitably

undergo a downturn, eliminating many jobs. Even without a down-turn, the influx of a million former welfare recipients into the low-wage labor market could depress wages by as much as 11.9 percent, according to the Economic Policy Institute (EPI) in Washington, D.C.

6   But is it really possible to make a living on the kinds of jobs currently available to unskilled people? Mathematically, the answer is no, as can be shown by taking $6 to $7 an hour, perhaps subtracting a dollar or two an hour for child care, multiplying by 160 hours a month, and comparing the result to the prevailing rents. According to the National Coalition for the Homeless, for example, in 1998 it took, on average nationwide, an hourly wage of $8.89 to afford a one-bedroom apartment, and the Preamble Center for Public Policy estimates that the odds against a typical welfare recipient's landing a job at such a "living wage" are about 97 to 1. If these numbers are right, low-wage work is not a solution to poverty and possibly not even to homelessness.

7   It may seem excessive to put this proposition to an experimental test. As certain family members keep unhelpfully reminding me, the viability of low-wage work could be tested, after a fashion, without ever leaving my study. I could just pay myself $7 an hour for eight hours a day, charge myself for room and board, and total up the numbers after a month. Why leave the people and work that I love? But I am an experimental scientist by training. In that business, you don't just sit at a desk and theorize; you plunge into the everyday chaos of nature, where surprises lurk in the most mundane measurements. Maybe, when I got into it, I would discover some hidden economies in the world of the low-wage worker. After all, if 30 percent of the workforce toils for less than $8 an hour, according to the EPI, they may have found some tricks as yet unknown to me. Maybe—who knows?—I would even to able to detect in myself the bracing psychological effects of getting out of the house, as promised by the welfare wonks at places like the Heritage Foundation. Or, on the other hand, maybe there would be unexpected costs—physical, mental, or financial—to throw off all my calculations. Ideally, I should do this with two small children in tow, that being the welfare average, but mine are grown and no one is willing to lend me theirs for a month-long vacation in penury. So this is not the perfect experiment, just a test of the best possible case: an unencumbered woman, smart and even strong, attempting to live more or less off the land.

8   On the morning of my first full day of job searching, I take a red pen to the want ads, which are auspiciously numerous. Everyone in Key West's booming "hospitality industry" seems to be looking for someone like me—trainable, flexible, and with suitably humble expectations as to pay. I know I possess certain traits that might be advanta-

geous—I'm white and, I like to think, well-spoken and poised—but I decide on two rules: One, I cannot use any skills derived from my education or usual work—not that there are a lot of want ads for satirical essayists anyway. Two, I have to take the best-paid job that is offered me and of course do my best to hold it; no Marxist rants or sneaking off to read novels in the ladies' room. In addition, I rule out various occupations for one reason or another. Hotel front-desk clerk, for example, which to my surprise is regarded as unskilled and pays around $7 an hour, gets eliminated because it involves standing in one spot for eight hours a day. Waitressing is similarly something I'd like to avoid, because I remember it leaving me bone tired when I was eighteen, and I'm decades of varicosities and back pain beyond that now. Telemarketing, one of the first refuges of the suddenly indigent, can be dismissed on grounds of personality. This leaves certain supermarket jobs, such as deli clerk, or housekeeping in Key West's thousands of hotel and guest rooms. Housekeeping is especially appealing, for reasons both atavistic and practical: it's what my mother did before I came along, and it can't be too different from what I've been doing part-time, in my own home, all my life.

9   So I put on what I take to be a respectful-looking outfit of ironed Bermuda shorts and scooped-neck T-shirt and set out for a tour of the local hotels and supermarkets. Best Western, Econo Lodge, and HoJo's all let me fill out application forms, and these are, to my relief, interested in little more than whether I am a legal resident of the United States and have committed any felonies. My next step is Winn-Dixie, the supermarket, which turns out to have a particularly onerous application process, featuring a fifteen-minute "interview" by computer since, apparently, no human on the premises is deemed capable of representing the corporate point of view. I am conducted to a large room decorated with posters illustrating how to look "professional" (it helps to be white and, if female, permed) and warning of the slick promises that union organizers might try to tempt me with. The interview is multiple choice: Do I have anything, such as child-care problems, that might make it hard for me to get to work on time? Do I think safety on the job is the responsibility of management? Then, popping up cunningly out of the blue: How many dollars' worth of stolen goods have I purchased in the last year? Would I turn in a fellow employee if I caught him stealing? Finally, "Are you an honest person?"

10   Apparently, I ace the interview, because I am told that all I have to do is show up in some doctor's office tomorrow for a urine test. This seems to be a fairly general rule: if you want to stack Cheerio boxes or vacuum hotel rooms in chemically fascist America, you have to be willing to squat down and pee in front of some health worker (who has no doubt had to do the same thing herself). The wages Winn-Dixie is

offering—$6 and a couple of dimes to start with—are not enough, I decide, to compensate for this indignity.[2]

11   I lunch at Wendy's, where $4.99 gets you unlimited refills at the Mexican part of the Superbar, a comforting surfeit of refried beans and "cheese sauce." A teenage employee, seeing me studying the want ads, kindly offers me an application form, which I fill out, though here, too, the pay is just $6 and change an hour. Then it's off for a round of the locally owned inns and guest-houses. At "The Palms," let's call it, a bouncy manager actually takes me around to see the rooms and meet the existing housekeepers, who, I note with satisfaction, look pretty much like me—faded ex-hippie types in shorts with long hair pulled back in braids. Mostly, though, no one speaks to me or even looks at me except to proffer an application form. At my last stop, a palatial B&B, I wait twenty minutes to meet "Max," only to be told that there are no jobs now but there should be one soon, since "nobody lasts more than a couple weeks." (Because none of the people I talked to knew I was a reporter, I have changed their names to protect their privacy and, in some cases perhaps, their jobs.)

12   Three days go by like this, and, to my chagrin, no one out of the approximately twenty places I've applied calls me for an interview. I had been vain enough to worry about coming across as too educated for the jobs I sought, but no one even seems interested in finding out how overqualified I am. Only later will I realize that the want ads are not a reliable measure of the actual jobs available at any particular time. They are, as I should have guessed from Max's comment, the employers' insurance policy against the relentless turnover of the low-wage workforce. Most of the big hotels run ads almost continually, just to build a supply of applicants to replace the current workers as they drift away or are fired, so finding a job is just a matter of being at the right place at the right time and flexible enough to take whatever is being offered that day. This finally happens to me at one of the big discount hotel chains, where I go, as usual, for housekeeping and am sent, instead, to try out as a waitress at the attached "family restaurant," a dismal spot with a counter and about thirty tables that looks out on a parking garage and features such tempting fare as "Pollish [sic] sausage and BBQ sauce" on 95-degree days. Phillip, the dapper young West Indian who introduces himself as the manager, interviews me with about as much enthusiasm as if he were a clerk processing me for Medicare, the principal questions being what shifts can I work and when can I start. I mutter something about being woefully out of practice as a waitress, but he's already on to the uniform: I'm to show up tomorrow wearing black slacks and black shoes; he'll provide the rust-colored polo shirt with HEARTHSIDE embroidered on it, though I might want to wear my own shirt to get to work, ha ha. At the word "tomorrow," something between fear and indignation rises in my chest. I

want to say, "Thank you for your time, sir, but this is just an experiment, you know, not my actual life."

13   So begins my career at the Hearthside, I shall call it, one small profit center within a global discount hotel chain, where for two weeks I work from 2:00 till 10:00 P.M. for $2.43 an hour plus tips.[3] In some futile bid for gentility, the management has barred employees from using the front door, so my first day I enter through the kitchen, where a red-faced man with shoulder-length blond hair is throwing frozen steaks against the wall and yelling, "Fuck this shit!" "That's just Jack," explains Gail, the wiry middle-aged waitress who is assigned to train me. "He's on the rag again"—a condition occasioned, in this instance, by the fact that the cook on the morning shift had forgotten to thaw out the steaks. For the next eight hours, I run after the agile Gail, absorbing bits of instruction along with fragments of personal tragedy. All food must be trayed, and the reason she's so tired today is that she woke up in a cold sweat thinking of her boyfriend, who killed himself recently in an upstate prison. No refills on lemonade. And the reason he was in prison is that a few DUIs caught up with him, that's all, could have happened to anyone. Carry the creamers to the table in a monkey bowl, never in your hand. And after he was gone she spent several months living in her truck, peeing in a plastic pee bottle and reading by candlelight at night, but you can't live in a truck in the summer, since you need to have the windows down, which means anything can get in, from mosquitoes on up.

14   At least Gail puts to rest any fears I had of appearing overqualified. From the first day on, I find that of all the things I have left behind, such as home and identity, what I miss the most is competence. Not that I have ever felt utterly competent in the writing business, in which one day's success augurs nothing at all for the next. But in my writing life, I at least have some notion of procedure: do the research, make the outline, rough out a draft, etc. As a server, though, I am beset by requests like bees: more iced tea here, ketchup over there, a to-go box for table fourteen, and where are the high chairs, anyway? Of the twenty-seven tables, up to six are usually mine at any time, though on slow afternoons or if Gail is off, I sometimes have the whole place to myself. There is the touch-screen computer-ordering system to master, which is, I suppose, meant to minimize server-cook contact, but in practice requires constant verbal fine-tuning: "That's gravy on the mashed, okay? None on the meatloaf," and so forth—while the cook scowls as if I were inventing these refinements just to torment him. Plus, something I had forgotten in the years since I was eighteen: about a third of a server's job is "side work" that's invisible to customers— sweeping, scrubbing, slicing, refilling, and restocking. If it isn't all done, every little bit of it, you're going to face the 6:00 P.M. dinner rush

defenseless and probably go down in flames. I screw up dozens of times at the beginning, sustained in my shame entirely by Gail's support—"It's okay, baby, everyone does that sometime"—because, to my total surprise and despite the scientific detachment I am doing my best to maintain, I care.

15   The whole thing would be a lot easier if I could just skate through it as Lily Tomlin in one of her waitress skits, but I was raised by the absurd Booker T. Washingtonian precept that says: If you're going to do something, do it well. In fact, "well" isn't good enough by half. Do it better than anyone has ever done it before. Or so said my father, who must have known what he was talking about because he managed to pull himself, and us with him, up from the mile-deep copper mines of Butte to the leafy suburbs of the Northeast, ascending from boilermakers to martinis before booze beat out ambition. As in most endeavors I have encountered in my life, doing it "better than anyone" is not a reasonable goal. Still, when I wake up at 4:00 A.M. in my own cold sweat, I am not thinking about the writing deadlines I'm neglecting; I'm thinking about the table whose order I screwed up so that one of the boys didn't get his kiddie meal until the rest of the family had moved on to their Key Lime pies. That's the other powerful motivation I hadn't expected—the customers, or "patients," as I can't help thinking of them on account of the mysterious vulnerability that seems to have left them temporarily unable to feed themselves. After a few days at the Hearthside, I feel the service ethic kick in like a shot of oxytocin, the nurturance hormone. The plurality of my customers are hard-working locals—truck drivers, construction workers, even housekeepers from the attached hotel—and I want them to have the closest to a "fine dining" experience that the grubby circumstances will allow. No "you guys" for me; everyone over twelve is "sir" or "ma'am." I ply them with iced tea and coffee refills; I return, mid-meal, to inquire how everything is; I doll up their salads with chopped raw mushrooms, summer squash slices, or whatever bits of produce I can find that have survived their sojourn in the cold-storage room mold-free.

16   There is Benny, for example, a short, tight-muscled sewer repairman, who cannot even think of eating until he has absorbed a half hour of air-conditioning and ice water. We chat about hyperthermia and electrolytes until he is ready to order some finicky combination like soup of the day, garden salad, and a side of grits. There are the German tourists who are so touched by my pidgin "Willkommen" and "Ist alles gut?" that they actually tip. (Europeans, spoiled by their trade-union-ridden, high-wage welfare states, generally do not know that they are supposed to tip. Some restaurants, the Hearthside included, allow servers to "grat" their foreign customers, or add a tip to the bill. Since this amount is added before the customers have a chance to tip or not tip, the practice amounts to an automatic penalty for imperfect Eng-

lish.) There are the two dirt-smudged lesbians, just off their construction shift, who are impressed enough by my suave handling of the fly in the piña colada that they take the time to praise me to Stu, the assistant manager. There's Sam, the kindly retired cop, who has to plug up his tracheotomy hole with one finger in order to force the cigarette smoke into his lungs.

17   Sometimes I play with the fantasy that I am a princess who, in penance for some tiny transgression, has undertaken to feed each of her subjects by hand. But the non-princesses working with me are just as indulgent, even when this means flouting management rules—concerning, for example, the number of croutons that can go on a salad (six). "Put on all you want," Gail whispers, "as long as Stu isn't looking." She dips into her own tip money to buy biscuits and gravy for an out-of-work mechanic who's used up all his money on dental surgery, inspiring me to pick up the tab for his milk and pie. Maybe the same high levels of agape can be found throughout the "hospitality industry." I remember the poster decorating one of the apartments I looked at, which said "If you seek happiness for yourself you will never find it. Only when you seek happiness for others will it come to you," or words to that effect—an odd sentiment, it seemed to me at the time, to find in the dank one-room basement apartment of a bellhop at the Best Western. At the Hearthside, we utilize whatever bits of autonomy we have to ply our customers with the illicit calories that signal our love. It is our job as servers to assemble the salads and desserts, pouring the dressings and squirting the whipped cream. We also control the number of butter patties our customers get and the amount of sour cream on their baked potatoes. So if you wonder why Americans are so obese, consider the fact that waitresses both express their humanity and earn their tips through the covert distribution of fats.

18   Ten days into it, this is beginning to look like a livable lifestyle. I like Gail, who is "looking at fifty" but moves so fast she can alight in one place and then another without apparently being anywhere between them. I clown around with Lionel, the teenage Haitian busboy, and catch a few fragments of conversation with Joan, the svelte fortyish hostess and militant feminist who is the only one of us who dares to tell Jack to shut the fuck up. I even warm up to Jack when, on a slow night and to make up for a particularly unwarranted attack on my abilities, or so I imagine, he tells me about his glory days as a young man at "coronary school"—or do you say "culinary"?—in Brooklyn, where he dated a knock-out Puerto Rican chick and learned everything there is to know about food. I finish up at 10:00 or 10:30, depending on how much side work I've been able to get done during the shift, and cruise home to the tapes I snatched up at random when I left my real home— Marianne Faithfull, Tracy Chapman, Enigma, King Sunny Ade, the Violent Femmes—just drained enough for the music to set my cranium

resonating but hardly dead. Midnight snack is Wheat Thins and Monterey Jack, accompanied by cheap white wine on ice and whatever AMC has to offer. To bed by 1:30 or 2:00, up at 9:00 or 10:00, read for an hour while my uniform whirls around in the landlord's washing machine, and then it's another eight hours spent following Mao's central instruction, as laid out in the Little Red Book, which was: Serve the people.

19   I could drift along like this, in some dreamy proletarian idyll, except for two things. One is management. If I have kept this subject on the margins thus far it is because I still flinch to think that I spent all those weeks under the surveillance of men (and later women) whose job it was to monitor my behavior for signs of sloth, theft, drug abuse, or worse. Not that managers and especially "assistant managers" in low-wage settings like this are exactly the class enemy. In the restaurant business, they are mostly former cooks or servers, still capable of pinch-hitting in the kitchen or on the floor, just as in hotels they are likely to be former clerks, and paid a salary of only about $400 a week. But everyone knows they have crossed over to the other side, which is, crudely put, corporate as opposed to human. Cooks want to prepare tasty meals; servers want to serve them graciously; but managers are there for only one reason—to make sure that money is made for some theoretical entity that exists far away in Chicago or New York, if a corporation can be said to have a physical existence at all. Reflecting on her career, Gail tells me ruefully that she had sworn, years ago, never to work for a corporation again. "They don't cut you no slack. You give and you give, and they take."

20   Managers can sit—for hours at a time if they want—but it's their job to see that no one else ever does, even when there's nothing to do, and this is why, for servers, slow times can be as exhausting as rushes. You start dragging out each little chore, because if the manager on duty catches you in an idle moment, he will give you something far nastier to do. So I wipe, I clean, I consolidate ketchup bottles and recheck the cheesecake supply, even tour the tables to make sure the customer evaluation forms are all standing perkily in their places—wondering all the time how many calories I burn in these strictly theatrical exercises. When, on a particularly dead afternoon, Stu finds me glancing at a USA Today a customer has left behind, he assigns me to vacuum the entire floor with the broken vacuum cleaner that has a handle only two feet long, and the only way to do that without incurring orthopedic damage is to proceed from spot to spot on your knees.

21   On my first Friday at the Hearthside there is a "mandatory meeting for all restaurant employees," which I attend, eager for insight into our overall marketing strategy and the niche (your basic Ohio cuisine

with a tropical twist?) we aim to inhabit. But there is no "we" at this meeting. Phillip, our top manager except for an occasional "consultant" sent out by corporate headquarters, opens it with a sneer: "The break room—it's disgusting. Butts in the ashtrays, newspapers lying around, crumbs." This windowless little room, which also houses the time clock for the entire hotel, is where we stash our bags and civilian clothes and take our half-hour meal breaks. But a break room is not a right, he tells us. It can be taken away. We should also know that the lockers in the break room and whatever is in them can be searched at any time. Then comes gossip; there has been gossip; gossip (which seems to mean employees talking among themselves) must stop. Off-duty employees are henceforth barred from eating at the restaurant, because "other servers gather around them and gossip." When Phillip has exhausted his agenda of rebukes, Joan complains about the condition of the ladies' room and I throw in my two bits about the vacuum cleaner. But I don't see any backup coming from my fellow servers, each of whom has subsided into her own personal funk; Gail, my role model, stares sorrowfully at a point six inches from her nose. The meeting ends when Andy, one of the cooks, gets up, muttering about breaking up his day off for this almighty bullshit.

22   Just four days later we are suddenly summoned into the kitchen at 3:30 P.M., even though there are live tables on the floor. We all—about ten of us—stand around Phillip, who announces grimly that there has been a report of some "drug activity" on the night shift and that, as a result, we are now to be a "drug-free" workplace, meaning that all new hires will be tested, as will possibly current employees on a random basis. I am glad that this part of the kitchen is so dark, because I find myself blushing as hard as if I had been caught toking up in the ladies' room myself: I haven't been treated this way—lined up in the corridor, threatened with locker searches, peppered with carelessly aimed accusations—since junior high school. Back on the floor, Joan cracks, "Next they'll be telling us we can't have sex on the job." When I ask Stu what happened to inspire the crackdown, he just mutters about "management decisions" and takes the opportunity to upbraid Gail and me for being too generous with the rolls. From now on there's to be only one per customer, and it goes out with the dinner, not with the salad. He's also been riding the cooks, prompting Andy to come out of the kitchen and observe—with the serenity of a man whose customary implement is a butcher knife—that "Stu has a death wish today."

23   Later in the evening, the gossip crystallizes around the theory that Stu is himself the drug culprit, that he uses the restaurant phone to order up marijuana and sends one of the late servers out to fetch it for him. The server was caught, and she may have ratted Stu out or at least said enough to cast some suspicion on him, thus accounting for his

pissy behavior. Who knows? Lionel, the busboy, entertains us for the rest of the shift by standing just behind Stu's back and sucking deliriously on an imaginary joint.

24   The other problem, in addition to the less-than-nurturing management style, is that this job shows no sign of being financially viable. You might imagine, from a comfortable distance, that people who live, year in and year out, on $6 to $10 an hour have discovered some survival stratagems unknown to the middle class. But no. It's not hard to get my co-workers to talk about their living situations, because housing, in almost every case, is the principal source of disruption in their lives, the first thing they fill you in on when they arrive for their shifts. After a week, I have compiled the following survey:

- Gail is sharing a room in a well-known downtown flophouse for which she and a roommate pay about $250 a week. Her roommate, a male friend, has begun hitting on her, driving her nuts, but the rent would be impossible alone.

- Claude, the Haitian cook, is desperate to get out of the two-room apartment he shares with his girlfriend and two other, unrelated, people. As far as I can determine, the other Haitian men (most of whom only speak Creole) live in similarly crowded situations.

- Annette, a twenty-year-old server who is six months pregnant and has been abandoned by her boyfriend, lives with her mother, a postal clerk.

- Marianne and her boyfriend are paying $170 a week for a one-person trailer.

- Jack, who is, at $10 an hour, the wealthiest of us, lives in a trailer he owns, paying only the $400-a-month lot fee.

- The other white cook, Andy, lives on his dry-docked boat, which, as far as I can tell from his loving descriptions, can't be more than twenty feet long. He offers to take me out on it, once it's repaired, but the offer comes with inquiries as to my marital status, so I do not follow up on it.

- Tina and her husband are paying $60 a night for a double room in a Days Inn. This is because they have no car and the Days Inn is within walking distance of the Hearthside. When Marianne, one of the breakfast servers, is tossed out of her trailer for subletting (which is against the trailer-park rules), she leaves her boyfriend and moves in with Tina and her husband.

- Joan, who had fooled me with her numerous and tasteful outfits (hostesses wear their own clothes), lives in a van she parks behind a shopping center at night and showers in Tina's motel room. The clothes are from thrift shops.[4]

25   It strikes me, in my middle-class solipsism, that there is gross improvidence in some of these arrangements. When Gail and I are wrapping silverware in napkins—the only task for which we are permitted to sit—she tells me she is thinking of escaping from her roommate by moving into the Days Inn herself. I am astounded: How can she even think of paying between $40 and $60 a day? But if I was afraid of sounding like a social worker, I come out just sounding like a fool. She squints at me in disbelief, "And where am I supposed to get a month's rent and a month's deposit for an apartment?" I'd been feeling pretty smug about my $500 efficiency, but of course it was made possible only by the $1,300 I had allotted myself for start-up costs when I began my low-wage life: $1,000 for the first month's rent and deposit, $100 for initial groceries and cash in my pocket, $200 stuffed away for emergencies. In poverty, as in certain propositions in physics, starting conditions are everything.

26   There are no secret economies that nourish the poor; on the contrary, there are a host of special costs. If you can't put up the two months' rent you need to secure an apartment, you end up paying through the nose for a room by the week. If you have only a room, with a hot plate at best, you can't save by cooking up huge lentil stews that can be frozen for the week ahead. You eat fast food, or the hot dogs and styrofoam cups of soup that can be microwaved in a convenience store. If you have no money for health insurance—and the Hearthside's niggardly plan kicks in only after three months—you go without routine care or prescription drugs and end up paying the price. Gail, for example, was fine until she ran out of money for estrogen pills. She is supposed to be on the company plan by now, but they claim to have lost her application form and need to begin the paperwork all over again. So she spends $9 per migraine pill to control the headaches she wouldn't have, she insists, if her estrogen supplements were covered. Similarly, Marianne's boyfriend lost his job as a roofer because he missed so much time after getting a cut on his foot for which he couldn't afford the prescribed antibiotic.

27   My own situation, when I sit down to assess it after two weeks of work, would not be much better if this were my actual life. The seductive thing about waitressing is that you don't have to wait for payday to feel a few bills in your pocket, and my tips usually cover meals and gas, plus something left over to stuff into the kitchen drawer I use as a bank. But as the tourist business slows in the summer heat, I sometimes leave work with only $20 in tips (the gross is higher, but servers share about 15 percent of their tips with the bus-boys and bartenders). With wages included, this amounts to about the minimum wage of $5.15 an hour. Although the sum in the drawer is piling up, at the present rate of accumulation it will be more than a hundred dollars short of my rent when the end of the month comes around. Nor can I see any expenses to cut. True, I haven't gone the lentil-stew route yet, but that's

because I don't have a large cooking pot, pot holders, or a ladle to stir with (which cost about $30 at Kmart, less at thrift stores), not to mention onions, carrots, and the indispensable bay leaf. I do make my lunch almost every day—usually some slow-burning, high-protein combo like frozen chicken patties with melted cheese on top and canned pinto beans on the side. Dinner is at the Hearthside, which offers its employees a choice of BLT, fish sandwich, or hamburger for only $2. The burger lasts longest, especially if it's heaped with gut-puckering jalapeños, but by midnight my stomach is growling again.

28   So unless I want to start using my car as a residence, I have to find a second, or alternative, job. I call all the hotels where I filled out housekeeping applications weeks ago—the Hyatt, Holiday Inn, Econo Lodge, Hojo's, Best Western, plus a half dozen or so locally run guesthouses. Nothing. Then I start making the rounds again, wasting whole mornings waiting for some assistant manager to show up, even dipping into places so creepy that the front-desk clerk greets you from behind bulletproof glass and sells pints of liquor over the counter. But either someone has exposed my real-life housekeeping habits—which are, shall we say, mellow—or I am at the wrong end of some infallible ethnic equation: most, but by no means all, of the working housekeepers I see on my job searches are African Americans, Spanish-speaking, or immigrants from the Central European post-Communist world, whereas servers are almost invariably white and monolingually English-speaking. When I finally get a positive response, I have been identified once again as server material. Jerry's, which is part of a well-known national family restaurant chain and physically attached here to another budget hotel chain, is ready to use me at once. The prospect is both exciting and terrifying, because, with about the same number of tables and counter seats, Jerry's attracts three or four times the volume of customers as the gloomy old Hearthside.

29   I start out with the beautiful, heroic idea of handling the two jobs at once, and for two days I almost do it: the breakfast/lunch shift at Jerry's, which goes till 2:00, arriving at the Hearthside at 2:10, and attempting to hold out until 10:00. In the ten minutes between jobs, I pick up a spicy chicken sandwich at the Wendy's drive-through window, gobble it down in the car, and change from khaki slacks to black, from Hawaiian to rust polo. There is a problem, though. When during the 3:00 to 4:00 P.M. dead time I finally sit down to wrap silver, my flesh seems to bond to the seat. I try to refuel with a purloined cup of soup, as I've seen Gail and Joan do dozens of times, but a manager catches me and hisses "No eating!" though there's not a customer around to be offended by the sight of food making contact with a server's lips. So I tell Gail I'm going to quit, and she hugs me and says she might just follow me to Jerry's herself.

30   But the chances of this are miniscule. She has left the flophouse and her annoying roommate and is back to living in her beat-up old truck. But guess what? she reports to me excitedly later that evening: Phillip has given her permission to park overnight in the hotel parking lot, as long as she keeps out of sight, and the parking lot should be totally safe, since it's patrolled by a hotel security guard! With the Hearthside offering benefits like that, how could anyone think of leaving?

31   True, I take occasional breaks from this life, going home now and then to catch up on e-mail and for conjugal visits (though I am careful to "pay" for anything I eat there), seeing *The Truman Show* with friends and letting them buy my ticket. And I still have those what-am-I-doing-here moments at work, when I get so homesick for the printed word that I obsessively reread the six-page menu. But as the days go by, my old life is beginning to look exceedingly strange. The e-mails and phone messages addressed to my former self come from a distant race of people with exotic concerns and far too much time on their hands. The neighborly market I used to cruise for produce now looks forbiddingly like a Manhattan yuppie emporium. And when I sit down one morning in my real home to pay bills from my past life, I am dazzled at the two- and three-figure sums owed to outfits like Club BodyTech and Amazon.com.

32   Management at Jerry's is generally calmer and more "professional" than at the Hearthside, with two exceptions. One is Joy, a plump, blowsy woman in her early thirties, who once kindly devoted several minutes to instructing me in the correct one-handed method of carrying trays but whose moods change disconcertingly from shift to shift and even within one. Then there's B.J., a.k.a. B.J.-the-bitch, whose contribution is to stand by the kitchen counter and yell, "Nita, your order's up, move it!" or, "Barbara, didn't you see you've got another table out there? Come on, girl!" Among other things, she is hated for having replaced the whipped-cream squirt cans with big plastic whipped-cream-filled baggies that have to be squeezed with both hands—because, reportedly, she saw or thought she saw employees trying to inhale the propellant gas from the squirt cans, in the hope that it might be nitrous oxide. On my third night, she pulls me aside abruptly and brings her face so close that it looks as if she's planning to butt me with her forehead. But instead of saying, "You're fired," she says, "You're doing fine." The only trouble is I'm spending time chatting with customers: "That's how they're getting you." Furthermore I am letting them "run me," which means harassment by sequential demands: you bring the ketchup and they decide they want extra Thousand Island; you bring that and they announce they now need a side of fries; and so on into distraction. Finally she tells me not to take her wrong. She tries to say things in a nice way, but you get into a mode, you know, because everything has to move so fast.[5]

33   I mumble thanks for the advice, feeling like I've just been stripped naked by the crazed enforcer of some ancient sumptuary law: No chatting for you, girl. No fancy service ethic allowed for the serfs. Chatting with customers is for the beautiful young college-educated servers in the downtown carpaccio joints, the kids who can make $70 to $100 a night. What had I been thinking? My job is to move orders from tables to kitchen and then trays from kitchen to tables. Customers are, in fact, the major obstacle to the smooth transformation of information into food and food into money—they are, in short, the enemy. And the painful thing is that I'm beginning to see it this way myself. There are the traditional asshole types—frat boys who down multiple Buds and then make a fuss because the steaks are so emaciated and the fries so sparse—as well as the variously impaired—due to age, diabetes, or literacy issues—who require patient nutritional counseling.

34   I make friends, over time, with the other "girls" who work my shift: Nita, the tattooed twenty-something who taunts us by going around saying brightly, "Have we started making money yet?" Ellen, whose teenage son cooks on the graveyard shift and who once managed a restaurant in Massachusetts but won't try out for management here because she prefers being a "common worker" and not "ordering people around." Easy-going fiftyish Lucy, with the raucous laugh, who limps toward the end of the shift because of something that has gone wrong with her leg, the exact nature of which cannot be determined without health insurance. We talk about the usual girl things—men, children, and the sinister allure of Jerry's chocolate peanut-butter cream pie—though no one, I notice, ever brings up anything potentially expensive, like shopping or movies. As at the Hearthside, the only recreation ever referred to is partying, which requires little more than some beer, a joint, and a few close friends. Still, no one here is homeless, or cops to it anyway, thanks usually to a working husband or boyfriend. All in all, we form a reliable mutual-support group: If one of us is feeling sick or overwhelmed, another one will "bev" a table or even carry trays for her. If one of us is off sneaking a cigarette or a pee,[6] the others will do their best to conceal her absence from the enforcers of corporate rationality.

35   But my saving human connection—my oxytocin receptor, as it were—George, the nineteen-year-old, fresh-off-the-boat Czech dishwasher. We get to talking when he asks me, tortuously, how much cigarettes cost at Jerry's. I do my best to explain that they cost over a dollar more here than at a regular store and suggest that he just take one from the half-filled packs that are always lying around on the break table. But that would be unthinkable. Except for the one tiny earring signaling his allegiance to some vaguely alternative point of view, George is a perfect straight arrow—crew-cut, hardworking, and hungry for eye contact. "Czech Republic," I ask, "or Slovakia?" and he

seems delighted that I know the difference. "Václav Havel," I try. "Velvet Revolution, Frank Zappa?" "Yes, yes, 1989," he says, and I realize we are talking about history.

36   My project is to teach George English. "How are you today, George?" I say at the start of each shift. "I am good, and how are you today, Barbara?" I learn that he is not paid by Jerry's but by the "agent" who shipped him over—$5 an hour, with the agent getting the dollar or so difference between that and what Jerry's pays dishwashers. I learn also that he shares an apartment with a crowd of other Czech "dishers," as he calls them, and that he cannot sleep until one of them goes off for his shift, leaving a vacant bed. We are having one of our ESL sessions late one afternoon when B.J. catches us at it and orders "Joseph" to take up the rubber mats on the floor near the dishwashing sinks and mop underneath. "I thought your name was George," I say loud enough for B.J. to hear as she strides off back to the counter. Is she embarrassed? Maybe a little, because she greets me back at the counter with "George, Joseph—there are so many of them!" I say nothing, neither nodding nor smiling, and for this I am punished later when I think I am ready to go and she announces that I need to roll fifty more sets of silverware and isn't it time I mixed up a fresh four-gallon batch of blue-cheese dressing? May you grow old in this place, B.J., is the curse I beam out at her when I am finally permitted to leave. May the syrup spills glue your feet to the floor.

37   I make the decision to move closer to Key West. First, because of the drive. Second and third, also because of the drive: gas is eating up $4 to $5 a day, and although Jerry's is as high-volume as you can get, the tips average only 10 percent, and not just for a newbie like me. Between the base pay of $2.15 an hour and the obligation to share tips with the busboys and dishwashers, we're averaging only about $7.50 an hour. Then there is the $30 I had to spend on the regulation tan slacks worn by Jerry's servers—a setback it could take weeks to absorb. (I had combed the town's two downscale department stores hoping for something cheaper but decided in the end that these marked-down Dockers, originally $49, were more likely to survive a daily washing.) Of my fellow servers, everyone who lacks a working husband or boyfriend seems to have a second job: Nita does something at a computer eight hours a day; another welds. Without the forty-five-minute commute, I can picture myself working two jobs and having the time to shower between them.

38   So I take the $500 deposit I have coming from my landlord, the $400 I have earned toward the next month's rent, plus the $200 reserved for emergencies, and use the $1,100 to pay the rent and deposit on trailer number 46 in the Overseas Trailer Park, a mile from the cluster of budget hotels that constitute Key West's version of an industrial park. Number 46 is about eight feet in width and shaped like a barbell

inside, with a narrow region—because of the sink and the stove—separating the bedroom from what might optimistically be called the "living" area, with its two-person table and half-sized couch. The bathroom is so small my knees rub against the shower stall when I sit on the toilet, and you can't just leap out of the bed, you have to climb down to the foot of it in order to find a patch of floor space to stand on. Outside, I am within a few yards of a liquor store, a bar that advertises "free beer tomorrow," a convenience store, and a Burger King—but no supermarket or, alas, laundromat. By reputation, the Overseas park is a nest of crime and crack, and I am hoping at least for some vibrant, multicultural street life. But desolation rules night and day, except for a thin stream of pedestrian traffic heading for their jobs at the Sheraton or 7-Eleven. There are not exactly people here but what amounts to canned labor, being preserved from the heat between shifts.

39   In line with my reduced living conditions, a new form of ugliness arises at Jerry's. First we are confronted—via an announcement on the computers through which we input orders—with the new rule that the hotel bar is henceforth off-limits to restaurant employees. The culprit, I learn through the grapevine, is the ultra-efficient gal who trained me—another trailer-home dweller and a mother of three. Something had set her off one morning, so she slipped out for a nip and returned to the floor impaired. This mostly hurts Ellen, whose habit it is to free her hair from its rubber band and drop by the bar for a couple of Zins before heading home at the end of the shift, but all of us feel the chill. Then the next day, when I go for straws, for the first time I find the dry-storage room locked. Ted, the portly assistant manager who opens it for me, explains that he caught one of the dishwashers attempting to steal something, and, unfortunately, the miscreant will be with us until a replacement can be found—hence the locked door. I neglect to ask what he had been trying to steal, but Ted tells me who he is—the kid with the buzz cut and the earring. You know, he's back there right now.

40   I wish I could say I rushed back and confronted George to get his side of the story. I wish I could say I stood up to Ted and insisted that George be given a translator and allowed to defend himself, or announced that I'd find a lawyer who'd handle the case pro bono. The mystery to me is that there's not much worth stealing in the dry-storage room, at least not in any fenceable quantity: "Is Gyorgi here, and am having 200—maybe 250—ketchup packets. What do you say?" My guess is that he had taken—if he had taken anything at all—some Saltines or a can of cherry-pie mix, and that the motive for taking it was hunger.

41   So why didn't I intervene? Certainly not because I was held back by the kind of moral paralysis that can pass as journalistic objectivity. On the contrary, something new—something loathsome and servile—

had infected me, along with the kitchen odors that I could still sniff on my bra when I finally undressed at night. In real life I am moderately brave, but plenty of brave people shed their courage in concentration camps, and maybe something similar goes on in the infinitely more congenial milieu of the low-wage American workplace. Maybe, in a month or two more at Jerry's, I might have regained my crusading spirit. Then again, in a month or two I might have turned into a different person altogether—say, the kind of person who would have turned George in. But this is not something I am slated to find out.

42   I can do this two-job thing, is my theory, if I can drink enough caffeine and avoid getting distracted by George's ever more obvious suffering.[7] The first few days after being caught he seemed not to understand the trouble he was in, and our chirpy little conversations had continued. But the last couple of shifts he's been listless and unshaven, and tonight he looks like the ghost we all know him to be, with dark half-moons hanging from his eyes. At one point, when I am briefly immobilized by the task of filling little paper cups with sour cream for baked potatoes, he comes over and looks as if he'd like to explore the limits of our shared vocabulary, but I am called to the floor for a table. I resolve to give him all my tips that night and to hell with the experiment in low-wage money management. At eight, Ellen and I grab a snack together standing at the mephitic end of the kitchen counter, but I can only manage two or three mozzarella sticks and lunch had been a mere handful of McNuggets. I am not tired at all, I assure myself, though it may be that there is simply no more "I" left to do the tiredness monitoring. What I would see, if I were more alert to the situation, is that the forces of destruction are already massing against me. There is only one cook on duty, a young man names Jesus ("Hay-Sue," that is) and he is new to the job. And there is Joy, who shows up to take over in the middle of the shift, wearing high heels and a long, clingy white dress and fuming as if she'd just been stood up in some cocktail bar.

43   Then it comes, the perfect storm. Four of my tables fill up at once. Four tables is nothing for me now, but only so long as they are obligingly staggered. As I bev table 27, tables 25, 28, and 24 are watching enviously. As I bev 25, 24 glowers because their bevs haven't even been ordered. Twenty-eight is four yuppyish types, meaning everything on the side and agonizing instructions as to the chicken Caesars. Twenty-five is a middle-aged black couple, who complain, with some justice, that the iced tea isn't fresh and the tabletop is sticky. But table 24 is the meteorological event of the century: ten British tourists who seem to have made the decision to absorb the American experience entirely by mouth. Here everyone has at least two drinks—iced tea and milk shake, Michelob and water (with lemon slice, please)—and a huge promiscuous orgy of breakfast specials, mozz sticks, chicken strips, quesadillas; burgers with cheese and without, sides of hash browns

with cheddar, with onions, with gravy, seasoned fries, plain fries, banana splits. Poor Jesus! Poor me! Because when I arrive with their first
tray of food—after three prior trips just to refill bevs—Princess Di refuses to eat her chicken strips with her pancake-and-sausage special,
since, as she now reveals, the strips were meant to be an appetizer.
Maybe the others would have accepted their meals, but Di, who is
deep into her third Michelob, insists that everything else go back while
they work on their "starters." Meanwhile, the yuppies are waving me
down for more decaf and the black couple looks ready to summon
the NAACP.

44   Much of what happened next is lost in the fog of war. Jesus starts
going under. The little printer on the counter in front of him is spew-
ing out orders faster than he can rip them off, much less produce the
meals. Even the invincible Ellen is ashen from stress. I bring table 24
their reheated main courses, which they immediately reject as either
too cold or fossilized by the microwave. When I return to the kitchen
with their trays (three trays in three trips), Joy confronts me with arms
akimbo: "What is this?" She means the food—the plates of rejected
pancakes, hash browns in assorted flavors, toasts, burgers, sausages,
eggs. "Uh, scrambled with cheddar," I try, "and that's . . ." "NO," she
screams in my face. "Is it a traditional, a super-scramble, an eye-
opener?" I pretend to study my check for a clue, but entropy has been
up to its tricks, not only on the plates but in my head, and I have to admit that the original order is beyond reconstruction. "You don't know
an eye-opener from a traditional?" she demands in outrage. All I know,
in fact, is that my legs have lost interest in the current venture and have
announced their intention to fold. I am saved by a yuppie (mercifully
not one of mine) who chooses this moment to charge into the kitchen
to bellow that his food is twenty-five minutes late. Joy screams at him
to get the hell out of her kitchen, please, and then turns on Jesus in a
fury, hurling an empty tray across the room for emphasis.

45   I leave. I don't walk out, I just leave. I don't finish my side work or
pick up my credit-card tips, if any, at the cash register or, of course, ask
Joy's permission to go. And the surprising thing is that you *can* walk
out without permission, that the door opens, that the thick tropical
night air parts to let me pass, that my car is still parked where I left it.
There is no vindication in this exit, no fuck-you surge of relief, just an
overwhelming, dank sense of failure pressing down on me and the entire parking lot. I had gone into this venture in the spirit of science, to
test a mathematical proposition, but somewhere along the line, in the
tunnel vision imposed by long shifts and relentless concentration, it
became a test of myself, and clearly I have failed. Not only had I
flamed out as a housekeeper/server, I had even forgotten to give
George my tips, and, for reasons perhaps best known to hardworking,

generous people like Gail and Ellen, this hurts. I don't cry, but I am in a position to realize, for the first time in many years, that the tear ducts are still there, and still capable of doing their job.

46   When I moved out of the trailer park, I gave the key to number 46 to Gail and arranged for my deposit to be transferred to her. She told me that Joan is still living in her van and that Stu had been fired from the Hearthside. I never found out what happened to George.

47   In one month, I had earned approximately $1,040 and spent $517 on food, gas, toiletries, laundry, phone, and utilities. If I had remained in my $500 efficiency, I would have been able to pay the rent and have $22 left over (which is $78 less than the cash I had in my pocket at the start of the month). During this time I bought no clothing except for the required slacks and no prescription drugs or medical care (I did finally buy some vitamin B to compensate for the lack of vegetables in my diet). Perhaps I could have saved a little on food if I had gotten to a supermarket more often, instead of convenience stores, but it should be noted that I lost almost four pounds in four weeks, on a diet weighted heavily toward burgers and fries.

48   How former welfare recipients and single mothers will (and do) survive in the low-wage workforce, I cannot imagine. Maybe they will figure out how to condense their lives—including child-raising, laundry, romance, and meals—into the couple of hours between full-time jobs. Maybe they will take up residence in their vehicles, if they have one. All I know is that I couldn't hold two jobs and I couldn't make enough money to live on with one. And I had advantages unthinkable to many of the long-term poor—health, stamina, a working car, and no children to care for and support. Certainly nothing in my experience contradicts the conclusion of Kathryn Edin and Laura Lein, in their recent book *Making Ends Meet: How Single Mothers Survive Welfare and Low-Wage Work*, that low-wage work actually involves more hardship and deprivation than life at the mercy of the welfare state. In the coming months and years, economic conditions for the working poor are bound to worsen, even without the almost inevitable recession. As mentioned earlier, the influx of former welfare recipients into the low-skilled workforce will have a depressing effect on both wages and the number of jobs available. A general economic downturn will only enhance these effects, and the working poor will of course be facing it without the slight, but nonetheless often saving, protection of welfare as a backup.

49   The thinking behind welfare reform was that even the humblest jobs are morally uplifting and psychologically buoying. In reality they are likely to be fraught with insult and stress. But I did discover one redeeming feature of the most abject low-wage work—the camaraderie

of people who are, in almost all cases, far too smart and funny and caring for the work they do and the wages they're paid. The hope, of course, is that someday these people will come to know what they're worth, and take appropriate action.

NOTES

1. According to the Department of Housing and Urban Development, the "fair-market rent" for an efficiency is $551 here in Monroe County, Florida. A comparable rent in the five boroughs of New York City is $704; in San Francisco, $713; and in the heart of Silicon Valley, $808. The fair-market rent for an area is defined as the amount that would be needed to pay rent plus utilities for "privately owned, decent, safe, and sanitary rental housing of a modest (non-luxury) nature with suitable amenities."

2. According to the *Monthly Labor Review* (November 1996), 28 percent of work sites surveyed in the service industry conduct drug tests (corporate workplaces have much higher rates), and the incidence of testing has risen markedly since the Eighties. The rate of testing is highest in the South (56 percent of work sites polled), with the Midwest in second place (50 percent). The drug most likely to be detected—marijuana, which can be detected in urine for weeks—is also the most innocuous, while heroin and cocaine are generally undetectable three days after use. Prospective employees sometimes try to cheat the tests by consuming excessive amounts of liquids and taking diuretics and even masking substances available through the Internet.

3. According to the Fair Labor Standards Act, employers are not required to pay "tipped employees," such as restaurant servers, more than $2.13 an hour in direct wages. However, if the sum of tips plus $2.13 an hour falls below the minimum wage, or $5.15 an hour, the employer is required to make up the difference. This fact was not mentioned by managers or otherwise publicized at either of the restaurants where I worked.

4. I could find no statistics on the number of employed people living in cars or vans, but according to the National Coalition for the Homeless' 1997 report, "Myths and Facts About Homelessness," nearly one in five homeless people (in twenty-nine cities across the nation) is employed in a full- or part-time job.

5. In *Workers in a Lean World: Unions in the International Economy* (Verso, 1997), Kim Moody cites studies finding an increase in stress-related workplace injuries and illness between the mid-1980s and the early 1990s. He argues that rising stress levels reflect a new system of "management by stress," in which workers in a variety of industries are being squeezed to extract maximum productivity, to the detriment of their health.

6. Until April 1998, there was no federally mandated right to bathroom breaks. According to Marc Linder and Ingrid Nygaard, authors of *Void Where Prohibited: Rest Breaks and the Right to Urinate on Company Time* (Cornell University Press, 1997), "The right to rest and void at work is not high on the list of social or political causes supported by professional or executive employees, who enjoy personal workplace liberties that millions of factory workers can only daydream about. . . . While we were dismayed to discover that workers lacked an acknowledged legal right to void at work, (the workers) were amazed by outsiders' naïve belief that their employers would permit them to perform this basic bodily function when necessary. . . . A factory worker, not allowed a break for six-hour stretches, voided into pads worn inside her uniform; and a kindergarten teacher in a school without aides had to take all twenty children with her to the bathroom and line them up outside the stall door when she voided."

7. In 1996, the number of persons holding two or more jobs averaged 7.8 million, or 6.2 percent of the workforce. It was about the same rate for men and for women (6.1 versus 6.2), though the kinds of jobs differ by gender. About two thirds of multiple jobholders work one job full-time and the other part-time. Only a heroic minority—4 percent of men and 2 percent of women—work two full-time jobs simultaneously. (From John F. Stinson Jr., "New Data on Multiple Jobholding Available from the CPS," in the *Monthly Labor Review,* March 1997.)

✧ *Evaluating the Text*

1. What kinds of hard choices does Ehrenreich have to make and what trade-offs is she constantly forced to consider in her no-win situation as an unskilled worker?

2. What insight does Ehrenreich's experience offer into the lives and conditions of the working poor? Which of her encounters did you find particularly surprising?

✧ *Exploring Different Perspectives*

1. Compare the very different motivations leading Ehrenreich and Tomoyuki Iwashita to quit their jobs.

2. Compare the real needs of low-wage workers described by Ehrenreich with the imagined needs of Taysoon and his wife in Catherine Lim's story.

✧ *Extending Viewpoints through Writing and Research*

1. Among the many issues that Ehrenreich touches upon—such as homelessness, drug testing in the workplace, and workers who need to hold two jobs in order to support themselves—which did you find the most interesting? Explore this topic in a short essay and support your observations with evidence drawn from the text and from library and Internet research.

2. How did reading this article change any preconceptions you may have had about the working poor in our society? Explain your answer.

3. Ehrenreich's work is discussed at http://www.cjr.org/issues/2003/6/ehren-sherman.asp.

What issues discussed by Ehrenreich does this photo illustrate?

Gerald W. Haslam

The Water Game

$\leftarrow\!\!\!\blacklozenge\!\!\!\rightarrow$

Gerald W. Haslam was born in Bakersfield, and raised in Oildale, in California's Great Central Valley. Much of his writing explores California's rural and small-town areas. He has worked as a farm laborer and an oilfield roughneck, and received a Ph.D. from Union Institute in 1961. "The Water Game" is drawn from Coming of Age in California: Personal Essays, *second edition (2000). The first edition was selected as one of the twentieth century's 100 top nonfiction books from the Western United States by a* San Francisco Chronicle *reader's poll.*

Before You Read

Consider how water is the most valuable natural resource, which makes everything else possible.

$\leftarrow\!\!\!\blacklozenge\!\!\!\rightarrow$

1   John Phoenix is acknowledged to have been one of the West's first great humorists. Phoenix was actually the nom de plume of a mischievous and talented graduate of West Point, George Horatio Derby. A topographical engineer for the United States Army, Derby wrote hilarious sketches even while on military assignments. In 1849, however, when he was dispatched to survey the Great Central Valley's farming potential, the wag turned grim.

2   The area north of Fresno—now the richest agricultural county in America—he reported, was "exceedingly barren, and singularly destitute of resources, except for a narrow strip on the borders of the stream; it was without timber and grass, and can never, in my estimation, be brought into requisition for agricultural purposes." Near present-day Bakersfield, in Kern County (the nation's second most productive), he found "the most miserable country that I ever beheld."

3   That same parched vale is now the most abundant agricultural cornucopia in the history of the world. Last year it produced over $15 billion in agriculture. How was that transformation possible? Distinguished historian W. H. Hutchinson says there were three principal reasons: "Water, water, and *more* water."

4   The control and manipulation of water in the arid West has been the key to everything from economics to politics here. Without water projects, there would be few Idaho potatoes; without water projects,

little Arizona cotton, no Utah alfalfa. There would also be no Phoenix, no Las Vegas, and no Los Angeles—not as we know them, anyway. There would be no Reno or El Paso or Albuquerque either, because they too have grown up in desiccated areas.

5   The American West is, in the main, arid to semiarid land. But the natural beauty and value of arid land have rarely been apparent to people whose ancestors migrated from green Europe, so enormous amounts of money have been spent and rapacious bureaucracies created in an effort to "make the desert bloom." Although only a tiny portion of the land has so far been "developed," that has bloomed abundantly.

6   Unfortunately, these efforts have also produced the seeds of their own doom: problems such as soil salinization, compaction, and subsidence; the leaching and concentrating of natural toxins from previously dry earth; the overuse of agricultural chemicals, which in turn concentrate in the environment; and the devastation of once huge aquifers in order to flood-irrigate crops better suited to other climates in other places. These developments now seem to have placed Westerners on a path trod by Assyrians, Mesopotamians, and Aztecs, desert peoples who also once challenged nature—and failed.

7   In the past year, ten photographers have embarked on a project to dramatize this long-ignored environmental crisis. "We've been managing water as an abstract legal right or a commodity," points out Robert Dawson, the Californian who initiated the endeavor, "rather than the most basic physical source of life. We believe that water is misused nationwide. We're focusing on the arid West because development here stands in high relief against the vast, open landscape. It's here that the impact of technology, government, and human ambition is most visible." Many major water policy decisions remain to be made, and only an informed public can do that.

8   Nowhere are the gains and losses associated with water manipulation more obvious than in Dawson's home region, the Great Central Valley of California, the physical and economic core of our richest state. All significant cities here, the state's heartland, grew near watercourses; it is an oasis civilization.

9   But it isn't the existence of cities that makes this area vital. It is the fact that 25 percent of all table food produced in the United States is grown in this single valley.

10   The climate here seems close to perfect for farming. Following a short, splendid spring, an extended summer develops. Sun prevails and the horizon seems to expand. Thanks to water pumped or imported, the list of crops grown in this natural hothouse is continually expanding as new varieties are planted: exotic herbs and condiments this year, kiwi fruit and frost-free berries next. Meanwhile, native

plants are rare and native animals—pronghorns, grizzlies, and condors—stand stuffed in local museums.

11   Here, too, a largely Hispanic work force toils on great farms owned by corporations, because this remains a place where the poor of any background can at least try to escape the cycle of poverty, one generation laboring that another might take advantage of the region's rich promise. But it isn't an easy climb; there has tended to be a direct link between centralized irrigation systems and centralized political and economic power, and that in turn has created a paternalistic, class-ridden society with nonwhites on the bottom.

12   Modern agribusiness is competitive, and Valley farmers and ranchers have been notable in inventing such agricultural devices as special adaptations of the clamshell dredge, peach defuzzers, olive pitters, wind machines to fight frost, hydraulic platforms for pruning, pneumatic tree-shakers for bringing down the fruit and nuts—a technological nascence of amazing creativity. But none of them would mean much without imported or pumped water.

13   Many farmers date their entry into Valley agriculture to the period just after World War I when the unregulated pumping of groundwater allowed fields to burgeon. Eventually farmers were pumping more and more from wells that had to be drilled deeper and deeper into unreplenishable aquifers. When the Central Valley Project and the California State Water Project—the two largest and most complex irrigation systems on earth—were completed, it seemed that at last the tapping of irreplaceable groundwater in the Valley could cease.

14   Today, more than 1,200 dams have been built, and thousands of miles of canals cross this onetime desert. Even that hasn't stopped subsurface pumping; it has actually expanded since those huge stores of surface water became available. Pumping now exceeds replenishment by more than half a *trillion* gallons annually, while ecosystems hundreds of miles to the north are threatened by the diversion of their rivers and creeks.

15   Writer Wallace Stegner has suggested that this area's—and by analogy, the West's—agriculture may have "to shrink back to something like the old, original scale, and maybe less than the original scale because there isn't the groundwater there anymore. It's actually more desert than it was when people first began to move in." Hutchinson adds, "We have to stop pretending we're frontiersmen dealing with unlimited water. There's too damn many of *us* and too damned little of *it*."

16   Giant agribusinesses in the Valley can buy that water for less than $10 per acre-foot, while northern California householders have paid well over $1,000 for the same acre-foot—with the difference subsidized by taxpayers. It seems to critics that such water is too cheap to use wisely and that both hubris and ignorance are manifest in the illusion

that moisture unused by humans is somehow squandered, the natural world be damned—and dammed. Ironically, most people—including most Westerners—seem to prefer not to be aware of all this, lest salads and beef suddenly become more expensive.

17   Irrigation is big business, and both of the vast water projects in California were justified, in part at least, as measures that would save existing family farms and perhaps increase the number of acres cultivated by small farmers. In fact, both have led to more and more acres coming under cultivation by huge corporations—Chevron U.S.A., Prudential Insurance Company, Shell Oil Company, Southern Pacific Railroad, J. G. Boswell Company, Getty Oil, among others.

18   How has the quest for water changed the West? Last year, driving in the southwest corner of the Central Valley, I decided to investigate Buena Vista Lake where I'd fished when I was a boy. I crossed the California Aqueduct, then drove west and finally stopped the car. An immense agricultural panorama opened before me, cultivated fields of various hues extending in all directions.

19   All its tributary streams have been diverted and its bed is now dry, so, ironically, Buena Vista Lake must be irrigated. As I gazed at this scene, a red-tailed hawk wheeled overhead, riding a thermal. Far to the east a yellow tractor shimmered through heat waves like a crawdad creeping across the old lake's floor. I saw no dwellings, few trees.

20   That hawk swung far over a green field where tiny fingers of water from elsewhere glistened through rows and where a lone brown man, an irrigator, leaned on a shovel.

21   Welcome to the real West, where agribusiness executives in corporate boardrooms, not cowboys or Indians or even irrigators, are the principal players.

✧ Evaluating the Text

1. How has control and manipulation of water in the West been the single most important factor in shaping the region's economy? What industries are completely dependent on a continual low-cost supply of water?

2. How have short-sighted policies in this regard created a potential crisis?

3. How is the credibility of this essay enhanced by Haslam's role as resident as well as reporter?

✧ Exploring Different Perspectives

1. How do the accounts by Haslam and Helena Norberg-Hodge reveal both the gains and loses of development in California and in the Himalayas?

2. To what extent has the seemingly endless availability of water discussed by Haslam created an illusion comparable to the prospect of easy riches in Catherine Lim's story, "Paper"?

✦ Extending Viewpoints through Writing and Research

1. Do a short research paper on the impact of water politics in your community in terms of cost to businesses versus cost to homeowners.

2. What other resource is indispensable in your community and how has its availability shaped local development?

Victor Villaseñor

Rain of Gold

◆

*Victor Villaseñor was born in 1940 in the barrio of Carlsbad, California,
to immigrant parents. He attended the University of San Diego and Santa
Clara University. Villaseñor was a construction worker in California
from 1965 to 1970 and has attained recognition as an authentic voice of
the Chicano community. Although he flunked English in college (because
of his fifth-grade reading ability), later trips to Mexico and introduction
to art, history, and works of literature by Homer, F. Scott Fitzgerald, and
James Joyce crystallized his decision to become a writer. Completely self-
taught, Villaseñor wrote for ten years, completing nine novels and sixty-
five short stories, and he received more than 260 rejections before he sold
his first book* Macho! *in 1973. He since has written an acclaimed work of
nonfiction,* Rain of Gold *(1992), from which the following excerpt is
drawn, and its sequel,* Wild Steps of Heaven *(1995), which is a saga of
the Villaseñor family. More recently, he has written a historical narrative,*
Authentic Family-Style Mexican Cooking *(1997), and* Burro Genius:
A Memoir *(2004).*

Before You Read

Notice how Villaseñor structures this account to build up to the ultimate
confrontation while at the same time giving an accurate picture of racial
attitudes in the early twentieth century.

◆

1   The weeks passed and Doña Margarita prayed to God, asking him
to heal her son's wounds. God heard her prayers and the bandages
came off. Juan could see in the broken bathroom mirror that he had a
long, swollen scar, thick as a worm, across his chin and all the way to
his left ear. Turning his head side to side, he discovered that if he lowered his chin and kept his head slightly turned to the left, the scar wasn't
quite as noticeable.

2   He decided to grow a beard and keep it until the red ridge of
swollen flesh went down. In some ways he'd been very lucky. It had
been such a clean, razor-sharp knife, the wound would eventually
disappear.

3   A couple of days later, Juan went to town to look for work. He was
broke. The two bastards had stolen all of his money. He had to get

some tortillas on the table before he went searching for those two sons-of-bitches to kill them.

4   In town, Juan found out that they were hiring at a local rock quarry, so he walked out to the quarry while the sun was still low. Getting there, Juan could see that there were at least fifty other Mexicans waiting to be hired ahead of him. The tall, lanky Anglo who was doing the hiring dropped the clipboard to his side. "Well, that's it for today," he said. "But you guys just all come on out tomorrow and maybe you'll get lucky."

5   Hearing the word, "lucky," Juan became suspicious. As a professional gambler, he never liked to leave anything to chance. He glanced around at his fellow countrymen, wondering what they were going to do about this. But he could see that they weren't going to do anything.

6   Juan took up ground. "Excuse me," he said. "But I'm new in town, so I'd like to know how you do your hiring. Should I give you my name for tomorrow, or do you only hire the same men every day?"

7   The tall Anglo smiled at him as if he'd said something ridiculous. "What's your name?" asked the Anglo.

8   "Juan Villa *señor*," said Juan, pronouncing the double "l's" of his name like a "y" and giving his name a dignified, natural sound.

9   "Well, Juan Vilee-senoreee," said the foreman, twisting his name into something ugly, "you just come on out here tomorrow if you want a job. That's all you gotta do. You ain't got to know no more. Catch my lingo, *amigo?*" And saying this, the man rocked back and forth on his feet and spit on the ground. Juan could see that the man was so mad that his jaw was twitching. But Juan said nothing. He simply lowered his eyes and turned to go. His heart was pounding. Why, this bastard had twisted his name into a piece of dog shit.

10   The other workmen moved aside, letting Juan pass by. Juan could feel the foreman's eyes burning into his back. But he already knew that he was never going to return. This bastard could take his job and stick it up his ass, as far as Juan was concerned.

11   But Juan had gone no more than a few yards when another Anglo came out of the office. "Doug!" he yelled at the man with the clipboard. "We need another powder man! Ask them if any of 'em has a license!"

12   "Hell, Jim, they ain't nothing but Mexicans," he said.

13   "Ask 'em," repeated the big, beefy man named Jim.

14   "*¡Oye! ¡Espérense!*" called Doug in perfectly good Spanish. "Do any of you have a powder license?"

15   Juan had a license to handle dynamite from the Copper Queen in Montana, but he glanced around to see if anyone had priority over him. No one raised his hand.

16   "I got one," said Juan.

17   "Where'd you get your license?" asked Doug.

18   "From the Copper Queen Mining Company," said Juan.

19   "Oh, in Arizona," said Jim.

20   "No, from Montana," said Juan.

21   The two Anglos glanced at each other. They were a long way from Montana.

22   "Let's see your license," said Doug.

23   Calmly, deliberately, Juan walked back to the two Anglos. They both towered over him. But Juan's mammoth neck and thick shoulders were wider than either of theirs.

24   He brought out his wallet and carefully took the paper out of his billfold that said he was licensed to do dynamite work. He handed it to Doug, who unfolded it, glanced it over, then handed it to Jim.

25   Reading it, Jim said, "Looks good to me," and he handed the paper back to Doug. "Hire him."

26   "All right, Juan Villa *señor*-eee," said Doug, pronouncing Juan's last name with less of a mean twist this time, "you got a job for the day. But just one little screw-up and you're out! Now go over to that shed and ask for Kenny. Show him your license and he'll fix you up."

27   "Sure," said Juan, taking back his license and going across the yard.

28   Everywhere were Mexicans bent over shovels and picks. It was a huge rock quarry. They looked like ants crawling about the great slab of rock that had been cut away from the mountain. Teams of horses and mules were moving the loads of rock, and the Mexicans drove these teams, too.

29   At the toolshed, Juan asked for Kenny. An old Anglo came up. He was chewing tobacco. He was short and thick and his eyes sparkled with humor. Juan liked him immediately. He didn't have that dried-out, sour-mean look of Doug's. He handed him his license.

30   "So how long you been a powder man, eh?" asked Kenny, looking over the license.

31   "Oh, three or four years," said Juan.

32   "All in Montana?" asked Kenny, walking over to the sledge hammers and bars.

33   Juan froze, but only for a moment. He'd originally learned his trade in prison at Turkey Flat, but he saw no reason for this man to know that. So he lied. "Yes," he said, "all in Montana."

34   "I see," said Kenny, coming forward with a sledge and a fistful of bars. He looked into Juan's eyes, but Juan didn't shy away. "Well," said the old man, handing Juan the tools, "where or how a man learned his trade ain't my concern." He spat a long stream of brown juice. "What interests me is the result," he added.

35   Walking around the shed, they headed for the cliff of cut rock in the distance. Climbing halfway up the face of the cliff, Kenny showed Juan where he wanted him to drill his holes to set the charges. Juan set

his tools down and slipped off his jacket. The other dynamite men were already hard at work, drilling their holes. They were all Anglos.

36   Juan glanced up at the sun and saw that it was already beginning to get hot. He slipped his shirt out of his pants so it would hang loose and the sweat could drip off him freely. He'd learned this trick from an old Greek when he'd worked in Montana. A big, loose shirt could work like an air conditioner. Once the sweat started coming fast, the garment would hold it and let the sun evaporate the sweat like a cooling unit.

37   Juan could feel the other powder men watching him. A couple of them had already stripped down to their waists and they were bare-chested to the sun. They were all huge, well-muscled men and towered over Juan. But Juan felt no need to hurry or show off. He'd worked with the best of them up in Montana before he'd gone to work for Duel. He knew his trade.

38   Spitting into the palms of his thick hands, Juan set his feet and picked up his short bar with his left hand and his sledge hammer with his right. He centered the point of the bar on the rock in front of him and he raised the sledge over his head, coming down real soft and easy on the head of the bar. He did this again and again, turning the bar each time with his left hand. He knew that Kenny and the other powder men were watching him, but he never let on. He just kept up a soft, steady, easy pace. He wasn't about to push the sledge. He would let the weight of the big hammer do the work for him all day long. Only a stupid, young fool pushed the iron. An experienced man let the iron do the work for him.

39   Kenny brought out his chew, cut off a piece, put it in his mouth and continued watching, but Juan still felt no nervousness. He'd worked at his trade for three months at Turkey Flat, and in Montana he'd done it for nearly three years, so he knew that he was good at his job. He wasn't one of these men who rushed in the morning to show off to the boss and then had nothing left to give in the afternoon. No, he could work all day long, from sunup until sundown, without ever slowing down. In fact, he was so steady and sure at his job that he'd won many a bet in Montana by placing a dime on the head of the bar and hitting it so smoothly that the dime wouldn't fall off, even after a hundred hits. An old Greek had also taught him this trick. Why, he could make the sledge and the bar sing, once he got going.

40   It was noon, and the sunlight was blinding hot on the great slab of rock. Juan had gone past all the Anglo powder men except one. This Anglo was huge. His name was Jack, and he wasn't just big, he was extremely well-muscled. But Juan wasn't impressed by this. He'd seen many big, strong men collapse under the hot, noon sun. And Jack had been one of the first to strip to the waist to show off his muscles, so he was now sweating fast and Juan knew that he wouldn't be able to keep up his pace all afternoon.

41   Juan decided to slow down and not push the man. He'd already proven himself. All he had to do now was give an honest day's work.

42   Then the horn blew, and it was time to eat lunch. The powder men all took their tools and put them in the shade so they wouldn't get too hot to handle when they came back to work.

43   Jack, the big man, came walking up close to Juan. It looked like he was going to say hello to him and shake his hand; but he didn't. He just laughed and turned away, joking with the other powder men. Juan didn't take offense, figuring that he was just having fun. He walked alongside Jack, hoping that maybe he and the big man could quit the competition that had started up between them and they could become friends. After all, he'd become friends with many Greeks and Anglos in Montana. But walking across the yard, the powder men acted as if Juan didn't exist.

44   Then, when they got in line to wash up before they ate, and it was Juan's turn to wash, the man in front of Juan didn't hand him the tin cup. No, he dropped it, instead. At first, Juan thought it was an accident, but then, when he bent over to pick up the cup, the man kicked it away.

45   Juan stood up and saw that all the powder men were sneering at him, especially Jack, who was grinning ear-to-ear. Quickly, Juan lowered his eyes so none of them would see what he was thinking. And he turned and walked away, tall and slow and with all the dignity he could muster. These smart-ass *gringos* had just made up his mind for him. This afternoon they were going to see a Greek-trained drilling machine.

46   He never once turned to glance back at them. No, he just kept going across the yard as slowly and proudly as he could. Getting to the Mexicans under the shade of a tree, he was given a cup when it was his turn to drink and wash up. But he had no lunch to eat, so he just sat down to rest.

47   Oh, it was a good thing that he hadn't brought his gun to work, or he would have been tempted to kill Jack and the seven other powder men. No one ridiculed him. Not even in prison when he'd been a child and they'd tried to rape him. He was his father's son when it came to having a terrible temper. He was truly of the crazy Villa *señors*. Why, he'd once seen his father grab a mule's leg that had kicked him and yank it up to bite it, dislocating the mule's hip. Then his father had beaten the mule to death with his bare fists.

48   Juan was sitting there, seething with rage, when a thick-necked Mexican named Julio called him over.

49   "*Amigo,*" he said, "come and eat with us."

50   Julio and several other Mexican men were sitting under a tree, heating their tacos on a shovel that they'd washed.

51   "No, *gracias,*" said Juan, "you go ahead and eat . . . to your health, my blessings." And saying this, Juan moved his hand, palm up, wel-

coming the man to fulfill himself. It was a very Mexican gesture, one especially common in the mountainous area of Jalisco.

52   "So you're from Jalisco, eh?" said Julio, turning over the bean tacos with a stick on the shovel.

53   "Why, yes, how did you know?" asked Juan.

54   Julio laughed. "Oh, I'm just a visionary from Guanajuato," he said, "who's seen that gesture of the hand too many times not to know a *tapatío.*" A *tapatío* was what the people from Jalisco were called.

55   "Come on, don't be so proud," said another Mexican named Rodolfo. "You got nothing to eat and you got to be strong for this afternoon." Rodolfo was tall and slender and had pockmarks all over his face, but he wasn't hard to look at. His eyes had a twinkle of mischief, and he had that confident air of a man who'd seen many battles. "We all saw that little movement of the cup across the yard. Those powder men, they're all *cabrones!*"[1]

56   "You saw it, eh?" said Juan, glancing across the yard to the powder men who were all sitting together and eating.

57   "Of course," said Rodolfo, "and we knew it was coming the moment we learned that one of our people had gotten a job so elevated."

58   "Go ahead," said Julio to Juan, taking the shovel off the little fire, "take a taco before this son-of-a-bitch schoolteacher from Monterrey eats all our lunches again." Saying this, Julio picked up one of the tacos with his fingertips from the hot shovel and tossed it to Juan, who reflexively caught it. "Eat, *hombre,*" he said to Juan good-naturedly, "so you can fart like a burro and screw those *gringo* sons-of-bitches this afternoon!"

59   "Which leads us to a very important question," said Rodolfo, the tall schoolteacher from Monterrey, "just how'd you ever get up there, anyway?"

60   "I have a powder license," said Juan, starting to eat.

61   "Oh, and how did you manage that miracle?" asked Rodolfo. "Hell, we got men here who know how to drill and set dynamite with the best of them, but none of them has been able to get a license." He ate his taco in two huge bites, working his big, lean jaws like a wolf.

62   "In Montana," said Juan, eating in small, courteous bites to show that he wasn't starving—but he was. "The Greeks up there, they'd never seen a Mexican, and so they'd thought I was Chinese and they made me a driller, thinking all Chinese know powder."

63   The Mexicans burst out laughing. But Rodolfo laughed the hardest of all.

64   "So that's how it's done, eh?" said Rodolfo. "We *Mejicanos* got to be Chinese!"

---

[1]*Cabrones* is a derogatory term that slanders masculinity.

65   "It worked for me," said Juan, laughing, too.

66   "I'll be damned," said the teacher, reaching for another taco. "Next you'll tell me that we'd be better off if we were Negroes, too."

67   "Shit, yes!" said Julio, who was very dark-skinned. "The blacker the better!"

68   They all laughed and ate together and Juan felt good to be back among his people. The jokes, the gestures, and the way they laughed with their heads thrown back and their mouths open, it was all so familiar.

69   Then the horn blew, and it was time to get back to work. The pock-faced man came close to Juan. "Be careful, my friend," he said. "That scar you wear may only be a small token compared to what awaits you this afternoon."

70   Juan nodded, having thought that no one could see his scar with his five-day-old beard. "*Gracias*," he said, "but I haven't gotten this far in life without being as wary as the chick with the coyote."

71   The tall man laughed, offering Juan his hand. "Rodolfo Rochin."

72   Juan took the schoolteacher's hand. "Juan Villa *señor*," he said.

73   "He's right," said Julio, coming up. "They're going to try and kill you. Hell, if they don't, soon we'll have all their jobs."

74   Juan nodded. "I'll be careful," he said.

75   "Good," said the thick man. "Julio Sanchez."

76   "Juan Villa *señor*," said Juan once again.

77   Then Juan turned and started across the open yard, and all the Mexicans watched after him. Not one of their people had ever worked up on the cliff before.

78   Picking up his tools, Juan walked by the powder men and climbed up the cliff. Jack came up and took his place alongside Juan, grinning at him. But Juan paid him no attention and went to work, iron singing at a good, steady pace.

79   Jack picked up his sledge and tore at the rock. He was still half a hole ahead of Juan and wanted to keep it like that. The big man pounded at the rock, arms pumping, iron pounding, and he tried to pull farther ahead of Juan. But Juan only smiled, glancing up at the hot sun, his ally.

80   The sun was going down, and it was the last hour of the day when Juan came up even with Jack. The other powder men stopped their work and watched. Jack grinned, still feeling confident, and began his new hole. He was huge and rippling with muscle, but Juan could see that he was all used up because he just didn't have the rhythm of the hammer down to a steady song.

81   Juan grinned back at Jack, spat into his hands, and began his new hole, too. But at a much slower pace. And the big man pulled ahead of him and the other powder men laughed, truly enjoying it. But Rodolfo and Julio and the other Mexicans down below knew what was coming.

So they stopped their work and looked up at the two men pounding the iron up on the tall cliff.

82   The muscles were standing on the big man's back, and his forearms were corded up into huge ropes. But still, Juan kept going at a slow, steady, easy pace, fully realizing that the boiling white sun was on his side and the *gringo* wouldn't be able to keep up his reckless pace for long.

83   Kenny saw what was going on, and he started for the cliff to bring the senseless competition to a stop when Doug came up behind him.

84   "Don't, Shorty," he said to Kenny. "Let that little bastard kill himself, trying to keep up with Big Jack."

85   Kenny never even smiled. Juan was his own size, so he just spat out a stream of tobacco, already knowing who was going to win. "Whatever you say, Doug," he said.

86   And Kenny and Doug took up watch, too.

87   Jack was pounding on, tearing into his bar with his big sledge, but he could see that Juan was keeping up with him at a much slower rhythm. It seemed like magic. Juan was going so easy and, yet, his iron was still drilling into the stone at a good pace.

88   Jack began to tire but he was tough, so he just forced his body to go harder. His lungs screamed for air, his huge muscles began to cramp, but he'd die before he gave up and let a Mexican beat him.

89   But then here came Juan, coming in for the kill, and he now picked up the pace, too. Juan was catching up to Jack, closing fast, and then going past him with good, steady power when, suddenly, a bunch of bars came sliding down the face of the cliff from above them.

90   "Watch out!" yelled Kenny.

91   Juan just managed to leap out of the way before the bars struck him.

92   Kenny turned to Doug and saw that he was grinning ear-to-ear. "All right!" barked Kenny. "No more of this horseshit! Now all of you, get back to work! You got thirty minutes to quitting time, damn it!"

93   Turning in their tools that afternoon, Kenny took Juan aside. "*Amigo,*" he said, "you and me, we're short, so we don't got to always go around being the big man. Jack, he's not so bad, believe me. I know him. It's just that a lot is expected of him." He cut a new chew with his pocket knife, offering Juan some, but Juan refused. "I like your work," he added, putting the new cut in his mouth, "you ease off *mañana* and I promise you that you got a job here as long as I'm powder foreman."

94   Juan looked into the old man's bright, blue eyes, blue like his own father's. "You got a deal," he said.

95   "Good," said Kenny, and he put his knife away and stuck out his hand and Juan took it.

96   This was the first time that Juan had ever met a man who had even bigger, thicker hands than his own. Why, Kenny's hands were monstrous, just like his own father's.

97   That day, Juan Salvador was paid two dollars, twice as much as the regular laborers. Walking back to town that afternoon with his people, Juan was a hero. He was the Mexican who screwed the *cabrón gringo*!

✧ *Evaluating the Text*

1. How do the initial reactions to Juan's request for work reveal the racial prejudice against Mexicans that existed in his father's time?

2. How does the encounter between Juan and Jack dramatize the separation of Anglos from Mexicans and the antagonism between them that was quite typical in the work gangs?

3. What means does Villaseñor use to structure the account in a suspenseful way?

✧ *Exploring Different Perspectives*

1. Discuss the struggle against stereotyping based on race or gender in the accounts by Villaseñor and Barbara Ehrenreich in "Nickel-and-Dimed."

2. How do the accounts of Villaseñor and Gerald W. Haslam offer insights into the contributions of Hispanic laborers who are trying to escape the cycle of poverty?

✧ *Extending Viewpoints through Writing and Research*

1. Did you ever have to prove yourself against prevailing stereotypes? What were they? Describe what happened?

2. In several places in Villaseñor's account, he makes a point of commenting on the more efficient way of working that his father had developed, which enabled him to outperform seemingly more powerful men. What techniques have you developed to make your work, including study habits, more efficient? Describe them and tell how you developed them.

3. The author's home page with related links is available at http://www.victoryvillasenor.com/.

Helena Norberg-Hodge

Learning from Ladakh

◆

Helena Norberg-Hodge was born in Sweden in 1946. She is a linguist by training, speaks six languages, and is the first Westerner to master the Ladakhi language. Ladakh, or "Little Tibet," is a desert land high up in the Western Himalayas that for more than a thousand years has been the home to a thriving culture based on frugality and cooperation. Encroachments by Western consumerism in the late 1970s and 1980s altered the natural balance and brought threats from pollution, inflation, unemployment, and greed.

She is the founder and director of the International Society for Ecology and Culture, and in 1986 she shared the Right Livelihood Award, known as the "Alternative Nobel Prize." Ancient Futures: Learning from Ladakh *(1992) from which the following selection has been taken has been translated into forty-two languages.*

Before You Read

Consider how a money-based economy could alter the relationships between people in a community that had been based on cooperative labor.

◆

We don't have any poverty here.

—Tsewang Paljor, 1975

If you could only help us Ladakhis, we're so poor.

—Tsewang Paljor, 1983

1   In the traditional culture, villagers provided for their basic needs without money. They had developed skills that enabled them to grow barley at 12,000 feet and to manage yaks and other animals at even higher elevations. People knew how to build houses with their own hands from the materials of the immediate surroundings. The only thing they actually needed from outside the region was salt, for which they traded. They used money in only a limited way, mainly for luxuries.

2   Now, suddenly, as part of the international money economy, Ladakhis find themselves ever more dependent—even for vital needs—on a system that is controlled by faraway forces. They are vulnerable to

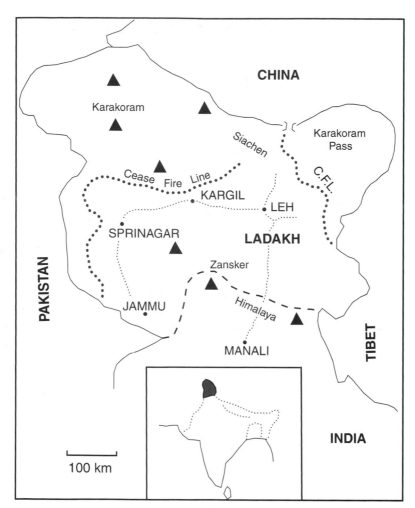

How does this map provide a geographical context for Norberg-Hodge's essay?

decisions made by people who do not even know that Ladakh exists. If the value of the dollar changes, it will ultimately have an effect on the Indian rupee. This means that Ladakhis who need money to survive are now under the control of the managers of international finance. Living off the land, they had been their own masters.

3   At first, people were not aware of the fact that the new economy creates dependence; money appeared to be only an advantage. Since it traditionally had been a good thing, bringing luxuries from far away, more of it seemed to be an unconditional improvement. Now you can buy all sorts of exotic things that you could not before, like three-minute noodles and digital watches.

4   As people find themselves dependent on a very different economic system for all their needs and vulnerable to the vagaries of inflation, it is not strange that they should become preoccupied with money. For two thousand years in Ladakh, a kilo of barley has been a kilo of barley, but now you cannot be sure of its value. If you have ten rupees today, it can buy two kilos of barley, but how do you know how much it will buy tomorrow? "It's terrible," Ladakhi friends would say to me, "everyone is getting so greedy. Money was never important before, but now it's all people can think about."

5   Traditionally, people were conscious of the limits of resources and of their personal responsibilities. I have heard older people say: "What on earth is going to happen if we start dividing the land and increasing in numbers? It can never work." But the new economy cuts people off from the earth. Paid work is in the city, where you cannot see the water and soil on which your life depends. In the village you can see with the naked eye how many mouths the land can support. A given area can only produce so much, so you know that it is important to keep the population stable. Not so in the city; there it is just a question of how much money you have, and the birth rate is no longer significant. More money will buy more food. And it can grow much faster than wheat or barley, which are dependent on nature with her own laws, rhythms, and limits. Money does not seem to have any limits; an advertisement for the local Jammu-Kashmir Bank says, "Your money grows quickly with us."

6   For centuries, people worked as equals and friends—helping one another by turn. Now that there is paid labor during the harvest, the person paying the money wants to pay as little as possible, while the person receiving wants to have as much as possible. Relationships change. The money becomes a wedge between people, pushing them further and further apart.

7   The house had a festive atmosphere whenever Tsering and Sonam Dolma's friends came to work with them as part of the traditional *lhangsde* practice. Sonam used to cook special food for the occasion. But in the last couple of years, the practice has gradually disappeared and their farm near Leh is increasingly dependent on paid labor. Sonam complains bitterly about rising prices and resents having to pay high wages. The festive atmosphere of friends working together has gone; these laborers are strangers, sometimes Nepalis or Indians from the plains who have no common language.

8   The changing economy makes it difficult to remain a farmer. Previously, with cooperative labor between people, farmers had no need for money. Now, unable to pay larger and larger wages for farm hands, some are forced to abandon the villages to earn money in the city. For those who stay, the pressure increases to grow food for profit, instead of food for themselves. Cash cropping becomes the norm as farmers

are pushed by the forces of development to become dependent on the market economy.

9   The new economy also increases the gap between rich and poor. In the traditional economy there were differences in wealth, but its accumulation had natural limits. You could only care for so many yaks or store so many kilos of barley. Money, on the other hand, is easily stored in the bank, and the rich get richer and the poor get poorer.

10   I knew a man named Lobzang who had an antique shop in Leh. Like many Ladakhi shopkeepers, he had given up farming and come to Leh to make money, but his wife and children still lived in the village. He wanted the best for his children, and as soon as he could afford the housing, he planned to bring them to town to get the benefits of an education and, in particular, to learn English.

11   I had just dropped into his shop to say hello when an old man from Lobzang's village came in to sell his butter jars. It was a full day's journey on foot and by bus from the village. The old man probably planned to spend a couple of days with relatives in Leh, buying supplies to take back to the village with the money from the butter jars. He looked dignified in his traditional burgundy woolen robes. He put two jars on the counter. They had the warm patina that comes from generations of constant handling. They were made of fine-grained apricot wood and had a simple elegance that would certainly appeal to tourists. "They're lovely," I said. "What will you keep your butter in without them?" "We keep it in used milk tins," he said.

12   They argued about the price. Apparently a few weeks earlier, Lobzang had promised him a much higher price than he was willing to offer now. He pointed to some cracks in the jars and refused to raise his offer. I knew he would get ten times as much when he sold the jars to the tourists. The old man threw me an imploring look, but what could I say? He left the shop with a disappointed stoop to his shoulders and enough money to buy a few kilos of sugar.

13   "You shouldn't have said they were lovely." Lobzang scolded me. "I had to give him more."

14   "But he's from your own village. Do you have to bargain so hard with him?"

15   "I hate it, but I have to. Besides, a stranger would have given him even less."

✧ *Evaluating the Text*

1. How has the introduction of a money-based economy distorted relationships between people and made them dependent on things they didn't even know existed?

2. How does the incident of the shopkeeper and his former neighbor illustrate the change for the worse that has overtaken the Ladakis since money became the medium of exchange?

✧ Exploring Different Perspectives

1. How does money override personal relationships in Norberg-Hodge's account and in Barbara Ehrenreich's article?

2. Discuss the distorting effect of materialism on the Ladakhis and on the characters in Catherine Lim's story.

✧ Extending Viewpoints through Writing and Research

1. Have you ever participated in a barter situation where you traded goods for services? How were your relationships different from those based solely on an exchange of money?

2. In your opinion, were the Ladakis better off before the introduction of money? Explain your answer.

3. The author's discussion of consumerism in Ladakh can be found at http://www.isec.org.uk/articles/pressure.html.

What does this picture tell you about the labor-based economy of Ladakh before consumerism took over?

Tomoyuki Iwashita

Why I Quit the Company

◆

Tomoyuki Iwashita signed on to work for a prominent Japanese corpora-
tion just after graduating from college. The life of the typical "salary-
man" did not appeal to him for reasons he explains in "Why I Quit the
Company," which originally appeared in The New Internationalist,
May 1992. He is currently a journalist based in Tokyo.

Before You Read

Consider the insights this piece offers into corporate life in Japan and why
a well-paid worker would drop out.

◆

1   When I tell people that I quit working for the company after only a
year, most of them think I'm crazy. They can't understand why I would
want to give up a prestigious and secure job. But I think I'd have been
crazy to stay, and I'll try to explain why.

2   I started working for the company immediately after graduating
from university. It's a big, well-known trading company with about
6,000 employees all over the world. There's a lot of competition to get
into this and other similar companies, which promise young people a
wealthy and successful future. I was set on course to be a Japanese
"yuppie."

3   I'd been used to living independently as a student, looking after
myself and organizing my own schedule. As soon as I started working
all that changed. I was given a room in the company dormitory, which
is like a fancy hotel, with a twenty-four-hour hot bath service and all
meals laid on. Most single company employees live in a dormitory like
this, and many married employees live in company apartments. The
dorm system is actually a great help because living in Tokyo costs
more than young people earn—but I found it stifling.

4   My life rapidly became reduced to a shuttle between the dorm and
the office. The working day is officially eight hours, but you can never
leave the office on time. I used to work from nine in the morning until
eight or nine at night, and often until midnight. Drinking with colleagues after work is part of the job; you can't say no. The company
building contained cafeterias, shops, a bank, a post office, a doctor's
office, a barber's. . . . I never needed to leave the building. Working,

drinking, sleeping, and standing on a horribly crowded commuter train for an hour and a half each way: This was my life. I spent all my time with the same colleagues; when I wasn't involved in entertaining clients on the weekend, I was expected to play golf with my colleagues. I soon lost sight of the world outside the company.

5   This isolation is part of the brainwashing process. A personnel manager said: "We want excellent students who are active, clever, and tough. Three months is enough to train them to be devoted businessmen." I would hear my colleagues saying: "I'm not making any profit for the company, so I'm not contributing." Very few employees claim all the overtime pay due to them. Keeping an employee costs the company 50 million yen ($400,000) a year, or so the company claims. Many employees put the company's profits before their own mental and physical well-being.

6   Overtiredness and overwork leave you little energy to analyze or criticize your situation. There are shops full of "health drinks," cocktails of caffeine and other drugs, which will keep you going even when you're exhausted. *Karoshi* (death from overwork) is increasingly common and is always being discussed in the newspapers. I myself collapsed from working too hard. My boss told me: "You should control your health; it's your own fault if you get sick." There is no paid sick leave; I used up half of my fourteen days' annual leave because of sickness.

7   We had a labor union, but it seemed to have an odd relationship with the management. A couple of times a year I was told to go home at five o'clock. The union representatives were coming around to investigate working hours; everyone knew in advance. If it was "discovered" that we were all working overtime in excess of fifty hours a month our boss might have had some problem being promoted; and our prospects would have been affected. So we all pretended to work normal hours that day.

8   The company also controls its employees' private lives. Many company employees under thirty are single. They are expected to devote all their time to the company and become good workers; they don't have time to find a girlfriend. The company offers scholarships to the most promising young employees to enable them to study abroad for a year or two. But unmarried people who are on these courses are not allowed to get married until they have completed the course! Married employees who are sent to train abroad have to leave their families in Japan for the first year.

9   In fact, the quality of married life is often determined by the husband's work. Men who have just gotten married try to go home early for a while, but soon have to revert to the norm of late-night work. They have little time to spend with their wives and even on the weekend are expected to play golf with colleagues. Fathers cannot find time

to communicate with their children and child rearing is largely left to mothers. Married men posted abroad will often leave their family behind in Japan; they fear that their children will fall behind in the fiercely competitive Japanese education system.

10   Why do people put up with this? They believe this to be a normal working life or just cannot see an alternative. Many think that such personal sacrifices are necessary to keep Japan economically successful. Perhaps, saddest of all, Japan's education and socialization processes do not equip people with the intellectual and spiritual resources to question and challenge the status quo. They stamp out even the desire for a different kind of life.

11   However, there are some signs that things are changing. Although many new employees in my company were quickly brainwashed, many others, like myself, complained about life in the company and seriously considered leaving. But most of them were already in fetters—of debt. Pleased with themselves for getting into the company and anticipating a life of executive luxury, these new employees throw their money around. Every night they are out drinking. They buy smart clothes and take a taxi back to the dormitory after the last train has gone. They start borrowing money from the bank and soon they have a debt growing like a snowball rolling down a slope. The banks demand no security for loans; it's enough to be working for a well-known company. Some borrow as much as a year's salary in the first few months. They can't leave the company while they have such debts to pay off.

12   I was one of the few people in my intake of employees who didn't get into debt. I left the company dormitory after three months to share an apartment with a friend. I left the company exactly one year after I entered it. It took me a while to find a new job, but I'm working as a journalist now. My life is still busy, but it's a lot better than it was. I'm lucky because nearly all big Japanese companies are like the one I worked for, and conditions in many small companies are even worse.

13   It's not easy to opt out of a life-style that is generally considered to be prestigious and desirable, but more and more young people in Japan are thinking about doing it. You have to give up a lot of superficially attractive material benefits in order to preserve the quality of your life and your sanity. I don't think I was crazy to leave the company. I think I would have gone crazy if I'd stayed.

✧ Evaluating the Text

1. What features of Iwashita's account address the crucial issue of his company's attempt to totally control the lives of employees?

2. What psychological effects led him to actually quit his secure job?

3. In what important respects do Japanese corporate employees differ from their American counterparts? In what ways are they similar?

✧ *Exploring Different Perspectives*

1. In what respects did Iwashita find himself being exploited in much the same way as the Ladakhis described in Helena Norberg-Hodge's account?

2. What parallels can you discover between Iwashita's situation in Japan and the low-wage workers in America in Barbara Ehrenreich's account?

✧ *Extending Viewpoints through Writing and Research*

1. Drawing on work experiences you have had, discuss any similarities and differences you found on the question of conformity and subservience to the company. Analyze the different motivations that drive Japanese and American workers.

2. If you were in Iwashita's situation, would you have made the same decision he did? Why or why not?

Catherine Lim

Paper

◆

Catherine Lim is one of Singapore's foremost writers. She currently works for the Curriculum Development Institute of Singapore, writing English-language instructional materials for use in the primary schools. Her widely praised collections of short stories include Little Ironies— Stories of Singapore *(1978), from which "Paper" is taken,* Or Else, The Lightning God and Other Stories *(1980), and* The Shadow of a Shadow of a Dream—Love Stories of Singapore *(1981). She is also the author of novels including* They Do Return *(1982),* The Serpent's Tooth *(1983),* The Teardrop Story Woman *(1998), and* Following the Wrong God Home *(2001). Her short stories have been compared to those of Guy de Maupassant for their accuracy of observation, clarity in presentation of character, and precise detail. Lim's stories reveal a wealth of information about the forces, customs, and pressures that shape the lives of the Chinese community in Singapore, a densely populated metropolis in which Chinese, Malay, and Indian cultures coexist and thrive. "Paper" is set against the turbulent background of the Singapore Stock Exchange, a volatile financial market reflecting the seemingly limitless possibilities of one of the world's most productive financial, industrial, and commercial centers. This story dramatically explores how the lure of easy money leads a man and his wife to tragic consequences.*

Before You Read

Notice the way in which the main characters fall victim to the intoxicating speculation of the Singapore Stock Exchange in ways not unlike those who were caught in the dot-com bubble.

◆

1   He wanted it, he dreamed of it, he hankered after it, as an addict after his opiate. Once the notion of a big beautiful house had lodged itself in his imagination, Tay Soon nurtured it until it became the consuming passion of his life. A house. A dream house such as he had seen on his drives with his wife and children along the roads bordering the prestigious housing estates on the island, and in the glossy pages of *Homes* and *Modern Living*. Or rather, it was a house which was an amalgam of the best, the most beautiful aspects of the houses he had seen. He knew every detail of his dream house already, from the aluminum

sliding doors to the actual shade of the dining room carpet to the shape of the swimming pool. Kidney. He rather liked that shape. He was not ashamed of the enthusiasm with which he spoke of the dream house, an enthusiasm that belonged to women only, he was told. Indeed, his enthusiasm was so great that it had infected his wife and even his children, small though they were. Soon his wife Yee Lian was describing to her sister Yee Yeng, the dream house in all its perfection of shape and decor, and the children were telling their cousins and friends, "My daddy says that when our house is ready . . . "

2   They talked of the dream house endlessly. It had become a reality stronger than the reality of the small terrace house which they were sharing with Tay Soon's mother, to whom it belonged. Tay Soon's mother, whose little business of selling bottled curries and vegetable preserves which she made herself, left her little time for dreams, clucked her tongue and shook her head and made sarcastic remarks about the ambitiousness of young people nowadays.

3   "What's wrong with this house we're staying in?" she asked petulantly. "Aren't we all comfortable in it?"

4   Not as long as you have your horrid ancestral altars all over the place, and your grotesque sense of colour—imagine painting the kitchen wall bright pink. But Yee Lian was tactful enough to keep the remarks to herself, or to make them only to her sister Yee Yeng, otherwise they were sure to reach the old lady, and there would be no end to her sharp tongue.

5   The house—the dream house—it would be a far cry from the little terrace house in which they were all staying now, and Tay Soon and Yee Lian talked endlessly about it, and it grew magnificently in their imaginations, this dream house of theirs with its timbered ceiling and panelled walls and sunken circular sitting room which was to be carpeted in rich amber. It was no empty dream, for there was much money in the bank already. Forty thousand dollars had been saved. The house would cost many times that, but Tay Soon and Yee Lian with their good salaries would be able to manage very well. Once they took care of the down payment, they would be able to pay back monthly over a period of ten years—fifteen, twenty—what did it matter how long it took as long as the dream house was theirs? It had become the symbol of the peak of earthly achievement, and all of Tay Soon's energies and devotion were directed towards its realisation. His mother said, "You're a show-off; what's so grand about marble flooring and a swimming pool? Why don't you put your money to better use?" But the forty thousand grew steadily, and after Tay Soon and Yee Lian had put in every cent of their annual bonuses, it grew to forty eight thousand, and husband and wife smiled at the smooth way their plans were going.

6   It was a time of growing interest in the stock market. The quotations for stocks and shares were climbing the charts, and the crowds in the rooms of the broking houses were growing perceptibly. Might we not do something about this? Yee Lian said to her husband. Do you know that Dr. Soo bought Rustan Banking for four dollars and today the shares are worth seven dollars each? The temptation was great. The rewards were almost immediate. Thirty thousand dollars' worth of NBE became fifty-five thousand almost overnight. Tay Soon and Yee Lian whooped. They put their remaining eighteen thousand in Far East Mart. Three days later the shares were worth twice that much. It was not to be imagined that things could stop here. Tay Soon secured a loan from his bank and put twenty thousand in OHTE. This was a particularly lucky share; it shot up to four times its value in three days.

7   "Oh, this is too much, too much," cried Yee Lian in her ecstasy, and she sat down with pencil and paper, and found after a few minutes' calculation that they had made a cool one hundred thousand in a matter of days.

8   And now there was to be no stopping. The newspapers were full of it, everybody was talking about it, it was in the very air. There was plenty of money to be made in the stock exchange by those who had guts—money to be made by the hour, by the minute, for the prices of stocks and shares were rising faster than anyone could keep track of them! Dr. Soo was said—he laughingly dismissed it as a silly rumour—Dr. Soo was said to have made two million dollars already. If he sold all his shares now, he would be a millionaire twice over. And Yee Yeng, Yee Lian's sister, who had been urged with sisterly goodwill to come join the others make money, laughed happily to find that the shares she had bought for four twenty on Tuesday had risen to seven ninety-five on Friday—she laughed and thanked Yee Lian who advised her not to sell yet, it was going further, it would hit the ten-dollar mark by next week. And Tay Soon both laughed and cursed—cursed that he had failed to buy a share at nine dollars which a few days later had hit seventeen dollars! Yee Lian said reproachfully, "I thought I told you to buy it, darling," and Tay Soon had beaten his forehead in despair and said, "I know, I know, why didn't I! Big fool that I am!" And he had another reason to curse himself—he sold five thousand West Parkes at sixteen twenty-three per share, and saw, to his horror, West Parkes climb to eighteen ninety the very next day!

9   "I'll never sell now," he vowed. "I'll hold on. I won't be so foolish." And the frenzy continued. Husband and wife couldn't talk or think of anything else. They thought fondly of their shares—going to be worth a million altogether soon. A million! In the peak of good humour, Yee Lian went to her mother-in-law, forgetting the past insults, and advised her to join the others by buying some shares; she would get her

broker to buy them immediately for her, there was sure money in it. The old lady refused curtly, and to her son later, she showed great annoyance, scolding him for being so foolish as to put all his money in those worthless shares. "Worthless!" exploded Tay Soon. "Do you know, Mother, if I sold all my shares today, I would have the money to buy fifty terrace houses like the one you have?"

10   His wife said, "Oh, we'll just leave her alone. I was kind enough to offer to help her make money. But since she's so nasty and ungrateful, we'll leave her alone." The comforting, triumphant thought was that soon, very soon, they would be able to purchase their dream house; it would be even more magnificent than the one they had dreamt of, since they had made almost a—Yee Lian preferred not to say the sum. There was the old superstitious fear of losing something when it is too often or too directly referred to, and Yee Lian had cautioned her husband not to make mention of their gains.

11   "Not to worry, not to worry," he said jovially, not superstitious like his wife. "After all, it's just paper gains so far."

12   The downward slide, or the bursting of the bubble as the newspapers dramatically called it, did not initially cause much alarm. For the speculators all expected the shares to bounce back to their original strength and thence continue the phenomenal growth, but that did not happen. The slide continued.

13   Tay Soon said nervously, "Shall we sell? Do you think we should sell?" but Yee Lian said stoutly, "There is talk that this decline is a technical thing only—it will be over soon, and then the rise will continue. After all, see what is happening in Hong Kong and London and New York. Things are as good as ever."

14   "We're still making, so not to worry," said Yee Lian after a few days. Their gains were pared by half. A few days later, their gains were pared to marginal.

15   There is talk of a recovery, insisted Yee Lian. Do you know, Tay Soon, Dr. Soo's wife is buying up some OHTE and West Parkes now? She says these two are sure to rise. She has some inside information that these two are going to climb past the forty-dollar mark—

16   Tay Soon sold all his shares and put the money in OHTE and West Parkes. OHTE and West Parkes crashed shortly afterwards. Some began to say the shares were not worth the paper of the certificates.

17   "Oh, I can't believe, I can't believe it," gasped Yee Lian, pale and sick. Tay Soon looked in mute horror at her.

18   "All our money was in OHTE and West Parkes," he said, his lips dry.

19   "That stupid Soo woman!" shrieked Yee Lian. "I think she deliberately led me astray with her advice! She's always been jealous of me— ever since she knew we were going to build a house grander than hers!"

20   "How are we going to get our house now?" asked Tay Soon in deep distress, and for the first time he wept. He wept like a child, for

the loss of all his money, for the loss of the dream house that he had never stopped loving and worshipping.

21   The pain bit into his very mind and soul, so that he was like a madman, unable to go to his office to work, unable to do anything but haunt the broking houses, watching with frenzied anxiety for the OHTE and West Parkes to show him hope. But there was no hope. The decline continued with gleeful rapidity. His broker advised him to sell, before it was too late, but he shrieked angrily, "What! Sell at a fraction at which I bought them! How can this be tolerated!"

22   And he went on hoping against hope.

23   He began to have wild dreams in which he sometimes laughed and sometimes screamed. His wife Yee Lian was afraid and she ran sobbing to her sister who never failed to remind her curtly that all her savings were gone, simply because when she wanted to sell, Yee Lian had advised her not to.

24   "But what is your sorrow compared to mine," wept Yee Lian, "see what's happening to my husband. He's cracking up! He talks to himself, he doesn't eat, he has nightmares, he beats the children. Oh, he's finished!"

25   Her mother-in-law took charge of the situation, while Yee Lian, wide-eyed in mute horror at the terrible change that had come over her husband, shrank away and looked to her two small children for comfort. Tight-lipped and grim, the elderly woman made herbal medicines for Tay Soon, brewing and straining for hours, and got a Chinese medicine man to come have a look at him.

26   "There is a devil in him," said the medicine man, and he proceeded to make him a drink which he mixed with the ashes of a piece of prayer paper. But Tay Soon grew worse. He lay in bed, white, haggard and delirious, seeming to be beyond the touch of healing. In the end, Yee Lian, on the advice of her sister and friends, put him in hospital.

27   "I have money left for the funeral," whimpered the frightened Yee Lian only a week later, but her mother-in-law sharply retorted, "You leave everything to me! I have the money for his funeral, and I shall give him the best! He wanted a beautiful house all his life; I shall give him a beautiful house now!"

28   She went to the man who was well-known on the island for his beautiful houses, and she ordered the best. It would come to nearly a thousand dollars, said the man, a thin, wizened fellow whose funereal gauntness and pallor seemed to be a concession to his calling.

29   That doesn't matter, she said, I want the best. The house is to be made of superior paper, she instructed, and he was to make it to her specifications. She recollected that he, Tay Soon, had often spoken of marble flooring, a timbered ceiling and a kidney-shaped swimming pool. Could he simulate all these in paper?

30   The thin, wizened man said, "I've never done anything like that before. All my paper houses for the dead have been the usual kind—I can put in paper furniture and paper cars, paper utensils for the kitchen and paper servants, all that the dead will need in the other world. But I shall try to put in what you've asked for. Only it will cost more."

31   The house when it was ready, was most beautiful to see. It stood seven feet tall, a delicate framework of wire and thin bamboo strips covered with finely worked paper of a myriad colours. Little silver flowers, scattered liberally throughout the entire structure, gave a carnival atmosphere. There was a paper swimming pool (round, as the man had not understood "kidney") which had to be fitted inside the house itself, as there was no provision for a garden or surrounding grounds. Inside the house were paper figures; there were at least four servants to attend to the needs of the master who was posed beside two cars, one distinctly a Chevrolet and the other a Mercedes.

32   At the appointed time, the paper house was brought to Tay Soon's grave and set on fire there. It burned brilliantly, and in three minutes was a heap of ashes on the grave.

✧ Evaluating the Text

1. To what extent are Tay Soon and his wife and children caught up in the idea of buying a magnificent dream house? How does the elaborate nature of the house Tay Soon wishes to own symbolize the peak of achievement?

2. What role does Tay Soon's wife, Yee Lian, play in contributing to the entire disaster? You might examine her actions both at the beginning of the story and later when the disastrous outcome might still have been averted.

3. How does the recurrent mention of the word *paper* (paper profits, certificates of paper, prayer paper, a paper house, and shares not worth the paper they are printed on) focus the reader's attention on one of the story's central themes?

✧ Exploring Different Perspectives

1. How does the contrast between the expectations of Tay Soon and his wife and those of Victor Villaseñor illustrate the difference between real needs and illusory desires?

2. Discuss the damaging and even tragic effects of materialism in Lim's story and in Helena Norberg-Hodge's account.

✧ *Extending Viewpoints through Writing and Research*

1. If you have ever been involved in a gambling venture in which the psychological dynamics of greed and fear were operating, describe your experiences.

2. What is your attitude toward deferring material gratification? Did you find yourself valuing the fantasies you had about a vacation, car, clothes, jewelry, or whatever, in ways comparable to the feelings of Tay Soon?

3. To discover what you really value, consider the following hypothetical situation: A raging fire has started where you live. You can save only one item other than another person or a pet. What item would you save? How does the value of this item (material, sentimental, or both) imply what is really important to you? Discuss your reactions.

Connecting Cultures

◆

Deborah Tannen, "Ritual Fighting"

Can the differences between Chinese and American speech style as described by Amy Tan in "The Language of Discretion" in Chapter 1 be viewed the same way as the differences in conversational style between men and women in the workplace as described by Tannen?

Barbara Ehrenreich, "Nickel-and-Dimed"

What parallels can you discover between the working poor in contemporary America in Ehrenreich's report and in Viramma's account, "A Pariah's Life" in southern India in Chapter 5?

Gerald W. Haslam, "The Water Game"

Discuss the ramifications of water use in raising cattle as described by Jeremy Rifkin (in "Big, Bad Beef" in Chapter 6) and the politics of water use in California as discussed by Haslam.

Victor Villaseñor, "Rain of Gold"

Discuss the theme of powerlessness versus overcoming odds in Villaseñor's narrative and Gloria Anzaldúa's story "Cervicide" in Chapter 7.

Helena Norberg-Hodge, "Learning from Ladakh"

Discuss how the pressures of consumerism distort age-old community ties as described by Norberg-Hodge with the distortion of parent-child relationships as analyzed by Eric Schlosser in "Kid Kustomers" in Chapter 6.

Tomoyuki Iwashita, "Why I Quit the Company"

What overall picture do you get of Japanese society after reading Iwashita's narrative and Kyoko Mori's "Polite Lies" in Chapter 7?

Catherine Lim, "Paper"

Discuss the different attitudes toward money and possessions in Lim's story and in Octavio Paz's analysis of the Mexican "Fiesta" in Chapter 8.

5

Race, Class, and Caste

Until there are no longer first-class and second-class citizens of any nation, until the color of a man's skin is of no more significance than the color of his eyes, me seh war.
   —Bob Marley (1945–1981) Jamaican reggae musician, "War," on the album *Rastaman Vibration* (1976)

———————◆———————

Every society can be characterized in terms of social class. Although the principles by which class is identified vary widely from culture to culture, from the amount of money you earn in the United States to what kind of accent you speak with in England to what religious caste you are born into in India, class serves to set boundaries around individuals in terms of opportunities and possibilities. The concept of class in its present form has been in force for only a few hundred years in Western cultures. In prior times, for example, in medieval Europe, your position and chances in life were determined at birth by the *estate* into which you were born, whether that of peasant, clergy, or noble.

Conflicts based on inequalities of social class are often intertwined with those of race, because minorities usually receive the least education, have the least political clout, earn the least income, and find work in occupations considered menial without the possibility of advancement. In some societies, such as that in India, for example, an oppressive caste system based on tradition has, until recently, been responsible for burdening the "untouchables" with the most onerous tasks.

Class conditions our entire lives by limiting—more than we might like to admit—who we can be friends with, what our goals are, and even who we can marry.

Class reflects the access one has to important resources, social privileges, choices, and a sense of control over one's own life. Although caste in India is something one cannot change, social stratification in the United States is less rigid and upward mobility is possible through a variety of means such as work, financial success, marriage, and education. More frequently, however, a *de facto* class system can be said to exist in terms of health care, salaries, housing, and opportunities for education that vary greatly for the rich and the poor.

The writers in this chapter explore many of the less obvious connections between social class and the control people exercise over their lives.

Martin Luther King Jr., in his famous speech "I Have a Dream," reminds his audience that the civil rights movement puts into action basic ideas contained in the Constitution. In "What's in a Name?" Itabari Njeri explains how adopting a name of African origin changed her life. Mary Crow Dog and Richard Erdoes, in "Civilize Them with a Stick," recount the racism experienced by Native Americans attending a government-run boarding school. A timeless story, "Désirée's Baby," by Kate Chopin, offers a complex and thoughtful exploration of the consequences of sexism and racism in turn-of-the-century Louisiana. Richard Rodriguez in "On Becoming a Chicano" compares the open Mexican-American culture of his childhood with the cloistered atmosphere of the academic world. Raymonde Carroll in "Sex, Money, and Success" investigates why money for Americans and sex for the French are used by each culture to establish social status.

Mahdokht Kashkuli, in "The Button," describes the circumstances of a family in modern-day Iran that force them to place one of their children in an orphanage. Although officially outlawed, the caste known as "untouchables" lead lives similar to that described by Viramma in her autobiographical account, "A Pariah's Life."

Martin Luther King Jr.

I Have a Dream

————◆————

Martin Luther King Jr. (1929–1968) was an influential figure in the civil rights movement. He was ordained a Baptist minister and received advanced degrees from Boston University (Ph.D., 1955; D.D., 1959). King founded the Southern Christian Leadership Conference and advocated nonviolent means for producing social change, which had been employed by the great Indian political leader Mahatma Gandhi. He led a series of sit-ins and mass marches that helped bring about the Civil Rights Act of 1964 and the Voting Rights Act of 1965. He received the Nobel Prize for Peace in 1964. His writings include Letter from Birmingham Jail *(1968) and* The Trumpet of Conscience *(1968). "I Have a Dream" (1963) is the speech King delivered to the nearly 250,000 people who had come to Washington, D.C., to commemorate the centennial of Lincoln's Emancipation Proclamation.*

Before You Read

Consider whether nonviolent protests are more effective or less effective than violent demonstrations to obtain rights that have been denied.

————◆————

1   I am happy to join with you today in what will go down in history as the greatest demonstration for freedom in the history of our nation.

2   Five score years ago, a great American, in whose symbolic shadow we stand today, signed the Emancipation Proclamation. This momentous decree came as a great beacon light of hope to millions of Negro slaves who had been seared in the flames of withering injustice. It came as a joyous daybreak to end the long night of their captivity. But one hundred years later, the Negro is still not free. One hundred years later, the life of the Negro is still sadly crippled by the manacles of segregation and the chains of discrimination. One hundred years later, the Negro lives on a lonely island of poverty in the midst of a vast ocean of material prosperity. One hundred years later, the Negro is still anguished in the corners of American society and finds himself in exile in his own land. And so we have come here today to dramatize a shameful condition.

3   In a sense we have come to our nation's capital to cash a check. When the architects of our republic wrote the magnificent words of the

Constitution and the Declaration of Independence, they were signing a promissory note to which every American was to fall heir. This note was the promise that all men—yes, Black men as well as white men— would be guaranteed the inalienable rights of life, liberty, and the pursuit of happiness.

4   It is obvious today that America has defaulted on this promissory note insofar as her citizens of color are concerned. Instead of honoring this sacred obligation, America has given the Negro people a bad check, a check which has come back marked "insufficient funds." But we refuse to believe that the bank of justice is bankrupt. We refuse to believe that there are insufficient funds in the great vaults of opportunity of this nation; and so we have come to cash this check, a check that will give us upon demand the riches of freedom and the security of justice.

5   We have also come to this hallowed spot to remind America of the fierce urgency of *now*. This is no time to engage in the luxury of cooling off or to take the tranquilizing drug of gradualism. *Now* is the time to make real the promises of democracy. *Now* is the time to rise from the dark and desolate valley of segregation to the sunlit patch of racial justice. *Now* is the time to lift our nation from the quicksands of racial injustice to the solid rock of brotherhood. *Now* is the time to make justice a reality for all of God's children.

6   It would be fatal for the nation to overlook the urgency of the moment. This sweltering summer of the Negro's legitimate discontent will not pass until there is an invigorating autumn of freedom and equality. Nineteen sixty-three is not an end, but a beginning. And those who hope that the Negro needed to blow off steam and will now be content will have a rude awakening if the nation returns to business as usual. There will be neither rest nor tranquility in America until the Negro is granted his citizenship rights. The whirlwinds of revolt will continue to shake the foundations of our nation until the bright day of justice emerges.

7   But there is something that I must say to my people who stand on the warm threshold which leads into the palace of justice. In the process of gaining our rightful place, we must not be guilty of wrongful deeds. Let us not seek to satisfy our thirst for freedom by drinking from the cup of bitterness and hatred. We must forever conduct our struggle on the high plane of dignity and discipline. We must not allow our creative protest to degenerate into physical violence. Again and again we must rise to the majestic heights of meeting physical force with soul force. And the marvelous new militancy which has engulfed the Negro community must not lead us to a distrust of all white people; for many of our white brothers, as evidenced by their presence here today, have come to realize that their destiny is tied up with our destiny, and they have come to realize that their freedom is inextricably bound to our freedom.

8   We cannot walk alone. And as we walk we must make the pledge that we shall always march ahead. We cannot turn back. There are those who are asking the devotees of civil rights, "When will you be satisfied?" We can never be satisfied as long as the Negro is the victim of the unspeakable horrors of police brutality. We can never be satisfied as long as our bodies, heavy with the fatigue of travel, cannot gain lodging in the motels of the highways and the hotels of the cities. We cannot be satisfied as long as the Negro's basic mobility is from a smaller ghetto to a larger one. We can never be satisfied as long as our children are stripped of their selfhood and robbed of their dignity by signs stating "For Whites Only." We cannot be satisfied as long as the Negro in Mississippi cannot vote and a Negro in New York believes he has nothing for which to vote. No, no, we are not satisfied, and we will not be satisfied until justice rolls down like waters and righteousness like a mighty stream.

9   I am not unmindful that some of you have come here out of great trials and tribulations. Some of you have come fresh from narrow jail cells. Some of you have come from areas where your quest for freedom left you battered by the storms of persecution and staggered by the winds of police brutality. You have been the veterans of creative suffering. Continue to work with the faith that unearned suffering is redemptive.

10   Go back to Mississippi, and go back to Alabama. Go back to South Carolina. Go back to Georgia. Go back to Louisiana. Go back to the slums and ghettos of our northern cities, knowing that somehow this situation can and will be changed. Let us not wallow in the valley of despair.

11   I say to you today, my friends, even though we face the difficulties of today and tomorrow, I still have a dream. It is a dream deeply rooted in the American dream. I have a dream that one day this nation will rise up and live out the true meaning of its creed: "We hold these truths to be self-evident, that all men are created equal." I have a dream that one day, on the red hills of Georgia, sons of former slaves and the sons of former slave owners will be able to sit down together at the table of brotherhood. I have a dream that one day even the state of Mississippi, a state sweltering with the heat of injustice, sweltering with the heat of oppression, will be transformed into an oasis of freedom and justice. I have a dream that my four little children will one day live in a nation where they will not be judged by the color of their skin, but by the content of their character.

12   I have a dream today. I have a dream that one day down in Alabama—with its vicious racists, with its governor's lips dripping with the words of interposition and nullification—one day right there in Alabama, little Black boys and Black girls will be able to join hands with little white boys and white girls as sisters and brothers.

13   I have a dream today. I have a dream that one day every valley shall be exalted and every hill and mountain shall be made low, the rough places will be made plain and the crooked places will be made straight, and the glory of the Lord shall be revealed, and all flesh shall see it together.

14   This is our hope. This is the faith that I go back to the South with. And with this faith we will be able to hew out of the mountain of despair a stone of hope. With this faith we will be able to transform the jangling discords of our nation into a beautiful symphony of brotherhood. With this faith we will be able to work together, to play together, to struggle together, to go to jail together, to stand up for freedom together, knowing that we will be free one day.

15   And this will be the day—this will be the day when all of God's children will be able to sing with new meaning.

> My country, 'tis of thee,
> Sweet land of liberty,
>   Of thee I sing;
> Land where my fathers died,
> Land of the Pilgrims' pride,
> From every mountainside
>   Let freedom ring.

And if America is to be a great nation, this must become true.

16   And so let freedom ring from the prodigious hilltops of New Hampshire. Let freedom ring from the mighty mountains of New York. Let freedom ring from the heightening Alleghenies of Pennsylvania. Let freedom ring from the snow-capped Rockies of Colorado. Let freedom ring from the curvaceous slopes of California.

17   But not only that. Let freedom ring from Stone Mountain of Georgia. Let freedom ring from Lookout Mountain of Tennessee. Let freedom ring from every hill and molehill of Mississippi. "From every mountainside let freedom ring."

18   And when this happens—when we allow freedom to ring, when we let it ring from every village and every hamlet, from every state and every city—we will be able to speed up that day when all of God's children, Black men and white men, Jews and Gentiles, Protestants and Catholics, will be able to join hands and sing in the words of the old Negro spiritual: "Free at last! Free at last! Thank God Almighty. We are free at last!"

✧ Evaluating the Text

1. How did the civil rights movement express ideas of equality and freedom that were already deeply rooted in the Constitution? How does King's affirmation of minority rights renew aspirations first stated by America's Founding Fathers?

2. What evidence is there that King was trying to reach many different groups of people, each with its own concerns? Where does he shift his attention from one group to another?

3. What importance does King place on the idea of nonviolent protest? How do King's references to the Bible and the Emancipation Proclamation enhance his speech?

✦ Exploring Different Perspectives

1. What political and social advances have occurred between the time Kate Chopin wrote "Désirée's Baby" and King wrote this speech?

2. Compare Itabari Njeri's aspirations with those of King and discuss any differences and similarities you discover.

✦ Extending Viewpoints through Writing and Research

1. Trace the rationale for nonviolent protest back to the roots of Thoreau and Gandhi. How was the principle of nonviolent protest adapted by King to meet the challenges faced by the civil rights movement in the 1960s?

2. Assess the changes made in the South since the 1960s and the extent to which the problems that King addressed have been remedied. For example, what part did race play in the response to Hurricane Katrina in New Orleans in August 2005?

How does this photo suggest Martin Luther King Jr.'s appeal to the audience who participated in the march on Washington, D.C.?

Itabari Njeri

What's in a Name?

———◆———

Itabari Njeri is an arts critic, essayist, and reporter whose memoir Every Goodbye Ain't Gone *(1990), an eloquent testimony to the African-American experience, won the American Book Award. She is also a talented professional singer as well as writer, and was named "Best New Pop Vocalist" by MGM records. From 1986 to 1992, she was a staff writer for the* Los Angeles Times Magazine, *where the following essay first appeared. Her most recent book is* The Last Plantation *(1997).*

Before You Read
Consider to what extent Njeri's decision to change her name is due to a desire to be an individual as well as to disengage herself from objectionable racial associations.

———◆———

1   The decade was about to end when I started my first newspaper job. The seventies might have been the disco generation for some, but it was a continuation of the Black Power, post–civil rights era for me. Of course in some parts of America it was still the pre–civil rights era. And that was the part of America I wanted to explore. As a good reporter I needed a sense of the whole country, not just the provincial Northeast Corridor in which I was raised.

2   I headed for Greenville ("Pearl of the Piedmont"), South Carolina.

3   "*Wheeere*," some people snarled, their nostrils twitching, their mouths twisted so their top lips went slightly to the right, the bottom ones way down and to the left, "did you get *that* name from?"

4   Itabiddy, Etabeedy. Etabeeree. Eat a berry. Mata Hari. Theda Bara. And one secretary in the office of the Greenville Urban League told her employer: "It's Ms. Idi Amin."

5   Then, and now, there are a whole bunch of people who greet me with: "Hi, Ita." They think "Bari" is my last name. Even when they don't, they still want to call me "Ita." When I tell them my first name is Itabari, they say, "Well, what do people call you for short?"

6   "They don't call me anything for short," I say. "The name is Itabari."

7   Sophisticated white people, upon hearing my name, approach me as would a cultural anthropologist finding a piece of exotica right in his own living room. This happens a lot, still, at cocktail parties.

8   "Oh, what an unusual and beautiful name. Where are you from?"

9   "Brooklyn," I say. I can see the disappointment in their eyes. Just
another home-grown Negro.

10   Then there are other white people, who, having heard my decid-
edly northeastern accent, will simply say, "What a lovely name," and
smile knowingly, indicating that they saw *Roots* and understand.

11   Then there are others, black and white, who for different reasons
take me through this number:

12   "What's your *real* name?"

13   "Itabari Njeri is my real, legal name," I explain.

14   "Okay, what's your original name?" they ask, often with eyes
rolling, exasperation in their voices.

15   After Malcolm X, Muhammad Ali, Kareem Abdul-Jabbar, Ntozake
Shange, and Kunta Kinte, who, I ask, should be exasperated by this
question-and-answer game?

16   Nevertheless, I explain, "Because of slavery, black people in the
Western world don't usually know their original names. What you really want to know is what my slave name was."

17   Now this is where things get tense. Four hundred years of bitter
history, culture, and politics between blacks and whites in America is
evoked by this one term, "slave name."

18   Some white people wince when they hear the phrase, pained
and embarrassed by this reminder of their ancestors' inhumanity. Further, they quickly scrutinize me and conclude that mine was a post–
Emancipation Proclamation birth. "You were never a slave."

19   I used to be reluctant to tell people my slave name unless I sur-
mised that they wouldn't impose their cultural values on me and
refuse to use my African name. I don't care anymore. When I changed
my name, I changed my life, and I've been Itabari for more years now
than I was Jill. Nonetheless, people will say: "Well, that's your *real*
name, you were born in America and that's what I am going to call
you." My mother tried a variation of this on me when I legalized my
traditional African name. I respectfully made it clear to her that I
would not tolerate it. Her behavior, and subsequently her attitude,
changed.

20   But many black folks remain just as skeptical of my name as my
mother was.

21   "You're one of those black people who changed their name, huh,"
they are likely to begin. "Well, I still got the old slave master's Irish
name," said one man named O'Hare at a party. This man's defensive
tone was a reaction to what I call the "blacker than thou" syndrome
perpetrated by many black nationalists in the sixties and seventies.
Those who reclaimed their African names made blacks who didn't do
the same thing feel like Uncle Toms.

22   These so-called Uncle Toms couldn't figure out why they should use an African name when they didn't know a thing about Africa. Besides, many of them were proud of their names, no matter how they had come by them. And it should be noted that after the Emancipation Proclamation in 1863, four million black people changed their names, adopting surnames such as Freeman, Freedman, and Liberty. They eagerly gave up names that slave masters had imposed upon them as a way of identifying their human chattel.

23   Besides names that indicated their newly won freedom, blacks chose common English names such as Jones, Scott, and Johnson. English was their language. America was their home, and they wanted names that would allow them to assimilate as easily as possible.

24   Of course, many of our European surnames belong to us by birthright. We are the legal as well as "illegitimate" heirs to the names Jefferson, Franklin, Washington, et al., and in my own family, Lord.

25   Still, I consider most of these names to be by-products of slavery, if not actual slave names. Had we not been enslaved, we would not have been cut off from our culture, lost our indigenous languages, and been compelled to use European names.

26   The loss our African culture is a tragic fact of history, and the conflict it poses is a profound one that has divided blacks many times since Emancipation: do we accept the loss and assimilate totally or do we try to reclaim our culture and synthesize it with our present reality?

27   A new generation of black people in America is reexamining the issues raised by the cultural nationalists and Pan-Africanists of the sixties and seventies: what are the cultural images that appropriately convey the "new" black aesthetic in literature and art?

28   The young Afro-American novelist Trey Ellis has asserted that the "New Black Aesthetic shamelessly borrows and reassembles across both race and class lines." It is not afraid to embrace the full implications of our hundreds of years in the New World. We are a new people who need not be tied to externally imposed or self-inflicted cultural parochialism. Had I understood that as a teenager, I might still be singing today.

29   Even the fundamental issue of identity and nomenclature, raised by Baraka and others twenty years ago, is back on the agenda: are we to call ourselves blacks or African-Americans?

30   In reality, it's an old debate. "Only with the founding of the American Colonization Society in 1816 did blacks recoil from using the term African in referring to themselves and their institutions," the noted historian and author Sterling Stuckey pointed out in an interview with me. They feared that using the term "African" would fuel white efforts to send them back to Africa. But they felt no white person had the right to send them back when they had slaved to build America.

31   Many black institutions retained their African identification, most notably the African Methodist Episcopal Church. Changes in black self-identification in America have come in cycles, usually reflecting the larger dynamics of domestic and international politics.

32   The period after World War II, said Stuckey, "culminating in the Cold War years of Roy Wilkins's leadership of the NAACP," was a time of "frenzied integrationism." And there was "no respectable black leader on the scene evincing any sort of interest in Africa—neither the NAACP or the Urban League."

33   This, he said, "was an example of historical discontinuity, the likes of which we, as a people, had not seen before." Prior to that, for more than a century and a half, black leaders were Pan-Africanists, including Frederick Douglass. "He recognized," said Stuckey, "that Africa was important and that somehow one had to redeem the motherland in order to be genuinely respected in the New World."

34   The Reverend Jesse Jackson has, of course, placed on the national agenda the importance of blacks in America restoring their cultural, historical, and political links with Africa.

35   But what does it really mean to be called an African-American?

36   "Black" can be viewed as a more encompassing term, referring to all people of African descent. "Afro-American" and "African-American" refer to a specific ethnic group. I use the terms interchangeably, depending on the context and the point I want to emphasize.

37   But I wonder: as the twenty-first century breathes down our necks—prodding us to wake up to the expanding mélange of ethnic groups immigrating in record numbers to the United States, inevitably intermarrying, and to realize the eventual reshaping of the nation's political imperatives in a newly multicultural society—will the term "African-American" be as much of a racial and cultural obfuscation as the term "black"? In other words, will we be the only people, in a society moving toward cultural pluralism, viewed to have no history and no culture? Will we just be a color with a new name: African-American?

38   Or will the term be—as I think it should—an ethnic label describing people with a shared culture who descended from Africans, were transformed in (as well as transformed) America, and are genetically intertwined with myriad other groups in the United States?

39   Such a definition reflects the historical reality and distances us from the fallacious, unscientific concept of separate races when there is only one: *Homo sapiens*.

40   But to comprehend what should be an obvious definition requires knowledge and a willingness to accept history.

41   When James Baldwin wrote *Nobody Knows My Name*, the title was a metaphor—at the deepest level of the collective African-American psyche—for the blighting of black history and culture before the nadir of slavery and since.

42   The eradication or distortion of our place in world history and culture is most obvious in the popular media. Liz Taylor—and, for an earlier generation, Claudette Colbert—still represent what Cleopatra— a woman of color in a multiethnic society, dominated at various times by blacks—looks like.

43   And in American homes, thanks to reruns and cable, a new generation of black kids grow up believing that a simpleton shouting "Dyno-mite!" is a genuine reflection of Afro-American culture, rather than a white Hollywood writer's stereotype.

44   More recently, *Coming to America*, starring Eddie Murphy as an African prince seeking a bride in the United States, depicted traditional African dancers in what amounted to a Las Vegas stage show, totally distorting the nature and beauty of real African dance. But with every burlesque-style pelvic thrust on the screen, I saw blacks in the audience burst into applause. They think that's African culture, too.

45   And what do Africans know of us, since blacks don't control the organs of communication that disseminate information about us?

46   "No!" screamed the mother of a Kenyan man when he announced his engagement to an African-American woman who was a friend of mine. The mother said marry a European, marry a white American. But please, not one of those low-down, ignorant, drug-dealing, murderous black people she had seen in American movies. Ultimately, the mother prevailed.

47   In Tanzania, the travel agent looked at me indignantly. "Njeri, that's Kikuyu. What are you doing with an African name?" he demanded.

48   I'd been in Dar es Salaam about a month and had learned that Africans assess in a glance the ethnic origins of the people they meet.

49   Without a greeting, strangers on the street in Tanzania's capital would comment, "Oh, you're an Afro-American or West Indian."

50   "Both."

51   "I knew it," they'd respond, sometimes politely, sometimes not.

52   Or, people I got to know while in Africa would mention, "I know another half-caste like you." Then they would call in the "mixed-race" person and say, "Please meet Itabari Njeri." The darker-complected African, presumably of unmixed ancestry, would then smile and stare at us like we were animals in the zoo.

53   Of course, this "half-caste" (which I suppose is a term preferable to "mulatto," which I hate, and which every person who understands its derogatory meaning—"mule"—should never use) was usually the product of a mixed marriage, not generations of ethnic intermingling. And it was clear from most "half-castes" I met that they did not like being compared to so mongrelized and stigmatized a group as Afro-Americans.

54   I had minored in African studies in college, worked for years with Africans in the United States, and had no romantic illusions as to how

I would be received in the motherland. I wasn't going back to find my roots. The only thing that shocked me in Tanzania was being called, with great disdain, a "white woman" by an African waiter. Even if the rest of the world didn't follow the practice, I then assumed everyone understood that any known or perceptible degree of African ancestry made one "black" in America by law and social custom.

55   But I was pleasantly surprised by the telephone call I received two minutes after I walked into my Dar es Salaam hotel room. It was the hotel operator. "Sister, welcome to Tanzania. . . . Please tell everyone in Harlem hello for us." The year was 1978, and people in Tanzania were wearing half-foot-high platform shoes and dancing to James Brown wherever I went.

56   Shortly before I left, I stood on a hill surrounded by a field of endless flowers in Arusha, near the border of Tanzania and Kenya. A toothless woman with a wide smile, a staff in her hand, and two young girls at her side, came toward me on a winding path. I spoke to her in fractured Swahili and she to me in broken English.

57   "I know you," she said smiling. "Wa-Negro." "Wa" is a prefix in Bantu languages meaning people. "You are from the lost tribe," she told me. "Welcome," she said, touching me, then walked down a hill that lay in the shadow of Mount Kilimanjaro.

58   I never told her my name, but when I told other Africans, they'd say: "*Emmmm* Itabari. Too long. How about I just call you Ita."

✧ Evaluating the Text

1. The variety of reactions Njeri's name elicits prompts her to make the case explaining why she changed her name to an African one. What were these reactions and how would this explain why she would want to justify her decision? Why was it ironic she met with the same responses in Tanzania as she did in Greenville, South Carolina?

2. What negative connotations did Njeri's given name have for her? By contrast, what positive associations does she have with her African name, Itabari?

✧ Exploring Different Perspectives

1. In what way do both Njeri's essay and Mary Crow Dog's account explore the predicament of being marginalized because of race?

2. How does Njeri's account raise issues of authenticity and identity in much the same way as Richard Rodriguez does in "On Becoming a Chicano"?

✧ *Extending Viewpoints through Writing and Research*

1. Evaluate Njeri's contention that the continued use of English-language names such as Jones, Scott, and Johnson perpetuates a legacy of slavery, whereas adoption of African names would allow African Americans to have their own identity?

2. Would you ever consider changing your name? If so, what would it be and what would it say about you that your present given name does not?

3. Describe the circumstances underlying the choice of your name. Do you like your given name or do you prefer to be called by a nickname you chose or others gave you?

4. African naming-practices are described at
http://www.slaveryinamerica.org/history/hs_es_names.htm.

Mary Crow Dog and Richard Erdoes

Civilize Them with a Stick

◆

Mary Crow Dog (who later took the name Mary Brave Bird) was born in 1956 and grew up on a South Dakota reservation in a one-room cabin without running water or electricity. She joined the new movement of tribal pride sweeping Native-American communities in the 1960s and 1970s and was at the siege of Wounded Knee, South Dakota, in 1973. She married the American Indian Movement (AIM) leader Leonard Crow Dog, the movement's chief medicine man. Her powerful autobiography Lakota Woman, *written with Richard Erdoes, one of America's leading writers on Native-American affairs and the author of eleven books, became a national best-seller and won the American Book Award for 1991. In it she describes what it was like to grow up a Sioux in a white-dominated society. Her second book,* Ohitka Woman *(1993), also written with Richard Erdoes, continues the story of a woman whose struggle for a sense of self and freedom is a testament to her will and spirit. In "Civilize Them with a Stick," from* Lakota Woman, *the author recounts her personal struggle as a young student at a boarding school run by the Bureau of Indian Affairs.*

Before You Read

Notice how the quote from the Department of Interior (1901) that precedes Mary Crow Dog's essay provides an ironic contrast to the conditions she describes.

◆

> *. . . Gathered from the cabin, the wickiup, and the tepee,*
> *partly by cajolery and partly by threats;*
> *partly by bribery and partly by force,*
> *they are induced to leave their kindred*
> *to enter these schools and take upon themselves*
> *the outward appearance of civilized life.*
> —Annual report of the Department of Interior, 1901

1   It is almost impossible to explain to a sympathetic white person what a typical old Indian boarding school was like; how it affected the Indian child suddenly dumped into it like a small creature from another world, helpless, defenseless, bewildered, trying desperately and

instinctively to survive and sometimes not surviving at all. I think such children were like the victims of Nazi concentration camps trying to tell average, middle-class Americans what their experience had been like. Even now, when these schools are much improved, when the buildings are new, all gleaming steel and glass, the food tolerable, the teachers well trained and well intentioned, even trained in child psychology—unfortunately the psychology of white children, which is different from ours—the shock to the child upon arrival is still tremendous. Some just seem to shrivel up, don't speak for days on end, and have an empty look in their eyes. I know of an eleven-year-old on another reservation who hanged herself, and in our school, while I was there, a girl jumped out of the window, trying to kill herself to escape an unbearable situation. That first shock is always there. . . .

2   The mission school at St. Francis was a curse for our family for generations. My grandmother went there, then my mother, then my sisters and I. At one time or other every one of us tried to run away. Grandma told me once about the bad times she had experienced at St. Francis. In those days they let students go home only for one week every year. Two days were used up for transportation, which meant spending just five days out of three hundred and sixty-five with her family. And that was an improvement. Before grandma's time, on many reservations they did not let the students go home at all until they had finished school. Anybody who disobeyed the nuns was severely punished. The building in which my grandmother stayed had three floors, for girls only. Way up in the attic were little cells, about five by five by ten feet. One time she was in church and instead of praying she was playing jacks. As punishment they took her to one of those little cubicles where she stayed in darkness because the windows had been boarded up. They left her there for a whole week with only bread and water for nourishment. After she came out she promptly ran away, together with three other girls. They were found and brought back. The nuns stripped them naked and whipped them. They used a horse buggy whip on my grandmother. Then she was put back into the attic—for two weeks.

3   My mother had much the same experiences but never wanted to talk about them, and then there I was, in the same place. The school is now run by the BIA—the Bureau of Indian Affairs—but only since about fifteen years ago. When I was there, during the 1960s, it was still run by the Church. The Jesuit fathers ran the boys' wing and the Sisters of the Sacred Heart ran us—with the help of the strap. Nothing had changed since my grandmother's days. I have been told recently that even in the '70s they were still beating children at that school. All I got out of school was being taught how to pray. I learned quickly that I would be beaten if I failed in my devotions or, God forbid, prayed the

wrong way, especially prayed in Indian to Wakan Tanka, the Indian Creator.

4   The girls' wing was built like an F and was run like a penal institution. Every morning at five o'clock the sisters would come into our large dormitory to wake us up, and immediately we had to kneel down at the sides of our beds and recite the prayers. At six o'clock we were herded into the church for more of the same. I did not take kindly to the discipline and to marching by the clock, left-right, left-right. I was never one to like being forced to do something. I do something because I feel like doing it. I felt this way always, as far as I can remember, and my sister Barbara felt the same way. An old medicine man once told me: "Us Lakotas are not like dogs who can be trained, who can be beaten and keep on wagging their tails, licking the hand that whipped them. We are like cats, little cats, big cats, wildcats, bobcats, mountain lions. It doesn't matter what kind, but cats who can't be tamed, who scratch if you step on their tails." But I was only a kitten and my claws were still small.

5   Barbara was still in the school when I arrived and during my first year or two she could still protect me a little bit. When Barb was a seventh-grader she ran away together with five other girls, early in the morning before sunrise. They brought them back in the evening. The girls had to wait for two hours in front of the mother superior's office. They were hungry and cold, frozen through. It was wintertime and they had been running the whole day without food, trying to make good their escape. The mother superior asked each girl, "Would you do this again?" She told them that as punishment they would not be allowed to visit home for a month and that she'd keep them busy on work details until the skin on their knees and elbows had worn off. At the end of her speech she told each girl, "Get up from this chair and lean over it." She then lifted the girls' skirts and pulled down their underpants. Not little girls either, but teenagers. She had a leather strap about a foot long and four inches wide fastened to a stick, and beat the girls, one after another, until they cried. Barb did not give her that satisfaction but just clenched her teeth. There was one girl, Barb told me, the nun kept on beating and beating until her arm got tired.

6   I did not escape my share of the strap. Once, when I was thirteen years old, I refused to go to Mass. I did not want to go to church because I did not feel well. A nun grabbed me by the hair, dragged me upstairs, made me stoop over, pulled my dress up (we were not allowed at the time to wear jeans), pulled my panties down, and gave me what they called "swats"—twenty-five swats with a board around which Scotch tape had been wound. She hurt me badly.

7   My classroom was right next to the principal's office and almost every day I could hear him swatting the boys. Beating was the common punishment for not doing one's homework, or for being late to

school. It had such a bad effect upon me that I hated and mistrusted every white person on sight, because I met only one kind. It was not until much later that I met sincere white people I could relate to and be friends with. Racism breeds racism in reverse.

8   The routine at St. Francis was dreary. Six A.M., kneeling in church for an hour or so; seven o'clock, breakfast; eight o'clock, scrub the floor, peel spuds, make classes. We had to mop the dining room twice every day and scrub the tables. If you were caught taking a rest, doodling on the bench with a fingernail or knife, or just rapping, the nun would come up with a dish towel and just slap it across your face, saying, "You're not supposed to be talking, you're supposed to be working!" Monday mornings we had cornmeal mush, Tuesday oatmeal, Wednesday rice and raisins, Thursday cornflakes, and Friday all the leftovers mixed together or sometimes fish. Frequently the food had bugs or rocks in it. We were eating hot dogs that were weeks old, while the nuns were dining on ham, whipped potatoes, sweet peas, and cranberry sauce. In winter our dorm was icy cold while the nuns' rooms were always warm.

9   I have seen little girls arrive at the school, first-graders, just fresh from home and totally unprepared for what awaited them, little girls with pretty braids, and the first thing the nuns did was chop their hair off and tie up what was left behind their ears. Next they would dump the children into tubs of alcohol, a sort of rubbing alcohol, "to get the germs off." Many of the nuns were German immigrants, some from Bavaria, so that we sometimes speculated whether Bavaria was some sort of Dracula country inhabited by monsters. For the sake of objectivity I ought to mention that two of the German fathers were great linguists and that the only Lakota–English dictionaries and grammars which are worth anything were put together by them.

10   At night some of the girls would huddle in bed together for comfort and reassurance. Then the nun in charge of the dorm would come in and say, "What are the two of you doing in bed together? I smell evil in this room. You girls are evil incarnate. You are sinning. You are going to hell and burn forever. You can act that way in the devil's frying pan." She would get them out of bed in the middle of the night, making them kneel and pray until morning. We had not the slightest idea what it was all about. At home we slept two and three in a bed for animal warmth and a feeling of security.

11   The nuns and the girls in the two top grades were constantly battling it out physically with fists, nails, and hair-pulling. I myself was growing from a kitten into an undersized cat. My claws were getting bigger and were itching for action. About 1969 or 1970 a strange young white girl appeared on the reservation. She looked about eighteen or twenty years old. She was pretty and had long, blond hair down to her waist, patched jeans, boots, and a backpack. She was different from

any other white person we had met before. I think her name was Wise. I do not know how she managed to overcome our reluctance and distrust, getting us into a corner, making us listen to her, asking us how we were treated. She told us that she was from New York. She was the first real hippie or Yippie we had come across. She told us of people called the Black Panthers, Young Lords, and Weathermen. She said, "Black people are getting it on. Indians are getting it on in St. Paul and California. How about you?" She also said, "Why don't you put out an underground paper, mimeograph it. It's easy. Tell it like it is. Let it all hang out." She spoke a strange lingo but we caught on fast.

12   Charlene Left Hand Bull and Gina One Star were two full-blood girls I used to hang out with. We did everything together. They were willing to join me in a Sioux uprising. We put together a newspaper which we called the *Red Panther*. In it we wrote how bad the school was, what kind of slop we had to eat—slimy, rotten, blackened potatoes for two weeks—the way we were beaten. I think I was the one who wrote the worst article about our principal of the moment, Father Keeler. I put all my anger and venom into it. I called him a goddam wa-sičun son of a bitch. I wrote that he knew nothing about Indians and should go back to where he came from, teaching white children whom he could relate to. I wrote that we knew which priests slept with which nuns and that all they ever could think about was filling their bellies and buying a new car. It was the kind of writing which foamed at the mouth, but which also lifted a great deal of weight from one's soul.

13   On Saint Patrick's Day, when everybody was at the big powwow, we distributed our newspapers. We put them on windshields and bulletin boards, in desks and pews, in dorms and toilets. But someone saw us and snitched on us. The shit hit the fan. The three of us were taken before a board meeting. Our parents, in my case my mother, had to come. They were told that ours was a most serious matter, the worst thing that had ever happened in the school's long history. One of the nuns told my mother, "Your daughter really needs to be talked to." "What's wrong with my daughter?" my mother asked. She was given one of our *Red Panther* newspapers. The nun pointed out its name to her and then my piece, waiting for mom's reaction. After a while she asked, "Well, what have you got to say to this? What do you think?"

14   My mother said, "Well, when I went to school here, some years back, I was treated a lot worse than these kids are. I really can't see how they can have any complaints, because we was treated a lot stricter. We could not even wear skirts halfway up our knees. These girls have it made. But you should forgive them because they are young. And it's supposed to be a free country, free speech and all that. I don't believe what they done is wrong." So all I got out of it was scrubbing six flights of stairs on my hands and knees, every day. And no boy-side privileges.

15   The boys and girls were still pretty much separated. The only time one could meet a member of the opposite sex was during free time, between four and five-thirty, in the study hall or on benches or the volleyball court outside, and that was strictly supervised. One day Charlene and I went over to the boys' side. We were on the ball team and they had to let us practice. We played three extra minutes, only three minutes more than we were supposed to. Here was the nuns' opportunity for revenge. We got twenty-five swats. I told Charlene, "We are getting too old to have our bare asses whipped that way. We are old enough to have babies. Enough of this shit. Next time we fight back." Charlene only said, "Hoka-hay!"

16   We had to take showers every evening. One little girl did not want to take her panties off and one of the nuns told her, "You take those underpants off—or else!" But the child was ashamed to do it. The nun was getting her swat to threaten the girl. I went up to the sister, pushed her veil off, and knocked her down. I told her that if she wanted to hit a little girl she should pick on me, pick one her own size. She got herself transferred out of the dorm a week later.

17   In a school like this there is always a lot of favoritism. At St. Francis it was strongly tinged with racism. Girls who were near-white, who came from what the nuns called "nice families," got preferential treatment. They waited on the faculty and got to eat ham or eggs and bacon in the morning. They got the easy jobs while the skins, who did not have the right kind of background—myself among them—always wound up in the laundry room sorting out ten bushel baskets of dirty boys' socks every day. Or we wound up scrubbing the floors and doing all the dishes. The school therefore fostered fights and antagonism between whites and breeds, and between breeds and skins. At one time Charlene and I had to iron all the robes and vestments the priests wore when saying Mass. We had to fold them up and put them into a chest in the back of the church. In a corner, looking over our shoulders, was a statue of the crucified Savior, all bloody and beaten up. Charlene looked up and said, "Look at that poor Indian. The pigs sure worked him over." That was the closest I ever came to seeing Jesus.

18   I was held up as a bad example and didn't mind. I was old enough to have a boyfriend and promptly got one. At the school we had an hour and a half for ourselves. Between the boys' and the girls' wings were some benches where one could sit. My boyfriend and I used to go there just to hold hands and talk. The nuns were very uptight about any boy-girl stuff. They had an exaggerated fear of anything having even the faintest connection with sex. One day in religion class, an all-girl class, Sister Bernard singled me out for some remarks, pointing me out as a bad example, an example that should be shown. She said that I was too free with my body. That I was holding hands which meant that I was not a good example to follow. She also said that I wore

unchaste dresses, skirts which were too short, too suggestive, shorter than regulations permitted, and for that I would be punished. She dressed me down before the whole class, carrying on and on about my unchastity.

19   I stood up and told her, "You shouldn't say any of those things, miss. You people are a lot worse than us Indians. I know all about you, because my grandmother and my aunt told me about you. Maybe twelve, thirteen years ago you had a water stoppage here in St. Francis. No water could get through the pipes. There are water lines right under the mission, underground tunnels and passages where in my grandmother's time only the nuns and priests could go, which were off-limits to everybody else. When the water backed up they had to go through all the water lines and clean them out. And in those huge pipes they found the bodies of newborn babies. And they were white babies. They weren't Indian babies. At least when our girls have babies, they don't do away with them that way, like flushing them down the toilet, almost.

20   "And that priest they sent here from Holy Rosary in Pine Ridge because he molested a little girl. You couldn't think of anything better than dump him on us. All he does is watch young women and girls with that funny smile on his face. Why don't you point him out for an example?"

21   Charlene and I worked on the school newspaper. After all we had some practice. Every day we went down to Publications. One of the priests acted as the photographer, doing the enlarging and developing. He smelled of chemicals which had stained his hands yellow. One day he invited Charlene into the darkroom. He was going to teach her developing. She was developed already. She was a big girl compared to him, taller too. Charlene was nicely built, not fat, just rounded. No sharp edges anywhere. All of a sudden she rushed out of the darkroom, yelling to me, "Let's get out of here! He's trying to feel me up. That priest is nasty." So there was this too to contend with—sexual harassment. We complained to the student body. The nuns said we just had a dirty mind.

22   We got a new priest in English. During one of his first classes he asked one of the boys a certain question. The boy was shy. He spoke poor English, but he had the right answer. The priest told him, "You did not say it right. Correct yourself. Say it over again." The boy got flustered and stammered. He could hardly get out a word. But the priest kept after him: "Didn't you hear? I told you to do the whole thing over. Get it right this time." He kept on and on.

23   I stood up and said, "Father, don't be doing that. If you go into an Indian's home and try to talk Indian, they might laugh at you and say, 'Do it over correctly. Get it right this time!'"

24   He shouted at me, "Mary, you stay after class. Sit down right now!"

25   I stayed after class, until after the bell. He told me, "Get over here!"

26   He grabbed me by the arm, pushing me against the blackboard, shouting, "Why are you always mocking us? You have no reason to do this."

27   I said, "Sure I do. You were making fun of him. You embarrassed him. He needs strengthening, not weakening. You hurt him. I did not hurt you."

28   He twisted my arm and pushed real hard. I turned around and hit him in the face, giving him a bloody nose. After that I ran out of the room, slamming the door behind me. He and I went to Sister Bernard's office. I told her, "Today I quit school. I'm not taking any more of this, none of this shit anymore. None of this treatment. Better give me my diploma. I can't waste any more time on you people."

29   Sister Bernard looked at me for a long, long time. She said, "All right, Mary Ellen, go home today. Come back in a few days and get your diploma." And that was that. Oddly enough, that priest turned out okay. He taught a class in grammar, orthography, composition, things like that. I think he wanted more respect in class. He was still young and unsure of himself. But I was in there too long. I didn't feel like hearing it. Later he became a good friend of the Indians, a personal friend of myself and my husband. He stood up for us during Wounded Knee and after. He stood up to his superiors, stuck his neck way out, became a real people's priest. He even learned our language. He died prematurely of cancer. It is not only the good Indians who die young, but the good whites, too. It is the timid ones who know how to take care of themselves who grow old. I am still grateful to that priest for what he did for us later and for the quarrel he picked with me—or did I pick it with him?—because it ended a situation which had become unendurable for me. The day of my fight with him was my last day in school.

✧ Evaluating the Text

1. What aspects of life at the government boarding school most clearly illustrate the government's desire to transform Native Americans? How did Mary Crow Dog react to the experiences to which she was subjected at the government-run school?

2. What historical insight did the experiences of Mary Crow Dog's mother and grandmother provide into those of Mary Crow Dog herself?

3. Why was the incident of the underground newspaper a crucial one for Mary Crow Dog?

✦ Exploring Different Perspectives

1. How do both Crow Dog's account and Mahdokht Kashkuli's story dramatize the effects of being raised by the state?

2. In what sense are Native Americans comparable to the untouchables or outcasts as described by Viramma?

✦ Extending Viewpoints through Writing and Research

1. What experiences have you had that made you aware of institutionalized racism?

2. How did this essay give you insight into the vast difference between the traditional culture of Native Americans and their lives in the present?

Kate Chopin

Désirée's Baby

—————◆—————

Kate Chopin (1851–1904) was born Katherine O'Flaherty, the daughter of a successful St. Louis businessman and his French Creole wife. After her father died in 1855, Kate was raised by her mother and great-grandmother. When she was nineteen, she married Oscar Chopin and accompanied him to New Orleans where he established himself as a cotton broker. After his business failed, they moved to his family plantation in Louisiana where he opened a general store. After his sudden death in 1883, Chopin managed the plantation for a year, but then decided to return to St. Louis with her six children. She began to submit stories patterned on the realistic fiction of Guy de Maupassant to local papers and national magazines, including the Saturday Evening Post *and* Atlantic Monthly. *Her stories of Creole life were widely praised for their realistic delineation of Creole manners and customs and were later collected in* Bayou Folk *(1894) and* A Night in Acadie *(1897). Her novel* The Awakening *(1899), although widely praised as a masterpiece for its frank depiction of its heroine's sexual awakening and need for self-fulfillment, created a public controversy. Chopin's uncompromising delineation of the pressures of class and race in Louisiana at the time are clearly seen in the poignant story "Désirée's Baby" (1899).*

Before You Read

Consider the extent to which the character of Désirée serves as a vehicle for the expression of Chopin's views on race and class.

—————◆—————

1   As the day was pleasant, Madame Valmondé drove over to L'Abri to see Désirée and the baby.

2   It made her laugh to think of Désirée with a baby. Why, it seems but yesterday that Désirée was little more than a baby herself; when Monsieur in riding through the gateway of Valmondé had found her lying asleep in the shadow of the big stone pillar.

3   The little one awoke in his arms and began to cry for "Dada." That was as much as she could do or say. Some people thought she might have strayed there of her own accord, for she was of the toddling age. The prevailing belief was that she had been purposely left by a party of Texans, whose canvas-covered wagons, late in the day, had crossed the ferry that Coton Maïs kept, just below the plantation. In time

Madame Valmondé abandoned every speculation but the one that Désirée had been sent to her by a beneficent Providence to be the child of her affection, seeing that she was without child of the flesh. For the girl grew to be beautiful and gentle, affectionate and sincere—the idol of Valmondé.

4   It was no wonder, when she stood one day against the stone pillar in whose shadow she had lain asleep, eighteen years before, that Armand Aubigny riding by and seeing her there, had fallen in love with her. That was the way all the Aubignys fell in love, as if struck by a pistol shot. The wonder was that he had not loved her before; for he had known her since his father brought him home from Paris, a boy of eight, after his mother died there. The passion that awoke in him that day, when he saw her at the gate, swept along like an avalanche, or like a prairie fire, or like anything that drives headlong over all obstacles.

5   Madame Valmondé bent her portly figure over Désirée and kissed her, holding her an instant tenderly in her arms. Then she turned to the child.

6   "This is not the baby!" she exclaimed, in startled tones. French was the language spoken at Valmondé in those days.

7   "I knew you would be astonished," laughed Désirée, "at the way he has grown. The little *cochon de lait!*[1] Look at his legs, mamma, and his hands and fingernails,—real fingernails. Zandrine had to cut them this morning. Isn't it true, Zandrine?"

8   The woman bowed her turbaned head majestically, "Mais si, Madame."

9   "And the way he cries," went on Désirée, "is deafening. Armand heard him the other day as far away as La Blanche's cabin."

10   Madame Valmondé had never removed her eyes from the child. She lifted it and walked with it over to the window that was lightest. She scanned the baby narrowly, then looked as searchingly at Zandrine, whose face was turned to gaze across the fields.

11   "Yes, the child has grown, has changed," said Madame Valmondé, slowly, as she replaced it beside its mother. "What does Armand say?"

12   Désirée's face became suffused with a glow that was happiness itself.

13   "Oh, Armand is the proudest father in the parish, I believe, chiefly because it is a boy, to bear his name; though he says not—that he would have loved a girl as well. But I know it isn't true. I know he says that to please me. And mamma," she added, drawing Madame Valmondé's head down to her, and speaking in a whisper, "he hasn't punished one of them—not one of them—since baby is born. Even Négrillon, who pretended to have burnt his leg that he might rest from work—he only laughed, and said Négrillon was a great scamp. Oh, mama, I'm so happy; it frightens me."

[1]*cochon de lait:* Literally "pig of milk"—a big feeder.

14   What Désirée said was true. Marriage, and later the birth of his son, had softened Armand Aubigny's imperious and exacting nature greatly. This was what made the gentle Désirée so happy, for she loved him desperately. When he frowned she trembled, but loved him. When he smiled, she asked no greater blessing of God. But Armand's dark, handsome face had not often been disfigured by frowns since the day he fell in love with her.

15   When the baby was about three months old, Désirée awoke one day to the conviction that there was something in the air menacing her peace. It was at first too subtle to grasp. It had only been a disquieting suggestion; an air of mystery among the blacks; unexpected visits from far-off neighbors who could hardly account for their coming. Then a strange, an awful change in her husband's manner, which she dared not ask him to explain. When he spoke to her, it was with averted eyes, from which the old love light seemed to have gone out. He absented himself from home; and when there, avoided her presence and that of her child, without excuse. And the very spirit of Satan seemed suddenly to take hold of him in his dealings with the slaves. Désirée was miserable enough to die.

16   She sat in her room, one hot afternoon, in her *peignoir*, listlessly drawing through her fingers the strands of her long, silky brown hair that hung about her shoulders. The baby, half naked, lay asleep upon her own great mahogany bed, that was like a sumptuous throne, with its satin-lined half canopy. One of La Blanche's little quadroon boys—half naked too—stood fanning the child slowly with a fan of peacock feathers. Désirée's eyes had been fixed absently and sadly upon the baby, while she was striving to penetrate the threatening mist that she felt closing about her. She looked from her child to the boy who stood beside him; and back again, over and over. "Ah!" It was a cry that she could not help, which she was not conscious of having uttered. The blood turned like ice in her veins, and a clammy moisture gathered upon her face.

17   She tried to speak to the little quadroon boy; but no sound would come, at first. When he heard his name uttered, he looked up, and his mistress was pointing to the door. He laid aside the great, soft fan, and obediently stole away, over the polished floor, on his bare tiptoes.

18   She stayed motionless, with gaze riveted upon her child, and her face the picture of fright.

19   Presently her husband entered the room, and without noticing her, went to a table and began to search among some papers which covered it.

20   "Armand," she called to him, in a voice which must have stabbed him, if he was human. But he did not notice. "Armand," she said again. Then she rose and tottered towards him. "Armand," she panted once more, clutching his arm, "look at our child. What does it mean? Tell me."

21   He coldly but gently loosened her fingers from about his arm and thrust the hand away from him. "Tell me what it means!" she cried despairingly.

22   "It means," he answered lightly, "that the child is not white; it means that you are not white."

23   A quick conception of all that this accusation meant for her nerved her with unwonted courage to deny it. "It is a lie; it is not true, I am white! Look at my hair, it is brown; and my eyes are gray, Armand, you know they are gray. And my skin is fair," seizing his wrist. "Look at my hand, whiter than yours, Armand," she laughed hysterically.

24   "As white as La Blanche's," he returned cruelly, and went away leaving her alone with their child.

25   When she could hold a pen in her hand, she sent a despairing letter to Madame Valmondé.

26   "My mother, they tell me I am not white. Armand has told me I am not white. For God's sake tell them it is not true. You must know it is not true. I shall die. I must die. I cannot be so unhappy, and live."

27   The answer that came was as brief:

28   "My own Désirée: Come home to Valmondé; back to your mother who loves you. Come with your child."

29   When the letter reached Désirée she went with it to her husband's study, and laid it open upon the desk before which he sat. She was like a stone image: silent, white, motionless after she placed it there.

30   In silence he ran his cold eyes over the written words. He said nothing. "Shall I go, Armand?" she asked in tones sharp with agonized suspense.

31   "Yes, go."

32   "Do you want me to go?"

33   "Yes, I want you to go."

34   He thought Almighty God had dealt cruelly and unjustly with him; and felt, somehow, that he was paying Him back in kind when he stabbed thus into his wife's soul. Moreover he no longer loved her, because of the unconscious injury she had brought upon his home and his name.

35   She turned away like one stunned by a blow, and walked slowly towards the door, hoping he would call her back.

36   "Good-by, Armand," she moaned.

37   He did not answer her. That was his last blow at fate.

38   Désirée went in search of her child. Zandrine was pacing the sombre gallery with it. She took the little one from the nurse's arms with no word of explanation, and descending the steps, walked away, under the live-oak branches.

39   It was an October afternoon; the sun was just sinking. Out in the still fields the Negroes were picking cotton.

40   Désirée had not changed the thin white garment nor the slippers which she wore. Her hair was uncovered and the sun's rays brought a golden gleam from its brown meshes. She did not take the broad, beaten road which led to the far-off plantation of Valmondé. She walked across a deserted field, where the stubble bruised her tender feet, so delicately shod, and tore her thin gown to shreds.

41   She disappeared among the reeds and willows that grew thick along the banks of the deep, sluggish bayou; and she did not come back again.

42   Some weeks later there was a curious scene enacted at L'Abri. In the centre of the smoothly swept back yard was a great bonfire. Armand Aubigny sat in the wide hallway that commanded a view of the spectacle; and it was he who dealt out to a half dozen negroes the material which kept this fire ablaze.

43   A graceful cradle of willow, with all its dainty furbishings, was laid upon the pyre, which had already been fed with the richness of a priceless *layette*. Then there were silk gowns, and velvet and satin ones added to these; laces, too, and embroideries; bonnets and gloves; for the *corbeille*[2] had been of rare quality.

44   The last thing to go was a tiny bundle of letters; innocent little scribblings that Désirée had sent to him during the days of their espousal. There was the remnant of one back in the drawer from which he took them. But it was not Désirée's; it was part of an old letter from his mother to his father. He read it. She was thanking God for the blessing of her husband's love:

45   "But, above all," she wrote, "night and day, I thank the good God for having so arranged our lives that our dear Armand will never know that his mother, who adores him, belongs to the race that is cursed with the brand of slavery."

✦ Evaluating the Text

1. What can you infer about Armand's character and his past behavior from the fact that he has not punished one slave since his baby was born? How does his behavior toward Désirée change after the baby is three months old? What causes this change in his behavior?

2. What did you assume Désirée would do when she realizes Armand values his social standing more than he does her? In retrospect, what clues would have pointed you toward the truth disclosed at the end of the story?

[2]*Corbeille:* a basket of linens, clothing, and accessories collected in anticipation of a baby's birth.

✧ *Exploring Different Perspectives*

1. How does race serve the same function in Chopin's story as caste does in India (see Viramma, "A Pariah's Life")?

2. How is success in Chopin's time defined in terms of whiteness as compared with the different criteria that prevail in modern-day America and France as discussed by Raymonde Carroll?

✧ *Extending Viewpoints through Writing and Research*

1. In a short essay, discuss the picture you formed of the society in which Chopin's story took place (late 1800s in Louisiana) and the extent to which race and class determined people's behavior.

2. At the end of the story, we discover that Armand is of mixed racial parentage and assume that Désirée is white. How would the impact of the story change if we also knew that Désirée was of a mixed racial background as well as Armand?

3. For an analysis of Kate Chopin's life and works consult http://www.empirezine.com/spotlight/chopin/chopin1.htm.

Richard Rodriguez

On Becoming a Chicano

———◆———

Richard Rodriguez was born in 1944 in San Francisco. After receiving his master's degree from Columbia in 1969, Rodriguez pursued his graduate studies at both the University of California at Berkeley and the Warburg Institute in London (1972–1973). Rodriguez was on a Fulbright fellowship in London, studying English Renaissance Literature, when he decided to leave the world of academic studies. His autobiography, Hunger of Memory: The Education of Richard Rodriguez *(1982), received the Christopher award. His latest work is* Brown: the Last Discovery of America *(2002). The following essay analyzes the predicament often encountered by those who acquire a new language and culture at the expense of the traditional culture in which they were raised. "On Becoming a Chicano" is Rodriguez's uncommonly sensitive account of how he found himself between two worlds, at home in neither.*

Before You Read

Consider whether getting a higher education automatically distances one from their roots.

———◆———

1   Today I am only technically the person I once felt myself to be—a Mexican-American, a Chicano. Partly because I had no way of comprehending my racial identity except in this technical sense, I gave up long ago the cultural consequences of being a Chicano.

2   The change came gradually but early. When I was beginning grade school, I noted to myself the fact that the classroom environment was so different in its styles and assumptions from my own family environment that survival would essentially entail a choice between both worlds. When I became a student, I was literally "remade"; neither I nor my teachers considered anything I had known before as relevant. I had to forget most of what my culture had provided, because to remember it was a disadvantage. The past and its cultural values became detachable, like a piece of clothing grown heavy on a warm day and finally put away.

3   Strangely, the discovery that I have been inattentive to my cultural past has arisen because others—student colleagues and faculty members—have started to assume that I am a Chicano. The ease with which the assumption is made forces me to suspect that the label is not meant

to suggest cultural, but racial, identity. Nonetheless, as a graduate student and a prospective university faculty member, I am routinely expected to assume intellectual leadership *as a member of a racial minority.* Recently, for example, I heard the moderator of a panel discussion introduce me as "Richard Rodriguez, a Chicano intellectual." I wanted to correct the speaker—because I felt guilty representing a non-academic cultural tradition that I had willingly abandoned. So I can only guess what it would have meant to have retained my culture as I entered the classroom, what it would mean for me to be today a "Chicano intellectual." (The two words juxtaposed excite me; for years I thought a Chicano had to decide between being one or the other.)

4   Does the fact that I barely spoke any English until I was nine, or that as a child I felt a surge of self-hatred whenever a passing teenager would yell a racial slur, or that I saw my skin darken each summer—do any of these facts shape the ideas which I have or am capable of having? Today, I suspect they do—in ways I doubt the moderator who referred to me as a "Chicano intellectual" intended. The peculiar status of being a "Chicano intellectual" makes me grow restless at the thought that I have lost at least as much as I have gained through education.

5   I remember when, 20 years ago, two grammar-school nuns visited my childhood home. They had come to suggest—with more tact than was necessary, because my parents accepted without question the church's authority—that we make a greater effort to speak as much English around the house as possible. The nuns realized that my brothers and I led solitary lives largely because we were barely able to comprehend English in a school where we were the only Spanish-speaking students. My mother and father complied as best they could. Heroically, they gave up speaking to us in Spanish—the language that formed so much of the family's sense of intimacy in an alien world—and began to speak a broken English. Instead of Spanish sounds, I began hearing sounds that were new, harder, less friendly. More important, I was encouraged to respond in English.

6   The change in language was the most dramatic and obvious indication that I would become very much like the "gringo"—a term which was used descriptively rather than pejoratively in my home—and unlike the Spanish-speaking relatives who largely constituted my preschool world. Gradually, Spanish became a sound freighted with only a kind of sentimental significance, like the sound of the bedroom clock I listened to in my aunt's house when I spent the night. Just as gradually, English became the language I came not to *hear* because it was the language I used every day, as I gained access to a new, larger society. But the memory of Spanish persisted as a reminder of the society I had left. I can remember occasions when I entered a room and my parents were speaking to one another in Spanish; seeing me, they shifted into their more formalized English. Hearing them speak to me

in English troubled me. The bonds their voices once secured were loosened by the new tongue.

7   This is not to suggest that I was being *forced* to give up my Chicano past. After the initial awkwardness of transition, I committed myself, fully and freely, to the culture of the classroom. Soon what I was learning in school was so antithetical to what my parents knew and did that I was careful about the way I talked about myself at the evening dinner table. Occasionally, there were moments of childish cruelty: a son's condescending to instruct either one of his parents about a "simple" point of English pronunciation or grammar.

8   Social scientists often remark, about situations such as mine, that children feel a sense of loss as they move away from their working-class identifications and models. Certainly, what I experienced, others have also—whatever their race. Like other generations of, say, Polish-American or Irish-American children coming home from college, I was to know the silence that ensues so quickly after the quick exchange of news and the dwindling of common interests.

9   In addition, however, education seemed to mean not only a gradual dissolving of familial and class ties but also a change of racial identity. The new language I spoke was only the most obvious reason for my associating the classroom with "gringo" society. The society I knew as Chicano was barely literate—in English *or* Spanish—and so impatient with either prolonged reflection or abstraction that I found the academic environment a sharp contrast. Sharpening the contrast was the stereotype of the Mexican as a mental inferior. (The fear of this stereotype has been so deep that only recently have I been willing to listen to those, like D. H. Lawrence, who celebrate the "non-cerebral" Mexican as an alternative to the rational and scientific European man.) Because I did not know how to distinguish the healthy non-rationality of Chicano culture from the mental incompetency of which Chicanos were unjustly accused, I was willing to abandon my non-mental skills in order to disprove the racist's stereotype.

10   I was wise enough not to feel proud of the person education had helped me to become. I knew that education had led me to repudiate my race. I was frequently labeled a *pocho*, a Mexican with gringo pretentions, not only because I could not speak Spanish but also because I would respond in English with precise and careful sentences. Uncles would laugh good-naturedly, but I detected scorn in their voices. For my grandmother, the least assimilated of my relations, the changes in her grandson since entering school were expecially troubling. She remains today a dark and silently critical figure in my memory, a reminder of the Mexican-Indian ancestry that somehow my educational success has violated.

11   Nonetheless, I became more comfortable reading or writing careful prose than talking to a kitchen filled with listeners, withdrawing from situations to reflect on their significance rather than grasping for

meaning at the scene. I remember, one August evening, slipping away from a gathering of aunts and uncles in the backyard, going into a bedroom tenderly lighted by a late sun, and opening a novel about life in nineteenth-century England. There, by an open window, reading, I was barely conscious of the sounds of laughter outside.

12   With so few fellow Chicanos in the university, I had no chance to develop an alternative consciousness. When I spent occasional weekends tutoring lower-class Chicano teenagers or when I talked with Mexican-American janitors and maids around the campus, there was a kind of sympathy—a sense, however privately held—that we knew something about one another. But I regarded them all primarily as people from my past. The maids reminded me of my aunts (similarly employed); the students I tutored reminded me of my cousins (who also spoke English with barrio accents).

13   When I was young, I was taught to refer to my ancestry as Mexican-American. *Chicano* was a word used among friends or relatives. It implied a familiarity based on shared experience. Spoken casually, the term easily became an insult. In 1968 the word *Chicano* was about to become a political term. I heard it shouted into microphones as Third World groups agitated for increased student and faculty representation in higher education. It was not long before I *became* a Chicano in the eyes of students and faculty members. My racial identity was assumed for only the simplest reasons: my skin color and last name.

14   On occasion I was asked to account for my interests in Renaissance English literature. When I explained them, declaring a need for cultural assimilation, on the campus, my listener would disagree. I sensed suspicion on the part of a number of my fellow minority students. When I could not imitate Spanish pronunciations or the dialect of the barrio, when I was plainly uninterested in wearing ethnic costumes and could not master a special handshake that minority students often used with one another, they knew I was different. And I was. I was assimilated into the culture of a graduate department of English. As a result, I watched how in less than five years nearly every minority graduate student I knew dropped out of school, largely for cultural reasons. Often they didn't understand the value of analyzing literature in professional jargon, which others around them readily adopted. Nor did they move as readily to lofty heights of abstraction. They became easily depressed by the seeming uselessness of the talk they heard around them. "It's not for real," I still hear a minority student murmur to herself and perhaps to me, shaking her head slowly, as we sat together in a class listening to a discussion on punctuation in a Renaissance epic.

15   I survived—thanks to the accommodation I had made long before. In fact, I prospered, partly as a result of the political movement designed to increase the enrollment of minority students less assimilated

than I in higher education. Suddenly grants, fellowships, and teaching offers became abundant.

16   In 1972 I went to England on a Fulbright scholarship. I hoped the months of brooding about racial identity were behind me. I wanted to concentrate on my dissertation, which the distractions of an American campus had not permitted. But the freedom I anticipated did not last for long. Barely a month after I had begun working regularly in the reading room of the British Museum, I was surprised, and even frightened, to have to acknowledge that I was not at ease living the rarefied life of the academic. With my pile of research file cards growing taller, the mass of secondary materials and opinions was making it harder for me to say anything original about my subject. Every sentence I wrote, every thought I had, became so loaded with qualifications and footnotes that it said very little. My scholarship became little more than an exercise in caution. I had an accompanying suspicion that whatever I did manage to write and call my dissertation would be of little use. Opening books so dusty that they must not have been used in decades, I began to doubt the value of writing what only a few people would read.

17   Obviously, I was going through the fairly typical crisis of the American graduate student. But with one difference: After four years of involvement with questions of racial identity, I now saw my problems as a scholar in the context of the cultural issues that had been raised by my racial situation. So much of what my work in the British Museum lacked, my parents' culture possessed. They were people not afraid to generalize or to find insights in their generalities. More important, they had the capacity to make passionate statements, something I was beginning to doubt my dissertation would ever allow me to do. I needed to learn how to trust the use of "I" in my writing the way they trusted its use in their speech. Thus developed a persistent yearning for the very Chicano culture that I had abandoned as useless.

18   Feelings of depression came occasionally but forcefully. Some days I found my work so oppressive that I had to leave the reading room and stroll through the museum. One afternoon, appropriately enough, I found myself in an upstairs gallery containing Mayan and Aztec sculptures. Even there the sudden yearning for a Chicano past seemed available to me only as nostalgia. One morning, as I was reading a book about Puritan autobiography, I overheard two Spaniards whispering to one another. I did not hear what they said, but I did hear the sound of their Spanish—and it embraced me, filling my mind with swirling images of a past long abandoned.

19   I returned from England, disheartened, a few months later. My dissertation was coming along well, but I did not know whether I wanted to submit it. Worse, I did not know whether I wanted a career in higher education. I detested the prospect of spending the rest of my life in

libraries and classrooms, in touch with my past only through the binoculars nostalgia makes available. I knew that I could not simply recreate a version of what I would have been like had I not become an academic. There was no possibility of going back. But if the culture of my birth was to survive, it would have to animate my academic work. That was the lesson of the British Museum.

20   I frankly do not know how my academic autobiography will end. Sometimes I think I will have to leave the campus, in order to reconcile my past and present. Other times, more optimistically, I think that a kind of negative reconciliation is already in progress, that I can make creative use of my sense of loss. For instance, with my sense of the cleavage between past and present, I can, as a literary critic, identify issues in Renaissance pastoral—a literature which records the feelings of the courtly when confronted by the alternatives of rural and rustic life. And perhaps I can speak with unusual feeling about the price we must pay, or have paid, as a rational society for confessing seventeenth-century Cartesian faiths. Likewise, because of my sense of cultural loss, I may be able to identify more readily than another the ways in which language has meaning simply as sound and what the printed word can and cannot give us. At the very least, I can point up the academy's tendency to ignore the cultures beyond its own horizons.

February 1974

21   On my job interview the department chairman has been listening to an oral version of what I have just written. I tell him he should be very clear about the fact that I am not, at the moment, confident enough to call myself a Chicano. Perhaps I never will be. But as I say all this, I look at the interviewer. He smiles softly. Has he heard what I have been trying to say? I wonder. I repeat: I have lost the ability to bring my past into my present; I do not know how to be a Chicano reader of Spenser or Shakespeare. All that remains is a desire for the past. He sighs, preoccupied, looking at my records. Would I be interested in teaching a course on the Mexican novel in translation? Do I understand that part of my duties would require that I become a counselor of minority students? What was the subject of that dissertation I did in England? Have I read the book on the same subject that was just published this month?

22   Behind the questioner, a figure forms in my imagination: my grandmother, her face solemn and still.

✧ Evaluating the Text

1. What qualities did Rodriguez feel he lost by moving from the open and confident Mexican-American culture of his childhood into the cloistered, self-critical atmosphere of the academic world?

2. How does the title, "On Becoming a Chicano," aptly express the point that Rodriguez had to consciously recover values he had discarded?

✧ Exploring Different Perspectives

1. In what way are both Rodriguez and Itabari Njeri seeking to find their authentic ethnic identities?

2. How is education for both Rodriguez and Mary Crow Dog, as she describes it in "Civilize Them with a Stick," an alienating experience because of being marginalized American citizens?

3. Why are the episodes concerning Rodriguez's grandmother central to understanding his sense of guilt over losing the values he learned in childhood?

✧ Extending Viewpoints through Writing and Research

1. Are any of Rodriguez's observations appropriate to describe your own experiences in attending college?

2. Write an essay discussing the advantages and disadvantages of bilingualism using either a point-by-point or subject-by-subject method of organization.

3. Richard Rodriguez's latest observations on Chicano identity are available at http://www.library.ca.gov/LDS/convo/convoc21 .html.

Raymonde Carroll

Sex, Money, and Success

◆

Why is bragging about sexual conquests as much a status symbol for the French as boasting about business success is for Americans? Raymonde Carroll has investigated this question and provides some surprising answers. Born in Tunisia, Carroll was educated in France and the United States. She was trained as an anthropologist and studied the culture of Micronesia while living for three years on the Pacific atoll Nukuoro. She presently teaches in the Department of Romance Languages at Oberlin College. This selection is drawn from her book, Cultural Misunderstandings: The French-American Experience *(translated by Carol Volk, 1988).*

Before You Read

Notice how Carroll integrates the speaking voices of both the French and the Americans into her analysis. Consider why sexual conquests and money are two time-honored indicators by which people measure personal success.

◆

1   Money. For a French person, the face of an American could easily be replaced by a dollar sign. A sign of "incurable materialism," of arrogance, of power, of "vulgar," unrefined pleasure . . . the list goes on. I have never read a book about Americans, including those written with sympathy, which did not speak of the "almighty dollar"; I have never had or heard a conversation about Americans which did not mention money.

2   Foreigners often discover with "horror" or "repulsion" that "everything in the United States is a matter of money." Indeed, one need only read the newspapers to find constant references to the price of things. Thus, a fire is not a news item but an entity (natural or criminal), the dimensions of which are calculated by what it has destroyed—for example, ". . . a house worth two hundred *thousand* dollars . . ." In fact, if it is at all possible to attach a price to something, as approximate as it may be, that price will surely be mentioned. Thus, a French woman became indignant toward her American brother-in-law: "He showed us the engagement ring he had just bought, and he just had to give us all the details about the deal he got in buying the diamond. . . . Talk about romantic!" I cannot even count the number of informants who had sim-

ilar stories to tell ("I was admiring the magnificent antique pieces in his living room, and do you know what he did? He gave me the price of each piece, with all kinds of details I hadn't asked for. I felt truly uncomfortable . . . really . . ."). Many French informants claimed to be shocked by the "constant showing off," the "lack of taste typical of nouveaux riches" and added, some not in so many words, "As for me, you know, I am truly repulsed by money."

3   On the other side, many Americans expressed surprise at the frequency with which French people spoke about money, only to say that "they weren't interested in it" ("so why talk about it?"), or at the frequency with which they say "it's too expensive" about all types of things. Some find the French to be "cheap" ("They always let you pay") or "hypocritical" ("Why, then, do the French sell arms to just anyone?"), too respectful of money to trifle with it, or too petty to take risks. The list of adjectives hurled from either side on this topic seems particularly long.

4   Yet a brief examination of certain ethnographic details left me puzzled. For instance, what is the American article, about the forest fire that destroyed the row of two-hundred-thousand-dollar homes in California, really saying? Living in the United States, I know that a house worth two hundred thousand dollars in California is far from a palace; on the contrary. Thus, if I took the price quoted literally, I would misinterpret the article as meaning that the fire had destroyed a row of quite ordinary houses—in which case the mention of the "price" is uninformative, uninteresting, and useless. Therefore, what this article conveys, by talking about hundreds of thousands of dollars, is the fact that the fire destroyed very valuable homes. This meaning is also conveyed by the use of the word "homes," which connotes individuality and uniqueness, rather than "houses," which suggests plain buildings. The mention of the price, therefore, carries meaning of a different nature: I think that this "price" serves only as a common point of reference; it does not represent the true monetary values but a symbolic value which can be grasped immediately by anyone reading this article. A French equivalent would be a reference to the period ("from the seventeenth century") with no mention of the state of the building.

5   Similarly, it is difficult to take the example of the engagement ring literally ("I'm a tightwad"; "I'm not romantic"); it is more comprehensible if we interpret it as a message with a different meaning. For the American in question, having obtained a discount in no way altered the true value of the diamond or the symbolic value of the gesture; this "feat" probably made the gesture even more significant because of the time and attention devoted to it (the worst gift is the one that demands no effort) and probably earned him the admiration and appreciation of his fiancée.

6   The study of cases in which money is mentioned would require an entire book. . . . I will content myself merely with raising the question here and will indicate the general orientation of my interpretation.

7   The striking thing is that money is charged with a multiplicity of meanings in American culture, that it has attained a level of abstraction difficult to imagine elsewhere. Money represents both good and bad, dependence and independence, idealism and materialism, and the list of opposites can go on indefinitely, depending on whom one speaks to. It is power, it is weakness, seduction, oppression, liberation, a pure gamble, a high-risk sport; a sign of intelligence, a sign of love, a sign of scorn; able to be tamed, more dangerous than fire; it brings people together, it separates them, it is constructive, it is destructive; it is reassuring, it is anxiety-producing; it is enchanting, dazzling, frightening; it accumulates slowly or comes in a windfall; it is displayed, it is invisible; it is solid, it evaporates. It is everything and nothing, it is sheer magic, it exists and does not exist at the same time; it is a mystery. The subject provokes hatred, scorn, or impassioned defense from Americans themselves, who are constantly questioning themselves on the topic.

8   I believe that one association remains incontestable, no matter how much resentment it provokes. Money symbolizes success. It is not enough to have money to be admired, but quite the contrary; there is no excuse for the playboy who squanders an inherited fortune. To earn money, a lot of money, and to spend it, is to give the most concrete, the most visible sign that one has been able to realize one's potential, that one has not wasted the "opportunities" offered by one's parents or by society, and that one always seeks to move on, not to stagnate, to take up the challenge presented in the premises shaping the education of children. . . .

9   As a result, money has become a common denominator. It is supposed to be accessible to all, independent of one's origins. And if it creates classes, it also allows free access to those classes to whoever wants to enter. (Let's not forget that we are talking here about "local verities," about cultural premises, and not about social realities.) Money is therefore the great equalizer, in the sense that the highest social class is, in principle, open to everyone, and that while those who are born into this social class have definite advantages, they must nonetheless deserve to remain there, must "prove themselves." And the newspapers are filled with enough stories of poor people turned millionaires to reinforce this conviction.

10   From this perspective, it is understandable that one does not hide one's success but displays it, shows it off. By making my humble origins known, by displaying my success, I am not trying to humiliate others (although it is possible that I, personally, am a real "stinker"), but I am showing others that it is possible, I am encouraging emulation through example, I am reaffirming a cultural truth: "if I can do it, you can do it."

Hence the constant copresence of dreams and success, that is to say, the constant reaffirmation that the impossible is possible, and that attaining the dream depends solely on me. The logical, and ironic, conclusion to all this is the essentially idealistic significance of money in American culture, which does not exclude its "materialistic" utilization.

11   I do not believe that the misunderstanding between the French and Americans concerning money can be resolved by performing a parallel analysis of the meaning of money in French culture, not because money is not a concern for the French, but because I believe that what Americans express through money is expressed by the French in another domain.

12   From this brief analysis, I will reiterate three points. The first is that money in America serves as a common point of reference, a shortcut for communication, a means of defining a context that is recognizable by all and comprehensible no matter what one's financial situation may be. The second is that it is not in bad taste to recount one's triumphs, one's success in this domain, whether it is a matter of having obtained a half-price diamond or of having accumulated a veritable fortune, insofar as this in no way implies that I wish to put down others, that I am conceited, and so on, characteristics which depend not on money but on my personality. And the third is that money is accessible to all, makes possible upward mobility, that is to say, access to any class.

13   To the extent that these three points I just made are not "true" for French culture—and that they might in fact provoke "real repulsion"—one must look in a realm other than that of money for what carries the same message. . . .

14   The repulsion with which many French people react to the "bad taste" of Americans who "brag about their wealth," "show off their money," and so on closely resembles the disgust with which many Americans speak of the "bad taste," the "vulgarity" of French people who "brag about their sexual exploits," "are proud of their sexual successes," which is a subject reserved by Americans for the "uncivilized" world of locker rooms, for the special and forced intimacy of these dressing rooms for athletes. (Although the expression "locker-room talk" traditionally evokes male conversation, it is just as applicable today to female locker-room talk.) The repugnance on the part of "tasteful" Americans to speak in public about their successes with men or women or their sexual "conquests" is interpreted, among the French, as additional proof of American "puritanism," whereas the French "modesty" concerning public conversations about money would tend to be interpreted by Americans as a type of French "puritanism."

15   This reciprocal accusation of "bad taste" led me to wonder if what was true for financial successes and conquests in American culture was not true for seduction, for amorous conquests, for sexual successes in French culture.

16   While it is not looked on favorably, in France, to show off one's money or titles, one may speak of one's amorous conquests without shocking anyone (unless one does it to belittle others with one's superiority, to insult them, etc., in which case it is not the subject that is important but the manner in which a particular person makes use of it). We have, in France, a great deal of indulgence and admiration for the "irresistible" man or woman, for "charmers" large and small of both cases. Seduction is an art which is learned and perfected.

17   Like money for Americans, amorous seduction is charged with a multiplicity of contradictory meanings for the French, depending on the person to whom one is speaking and the moment one raises the topic. Nonetheless, if a (French) newspaper article defines a particular person as *séduisante*, the term does not refer to indisputable characteristics but to a category recognizable by all, to a common point of reference, to a comprehensible descriptive shortcut. (It is interesting to note that the American translation of *séduisante* would be "attractive," a word which, as opposed to the French, evokes identifiable and predictable characteristics. The word *seductive*—not an adequate translation—evokes manipulation and the negative connotations attached to taking advantage of naiveté.)

18   Seduction, as I have said, is an art for the French. It is not enough to be handsome or beautiful to seduce; a certain intelligence and expertise are necessary, which can only be acquired through a long apprenticeship, even if this apprenticeship begins in the most tender infancy. (Thus, an ad for baby clothing, a double spread in the French version of the magazine *Parents*, shows the perfect outfit for the "heartbreak girl" and for the "playboy"; this is an indication of the extent to which this quality is desirable, since I assume the ad is geared toward the parents who provide for and teach these babies, and not toward the babies themselves.) It is therefore "normal" for me to be proud of my successes, for me to continually take up the challenge of new conquests, for me never to rest on my laurels, for me not to waste my talent. It is therefore not in "bad taste" to talk about it (bad taste and seduction are, in a sense, mutually exclusive in French). What is more, I can "freely" share my secrets and my "reflections" on the subject of men or women—a topic I have thoroughly mastered.

19   Like money for Americans, seduction for the French may be the only true class equalizer. In fact, one of the greatest powers of amorous seduction is precisely the fact that it permits the transgression of class divisions. The French myths of the "kept woman," of the attractiveness of the *midinette* (a big-city shopgirl or office clerk, who is supposed to be very sentimental), of the seductive powers of "P'tit Louis" (a "hunk," a good dancer, from the working class), and the innumerable seducers of both sexes in French novels, songs, and films are sufficient proof.

20   The interest of a parallel such as the one I have just established is that it shows how astonishingly similar meanings can be expressed in areas which seem to be completely unrelated. Yet the greatest attraction of cultural analysis, for me, is the possibility of replacing a dull exchange of invectives with an exploration that is, at the very least, fascinating—a true feast to which I hereby invite you.

✧ Evaluating the Text

1. What culturally based misunderstandings do the French and Americans have about each other in terms of money and sex?

2. How is the approach Carroll takes that of an anthropologist who is interested in why success is measured in such different ways in France and the United States?

3. The playboy (womanizer) in France is regarded very differently from his American counterpart. What differences in cultural values between the two countries explain this perception?

✧ Exploring Different Perspectives

1. What different forms does social mobility take in Carroll's acount and in Richard Rodriguez's narrative, "On Becoming a Chicano"?

2. Are race and ethnicity the primary markers of social class in Carroll's essay and in Itabari Njeri's account? Why or why not?

✧ Extending Viewpoints through Writing and Research

1. Write a short essay in which you support or challenge Carroll's claim by exploring the way in which the subjects of money and sex are treated in a range of magazines. In what ways do magazines devoted to money (such as *Money* and *Forbes*) focus on business success in the same way that magazines devoted to sex (such as *Playboy*) commodify seduction?

2. Carroll asserts that seduction in France and money in America signify social mobility. Write a short rebuttal to Carroll's argument in which you give equal importance to race and ethnicity as indicators of social class.

3. Resources for studying French culture can be found at http://www.gofrance.about.com/od/culture/.

Mahdokht Kashkuli

The Button

◆

Mahdokht Kashkuli was born in 1950 in Teheran, Iran. She was married at age fourteen and, unlike similar marriages, hers did not prevent her from pursuing an education. She succeeded in obtaining her bachelor of arts in performing literature from Teheran University. By 1982 she had completed two master's degrees, one in library science and one in linguistics, and a doctorate in the language, culture, and religion of ancient Iran from the same university. She started her career first as a researcher for Iranian Educational Television from 1975 to 1985 and then as a professor of performing literature at Teheran University. Her short stories, including "The Fable of Rain in Iran," "The Fable of Creation in Iran," "Our Customs, Our Share," "The Pearl and the Moon," and "Tears and Water," have won her national recognition. "The Button," translated by Soraya Sullivan, was first published in the summer of 1978 in the periodical Arash. *This short story explores the heartbreaking consequences of a family's poverty in contemporary Iran.*

Before You Read

Observe the clues as to the harsh economic circumstances of this poverty-stricken family in Iran and the extent to which Kashkuli is critical of religious fatalism.

◆

1   My sister was perched in the doorway, sobbing bitterly; her curly, russet hair was stuck to her sweaty forehead. My mother was doing her wash by the pond, paying no attention to my sister's sobs or my father's shouts, "Hurry up Reza! Move it!" I was holding on to the edge of the mantle shelf tightly, wishing that my hand would remain glued there permanently. It was only a few nights ago that I had heard, with my own ears, my father's voice whispering to my mother, "Woman, stop grumbling! God knows that my heart is aching too, but we don't have a choice. I can't even provide them with bread. What else can I do? This way, we'll have one less mouth to feed." I had cocked my ears to hear who that "one less mouth to feed" was. I remained frozen, holding my breath for a few minutes; then I heard my father say, "Reza is the naughtiest of all; the most restless. Akbar and Asghar are more tame, and we can't send the girls away. It's not wise." Suddenly a dry

cough erupted from my mouth. My father called out, "Reza! Reza! Are you awake?" I did not answer him. He fell silent, and then my mother's snorts followed the awkward silence. My father went on, "Woman, who said the orphanage is a bad place? They teach the kids, they feed them, they clothe them. At least this one will have a chance to live a good life." My mother's snorts stopped. She groaned, "I don't know. I don't know anything. Just do what you think is best." And then there was silence.

2   Why are they going to make me the "one less mouth to feed"? What is an orphanage? I wish I hadn't nibbled the bread on my way home from the bakery; I wish I hadn't quarreled with Asghar; I wish I hadn't messed around with my mother's yarn, as if it were a ball; I wish I hadn't pulled the bottle out of Kobra's mouth, and drunk her milk; I wish I could stay still, like the mannequin in the clothing store at the corner. Then they wouldn't make me the "one less mouth to feed." My pillow was soaked with tears.

3   I ran outside with puffy eyes the next morning. Ahmad was standing at the other end of the alley, keeping watch for Husain so he could pick a fight with him. I yelled, "Ahmad, Ahmad! What's an orphanage?" Keeping his eyes still on the door to Husain's house, Ahmad said, "It's a place where they put up poor people's children." "Have you been there?" I asked. He shouted indignantly, "Listen to this goddamn wretch! You can't be nice to anyone these days!" I ran back to the house, scared. If Ahmad hadn't been waiting for Husain, he surely would have beaten me up.

4   My father's screams shot up again, "Are you deaf? Hurry up, it's late!" I released my grip on the shelf and went down the stairs. The saltiness of my tears burned my face. My father said, "What's wrong? Why are you crying? Come, my boy! Come wash your face!" Then he took my hand and led me to the pond and splashed a handful of the murky water on my face. He wiped my face with his coat lining. I became uneasy. My father seldom showed signs of affection; I suspected that he was being affectionate because he had decided to make me the "one less mouth to feed." We walked towards the door. He pulled aside the old cotton rug hanging before the door with his bony hands. Then he said, in a tone as if he were talking to himself, "One thousand . . . God knows, I had to pull a thousand strings before they agreed to admit you."

5   I asked, while I kept my head down, "Why?" My father screamed angrily, "He asks why again! Because!" I lowered my head. My eyes met his shoes. They were strangely crooked and worn out; maybe he had them on wrong. . . . The lower part of his long underwear showed from beneath his pants. He was wearing a belt to hold his loose pants up, and they creased like my mother's skirt. "I'm telling you, Reza, a

thousand strings," he repeated. "You must behave when you get there." I didn't look at him but said grudgingly, "I don't want to behave!"

6   He threw a darting glance at me and raved, his hand rising to cuff me on the back of the neck but he changed his mind and said instead, "They'll teach you how to behave yourself." Indignantly I said, "I don't want to go to an orphanage, and if you take me there, I'll run away." I pulled my hand out of his quickly and ran ahead, knowing that he'd hit me this time. But he didn't. He only said, "You think they admit everyone? I've been running around for a year, resorting to everyone I know." I said, "Dad, I don't want to go to the orphanage. They keep poor children there." "What do you think you are, rich?" my father said. "Listen to him use words bigger than his mouth!" And he broke out laughing. When he laughed I saw his gold teeth. There were two of them. I thought to myself, "What does it take to be rich? My father has gold teeth, my mother has gold teeth, and my brother has a fountain pen." I looked at his face. He wasn't laughing anymore; his face had turned gray. I said spontaneously, "Dad, is the landlord rich?" He didn't hear me, or it seemed he didn't, and said absentmindedly, "What?" I said, "Nothing."

7   I thought about the landlord. He sends his oldest son or his young daughter to collect the rent two weeks before the rent is due. His oldest son enters my father's shop and stands in the front of the mirror, scrutinizing himself, resting one hand on his waist. My father rushes to him and says, "Do you want a haircut?" The landlord's son responds, "No. You just gave me one on Thursday." My father says politely, "What can I do for you, then?" The landlord's son says, "Is the rent ready?" My father answers, "Give me a few more days. Tell Haji Agha I'll pay before the due date." And the next day his young daughter shows up in the shop. She is so small that she can hardly see herself in the mirror. She holds her veil tightly under her chin with those tiny, delicate hands, and says, "Hello!" My father smiles and says, "Hello, cutie pie! What can I do for you?" The girl laughs cheerfully and says, "My father sent me after the rent. If it's ready, give it to me." My father picks a sugar cube out of the sugar bowl, puts it gently in her palm, and says, "Tell Haji Agha, fine!"

8   We reached the intersection. My father held my hand in his tightly and stopped to look around. We then crossed the street. He was mumbling to himself, "The damn thing is so far away. . . ."

9   I felt sick. I said, "Wait a minute!" He eyed me curiously and said, "Why, what's wrong?" I said, "I'm tired; I don't want to go to the orphanage." He mimicked me, pursing his lips, and said, "You don't understand! You were always dumb, dense!"

10   I remembered that my father was always unhappy with me, although I swept the shop every day and watered the China roses he had planted in front of the shop. I would take my shirt off on hot summer

afternoons and jump in the brook with my underpants. The elastic of my pants was always loose and I always tried to tie it into a knot, never succeeding to make it tight enough to stay. In the brook, I held my pants with one hand while I watered the China roses with a small bowl. It felt nice and cool there. Flies would gather around my shoulders and arms. Grandmother used to say, "God made flies out of wax." But I didn't understand why they didn't melt in the hot sun; they flew off my body and landed on the China rose flowers and I shook the branches with my bowl to disperse them. The flowers were my father's and no fly was allowed to sit on them. In spite of all my efforts, my father was always unhappy with me; he was unhappy with my mother, with my sisters and brothers, with the landlord, and with the neighbors. But he was happy with one person: God. He would sigh, tap himself hard on the forehead, and say, "Thank God!"

11   I said to him one day, "Why are you thanking God, Dad?" Suddenly, he hit me in the mouth with the back of his hand. My upper lip swelled and my mouth tasted bloody. I was used to the taste of blood because whenever I bled in the nose, I tasted blood in my mouth. I covered my mouth, walked to the garden and spat in the dirt. I looked at the bubbles on my spittle, tapped myself on the forehead and said, "Thank God!" Then I picked up a piece of watermelon skin lying on the brook and smacked it on the head of a yellow dog that always used to nap by the electric post. The yellow dog only opened its eyes, looked at me indifferently, and shut its eyes again, thanking God, perhaps.

12   We passed another street before we got to the bus station. A few people were waiting in line; one of them was sitting at the edge of the brook. My father took my hand and led me to the front of the bus line. Someone said, "This is not the end of the line, old man!" I only looked at my father.

13   He said to me, "Ignore him. Just stay right here!" The bus came and my father pushed me towards it. I tore my feet off the ground and jumped on the coach-stop, feeling as if I were floating in the air. Someone said, "Old man, the end of the line is on the other side! Look how people give you a headache on a Monday morning!" My father didn't hear him; he pushed me forward. I was stuck between a seat and the handle bar. . . . So, today is Monday. . . . Every week on Monday my mother does her wash. The clothesline spread around the entire yard. I liked the smell of damp clothes. In spite of my mother's curses, I liked cupping my hands underneath the dripping clothes so that the water that dripped could tickle my palms. Every Monday we had yogurt soup for lunch. My brother and I would take a bowl to the neighborhood dairy store to buy yogurt. On the way back, we took turns licking the surface of the yogurt. When we handed the bowl to my mother, she would scream at us and beat the first one of us she could get her hands on. . . . I felt depressed. I wished I could jump out the window.

14   The bus stopped at a station and we got off. My father walked ahead of me while I dragged my feet along behind him.

15   He waited for me to catch up, then he said, "Move it! He walks like a corpse. Hurry up, it's late!" I stopped momentarily and said, "Dad, I don't want to go. I don't want to go to the orphanage." My father froze in his spot. He said incredulously, "What did you say? You think you know what's good for you? Don't you want to become a decent human being some day? They have rooms, there. They have food, and they'll teach you everything you need to learn to get a decent job." I sobbed, "To hell with anyone who has a decent job. To hell with decent jobs. I don't want one! I like staying home. I like playing with Asghar and Akbar. I want to sell roasted corn with the kids from the neighborhood in the summer. I want to help you out in the shop. I don't want to go."

16   My father sprang towards me, but suddenly retreated and became affectionate. He said, "Let's go, good boy! We're almost there." I felt sorry for him because every time he was kind he looked miserable. My father was walking ahead of me and I was following him, dragging my feet on the street like that yellow dog. On the next street, we stopped in front of a big metal door. A chair was placed inside the door to keep it ajar. A man was sitting on the chair, playing with a ring of prayer beads. He had on a navy blue coat with metal buttons. His eyes were half-closed and his mouth was open. His cheeks were puffy, as if he had a toothache. My father greeted him and said, "Mr. Guard!" The man opened his eyes. Strands of blood ran through the white of his eyes. He said with a gloomy voice, "What is it, what do you want?" My father thrust his hand in both his pockets, took out an envelope and extended it toward the guard with both hands. The man looked at my father, then threw a threatening glance at me. He yawned, stared at the envelope for a while (I didn't believe he could read), shook his head, coughed, and said, "They won't leave you alone; one leaves, another comes!" Then he pushed the door with the tip of his shoes. The door opened just enough to let me in.

17   After my father walked through the doorway behind me, the guard gave him the envelope and said, "The first door!" My father was walking fast, and when he opened the hallway door, my heart started beating violently and I started to cry. He said, "My boy, my sweet Reza, this is a nice place. The people here are nice, the kids are all your own age. . . ."

18   He didn't finish his sentence. He pushed on the door. The door opened and I saw a woman inside the room. I wished she were my mother, but she was heavier than my mother, with a deep vertical wrinkle between her eyebrows. She wore a blue uniform and her hair was a bleached blonde.

19   My father pushed me further in and said, "Greet her, Reza! Greet her!" I didn't feel like greeting anyone.

20   My father handed the woman the envelope. She opened it, pulled the letter out halfway, and started reading it. Then she turned to my father and said, "Go to the office so they can complete his file."

21   My father leaped and ran out the door. Then, as though he had remembered something, he returned and stood in front of the door, rubbing his hand on the wood frame of the door. He raised one hand to tap on his forehead and say, "Thank God," but stopped, rubbed his forehead gently and sighed. His eyes were as moist and shiny as the eyes of the yellow dog hanging around his shop. Her head still lowered on the letter, the woman said, "Go, old man! What are you waiting for? Go to the office!" Father took a few steps backwards, then tore himself from the door and disappeared into the corridor.

22   The woman looked at me, then turned her gaze toward the window and fixed it there. While she had her back to me, she said, "Don't cry, boy! Please don't, I'm not in the mood!" Then she turned around and put her hands on my shoulders. Her hands were as heavy as my mother's but not as warm. She took my hand and walked me toward the door. We passed one corridor, and entered another. Then we entered a room, then another corridor and another room. There were a few people in the room. One was sitting in the doorway, whistling; one was leaning against the desk; one was sitting in a chair writing something. Although the room was furnished with chairs and desks, it was not warm. The woman said, "Say hello to these people!" I looked at her but didn't say anything. I didn't feel like talking to them. I didn't hear what they said to each other, either. I only wanted to sit still and look at them. We left that room and went into another. There was another woman there. I wished she were my mother. She was wearing a blue uniform and had a red scarf around her neck. I think she had a cold because she sniffled constantly. As soon as she saw me, she checked me out thoroughly and spoke with a nasal voice, "Is he new here? I don't know where we're going to put him." She then opened a closet, took out a uniform and said to me, "Take your jacket off and wear this!" Then she continued, "Take your shirt off, too. How long has it been since your last shower?" I didn't answer. Her words hit my ears and bounced right off. She went toward the closet again and asked, "Are you done?" I looked around and then looked at myself, my eyes becoming fixed on my jacket. It had only one button. The button had belonged to my mother's jacket before she used it to replace my missing button. The woman's voice went on, "Quit stalling, boy! Hurry up, I have tons of work to do!"

23   I put my hand on the button and pulled it out, then hid it in my palm. The woman said, "Are you done?" I said, "Yes!"

24   I thrust the button in my uniform pocket and wiped my tears with the back of my hand.

✧ *Evaluating the Text*

1. Of what imagined crimes does the narrator accuse himself that might explain why he is the one to be sent to an orphanage instead of one of his three siblings?

2. How would you characterize the boy's relationship with his father? In your view, what has caused the father to choose him to be the one out of his four children to be sent to an orphanage?

3. How does Reza's attitude toward the button reveal his feelings and emotions?

✧ *Exploring Different Perspectives*

1. In what ways do the stories by Kashkuli and Kate Chopin (Désirée's Baby") focus on children who come to be seen as liabilities?

2. What parallels can you discover between the circumstances that led Mary Crow Dog to be placed in a government-run school and those of the little boy in Kashkuli's story?

✧ *Extending Viewpoints through Writing and Research*

1. What insight does this story provide into the prevailing economic and social conditions in modern Iranian society?

2. Write about one of your grandparents or parents through an object you connect with him or her. Under what circumstances did you first come across this object? What associations connect this object with your parent or grandparent?

Viramma

A Pariah's Life

◆

Viramma is an agricultural worker and midwife in Karani, a village in southeast India. She is a member of the caste known as Untouchables. She has told her life story over a period of ten years to Josiane and Jean-Luc Racine. She communicates an impression of great strength and fatalism (of her twelve children, only three survive) and her account, translated by Will Hobson, which first appeared in GRANTA, Spring 1997, is a vivid portrait of one at the margin of society.

Before You Read

Consider the unusual superstitions and rituals by which Viramma lives her life and her status as an Untouchable in Indian society.

◆

1   I am the midwife here. I was born in the village of Velpakkam in Tamil Nadu, and when I married, I came to Karani, my husband's village. I was still a child then. I am a farm worker and, like all my family, I am a serf, bonded to Karani's richest landowner. We are Pariahs. We live apart from the other castes; we eat beef, we play the drums at funerals and weddings because only we can touch cow hide; we work the land. My son Anbin corrects me when I say "Pariah"; he says we should use the word "Harijan."[1] Every day people from the political parties come to the village and tell us to demand higher wages, to fight the caste system. And they mean well. But how would we survive? We have no land, not even a field.

2   We midwives help women during labour and are paid twenty rupees a month by the state. When a woman goes into labour, her relatives come and find me: "Eldest sister-in-law! The woman's in pain at home!" So I drop everything; I go and see her, examine her, turn her round one way, then the other; I pester her a bit and then tell her more or less when the child is going to be born. And it always turns out as I said it would. When the child is born, I cut the cord with a knife and tell one of the other women attending to find a hoe and a crowbar and to dig a hole in the channel near the house. I wait for the placenta to

---

[1]*Harijan* means "loved ones of God." The name change was suggested by Mahatma Gandhi.

come out and go and bury it immediately. Then I take care of the mother. I stretch her out on a mat, propped up with pillows, wash the baby with soap and hot water and lay it down next to its mother. Then I put a sickle and some margosa leaves at the head of the mat, so spirits don't come near them—those rogue spirits love to prowl around the lanes in the evening or at night, eating any food left lying on the ground and trying to possess people.

3   It's well known that they follow us everywhere we go, when we're hoeing or planting out; when we're changing our sanitary towels; when we're washing our hair. They sense that we're going to visit a woman in labour and then they possess us. That's why we put down the sickle and the margosa leaves. After the birth I'll visit the mother quite often, to make sure everything's going all right. If impurities have stayed in the womb, I'll cook the leaves of the "cow's itch" plant, extract the juice and make the mother drink it three times.

4   That's how a birth happens here. We Pariahs prefer to have babies at home. I tell the nurse if the newborns are boys or girls, and she goes and enters them in the registers at Pondicherry hospital. In the past, we'd take women to hospital only in emergencies. We went there in an ox-cart or a rickshaw, and often the woman died on the way. Nowadays doctors visit the villages and give medicines and tonics to women when they become pregnant. In the sixth or seventh month they're meant to go to the dispensary for a check-up. A nurse also comes to the village. Yes, everything has changed now.

5   I had my twelve children alone; I didn't let anyone near me. "Leave me in peace," I always said to the nurses. "It will come out on its own! Why do you want to rummage around in there?" I always give birth very gently—like stroking a rose. It never lasts long: I'm not one of those women whose labours drag on all night, for days even.

6   When I'm giving birth I first make a point of preparing a tray for Ettiyan—the god of death's assistant—and his huge men, with their thick moustaches and muscly shoulders. On the tray I put green mangoes, coconuts and other fruit as well as some tools: a hoe, a crowbar, a basket, so that they can set to work as soon as the child comes out of the sack in our womb. Yes! I've seen enough to know what I'm talking about. I've had a full bushel of children! Everything we eat goes into that sack: that's how the child grows. Just think what a mystery it is. With the blood he collects over ten months, Isvaran [the god Siva] moulds a baby in our womb. Only he can do that. Otherwise how could a sperm become a child?

7   I've always had plenty of milk. It used to flow so much that the front of my sari was all stiff. It's well known that we breastfeed our children for a long time. That prevents us from having another child immediately. If we were always pregnant, how could we work and eat? Rich women can stretch their legs and take a rest. But to get my rice, I have

to work: planting out, hoeing, grazing the cows, collecting wood. When we've got a little one in our arms, it's the same: we take it everywhere, and we worry, because while we're working we don't really know what it's doing, where it is. That's why we try to wait at least three years, until the child grows up, walks and can say, "Dad," "Mum," "That's our cow." That's what we take as a sign. Then we can start "talking" again, "doing it." If we time it like this, the child will be strong and chubby.

8   But Isvaran has given me a baby a year. Luckily my blood has stayed the same; it hasn't turned, and my children have never been really emaciated. Of course that also depends on the way you look after them. For me, that used to be my great worry! I managed to feed them well. As soon as I had a little money, I'd buy them sweets. I'd make them rice whenever I could, some *dosai,* some *idli.* I'd put a little sugar in cow's milk. . . . That's how I took care of them. There are some women who just let their children be without giving them regular meals. Human beings can only live if you put at least a little milk in their mouths when they're hungry! It happens with us that some women skip their children's mealtimes when they're working. But how do you expect them to grow that way?

9   Isvaran has done his work well; he's put plenty of children in my womb: beautiful children, born in perfect health. It's only afterwards that some have died. One of diarrhea, another of apoplexy. All of them have walked! Two of my children even came to the peanut harvest. I pierced their noses to put a jewel in. I plaited their hair and put flowers in it and pretty *potteu* on their foreheads, made with paste. I took good care of my little ones. I never neglected them. I dressed them neatly. If high-caste people saw them running in the street, they'd talk to them kindly, thinking that they were high-caste children.

10   How many children have I had? Wait . . . I've had twelve. The first was a girl, Muttamma. Then a boy, Ganesan. After that, a girl, Arayi. *Ayo!* After that I don't remember any more. But I've definitely had twelve: we registered them at the registry office. Yes, when there's a birth, you have to go there and declare it. "Here Sir, I've had a boy or a girl and I name it Manivelu, Nataraja or Perambata." Down there they enter all that into a big ledger. *Ayo!* If we went to that office, perhaps they could tell us how many children I've had and their names as well. *Ayo!* Look at that, I don't remember any more. They're born; they die. I haven't got all my children's names in my head: all I have left are Miniyamma, my fourth child; Anbin, my eighth; and Sundari, my eleventh.

11   A pregnant woman is prey to everything that roams around her: ghosts, ghouls, demons, the evil spirits of people who have committed suicide or died violent deaths. She has to be very careful, especially if she is a Pariah. We Pariah women have to go all over the place, grazing the cattle, collecting wood. We're outside the whole time, even

when the sun's at its height. Those spirits take advantage of this: they grab us and possess us so we fall ill, or have miscarriages. Something like that happened to me when I was pregnant with my second child.

12 One of my nephews died suddenly, the day after his engagement. One night when I was asleep I saw him sitting on me—I felt him! My husband told me that I had squeezed him very tight in my arms, that I'd been delirious and mumbling something. The following day we decided that the boy needed something, and that's why he'd come. My husband went to get bottles of arrack and palm wine. I arranged the offerings in the middle of the house: betel, areca nuts, lime, a big banana leaf with a mountain of rice, some salt fish, some toast, a cigar, bottles of alcohol, a jar of water and a beautiful oil lamp. In the meantime my husband went to find the priest from the temple of Perumal [Vishnu]— he's the one responsible for funerals. The priest asked us to spread river sand next to the offerings. He called on Yama, the god of death, and drew the sign of Yama in the sand. We ate that evening as usual and went to sleep in a corner. You must never sleep opposite the door, because a spirit might slap you when it comes in if it finds you in its way. You have to be brave when a spirit arrives! In fact you won't see it; you only hear its footsteps, like the sound of little bells, *djang, djang,* when an ox-cart goes by. It goes *han! han! han!* as if it's craving something. It always comes with its messengers, all tied to each other with big ropes. You hear them walking with rhythmic, heavy steps: *ahum! ahum! ahum!*

13 We were very afraid. As soon as the spirit came in, the lamp went out in a flash, even though it was full of oil. We heard it walking about and eating its fill and then suddenly it fled. We heard it running away very fast. When day broke soon after it had gone, we rushed to see what had happened. The rice was scattered, everywhere. On the sand we found a cat's paw-print, and part of Yama's sign had been rubbed out. The spirit had come in the form of a cat! While we were waiting for the priest to come, we collected the offerings in a big wicker basket. The priest himself was very satisfied and said that the spirit wouldn't come back. But I fell ill soon after and had a miscarriage.

14 There are worse spirits, though: the *katteri,* for example, who spy on women when they are pregnant. You have to be very careful with them. There are several sorts of *katteri:* Rana Katteri, who has bleeding wounds and drinks blood; or Irsi Katteri, the foetus eater—she's the one who causes miscarriages. As soon as she catches the smell of a foetus in a woman's womb, she's there, spying, waiting for her chance. We can tell immediately that it's that bitch at work if there are black clots when a baby aborts: she sucks up the good blood and leaves only the bad.

15 My first three children were born at my mother's house. Their births went well, and they died in good shape. It was the spirit living in that house who devoured them. My grandfather knew about sor-

cery. People came to see him; they used to say that he called up the spirit, talked to it and asked it to go along with him when he went out. It lived with him, basically. When my grandfather died, we tried to drive it away but it was no use; it used to come back in the form of my grandfather; it joined in conversations, calling my grandmother by her name like her dead husband used to. And my grandmother used to answer back, "Ah! The only answer I'll give you is with my broom, you dog! I recognize you! I know who you are! Get out of here!" It would just throw tamarind seeds at her face. When a sorcerer came from Ossur to try and get rid of it, it turned vicious. The sorcerer told us he couldn't do anything against it. The spirit had taken root in that ground. It was old and cunning: we were the ones who had to go. It destroyed everything! Everything! A garlic clove couldn't even grow! My father had to sell his paddy field. I gave birth three times there: none of those children survived. The spirit ate them as and when they were born. Nothing prospered. That's how it is with the spirits.

16   All my children have been buried where they died: the first ones at Velpakkam, the others at Karani. My mother insisted we burn the first-born and throw her ashes in the river so a sorcerer didn't come and get them. The ashes or bones of first-borns are coveted by magicians. A tiny bit of ash or hair is enough for them. You see them with a hoe on their shoulder prowling around where a first-born has been burnt or buried. We made sure that everything disappeared. We have a saying that if you dissolve the ashes completely in water, you'll immediately have another child.

17   Until they grow up, we mothers always have a fire in our belly for our children: we must feed them, keep them from sickness, raise them to become men or women who can work. One of my three sisters died of a kind of tuberculosis. She had been married and she left a son. I brought him up after her death, but like his mother, he was often ill. Before she died, my sister had prayed that he would become strong, so I took up her prayers. I went into three houses and in each one I asked for a cubit of fabric. I put the three bits of fabric on the ground and laid the child on them. Then I went into three other houses and exchanged the child for three measures of barley, saying, "The child is yours; the barley is mine." Of course afterwards I would get the child back. Then I went to three other houses to collect handfuls of dirt. I mixed the three handfuls, spread them out and rolled the baby in them, saying, "Your name will be Kuppa! You are Kuppa! You have been born of dirt!" Then I pierced his nostril with a silver thread which I twisted into a ring. That worked very well for him! He's still alive and he still wears that ring in his nose today.

18   What is more important for us women than children? If we don't draw anything out of our womb, what's the use of being a woman?

A woman who has no son to put a handful of rice in her mouth, no daughter to close her eyes, is an unhappy woman. She or her parents must have failed in their dharma. I have been blessed in that way: Isvaran has filled my womb. Ah, if all my children were alive, they'd do all the trades in the world! One would be a labourer, another a carpenter. I would have made one of them study. We could have given two daughters away in marriage and enjoyed our grandchildren. I would be able to go and rest for a month with each of my sons. Yes, we would have been proud of our children.

✧ Evaluating the Text

1. In what specific ways does the caste into which Viramma was born determine every aspect of her life?

2. Folk beliefs and superstitions play a very important role in Viramma's world. What are some of these and how does her belief in them provide an explanation for the things that have happened to her?

3. From a Western perspective, Viramma's attitude toward childbearing is unusual. However, she earns her living as a midwife and has become reconciled to the death of most of her own children. What cultural values unique to India does she embody?

✧ Exploring Different Perspectives

1. Would Viramma have ever considered placing one of her children in an orphanage as did the parents in Mahdokht Kashkuli's story, "The Button"? Why or why not?

2. Compare Viramma's acceptance of the caste structure in India to Mary Crow Dog's rebellion in "Civilize Them With a Stick."

✧ Extending Viewpoints through Writing and Research

1. Have you ever known anyone whose explanation for events was rooted in superstition? What were the events and what were the superstitions that explained them?

2. What is your own attitude toward having large families? Do you think people should have as many children as they want? Why or why not? As a research project, you might investigate the one-child policy in China.

3. For information on the caste known as Untouchables, see http://www.dalits.org/default.htm.

*How does this image suggest the marginal life of the
"untouchables" that Viramma describes?*

Connecting Cultures

◆

Martin Luther King Jr., "I Have a Dream"

Examine the issues discussed by Gayle Pemberton (see "Antidisestablishmentarianism" in Chapter 1) in the context of King's epochal speech.

Itabari Njeri, "What's in a Name?"

How does the issue of achieving self-worth in a white society underlie Njeri's analysis and Gayle Pemberton's account in "Antidisestablishmentarianism" in Chapter 1?

Mary Crow Dog and Richard Erdoes, "Civilize Them with a Stick"

What parallels can you discover in the way race-based propaganda is used in education in the accounts of Crow Dog and Ngũgĩ wa Thiong'o (see "Decolonising the Mind" in Chapter 7)?

Kate Chopin, "Désirée's Baby"

Contrast Chopin's depiction of Désirée in the nineteenth century with Judith Ortiz Cofer's reaction (see "The Myth of the Latin Woman" in Chapter 3) to sexual and racial stereotyping in today's world.

Richard Rodriguez, "On Becoming a Chicano"

How do the issues of class and empowerment among Mexican Americans enter into Rodriguez's account and Gloria Anzaldúa's story "Cervicide" in Chapter 7?

Raymonde Carroll, "Sex, Money, and Success"

Although Carroll depicts Americans as being obsessed by achieving monetary success, how does Catherine Lim's story "Paper" (Chapter 4) reveal the same theme in Singapore?

Mahdokht Kashkuli, "The Button"

How does the "button" in Kashkuli's story and the "Persian carpet" in Hanan Al-Shaykh's story (Chapter 2) symbolize the emotional states of the children?

Viramma, "A Pariah's Life"

Compare the superstitions and cultural beliefs in Viramma's account with those described by Gino Del Guercio in "The Secrets of Haiti's Living Dead" in Chapter 7.

6

Social and Political Issues

Two things only the people anxiously desire, Bread and the Circus games.

—Juvenal (A.D. 60–140), Roman satirical poet, *Satire* X. 77–80

◆

The landscape of our society is dominated by contemporary concerns that are touched on by essays in this chapter. For example, Philip Slater, in "Want-Creation Fuels Americans' Addictiveness," investigates whether the national predisposition to "quick fixes" is the cause of the rising trend in drug use. Jeremy Rifkin, in "Big, Bad Beef," sees our addiction to beef as an environmental threat and Eric Schlosser, in "Kid Kustomers," reveals how corporations get an early start in building brand loyalty.

In the political sphere, no conflicts between different points of view are more dramatic than those between individuals and the governments to which they relinquish a certain degree of freedom in exchange for the benefits that can be achieved only through collective political and social institutions, such as the military and the legal, health care, and educational systems. The allegiance individuals owe their governments (and the protection of individual rights citizens expect in return) has been the subject of intense analysis through the ages by such figures as Socrates in Plato's *Apology* and *Crito*, Henry David Thoreau in *Civil Disobedience*, and Martin Luther King Jr. in his letters and speeches. The readings that follow continue this debate. Through accounts drawn from many different societies we view assumptions that are very different, in some cases, from those that characterize our own form of government.

The Chilean author, Luis Sepulveda, in "Daisy," displays an unusual ironic detachment in his account of having to cope with the literary pretensions of his prison guard. Stephen Chapman, in "The

Prisoner's Dilemma" examines how practices of punishment in Eastern cultures differ from those in the West.

Based on a real incident in Cyprus, Panos Ioannides's story, "Gregory," explores the question of conscience during wartime. With unusual honesty, Rae Yang, in "At the Center of the Storm," tells how she and the other Red Guards tyrannized school teachers and others who had been authority figures before Mao Tse Tung's Cultural Revolution.

Philip Slater

Want-Creation Fuels Americans' Addictiveness

————◆————

Philip Slater (b. 1927) was a professor of sociology at Harvard and is author of The Pursuit of Loneliness *(1970) and* Wealth-Addiction *(1980). Slater argues that the premium Americans put on success causes many people to resort to drugs to feel better about themselves and to cope with feelings of inadequacy. Slater cites a broad range of examples from everyday life to demonstrate that advertisers exploit societal pressures in order to sell products. The following article first appeared in the* St. Paul Pioneer Press Dispatch *(September 6, 1984). His latest book is* The Temporary Society *(revised edition with Warren G. Bennis, 1998).*

Before You Read

Consider the extent to which a "quick fix" mentality could be responsible for the prevalence of addictions in America.

————◆————

1   Imagine what life in America would be like today if the surgeon general convinced Congress that cigarettes, as America's most lethal drug, should be made illegal.

2   The cost of tobacco would increase 5,000 percent. Law enforcement budgets would quadruple but still be hopelessly inadequate to the task. The tobacco industry would become mob-controlled, and large quantities of Turkish tobacco would be smuggled into the country through New York and Miami.

3   Politicians would get themselves elected by inveighing against tobacco abuse. Some would argue shrewdly that the best enforcement strategy was to go after the growers and advertisers—making it a capital offense to raise or sell tobacco. And a great many Americans would try smoking for the first time.

4   Americans are individualists. We like to express our opinions much more than we like to work together. Passing laws is one of the most popular pastimes, and enforcing them one of the least. We make laws like we make New Year's resolutions—the impulse often exhausted by giving voice to it. Who but Americans would have their food grown and harvested by people who were legally forbidden to be in the country?

5   We are a restless, inventive, dissatisfied people. We like novelty. We like to try new things. We may not want to change in any basic sense, any more than other people, but we like the illusion of movement.

6   We like anything that looks like a quick fix—a new law, a new road, a new pill. We like immediate solutions. We want the pain to stop, the dull mood to pass, the problem to go away. The quicker the action, the better we like it. We like confrontation better than negotiation, antibiotics better than slow healing, majority rule better than community consensus, demolition better than renovation.

7   When we want something we want it fast and we want it cheap. Obstacles and complications annoy us. We don't want to stop to think about side effects, the Big Picture, or how it's going to make things worse in the long run. We aren't too interested in the long run, as long as something brings more money, a promotion or a new status symbol in the short.

8   Our model for problem-solving is the 30-second TV commercial, in which change is produced instantaneously and there is always a happy ending. The side effects, the pollution, the wasting diseases, the slow poisoning—all these unhappy complications fall into the great void outside that 30-second frame.

9   Nothing fits this scenario better than drugs—legal and illegal. The same impatience that sees an environmental impact report as an annoying bit of red tape makes us highly susceptible to any substance that can make us feel better within minutes after ingesting it—whose immediate effects are more or less predictable and whose negative aspects are generally much slower to appear.

10   People take drugs everywhere, of course, and there is no sure way of knowing if the United States has more drug abusers than other countries. The term "abuse" itself is socially defined.

11   The typical suburban alcoholic of the '40s and '50s and the wealthy drunks glamorized in Hollywood movies of that period were not considered "drug abusers." Nor is the ex-heroin addict who has been weaned to a lifetime addiction to Methadone.

12   In the 19th century, morphine addicts (who were largely middle-aged, middle-class women) maintained their genteel but often heavy addictions quite legally, with the aid of the family doctor and local druggist. Morphine only became illegal when its use spread to young, poor, black males. (This transition created some embarrassment for political and medical commentators, who argued that a distinction had to be made between "drug addicts" and "dope fiends.")

13   Yet addiction can be defined in a way that overrides these biases. Anyone who cannot or will not let a day pass without ingesting a substance should be considered addicted to it, and by this definition Americans are certainly addiction-prone.

14   It would be hard to find a society in which so great a variety of different substances have been "abused" by so many different kinds of people. There are drugs for every group, philosophy and social class: marijuana and psychedelics for the '60s counter-culture, heroin for the hopeless of all periods, PCP for the angry and desperate, and cocaine for modern Yuppies and Yumpies.[1]

15   Drugs do, after all, have different effects, and people select the effects they want. At the lower end of the social scale people want a peaceful escape from a hopeless and depressing existence, and for this heroin is the drug of choice. Cocaine, on the other hand, with its energized euphoria and illusion of competence is particularly appealing to affluent achievers—those both obsessed and acquainted with success.

16   Addiction among the affluent seems paradoxical to outsiders. From the viewpoint of most people in the world an American man or woman making over $50,000 a year has everything a human being could dream of. Yet very few such people—even those with hundreds of millions of dollars—feel this way themselves. While they may not suffer the despair of the very poor, there seems to be a kind of frustration and hopelessness that seeps into all social strata in our society. The affluent may have acquired a great deal, but they seem not to have acquired what they wanted.

17   Most drugs—heroin, alcohol, cocaine, speed, tranquilizers, barbiturates—virtually all of them except the psychedelics and to some extent marijuana—have a numbing effect. We might then ask: Why do so many Americans need to numb themselves?

18   Life in modern society is admittedly harsh and confusing considering the pace for which our bodies were designed. Noise pollution alone might justify turning down our sensory volume: It's hard today even in a quiet suburb or rural setting to find respite from the harsh sound of "labor-saving" machines.

19   But it would be absurd to blame noise pollution for drug addiction. This rasping clamor that grates daily on our ears is only a symptom—one tangible consequence of our peculiar lifestyle. For each of us wants to be able to exert his or her will and control without having to negotiate with anyone else.

20   "I have a right to run my machine and do my work" even if it makes your rest impossible. "I have a right to hear my music" even if this makes it impossible to hear your music, or better yet, enjoy that most rare and precious of modern commodities: silence. "I have a right to make a profit" even if it means poisoning you, your children and your children's children. "I have a right to have a drink when I want to and drive my car when I want to" even if it means totaling your car and crippling your life.

[1]*Yumpies:* young, upper-middle-class professionals.

21   This intolerance of any constraint or obstacle makes our lives rich in conflict and aggravation. Each day we encounter the noise, distress and lethal fallout of the dilemmas we brushed aside so impatiently the day before. Each day the postponed problems multiply, proliferate, metastasize—but this only makes us more aggravated and impatient than we were before. And since we're unwilling to change our ways it becomes more and more necessary to anesthetize ourselves to the havoc we've wrought.

22   We don't like the thought of attuning ourselves to nature or to a group or community. We like to fantasize having control over our lives, and drugs seem to make this possible. With drugs you are not only master of your fate and captain of your soul, you are dictator of your body as well.

23   Unwilling to respond to its own needs and wants, you goad it into activity with caffeine in the morning and slow it down with alcohol at night. If the day goes poorly, a little cocaine will set it right, and if quiet relaxation and sensual enjoyment is called for, marijuana.

24   Cocaine or alcohol makes a party or a performance go well. Nothing is left to chance. The quality of experience is measured by how many drugs or drinks were consumed rather than by the experience itself. Most of us are unwilling to accept the fact that life has good days and bad days. We attempt—unsuccessfully but valiantly—to postpone all the bad days until that fateful moment when the body presents us with all our IOUs, tied up in a neat bundle called cancer, heart disease, cirrhosis or whatever.

25   Every great sage and spiritual leader throughout history has emphasized that happiness comes not from getting more but from learning to want less. Clearly this is a hard lesson for humans, since so few have learned it.

26   But in our society we spend billions each year creating want. Covetousness, discontent and greed are taught to our children, drummed into them—they are bombarded with it. Not only through advertising, but in the feverish emphasis on success, on winning at all costs, on being the center of attention through one kind of performance or another, on being the first at something—no matter how silly or stupid (*The Guinness Book of Records*). We are an addictive society.

27   Addiction is a state of wanting. It is a condition in which the individual feels he or she is incomplete, inadequate, lacking, not whole, and can only be made whole by the addition of something external.

28   This need not be a drug. It can be money, food, fame, sex, responsibility, power, good deeds, possessions, cleaning—the addictive impulse can attach itself to anything, real or symbolic. You're addicted to something whenever you feel it completes you—that you wouldn't be a whole person without it. When you try to make sure it's always there, that there's always a good supply on hand.

29   Most of us are a little proud of the supposed personality defects
that make addiction "necessary"—the "I can't . . . ," "I have to . . . ," "I
always . . . ," "I never . . ." But such "lacks" are all delusional. It's fun
to brag about not being able to live without something but it's just
pomposity. We are all human, and given water, a little food, and a little
warmth, we'll survive.

30   But it's very hard to hang onto this humanity when we're told
every day that we're ignorant, misguided, inadequate, incompetent
and undesirable and that we will emerge from this terrible condition
only if we eat or drink or buy something, at which point we'll magically and instantly feel better.

31   We may be smart enough not to believe the silly claims of the individual ad, but can we escape the underlying message on which all of
them agree? That you can only be made whole and healthy by buying
or ingesting something? Can we reasonably complain about the
amount of addiction in our society when we teach it every day?

32   A Caribbean worker once said, apropos of the increasing role of
Western products in the economy of his country: "Your corporations
are like mosquitoes. I don't so much mind their taking a little of my
blood, but why do they have to leave that nasty itch in its place?"

33   It seems futile to spend hundreds of billions of dollars trying to
intercept the flow of drugs—arresting and imprisoning those who
meet the demand for them, when we activate and nourish that demand every day. Until we get tired of encouraging the pursuit of illusory fixes and begin to celebrate and refine what we already are and
have, addictive substances will always proliferate faster than we can
control them.

✧ *Evaluating the Text*

1. In Slater's view, how is the quick fix mentality responsible for
   rampant drug use and addiction in the United States?

2. Consider the definition of addiction that Slater presents. Do you
   agree or disagree with the way he frames the debate? Why or why
   not?

✧ *Exploring Different Perspectives*

1. What symbolic cultural value does beef have, according to Jeremy
   Rifkin, that makes it part of the problem in an addictive culture
   described by Slater?

2. How does "want-creation" as defined by Slater now begin with the
   small children that Eric Schlosser discusses in "Kid Kustomers"?

✧ *Extending Viewpoints through Writing and Research*

1. What current ads set up hypothetically stressful situations and then push products as a quick and easy way to relieve the stress? Analyze a few of these ads.

2. To what extent have performance-enhancing drugs or steroids become an important component of sports? In your opinion, are athletes coerced into taking these drugs in order to remain competitive? Why or why not?

3. To evaluate Philip Slater's thesis in light of recent Super Bowl ads see http://www.adage.com/reports.cms.

Jeremy Rifkin

Big, Bad Beef

◆

Jeremy Rifkin is the head of the Foundation on Economic Trends, Washington, D.C. He has written extensively on the impact of scientific and technological changes on the economy, the workforce, society, and the environment. His recent books include The Age of Access *(2000),* The Hydrogen Economy *(2002), and* The European Dream *(2004). The following article was first published in the March 23, 1992 issue of the* New York Times.

Before You Read

Consider whether the consumption of beef has become excessive in the United States.

◆

1   In the U.S., beef is king. More than six billion hamburgers were sold last year at fast-food restaurants alone. The average American consumes the meat of seven 1,100-pound steers in a lifetime. Some 100,000 cows are slaughtered every 24 hours. In South America, the cattle population is approaching the human population. In Australia, cattle outnumber people.

2   Beef has been central to the American experience. Entrance into the beef culture was viewed by many immigrants as a rite of passage into the middle class. Commenting on the failure of European socialism to gain a foothold in America, Werner Sombart, the German economist, wrote, "On the shoals of roast beef and apple pie, all socialist utopias founder."

3   Now, the good life promised by the beef culture has metamorphosed into an environmental and social nightmare for the planet.

4   Cattle raising is a major factor in the destruction of remaining rain forests. Since 1960, more than a quarter of Central American forests have been razed to make cattle pastures. In South America, 38 percent of the Amazon forest cleared has been for ranching.

5   The impact of cattle extends well beyond rain forests. According to a 1991 report for the UN, as much as 85 percent of rangeland in the Western U.S. is being destroyed, largely by overgrazing. Nearly half the water used each year in the U.S. goes to grow feed for cattle and other livestock. A 1992 study by the California Department of Water Resources reported that more than 1,200 gallons of water are required to produce an eight-ounce boneless steak in California.

6   Cattle raising is even a significant factor in global warming. The burning of tropical forests to clear land for pasture releases millions of tons of carbon dioxide into the atmosphere each year. In addition, it is estimated that the earth's 1.28 billion cattle and other cud-chewing animals are responsible for 12 percent of the methane emitted into the atmosphere.

7   The beef addiction of the U.S. and other industrialized nations has also contributed to the global food crisis. Cattle and other livestock consume more than 70 percent of the grain produced in the U.S. and about a third of the world's total grain harvest—while nearly a billion people suffer from chronic under-nutrition. If the U.S. land now used to grow livestock feed were converted to grow grain for human consumption, we could feed an additional 400 million people.

8   Despite the grim facts, the government continues to pursue policies that support cattle production and beef consumption. For example, at the same time the Surgeon General is warning Americans to reduce their consumption of saturated fat, the Agriculture Department's Beef Promotion and Research Board is trying to persuade Americans to eat more beef. This year, the board is expected to spend $45 million on advertising.

9   Equally troubling is the government's grading system to measure the value of beef. Established in 1927, the system grades beef on its fat content: the higher the fat "marbling," the better the beef. By favoring fat over lean beef, the Agriculture Department has helped promote greater amounts of saturated fat in the American diet and, in so doing, has contributed to rising health care costs.

10   Finally, the government has been virtually subsidizing Western cattle ranchers, providing them with cheap access to millions of acres of public land. Today, 30,000 ranchers in 11 Western states pay less than $1.92 a month per cow for the right to graze cattle on nearly 300 million acres of public land.

11   In 1986, the Reagan Administration estimated the market value for pasturing cattle on the same grasslands to be between $6.40 and $9.50 a month. This giveaway program has resulted in land erosion and the destruction of native habitats and wildlife.

12   The government's antiquated cattle and beef policies must be overhauled. The Agriculture Department needs to shift its priorities from promoting beef consumption to promoting a more balanced diet. Last year, the agency tried to do this by recommending a new "eating right" pyramid, which emphasized vegetables, fruit and grains. The effort was abandoned under pressure from the meat industry. The department's grading system should also be restructured, with new classifications that elevate the status of leaner cuts of beef.

13   In addition, Congress must pass legislation to insure that ranchers pay the market value for leased public lands. It should also reduce the

public acreage available to ranchers, to help restore the Western grass-lands and preserve the native wildlife and habitat.

14   If we reduce our beef consumption by at least 50 percent, we can help restore the global environment, free up arable land to grow food for hungry people, protect our own health and reduce the suffering of cattle and other animals.

✧ Evaluating the Text

1. What purpose is served by Rifkin's statement that "entrance into the beef culture was viewed by many immigrants as a rite of pas-sage into the middle class"? By stating it in this way, does Rifkin hope to distance his audience from a value that once was appro-priate but is now outdated?

2. How compelling do you find the evidence that Rifkin advances to support his contention that beef eating has become "an environ-mental and social nightmare for the planet"? Is the evidence ade-quate to support such a far-reaching claim?

✧ Exploring Different Perspectives

1. How are the essays by Rifkin and Philip Slater constructed as causal arguments?

2. What role does cultural programming play in the analyses by Rifkin and Eric Schlosser?

✧ Extending Viewpoints through Writing and Research

1. Which of Rifkin's arguments seem most and least compelling? If you don't agree with him, what counterarguments or compro-mise proposals can you offer that would offset his analysis and conclusions?

2. Would any of Rifkin's arguments persuade you to become a vege-tarian or vegan? Why or why not? What other arguments (eco-nomic, philosophical, religious, or health related) would convince you to stop eating beef?

3. The environmental impact of beef consumption is analyzed at http://www.earthsave.org/environment/foodchoices.htm.

Eric Schlosser

Kid Kustomers

◆

Eric Schlosser is a contributing editor of The Atlantic. *His articles on marijuana and the law (August and September 1994) won a National Magazine Award for reporting. He has appeared on* 60 Minutes. *In "Kid Kustomers," from* Fast Food Nation: The Dark Side of the All-American Meal *(2001), Schlosser reveals how advertisers are becoming more savvy in marketing their products toward children. His latest work is* Reefer Madness: Sex, Drugs, and Cheap Labor in the American Black Market *(2003).*

Before You Read

Consider whether the children you know are heavily influenced by advertising directed toward them.

◆

1   Twenty-five years ago, only a handful of American companies directed their marketing at children—Disney, McDonald's, candy makers, toy makers, manufacturers of breakfast cereal. Today children are being targeted by phone companies, oil companies, and automobile companies as well as clothing stores and restaurant chains. The explosion in children's advertising occurred during the 1980s. Many working parents, feeling guilty about spending less time with their kids, started spending more money on them. One marketing expert has called the 1980s "the decade of the child consumer." After largely ignoring children for years, Madison Avenue began to scrutinize and pursue them. Major ad agencies now have children's divisions, and a variety of marketing firms focus solely on kids. These groups tend to have sweet-sounding names: Small Talk, Kid Connection, Kid2Kid, the Gepetto Group, Just Kids, Inc. At least three industry publications—*Youth Market Alert, Selling to Kids,* and *Marketing to Kids Report*—cover the latest ad campaigns and market research. The growth in children's advertising has been driven by efforts to increase not just current, but also future, consumption. Hoping that nostalgic childhood memories of a brand will lead to a lifetime of purchases, companies now plan "cradle-to-grave" advertising strategies. They have come to believe what Ray Kroc and Walt Disney realized long ago—a person's "brand loyalty" may begin as early as the age of two. Indeed, market research

has found that children often recognize a brand logo before they can recognize their own name.

2   The discontinued Joe Camel ad campaign, which used a hip cartoon character to sell cigarettes, showed how easily children can be influenced by the right corporate mascot. A 1991 study published in the *Journal of the American Medical Association* found that nearly all of America's six-year-olds could identify Joe Camel, who was just as familiar to them as Mickey Mouse. Another study found that one-third of the cigarettes illegally sold to minors were Camels. More recently, a marketing firm conducted a survey in shopping malls across the country, asking children to describe their favorite TV ads. According to the CME KidCom Ad Traction Study II, released at the 1999 Kids' Marketing Conference in San Antonio, Texas, the Taco Bell commercials featuring a talking chihuahua were the most popular fast food ads. The kids in the survey also like Pepsi and Nike commercials, but their favorite television ad was for Budweiser.

3   The bulk of the advertising directed at children today has an immediate goal. "It's not just getting kids to whine," one marketer explained in *Selling to Kids*, "it's giving them a specific reason to ask for the product." Years ago sociologist Vance Packard described children as "surrogate salesmen" who had to persuade other people, usually their parents, to buy what they wanted. Marketers now use different terms to explain the intended response to their ads—such as "leverage," "the nudge factor," "pester power." The aim of most children's advertising is straightforward: Get kids to nag their parents and nag them well.

4   James U. McNeal, a professor of marketing at Texas A&M University, is considered America's leading authority on marketing to children. In his book *Kids As Customers* (1992), McNeal provides marketers with a thorough analysis of "children's requesting styles and appeals." He classifies juvenile nagging tactics into seven major categories. A *pleading* nag is one accompanied by repetitions of words like "please" or "mom, mom, mom." A *persistent* nag involves constant requests for the coveted product and may include the phrase "I'm gonna ask just one more time." *Forceful* nags are extremely pushy and may include subtle threats, like "Well, then, I'll go and ask Dad." *Demonstrative* nags are the most high-risk, often characterized by full-blown tantrums in public places, breath-holding, tears, a refusal to leave the store. *Sugar-coated* nags promise affection in return for a purchase and may rely on seemingly heartfelt declarations like "You're the best dad in the world." *Threatening* nags are youthful forms of blackmail, vows of eternal hatred and of running away if something isn't bought. *Pity* nags claim the child will be heartbroken, teased, or socially stunted if the parent refuses to buy a certain item. "All of these appeals and styles may be used in combination," McNeal's research has discovered, "but

kids tend to stick to one or two of each that proved most effective . . . for their own parents."

5   McNeal never advocates turning children into screaming, breath-holding monsters. He has been studying "Kid Kustomers" for more than thirty years and believes in a more traditional marketing approach. "The key is getting children to see a firm . . . in much the same way as [they see] mom or dad, grandma or grandpa," McNeal argues. "Likewise, if a company can ally itself with universal values such as patriotism, national defense, and good health, it is likely to nurture belief in it among children."

6   Before trying to affect children's behavior, advertisers have to learn about their tastes. Today's market researchers not only conduct surveys of children in shopping malls, they also organize focus groups for kids as young as two or three. They analyze children's artwork, hire children to run focus groups, stage slumber parties and then question children into the night. They send cultural anthropologists into homes, stores, fast food restaurants, and other places where kids like to gather, quietly and surreptitiously observing the behavior of prospective customers. They study the academic literature on child development, seeking insights from the work of theorists such as Erik Erikson and Jean Piaget. They study the fantasy lives of young children, they apply the findings in advertisements and product designs.

7   Dan S. Acuff—the president of Youth Market System Consulting and the author of *What Kids Buy and Why* (1997)—stresses the importance of dream research. Studies suggest that until the age of six, roughly 80 percent of children's dreams are about animals. Rounded, soft creatures like Barney, Disney's animated characters, and the Teletubbies therefore have an obvious appeal to young children. The Character Lab, a division of Youth Market System Consulting, uses a proprietary technique called Character Appeal Quadrant analysis to help companies develop new mascots. The technique purports to create imaginary characters who perfectly fit the targeted age group's level of cognitive and neurological development.

8   Children's clubs have for years been considered an effective means of targeting ads and collecting demographic information; the clubs appeal to a child's fundamental need for status and belonging. Disney's Mickey Mouse Club, formed in 1930, was one of the trailblazers. During the 1980s and 1990s, children's clubs proliferated, as corporations used them to solicit the names, addresses, zip codes, and personal comments of young customers. "Marketing messages sent through a club not only can be personalized," James McNeal advises, "they can be tailored for a certain age or geographical group." A well-designed and well-run children's club can be extremely good for business. According to one Burger King executive, the creation of a Burger King

Kids Club in 1991 increased the sales of children's meals as much as 300 percent.

9   The Internet has become another powerful tool for assembling data about children. In 1998 a federal investigation of Web sites aimed at children found that 89 percent requested personal information from kids; only 1 percent required that children obtain parental approval before supplying the information. A character on the McDonald's Web site told children that Ronald McDonald was "the ultimate authority in everything." The site encouraged kids to send Ronald an e-mail revealing their favorite menu item at McDonald's, their favorite book, their favorite sports team—and their name. Fast food Web sites no longer ask children to provide personal information without first gaining parental approval; to do so is now a violation of federal law, thanks to the Children's Online Privacy Protection Act, which took effect in April of 2000.

10   Despite the growing importance of the Internet, television remains the primary medium for children's advertising. The effects of these TV ads have long been a subject of controversy. In 1978, the Federal Trade Commission (FTC) tried to ban all television ads directed at children seven years old or younger. Many studies had found that young children often could not tell the difference between television programming and television advertising. They also could not comprehend the real purpose of commercials and trusted that advertising claims were true. Michael Pertschuk, the head of the FTC, argued that children need to be shielded from advertising that preys upon their immaturity. "They cannot protect themselves," he said, "against adults who exploit their present-mindedness."

11   The FTC's proposed ban was supported by the American Academy of Pediatrics, the National Congress of Parents and Teachers, the Consumers Union, and the Child Welfare League, among others. But it was attacked by the National Association of Broadcasters, the Toy Manufacturers of America, and the Association of National Advertisers. The industry groups lobbied Congress to prevent any restrictions on children's ads and sued in federal court to block Pertschuk from participating in future FTC meetings on the subject. In April of 1981, three months after the inauguration of President Ronald Reagan, an FTC staff report argued that a ban on ads aimed at children would be impractical, effectively killing the proposal. "We are delighted by the FTC's reasonable recommendation," said the head of the National Association of Broadcasters.

12   The Saturday-morning children's ads that caused angry debates twenty years ago now seem almost quaint. Far from being banned, TV advertising aimed at kids is now broadcast twenty-four hours a day, closed-captioned and in stereo. Nickelodeon, the Disney Channel, the Cartoon Network, and the other children's cable networks are now

responsible for about 80 percent of all television viewing by kids. None of these networks existed before 1979. The typical American child now spends about twenty-one hours a week watching television—roughly one and a half months of TV every year. That does not include the time children spend in front of a screen watching videos, playing video games, or using the computer. Outside of school, the typical American child spends more time watching television than doing any other activity except sleeping. During the course of a year, he or she watches more than thirty thousand TV commercials. Even the nation's youngest children are watching a great deal of television. About one-quarter of American children between the ages of two and five have a TV in their room.

✧ Evaluating the Text

1. What factors led to an upsurge in advertising directed toward children, and how is "pester power" used to influence what parents buy?

2. How does Schlosser use examples of the extraordinary lengths to which advertisers will go to obtain marketing data on what children want?

✧ Exploring Different Perspectives

1. Do corporations play the same role for children, as discussed by Schlosser, as Mao's Cultural Revolution did for the Red Guards as discussed by Rae Yang in "At the Center of the Storm?" To what extent has Ronald McDonald replaced Chairman Mao?

2. How does Schlosser's analysis suggest that addictive behavior, as Philip Slater describes it, begins in childhood in America?

✧ Extending Viewpoints through Writing and Research

1. Advertising for children can be studied in different ways: (1) you might watch a Saturday morning cartoon show and observe the connection between the characters in the show and the products directly linked to them, or (2) you might study an ad specifically targeted for children and in a few paragraphs analyze the components that contribute to its effectiveness.

2. Should advertisments geared to children be more closely regulated by the government? Why or why not? This might be a good subject for a class debate.

What does this photo suggest about McDonald's global marketing strategy for "kid kustomers"?

Luis Sepulveda

Daisy

◆

The Chilean expatriot novelist Luis Sepulveda takes us inside the prison where he was confined and reveals, with surprising good humor, one of his experiences. This chapter, translated by Chris Andrews and drawn from Full Circle: A South American Journey, *reveals Sepulveda's ironic sensibility as he tries to evade torture and remain an honest critic of his jailer's literary efforts. His works include his acclaimed detective novel* The Old Man Who Read Love Stories *(1992) and* The Name of the Bullfighter *(1996). He is also the author of a novel,* Zorba and Lucky *(1998), for which he wrote the screenplay, and* Hot Line *(2002).*

Before You Read
Consider the unusual importance that literature takes on in this most unlikely environment.

◆

1   The military had rather inflated ideas of our destructive capacity. They questioned us about plans to assassinate all the officers in American military history, to blow up bridges and seal off tunnels, and to prepare for the landing of a terrible foreign enemy whom they could not identify.

2   Temuco is a sad, grey, rainy city. No-one would call it a tourist attraction, and yet the barracks of the Tucapel regiment came to house a sort of permanent international convention of sadists. The Chileans, who were the hosts, after all, were assisted in the interrogations by primates from Brazilian military intelligence—they were the worst—North Americans from the State Department, Argentinian paramilitary personnel, Italian neo-fascists and even some agents of Mossad.

3   I remember Rudi Weismann, a Chilean with a passion for the South and sailing, who was tortured and interrogated in the gentle language of the synagogues. This infamy was too much for Rudi, who had thrown in his lot with Israel: he had worked on a kibbutz, but in the end his nostalgia for Tierra del Fuego had brought him back to Chile. He simply could not understand how Israel could support such a gang of criminals, and though till then he had always been a model of good humour, he dried up like a neglected plant. One morning we found him dead in his sleeping bag. No need for an autopsy, his face made it clear: Rudi Weismann had died of sadness.

353

4   The commander of the Tucapel regiment—a basic respect for paper prevents me from writing his name—was a fanatical admirer of Field Marshal Rommel. When he found a prisoner he liked, he would invite him to recover from the interrogations in his office. After assuring the prisoner that everything that happened in the barracks was in the best interests of our great nation, the commander would offer him a glass of Korn—somebody used to send him this insipid, wheat-based liquor from Germany—and make him sit through a lecture on the Afrika Korps. The guy's parents or grandparents were German, but he couldn't have looked more Chilean: chubby, short-legged, dark untidy hair. You could have mistaken him for a truck driver or a fruit vendor, but when he talked about Rommel he became the caricature of a Nazi guard.

5   At the end of the lecture he would dramatise Rommel's suicide, clicking his heels, raising his right hand to his forehead to salute an invisible flag, muttering "Adieu geliebtes Vaterland," and pretending to shoot himself in the mouth. We all hoped that one day he would do it for real.

6   There was another curious officer in the regiment: a lieutenant struggling to contain a homosexuality that kept popping out all over the place. The soldiers had nicknamed him Daisy, and he knew it.

7   We could all tell that it was a torment for Daisy not to be able to adorn his body with truly beautiful objects, and the poor guy had to make do with the regulation paraphernalia. He wore a .45 pistol, two cartridge clips, a commando's curved dagger, two hand grenades, a torch, a walkie-talkie, the insignia of his rank and the silver wings of the parachute corps. The prisoners and the soldiers thought he looked like a Christmas tree.

8   This individual sometimes surprised us with generous and apparently disinterested acts—we didn't know that the Stockholm syndrome could be a military perversion. For example, after the interrogations he would suddenly fill our pockets with cigarettes or the highly prized aspirin tablets with vitamin C. One afternoon he invited me to his room.

9   "So you're a man of letters," he said, offering me a can of Coca-Cola.

10   "I've written a couple of stories. That's all," I replied.

11   "You're not here for an interrogation. I'm very sorry about what's happening, but that's what war is like. I want us to talk as one writer to another. Are you surprised? The army has produced some great men of letters. Think of Don Alonso de Ercilla y Zúñiga, for example."

12   "Or Cervantes," I added.

13   Daisy included himself among the greats. That was his problem. If he wanted adulation, he could have it. I drank the Coca-Cola and thought about Garcés, or rather, about his chicken, because, incredible as it seems, the cook had a chicken called Dulcinea, the name of Don Quixote's mistress.

14   One morning it jumped the wall which separated the common-law prisoners from the POWs, and it must have been a chicken with deep political convictions, because it decided to stay with us. Garcés caressed it and sighed, saying: "If I had a pinch of pepper and a pinch of cumin, I'd make you a chicken marinade like you've never tasted."

15   "I want you to read my poems and give me your opinion, your honest opinion," said Daisy, handing me a notebook.

16   I left that room with my pockets full of cigarettes, caramel sweets, tea bags and a tin of US Army marmalade. That afternoon I started to believe in the brotherhood of writers.

17   They transported us from the prison to the barracks and back in a cattle truck. The soldiers made sure there was plenty of cow shit on the floor of the truck before ordering us to lie face down with our hands behind our necks. We were guarded by four of them, with North American machine guns, one in each corner of the truck. They were almost all young guys brought down from northern garrisons, and the harsh climate of the South kept them flu-ridden and in a perpetually filthy mood. They had orders to fire on the bundles—us—at the slightest suspect movement, or on any civilian who tried to approach the truck. But as time wore on, the discipline gradually relaxed and they turned a blind eye to the packet of cigarettes or piece of fruit thrown from a window, or the pretty and daring girl who ran beside the truck blowing us kisses and shouting: "Don't give up, comrades! We'll win!"

18   Back in prison, as always, we were met by the welcoming committee organised by Doctor "Skinny" Pragnan, now an eminent psychiatrist in Belgium. First he examined those who couldn't walk and those who had heart problems, then those who had come back with a dislocation or with ribs out of place. Pragnan was expert at estimating how much electricity had been put into us on the grill, and patiently determined who would be able to absorb liquids in the next few hours. Then finally it was time to take communion: we were given the aspirin with vitamin C and an anticoagulant to prevent internal haematomas.

19   "Dulcinea's days are numbered," I said to Garcés, and looked for a corner in which to read Daisy's notebook.

20   The elegantly inscribed pages were redolent of love, honey, sublime suffering and forgotten flowers. By the third page I knew that Daisy hadn't even gone to the trouble of reusing the ideas of the Mexican poet Amado Nervo—he'd simply copied out his poems word for word.

21   I called out to Peyuco Gálvez, a Spanish teacher, and read him a couple of lines.

22   "What do you think, Peyuco?"

23   "Amado Nervo. The book is called *The Interior Gardens*."

24   I had got myself into a real jam. If Daisy found out that I knew the work of this sugary poet Nervo, then it wasn't Garcés's chicken whose

days were numbered, but mine. It was a serious problem, so that night I presented it to the Council of Elders.

25 "Now, Daisy, would he be the passive or the active type?" enquired Iriarte.

26 "Stop it, will you. My skin's at risk here," I replied.

27 "I'm serious. Maybe our friend wants to have an affair with you, and giving you the notebook was like dropping a silk handkerchief. And like a fool you picked it up. Perhaps he copied out the poems for you to find a message in them. I've known queens who seduced boys by lending them *Demian* by Hermann Hesse. If Daisy is the passive type, this business with Amado Nervo means he wants to test your nerve, so to speak. And if he's the active type, well, it would have to hurt less than a kick in the balls."

28 "Message my arse. He gave you the poems as his own, and you should say you liked them a lot. If he was trying to send a message, he should have given the notebook to Garcés; he's the only one who has an interior garden. Or maybe Daisy doesn't know about the pot plant," remarked Andrés Müller.

29 "Let's be serious about this. You have to say something to him, and Daisy mustn't even suspect that you know Nervo's poems," declared Pragnan.

30 "Tell him you liked the poems, but that the adjectives strike you as a bit excessive. Quote Huidobro: when an adjective doesn't give life, it kills. That way you'll show him that you read his poems carefully and that you are criticising his work as a colleague," suggested Gálvez.

31 The Council of Elders approved of Gálvez's idea, but I spent two weeks on tenterhooks. I couldn't sleep. I wished they would come and take me to be kicked and electrocuted so I could give the damned notebook back. In those two weeks I came to hate good old Garcés:

32 "Listen, mate, if everything goes well, and you get a little jar of capers as well as the cumin and the pepper, we'll have such a feast with that chicken."

33 After a fortnight, I found myself at last stretched out face down on the mattress of cowpats with my hands behind my neck. I thought I was going mad: I was happy to be heading towards a session of the activity known as torture.

34 Tucapel barracks. Service Corps. In the background, the perpetual green of Cerro Ñielol, sacred to the Mapuche Indians. There was a waiting room outside the interrogation cell, like at the doctor's. There they made us sit on a bench with our hands tied behind our backs and black hoods over our heads. I never understood what the hoods were for, because once we got inside they took them off, and we could see the interrogators—the toy soldiers who, with panic-stricken faces, turned the handle of the generator, and the health officers who attached the electrodes to our anuses, testicles, gums and tongue, and

then listened with stethoscopes to see who was faking and who had really passed out on the grill.

35   Lagos, a deacon of the Emmaus International ragmen, was the first to be interrogated that day. For a year they had been working him over to find out how the organisation had come by a couple of dozen old military uniforms which had been found in their warehouses. A trader who sold army surplus gear had donated them. Lagos screamed in pain and repeated over and over what the soldiers wanted to hear: the uniforms belonged to an invading army which was preparing to land on the Chilean coast.

36   I was waiting for my turn when someone took off the hood. It was Lieutenant Daisy.

37   "Follow me," he ordered.

38   We went into an office. On the desk I saw a tin of cocoa and a carton of cigarettes which were obviously there to reward my comments on his literary work.

39   "Did you read my poesy?" he asked, offering me a seat.

40   Poesy. Daisy said poesy, not poetry. A man covered with pistols and grenades can't say "poesy" without sounding ridiculous and effete. At that moment he revolted me, and I decided that even if it meant pissing blood, hissing when I spoke and being able to charge batteries just by touching them, I wasn't going to lower myself to flattering a plagiarising faggot in uniform.

41   "You have pretty handwriting, Lieutenant. But you know these poems aren't yours," I said, giving him back the notebook.

42   I saw him begin to shake. He was carrying enough arms to kill me several times over, and if he didn't want to stain his uniform, he could order someone else to do it. Trembling with anger he stood up, threw what was on the desk onto the floor and shouted:

43   "Three weeks in the cube. But first, you're going to visit the chiropodist, you piece of subversive shit!"

44   The chiropodist was a civilian, a landholder who had lost several thousand hectares in the land reform, and who was getting his revenge by participating in the interrogations as a volunteer. His speciality was peeling back toenails, which led to terrible infections.

45   I knew the cube. I had spent my first six months of prison there in solitary confinement: it was an underground cell, one and a half metres wide by one and a half metres long by one and a half metres high. In the old days there had been a tannery in the Temuco jail, and the cube was used to store fat. The walls still stank of fat, but after a week your excrement fixed that, making the cube very much a place of your own.

46   You could only stretch out across the diagonal, but the low temperatures of southern Chile, the rainwater and the soldiers' urine made you want to curl up hugging your legs and stay like that wishing yourself smaller and smaller, so that eventually you could live on one of the

islands of floating shit, which conjured up images of dream holidays. I was there for three weeks, running through Laurel and Hardy films, remembering the books of Salgari, Stevenson and London word by word, playing long games of chess, licking my toes to protect them from infection. In the cube I swore over and over again never to become a literary critic.

✧ *Evaluating the Text*

1. To what paradoxical aspects of prison life does Sepulveda have to adapt in order to survive?

2. What unusual mixture of character traits and aspirations does Daisy display, given his role as prison guard and torturer? What kind of relationship does Sepulveda have with Daisy?

3. In what ways is Sepulveda's style unusual, given his predicament? In what sense might his style itself be a way of coping with the dangerous circumstances with which he was confronted?

✧ *Exploring Different Perspectives*

1. Compare Sepulveda's narrative with Panos Ioannides's story "Gregory" in terms of the moral dilemmas involved.

2. What similarities can you discover between the punishments for a political crime that face Sepulveda and those Stephen Chapman describes in his essay, "The Prisoner's Dilemma"?

✧ *Extending Viewpoints through Writing and Research*

1. If you had been in the same situation as Sepulveda, would you have been as honest as he was? Why or why not?

2. Plagiarism is a moral problem with which students are often confronted. What experiences have you had either directly or indirectly? Tell what happened.

3. A history of Chile's dictatorship from 1973 to 1990 can be found at http://www.chipsites.com/derechos/dictadura_eng.html.

Stephen Chapman

The Prisoner's Dilemma

◆

Stephen Chapman (b. 1954) has served as the associate editor of the New
Republic *and is currently a columnist and editorial writer with the*
Chicago Tribune. *He is a native of Texas who attended Harvard. In "The
Prisoner's Dilemma" (which first appeared in the* New Republic *on
March 8, 1980), Chapman calls into question the widely held assumption
that the system of imprisonment as punishment employed in the West is
more humane and less barbaric than the methods of punishment (including
flogging, stoning, and amputation) practiced in Eastern Islamic nations.*

Before You Read

As you read, notice the very different objectives punishment serves in
Eastern and Western cultures.

◆

*If the punitive laws of Islam were applied for only one year,
all the devastating injustices would be uprooted. Misdeeds
must be punished by the law of retaliation; cut off the hands
of the thief; kill the murderers; flog the adulterous woman
or man. Your concerns, your "humanitarian" scruples are
more childish than reasonable. Under the terms of Koranic
law, any judge fulfilling the seven requirements (that he
have reached puberty, be a believer, know the Koranic laws
perfectly, be just, and not be affected by amnesia, or be a
bastard, or be of the female sex) is qualified to be a judge in
any type of case. He can thus judge and dispose of twenty
trials in a single day, whereas the Occidental justice may
take years to argue them out.*
—from Sayings of the Ayatollah Khomeni (Bantam Books)

1   One of the amusements of life in the modern West is the opportunity to observe the barbaric rituals of countries that are attached to the
customs of the dark ages. Take Pakistan, for example, our newest ally
and client state in Asia. Last October President Zia, in harmony with
the Islamic fervor that is sweeping his part of the world, revived the
traditional Moslem practice of flogging lawbreakers in public. In Pakistan, this qualified as mass entertainment, and no fewer than 10,000
law-abiding Pakistanis turned out to see justice done to 26 convicts. To

Western sensibilities the spectacle seemed barbaric—both in the sense of cruel and in the sense of pre-civilized. In keeping with Islamic custom each of the unfortunates—who had been caught in prostitution raids the previous night and summarily convicted and sentenced— was stripped down to a pair of white shorts, which were painted with a red stripe across the buttocks (the target). Then he was shackled against an easel, with pads thoughtfully placed over the kidneys to prevent injury. The floggers were muscular, fierce-looking sorts—convicted murderers, as it happens—who paraded around the flogging platform in colorful loincloths. When the time for the ceremony began, one of the floggers took a running start and brought a five-foot stave down across the first victim's buttocks, eliciting screams from the convict and murmurs from the audience. Each of the 26 received from five to 15 lashes. One had to be carried from the stage unconscious.

2   Flogging is one of the punishments stipulated by Koranic law, which has made it a popular penological device in several Moslem countries, including Pakistan, Saudi Arabia, and, most recently, the ayatollah's Iran. Flogging, or *Tá zir,* is the general punishment prescribed for offenses that don't carry an explicit Koranic penalty. Some crimes carry automatic *hadd* punishments—stoning or scourging (a severe whipping) for illicit sex, scourging for drinking alcoholic beverages, amputation of the hands for theft. Other crimes—as varied as murder and abandoning Islam—carry the death penalty (usually carried out in public). Colorful practices like these have given the Islamic world an image in the West, as described by historian G. H. Jansen, "of blood dripping from the stumps of amputated hands and from the striped backs of malefactors, and piles of stones barely concealing the battered bodies of adulterous couples." Jansen, whose book *Militant Islam* is generally effusive in its praise of Islamic practices, grows squeamish when considering devices like flogging, amputation, and stoning. But they are given enthusiastic endorsement by the Koran itself.

3   Such traditions, we all must agree, are no sign of an advanced civilization. In the West, we have replaced these various punishments (including the death penalty in most cases) with a single device. Our custom is to confine criminals in prison for varying lengths of time. In Illinois, a reasonably typical state, grand theft carries a punishment of three to five years; armed robbery can get you from six to 30. The lowest form of felony theft is punishable by one to three years in prison. Most states impose longer sentences on habitual offenders. In Kentucky, for example, habitual offenders can be sentenced to life in prison. Other states are less brazen, preferring the more genteel sounding "indeterminate sentence," which allows parole boards to keep inmates locked up for as long as life. It was under an indeterminate sentence of one to 14 years that George Jackson served 12 years in California prisons for committing a $70 armed robbery. Under a Texas law

imposing an automatic life sentence for a third felony conviction, a man was sent to jail for life last year because of three thefts adding up to less than $300 in property value. Texas also is famous for occasionally imposing extravagantly long sentences, often running into hundreds or thousands of years. This gives Texas a leg up on Maryland, which used to sentence some criminals to life plus a day—a distinctive if superfluous flourish.

4   The punishment *intended* by Western societies in sending their criminals to prison is the loss of freedom. But, as everyone knows, the actual punishment in most American prisons is of a wholly different order. The February 2 riot at New Mexico's state prison in Santa Fe, one of several bloody prison riots in the nine years since the Attica bloodbath, once again dramatized the conditions of life in an American prison. Four hundred prisoners seized control of the prison before dawn. By sunset the next day 33 inmates had died at the hands of other convicts and another 40 people (including five guards) had been seriously hurt. Macabre stories came out of prisoners being hanged, murdered with blowtorches, decapitated, tortured, and mutilated in a variety of gruesome ways by drug-crazed rioters.

5   The Santa Fe penitentiary was typical of most maximum-security facilities, with prisoners subject to overcrowding, filthy conditions, and routine violence. It also housed first-time, non-violent offenders, like check forgers and drug dealers, with murderers serving life sentences. In a recent lawsuit, the American Civil Liberties Union called the prison "totally unfit for human habitation." But the ACLU says New Mexico's penitentiary is far from the nation's worst.

6   That American prisons are a disgrace is taken for granted by experts of every ideological stripe. Conservative James Q. Wilson has criticized our "crowded, antiquated prisons that require men and women to live in fear of one another and to suffer not only deprivation of liberty but a brutalizing regimen." Leftist Jessica Mitford has called our prisons "the ultimate expression of injustice and inhumanity." In 1973 a national commission concluded that "the American correctional system today appears to offer minimum protection to the public and maximum harm to the offender." Federal courts have ruled that confinement in prisons in 16 different states violates the constitutional ban on "cruel and unusual punishment."

7   What are the advantages of being a convicted criminal in an advanced culture? First there is the overcrowding in prisons. One Tennessee prison, for example, has a capacity of 806, according to accepted space standards, but it houses 2300 inmates. One Louisiana facility has confined four and five prisoners in a single six-foot-by-six-foot cell. Then there is the disease caused by overcrowding, unsanitary conditions, and poor or inadequate medical care. A federal appeals court

noted that the Tennessee prison had suffered frequent outbreaks of infectious diseases like hepatitis and tuberculosis. But the most distinctive element of American prison life is its constant violence. In his book *Criminal Violence, Criminal Justice,* Charles Silberman noted that in one Louisiana prison, there were 211 stabbings in only three years, 11 of them fatal. There were 15 slayings in a prison in Massachusetts between 1972 and 1975. According to a federal court, in Alabama's penitentiaries (as in many others), "robbery, rape, extortion, theft and assault are everyday occurrences."

8   At least in regard to cruelty, it's not at all clear that the system of punishment that has evolved in the West is less barbaric than the grotesque practices of Islam. Skeptical? Ask yourself: would you rather be subjected to a few minutes of intense pain and considerable public humiliation, or to be locked away for two or three years in a prison cell crowded with ill-tempered sociopaths? Would you rather lose a hand or spend 10 years or more in a typical state prison? I have taken my own survey on this matter. I have found no one who does not find the Islamic system hideous. And I have found no one who, given the choices mentioned above, would not prefer its penalties to our own.

9   The great divergence between Western and Islamic fashions in punishment is relatively recent. Until roughly the end of the 18th century, criminals in Western countries rarely were sent to prison. Instead they were subjected to an ingenious assortment of penalties. Many perpetrators of a variety of crimes simply were executed, usually by some imaginative and extremely unpleasant method involving prolonged torture, such as breaking on the wheel, burning at the stake, or drawing and quartering. Michel Foucault's book *Discipline and Punishment: The Birth of the Prison* notes one form of capital punishment in which the condemned man's "belly was opened up, his entrails quickly ripped out, so that he had time to see them, with his own eyes, being thrown on the fire; in which he was finally decapitated and his body quartered." Some criminals were forced to serve on slave galleys. But in most cases various corporal measures such as pillorying, flogging, and branding sufficed.

10   In time, however, public sentiment recoiled against these measures. They were replaced by imprisonment, which was thought to have two advantages. First, it was considered to be more humane. Second, and more important, prison was supposed to hold out the possibility of rehabilitation—purging the criminal of his criminality—something that less civilized punishments did not even aspire to. An 1854 report by inspectors of the Pennsylvania prison system illustrates the hopes nurtured by humanitarian reformers:

> Depraved tendencies, characteristic of the convict, have been restrained by the absence of vicious association, and in the mild teaching of Christianity, the unhappy criminal finds a solace for an

involuntary exile from the comforts of social life. If hungry, he is fed; if naked, he is clothed; if destitute of the first rudiments of education, he is taught to read and write; and if he has never been blessed with a means of livelihood, he is schooled in a mechanical art, which in after life may be to him the source of profit and respectability. Employment is not his toil nor labor, weariness. He embraces them with alacrity, as contributing to his moral and mental elevation.

11   Imprisonment is now the universal method of punishing criminals in the United States. It is thought to perform five functions, each of which has been given a label by criminologists. First, there is simple *retribution:* punishing the lawbreaker to serve society's sense of justice and to satisfy the victims' desire for revenge. Second, there is *specific deterrence:* discouraging the offender from misbehaving in the future. Third, *general deterrence:* using the offender as an example to discourage others from turning to crime. Fourth, *prevention:* at least during the time he is kept off the streets, the criminal cannot victimize other members of society. Finally, and most important, there is *rehabilitation:* reforming the criminal so that when he returns to society he will be inclined to obey the laws and able to make an honest living.

12   How satisfactorily do American prisons perform by these criteria? Well, of course, they do punish. But on the other scores they don't do so well. Their effect in discouraging future criminality by the prisoner or others is the subject of much debate, but the soaring rates of the last 20 years suggest that prisons are not a dramatically effective deterrent to criminal behavior. Prisons do isolate convicted criminals, but only to divert crime from ordinary citizens to prison guards and fellow inmates. Almost no one contends anymore that prisons rehabilitate their inmates. If anything, they probably impede rehabilitation by forcing inmates into prolonged and almost exclusive association with other criminals. And prisons cost a lot of money. Housing a typical prisoner in a typical prison costs far more than a stint at a top university. This cost would be justified if prisons did the job they were intended for. But it is clear to all that prisons fail on the very grounds—humanity and hope of rehabilitation—that caused them to replace earlier, cheaper forms of punishment.

13   The universal acknowledgment that prisons do not rehabilitate criminals has produced two responses. The first is to retain the hope of rehabilitation but do away with imprisonment as much as possible and replace it with various forms of "alternative treatment," such as psychotherapy, supervised probation, and vocational training. Psychiatrist Karl Menninger, one of the principal critics of American penology, has suggested even more unconventional approaches, such as "a new job opportunity or a vacation trip, a course of reducing exercises, a cosmetic surgical operation or a herniotomy, some night school courses, a

wedding in the family (even one for the patient!), an inspiring sermon." The starry-eyed approach naturally has produced a backlash from critics on the right, who think that it's time to abandon the goal of rehabilitation. They argue that prisons perform an important service just by keeping criminals off the streets, and thus should be used with that purpose in mind.

14   So the debate continues to rage in all the same old ruts. No one, of course, would think of copying the medieval practices of Islamic nations and experimenting with punishments such as flogging and amputation. But let us consider them anyway. How do they compare with our American prison system in achieving the ostensible objectives of punishment? First, do they punish? Obviously they do, and in a uniquely painful and memorable way. Of course any sensible person, given the choice, would prefer suffering these punishments to years of incarceration in a typical American prison. But presumably no Western penologist would criticize Islamic punishments on the grounds that they are not barbaric enough. Do they deter crime? Yes, and probably more effectively than sending convicts off to prison. Now we read about a prison sentence in the newspaper, then think no more about the criminal's payment for his crimes until, perhaps, years later we read a small item reporting his release. By contrast, one can easily imagine the vivid impression it would leave to be wandering through a local shopping center and to stumble onto the scene of some poor wretch being lustily flogged. And the occasional sight of an habitual offender walking around with a bloody stump at the end of his arm no doubt also would serve as a forceful reminder that crime does not pay.

15   Do flogging and amputation discourage recidivism? No one knows whether the scars on his back would dissuade a criminal from risking another crime, but it is hard to imagine that corporal measures could stimulate a higher rate of recidivism than already exists. Islamic forms of punishment do not serve the favorite new right goal of simply isolating criminals from the rest of society, but they may achieve the same purpose of making further crimes impossible. In the movie *Bonnie and Clyde,* Warren Beatty successfully robs a bank with his arm in a sling, but this must be dismissed as artistic license. It must be extraordinarily difficult, at the very least, to perform much violent crime with only one hand.

16   Do the medieval forms of punishment rehabilitate the criminal? Plainly not. But long prison terms do not rehabilitate either. And it is just as plain that typical Islamic punishments are no crueler to the convict than incarceration in the typical American state prison.

17   Of course there are other reasons besides its bizarre forms of punishment that the Islamic system of justice seems uncivilized to the Western mind. One is the absence of due process. Another is the long list of offenses—such as drinking, adultery, blasphemy, "profiteering,"

and so on—that can bring on conviction and punishment. A third is all the ritualistic mumbojumbo in pronouncements of Islamic law (like that talk about puberty and amnesia in the ayatollah's quotation at the beginning of this article). Even in these matters, however, a little cultural modesty is called for. The vast majority of American criminals are convicted and sentenced as a result of plea bargaining, in which due process plays almost no role. It has been only half a century since a wave of religious fundamentalism stirred this country to outlaw the consumption of alcoholic beverages. Most states also still have laws imposing austere constraints on sexual conduct. Only two weeks ago the *Washington Post* reported that the FBI had spent two and a half years and untold amounts of money to break up a nationwide pornography ring. Flogging the clients of prostitutes, as the Pakistanis did, does seem silly. But only a few months ago Mayor Koch of New York was proposing that clients caught in his own city have their names broadcast by radio stations. We are not so far advanced on such matters as we often like to think. Finally, my lawyer friends assure me that the rules of jurisdiction for American courts contain plenty of petty requirements and bizarre distinctions that would sound silly enough to foreign ears.

18   Perhaps it sounds barbaric to talk of flogging and amputation, and perhaps it is. But our system of punishment also is barbaric, and probably more so. Only cultural smugness about their system and willful ignorance about our own make it easy to regard the one as cruel and the other as civilized. We inflict our cruelties away from public view, while nations like Pakistan stage them in front of 10,000 onlookers. Their outrages are visible; ours are not. Most Americans can live their lives for years without having their peace of mind disturbed by the knowledge of what goes on in our prisons. To choose imprisonment over flogging and amputation is not to choose human kindness over cruelty, but merely to prefer that our cruelties be kept out of sight, and out of mind.

19   Public flogging and amputation may be more barbaric forms of punishment than imprisonment, even if they are not more cruel. Society may pay a higher price for them, even if the particular criminal does not. Revulsion against officially sanctioned violence and infliction of pain derives from something deeply ingrained in Western conscience, and clearly it is something admirable. Grotesque displays of the sort that occur in Islamic countries probably breed a greater tolerance for physical cruelty, for example, which prisons do not do precisely because they conceal their cruelties. In fact it is our admirable intolerance for calculated violence that makes it necessary for us to conceal what we have not been able to do away with. In a way this is a good thing, since it holds out the hope that we may eventually find a

way to do away with it. But in another way it is a bad thing, since it permits us to congratulate ourselves on our civilized humanitarianism while violating its norms in this one area of our national life.

✧ Evaluating the Text

1. What are the five objectives that imprisonment is supposed to achieve in Western culture? How satisfactorily do American prisons perform these functions?

2. How do the practices of punishment in Eastern cultures differ from those in Western societies? What is Chapman's attitude toward these practices in comparison with Western methods of punishment?

3. How does Chapman use comparison and contrast to more clearly illustrate the differences between them?

✧ Exploring Different Perspectives

1. Evaluate the choices facing the hypothetical prisoner in Chapman's essay with the no-win situation that faces the narrator in "Gregory."

2. Which system of punishment as described by Chapman is closer to that of Chinese Communism under Mao Tse Tung, as described by Rae Yang in "At the Center of the Storm"?

✧ Extending Viewpoints through Writing and Research

1. Write a short essay that answers Chapman's question, "Would you rather be subjected to a few minutes of intense pain and considerable public humiliation, or be locked away for two or three years in a prison cell crowded with ill-tempered sociopaths?"

2. In your opinion, what is the significance of the fact that in the West punishment is private and follows secular guidelines whereas in Eastern cultures punishment is public and follows Islamic law?

Panos Ioannides

Gregory

◆——————

Panos Ioannides was born in Cyprus in 1935 and was educated in Cyprus, the United States, and Canada. He has been the head of TV programs at Cyprus Broadcasting Corporation. Ioannides is the author of many plays, which have been staged or telecast internationally, and has written novels, short stories, and radio scripts. "Gregory" was written in 1963 and first appeared in The Charioteer, *a* Review of Modern Greek Literature *(1965). The English translation is by Marion Byron and Catherine Raisiz. This compelling story is based on a true incident that took place during the Cypriot Liberation struggle against the British in the late 1950s. Ioannides takes the unusual approach of letting the reader experience the torments of a soldier ordered to shoot a prisoner, Gregory, who had saved his life and was his friend.*

Before You Read

Evaluate to what extent the story is more effective because it is told from the perspective of the narrator/executioner rather than Gregory.

——————◆——————

1   My hand was sweating as I held the pistol. The curve of the trigger was biting against my finger.

2   Facing me, Gregory trembled.

3   His whole being was beseeching me, "Don't!"

4   Only his mouth did not make a sound. His lips were squeezed tight. If it had been me, I would have screamed, shouted, cursed.

5   The soldiers were watching. . . .

6   The day before, during a brief meeting, they had each given their opinions: "It's tough luck, but it has to be done. We've got no choice."

7   The order from Headquarters was clear: "As soon as Lieutenant Rafel's execution is announced, the hostage Gregory is to be shot and his body must be hanged from a telegraph pole in the main street as an exemplary punishment."

8   It was not the first time that I had to execute a hostage in this war. I had acquired experience, thanks to Headquarters which had kept entrusting me with these delicate assignments. Gregory's case was precisely the sixth.

9   The first time, I remember, I vomited. The second time I got sick and had a headache for days. The third time I drank a bottle of rum.

The fourth, just two glasses of beer. The fifth time I joked about it, "This little guy, with the big pop-eyes, won't be much of a ghost!"

10   But why, dammit, when the day came did I have to start thinking that I'm not so tough, after all? The thought had come at exactly the wrong time and spoiled all my disposition to do my duty.

11   You see, this Gregory was such a miserable little creature, such a puny thing, such a nobody, damn him.

12   That very morning, although he had heard over the loudspeakers that Rafel had been executed, he believed that we would spare his life because we had been eating together so long.

13   "Those who eat from the same mess tins and drink from the same water canteen," he said, "remain good friends no matter what."

14   And a lot more of the same sort of nonsense.

15   He was a silly fool—we had smelled that out the very first day Headquarters gave him to us. The sentry guarding him had got dead drunk and had dozed off. The rest of us with exit permits had gone from the barracks. When we came back, there was Gregory sitting by the sleeping sentry and thumbing through a magazine.

16   "Why didn't you run away, Gregory?" we asked, laughing at him, several days later.

17   And he answered, "Where would I go in this freezing weather? I'm O.K. here."

18   So we started teasing him.

19   "You're dead right. The accommodations here are splendid. . . . "

20   "It's not so bad here," he replied. "The barracks where I used to be are like a sieve. The wind blows in from every side. . . . "

21   We asked him about his girl. He smiled.

22   "Maria is a wonderful person," he told us. "Before I met her she was engaged to a no-good fellow, a pig. He gave her up for another girl. Then nobody in the village wanted to marry Maria. I didn't miss my chance. So what if she is second-hand. Nonsense. Peasant ideas, my friend. She's beautiful and good-hearted. What more could I want? And didn't she load me with watermelons and cucumbers every time I passed by her vegetable garden? Well, one day I stole some cucumbers and melons and watermelons and I took them to her. 'Maria,' I said, 'from now on I'm going to take care of you.' She started crying and then me, too. But ever since that day she has given me lots of trouble— jealousy. She wouldn't let me go even to my mother's. Until the day I was recruited, she wouldn't let me go far from her apron strings. But that was just what I wanted. . . . "

23   He used to tell this story over and over, always with the same words, the same commonplace gestures. At the end he would have a good laugh and start gulping from his water jug.

24   His tongue was always wagging! When he started talking, nothing could stop him. We used to listen and nod our heads, not saying a word. But sometimes, as he was telling us about his mother and family

problems, we couldn't help wondering, "Eh, well, these people have the same headaches in their country as we've got."

25   Strange, isn't it!

26   Except for his talking too much, Gregory wasn't a bad fellow. He was a marvelous cook. Once he made us some apple tarts, so delicious we licked the platter clean. And he could sew, too. He used to sew on all our buttons, patch our clothes, darn our socks, iron our ties, wash our clothes. . . .

27   How the devil could you kill such a friend?

28   Even though his name was Gregory and some people on his side had killed one of ours, even though we had left wives and children to go to war against him and his kind—but how can I explain? He was our friend. He actually liked us! A few days before, hadn't he killed with his own bare hands a scorpion that was climbing up my leg? He could have let it send me to hell!

29   "Thanks, Gregory!" I said then, "Thank God who made you. . . . "

30   When the order came, it was like a thunderbolt. Gregory was to be shot, it said, and hanged from a telegraph pole as an exemplary punishment.

31   We got together inside the barracks. We sent Gregory to wash some underwear for us.

32   "It ain't right."

33   "What is right?"

34   "Our duty!"

35   "Shit!"

36   "If you dare, don't do it! They'll drag you to court-martial and then bang-bang. . . . "

37   Well, of course. The right thing is to save your skin. That's only logical. It's either your skin or his. His, of course, even if it was Gregory, the fellow you've been sharing the same plate with, eating with your fingers, and who was washing your clothes that very minute.

38   What could I do? That's war. We had seen worse things.

39   So we set the hour.

40   We didn't tell him anything when he came back from the washing. He slept peacefully. He snored for the last time. In the morning, he heard the news over the loudspeaker and he saw that we looked gloomy and he began to suspect that something was up. He tried talking to us, but he got no answers and then he stopped talking.

41   He just stood there and looked at us, stunned and lost. . . .

Now, I'll squeeze the trigger. A tiny bullet will rip through his chest. Maybe I'll lose my sleep tonight but in the morning I'll wake up alive.

Gregory seems to guess my thoughts. He puts out his hand and asks, "You're kidding, friend! Aren't you kidding?"

What a jackass! Doesn't he deserve to be cut to pieces? What a thing to ask at such a time. Your heart is about to burst and he's asking if you're kidding. How can a body be kidding about such a thing? Idiot! This is no time for jokes. And you, if you're such a fine friend, why don't you make things easier for us? Help us kill you with fewer qualms? If you would get angry—curse our Virgin, our God—if you'd try to escape it would be much easier for us and for you.

So it is *now.*

Now, Mr. Gregory, you are going to pay for your stupidities wholesale. Because you didn't escape the day the sentry fell asleep; because you didn't escape yesterday when we sent you all alone to the laundry—we did it on purpose, you idiot! Why didn't you let me die from the sting of the scorpion?

So now don't complain. It's all your fault, nitwit.

Eh? What's happening to him now?

Gregory is crying. Tears flood his eyes and trickle down over his cleanshaven cheeks. He is turning his face and pressing his forehead against the wall. His back is shaking as he sobs. His hands cling, rigid and helpless, to the wall.

Now is my best chance, now that he knows there is no other solution and turns his face from us.

I squeeze the trigger.

Gregory jerks. His back stops shaking up and down.

I think I've finished him! How easy it is. . . . But suddenly he starts crying out loud, his hands claw at the wall and try to pull it down. He screams, "No, no. . . . "

I turn to the others. I expect them to nod, "That's enough."

They nod, "What are you waiting for?"

I squeeze the trigger again.

The bullet smashed into his neck. A thick spray of blood spurts out.

Gregory turns. His eyes are all red. He lunges at me and starts punching me with his fists.

"I hate you, hate you. . . ," he screams.

I emptied the barrel. He fell and grabbed my leg as if he wanted to hold on.

42   He died with a terrible spasm. His mouth was full of blood and so were my boots and socks.

43   We stood quietly, looking at him.

44   When we came to, we stooped and picked him up. His hands were frozen and wouldn't let my legs go.

45   I still have their imprints, red and deep, as if made by a hot knife.

46   "We will hang him tonight," the men said.

47　　"Tonight or now?" they said.

48　　I turned and looked at them one by one.

49　　"Is that what you all want?" I asked.

50　　They gave me no answer.

51　　"Dig a grave," I said.

52　　Headquarters did not ask for a report the next day or the day after. The top brass were sure that we had obeyed them and had left him swinging from a pole.

53　　They didn't care to know what happened to that Gregory, alive or dead.

✧ Evaluating the Text

1. Much of the story's action takes place during the few seconds when the narrator must decide whether to pull the trigger. Why do you think Ioannides chooses to tell the story from the executioner's point of view rather than from Gregory's? What in the narrator's past leads his superiors (and the narrator himself) to conclude that he is the one best-suited to kill Gregory?

2. What details illustrate that Gregory has become a friend to the narrator and other soldiers? In what way does he embody the qualities of humanity, decency, and domestic life that the soldiers were forced to leave behind? Why is his innocence a source of both admiration and irritation? How does Gregory's decision to marry Maria suggest the kind of person he is and answer the question as to why he doesn't try to escape when he is told he is going to be killed? What explains why he doesn't perceive the threat to his life even at the moment the narrator points a gun at his head?

3. Discuss the psychological process that allows the narrator to convert his anguish at having to shoot Gregory into a justification for doing so.

4. When the narrator fires the first shot, why does he hope the other soldiers will stop him from firing again? Why don't they stop him? At the end, how does the narrator's order not to hang Gregory's body reveal his distress after shooting Gregory? Why is it ironic that the higher-ups never inquire whether their orders have been carried out? What does this imply and why does it make the narrator feel even worse?

✧ Exploring Different Perspectives

1. What role does political coercion play in "Gregory" and in Rae Yang's account in terms of qualms that each protagonist feels?

2. How does public punishment become an important theme in "Gregory" and in Stephen Chapman's analysis in "The Prisoner's Dilemma"?

✧ *Extending Viewpoints through Writing and Research*

1. In your opinion, is Gregory a good person or just a fool who is stupid enough to get killed when he does not have to die?

2. If you were in the narrator's shoes, what would you have done? Do you think you would have made yourself hate Gregory, as the narrator did, in order to be able to kill him?

Rae Yang

At the Center of the Storm

———◆———

Rae Yang, who teaches East Asian Studies at Dickinson College, offers an unusual perspective of one who grew up in China and, at the age of fifteen, joined the Red Guards in Beijing. Her account of her life working on a pig farm and the political and moral crises that she experienced as a result of the Cultural Revolution offers a unique portrait of someone who was a committed, and even fanatic, revolutionary, who only later had misgivings about what the Red Guards had done. The following chapter is drawn from Spider Eaters *(1997). Her latest work is* China: Fifty Years Inside the People's Republic *(1999).*

China's modern history has been characterized by cycles of liberalization followed by violent oppression. In 1957, reaction against the so-called "let a hundred flowers bloom" period led to a crackdown against intellectuals. In 1966, Mao launched the Cultural Revolution to purge the government and society of liberal elements. Revolutionary Red Guards composed of ideologically motivated young men and women acted with the army to attack so-called bourgeois elements in the government and in the culture at large. After Mao's death in 1976, a backlash led to the imprisoning of Mao's wife, Jiang Qing, and three colleagues (the "Gang of Four").

Before You Read

As you read consider the insight you gain as to why Mao Tse Tung chose young people to spearhead his Cultural Revolution.

———◆———

1   From May to December 1966, the first seven months of the Cultural Revolution left me with experiences I will never forget. Yet I forgot things almost overnight in that period. So many things were happening around me. The situation was changing so fast. I was too excited, too jubilant, too busy, too exhausted, too confused, too uncomfortable. . . . The forgotten things, however, did not all go away. Later some of them sneaked back into my memory, causing me unspeakable pain and shame. So I would say that those seven months were the most terrible in my life. Yet they were also the most wonderful! I had never felt so good about myself before, nor have I ever since.

2   In the beginning, the Cultural Revolution exhilarated me because suddenly I felt that I was allowed to think with my own head and say

what was on my mind. In the past, the teachers at 101 had worked hard to make us intelligent, using the most difficult questions in mathematics, geometry, chemistry, and physics to challenge us. But the mental abilities we gained, we were not supposed to apply elsewhere. For instance, we were not allowed to question the teachers' conclusions. Students who did so would be criticized as "disrespectful and conceited," even if their opinions made perfect sense. Worse still was to disagree with the leaders. Leaders at various levels represented the Communist Party. Disagreeing with them could be interpreted as being against the Party, a crime punishable by labor reform, imprisonment, even death.

3   Thus the teachers created a contradiction. On the one hand, they wanted us to be smart, rational, and analytical. On the other hand, they forced us to be stupid, to be "the teachers' little lambs" and "the Party's obedient tools." By so doing, I think, they planted a sick tree; the bitter fruit would soon fall into their own mouths.

4   When the Cultural Revolution broke out in late May 1966, I felt like the legendary monkey Sun Wukong, freed from the dungeon that had held him under a huge mountain for five hundred years. It was Chairman Mao who set us free by allowing us to rebel against authorities. As a student, the first authority I wanted to rebel against was Teacher Lin, our homeroom teacher—in Chinese, *banzhuren*. As *banzhuren*, she was in charge of our class. A big part of her duty was to make sure that we behaved and thought correctly.

5   Other students in my class might have thought that I was Teacher Lin's favorite. As our Chinese teacher, she read my papers in front of the class once in a while. That was true. (Only she and I knew that the grades I got for those papers rarely went above 85. I could only imagine what miserable grades she gave to others in our class.) She also chose me to be the class representative for Chinese, which meant if others had difficulties with the subject, I was to help them. In spite of all these, I did not like Teacher Lin! She had done me a great wrong in the past. I would never forget it.

6   In my opinion, Lin was exactly the kind of teacher who, in Chairman Mao's words, "treated the students as their enemies." In 1965, we went to Capital Steel and Iron Company in the far suburb of Beijing to do physical labor. One night there was an earthquake warning. We were made to stay outdoors to wait for it. By midnight, no earthquake had come. Two o'clock, still all quiet. Three o'clock, four o'clock, five. . . . The night was endless. Sitting on the cold concrete pavement for so many hours, I was sleepy. I was exhausted. My only wish at the moment was to be allowed to go into the shack and literally "hit the hay." Without thinking I grumbled: "Ai! How come there is still no earthquake?"

7   Who should have thought that this remark was overheard by Teacher Lin? All of a sudden she started criticizing me in a loud voice.

8   "The workers and the poor and lower-middle peasants would never say such a thing! Think of all the property that will be damaged by an earthquake. Think of all the lives that may be lost! Now you are looking forward to an earthquake! Only class enemies look forward to earthquakes! Where did your class feelings go? Do you have any proletarian feelings at all? . . . "

9   She went on and on. Her shrill voice woke up everybody, my classmates as well as students in the other five parallel classes. All were sitting outside at the moment. Everybody turned to watch us. Three hundred pairs of eyes! It was such a shame! I felt my cheeks burning. I wanted to defend myself. I wanted to tell Teacher Lin that although there might be some truth in what she said, I had never been in an earthquake. I was merely tired and wished the whole thing over. Besides, I was only half awake when I said that. I was not looking forward to an earthquake!

10   In fact, what I really wanted to tell her was that I knew why she was making such a fuss about my remark, which if she had not seized would have drifted away and scattered in the morning breeze like a puff of vapor: she was using this as an opportunity to show off her political correctness in front of all these teachers and students. At my cost! Later she might be able to cash in on it, using it as her political capital. . . .

11   But of course I knew it would be crazy for me to talk back like that. Contradicting the teacher would only lead me into more trouble. So I swallowed the words that were rolling on the tip of my tongue and lowered my head. Hot tears assaulted my eyes. Tears of anger. Tears of shame. I bit my lips to force them back. *Let's wait and see, Teacher Lin. Someday I will have my revenge. On you!*

12   Now the time had come for the underdogs to speak up, to seek justice! Immediately I took up a brush pen, dipped it in black ink and wrote a long *dazibao* (criticism in big characters). Using some of the rhetorical devices Teacher Lin had taught us, I accused her of lacking proletarian feelings toward her students, of treating them as her enemies, of being high-handed, and suppressing different opinions. When I finished and showed it to my classmates, they supported me by signing their names to it. Next, we took the *dazibao* to Teacher Lin's home nearby and pasted it on the wall of her bedroom for her to read carefully day and night. This, of course, was not personal revenge. It was answering Chairman Mao's call to combat the revisionist educational line. If in the meantime it caused Teacher Lin a few sleepless nights, so be it! This revolution was meant to "touch the soul" of people, an unpopular teacher in particular.

13   Teacher Lin, although she was not a good teacher in my opinion, was not yet the worst. Teacher Qian was even worse. He was the political teacher who had implemented the Exposing Third Layer of

Thoughts campaign. In the past many students believed that he could read people's minds. Now a *dazibao* by a student gave us a clue as to how he acquired this eerie ability. Something I would not have guessed in a thousand years! He had been reading students' diaries in class breaks, while we were doing physical exercise on the sports ground. The student who wrote the *dazibao* felt sick one day and returned to his classroom earlier than expected. There he had actually seen Qian sneak a diary from a student's desk and read it. The student kept his silence until the Cultural Revolution, for Qian was his *banzhuren*.

14   So this was Qian's so-called "political and thought work"! What could it teach us but dishonesty and hypocrisy? Such a "glorious" example the school had set for us, and in the past we had revered him so much! Thinking of the nightmare he gave me, I was outraged. "Take up a pen, use it as a gun." I wrote another *dazibao* to denounce Teacher Qian.

15   Within a few days *dazibao* were popping up everywhere like bamboo shoots after a spring rain, written by students, teachers, administrators, workers, and librarians. Secrets dark and dirty were exposed. Everyday we made shocking discoveries. The sacred halo around the teachers' heads that dated back two thousand five hundred years to the time of Confucius disappeared. Now teachers must drop their pretentious airs and learn a few things from their students. Parents would be taught by their kids instead of vice versa, as Chairman Mao pointed out. Government officials would have to wash their ears to listen to the ordinary people. Heaven and earth were turned upside down. The rebellious monkey with enormous power had gotten out. A revolution was underway.

16   Looking back on it, I should say that I felt good about the Cultural Revolution when it started. It gave me a feeling of superiority and confidence that I had never experienced before. Yet amidst the new freedom and excitement, I ran into things that made me very uncomfortable.

17   I remember one day in July, I went to have lunch at the student dining hall. On the way I saw a crowd gathering around the fountain. I went over to take a look. The fountain had been a pleasant sight in the past. Sparkling water swaying in the wind among green willow twigs, making the air fresh and clean. In Beijing it was a luxury ordinary middle schools did not enjoy. When the Cultural Revolution broke out, the water was turned off. Now the bottom of the fountain was muddy, littered with wastepaper and broken glass.

18   On this day I saw a teacher in the fountain, a middle-aged man. His clothes were muddy. Blood was streaming down his head, as a number of students were throwing bricks at him. He tried to dodge the bricks. While he did so, without noticing it, he crawled in the fountain, round and round, like an animal in the zoo. Witnessing such a scene, I suddenly felt sick to my stomach. I would have vomited, if I had not

quickly turned round and walked away. Forget about lunch. My appetite was gone.

19   Sitting in an empty classroom, I wondered why this incident upset me so much: *This is the first time I've seen someone beaten. Moreover this person isn't a stranger. He's a teacher at 101. Do I pity him? Maybe a little? Maybe not. After all I don't know anything about him. He might be a counterrevolutionary or a bad element. He might have done something very bad; thus he deserved the punishment. Something else bothers me, then—not the teacher. What is it?*

20   Then it dawned on me that I was shocked by the ugliness of the scene. *Yes. That's it! In the past when I read about torture in revolutionary novels, saw it in movies, and daydreamed about it, it was always so heroic, so noble; therefore it was romantic and beautiful. But now, in real life, it happened in front of me. It's so sordid! I wish I'd seen none of it! I don't want the memory to destroy my hero's dream.*

21   This teacher survived; another was not so fortunate. Teacher Chen, our art teacher, was said to resemble a spy in the movies. He was a tall, thin man with sallow skin and long hair, which was a sign of decadence. Moreover, he seemed gloomy and he smoked a lot. "If a person weren't scheming or if he didn't feel very unhappy in the new society, why would he smoke like that?" a classmate asked me, expecting nothing but heartfelt consent from me. "Not to say that in the past he had asked students to draw naked female bodies in front of plaster statues to corrupt them!" For these "crimes," he was beaten to death by a group of senior students.

22   When I heard this, I felt very uncomfortable again. The whole thing seemed a bad joke to me. Yet it was real! Teacher Chen had taught us the year before and unlike Teacher Lin and Teacher Qian, he had never treated students as his enemies. He was polite and tolerant. If a student showed talent in painting, he would be delighted. On the other hand, he would not embarrass a student who "had no art cells." I had never heard complaints about him before. Yet somehow he became the first person I knew who was killed in the Cultural Revolution.

23   Living next door to Teacher Chen was Teacher Jiang, our geography teacher. While Teacher Chen was tall and lean, Teacher Jiang was short and stout. Both were old bachelors, who taught auxiliary courses. Before the Cultural Revolution Teacher Jiang was known for two things. One was his unkempt clothes. The other was the fact that he never brought anything but a piece of chalk to class. Yet many students said that he was the most learned teacher at 101. He had many maps and books stored in his funny big head.

24   If Teacher Jiang had been admired by students before, he became even more popular after the revolution started and Teacher Chen was killed. Since August 1966 Red Guards were allowed to travel free of charge to places all over China. Before we set off, everybody wanted to

get a few tips from him, and afterwards we'd love to tell him a few stories in return. It was our chance to show off what we had learned from the trips. Thus from August to December, Teacher Jiang had many visitors. Happy voices and laughter were heard from across the lotus pond in front of his dorm house. At night lights shone through his windows often into the small hours. Geography turned out a true blessing for Teacher Jiang, while art doomed Teacher Chen.

25   In contrast to the teachers who lost control over their lives in 1966, we students suddenly found power in our hands. Entrance examinations for senior middle school and college were canceled. Now it was entirely up to us to decide what we would do with our time. This was a big change. In the past, decisions had always been made for us by our parents, teachers, and leaders. At school, all courses were required and we took them according to a fixed schedule, six classes a day, six days a week. College was the same as middle schools. After college, the state would assign everybody a job, an iron rice bowl. Like it or not, it would be yours for life.

26   Now those who had made decisions for us—teachers, parents, administrators—were swept aside by the storm. We were in charge. We could do things on our own initiative. We made plans. We carried them out. So what did we do? Instead of routine classes, we organized meetings at which we shared our family history. (People who spoke up at such meetings were of course revolutionary cadres' children. Others could only listen.) I remember Wu, a girl from a high-ranking cadre's family, told a story that left a deep impression on me.

27   In 1942 Japanese troops raided the Communist base in the north. At this time Wu's older brother was only several months old. He was a beautiful baby boy, with a chubby face and the mother's large brown eyes. The mother gave him the name Precious. Day and night she longed for the father to come back from the front to meet his firstborn.

28   But before the father returned, the Japanese invaders came. Wu's mother took the baby and fled to the mountains. She and many others hid in a cavern. The enemy soldiers came near, searching for them. At this moment the baby woke up and was about to cry. Her mother had no choice but to cover his mouth with her own hand. Or else all would have been found and killed by the Japanese.

29   The baby was in agony. He struggled with all his might for his life. His lovely little face turned red and then blue. His tiny hands grabbed at his mother's, desperately trying to push it away so that he could breathe. His plump little feet kicked helplessly. The mother's heart was pierced by ten thousand arrows, but she did not dare loosen her grip. Finally the Japanese went away. By then the baby had turned cold in her arms.

30   Wu burst into tears and we all cried with her.

31   *Why does she cry like that? Yes. I understand. The brother! Because he died so tragically, he will always be loved most by the parents. The perfect*

child. The most "precious" one, the one they sacrificed for the revolution. Wu and her other siblings cannot rival him, no matter how good they are . . .

32   But of course that was not why she cried or why we cried with her on that day. We cried because we were deeply moved by the heroic struggle and tremendous sacrifice made by our parents and older brothers and sisters. The stories we told at such meetings convinced us that our lives were on the line: if we should allow the revolution to deteriorate, the evil imperialists and beastly Nationalists would come back. As a slogan of the thirties went, "Cut the grass and eliminate the roots"—if we did not act, they would kill our parents who were revolutionary cadres and make sure that none of us would survive to seek revenge on them.

33   Suddenly I felt that these classmates of mine were dearer to me than my own brothers and sisters. I loved them! They loved me! Today we shed tears in the same room. Tomorrow we would shed blood in the same ditch. I was willing to sacrifice my life for any of them, while before the Cultural Revolution I mistrusted them, seeing them as nothing but my rivals.

34   In fact, it was not fear for our lives but pride and a sense of responsibility that fired us up. Chairman Mao had said that we were the morning sun. We were the hope. The future of China and the fate of humankind depended on us. The Soviet Union and East European countries had changed colors. Only China and Albania remained true to Marxism and Leninism. By saving the revolution in China, we were making history. We must uproot bureaucracy and corruption in China, abolish privileges enjoyed by government officials and the intelligentsia, reform education, reform art and literature, reform government organizations. . . . In short, we must purify China and make it a shining example. Someday the whole world would follow us onto this new path.

35   Aside from sharing family history, we biked to universities and middle schools all over Beijing to read *dazibao* and attend mass rallies where Lin Biao, Zhou Enlai, and Mao's wife, Jiang Qing, showed up to give speeches. I first heard the term "Red Guard" in late June at Middle School attached to Qinghua University, two months before most Chinese would hear of it. It was an exciting idea. On our way back, my schoolmates and I were so preoccupied with the notion that our bikes stopped on a riverbank. Next thing I remember, we were tearing up our red scarves, which only a month before had been the sacred symbol of the Young Pioneers. Now they represented the revisionist educational line and to tear them up was a gesture of rebellion. We tied the strips of red cloth around our left arms in the style of workers' pickets of the 1920s. When we rode away from the spot, we had turned ourselves into Red Guards.

36   People in the street noticed our new costume: faded army uniforms that had been worn by our parents, red armbands, wide canvas

army belts, army caps, the peaks pulled down low by girls in the style of the boys. . . . Some people smiled at us. Some waved their hands. Their eyes showed surprise, curiosity, excitement, admiration. I don't think I saw fear. Not yet.

37 When people smiled at us, we smiled back, proud of ourselves. Our eyes were clear and bright. Our cheeks rosy and radiant. Red armbands fluttered in the wind. We pedaled hard. We pedaled fast. All of us had shiny new bikes, a luxury most Chinese could not afford at the time. (In my case, Father had bought me a new bike so as to show his support for the Cultural Revolution. Being a dreamer himself, he believed, or at least hoped, that the Cultural Revolution would purify the Communist Party and save the revolution.)

38 When we rang the bells, we rang them in unison, for a long time. It was not to warn people to get out of our way. It was to attract their attention. Or maybe we just wanted to listen to the sound. The sound flew up, crystal clear and full of joy, like a flock of white doves circling in the blue sky. At the time, little did I know that this was the first stir of a great storm that would soon engulf the entire country.

39 On August 18, 1966, I saw Chairman Mao for the first time. The night before, we set off from 101 on foot a little after midnight and arrived at Tian'anmen Square before daybreak. In the dark we waited anxiously. Will Chairman Mao come? was the question in everybody's mind. Under a starry sky, we sang.

40 "Lifting our heads we see the stars of Beidou [the Big Dipper], lowering our heads we are longing for Mao Zedong, longing for Mao Zedong. . . . "

41 We poured our emotions into the song. Chairman Mao who loved the people would surely hear it, for it came from the bottom of our hearts.

42 Perhaps he did. At five o'clock, before sunrise, like a miracle he walked out of Tian'anmen onto the square and shook hands with people around him. The square turned into a jubilant ocean. Everybody was shouting "Long live Chairman Mao!" Around me girls were crying; boys were crying too. With hot tears streaming down my face, I could not see Chairman Mao clearly. He had ascended the rostrum. He was too high, or rather, the stands for Red Guard representatives were too low.

43 Earnestly we chanted: "We-want-to-see-Chair-man-Mao!" He heard us! He walked over to the corner of Tian'anmen and waved at us. Now I could see him clearly. He was wearing a green army uniform and a red armband, just like all of us. My blood was boiling inside me. I jumped and shouted and cried in unison with a million people in the square. At that moment, I forgot myself; all barriers that existed between me and others broke down. I felt like a drop of water that finally joined the mighty raging ocean. I would never be lonely again.

44   The night after, we celebrated the event at 101. Everybody joined the folk dance called *yangge* around bonfires. No one was shy. No one was self-conscious. By then, we had been up and awake for more than forty hours, but somehow I was still bursting with energy. Others seemed that way too. After dancing a couple of hours, I biked all the way home to share the happiness with my parents. By this time, they no longer minded that I woke them up at three o'clock in the morning. In fact, they had urged me to wake them up whenever I got home so that they could hear the latest news from me about the revolution.

45   Seeing Chairman Mao added new fuel to the flame of our revolutionary zeal. The next day, my fellow Red Guards and I held a meeting to discuss our next move. Obviously if we loved Chairman Mao, just shouting slogans was not enough. We must do something. But what could we do? By mid-August the teachers at 101 had been criticized and some were detained in "cow sheds." Even the old school principal, Wang Yizhi, had been "pulled down from the horse" because of her connection with Liu Shaoqi, the biggest capitalist-roader in the Party. On campus, little was left for us to rebel against. Therefore, many Red Guards had walked out of schools to break "four olds" (old ideas, old culture, old customs and old habits) in the city.

46   This was what we should do. Only first we had to pinpoint some "four olds." I suggested that we go to a nearby restaurant to get rid of some old practices. Everybody said: "Good! Let's do it!" So we jumped onto our bikes and rushed out like a gust of wind.

47   Seeing a group of Red Guards swarming in, everybody in the restaurant tensed up. In August, people began to fear Red Guards who summoned the wind, raised the storm, and spread terror all over China. Small talk ceased. All eyes were fastened on us.

48   I stepped forward and began ritualistically: "Our great leader Chairman Mao teaches us, 'Corruption and waste are very great crimes.'" After that, I improvised: "Comrades! In today's world there are still many people who live in poverty and have nothing to eat. So we should not waste food. Nor should we behave like bourgeois ladies and gentlemen who expect to be waited on by others in a restaurant. From now on, people who want to eat in this restaurant must follow new rules: One, go to the window to get your own food. Two, carry it to the table yourselves. Three, wash your own dishes. Four, you must finish the food you ordered. Otherwise you may not leave the restaurant!"

49   While I said this, I saw some people change color and sweat broke out on their foreheads. They had ordered too much food. Now they had to finish it under the watchful eyes of a group of Red Guards. This was not an enviable situation. But nobody in the restaurant protested. Contradicting a Red Guard was asking for big trouble. It was like playing with thunderbolts and dynamite. So people just lowered their heads and swallowed the food as fast as they could. Some of them

might develop indigestion afterwards, but I believed it was their own fault. By showing off their wealth at a restaurant, they wasted the blood and sweat of the peasants. Now they got caught and lost face. This should teach them a lesson!

50   While my comrades and I were breaking "four olds" at restaurants, other Red Guards were raiding people's homes all over the city. News of victory poured in: Red Guards discovered guns, bullets, old deeds, gold bars, foreign currency, yellow books and magazines (pornography). . . . Hearing this, people in my group became restless. But somehow I was not eager to raid homes, and I did not ask myself why. "We are busy making revolution at restaurants, aren't we?"

51   Then one day an old woman stopped us in the street and insisted that we go with her to break some "four olds" in the home of a big capitalist. None of us could say No to this request. So she led us to the home of a prominent overseas Chinese, where the "four olds" turned out to be flowers.

52   The courtyard we entered was spacious. A green oasis of cool shade, drifting fragrance, and delicate beauty: tree peonies and bamboo were planted next to Tai Lake rocks. Orchids and chrysanthemums grew along a winding path inlaid with cobblestones. A trellis of wisteria stood next to a corridor. Goldfish swam under water lilies in antique vats. . . .

53   *Strange! Why does this place look familiar? I am sure I've never been here before. Could it be I've seen it in a dream? . . .*

54   Suddenly the answer dawned on me: *this place looks just like Nainai's home. Nainai's home must have been raided. Maybe several times by now. Is she still there? Did they kick her out? Is she all right? And what happened to the beautiful flowers she and Third Aunt planted?. . . No use thinking about such things! I can't help her anyway. She is a capitalist. I am a Red Guard. I have nothing to do with her!*

55   *The question in front of me now is what to do with these flowers. Smash them! Uproot them! Trample them to the ground! Flowers, plants, goldfish, birds, these are all bourgeois stuff. The new world has no place for them. My fellow Red Guards have already started. I mustn't fall behind.*

56   So I lifted up a flowerpot and dropped it against a Tai Lake rock. Bang! The sound was startling. *Don't be afraid. The first step is always the most difficult.* Bang! Bang! *Actually it isn't so terrible. Now I've started, I can go on and on. To tell the truth, I even begin to enjoy breaking flowerpots! Who would have thought of that?. . .*

57   After a while, we were all out of breath. So we ordered the family to get rid of the remaining flowers in three days, pledging that we'd come back to check on them. Then we left. Behind us was a world of broken pots, spilled soil, fallen petals, and bare roots. Another victory of Mao Zedong thought.

58   On my way home, surprise caught up with me. I was stopped by a group of Red Guards whom I did not know. They told me that my long braids were also bourgeois stuff. Hearing this, I looked around and

saw Red Guards stand on both sides of the street with scissors in their hands. Anyone who had long or curly hair would be stopped by them, their hair cut off on the spot in front of jeering kids. Suddenly I felt my cheeks burning. To have my hair cut off in the street was to lose face. So I pleaded with them, vowing that I would cut my braids as soon as I got home. They let me go. For the time being, I coiled my braids on top of my head and covered them with my army cap.

59   Fearing that other surprises might be in store for me in the street, I went straight home. There I found Aunty in dismay. It turned out that she too had seen Red Guards cutting long hair in the street. So she did not dare leave home these couple of days and we were about to run out of groceries.

60   "What shall I do?" she asked me. "If I cut my hair, won't I look like an old devil, with short white hair sticking up all over my head?" Her troubled look reminded me that since her childhood, Aunty always had long hair. Before she was married, it was a thick, long braid. Then a bun, for a married woman, which looked so elegant on the back of her head. Even in Switzerland, she had never changed her hairstyle. But now neither she nor I had any choice. If we did not want to lose face in the street, we'd better do it ourselves at home.

61   While Aunty and I were cutting each other's hair, my parents were burning things in the bathroom. The idea was the same: to save face and avoid trouble, better destroy all the "four olds" we had before others found them out. So they picked out a number of Chinese books, burned them together with all the letters they had kept and some old photographs. The ash was flushed down the toilet. Repair the house before it rains. That was wise. No one could tell whose home would be raided next. Better be prepared for the worst.

62   Now suddenly it seemed everybody in my family had trouble, including Lian, who was eleven. His problem was our cat, Little Tiger. Lian found him three years ago playing hide and seek in a lumber yard. Then he was a newborn kitten. So little that he did not even know how to drink milk. Aunty taught us how to feed him. Put milk in a soupspoon. Tilt it to make the milk flow slowly through the depression in the middle of the handle. Put the tip of the handle into the kitten's tiny mouth. He tasted the milk. He liked it. He began to drink it. By and by the kitten grew into a big yellow cat with black stripes. On his forehead, three horizontal lines formed the Chinese character *wang*, which means king. We called him Little Tiger because in China the tiger is king of all animals.

63   Little Tiger's life was in danger now, for pets were considered bourgeois too. This morning Lian had received an ultimatum from kids who were our neighbors. It said we had to get rid of Little Tiger in three days or else they would come and take revolutionary action. This time we could not solve the problem by doing it ourselves. Little Tiger was a member of our family. We had to think of a way to save his life.

64   Aunty suggested that we hide him in a bag, take him out to a far-away place, and let him go. He would become a wild cat. Good idea. Only I did not want to do this. What would people say if they found that I, a Red Guard, was hiding a cat in my bag? So I told Lian to do it and went back to school. Since the Cultural Revolution started, I had a bed in the student dormitory and spent most of the nights there.

65   A few days later when I came back home, Aunty told me what had happened to Little Tiger. (Lian himself wouldn't talk about it.) When Lian took him out, he was spotted by the boys who had given him the ultimatum. Noticing something was moving in his bag, they guessed it was the cat. They grabbed the bag, swung it round, and hit it hard against a brick wall. "Miao!" Little Tiger mewed wildly. The boys laughed. It was fun. They continued to hit him against the wall. Lian started to cry and he begged them to stop. Nobody listened to him. Little Tiger's blood stained the canvas bag, leaving dark marks on the brick wall. But he was still alive. Only his mewing became weak and pitiable. Too bad a cat had nine lives! It only prolonged his suffering and gave the boys more pleasure. Bang! Bang! Little Tiger was silent. Dead at last. Lian ran back and cried in Aunty's arms for a long time.

66   A week after our cat was killed by the boys, a neighbor whom I called Guma killed herself. On that day, I happened to be home. I heard a commotion outside and looked. Many people were standing in front of our building. When I went out, I saw clearly that Guma was hanging from a pipe in the bathroom. Another gruesome sight I could not wipe from my memory.

67   Why did she kill herself? Nobody knew the answer. Before she died, she was a typist at the college. A quiet little woman. She had no enemies; no historical problems. Nobody had struggled against her. So people assumed that she killed herself for her husband's sake.

68   The love story between her and her husband must have been quite dramatic. Mother said a writer had interviewed them because he wanted to write a book about it. Guma's husband, whom I called Guzhang, was a professor in the French department. I used to like him a lot because of his refined, gentle manner and the many interesting books he owned. Recently, however, it became known that Guzhang had serious historical problems. In his youth he had studied in France and joined the Communist Party there. Later somehow he dropped out of the Party and turned away from politics. Because of this, he was accused of being a renegade. A renegade he seemed to me, like one who was a coward in revolutionary novels and movies. The following story would prove my point.

69   After Guma killed herself, Guzhang wanted to commit suicide too. He went to the nearby Summer Palace and jumped into the lake. But the place he jumped was too shallow. After a while he climbed out, saying the water was too cold. When people at the college heard this

story, he became a laughingstock. Even Aunty remarked: "You may know people for a long time and still you don't know their hearts. Who should have thought that Guma, a woman so gentle and quiet, was so resolute, while Guzhang, a big man, did not have half her courage."

70   These words seemed sinister. To tell the truth, I was alarmed by them. Just a couple of days before a nanny had killed herself at the nearby University of Agriculture. The old woman was a proletarian pure and simple. So why did she kill herself?

71   Her death was caused by a new chapter in the breaking "four olds" campaign. The idea was actually similar to mine: in the past bourgeois ladies and gentlemen were waited on hand and foot by the working people. In the new society such practices should be abolished. The working people would no longer serve and be exploited by bourgeois ladies and gentlemen. Thus the new rule said those who were labeled bourgeois ladies and gentlemen were not allowed to use nannies. As for those who were not labeled bourgeois ladies and gentlemen, they were not allowed to use nannies either. Because if they used nannies, it was proof enough that they were bourgeois ladies and gentlemen, and bourgeois ladies and gentlemen were not allowed to use nannies. Thus according to the new rule, no family was allowed to use nannies.

72   As a result, the old woman killed herself, because she lost her job and had no children to support her. Though she had saved some money for her old age, another new rule had it all frozen in the bank.

73   Aunty was in exactly the same situation. When she first came to work for us, she was forty-six. Then her son died. Now she was sixty-two, an old woman by traditional standards. Right now all her savings were frozen in the bank. Whether someday she might get them back or not, and if yes when, was anybody's guess. Now the deadline set by the Red Guards of the college for all the nannies to leave was drawing near. Recently Aunty made me uneasy. I was frightened by her eyes. They were so remote, as if they were in a different world. I could not get in touch with them. Then she made that strange comment about being resolute. Could she mean. . . ?

74   On the evening before Aunty left (fortunately she had kept her old home in the city, to which now she could return), Father gathered our whole family together. Solemnly he made a pledge to her. He said that he would continue to support her financially for as long as she lived. Although for the time being she had to leave, she would always be a member of our family. She needn't worry about her old age.

75   That was, in my opinion, the exact right thing to say at the right moment. Even today when I look back on it, I am proud of Father for what he said on that hot summer evening thirty years ago. By then tens of thousands of nannies were being driven out of their employers' homes in Beijing, and who knows how many in the whole country. But few people had the kindness and generosity to say what Father said.

76   Aunty said nothing in return. But she was moved. From then on, she took our family to be her own. Instead of a burden, she became a pillar for our family through one storm after another. She did not quit until all her strength was used up.

✧ Evaluating the Text

1. As a result of the Cultural Revolution, how did personal animosities, jealousies, and the desire for revenge become legitimized in the new political environment?

2. What principles motivated the Red Guards? What different areas of society were touched by them? Why were most of their activities involved with destruction of every kind—even including cutting off Yang's braids?

3. As her narrative proceeds, Yang has several experiences that lead her to question her initial zeal. What are some of these and how do they change her attitude?

✧ Exploring Different Perspectives

1. Compare Yang's account in terms of the narrator's sense of conscience and remorse for following orders from authority figures with the narrator's predicament in Ioannides's story.

2. To what extent was Yang turned into a surrogate defender of Maoism, just at American children are turned into surrogate promoters by corporations as depicted by Eric Schlosser?

✧ Extending Viewpoints through Writing and Research

1. Yang is completely honest in admitting the excesses in which she participated and about which she was very enthusiastic. Did you ever have a change of heart about something about which you were at one time zealous? Describe your experience. What caused you to change your attitude?

2. Yang presents a comprehensive picture of the topsy-turvy effect the Cultural Revolution had on Chinese society when it imbued the Red Guards with power over teachers, parents, administrators, and others who once had power over them. What scenario can you imagine would occur in American society if a comparable table-turning revolution took place?

3. An account of the Cultural Revolution is available at http://www .historylearningsite.co.uk/cultural_revolution.

How does this image of the Red Guards communicate the fervor that Yang felt?

Connecting Cultures

◆

Philip Slater, "Want-Creation Fuels Americans' Addictiveness"

Are the ever-recurring fiestas in Mexico (see Octavio Paz, "Fiesta" in Chapter 8) signs of a cultural addiction comparable to the "quick fix" syndrome in American culture as analyzed by Slater?

Jeremy Rifkin, "Big, Bad Beef"

Why is it ironic that only the untouchables in India as reported by Viramma in "A Pariah's Life" (Chapter 5) can work with beef products?

Eric Schlosser, "Kid Kustomers"

Compare the experiences of children in a culture of surplus in America, as discussed by Schlosser, with the choices available to a child from a highly privileged family as described by Gayatri Devi (see "A Princess Remembers" in Chapter 1).

Luis Sepulveda, "Daisy"

What role does using language as a form of rebellion play in "Daisy" and in Ngũgĩ wa Thiong'o's "Decolonising the Mind" in Chapter 7?

Stephen Chapman, "The Prisoner's Dilemma"

Discuss the paradox of women being veiled (see Elizabeth W. and Robert A. Fernea, "A Look Behind the Veil" in Chapter 3) in Middle Eastern countries while in the same societies punishment is public.

Panos Ioannides, "Gregory"

Discuss the moral choices that come about because of political coercion in this story and in Gloria Anzaldúa's "Cervicide" in Chapter 7.

Rae Yang, "At the Center of the Storm"

Why is it ironic that the political turmoil Yang discusses ultimately produced the situation in China described by Daniela Deane (see "The Little Emperors" in Chapter 1)?

7

The Other

*I am an invisible man. . . . I am a man of substance, of flesh
and bone, fiber and liquids—and I might even be said to
possess a mind. I am invisible, understand, simply because
people refuse to see me.*

—Ralph Ellison (1914–1994) African-American author,
The narrator, in Prologue, *The Invisible Man*, 1952

In some ways, our age—the age of the displaced person, and those whom society considers deviant, abnormal, or simply different—is defined by the condition of exile and otherness. Being brought up in one world and then emigrating to a different culture inevitably produces feelings of alienation. Moving to another country involves living among people who dress differently, eat unfamiliar foods, have puzzling customs, and speak another language. Without insight into the norms that govern behavior in a new environment, it is often difficult for immigrants to interpret the actions of others—to know what particular facial expressions and gestures might mean, what assumptions govern physical contact, how people express and resolve conflicts, or what topics of conversation are deemed appropriate.

The works in this chapter offer insights into how various groups are designated as the "other" and are often stigmatized and ostracized. Temple Grandin, one of the few to break out of the limitations of autism, shares her experiences in "Thinking in Pictures." The Chicana writer Gloria Anzaldúa, in "Cervicide," tells a poignant story of a Mexican-American family living on the Texas border. Poranee Natadecha-Sponsel, in "Individualism as an American Cultural Value," describes the often perplexing cultural differences that she experienced after moving to America from Thailand. Gino Del Guercio's "The Secrets of Haiti's Living Dead" reveals that, in contrast to its stereotyped image, voodoo is part of a cohesive system of social control in Haiti.

Speaking from a postcolonial perspective in Kenya, Ngũgĩ wa Thiong'o, in "Decolonising the Mind," analyzes the damaging psychological consequences of having been forbidden to write or speak in his native language while at school. In "Polite Lies" Kyoko Mori describes how the protocols that govern conversation in Japanese society became intolerable when she returned to visit. David R. Counts, in "Too Many Bananas," reveals the many lessons about reciprocity he learned while doing fieldwork in New Guinea.

Temple Grandin

Thinking in Pictures

◆

Temple Grandin has a Ph.D. in animal science from the University of Illinois. She has designed many of the livestock-handling facilities in the United States and in other countries. What makes her achievement astounding is the fact that she is autistic (a condition characterized by difficulty in communicating, repetitive gestures, and withdrawal into fantasy) and is one of the few who have overcome this neurological impairment enough to communicate with others. The following selection is drawn from her autobiography, Thinking in Pictures: And Other Reports from My Life with Autism *(1996). She has also written (with Catherine Johnson)* Animals in Translation: Using the Mysteries of Autism to Decode Animal Behavior *(2005).*

Before You Read

How do you understand the nature of autism and the way it severely limits those who suffer from it?

◆

Processing Nonvisual Information

1 Autistics have problems learning things that cannot be thought about in pictures. The easiest words for an autistic child to learn are nouns, because they directly relate to pictures. Highly verbal autistic children like I was can sometimes learn how to read with phonics. Written words were too abstract for me to remember, but I could laboriously remember the approximately fifty phonetic sounds and a few rules. Lower-functioning children often learn better by association, with the aid of word labels attached to objects in their environment. Some very impaired autistic children learn more easily if words are spelled out with plastic letters they can feel.

2 Spatial words such as "over" and "under" had no meaning for me until I had a visual image to fix them in my memory. Even now, when I hear the word "under" by itself, I automatically picture myself getting under the cafeteria tables at school during an air-raid drill, a common occurrence on the East Coast during the early fifties. The first memory that any single word triggers is almost always a childhood memory. I can remember the teacher telling us to be quiet and walking single-file into the cafeteria, where six or eight children huddled under

each table. If I continue on the same train of thought, more and more associative memories of elementary school emerge. I can remember the teacher scolding me after I hit Alfred for putting dirt on my shoe. All of these memories play like videotapes in the VCR in my imagination. If I allow my mind to keep associating, it will wander a million miles away from the word "under," to submarines under the Antarctic and the Beatles song "Yellow Submarine." If I let my mind pause on the picture of the yellow submarine, I then hear the song. As I start humming the song and get to the part about people coming on board, my association switches to the gangway of a ship I saw in Australia.

3   I also visualize verbs. The word "jumping" triggers a memory of jumping hurdles at the mock Olympics held at my elementary school. Adverbs often trigger inappropriate images—"quickly" reminds me of Nestle's Quik—unless they are paired with a verb, which modifies my visual image. For example, "he ran quickly" triggers an animated image of Dick from the first-grade reading book running fast, and "he walked slowly" slows the image down. As a child, I left out words such as "is," "the," and "it," because they had no meaning by themselves. Similarly, words like "of" and "an" made no sense. Eventually I learned how to use them properly, because my parents always spoke correct English and I mimicked their speech patterns. To this day certain verb conjugations, such as "to be," are absolutely meaningless to me.

4   When I read, I translate written words into color movies or I simply store a photo of the written page to be read later. When I retrieve the material, I see a photocopy of the page in my imagination. I can then read it like a TelePrompTer. It is likely that Raymond, the autistic savant depicted in the movie *Rain Man,* used a similar strategy to memorize telephone books, maps, and other information. He simply photocopied each page of the phone book into his memory. When he wanted to find a certain number, he just scanned pages of the phone book that were in his mind. To pull information out of my memory, I have to replay the video. Pulling facts up quickly is sometimes difficult, because I have to play bits of different videos until I find the right tape. This takes time.

5   When I am unable to convert text to pictures, it is usually because the text has no concrete meaning. Some philosophy books and articles about the cattle futures market are simply incomprehensible. It is much easier for me to understand written text that describes something that can be easily translated into pictures. The following sentence from a story in the February 21, 1994, issue of *Time* magazine, describing the Winter Olympics figure-skating championships, is a good example: "All the elements are in place—the spotlights, the swelling waltzes and jazz tunes, the sequined sprites taking to the air." In my imagination, I see the skating rink and skaters. However, if I ponder too long on the word "elements," I will make the inappropriate associ-

ation of a periodic table on the wall of my high school chemistry classroom. Pausing on the word "sprite" triggers an image of a Sprite can in my refrigerator instead of a pretty young skater.

6   Teachers who work with autistic children need to understand associative thought patterns. An autistic child will often use a word in an inappropriate manner. Sometimes these uses have a logical associative meaning and other times they don't. For example, an autistic child might say the word "dog" when he wants to go outside. The word "dog" is associated with going outside. In my own case, I can remember both logical and illogical use of inappropriate words. When I was six, I learned to say "prosecution." I had absolutely no idea what it meant, but it sounded nice when I said it, so I used it as an exclamation every time my kite hit the ground. I must have baffled more than a few people who heard me exclaim "Prosecution!" to my downward-spiraling kite.

7   Discussions with other autistic people reveal similar visual styles of thinking about tasks that most people do sequentially. An autistic man who composes music told me that he makes "sound pictures" using small pieces of other music to create new compositions. A computer programmer with autism told me that he sees the general pattern of the program tree. After he visualizes the skeleton for the program, he simply writes the code for each branch. I use similar methods when I review scientific literature and troubleshoot at meat plants. I take specific findings or observations and combine them to find new basic principles and general concepts.

8   My thinking pattern always starts with specifics and works toward generalization in an associational and nonsequential way. As if I were attempting to figure out what the picture on a jigsaw puzzle is when only one third of the puzzle is completed, I am able to fill in the missing pieces by scanning my video library. Chinese mathematicians who can make large calculations in their heads work the same way. At first they need an abacus, the Chinese calculator, which consists of rows of beads on wires in a frame. They make calculations by moving the rows of beads. When a mathematician becomes really skilled, he simply visualizes the abacus in his imagination and no longer needs a real one. The beads move on a visualized video abacus in his brain.

Abstract Thought

9   Growing up, I learned to convert abstract ideas into pictures as a way to understand them. I visualized concepts such as peace or honesty with symbolic images. I thought of peace as a dove, an Indian peace pipe, or TV or newsreel footage of the signing of a peace agreement. Honesty was represented by an image of placing one's hand on the Bible in court. A news report describing a person returning a wallet with all the money in it provided a picture of honest behavior.

10   The Lord's Prayer was incomprehensible until I broke it down into specific visual images. The power and the glory were represented by a semicircular rainbow and an electrical tower. These childhood visual images are still triggered every time I hear the Lord's Prayer. The words "thy will be done" had no meaning when I was a child, and today the meaning is still vague. Will is a hard concept to visualize. When I think about it, I imagine God throwing a lightning bolt. Another adult with autism wrote that he visualized "Thou art in heaven" as God with an easel above the clouds. "Trespassing" was pictured as black and orange no trespassing signs. The word "Amen" at the end of the prayer was a mystery: a man at the end made no sense.

11   As a teenager and young adult I had to use concrete symbols to understand abstract concepts such as getting along with people and moving on to the next steps of my life, both of which were always difficult. I knew I did not fit in with my high school peers, and I was unable to figure out what I was doing wrong. No matter how hard I tried, they made fun of me. They called me "workhorse," "tape recorder," and "bones" because I was skinny. At the time I was able to figure out why they called me "workhorse" and "bones," but "tape recorder" puzzled me. Now I realize that I must have sounded like a tape recorder when I repeated things verbatim over and over. But back then I just could not figure out why I was such a social dud. I sought refuge in doing things I was good at, such as working on reroofing the barn or practicing my riding prior to a horse show. Personal relationships made absolutely no sense to me until I developed visual symbols of doors and windows. It was then that I started to understand concepts such as learning the give-and-take of a relationship. I still wonder what would have happened to me if I had not been able to visualize my way in the world.

✧ Evaluating the Text

1. What limitations does Grandin confront in trying to understand abstract ideas and to communicate with other people? What problems did she encounter in high school because of this limitation?

2. In order to explain the radical difference of the way people with autism think about things and understand words, Grandin uses analogies. Which of these analogies did you find most effective?

✧ Exploring Different Perspectives

1. How does the theme of the acquisition of language play an important role in the accounts by Grandin and Ngũgĩ wa Thiong'o? (see "Decolonising the Mind")?

2. What different factors impede communication in the accounts by Grandin and by Kyoko Mori in "Polite Lies"?

✦ *Extending Viewpoints through Writing and Research*

1. Try to translate a passage about an abstract idea (for example, charity or love) by thinking in pictures instead of words. What images did you use to represent these abstract ideas? What insight did this exercise give you into the world of autism?

2. How have new statistics regarding the frequency of autism (one in 166 children whereas a decade ago it was one in 2,500) in the United States increased public recognition of this fast-growing developmental disability with no known cure? Research this issue on the Internet and write a few paragraphs summarizing your findings. An intriguing new study linking childhood vaccinations with autism is David Kirby's *Evidence of Harm* (2005).

3. The use of mercury in vaccines and its role as a possible cause of autism is investigated at http://www.lewrockwell.com/miller/miller14.html.

How does this magazine cover illustrate public awareness of this escalating disability?

Gloria Anzaldúa

Cervicide[1]

———————◆———————

Gloria Anzaldúa (1942–2004) was a Chicana poet and fiction writer who grew up in south Texas. She edited several highly praised anthologies. This Bridge Called My Back: Writings by Radical Women of Color *won the 1986 Before Columbus Foundation American Book Award.* Borderlands—La Frontera, the New Mestiza *was selected as one of the best books of 1987 by* Library Journal. *Her recent works include* Making Face, Making Soul *(1990),* La Prieta *(1991),* Interviews = Entrevistas *(2000), and a children's book,* Friends from the Other Side *(1993). She was a contributing editor for* Sinister Wisdom *and taught Chicano studies, feminist studies, and creative writing at the University of Texas at Austin, San Francisco State University, and the University of California, Santa Cruz. "Cervicide" first appeared in* Labyris *(vol. 4, no. 11, Winter 1983). In it, Anzaldúa tells the poignant story of a Mexican-American family living on the Texas border who are forced to kill a pet deer whose detection by the game warden would result in an unaffordable fine or the father's imprisonment.*

Before You Read

Consider how Anzaldúa enhances the sense of urgency in what proves to be a no-win situation for Prieta.

———————◆———————

1   *La venadita.* The small fawn. They had to kill their pet, the fawn. The game warden was on the way with his hounds. The penalty for being caught in possession of a deer was $250 or jail. The game warden would put *su papí en la cárcel.*[2]

2   How could they get rid of the fawn? Hide it? No, *la guardia's*[3] hounds would sniff Venadita out. Let Venadita loose in the *monte?* They had tried that before. The fawn would leap away and seconds later return. Should they kill Venadita? The mother and Prieta looked toward *las carabinas* propped against the wall behind the kitchen door—the shiny barrel of the .22, the heavy metal steel of the 40-40.

---

[1]*Cervicide*—the killing of a deer. In archetypal symbology the Self appears as a deer for women.

[2]*su papí en la cárcel*—her father in jail.

[3]*monte*—the woods.

No, if *they* could hear his pickup a mile and a half down the road, he would hear the shot.

3   Quick, they had to do something. Cut Venadita's throat? Club her to death? The mother couldn't do it. She, Prieta,[4] would have to be the one. The game warden and his *perros*[5] were a mile down the road. Prieta loved her *papí*.

4   In the shed behind the corral, where they'd hidden the fawn, Prieta found the hammer. She had to grasp it with both hands. She swung it up. The weight folded her body backwards. A thud reverberated on Venadita's skull, a wave undulated down her back. Again, a blow behind the ear. Though Venadita's long lashes quivered, her eyes never left Prieta's face. Another thud, another tremor. *La guardia* and his hounds were driving up the front yard. The *venadita* looked up at her, the hammer rose and fell. Neither made a sound. The tawny, spotted fur was the most beautiful thing Prieta had ever seen. She remembered when they had found the fawn. She had been a few hours old. A hunter had shot her mother. The fawn had been shaking so hard, her long thin legs were on the edge of buckling. Prieta and her sister and brothers had bottle-fed Venadita, with a damp cloth had wiped her skin, had watched her tiny, perfectly formed hooves harden and grow.

5   Prieta dug a hole in the shed, a makeshift hole. She could hear the warden talking to her mother. Her mother's English had suddenly gotten bad—she was trying to stall *la guardia*. Prieta rolled the fawn into the hole, threw in the empty bottle. With her fingers raked in the dirt. Dust caked on her arms and face where tears had fallen. She patted the ground flat with her hands and swept it with a dead branch. The game warden was strutting toward her. His hounds sniffing, sniffing, sniffing the ground in the shed. The hounds pawing pawing the ground. The game warden, straining on the leashes *les dio un tirón, sacó los perros*.[6] He inspected the corrals, the edge of the woods, then drove away in his pickup.

✧ *Evaluating the Text*

1. To what pressures is the family subject because they are illegal immigrants?

2. Discuss the consequences for the narrator of having to make such a choice and perform such an action. In your opinion, how will she be different from then on? In what sense might the deer symbolize the self that can no longer exist?

[4]*Prieta*—literally one who is dark-skinned, a nickname.
[5]*perros*—dogs.
[6]*les dio un tirón, sacó los perros*—jerked the dogs out.

3. How does being forced to choose between a deer she loves and her loyalty to her father illustrate the kind of predicament in which those without power find themselves?

✧ Exploring Different Perspectives

1. In what way does Prieta in Anzaldúa's story find herself in an alien culture just as David R. Counts ("Too Many Bananas") does in New Guinea?

2. How are the families in Anzaldúa's story and in Ngũgĩ wa Thiong'o's "Decolonising the Mind" both oppressed by political regimes?

✧ Extending Viewpoints through Writing and Research

1. What actions did a pet of yours take that led you to believe it showed evidence of consciousness, motivation, and intelligence? What could your pet say about you that no human being knows?

2. Describe your search for a name for your pet. What character traits important to you or your family does this name reveal?

Poranee Natadecha-Sponsel

Individualism as an American Cultural Value

◆

Poranee Natadecha-Sponsel was born and raised in a multiethnic Thai and Malay region in the southern part of Thailand. She received her B.A. with honors in English and philosophy from Chulalongkorn University in Bangkok, Thailand, in 1969. She has lived in the United States for more than fifteen years, earning her M.A. in philosophy at Ohio University, in Athens, in 1973 and her Ed.D. in 1991 from the University of Hawaii at Manoa. She currently teaches interdisciplinary courses in women's studies and coordinates the mentoring program for new women faculty at the University of Hawaii at Manoa.

Before You Read

Consider the different cultural assumptions that govern what Thai people consider appropriate to ask strangers.

◆

1   "Hi, how are you?" "Fine, thank you, and you?" These are greetings that everybody in America hears and says every day—salutations that come ready-made and packaged just like a hamburger and fries. There is no real expectation for any special information in response to these greetings. Do not, under any circumstances, take up anyone's time by responding in depth to the programmed query. What or how you may feel at the moment is of little, if any, importance. Thai people would immediately perceive that our concerned American friends are truly interested in our welfare, and this concern would require polite reciprocation by spelling out the details of our current condition. We become very disappointed when we have had enough experience in the United States to learn that we have bored, amused, or even frightened many of our American acquaintances by taking the greeting "How are you?" so literally. We were reacting like Thai, but in the American context where salutations have a different meaning, our detailed reactions were inappropriate. In Thai society, a greeting among acquaintances usually requests specific information about the other person's condition, such as "Where are you going?" or "Have you eaten?"

2   One of the American contexts in which this greeting is most confusing and ambiguous is at the hospital or clinic. In these sterile and
ritualistic settings, I have always been uncertain exactly how to answer
when the doctor or nurse asks "How are you?" If I deliver a packaged
answer of "Fine," I wonder if I am telling a lie. After all, I am there in
the first place precisely because I am not so fine. Finally, after debating
for some time, I asked one nurse how she expected a patient to answer
the query "How are you?" But after asking this question, I then wondered if it was rude to do so. However, she looked relieved after I explained to her that people from different cultures have different ways
to greet other people and that for me to be asked how I am in the hospital results in awkwardness. Do I simply answer, "Fine, thank you,"
or do I reveal in accurate detail how I really feel at the moment? My
suspicion was verified when the nurse declared that "How are you?"
was really no more than a polite greeting and that she didn't expect
any answer more elaborate than simply "Fine." However, she told me
that some patients do answer her by describing every last ache and
pain from which they are suffering.

3   A significant question that comes to mind is whether the verbal
pattern of greetings reflects any social relationship in American culture.
The apparently warm and sincere greeting may initially suggest interest in the person, yet the intention and expectations are, to me, quite
superficial. For example, most often the person greets you quickly and
then walks by to attend to other business without even waiting for
your response! This type of greeting is just like a package of American
fast food! The person eats the food quickly without enjoying the taste.
The convenience is like many other American accoutrements of living
such as cars, household appliances, efficient telephones, or simple,
systematic, and predictable arrangements of groceries in the supermarket. However, usually when this greeting is delivered, it seems to lack
a personal touch and genuine feeling. It is little more than ritualized
behavior.

4   I have noticed that most Americans keep to themselves even at social gatherings. Conversation may revolve around many topics, but little, if anything, is revealed about oneself. Without talking much about
oneself and not knowing much about others, social relations seem to
remain at an abbreviated superficial level. How could one know a person without knowing something about him or her? How much does
one need to know about a person to really know that person?

5   After living in this culture for more than a decade, I have learned
that there are many topics that should not be mentioned in conversations with American acquaintances or even close friends. One's personal life and one's income are considered to be very private and even
taboo topics. Unlike my Thai culture, Americans do not show interest

or curiosity by asking such personal questions, especially when one just meets the individual for the first time. Many times I have been embarrassed by my Thai acquaintances who recently arrived at the University of Hawaii and the East-West Center. For instance, one day I was walking on campus with an American friend when we met another Thai woman to whom I had been introduced a few days earlier. The Thai woman came to write her doctoral dissertation at the East-West Center where the American woman worked, so I introduced them to each other. The American woman greeted my Thai companion in Thai language, which so impressed her that she felt immediately at ease. At once, she asked the American woman numerous personal questions such as, How long did you live in Thailand? Why were you there? How long were you married to the Thai man? Why did you divorce him? How long have you been divorced? Are you going to marry a Thai again or an American? How long have you been working here? How much do you earn? The American was stunned. However, she was very patient and more or less answered all those questions as succinctly as she could. I was so uncomfortable that I had to interrupt whenever I could to get her out of the awkward situation in which she had been forced into talking about things she considered personal. For people in Thai society, such questions would be appropriate and not considered too personal let alone taboo.

6   The way Americans value their individual privacy continues to impress me. Americans seem to be open and yet there is a contradiction because they are also aloof and secretive. This is reflected in many of their behavior patterns. By Thai standards, the relationship between friends in American society seems to be somewhat superficial. Many Thai students, as well as other Asians, have felt that they could not find genuine friendship with Americans. For example, I met many American classmates who were very helpful and friendly while we were in the same class. We went out, exchanged phone calls, and did the same things as would good friends in Thailand. But those activities stopped suddenly when the semester ended.

7   Privacy as a component of the American cultural value of individualism is nurtured in the home as children grow up. From birth they are given their own individual, private space, a bedroom separate from that of their parents. American children are taught to become progressively independent, both emotionally and economically, from their family. They learn to help themselves at an early age. In comparison, in Thailand, when parents bring a new baby home from the hospital, it shares the parents' bedroom for two to three years and then shares another bedroom with older siblings of the same sex. Most Thai children do not have their own private room until they finish high school, and some do not have their own room until another sibling moves out, usually when the sibling gets married. In Thailand, there are strong

bonds within the extended family. Older siblings regularly help their parents to care for younger ones. In this and other ways, the Thai family emphasizes the interdependence of its members.

8 I was accustomed to helping Thai babies who fell down to stand up again. Thus, in America when I saw babies fall, it was natural for me to try to help them back on their feet. Once at a summer camp for East-West Center participants, one of the supervisors brought his wife and their ten-month-old son with them. The baby was so cute that many students were playing with him. At one point he was trying to walk and fell, so all the Asian students, males and females, rushed to help him up. Although the father and mother were nearby, they paid no attention to their fallen and crying baby. However, as the students were trying to help and comfort him, the parents told them to leave him alone; he would be all right on his own. The baby did get up and stopped crying without any assistance. Independence is yet another component of the American value of individualism.

9 Individualism is even reflected in the way Americans prepare, serve, and consume food. In a typical American meal, each person has a separate plate and is not supposed to share or taste food from other people's plates. My Thai friends and I are used to eating Thai style, in which you share food from a big serving dish in the middle of the table. Each person dishes a small amount from the serving dish onto his or her plate and finishes this portion before going on with the next portion of the same or a different serving dish. With the Thai pattern of eating, you regularly reach out to the serving dishes throughout the meal. But this way of eating is not considered appropriate in comparison to the common American practice where each person eats separately from his or her individual plate.

10 One time my American host, a divorcée who lives alone, invited a Thai girlfriend and myself to an American dinner at her home. When we were reaching out and eating a small portion of one thing at a time in Thai style, we were told to dish everything we wanted onto our plates at one time and that it was not considered polite to reach across the table. The proper American way was to have each kind of food piled up on your plate at once. If we were to eat in the same manner in Thailand, eyebrows would have been raised at the way we piled up food on our plates, and we would have been considered to be eating like pigs, greedy and inconsiderate of others who shared the meal at the table.

11 Individualism as a pivotal value in American culture is reflected in many other ways. Material wealth is not only a prime status marker in American society but also a guarantee and celebration of individualism—wealth allows the freedom to do almost anything, although usually within the limits of law. The pursuit of material wealth through individual achievement is instilled in Americans from the youngest age. For example, I was surprised to see an affluent American couple,

who own a large ranch house and two BMW cars, send their nine-year-old son to deliver newspapers. He has to get up very early each morning to deliver the papers, even on Sunday! During summer vacation, the boy earns additional money by helping in his parents' gift shop from 10 A.M. to 5 P.M. His thirteen-year-old sister often earns money by babysitting, even at night.

12   In Thailand, only children from poorer families work to earn money to help the household. Middle- and high-income parents do not encourage their children to work until after they have finished their education. They provide economic support in order to free their children to concentrate on and excel in their studies. Beyond the regular schooling, families who can afford it pay for special tutoring as well as training in music, dance, or sports. However, children in low- and middle-income families help their parents with household chores and the care of younger children.

13   Many American children have been encouraged to get paid for their help around the house. They rarely get any gifts free of obligations. They even have to be good to get Santa's gifts at Christmas! As they grow up, they are conditioned to earn things they want; they learn that "there is no such thing as a free lunch." From an early age, children are taught to become progressively independent economically from their parents. Also, most young people are encouraged to leave home at college age to be on their own. From my viewpoint as a Thai, it seems that American family ties and closeness are not as strong as in Asian families whose children depend on family financial support until joining the work force after college age. Thereafter, it is the children's turn to help support their parents financially.

14   Modern American society and economy emphasize individualism in other ways. The nuclear family is more common than the extended family, and newlyweds usually establish their own independent household rather than initially living with either the husband's or the wife's parents. Parents and children appear to be close only when the children are very young. Most American parents seem to "lose" their children by the teenage years. They don't seem to belong to each other as closely as do Thai families. Even though I have seen more explicit affectionate expression among American family members than among Asian ones, the close interpersonal spirit seems to be lacking. Grandparents have relatively little to do with the grandchildren on any regular basis, in contrast to the extended family, which is more common in Thailand. The family and society seem to be graded by age to the point that grandparents, parents, and children are separated by generational subcultures that are evidently alienated from one another. Each group "does its own thing." Help and support are usually limited to whatever does not interfere with one's own life. In America, the locus of responsibility is more on the individual than on the family.

15   In one case I know of, a financially affluent grandmother with Alzheimer's disease is taken care of twenty-four hours a day by hired help in her own home. Her daughter visits and relieves the helper occasionally. The mature granddaughter, who has her own family, rarely visits. Yet they all live in the same neighborhood. However, each lives in a different house, and each is very independent. Although the mother worries about the grandmother, she cannot do much. Her husband also needs her, and she divides her time between him, her daughters and their children, and the grandmother. When the mother needs to go on a trip with her husband, a second hired attendant is required to care for the grandmother temporarily. When I asked why the granddaughter doesn't temporarily care for the grandmother, the reply was that she has her own life, and it would not be fair for the granddaughter to take care of the grandmother, even for a short period of time. Yet I wonder if it is fair for the grandmother to be left out. It seems to me that the value of individualism and its associated independence account for these apparent gaps in family ties and support.

16   In contrast to American society, in Thailand older parents with a long-term illness are asked to move in with their children and grandchildren if they are not already living with them. The children and grandchildren take turns attending to the grandparent, sometimes with help from live-in maids. Living together in the same house reinforces moral support among the generations within an extended family. The older generation is respected because of the previous economic, social, and moral support for their children and grandchildren. Family relations provide one of the most important contexts for being a "morally good person," which is traditionally the principal concern in the Buddhist society of Thailand.

17   In America, being young, rich, and/or famous allows one greater freedom and independence and thus promotes the American value of individualism. This is reflected in the mass appeal of major annual television events like the Super Bowl and the Academy Awards. The goal of superachievement is also seen in more mundane ways. For example, many parents encourage their children to take special courses and to work hard to excel in sports as a shortcut to becoming rich and famous. I know one mother who has taken her two sons to tennis classes and tournaments since the boys were six years old, hoping that at least one of them will be a future tennis star like Ivan Lendl. Other parents focus their children on acting, dancing, or musical talent. The children have to devote much time and hard work as well as sacrifice the ordinary activities of youth in order to develop and perform their natural talents and skills in prestigious programs. But those who excel in the sports and entertainment industries can become rich and famous, even at an early age, as for example Madonna, Tom Cruise, and Michael Jackson. Television and other media publicize these celebrities

and thereby reinforce the American value of individualism, including personal achievement and financial success.

18   Although the American cultural values of individualism and the aspiration to become rich and famous have had some influence in Thailand, there is also cultural and religious resistance to these values. Strong social bonds, particularly within the extended family, and the hierarchical structure of the kingdom run counter to individualism. Also, youth gain social recognition through their academic achievement. From the perspective of Theravada Buddhism, which strongly influences Thai culture, aspiring to be rich and famous would be an illustration of greed, and those who have achieved wealth and fame do not celebrate it publicly as much as in American society. Being a good, moral person is paramount, and ideally Buddhists emphasize restraint and moderation.

19   Beyond talent and skill in the sports and entertainment industries, there are many other ways that young Americans can pursue wealth. Investment is one route. One American friend who is only a sophomore in college has already invested heavily in the stock market to start accumulating wealth. She is just one example of the 1980s trend for youth to be more concerned with their individual finances than with social, political, and environmental issues. With less attention paid to public issues, the expression of individualism seems to be magnified through emphasis on lucrative careers, financial investment, and material consumption—the "Yuppie" phenomenon. This includes new trends in dress, eating, housing (condominiums), and cars (expensive European imports). Likewise, there appears to be less of a long-term commitment to marriage. More young couples are living together without either marriage or plans for future marriage. When such couples decide to get married, prenuptial agreements are made to protect their assets. Traditional values of marriage, family, and sharing appear to be on the decline.

20   Individualism as one of the dominant values in American culture is expressed in many ways. This value probably stems from the history of the society as a frontier colony of immigrants in search of a better life with independence, freedom, and the opportunity for advancement through personal achievement. However, in the beliefs and customs of any culture there are some disadvantages as well as advantages. Although Thais may admire the achievements and material wealth of American society, there are costs, especially in the value of individualism and associated social phenomena.

✧ Evaluating the Test

1. For the Thais, what are the kinds of private topics about which it would be rude to inquire? How do these differ from the topics that are taboo among Americans?

2. How do concepts of friendship and privacy differ in Natadecha-Sponsel's experience with the Thai and American cultures?

3. How do the examples involving the child who has fallen, the way food is served and eaten, and the newspaper route provide the author with significant insights into American cultural values? Do you agree with her interpretations?

✧ Exploring Different Perspectives

1. How do the accounts by Natadecha-Sponsel and Ngũgĩ wa Thiong'o ("Decolonising the Mind") dramatize the relationship between language and identity for Thai immigrants in America and the natives of Kenya under British rule?

2. How is the deciphering of language codes an important issue in Natadecha-Sponsel's analysis and in Kyoko Mori's account ("Polite Lies")?

✧ Extending Viewpoints through Writing and Research

1. How do concepts of the care of the elderly and Buddhist philosophy provide strikingly different models for behavior in Thailand and in the United States?

2. What incidents in your own experience illustrate the value placed on individualism in American culture, a value that those from other cultures might find strange?

Gino Del Guercio

The Secrets of Haiti's Living Dead

✦

Gino Del Guercio is a national science writer for United Press Interna-
tional and was a MACY fellow at Boston's television station WGBH. He
is currently a documentary filmmaker, specializing in scientific and med-
ical subjects, for Boston Science Communications, Inc. "The Secrets of
Haiti's Living Dead" was first published in Harvard Magazine *(Janu-*
ary/February 1986). In 1982, Wade Davis, a Harvard-trained ethnob-
otanist, whose exploits formed the basis for this article, traveled into the
Haitian countryside to investigate accounts of zombies—the infamous
living dead of Haitian folklore. Davis's research led him to obtain the poi-
son associated with the process. His findings were first presented in The
Serpent and the Rainbow *(1988), a work that served as the basis for the*
movie of the same name, directed by Wes Craven, and later in Passage of
Darkness *(1988). Del Guercio's report reveals the extent to which Hai-*
tian life is controlled by voodoo, a religious belief, West African in origin,
that is characterized by induced trances and magical rituals. Until this
century, voodoo was the state religion and continues to flourish despite
opposition from Roman Catholicism, the other major religion in Haiti.

Before You Read

Consider the extent to which your concept of zombies is influenced by
films and television.

✦

1   Five years ago, a man walked into l'Estére, a village in central
Haiti, approached a peasant woman named Angelina Narcisse, and
identified himself as her brother Clairvius. If he had not introduced
himself using a boyhood nickname and mentioned facts only intimate
family members knew, she would not have believed him. Because,
eighteen years earlier, Angelina had stood in a small cemetery north of
her village and watched as her brother Clairvius was buried.

2   The man told Angelina he remembered that night well. He knew
when he was lowered into his grave, because he was fully conscious,
although he could not speak or move. As the earth was thrown over
his coffin, he felt as if he were floating over the grave. The scar on his
right cheek, he said, was caused by a nail driven through his casket.

3   The night he was buried, he told Angelina, a voodoo priest raised him from the grave. He was beaten with a sisal whip and carried off to a sugar plantation in northern Haiti where, with other zombies, he was forced to work as a slave. Only with the death of the zombie master were they able to escape, and Narcisse eventually returned home.

4   Legend has it that zombies are the living dead, raised from their graves and animated by malevolent voodoo sorcerers, usually for some evil purpose. Most Haitians believe in zombies, and Narcisse's claim is not unique. At about the time he reappeared, in 1980, two women turned up in other villages saying they were zombies. In the same year, in northern Haiti, the local peasants claimed to have found a group of zombies wandering aimlessly in the fields.

5   But Narcisse's case was different in one crucial respect; it was documented. His death had been recorded by doctors at the American-directed Schweitzer Hospital in Deschapelles. On April 30, 1962, hospital records show, Narcisse walked into the hospital's emergency room spitting up blood. He was feverish and full of aches. His doctors could not diagnose his illness, and his symptoms grew steadily worse. Three days after he entered the hospital, according to the records, he died. The attending physicians, an American among them, signed his death certificate. His body was placed in cold storage for twenty hours, and then he was buried. He said he remembered hearing his doctors pronounce him dead while his sister wept at his bedside.

6   At the Centre de Psychiatrie et Neurologie in Port-au-Prince, Dr. Lamarque Douyon, a Haitian-born, Canadian-trained psychiatrist, has been systematically investigating all reports of zombies since 1961. Though convinced zombies were real, he had been unable to find a scientific explanation for the phenomenon. He did not believe zombies were people raised from the dead, but that did not make them any less interesting. He speculated that victims were only made to *look* dead, probably by means of a drug that dramatically slowed metabolism. The victim was buried, dug up within a few hours, and somehow reawakened.

7   The Narcisse case provided Douyon with evidence strong enough to warrant a request for assistance from colleagues in New York. Douyon wanted to find an ethnobotanist, a traditional-medicines expert, who could track down the zombie potion he was sure existed. Aware of the medical potential of a drug that could dramatically lower metabolism, a group organized by the late Dr. Nathan Kline—a New York psychiatrist and pioneer in the field of psychopharmacology—raised the funds necessary to send someone to investigate.

8   The search for that someone led to the Harvard Botanical Museum, one of the world's foremost institutes of ethnobiology. Its director, Richard Evans Schultes, Jeffrey professor of biology, had spent thirteen years in the tropics studying native medicines. Some of his best-known

work is the investigation of curare, the substance used by the nomadic people of the Amazon to poison their darts. Refined into a powerful muscle relaxant called D-tubocurarine, it is now an essential component of the anesthesia used during almost all surgery.

9   Schultes would have been a natural for the Haitian investigation, but he was too busy. He recommended another Harvard ethnobotanist for the assignment, Wade Davis, a 28-year-old Canadian pursuing a doctorate in biology.

10   Davis grew up in the tall pine forests of British Columbia and entered Harvard in 1971, influenced by a *Life* magazine story on the student strike of 1969. Before Harvard, the only Americans he had known were draft dodgers, who seemed very exotic. "I used to fight forest fires with them," Davis says. "Like everybody else, I thought America was where it was at. And I wanted to go to Harvard because of that *Life* article. When I got there, I realized it wasn't quite what I had in mind."

11   Davis took a course from Schultes, and when he decided to go to South America to study plants, he approached his professor for guidance. "He was an extraordinary figure," Davis remembers. "He was a man who had done it all. He had lived alone for years in the Amazon." Schultes sent Davis to the rain forest with two letters of introduction and two pieces of advice: wear a pith helmet and try ayahuasca, a powerful hallucinogenic vine. During that expedition and others, Davis proved himself an "outstanding field man," says his mentor. Now, in early 1982, Schultes called him into his office and asked if he had plans for spring break.

12   "I always took to Schultes's assignments like a plant takes to water," says Davis, tall and blond, with inquisitive blue eyes. "Whatever Schultes told me to do, I did. His letters of introduction opened up a whole world." This time the world was Haiti.

13   Davis knew nothing about the Caribbean island—and nothing about African traditions, which serve as Haiti's cultural basis. He certainly did not believe in zombies. "I thought it was a lark," he says now.

14   Davis landed in Haiti a week after his conversation with Schultes, armed with a hypothesis about how the zombie drug—if it existed— might be made. Setting out to explore, he discovered a country materially impoverished, but rich in culture and mystery. He was impressed by the cohesion of Haitian society; he found none of the crime, social disorder, and rampant drug and alcohol abuse so common in many of the other Caribbean islands. The cultural wealth and cohesion, he believes, spring from the country's turbulent history.

15   During the French occupation of the late eighteenth century, 370,000 African-born slaves were imported to Haiti between 1780 and 1790. In 1791, the black population launched one of the few successful slave revolts in history, forming secret societies and overcoming first the French plantation owners and then a detachment of troops from

Napoleon's army, sent to quell the revolt. For the next hundred years Haiti was the only independent black republic in the Caribbean, populated by people who did not forget their African heritage. "You can almost argue that Haiti is more African than Africa," Davis says. "When the west coast of Africa was being disrupted by colonialism and the slave trade, Haiti was essentially left alone. The amalgam of beliefs in Haiti is unique, but it's very, very African."

16   Davis discovered that the vast majority of Haitian peasants practice voodoo, a sophisticated religion with African roots. Says Davis, "It was immediately obvious that the stereotypes of voodoo weren't true. Going around the countryside, I found clues to a whole complex social world." Vodounists believe they communicate directly with, indeed are often possessed by, the many spirits who populate the everyday world. Vodoun society is a system of education, law, and medicine; it embodies a code of ethics that regulates social behavior. In rural areas, secret vodoun societies, much like those found on the west coast of Africa, are as much or more in control of everyday life as the Haitian government.

17   Although most outsiders dismissed the zombie phenomenon as folklore, some early investigators, convinced of its reality, tried to find a scientific explanation. The few who sought a zombie drug failed. Nathan Kline, who helped finance Davis's expedition, had searched unsuccessfully, as had Lamarque Douyon, the Haitian psychiatrist. Zora Neale Hurston, an American black woman, may have come closest. An anthropological pioneer, she went to Haiti in the Thirties, studied vodoun society, and wrote a book on the subject, *Tell My Horse*, first published in 1938. She knew about the secret societies and was convinced zombies were real, but if a powder existed, she too failed to obtain it.

18   Davis obtained a sample in a few weeks.

19   He arrived in Haiti with the names of several contacts. A BBC reporter familiar with the Narcisse case had suggested he talk with Marcel Pierre. Pierre owned the Eagle Bar, a bordello in the city of Saint Marc. He was also a voodoo sorcerer and had supplied the BBC with a physiologically active powder of unknown ingredients. Davis found him willing to negotiate. He told Pierre he was a representative of "powerful but anonymous interests in New York," willing to pay generously for the priest's services, provided no questions were asked. Pierre agreed to be helpful for what Davis will only say was a "sizable sum." Davis spent a day watching Pierre gather the ingredients—including human bones—and grind them together with mortar and pestle. However, from his knowledge of poison, Davis knew immediately that nothing in the formula could produce the powerful effects of zombification.

20   Three weeks later, Davis went back to the Eagle Bar, where he found Pierre sitting with three associates. Davis challenged him. He

called him a charlatan. Enraged, the priest gave him a second vial, claiming that this was the real poison. Davis pretended to pour the powder into his palm and rub it into his skin. "You're a dead man," Pierre told him, and he might have been, because this powder proved to be genuine. But, as the substance had not actually touched him, Davis was able to maintain his bravado, and Pierre was impressed. He agreed to make the poison and show Davis how it was done.

21   The powder, which Davis keeps in a small vial, looks like dry black dirt. It contains parts of toads, sea worms, lizards, tarantulas, and human bones. (To obtain the last ingredient, he and Pierre unearthed a child's grave on a nocturnal trip to the cemetery.) The poison is rubbed into the victim's skin. Within hours he begins to feel nauseated and has difficulty breathing. A pins-and-needles sensation afflicts his arms and legs, then progresses to the whole body. The subject becomes paralyzed; his lips turn blue for lack of oxygen. Quickly—sometimes within six hours—his metabolism is lowered to a level almost indistinguishable from death.

22   As Davis discovered, making the poison is an inexact science. Ingredients varied in the five samples he eventually acquired, although the active agents were always the same. And the poison came with no guarantee. Davis speculates that sometimes instead of merely paralyzing the victim, the compound kills him. Sometimes the victim suffocates in the coffin before he can be resurrected. But clearly the potion works well enough often enough to make zombies more than a figment of Haitian imagination.

23   Analysis of the powder produced another surprise. "When I went down to Haiti originally," says Davis, "my hypothesis was that the formula would contain *concombre zombi*, the 'zombie's cucumber,' which is a *Datura* plant. I thought somehow *Datura* was used in putting people down." *Datura* is a powerful psychoactive plant, found in West Africa as well as other tropical areas and used there in ritual as well as criminal activities. Davis had found *Datura* growing in Haiti. Its popular name suggested the plant was used in creating zombies.

24   But, says Davis, "there were a lot of problems with the *Datura* hypothesis. Partly it was a question of how the drug was administered. *Datura* would create a stupor in huge doses, but it just wouldn't produce the kind of immobility that was key. These people had to appear dead, and there aren't many drugs that will do that."

25   One of the ingredients Pierre included in the second formula was a dried fish, a species of puffer or blowfish, common to most parts of the world. It gets its name from its ability to fill itself with water and swell to several times its normal size when threatened by predators. Many of these fish contain a powerful poison known as tetrodotoxin. One of the most powerful nonprotein poisons known to man, tetrodotoxin turned up in every sample of zombie powder that Davis acquired.

26   Numerous well-documented accounts of puffer fish poisoning exist, but the most famous accounts come from the Orient, where *fugu* fish, a species of puffer, is considered a delicacy. In Japan, special chefs are licensed to prepare *fugu*. The chef removes enough poison to make the fish nonlethal, yet enough remains to create exhilarating physiological effects—tingles up and down the spine, mild prickling of the tongue and lips, euphoria. Several dozen Japanese die each year, having bitten off more than they should have.

27   "When I got hold of the formula and saw it was the *fugu* fish, that suddenly threw open the whole Japanese literature," says Davis. Case histories of *fugu* poisoning read like accounts of zombification. Victims remain conscious but unable to speak or move. A man who had "died" after eating *fugu* recovered seven days later in the morgue. Several summers ago, another Japanese poisoned by *fugu* revived after he was nailed into his coffin. "Almost all of Narcisse's symptoms correlated. Even strange things such as the fact that he said he was conscious and could hear himself pronounced dead. Stuff that I thought had to be magic, that seemed crazy. But, in fact, that is what people who get *fugu*-fish poisoning experience."

28   Davis was certain he had solved the mystery. But far from being the end of his investigation, identifying the poison was, in fact, its starting point. "The drug alone didn't make zombies," he explains. "Japanese victims of puffer-fish poisoning don't become zombies, they become poison victims. All the drug could do was set someone up for a whole series of psychological pressures that would be rooted in the culture. I wanted to know why zombification was going on," he says.

29   He sought a cultural answer, an explanation rooted in the structure and beliefs of Haitian society. Was zombification simply a random criminal activity? He thought not. He had discovered that Clairvius Narcisse and "Ti Femme," a second victim he interviewed, were village pariahs. Ti Femme was regarded as a thief. Narcisse had abandoned his children and deprived his brother of land that was rightfully his. Equally suggestive, Narcisse claimed that his aggrieved brother had sold him to a *bokor,* a voodoo priest who dealt in black magic; he made cryptic reference to having been tried and found guilty by the "masters of the land."

30   Gathering poisons from various parts of the country, Davis had come into direct contact with the vodoun secret societies. Returning to the anthropological literature on Haiti and pursuing his contacts with informants, Davis came to understand the social matrix within which zombies were created.

31   Davis's investigations uncovered the importance of the secret societies. These groups trace their origins to the bands of escaped slaves that organized the revolt against the French in the late eighteenth century. Open to both men and women, the societies control specific

territories of the country. Their meetings take place at night, and in many rural parts of Haiti the drums and wild celebrations that characterize the gatherings can be heard for miles.

32   Davis believes the secret societies are responsible for policing their communities, and the threat of zombification is one way they maintain order. Says Davis, "Zombification has a material basis, but it also has a societal logic." To the uninitiated, the practice may appear a random criminal activity, but in rural vodoun society, it is exactly the opposite—a sanction imposed by recognized authorities, a form of capital punishment. For rural Haitians, zombification is an even more severe punishment than death, because it deprives the subject of his most valued possessions: his free will and independence.

33   The vodounists believe that when a person dies, his spirit splits into several different parts. If a priest is powerful enough, the spiritual aspect that controls a person's character and individuality, known as *ti bon ange*, the "good little angel," can be captured and the corporeal aspect, deprived of its will, held as a slave.

34   From studying the medical literature on tetrodotoxin poisoning, Davis discovered that if a victim survives the first few hours of the poisoning, he is likely to recover fully from the ordeal. The subject simply revives spontaneously. But zombies remain without will, in a trance-like state, a condition vodounists attribute to the power of the priest. Davis thinks it possible that the psychological trauma of zombification may be augmented by *Datura* or some other drug; he thinks zombies may be fed a *Datura* paste that accentuates their disorientation. Still, he puts the material basis of zombification in perspective: "Tetrodotoxin and *Datura* are only templates on which cultural forces and beliefs may be amplified a thousand times."

35   Davis has not been able to discover how prevalent zombification is in Haiti. "How many zombies there are is not the question," he says. He compares it to capital punishment in the United States: "It doesn't really matter how many people are electrocuted, as long as it's a possibility." As a sanction in Haiti, the fear is not of zombies, it's of becoming one.

36   Davis attributes his success in solving the zombie mystery to his approach. He went to Haiti with an open mind and immersed himself in the culture. "My intuition unhindered by biases served me well," he says. "I didn't make any judgments." He combined this attitude with what he had learned earlier from his experiences in the Amazon. "Schultes's lesson is to go and live with the Indians as an Indian." Davis was able to participate in the vodoun society to a surprising degree, eventually even penetrating one of the Bizango societies and dancing in their nocturnal rituals. His appreciation of Haitian culture is apparent. "Everybody asks me how did a white person get this information? To ask the question means you don't understand Haitians—they don't judge you by the color of your skin."

37   As a result of the exotic nature of his discoveries, Davis has gained a certain notoriety. He plans to complete his dissertation soon, but he has already finished writing a popular account of his adventures. To be published in January by Simon and Schuster, it is called *The Serpent and the Rainbow,* after the serpent that vodounists believe created the earth and the rainbow spirit it married. Film rights have already been optioned; in October Davis went back to Haiti with a screenwriter. But Davis takes the notoriety in stride. "All this attention is funny," he says. "For years, not just me, but all Schultes's students have had extraordinary adventures in the line of work. The adventure is not the end point, it's just along the way of getting the data. At the Botanical Museum, Schultes created a world unto itself. We didn't think we were doing anything above the ordinary. I still don't think we do. And you know," he adds, "the Haiti episode does not begin to compare to what others have accomplished—particularly Schultes himself."

✧ Evaluating the Text

1. To what extent does Del Guercio's account gain credibility because he begins with the mysterious case of Clairvius Narcisse? How is Narcisse's identification by his sister intended to put the case beyond all doubt and leave the process of zombification as the only possible explanation for his otherwise inexplicable "death"?

2. Why is it important to Guercio's account that he mentions physicians from the United States as well as Haitian doctors who certified the "death" of Clairvius Narcisse? What is Del Guercio's attitude toward this phenomenon? How is this attitude revealed in the way he constructs his report?

3. How does the threat of zombification serve as a preventive measure that ensures social control in deterring crimes against the community? How did it operate in the cases of Clairvius Narcisse and "Ti Femme"? In what way is the reality of the social mechanism of zombification quite different from how it has been presented in movies and popular culture?

4. What kind of independent confirmation of the effects of tetrodotoxin, a potent neurotoxin that drastically reduces metabolism and produces paralysis, did Davis discover in his research on the effects of Japanese victims of *fugu* fish poisoning?

✧ Exploring Different Perspectives

1. Compare the discoveries made by Wade Davis and by David R. Counts, in "Too Many Bananas," as they venture into the unfamiliar territories of Haiti and New Guinea.

2. Discuss the social conditioning that results in someone being designated as an outcast in Del Guercio's account with Temple Grandin's experiences, as told in "Thinking in Pictures."

✧ *Extending Viewpoints through Writing and Research*

1. If you are familiar with or interested in the processes by which various religious cults enlist and program their members, you might compare their methods to those of the vodoun priests in terms of positive and negative reinforcement of psychological, sociological, and physiological conditioning.

2. If you have had the opportunity to see the movie *The Serpent and the Rainbow* (1988), directed by Wes Craven, you might wish to compare its representation of the events described in this article with Wade Davis's book *The Serpent and the Rainbow* (1985). For further research on this subject, you might consult Wade Davis, *Passage of Darkness: The Ethnobiology of the Haitian Zombie* (1988), an in-depth study of the political, social, and botanical mechanisms of zombification.

3. The African origins of voodoo are described in-depth at http://www.swagga.com/voodoo.htm.

How does this image illustrate the way rituals enhance the belief system of voodoo?

Ngũgĩ wa Thiong'o

Decolonising the Mind

◆

Ngũgĩ wa Thiong'o is regarded as one of the most important contemporary writers on the African continent. He wrote his first novels, Weep Not, Child *(1964) and* The River Between *(1965), in English, and* Caitaani Mũtharava-Ini *(translated as* Devil on the Cross, *1982) in his native language, Gĩkũyũ. He was chairman of the department of literature at the University of Nairobi until his detention without trial by the Kenyan authorities in 1977, an account of which appeared under the title* Detained: A Writer's Prison Diary *(1981). The international outcry over his imprisonment eventually produced his release. This selection comes from* Decolonising the Mind: The Politics of Language in African Literature *(1986). A recent work is* Penpoints, Gunpoints, and Dreams: Toward a Critical Theory of the Arts and the State in Africa *(1998).*

Black Africans of forty different ethnic groups make up 97 percent of the population of Kenya. The official languages are Swahili and English. The situation described by Thiong'o has changed to the extent that children are now taught in their native languages for the first three years of school, after which instruction is exclusively in English.

Before You Read

Underline the key points in Thiong'o's analysis and the supporting examples that clarify his thesis.

◆

1   I was born into a large peasant family: father, four wives and about twenty-eight children. I also belonged, as we all did in those days, to a wider extended family and to the community as a whole.

2   We spoke Gĩkũyũ as we worked in the fields. We spoke Gĩkũyũ in and outside the home. I can vividly recall those evenings of storytelling around the fireside. It was mostly the grown-ups telling the children but everybody was interested and involved. We children would re-tell the stories the following day to other children who worked in the fields picking the pyrethrum flowers, tea-leaves or coffee beans of our European and African landlords.

3   The stories, with mostly animals as the main characters, were all told in Gĩkũyũ. Hare, being small, weak but full of innovative wit and

cunning, was our hero. We identified with him as he struggled against the brutes of prey like lion, leopard, hyena. His victories were our victories and we learnt that the apparently weak can outwit the strong. We followed the animals in their struggle against hostile nature— drought, rain, sun, wind—a confrontation often forcing them to search for forms of co-operation. But we were also interested in their struggles amongst themselves, and particularly between the beasts and the victims of prey. These twin struggles, against nature and other animals, reflected real-life struggles in the human world.

4   Not that we neglected stories with human beings as the main characters. There were two types of characters in such human-centred narratives: the species of truly human beings with qualities of courage, kindness, mercy, hatred of evil, concern for others; and a man-eat-man two-mouthed species with qualities of greed, selfishness, individualism and hatred of what was good for the larger co-operative community. Co-operation as the ultimate good in a community was a constant theme. It could unite human beings with animals against ogres and beasts of prey, as in the story of how dove, after being fed with castor-oil seeds, was sent to fetch a smith working far away from home and whose pregnant wife was being threatened by these man-eating two-mouthed ogres.

5   There were good and bad story-tellers. A good one could tell the same story over and over again, and it would always be fresh to us, the listeners. He or she could tell a story told by someone else and make it more alive and dramatic. The differences really were in the use of words and images and the inflexion of voices to effect different tones.

6   We therefore learnt to value words for their meaning and nuances. Language was not a mere string of words. It had a suggestive power well beyond the immediate and lexical meaning. Our appreciation of the suggestive magical power of language was reinforced by the games we played with words through riddles, proverbs, transpositions of syllables, or through nonsensical but musically arranged words.[1] So we learnt the music of our language on top of the content. The language, through images and symbols, gave us a view of the world, but it had a beauty of its own. The home and the field were then our pre-primary school but what is important, for this discussion, is that the language of our evening teach-ins, and the language of our immediate and wider community, and the language of our work in the fields were one.

7   And then I went to school, a colonial school, and this harmony was broken. The language of my education was no longer the language of my culture. I first went to Kamaandura, missionary run, and then to another called Maanguuũ run by nationalists grouped around the Gĩkũyũ Independent and Karinga Schools Association. Our language of education was still Gĩkũyũ. The very first time I was ever given an

ovation for my writing was over a composition in Gĩkũyũ. So for my first four years there was still harmony between the language of my formal education and that of the Limuru peasant community.

8   It was after the declaration of a state of emergency over Kenya in 1952 that all the schools run by patriotic nationalists were taken over by the colonial regime and were placed under District Education Boards chaired by Englishmen. English became the language of my formal education. In Kenya, English became more than a language: it was *the* language, and all the others had to bow before it in deference.

9   Thus one of the most humiliating experiences was to be caught speaking Gĩkũyũ in the vicinity of the school. The culprit was given corporal punishment—three to five strokes of the cane on bare buttocks—or was made to carry a metal plate around the neck with inscriptions such as I AM STUPID or I AM A DONKEY. Sometimes the culprits were fined money they could hardly afford. And how did the teachers catch the culprits? A button was initially given to one pupil who was supposed to hand it over to whoever was caught speaking his mother tongue. Whoever had the button at the end of the day would sing who had given it to him and the ensuing process would bring out all the culprits of the day. Thus children were turned into witch-hunters and in the process were being taught the lucrative value of being a traitor to one's immediate community.

10   The attitude to English was the exact opposite: any achievement in spoken or written English was highly rewarded; prizes, prestige, applause; the ticket to higher realms. English became the measure of intelligence and ability in the arts, the sciences, and all the other branches of learning. English became *the* main determinant of a child's progress up the ladder of formal education.

11   As you may know, the colonial system of education in addition to its apartheid racial demarcation had the structure of a pyramid: a broad primary base, a narrowing secondary middle, and an even narrower university apex. Selections from primary into secondary were through an examination, in my time called Kenya African Preliminary Examination, in which one had to pass six subjects ranging from Maths to Nature Study and Kiswahili. All the papers were written in English. Nobody could pass the exam who failed the English language paper no matter how brilliantly he had done in the other subjects. I remember one boy in my class of 1954 who had distinctions in all subjects except English, which he had failed. He was made to fail the entire exam. He went on to become a turn boy in a bus company. I who had only passes but a credit in English got a place at the Alliance High School, one of the most elitist institutions for Africans in colonial Kenya. The requirements for a place at the University, Makerere University College, were broadly the same: nobody could go on to wear the undergraduate red gown, no matter how brilliantly they had performed in

all the other subjects unless they had a credit—not even a simple pass!—in English. Thus the most coveted place in the pyramid and in the system was only available to the holder of an English language credit card. English was the official vehicle and the magic formula to colonial elitedom.

12   Literary education was now determined by the dominant language while also reinforcing that dominance. Orature (oral literature) in Kenyan languages stopped. In primary school I now read simplified Dickens and Stevenson alongside Rider Haggard. Jim Hawkins, Oliver Twist, Tom Brown—not Hare, Leopard, and Lion—were now my daily companions in the world of imagination. In secondary school, Scott and G. B. Shaw vied with more Rider Haggard, John Buchan, Alan Paton, Captain W. E. Johns. At Makerere I read English: from Chaucer to T. S. Eliot with a touch of Graham Greene.

13   Thus language and literature were taking us further and further from ourselves to other selves, from our world to other worlds.

14   What was the colonial system doing to us Kenyan children? What were the consequences of, on the one hand, this systematic suppression of our languages and the literature they carried, and on the other the elevation of English and the literature it carried? To answer those questions, let me first examine the relationship of language to human experience, human culture, and the human perception of reality.

15   Language, any language, has a dual character: it is both a means of communication and a carrier of culture. Take English. It is spoken in Britain and in Sweden and Denmark. But for Swedish and Danish people English is only a means of communication with non-Scandinavians. It is not a carrier of their culture. For the British, and particularly the English, it is additionally, and inseparably from its use as a tool of communication, a carrier of their culture and history. Or take Swahili in East and Central Africa. It is widely used as a means of communication across many nationalities. But it is not the carrier of a culture and history of many of those nationalities. However in parts of Kenya and Tanzania, and particularly in Zanzibar, Swahili is inseparably both a means of communication and a carrier of the culture of those people to whom it is a mother-tongue.

16   Culture transmits or imparts those images of the world and reality through the spoken and the written language, that is through a specific language. In other words, the capacity to speak, the capacity to order sounds in a manner that makes for mutual comprehension between human beings is universal. This is the universality of language, a quality specific to human beings. It corresponds to the universality of the struggle against nature and that between human beings. But the particularity of the sounds, the words, the word order into phrases and

sentences, and the specific manner, or laws, of their ordering is what distinguishes one language from another. Thus a specific culture is not transmitted through language in its universality but in its particularity as the language of a specific community with a specific history. Written literature and orature are the main means by which a particular language transmits the images of the world contained in the culture it carries.

17   Language as communication and as culture are then products of each other. Communication creates culture: culture is a means of communication. Language carries culture, and culture carries, particularly through orature and literature, the entire body of values by which we come to perceive ourselves and our place in the world. How people perceive themselves affects how they look at their culture, at their politics and at the social production of wealth, at their entire relationship to nature and to other beings. Language is thus inseparable from ourselves as a community of human beings with a specific form and character, a specific history, a specific relationship to the world.

18   So what was the colonialist imposition of a foreign language doing to us children?

19   The real aim of colonialism was to control the people's wealth: what they produced, how they produced it, and how it was distributed; to control, in other words, the entire realm of the language of real life. Colonialism imposed its control of the social production of wealth through military conquest and subsequent political dictatorship. But its most important area of domination was the mental universe of the colonised, the control, through culture, of how people perceived themselves and their relationship to the world. Economic and political control can never be complete or effective without mental control. To control a people's culture is to control their tools of self-definition in relationship to others.

20   For colonialism this involved two aspects of the same process: the destruction or the deliberate undervaluing of a people's culture, their art, dances, religions, history, geography, education, orature and literature, and the conscious elevation of the language of the coloniser. The domination of a people's language by the languages of the colonising nations was crucial to the domination of the mental universe of the colonised.

21   Take language as communication. Imposing a foreign language, and suppressing the native languages as spoken and written, were already breaking the harmony previously existing between the African child and the three aspects of language. Since the new language as a means of communication was a product of and was reflecting the 'real language of life' elsewhere, it could never as spoken or written properly reflect or imitate the real life of that community. This may in part

explain why technology always appears to us as slightly external, *their* product and not *ours*. The word "missile" used to hold an alien far-away sound until I recently learnt its equivalent in Gĩkũyũ, *ngurukuhĩ*, and it made me apprehend it differently. Learning, for a colonial child, became a cerebral activity and not an emotionally felt experience.

22   But since the new, imposed languages could never completely break the native languages as spoken, their most effective area of domination was the third aspect of language as communication, the written. The language of an African child's formal education was foreign. The language of the books he read was foreign. The language of his conceptualisation was foreign. Thought, in him, took the visible form of a foreign language. So the written language of a child's upbringing in the school (even his spoken language within the school compound) became divorced from his spoken language at home. There was often not the slightest relationship between the child's written world, which was also the language of his schooling, and the world of his immediate environment in the family and the community. For a colonial child, the harmony existing between the three aspects of language as communication was irrevocably broken. This resulted in the disassociation of the sensibility of that child from his natural and social environment, what we might call colonial alienation. The alienation became reinforced in the teaching of history, geography, music, where bourgeois Europe was always the centre of the universe.

23   This disassociation, divorce, or alienation from the immediate environment becomes clearer when you look at colonial language as a carrier of culture.

24   Since culture is a product of the history of a people which it in turn reflects, the child was now being exposed exclusively to a culture that was a product of a world external to himself. He was being made to stand outside himself to look at himself. *Catching Them Young* is the title of a book on racism, class, sex, and politics in children's literature by Bob Dixon. "Catching them young" as an aim was even more true of a colonial child. The images of this world and his place in it implanted in a child take years to eradicate, if they ever can be.

25   Since culture does not just reflect the world in images but actually, through those very images, conditions a child to see that world in a certain way, the colonial child was made to see the world and where he stands in it as seen and defined by or reflected in the culture of the language of imposition.

26   And since those images are mostly passed on through orature and literature it meant the child would now only see the world as seen in the literature of his language of adoption. From the point of view of alienation, that is of seeing oneself from outside oneself as if one was another self, it does not matter that the imported literature carried the great humanist tradition of the best in Shakespeare, Goethe, Balzac,

Tolstoy, Gorky, Brecht, Sholokhov, Dickens. The location of this great mirror of imagination was necessarily Europe and its history and culture and the rest of the universe was seen from the centre.

27   But obviously it was worse when the colonial child was exposed to images of his world as mirrored in the written languages of his coloniser. Where his own native languages were associated in his impressionable mind with low status, humiliation, corporal punishment, slow-footed intelligence and ability or downright stupidity, non-intelligibility and barbarism, this was reinforced by the world he met in the works of such geniuses of racism as a Rider Haggard or a Nicholas Monsarrat; not to mention the pronouncement of some of the giants of western intellectual and political establishment, such as Hume (". . . the negro is naturally inferior to the whites . . . "),[2] Thomas Jefferson (". . . the blacks . . . are inferior to the whites on the endowments of both body and mind . . . "),[3] or Hegel with his Africa comparable to a land of childhood still enveloped in the dark mantle of the night as far as the development of self-conscious history was concerned. Hegel's statement that there was nothing harmonious with humanity to be found in the African character is representative of the racist images of Africans and Africa such a colonial child was bound to encounter in the literature of the colonial languages.[4] The results could be disastrous.

28   In her paper read to the conference on the teaching of African literature in schools held in Nairobi in 1973,[5] entitled "Written Literature and Black Images," the Kenyan writer and scholar Professor Mĩcere Mũgo related how a reading of the description of Gagool as an old African woman in Rider Haggard's *King Solomon's Mines* had for a long time made her feel mortal terror whenever she encountered old African women. In his autobiography *This Life*, Sydney Poitier describes how, as a result of the literature he had read, he had come to associate Africa with snakes. So on arrival in Africa and being put up in a modern hotel in a modern city, he could not sleep because he kept on looking for snakes everywhere, even under the bed. These two have been able to pinpoint the origins of their fears. But for most others the negative image becomes internalised and it affects their cultural and even political choices in ordinary living.

NOTES

1. Example from a tongue twister: "Kaana ka Nikoora koona koora: na ko koora koona kaana ka Nikoora koora koora." I'm indebted to Wangui wa Goro for this example. 'Nichola's child saw a baby frog and ran away: and when the baby frog saw Nichola's child it also ran away.' A Gĩkũyũ-speaking child has to get the correct tone and length of vowel and pauses to get it right. Otherwise it becomes a jumble of k's and r's and na's.
2. Quoted in Eric Williams, *A History of the People of Trinidad and Tobago*, London 1964, p. 32.
3. Ibid, p. 31.

4. In references to Africa in the introduction to his lectures in *The Philosophy of History*, Hegel gives historical, philosophical, rational expression and legitimacy to every conceivable European racist myth about Africa. Africa is even denied her own geography where it does not correspond to myth. Thus Egypt is not part of Africa; and North Africa is part of Europe. Africa proper is the especial home of ravenous beasts, snakes of all kinds. The African is not part of humanity. Only slavery to Europe can raise him, possibly, to the lower ranks of humanity. Slavery is good for the African. "Slavery is in and for itself *injustice,* for the essence of humanity is *freedom;* but for this man must be matured. The gradual abolition of slavery is therefore wiser and more equitable than its sudden removal." (Hegel, *The Philosophy of History,* Dover edition, New York: 1956, pp. 91–9.) Hegel clearly reveals himself as the nineteenth-century Hitler of the intellect.

5. The paper is now in Akivaga and Gachukiah's *The Teaching of African Literature in Schools,* published by Kenya Literature Bureau.

✧ Evaluating the Text

1. In what way would stories involving animals as heroes be especially important to the children to whom they were told? How might the nature of the conflicts in the animal stories better prepare children to deal with conflicts in real life? To what extent do these stories transmit cultural values by stressing the importance of resourcefulness, self-esteem, a connection to the past, and a pride in one's culture?

2. In addition to transmitting cultural values, how did hearing these stories, along with riddles and proverbs, imbue children with a love of the language of Gĩkũyũ and enhance their responsiveness to and skill with features of narrative, imagery, inflection, and tone? How did hearing different people tell the same stories contribute to their development of critical abilities in distinguishing whether a given story was told well or poorly?

3. Describe the disruption Thiong'o experienced when he first attended a colonial school, where he was forbidden to speak the language of the community from which he came. How do the kinds of punishments meted out for speaking Gĩkũyũ give you some insight into how psychologically damaging such an experience could be for a child? Which of the examples Thiong'o gives, in your opinion, most clearly reveals the extent to which speaking English was rewarded? In what way was the knowledge of English the single most important determinant of advancement?

4. Explain how the British as colonizers of Kenya sought to achieve dominance by (1) devaluing native speech, dance, art, and traditions and (2) promoting the worth of everything British, including the speaking of English. How does changing the language a people are allowed to speak change the way they perceive themselves and their relationship to those around them? Why did the British try to

make it impossible for Kenyans to draw on the cultural values and traditions embodied in their language, Gĩkũyũ? Why was it also in the British interest to encourage and even compel Kenyans to look at themselves only through a British perspective? How was this view reinforced by teaching Kenyans British literature?

✧ Exploring Different Perspectives

1. Compare the accounts by Thiong'o and Gino Del Guercio ("The Secrets of Haiti's Living Dead") in terms of reprogramming citizens to accept a "correct" ideology whether that of British colonialism or of the soulless zombie.

2. Discuss the adequacy of education in meeting the needs of children in Kenya during the British occupation and the programs for autistics that Temple Grandin encountered, as told in "Thinking in Pictures."

✧ Extending Viewpoints through Writing and Research

1. For a research project, you might compare Thiong'o's discussion of the stories he heard as a child with Bruno Bettleheim's study *The Uses of Enchantment: The Meaning and Importance of Fairy Tales* (1976). Bettleheim suggests that these traditional forms of storytelling help children build inner strength by acknowledging that real evil exists while offering hope that those who are resourceful can overcome the evil.

2. Discuss the extent to which Thiong'o's argument expresses a rationale similar to that advanced by proponents of bilingualism. You might also wish to consider the similarities and differences in political terms between the situation Thiong'o describes and that of a Hispanic or Chinese child in the United States. If you come from a culture where English was not your first language, to what extent did your experiences match Thiong'o's when you entered a school where English was the required language?

Kyoko Mori

Polite Lies

——————◆——————

Kyoko Mori was born in Japan in 1957 and emigrated to the United States when she was twenty. She currently teaches creative writing at St. Norbert's College in De Pere, Wisconsin. She has written two volumes of fiction for young adults, Shizuko's Daughter *(1993) and* One Bird *(1995). Her acclaimed memoir,* The Dream of Water *(1995), delves into her traumatic experiences as a child in Japan: her mother committed suicide, and her father was emotionally abusive. In the following selection from her 1997 book,* Polite Lies: On Being a Woman Caught between Cultures, *Mori expands on what she sees as a defining feature of Japanese culture: courtesy intertwined with pretense. Mori has recently written* Stone Field, True Arrow *(2000).*

Before You Read

Consider under what circumstances courtesy can be used as a form of evasion.

——————◆——————

1   I don't like to go to Japan because I find it exhausting to speak Japanese all day, every day. What I am afraid of is the language, not the place. Even in Green Bay, when someone insists on speaking to me in Japanese, I clam up after a few words of general greetings, unable to go on.

2   I can only fall silent because thirty seconds into the conversation, I have already failed at an important task: while I was bowing and saying hello, I was supposed to have been calculating the other person's age, rank, and position in order to determine how polite I should be for the rest of the conversation. In Japanese conversations, the two speakers are almost never on an equal footing: one is senior to the other in age, experience, or rank. Various levels of politeness and formality are required according to these differences: it is rude to be too familiar, but people are equally offended if you are too formal, sounding snobbish and untrusting. Gender is as important as rank. Men and women practically speak different languages; women's language is much more indirect and formal than men's. There are words and phrases that women are never supposed to say, even though they are not crude or obscene. Only a man can say *damare* (shut up). No matter how angry she is, a woman must say, *shizukani* (quiet).

3   Until you can find the correct level of politeness, you can't go on
with the conversation: you won't even be able to address the other person properly. There are so many Japanese words for the pronoun *you*.
Anata is a polite but intimate *you* a woman would use to address her
husband, lover, or a very close woman friend, while a man would say
kimi, which is informal, or *omae,* which is so informal that a man would
say this word only to a family member; *otaku* is informal but imper-
sonal, so it should be used with friends rather than family. Though
there are these various forms of *you,* most people address each other in
the third person—it is offensive to call someone *you* directly. To a
woman named Hanako Maeda, you don't say, "Would you like to go
out for lunch?" You say, "Would Maeda-san (Miss Maeda) like to go
out for lunch?" But if you had known Hanako for a while, maybe you
should call her Hanako-san instead of Maeda-san, especially if you are
also a woman and not too much younger than she. Otherwise, she
might think that you are too formal and unfriendly. The word for *lunch*
also varies: *hirumeshi* is another casual word only a man is allowed to
say, *hirugohan* is informal but polite enough for friends, *ohirugohan* is a
little more polite, *chushoku* is formal and businesslike, and *gochushoku*
is the most formal and businesslike.

4   All these rules mean that before you can get on with any conversation beyond the initial greetings, you have to agree on your relationship—which one of you is superior, how close you expect to be, who
makes the decisions and who defers. So why even talk, I always wonder. The conversation that follows the mutual sizing-up can only be an
empty ritual, a careful enactment of our differences rather than a
chance to get to know each other or to exchange ideas.

5   Talking seems especially futile when I have to address a man in
Japanese. Every word I say forces me to be elaborately polite, indirect,
submissive, and unassertive. There is no way I can sound intelligent,
clearheaded, or decisive. But if I did not speak a "proper" feminine language, I would sound stupid in another way—like someone who is uneducated, insensitive, and rude, and therefore cannot be taken seriously.
I never speak Japanese with the Japanese man who teaches physics at
the college where I teach English. We are colleagues, meant to be equals.
The language I use should not automatically define me as second best.

6   Meeting Japanese-speaking people in the States makes me nervous
for another reason. I have nothing in common with these people except
that we speak Japanese. Our meeting seems random and artificial, and
I can't get over the oddness of addressing a total stranger in Japanese.
In the twenty years I lived in Japan, I rarely had a conversation with
someone I didn't already know. The only exception was the first day of
school in seventh grade, when none of us knew one another, or when I
was introduced to my friends' parents. Talking to clerks at stores
scarcely counts. I never chatted with people I was doing business with.

This is not to say that I led a particularly sheltered life. My experience was typical of anyone—male or female—growing up in Japan.

7　In Japan, whether you are a child or an adult, ninety-five percent of the people you talk to are your family, relatives, old friends, neighbors, and people you work or go to school with every day. The only new people you meet are connected to these people you already know—friends of friends, new spouses of your relatives—and you are introduced to them formally. You don't all of a sudden meet someone new. My friends and I were taught that no "nice" girl would talk to strangers on trains or at public places. It was bad manners to gab with shopkeepers or with repair people, being too familiar and keeping them from work. While American children are cautioned not to speak with strangers for reasons of safety, we were taught not to do so because it wasn't "nice." Even the most rebellious of us obeyed. We had no language in which we could address a stranger even if we had wanted to.

8　Traveling in Japan or simply taking the commuter train in Kobe now, I notice the silence around me. It seems oppressive that you cannot talk to someone who is looking at your favorite painting at a museum or sitting next to you on the train, reading a book that you finished only last week. In Japan, you can't even stop strangers and ask for simple directions when you are lost. If you get lost, you look for a policeman, who will help you because that is part of his job.

9　A Japanese friend and I got lost in Yokohama one night after we came out of a restaurant. We were looking for the train station and had no idea where it was, but my friend said, "Well, we must be heading in the right direction, since most people seem to be walking that way. It's late now. They must be going back to the station, too." After about ten minutes—with no train station in sight yet—my friend said that if she had been lost in New York or Paris, she would have asked one of the people we were following. But in her own country, in her own language, it was unthinkable to approach a stranger.

10　For her, asking was not an option. That's different from when people in the Midwest choose not to stop at a gas station for directions or flag down a store clerk to locate some item on the shelves. Midwestern people don't like to ask because they don't want to call attention to themselves by appearing stupid and helpless. Refusing to ask is a matter of pride and self-reliance—a matter of choice. Even the people who pride themselves on never asking know that help is readily available. In Japan, approaching a stranger means breaking an unspoken rule of public conduct.

11　The Japanese code of silence in public places does offer a certain kind of protection. In Japan, everyone is shielded from unwanted intrusion or attention, and that isn't entirely bad. In public places in the States, we all wish, from time to time, that people would go about their business in silence and leave us alone. Just the other day in the weight room of the YMCA, a young man I had never met before told me that he had been working out for the last two months and gained fifteen pounds. "I've always been too thin," he explained. "I want to gain twenty more pounds, and I'm going to put it all up here." We were sitting side by side on different machines. He indicated his shoulders and chest by patting them with his hand. "That's nice," I said, noncommittal but polite. "Of course," he continued, "I couldn't help putting some of the new weight around my waist, too." To my embarrassment, he lifted his shirt and pointed at his stomach. "Listen," I told him. "You don't have to show it to me or anything." I got up from my machine even though I wasn't finished. Still, I felt obligated to say, "Have a nice workout," as I walked away.

12   I don't appreciate discussing a complete stranger's weight gain and being shown his stomach, and it's true that bizarre conversations like that would never happen in a Japanese gym. Maybe there is comfort in knowing that you will never have to talk to strangers—that you can live your whole life surrounded by friends and family who will understand what you mean without your saying it. Silence can be a sign of harmony among close friends or family, but silent harmony doesn't help people who disagree or don't fit in. On crowded trains in Kobe or Tokyo, where people won't even make eye contact with strangers, much less talk to them, I feel as though each one of us were sealed inside an invisible capsule, unable to breathe or speak out. It is just like my old dream of being stuck inside a spaceship orbiting the earth. I am alarmed by how lonely I feel—and by how quietly content everyone else seems to be.

✧ Evaluating the Text

1. Why is having to speak Japanese on her return to Japan a stressful experience for Mori? What sorts of things does a Japanese speaker evaluate at the start of a conversation?

2. Provide some examples of how conversations in Japan differ from those in the United States. What aspects of American conversations does Mori find embarrassing?

3. Why is having a sense of private space important to the Japanese? How does the code of silence in public contribute to this? In what way does Mori's recurrent dream serve as a metaphor for her return trips to Japan?

✧ Exploring Different Perspectives

1. In what sense was Mori an outsider when she visited Japan just as David R. Counts ("Too Many Bananas") was an outsider trying to decode the cultural mores in New Guinea?

2. What parallels can you discover in Mori's experiences in Japan and in America with Poranee Natadecha-Sponsel's discussion in "Individualism as an American Cultural Value" regarding the differences between Thai and American cultural values?

✧ Extending Viewpoints through Writing and Research

1. The next time you are in an elevator, observe the protocols that govern conversations and interactions between strangers and compare them with those that prevail in Japan. For information about the latter, see the report by Terry Caesar in "In and Out of Elevators in Japan" (February 2000) in the online *Journal of Mundane Behavior* at http://www.mundanebehavior.org/issues/v1n1/caesar.htm. (This journal provides analyses of ordinary events in the lives of people in different societies.) Discuss your conclusions in a short essay.

2. Do you prefer people who say exactly what they think or those who are polite but leave you wondering what they really think? To what extent are these different styles culturally based? Make a case for one style over the other.

3. For an analysis of politeness in Japanese culture, see http://www.apmforum.com/columns/boye29.htm.

David R. Counts

Too Many Bananas

◆

David R. Counts teaches in the anthropology department at McMaster University in Ontario, Canada. Together with his wife, Dorothy A. Counts, he has edited a number of works, including Coping with the Final Tragedy: Dying and Grieving in Cross-Cultural Perspective *(1991) and* Aging and Its Transformations: Moving Toward Death in Pacific Societies *(1992). This selection is drawn from his book* The Humbled Anthropologist: Tales from the Pacific *(1990). A recent work is* Over the Next Hill: An Ethnography of RVing Seniors in North America *(2001).*

New Guinea, the world's second-largest island after Greenland, is located in the southwestern Pacific Ocean north of Australia. The western half of the island, known as Irian Jaya, is administered by Indonesia. Papua, which occupies the eastern half of New Guinea, was formerly a territory of Australia. It became the independent nation of Papua New Guinea in 1975. As one might gather from David R. Counts's article, the chief food crops are bananas, taro roots, and yams. The economy of New Guinea is one of the least developed of any area in the world. Most of the people farm land and grow their own food.

Before You Read

Counts's essay is divided into three sections. Take a moment after reading each section to write a brief summary of the new information in that part about the role of food in a barter society.

◆

No Watermelon at All

1   The woman came all the way through the village, walking between the two rows of houses facing each other between the beach and the bush, to the very last house standing on a little spit of land at the mouth of the Kaini River. She was carrying a watermelon on her head, and the house she came to was the government "rest house," maintained by the villagers for the occasional use of visiting officials. Though my wife and I were graduate students, not officials, and had asked for permission to stay in the village for the coming year, we were living in the rest house while the debate went on about where a house would be built for us. When the woman offered to sell us the water-

melon for two shillings, we happily agreed, and the kids were de-lighted at the prospect of watermelon after yet another meal of rice and bully beef. The money changed hands and the seller left to return to her village, a couple of miles along the coast to the east.

2   It seemed only seconds later that the woman was back, reluctantly accompanying Kolia, the man who had already made it clear to us that he was the leader of the village. Kolia had no English, and at that time, three or four days into our first stay in Kandoka Village on the island of New Britain in Papua New Guinea, we had very little Tok Pisin. Lan-guage difficulties notwithstanding, Kolia managed to make his mes-sage clear: The woman had been outrageously wrong to sell us the watermelon for two shillings and we were to return it to her and reclaim our money immediately. When we tried to explain that we thought the price to be fair and were happy with the bargain, Kolia explained again and finally made it clear that we had missed the point. The problem wasn't that we had paid too much; it was that we had paid at all. Here he was, a leader, responsible for us while we were living in his village, and we had shamed him. How would it look if he let guests in his vil-lage *buy* food? If we wanted watermelons, or bananas, or anything else, all that was necessary was to let him know. He told us that it would be all right for us to give little gifts to people who brought food to us (and they surely would), but *no one* was to sell food to us. If anyone were to try—like this woman from Lauvore—then we should refuse. There would be plenty of watermelons without us buying them.

3   The woman left with her watermelon, disgruntled, and we were left with our two shillings. But we had learned the first lesson of many about living in Kandoka. We didn't pay money for food again that whole year, and we did get lots of food brought to us . . . but we never got another watermelon. That one was the last of the season.

LESSON 1: *In a society where food is shared or gifted as part of social life, you may not buy it with money.*

Too Many Bananas

4   In the couple of months that followed the watermelon incident, we managed to become at least marginally competent in Tok Pisin, to nego-tiate the construction of a house on what we hoped was neutral ground, and to settle into the routine of our fieldwork. As our village leader had predicted, plenty of food was brought to us. Indeed, seldom did a day pass without something coming in—some sweet potatoes, a few taro, a papaya, the occasional pineapple, or some bananas—lots of bananas.

5   We had learned our lesson about the money, though, so we never even offered to buy the things that were brought, but instead made gifts, usually of tobacco to the adults or chewing gum to the children.

Nor were we so gauche as to haggle with a giver over how much of a return gift was appropriate, though the two of us sometimes conferred as to whether what had been brought was a "two-stick" or a "three-stick" stalk, bundle, or whatever. A "stick" of tobacco was a single large leaf, soaked in rum and then twisted into a ropelike form. This, wrapped in half a sheet of newsprint (torn for use as cigarette paper), sold in the local trade stores for a shilling. Nearly all of the adults in the village smoked a great deal, and they seldom had much cash, so our stocks of twist tobacco and stacks of the Sydney *Morning Herald* (all, unfortunately, the same day's issue) were seen as a real boon to those who preferred "stick" to the locally grown product.

6   We had established a pattern with respect to the gifts of food. When a donor appeared at our veranda we would offer our thanks and talk with them for a few minutes (usually about our children, who seemed to hold a real fascination for the villagers and for whom most of the gifts were intended) and then we would inquire whether they could use some tobacco. It was almost never refused, though occasionally a small bottle of kerosene, a box of matches, some laundry soap, a cup of rice, or a tin of meat would be requested instead of (or even in addition to) the tobacco. Everyone, even Kolia, seemed to think this arrangement had worked out well.

7   Now, what must be kept in mind is that while we were following their rules—or seemed to be—we were *really still buying food*. In fact we kept a running account of what came in and what we "paid" for it. Tobacco as currency got a little complicated, but since the exchange rate was one stick to one shilling, it was not too much trouble as long as everyone was happy, and meanwhile we could account for the expenditure of "informant fees" and "household expenses." Another thing to keep in mind is that not only did we continue to think in terms of our buying the food that was brought, we thought of them as *selling it*. While it was true they never quoted us a price, they also never asked us if we needed or wanted whatever they had brought. It seemed clear to us that when an adult needed a stick of tobacco, or a child wanted some chewing gum (we had enormous quantities of small packets of Wrigley's for just such eventualities) they would find something surplus to their own needs and bring it along to our "store" and get what they wanted.

8   By late November 1966, just before the rainy season set in, the bananas were coming into flush, and whereas earlier we had received banana gifts by the "hand" (six or eight bananas in a cluster cut from the stalk), donors now began to bring bananas, "for the children," by the *stalk!* The Kaliai among whom we were living are not exactly specialists in banana cultivation—they only recognize about thirty varieties, while some of their neighbors have more than twice that many—but the kinds they produce differ considerably from each other in size,

shape, and taste, so we were not dismayed when we had more than one stalk hanging on our veranda. The stalks ripen a bit at the time, and having some variety was nice. Still, by the time our accumulation had reached *four* complete stalks, the delights of variety had begun to pale a bit. The fruits were ripening progressively and it was clear that even if we and the kids ate nothing but bananas for the next week, some would still fall from the stalk onto the floor in a state of gross overripeness. This was the situation as, late one afternoon, a woman came bringing yet another stalk of bananas up the steps of the house.

9 Several factors determined our reaction to her approach: one was that there was literally no way we could possibly use the bananas. We hadn't quite reached the point of being crowded off our veranda by the stalks of fruit, but it was close. Another factor was that we were tired of playing the gift game. We had acquiesced in playing it—no one was permitted to sell us anything, and in turn we only gave things away, refusing under any circumstances to sell tobacco (or anything else) for money. But there had to be a limit. From our perspective what was at issue was that the woman wanted something and she had come to trade for it. Further, what she had brought to trade was something we neither wanted nor could use, and it should have been obvious to her. So we decided to bite the bullet.

10 The woman, Rogi, climbed the stairs to the veranda, took the stalk from where it was balanced on top of her head, and laid it on the floor with the words, "Here are some bananas for the children." Dorothy and I sat near her on the floor and thanked her for her thought but explained, "You know, we really have too many bananas—we can't use these; maybe you ought to give them to someone else. . . ." The woman looked mystified, then brightened and explained that she didn't want anything for them, she wasn't short of tobacco or anything. They were just a gift for the kids. Then she just sat there, and we sat there, and the bananas sat there, and we tried again. "Look," I said, pointing up to them and counting, "we've got four stalks already hanging here on the veranda—there are too many for us to eat now. Some are rotting already. Even if we eat only bananas, we can't keep up with what's here!"

11 Rogi's only response was to insist that these were a gift, and that she didn't want anything for them, so we tried yet another tack: "Don't *your* children like bananas?" When she admitted that they did, and that she had none at her house, we suggested that she should take them there. Finally, still puzzled, but convinced we weren't going to keep the bananas, she replaced them on her head, went down the stairs, and made her way back through the village toward her house.

12 As before, it seemed only moments before Kolia was making his way up the stairs, but this time he hadn't brought the woman in tow. "What was wrong with those bananas? Were they no good?" he demanded. We explained that there was nothing wrong with the

bananas at all, but that we simply couldn't use them and it seemed foolish to take them when we had so many and Rogi's own children had none. We obviously didn't make ourselves clear because Kolia then took up the same refrain that Rogi had—he insisted that we shouldn't be worried about taking the bananas, because they were a gift for the children and Rogi hadn't wanted anything for them. There was no reason, he added, to send her away with them—she would be ashamed. I'm afraid we must have seemed as if we were hard of hearing or thought he was, for our only response was to repeat our reasons. We went through it again—there they hung, one, two, three, *four* stalks of bananas, rapidly ripening and already far beyond our capacity to eat— we just weren't ready to accept any more and let them rot (and, we added to ourselves, pay for them with tobacco, to boot).

13   Kolia finally realized that we were neither hard of hearing nor intentionally offensive, but merely ignorant. He stared at us for a few minutes, thinking, and then asked: "Don't you frequently have visitors during the day and evening?" We nodded. Then he asked, "Don't you usually offer them cigarettes and coffee or milo?" Again, we nodded. "Did it ever occur to you to suppose," he said, "that your visitors might be hungry?" It was at this point in the conversation, as we recall, that we began to see the depth of the pit we had dug for ourselves. We nodded, hesitantly. His last words to us before he went down the stairs and stalked away were just what we were by that time afraid they might be. "When your guests are hungry, *feed them bananas!*"

LESSON 2: *Never refuse a gift, and never fail to return a gift. If you cannot use it, you can always give it away to someone else—there is no such thing as too much—there are never too many bananas.*

Not Enough Pineapples

14   During the fifteen years between that first visit in 1966 and our residence there in 1981 we had returned to live in Kandoka village twice during the 1970s, and though there were a great many changes in the village, and indeed for all of Papua New Guinea during that time, we continued to live according to the lessons of reciprocity learned during those first months in the field. We bought no food for money and refused no gifts, but shared our surplus. As our family grew, we continued to be accompanied by our younger children. Our place in the village came to be something like that of educated Kaliai who worked far away in New Guinea. Our friends expected us to come "home" when we had leave, but knew that our work kept us away for long periods of time. They also credited us with knowing much more about the rules of their way of life than was our due. And we sometimes shared the delusion that we understood life in the village, but even fif-

teen years was not long enough to relieve the need for lessons in learning to live within the rules of gift exchange.

15   In the last paragraph I used the word *friends* to describe the villagers intentionally, but of course they were not all our friends. Over the years some really had become friends, others were acquaintances, others remained consultants or informants to whom we turned when we needed information. Still others, unfortunately, we did not like at all. We tried never to make an issue of these distinctions, of course, and to be evenhanded and generous to all, as they were to us. Although we almost never actually refused requests that were made of us, over the long term our reciprocity in the village was balanced. More was given to those who helped us the most, while we gave assistance or donations of small items even to those who were not close or helpful.

16   One elderly woman in particular was a trial for us. Sara was the eldest of a group of siblings and her younger brother and sister were both generous, informative, and delightful persons. Her younger sister, Makila, was a particularly close friend and consultant, and in deference to that friendship we felt awkward in dealing with the elder sister.

17   Sara was neither a friend nor an informant, but she had been, since she returned to live in the village at the time of our second trip in 1971, a constant (if minor) drain on our resources. She never asked for much at a time. A bar of soap, a box of matches, a bottle of kerosene, a cup of rice, some onions, a stick or two of tobacco, or some other small item was usually all that was at issue, but whenever she came around it was always to ask for something—or to let us know that when we left, we should give her some of the furnishings from the house. Too, unlike almost everyone else in the village, when she came, she was always empty-handed. We ate no taro from her gardens, and the kids chewed none of her sugarcane. In short, she was, as far as we could tell, a really grasping, selfish old woman—and we were not the only victims of her greed.

18   Having long before learned the lesson of the bananas, one day we had a stalk that was ripening so fast we couldn't keep up with it, so I pulled a few for our own use (we only had one stalk at the time) and walked down through the village to Ben's house, where his five children were playing. I sat down on his steps to talk, telling him that I intended to give the fruit to his kids. They never got them. Sara saw us from across the open plaza of the village and came rushing over, shouting, "My bananas!" Then she grabbed the stalk and went off gorging herself with them. Ben and I just looked at each other.

19   Finally it got to the point where it seemed to us that we had to do something. Ten years of being used was long enough. So there came the afternoon when Sara showed up to get some tobacco—again. But this time, when we gave her the two sticks she had demanded, we confronted her.

20   First, we noted the many times she had come to get things. We didn't mind sharing things, we explained. After all, we had plenty of tobacco and soap and rice and such, and most of it was there so that we could help our friends as they helped us, with folktales, information, or even gifts of food. The problem was that she kept coming to get things, but never came to talk, or to tell stories, or to bring some little something that the kids might like. Sara didn't argue—she agreed. "Look," we suggested, "it doesn't have to be much, and we don't mind giving you things—but you can help us. The kids like pineapples, and we don't have any—the next time you need something, bring some-thing—like maybe a pineapple." Obviously somewhat embarrassed, she took her tobacco and left, saying that she would bring something soon. We were really pleased with ourselves. It had been a very diffi-cult thing to do, but it was done, and we were convinced that either she would start bringing things or not come. It was as if a burden had lifted from our shoulders.

21   It worked. Only a couple of days passed before Sara was back, bringing her bottle to get it filled with kerosene. But this time, she came carrying the biggest, most beautiful pineapple we had seen the entire time we had been there. We had a friendly talk, filled her kerosene container, and hung the pineapple up on the veranda to ripen just a little further. A few days later we cut and ate it, and whether the satisfaction it gave came from the fruit or from its source would be hard to say, but it was delicious. That, we assumed, was the end of that irritant.

22   We were wrong, of course. The next afternoon, Mary, one of our best friends for years (and no relation to Sara), dropped by for a visit. As we talked, her eyes scanned the veranda. Finally she asked whether we hadn't had a pineapple there yesterday. We said we had, but that we had already eaten it. She commented that it had been a really nice-looking one, and we told her that it had been the best we had eaten in months. Then, after a pause, she asked, "Who brought it to you?" We smiled as we said, "Sara!" because Mary would appreciate our coup—she had commented many times in the past on the fact that Sara only *got* from us and never gave. She was silent for a moment, and then she said, "Well, I'm glad you enjoyed it—my father was waiting until it was fully ripe to harvest it for you, but when it went missing I thought maybe it was the one you had here. I'm glad to see you got it. I thought maybe a thief had eaten it in the bush."

LESSON 3: *Where reciprocity is the rule and gifts are the idiom, you cannot de-mand a gift, just as you cannot refuse a request.*

23   It says a great deal about the kindness and patience of the Kaliai people that they have been willing to be our hosts for all these years

despite our blunders and lack of good manners. They have taught us a lot, and these three lessons are certainly not the least important things we learned.

✧ Evaluating the Text

1. How does Counts's initial experience of offering money for watermelon teach him his first important lesson about the culture of New Guinea?

2. How does the idea of "too many bananas" sum up the important principle of reciprocity that Counts learns? In your own words, describe the principle involved.

3. How does the experience Counts has with Sara lead to his ironic realization of the third lesson about the culture of New Guinea?

✧ Exploring Different Perspectives

1. Compare the lessons Counts learns about reciprocity in New Guinea with what Porance Natadecha-Sponsel learns about individualism in America, as told in "Individualism as an American Cultural Value."

2. How did Counts's experiences as an anthropologist resemble that of Wade Davis in Haiti, as reported by Gino Del Guercio in "The Secrets of Haiti's Living Dead," in terms of changing perspectives on native cultures?

✧ Extending Viewpoints through Writing and Research

1. What experiences have you had that involved the principle of reciprocity in your relationship with another? Discuss an incident and the lesson you learned.

2. If you were a "stranger in a strange land," would you feel more comfortable if you had many of your material possessions with you? Why or why not?

Connecting Cultures

———————◆———————

Temple Grandin, "Thinking in Pictures"

What insights into the acquisition of language are offered by Grandin and Amy Tan in "The Language of Discretion" in Chapter 1?

Gloria Anzaldúa, "Cervicide"

How do the stories by Anzaldúa and Mahdokht Kashkuli (see "The Button" in Chapter 5) dramatize the predicament of families faced with dehumanizing choices?

Poranee Natadecha-Sponsel, "Individualism as an American Cultural Value"

Discuss the importance of individual choices in American society as discussed by Natadecha-Sponsel and Steve Sailer (see "The Cousin Marriage Conundrum" in Chapter 1).

Gino Del Guercio, "The Secrets of Haiti's Living Dead"

How do both Del Guercio and Nabil Gorgy (see "Cairo Is a Small City" in Chapter 8) provide insight into cultural mechanisms for obtaining justice?

Ngũgĩ wa Thiong'o, "Decolonising the Mind"

Compare the accounts by Thiong'o and Rae Yang (see "At the Center of the Storm" in Chapter 6) in terms of conditioning citizens to accept a "correct" ideology.

Kyoko Mori, "Polite Lies"

Compare the role of the "perfect" wife in Mori's narrative and in Shirley Saad's story, "Amina," in Chapter 3.

David R. Counts, "Too Many Bananas"

Compare the way sex and money solidify social ties as discussed by Raymonde Carroll in "Sex, Money, and Success" in Chapter 5 with the way reciprocal gifts of food and goods function in New Guinua as described by Counts.

8

Customs, Rituals, and Values

*Every country gets the circus it deserves. Spain gets
bullfights. Italy gets the Catholic Church. America gets
Hollywood.*

> —Erica Jong (b. 1942, U.S. fiction and nonfiction
> writer), *How to Save Your Own Life* (1977)

———————◆———————

In the customs, rituals, and values that a society embraces, we can see
most clearly the hidden cultural logic and unconscious assumptions
people in that society rely on to interpret everything that goes on in
their world. Customs and rituals that may seem bizarre or strange to
an outsider appear entirely normal and natural to those within the culture. Unfortunately, the potential for conflict exists as soon as people
from different cultures whose "natural" ways do not coincide make
contact with each other.

As communications, immigration, and travel make the world
smaller, the potential for cross-cultural misunderstanding accelerates.
Correspondingly, the need grows to become aware of the extent to
which our own and other people's conclusions about the world are
guided by different cultural presuppositions. Analysis of the customs
of culture other than our own allows us to temporarily put aside
our taken-for-granted ways of seeing the world and—even if we are
normally unaware of the extent to which we rely on these implicit
premises—to understand that the meanings we give to events, actions,
and statements are not their only possible meanings.

The range and diversity of the selections in this chapter will allow
you to temporarily replace your own way of perceiving the world and
become aware, perhaps for the first time, of the cultural assumptions
that govern your interpretations of the world.

Harold Miner in "Body Ritual Among the Nacirema" describes the
strange obsessions of a little-known North American tribe. Mary Brave

Bird of the Lakota tribe, in "The Granddaddy of Them All," provides a behind-the-scenes account of the preparations for the sun dance, the most sacred religious ceremony of the Plains Indians. Jennifer Fisher, in *"Nutcracker* Nation," relates the many-faceted adaptations of this ubiquitous and popular ballet. Octavio Paz, in "Fiesta," explores the important role fiestas play in Mexican culture and their relationship to the Mexican national character. In "The Shopping Mall and the Formal Garden" Richard Keller Simon examines how the modern mall incorporates many designs modeled on gardens of the past to create a shopper's paradise.

The Egyptian writer, Nabil Gorgy, in "Cairo Is a Small City," tells how a ruthless engineer is held accountable to the traditional Bedouin concept of justice in modern-day Egypt. Liza Dalby, the first non-Japanese to live as a geisha explains, in "Kimono," that the garment constitutes "a social code" replete with meanings about the wearer's social class and marital status. Valerie Steele and John S. Major, in "China Chic: East Meets West," analyze the hidden political and social meanings of the custom of foot binding in ancient China.

Harold Miner

Body Ritual Among the Nacirema

◆

Horace Mitchell (Harold) Miner (1912-1993) studied at the University of Chicago and taught at the University of Michigan (1946-1985). An early work is St. Denis: A French Canadian Parish *(1936). This classic essay (written as a spoof) was originally published in the* American Anthropologist, *June 1956 and has become a defining work in an ever-expanding field devoted to research on this little known North American tribe.*

Before You Read

Consider how an everyday ritual of yours might be viewed as an anthropological curiosity.

◆

1   The anthropologist has become so familiar with the diversity of ways in which different peoples behave in similar situations that he is not apt to be surprised by even the most exotic customs. In fact, if all of the logically possible combinations of behavior have not been found somewhere in the world, he is apt to suspect that they must be present in some yet undescribed tribe. This point has, in fact, been expressed with respect to clan organization by Murdock (1949: 71). In this light, the magical beliefs and practices of the Nacirema present such unusual aspects that it seems desirable to describe them as an example of the extremes to which human behavior can go.

2   Professor Linton first brought the ritual of the Nacirema to the attention of anthropologists twenty years ago (1936: 326), but the culture of this people is still very poorly understood. They are a North American group living in the territory between the Canadian Cree, the Yaqui and Tarahumare of Mexico, and the Carib and Arawak of the Antilles. Little is known of their origin, though tradition states that they came from the east. According to Nacirema mythology, their nation was originated by a culture hero, Notgnishaw, who is otherwise known for two great feats of strength—the throwing of a piece of wampum across the river Pa-To-Mac and the chopping down of a cherry tree in which the Spirit of Truth resided.

3   Nacirema culture is characterized by a highly developed market economy which has evolved in a rich natural habitat. While much of the people's time is devoted to economic pursuits, a large part of the

fruits of these labors and a considerable portion of the day are spent in ritual activity. The focus of this activity is the human body, the appearance and health of which loom as a dominant concern in the ethos of the people. While such a concern is certainly not unusual, its ceremonial aspects and associated philosophy are unique.

4   The fundamental belief underlying the whole system appears to be that the human body is ugly and that its natural tendency is to debility and disease. Incarcerated in such a body, man's only hope is to avert these characteristics through the use of the powerful influences of ritual and ceremony. Every household has one or more shrines devoted to this purpose. The more powerful individuals in the society have several shrines in their houses and, in fact, the opulence of a house is often referred to in terms of the number of such ritual centers it possesses. Most houses are of wattle and daub construction, but the shrine rooms of the more wealthy are walled with stone. Poorer families imitate the rich by applying pottery plaques to their shrine walls.

5   While each family has at least one such shrine, the rituals associated with it are not family ceremonies but are private and secret. The rites are normally only discussed with children, and then only during the period when they are being initiated into these mysteries. I was able, however, to establish sufficient rapport with the natives to examine these shrines and to have the rituals described to me.

6   The focal point of the shrine is a box or chest which is built into the wall. In this chest are kept the many charms and magical potions without which no native believes he could live. These preparations are secured from a variety of specialized practitioners. The most powerful of these are the medicine men, whose assistance must be rewarded with substantial gifts. However, the medicine men do not provide the curative potions for their clients, but decide what the ingredients should be and then write them down in an ancient and secret language. This writing is understood only by the medicine men and by the herbalists who, for another gift, provide the required charm.

7   The charm is not disposed of after it has served its purpose, but is placed in the charm-box of the household shrine. As these magical materials are specific for certain ills, and the real or imagined maladies of the people are many, the charm-box is usually full to overflowing. The magical packets are so numerous that people forget what their purposes were and fear to use them again. While the natives are very vague on this point, we can only assume that the idea in retaining all the old magical materials is that their presence in the charm-box, before which the body rituals are conducted, will in some way protect the worshipper.

8   Beneath the charm-box is a small font. Each day every member of the family, in succession, enters the shrine room, bows his head before the charm-box, mingles different sorts of holy water in the font, and proceeds with a brief rite of ablution. The holy waters are secured from

the Water Temple of the community, where the priests conduct elaborate ceremonies to make the liquid ritually pure.

9   In the hierarchy of magical practitioners, and below the medicine men in prestige, are specialists whose designation is best translated "holy-mouth-men." The Nacirema have an almost pathological horror and fascination with the mouth, the condition of which is believed to have a supernatural influence on all social relationships. Were it not for the rituals of the mouth, they believe that their teeth would fall out, their gums bleed, their jaws shrink, their friends desert them, and their lovers reject them. (They also believe that a strong relationship exists between oral and moral characteristics. For example, there is a ritual ablution of the mouth for children which is supposed to improve their moral fiber.)

10   The daily body ritual performed by everyone includes a mouth-rite. Despite the fact that these people are so punctilious about care of the mouth, this rite involves a practice which strikes the uninitiated stranger as revolting. It was reported to me that the ritual consists of inserting a small bundle of hog hairs into the mouth, along with certain magical powders, and then moving the bundle in a highly formalized series of gestures.

11   In addition to the private mouth-rite, the people seek out a holy-mouth-man once or twice a year. These practitioners have an impressive set of paraphernalia, consisting of a variety of augers, awls, probes, and prods. The use of these objects in the exorcism of the evils of the mouth involves almost unbelievable ritual torture of the client. The holy-mouth-man opens the client's mouth and, using the above mentioned tools, enlarges any holes which decay may have created in the teeth. Magical materials are put into these holes. If there are no naturally occurring holes in the teeth, large sections of one or more teeth are gouged out so that the supernatural substance can be applied. In the client's view, the purpose of these ministrations is to arrest decay and to draw friends. The extremely sacred and traditional character of the rite is evident in the fact that the natives return to the holy-mouth-men year after year, despite the fact that their teeth continue to decay.

12   It is to be hoped that, when a thorough study of the Nacirema is made, there will be a careful inquiry into the personality structure of these people. One has but to watch the gleam in the eye of a holy-mouth-man, as he jabs an awl into an exposed nerve, to suspect that a certain amount of sadism is involved. If this can be established, a very interesting pattern emerges, for most of the population shows definite masochistic tendencies. It was to these that Professor Linton referred in discussing a distinctive part of the daily body ritual which is performed only by men. This part of the rite involves scraping and lacerating the surface of the face with a sharp instrument. Special women's rites are performed only four times during each lunar month, but what they lack in frequency is made up in barbarity. As part of this ceremony,

women bake their heads in small ovens for about an hour. The theoretically interesting point is that what seems to be a preponderantly masochistic people have developed sadistic specialists.

13   The medicine men have an imposing temple, or *latipso*, in every community of any size. The more elaborate ceremonies required to treat very sick patients can only be performed at this temple. These ceremonies involve not only the thaumaturge but a permanent group of vestal maidens who move sedately about the temple chambers in distinctive costume and headdress.

14   The *latipso* ceremonies are so harsh that it is phenomenal that a fair proportion of the really sick natives who enter the temple ever recover. Small children whose indoctrination is still incomplete have been known to resist attempts to take them to the temple because "that is where you go to die." Despite this fact, sick adults are not only willing but eager to undergo the protracted ritual purification, if they can afford to do so. No matter how ill the supplicant or how grave the emergency, the guardians of many temples will not admit a client if he cannot give a rich gift to the custodian. Even after one has gained admission and survived the ceremonies, the guardians will not permit the neophyte to leave until he makes still another gift.

15   The supplicant entering the temple is first stripped of all his or her clothes. In every-day life the Nacirema avoids exposure of his body and its natural functions. Bathing and excretory acts are performed only in the secrecy of the household shrine, where they are ritualized as part of the body-rites. Psychological shock results from the fact that body secrecy is suddenly lost upon entry into the *latipso*. A man, whose own wife has never seen him in an excretory act, suddenly finds himself naked and assisted by a vestal maiden while he performs his natural functions into a sacred vessel. This sort of ceremonial treatment is necessitated by the fact that the excreta are used by a diviner to ascertain the course and nature of the client's sickness. Female clients, on the other hand, find their naked bodies are subjected to the scrutiny, manipulation, and prodding of the medicine men.

16   Few supplicants in the temple are well enough to do anything but lie on their hard beds. The daily ceremonies, like the rites of the holy-mouth-men, involve discomfort and torture. With ritual precision, the vestals awaken their miserable charges each dawn and roll them about on their beds of pain while performing ablutions, in the formal movements of which the maidens are highly trained. At other times they insert magic wands in the supplicant's mouth or force him to eat substances which are supposed to be healing. From time to time the medicine men come to their clients and jab magically treated needles into their flesh. The fact that these temple ceremonies may not cure, and may even kill the neophyte, in no way decreases the people's faith in the medicine men.

17   There remains one other kind of practitioner, known as a "listener." This witch-doctor has the power to exorcise the devils that lodge in the heads of people who have been bewitched. The Nacirema believe that parents bewitch their own children. Mothers are particularly suspected of putting a curse on children while teaching them the secret body rituals. The counter-magic of the witch-doctor is unusual in its lack of ritual. The patient simply tells the "listener" all his troubles and fears, beginning with the earliest difficulties he can remember. The memory displayed by the Nacirema in these exorcism sessions is truly remarkable. It is not uncommon for the patient to bemoan the rejection he felt upon being weaned as a babe, and a few individuals even see their troubles going back to the traumatic effects of their own birth.

18   In conclusion, mention must be made of certain practices which have their base in native esthetics but which depend upon the pervasive aversion to the natural body and its functions. There are ritual fasts to make fat people thin and ceremonial feasts to make thin people fat. Still other rites are used to make women's breasts large if they are small, and smaller if they are large. General dissatisfaction with breast shape is symbolized in the fact that the ideal form is virtually outside the range of human variation. A few women afflicted with almost inhuman hyper-mammary development are so idolized that they make a handsome living by simply going from village to village and permitting the natives to stare at them for a fee.

19   Reference has already been made to the fact that excretory functions are ritualized, routinized, and relegated to secrecy. Natural reproductive functions are similarly distorted. Intercourse is taboo as a topic and scheduled as an act. Efforts are made to avoid pregnancy by the use of magical materials or by limiting intercourse to certain phases of the moon. Conception is actually very infrequent. When pregnant, women dress so as to hide their condition. Parturition takes place in secret, without friends or relatives to assist, and the majority of women do not nurse their infants.

20   Our review of the ritual life of the Nacirema has certainly shown them to be a magic-ridden people. It is hard to understand how they have managed to exist so long under the burdens which they have imposed upon themselves. But even such exotic customs as these take on real meaning when they are viewed with the insight provided by Malinowski when he wrote (1948: 70):

> Looking from far and above, from our high places of safety in the developed civilization, it is easy to see all the crudity and irrelevance of magic. But without its power and guidance early man could not have mastered his practical difficulties as he has done, nor could man have advanced to the higher stages of civilization.

REFERENCES

Linton, Ralph. 1936. *The Study of Man.* New York, D. Appleton-Century Co.
Malinowski, Bronislaw. 1948. *Magic, Science, and Religion.* Glencoe, The Free Press.
Murdock, George P. 1949. *Social Structure.* New York, The Macmillan Co.

✧ *Evaluating the Text*

1. What bizarre attitude do the Nacirema have toward the human body?

2. What different kinds of body rituals, shrines, and practioners do the Nacirema resort to based on their obsession with the human body?

✧ *Exploring Different Perspectives*

1. What rituals when viewed objectively are as bizarre among the Nacirema as foot binding was for the Chinese as described by Valerie Steele and John S. Major in "China Chic: East Meets West"?

2. What obsessions and rituals characterize the Nacirema, and how do they differ from those practiced in Mexico as described by Octavio Paz in "Fiesta"?

✧ *Extending Viewpoints through Writing and Research*

1. Have you ever heard of the Nacirema or their hero Notgnishaw? Which of their rituals might well be commonplace in our culture?

2. How would an objective observer describe any commonplace obsessive ritual in our culture other than those described by Miner—for example, fitness clubs, yoga, pilates, teeth whitening?

3. Resources on the Nacirema people are available at http://www .beadsland.com/nacirema/.

Mary Brave Bird

The Granddaddy of Them All

◆

Mary Brave Bird (aka Mary Crow Dog) was born on the Rosebud reservation in South Dakota. She is known for her autobiographies Lakota Woman *(1990) and* Ohitika Woman *(1993). She is a political activist and joined the American Indian Movement (AIM) in 1971. In this chapter from* Ohitika Woman *(1993), Mary Brave Bird describes the significance of the four-day sun dance, the most sacred religious ceremony of the Plains Indians. Her account provides unequaled insight into the elaborate preparations necessary for the ceremony, the meaning of the voluntary physical piercings and mutilations to which the dancers subject themselves, and the role this purification ritual plays in the cultural and religious life of Native Americans.*

Before You Read

Consider the role that purification rituals play in important religious ceremonies.

◆

1   I knew an old medicine man who called the sun dance the granddaddy of all our ceremonies. It is the foremost, the most solemn, the most sacred of all our rituals. It is a celebration of life, of the sun, the buffalo, the eagle. It is a self-sacrifice, a suffering for someone you love, to take his or her pain upon yourself. It is not an initiation rite or a way to prove one's courage as was shown in the movie *A Man Called Horse.* That was a misrepresentation of what the dance is about. I don't want to talk here about the innermost meanings and details of rituals of the sun dance. That should be for a respected medicine man to do (or not to do). I want to talk about the basics as I have experienced them, year after year, at Crow Dog's Paradise, such down-to-earth aspects as the part I played as a woman and wife of the sun dance director. I'll start with the everyday things going on during a sun dance, the work and the never-ending tasks, and not the things directly involved with the ritual. First of all, people going to the sun dance, even if they are not dancers themselves, should refrain from sexual intercourse, drinking, smoking weed, and from all common pleasures. They should refrain from all worldly things for two weeks before the dance until four days after it is over.

2   The hard thing for me was maintaining the kitchen and caring for the people who would come around and camp. Some of them would stay to help build the arbor and get things ready for the sun dance. So I'd have to get wood, cook outside, haul water, feed them, do all the dishes, and fry bread over the hot fire. I was constantly getting that black soot all over my clothes. It took a pretty good toll on me—by the time you got one meal finished and got things cleaned up, it was already time for the next meal. This went on from sunrise to sundown. That took up all my time. On top of it I had to take care of the kids, getting their hair brushed, getting them cleaned up for the day. People would come and bring Crow Dog tobacco, or the pipe, and they'd want to talk to him, so whatever I was doing I had to put off, just to accommodate the people. There were always people arriving and you had to offer them coffee. Then I had to go to town, check the mail, run to the store, all these little things that took up my time. Crow Dog's daughter Bernadette was always helpful. I think she was as old as Jenny is now when I first met her. So we kind of grew up there together in the kitchen. She was usually the one who kept the coffee going, and she was always there when I needed help. I could always depend on her. Sometimes different women would come over and offer to help, but then we would have too many people in the kitchen and it would get to be a mess—people cooked different ways, which led to arguments. Every day we'd make two big old pots of soup, and we'd put beef in one pot and vegetables in the other. And every day we'd feed everybody in the camp. We'd make frybread over the open fire constantly. So the sweating was going on constantly, and the eating, too. The kitchen was constantly open. Sometimes I'd have the morning meals done when the sun was up. We'd cook on an open fire and make things like cornmeal, or pancakes. Just when you thought you were through, somebody would show up from a long way off, so you'd have to cook for them.

3   Then I had to care for the sick. A lot of people drink from the little river that runs through the Paradise and they come down with a tremendous case of the shits. They think because they are on Indian land the water must be pure, but it was already polluted from way upstream outside the res. Others wander off into the woods and they get a bad case of poison ivy. We always have a case or two of sunstroke to deal with. Last summer a white woman went to the outhouse and there was a big, fat rattlesnake coiled up on the seat. That was one encounter the lady could have done without. There's never a dull moment.

4   There's a lot of preparation for the sun dance. A lot of work goes into making the arbor, which is built around a circle, with a door to the east where the people come and sit, and usually on the west side there's a place where the dancers rest. Then we have to put up the sweat lodges, which are made out of fresh willows. There are at least

two main lodges—one for the men and one for the women. Another major task is bringing in a lot of firewood. The main fire is lit before sunrise on purification morning. There's always someone there, the main fire person, to watch it and to keep it burning until the last day, the last sweat lodge. Then there is the sun dance tree, which is sacred. It is the tree of life. In the old days scouts were sent out to pick a flawless cottonwood. The scouts would count coup upon it as if it were a brave enemy.

5   Then there is the ceremony of putting up the tree. The way I know it, the tree, which has been left standing for a year, is taken out of its spot to be replaced by a new tree. They put the old one in a place where nobody will bother it, because it still has the offerings from the previous year on it.

6   On the last day of purification—the sun dance usually starts on a Sunday and ends on Wednesday—the old tree is taken out and the dancers are asked to clean inside and under the arbor and to get their things ready. Then the dancers go and get another tree, sometimes accompanied by their families. The only people who stay behind are the old people. So they go and get a tree, which is usually picked ahead of time by a medicine man or elder, who then marks it with the four directions, with wasé, red paint. A young girl, who has to be a virgin before her puberty, is given an axe, and she'll cut the tree, to mark it, in each direction. After that each sun dancer takes a turn chopping, with one swing each, until it comes down. Usually the men do this. It goes pretty fast. When the tree is down, they catch it and make sure it doesn't touch the ground. Then they trim it just a little bit from the bottom. When the tree is ready to go up they carry it with the leaves toward the front to the sun dance ground. When the dancers enter the camp, there is usually a warrior who will make a yell, the ageesha, and he'll do it four times by the time they get to the arbor. Then they bring the tree in, and that's the only time it is set down, very carefully. Then somebody puts the chokecherry branches in the crotch of the tree, along with the figure of a man and a buffalo made out of buffalo hide. From there they'll put on the flags in the Four Direction colors. Then the dancers all put their offerings on the tree. Before they bring the tree in they sing songs to greet its arrival. When all this has been done, they put the spiritual food into the hole in the ground into which the tree will be planted. We feed the tree with water, corn, papa, and chokecherries. Some use buffalo and kidney fat in the papa. Then they place the tree in the hole and the dancers raise it by pulling on ropes attached to its top. They have to steady the tree with the ropes, because it is big. In the old days a song was chanted after the tree had been raised:

At the center of the earth
You stand,

Looking around you,
Beholding the people,
Who stand in awe.
They wish to live.

7   During the purification days you're asked to get fresh sage. It's used for the wreaths around the dancers' heads, wrists, and ankles. They line the sweat lodges with sage, and they also put some under the tree. Whoever is piercing will lie on that bed of sage. So it takes a lot of people to gather all the sage. People get their eagle-bone whistles ready. And they get the last-minute things they need on their sun dance outfits. During purification, sweat lodges are run constantly. So a lot of rocks are needed. Then there's the water—you usually have to go to the tribal headquarters and get a water truck so there'll be enough. Also during this time, a lot of people are taken up on the hill to fast. By the time they come down they go right into the dance, so some dancers fast for four days and go into the dance, making it an eight-day ritual. During this time, also, campers are coming in, setting up tipis, and settling down.

8   Now the four days of the dance start. If there are many dancers, they'll start piercing from the first day on. Usually the dancers have made a vow the year before to pierce.

9   At the time of the piercing they ask that any women on their moon stay away from the arbor, or the sweat lodges, or any sacred things. Last year they asked women on their moon to leave the camp. When women on their moon come around the dancers, the dancers get real sick. Most women respect the rule, but sometimes there's young girls who don't realize this.

10   It's the dancers' choice how they want to pierce. I've seen some that were pierced with eagle claws. I've heard men say that they pierce because women have pain during childbirth; so they pierce for their children and their families and the women who've suffered bringing the generations into life. It's an honorable thing to do, to offer oneself in sacrifice. Some people pierce on their chest or on their back, and they'll pierce not from the tree, but they'll put the rope through the tree, over the crotch, and the horse will pull them. Women pierce now. Some do flesh offerings, some will pierce with feathers in their arms, some will pierce and drag a buffalo skull. I remember a sun dancer from Pine Ridge, Loretta Whirlwind Horse. Her father was sick and couldn't move his legs, so she danced for him. He later told in a meeting that while she was dancing for him, suffering, he could move his legs, and feel them, where he couldn't before.

11   When the women pierce with a feather, they pierce their arms and tie the feather on with a piece of sinew. Some will keep it on for four days. On the last day they'll make their last prayer. Then they'll have it

pulled off. I have old scars where I've been pierced on my arms—Bill Eagle Feathers did the piercing, and he cut my arms for flesh offerings. That year I pierced with wooden pegs. Bill is one man that I really miss. At the sun dance he'd always make a coyote yell. Usually eagles come and circle around the arbor and the camp, as if they know they are wanted. They hear the dancers' eagle-bone whistles. It's our belief that Tunkashila communicates with the eagle, our relative. When you're given a whistle you're supposed to take care of it.

12   All of the dancers' pipes have to be smoked in one day. When one dance round is over, all the dancers face south in rows, and the first row will go and get their pipes from where they put them in the morning on the west side of the arbor, where all the pipes are laid when the dancers first come in. So they go over there and they pick up their pipes from the racks, and they go around the tree, and then back in the row. At the same time there'll be helpers that will pick out certain people from under the arbor to accept the dancers' pipes. The dancers will go back and forth four times, and the fourth time they'll give those people the pipes. When they hand them their pipes, the singing stops. The round is over, and the people who were picked will go back, in formation, to their place under the arbor where they smoke the dancers' pipes. The dancers have to keep their pipes real clean, so the people who smoke the pipes for them won't have any problems lighting them. I was sitting under the arbor with Rocky, and she said: "Why are white people dancing this year?" I said: "This is the year for reconciliation." There are some real sincere, dedicated people there, but I'm worried that once you let them in the door, they might try to take over, or to exploit it.

13   Different women will take turns running the sweat lodge. The guys sweat all the time, constantly, at late-night and early-morning sweats. We have children's sweats, too. The little boys will have sweats. My kids always sweat. June Bug said: "I'm going to sweat, but it's going to be a man's sweat. I'm not sweating with any girls." He was at that age. But it's really nice to see kids sweating and praying. They run the sweats themselves, and they'll say their prayers and express themselves. They conduct themselves in a good way.

14   After the last round of piercing, when it's time for the sun dance to end, they'll put some water on the buffalo skull, our altar. The helper will get the flags from each direction and all the dancers will gather their pipes. The leaders go out first. They dance in formation toward the east door, stopping four times. It's a beautiful sight. People will gather outside the arbor to shake the dancers' hands as they leave. The dancers go to the sweat lodge to do their last sweat. During the breaks in the dance there are ceremonies that go on too. Marriages are performed, girls' ears are pierced. After the dance, the feast begins. During this time, if a family has someone who has danced four years in a

row and is finished with his four vows, they'll have a giveaway in his honor. Sometimes naming ceremonies are going on too, and we have special songs for that. Also during this time, people who want to dance the next year are asked to make their vows. And we honor the singers and drummers. From the time when they bring in the tree to the end of the dance they've been singing the songs. And if they do an honoring song, money is donated to them. It's hard to sit there and sing for four days straight.

15   When I danced, I suffered for my children, for the Lakota people, for my Diné friends facing relocation at Big Mountain. They cut my flesh from where I had pierced, and put it in a little tobacco pouch and offered it to the tree, to the spirit. After having pierced for the first time, I was asked to speak. I spoke about my friends who had gone to another world, about Annie Mae Aquash, who had sun danced, who believed in the pipe and the sacred medicine.

16   I wanted to dance last summer at the Paradise but was still too weak from my car accident. I went to the drum to sing along in the wicaglata way, echoing the male singers, and I grew faint and had to sit down, but I am sure that, sometime in the future, I will dance again.

17   Good things happen during the sun dance, you could maybe call them spiritual. There were two men who had been bitter enemies some twenty years ago, and one of them had shot the other and nearly killed him. Then two years ago, in the spirit of the sacred dance, they not only forgave each other, but became friends and even pierced each other. It really touched my heart.

18   There is a Chicano who walks hundreds of miles on foot, all the way from Mexico, to come to the sun dance. They call him "So Happy." Years ago, he was a survivor of that horrible incident where a train car full of wetbacks were tricked out of their money and left in the car to suffocate.

19   At the last sun dance, in 1991, they flew the Stars and Stripes right-side up for the first time. That came as a shock to me. The only way I had ever seen the flag used by AIM people was upside down, the way ghost dancers used to wrap themselves in the flag as a sign of distress and mourning, and the way AIM used it as a sign of protest. But things are changing and getting more mellow. They flew the flag the right way to honor our own veterans who have fought in every war the United States was involved in—World War I, World War II, Korea, Vietnam, and Desert Storm. Sioux men were fighting in all those far-away places, though some who had been in Nam said later that they felt like the Crows and Arikaras scouting for Custer, scouting for the whites against nonwhite people. Still, many Sioux gave their lives in distant lands and so now we have a respect for the American flag. In a way it's good to come to an understanding, particularly as those

flags last year were flown to honor Francis Primeaux, an old veteran and roadman of the Native American Church, who had died a short time before.

20   Also at the last sun dance, Archie Fire Lame Deer allowed some heyokas, the contrary, "forwards-backwards thunder dreamers," to dance. That was the second time they came and pierced. Being heyokas, they dress different than the other dancers. One was painted with black and white polka dots; another had his face hidden by a shawl; a third had a sort of fantastic many-colored outfit on and a bunch of feathers from various birds on his head. Everyone dressed according to his vision. They were very strong dancers.

21   And at last year's sun dance people encouraged me: "Sister, hold your head up!" We embraced and laughed and cried together. And there was the cry: "All you Wounded Knee veterans, stand up!" And so we stood there—Clyde and Crow Dog, Carla and Ron and Carter and myself—and they sang the honoring song for us. They say the movement is dead, but it isn't. We're still working for the people; we are still here. You can't stop us now. When they sang the honoring song for me and my sisters and brothers, I felt really good.

✧ Evaluating the Text

1. What role does the sun dance play among the Lakota? What misconceptions does Mary Brave Bird wish to correct about the nature and purpose of these ceremonies?

2. What part does purification, the burning of sage, and piercing the flesh play in the ritual of the sun dance? What is so unusual about the way in which voluntary suffering is viewed?

3. How does this account suggest that the sun dance has a political as well as religious meaning for Mary Brave Bird?

✧ Exploring Different Perspectives

1. Compare the way the sun dance creates it own world—involving costumes, ceremonies, and piercings, not normally encouraged in everyday life—with the ritual of going to the shopping mall described by Richard Keller Simon in "The Shopping Mall and the Formal Garden."

2. Compare the spiritual values that are important to Native Americans with the body-centered rituals that are important to the Nacirema, as described by Harold Miner in "Body Ritual Among the Nacirema.

❖ *Extending Viewpoints through Writing and Research*

1. Have you ever participated in a religious ceremony that entailed deprivation, fasting, or other voluntary suffering? Describe the meaning and purpose of the ritual.

2. Is there one ceremony that expresses the core of religious values for your community? If so, describe it.

3. For more information on the sun dance, see http://www.angelfire .com/co/medicinewolf/lakota/sundance.html.

How does this photo suggest that the sun dance is not only a religious cere-mony but a social one as well?

Jennifer Fisher

Nutcracker *Nation*

◆

Jennifer Fisher holds a master's degree in dance from York University in Toronto and a Ph.D. in Dance History and Theory from the University of California at Riverside. A former dancer and actor, she has previously taught at York University and Pomona College. She is currently an Assistant Professor of Dance at the University of California at Irvine. The following selection is drawn from Nutcracker Nation: How an Old World Ballet Became a Christmas Tradition in the New World *(2003).*

Before You Read

Consider whether you have ever participated in, or seen, a performance of Tchaikovsky's ballet, *The Nutcracker*. You have no doubt heard of it; speculate on its popularity.

◆

1   At the Clinton White House, back in 1994, *The Nutcracker* was chosen as the official Christmas decorating theme, and suddenly effigies of the Nutcracker Prince, Clara, and the Sugar Plum Fairy were hanging off trees and mantles all over the building. There was even a needlepoint Christmas stocking on which two nutcracker soldiers were pictured guarding the Capitol, thus accomplishing the difficult feat of linking Christmas cheer to national defense. This wasn't the first time a nutcracker had been drafted to serve as a symbol of U.S. patriotism. The German nutcracker carving industry long ago recognized the American market by offering figurines carved in the image of U.S. presidents, Uncle Sam, and Civil War soldiers. But this was the first time the ballet named for a nutcracker had taken up residence, symbolically at least, in the White House.

2   It was a moment the immigrant *Nutcracker* had been preparing for its whole life in the New World—all those children and soldiers marching across stages all over the country, all that hobnobbing with the common people to get their support. Finally it was being recognized as a national icon. If the immigrant *Nutcracker* had been gradually earning naturalized citizenship, this was official notification. The reason for its visibility in the nation's capital in the mid-1990s wasn't hard to figure out. In the time-honored tradition of getting to the top because you

know the right people, *The Nutcracker* ended up in the White House because of personal connections—the Clintons had a child in the ballet. Not that anyone would have complained about undue influence; by then, so many Americans were involved in *The Nutcracker,* the ballet could have easily won an election on its own merits.

3   The Clinton's experience was much like that of any other *Nutcracker* family, except that Chelsea had her progress through the corps de ballet ranks tracked by CNN and flashed on the national news every Christmas. It's hard to know whether or not this TV exposure piqued more interest in *The Nutcracker* than usual, but the presidential emphasis on the ballet was new—and fortunately occurred in the years before Clinton's image as a family man was tarnished. The first daughter appeared in the Washington Ballet's production for several seasons, playing the "Favorite Aunt" in the party scene, or one of the court ladies who welcome Clara to the Land of the Sweets. Her parents dutifully came to see her each year, the president sometimes stealing in to see a second performance, standing at the back of the house so as not to draw attention away from the stage. In the official White House booklet describing the *Nutcracker* decorations, a warm personal message from Bill and Hillary made the link between the ballet and nationhood by noting that *The Nutcracker* had inspired American artisans all over the country to create holiday ornaments and trimmings that all Americans could enjoy. It rather sealed the deal on what might be termed "patriotic seasonal family togetherness."

4   This was not, of course, a sudden elevation to citizenship; the hearts and minds of Americans were won over a period of years, during which various versions were threaded into the fabric of many communities. *The Nutcracker* was a bit like a franchise operation, except that no one was technically in charge, so it never fell into the comfortable but bland consistency that results from licensing agreements. *The Nutcracker* just seemed to sprout up all over, in some ways like any ballet that travels; plots and steps from the classics have always been stolen or borrowed and reworked by itinerant choreographers and dancers. But the kinds of changes *The Nutcracker* underwent over the years resulted not only in adaptation but in virtual adoption, and the ballet often started to look like its new parents. Hulas were added in Hawaii, cowboys in Arizona, hockey players in Winnipeg, Cajun food in Louisiana. Many productions tried to recreate elements of the original *Nutcracker,* or at least stick with traditional stagings, but often the process involved the intertwining strategies of nationalization and localization. For *The Nutcracker,* fitting in to its new home was a many splendored thing.

5   Clara, it turns out, might have moved from Germany to Georgia, and she might be a jazz dancer, or a student of *ballet folklórico* or *bharata*

natyam, a classical dance form from southern India. She could be your neighbor's six-year-old or a teenager you recognize, or she could be played by a ballerina from Beijing who joins the resident ballet company and tries to figure out why *The Nutcracker* is such a big deal in North America. Clara has also been envisioned as an older woman remembering her youth; and, of course, she is often called Marie, as in the original story and the Balanchine version, or Masha, or maybe Claire or Marcy or just plain Mary, if she's trying to seem less foreign than usual. No one formula has guaranteed financial or critical success, but renovations and adaptations seem to keep the ballet alive. Never very secure about its identity back in Russia, *The Nutcracker* has always been a good sport abroad, especially when it came to the satiric nutty-*Nuts* and naughty *Nutcracker*s that were a byproduct of the ballet's establishment as an iconic yearly tradition. Making Clara an illegal alien or a cross-dresser, or having the Sugar Plum Fairy and her Prince duke it out in a boxing ring are merely alternate ways of having the ballet reflect a particular community. From sea to shining sea, the obliging *Nutcracker* gradually became a ballet on which desires, identities, and agendas are projected.

6　　　Among traditional productions, an early example of *Nutcracker* relocation occurred in Ohio in 1974, when the Cincinnati Ballet took advantage of the ballet's German setting by soliciting the support of descendants of German immigrants who had settled in Cincinnati. It was found that one could easily imagine the Stahlbaum family in the Ohio Valley instead of the old country, and the production (which has since been renovated) featured set details taken from local landmarks. Several prominent local businesses owned by families of German descent were happy to provide funds for a respected, family-oriented holiday ballet, eventually establishing an endowment ear-marked especially for *Nutcracker* performances. Until recently, the indebted Cincinnati Ballet called their production *The Frisch's Nutcracker,* after a restaurant chain owned by the Maier family. (The Frisch's people relinquished this name, reputedly because some unsavory double entendres about cracking nuts became popular, and the title is now a slightly less proprietary *"The Nutcracker,* sponsored by Frisch's.")

7　　　In other cities, different European immigrant groups have sometimes been substituted. Scots have proved popular in the party scene, from an amateur version in St. John's, Newfoundland, where kilts and Scottish country dancing dot the scene, to a production in Alma, Michigan—a town nicknamed "Scotland, U.S.A."—which is set in the Edinburgh of 1905. In the latter case, Clara is part of the MacMillan clan, her brother Fritz is rechristened Jamie, and bagpipes are added without shifting the essentials of the plot.

8　　　When localizing liberties are taken, the name of the ballet sometimes changes, a strategy that works as a bonding agent for many audiences and ballet companies. "People want to feel as if their version belongs to them," is a refrain heard round the *Nutcracker* realm. The obliging ballet has seemingly never met a relocation scheme it wouldn't try. Cajun country? It calls for a *Bayou Nutcracker*. The Baton Rouge Ballet Theatre set its version in antebellum Louisiana and was lauded for preserving local heritage. And for those who have no patience with Old World nostalgia, there are at least two *Urban Nutcrackers,* one set in contemporary Cleveland, with a character called "Drosselmorgan," who is a Web master; and one that takes place in the Atlanta of the 1940s, featuring soldiers dressed as civil rights champion Marcus Garvey to provide a little black history reinforcement. The New York-based Dances Patrelle places its *Yorkville Nutcracker* in turn-of-the-century New York, using local landmarks like Central Park, Gracie Mansion, and the Bronx Botanical Gardens, as well as some historical characters (Theodore Roosevelt takes a night off from running the police board to attend a Christmas Eve party at Gracie Mansion). Coyotes and rattlesnakes show up in the Tucson Regional Ballet's *Southwest Nutcracker,* set in 1880s Arizona. Farther west, the proximity of the film industry inspired the Santa Barbara-based State Street Ballet to do *The Hollywood Nutcracker,* in which first-act party guests have just finished shooting a movie and are attending a Christmas Eve wrap party at the producer's house. In this one, Clara wants to be a movie star and idolizes a femme fatale Sugar Plum character.

9   Often, a dance company adopts a specialized movement vocabulary to match its theme, or at least to provide some unique gestural detail for ballet steps. Not always, though—the Hartford Ballet adopted the name *American Nutcracker* in 1997 without altering the choreography of its previous production. It became "American" mainly through renaming strategies and new costume and set designs, all of which came about in conjunction with a substantial grant from the council of the Mashantucket Pequot Tribal Nation, also located in Connecticut. The setting was switched to America's Gold Rush era, and the Stahlbaum family replaced with a collection of disparate historical figures. They all showed up in northern California at Kings Canyon National Park, where the giant sequoia named "General Grant" served as a Christmas tree.

✧ Evaluating the Text

1. In what ways has *The Nutcracker* come to represent a nondenominational seasonal festival that bridges the gap between high art and popular culture?

2. How does Fisher use examples of multicultural or local adaptions to emphasize *The Nutcracker*'s universality?

❖ *Exploring Different Perspectives*

1. Compare the cultural meanings of performances of *The Nutcracker* with the sun dance as described by Mary Brave Bird in "Granddaddy of Them All."

2. In what way has *The Nutcracker* been adapted for regional performances throughout America in much the same way as fiestas are celebrated throughout Mexico (see Octavio Paz's "Fiestas")?

❖ *Extending Viewpoints through Writing and Research*

1. Which performances of *The Nutcracker* have you seen, either live or on television, and how did it transcend being simply a ballet and become a cultural event?

2. When you were a child would you have wanted to be in *The Nutcracker*? Why or why not?

Octavio Paz

Fiesta

———◆———

Octavio Paz (1914–1998), born in Mexico City, was a poet, essayist, and unequaled observer of Mexican society. He served as a Mexican diplomat in France and Japan and as Ambassador to India before resigning from the diplomatic service to protest the Tlatelolco Massacre (government massacre of 300 students in Mexico City) in 1968. His many volumes of poetry include Sun Stone *(1958), a new reading of the Aztec myths;* Marcel Duchamp *(1968);* The Children of the Mire *(1974); and* The Monkey Grammarian *(1981). In 1990, Paz was awarded the Nobel Prize for Literature. As an essayist whose works have helped redefine the concept of Latin American culture, Paz wrote* The Other Mexico *(1972) and* The Labyrinth of Solitude, *translated by Lysander Kemp (1961), from which "Fiesta" is taken. In the following essay, Paz offers insight, conveyed with his typical stylistic grace and erudition, into the deep psychological needs met by fiestas in Mexican culture.*

Before You Read

While you read, evaluate how the noncompetitive and communal nature of Mexican fiestas differs from their American counterparts.

———◆———

1   The solitary Mexican loves fiestas and public gatherings. Any occasion for getting together will serve, any pretext to stop the flow of time and commemorate men and events with festivals and ceremonies. We are a ritual people, and this characteristic enriches both our imaginations and our sensibilities, which are equally sharp and alert. The art of the fiesta has been debased almost everywhere else, but not in Mexico. There are few places in the world where it is possible to take part in a spectacle like our great religious fiestas with their violent primary colors, their bizarre costumes and dances, their fireworks and ceremonies and their inexhaustible welter of surprises: the fruit, candy, toys and other objects sold on these days in the plazas and open-air markets.

2   Our calendar is crowded with fiestas. There are certain days when the whole country, from the most remote villages to the largest cities, prays, shouts, feasts, gets drunk and kills, in honor of the Virgin of Guadalupe or Benito Juaréz. Each year on the fifteenth of September, at

eleven o'clock at night, we celebrate the fiesta of the *Grito*[1] in all the plazas of the Republic, and the excited crowds actually shout for a whole hour . . . the better, perhaps, to remain silent for the rest of the year. During the days before and after the twelfth of December,[2] time comes to a full stop, and instead of pushing us toward a deceptive tomorrow that is always beyond our reach, offers us a complete and perfect today of dancing and revelry, of communion with the most ancient and secret Mexico. Time is no longer succession, and becomes what it originally was and is: the present, in which past and future are reconciled.

3   But the fiestas which the Church and State provide for the country as a whole are not enough. The life of every city and village is ruled by a patron saint whose blessing is celebrated with devout regularity. Neighborhoods and trades also have their annual fiestas, their ceremonies and fairs. And each one of us—atheist, Catholic, or merely indifferent—has his own saint's day, which he observes every year. It is impossible to calculate how many fiestas we have and how much time and money we spend on them. I remember asking the mayor of a village near Mitla, several years ago, "What is the income of the village government?" "About 3,000 pesos a year. We are very poor. But the Governor and the Federal Government always help us to meet our expenses." "And how are the 3,000 pesos spent?" "Mostly on fiestas, señor. We are a small village, but we have two patron saints."

4   This reply is not surprising. Our poverty can be measured by the frequency and luxuriousness of our holidays. Wealthy countries have very few: there is neither the time nor the desire for them, and they are not necessary. The people have other things to do, and when they amuse themselves they do so in small groups. The modern masses are agglomerations of solitary individuals. On great occasions in Paris or New York, when the populace gathers in the squares or stadiums, the absence of people, in the sense of *a* people, is remarkable: there are couples and small groups, but they never form a living community in which the individual is at once dissolved and redeemed. But how could a poor Mexican live without the two or three annual fiestas that make up for his poverty and misery? Fiestas are our only luxury. They replace, and are perhaps better than, the theater and vacations, Anglo-Saxon weekends and cocktail parties, the bourgeois reception, the Mediterranean café.

5   In all of these ceremonies—national or local, trade or family—the Mexican opens out. They all give him a chance to reveal himself and to converse with God, country, friends or relations. During these days the silent Mexican whistles, shouts, sings, shoots off fireworks, discharges

---

[1]Padre Hildalgo's call-to-arms against Spain, 1810.—*Tr.*
[2]Fiesta of the Virgin of Guadalupe.—*Tr.*

his pistol into the air. He discharges his soul. And his shout, like the rockets we love so much, ascends to the heavens, explodes into green, red, blue, and white lights, and falls dizzily to earth with a trail of golden sparks. This is the night when friends who have not exchanged more than the prescribed courtesies for months get drunk together, trade confidences, weep over the same troubles, discover that they are brothers, and sometimes, to prove it, kill each other. The night is full of songs and loud cries. The lover wakes up his sweetheart with an orchestra. There are jokes and conversations from balcony to balcony, sidewalk to sidewalk. Nobody talks quietly. Hats fly in the air. Laughter and curses ring like silver pesos. Guitars are brought out. Now and then, it is true, the happiness ends badly, in quarrels, insults, pistol shots, stabbings. But these too are part of the fiesta, for the Mexican does not seek amusement: he seeks to escape from himself, to leap over the wall of solitude that confines him during the rest of the year. All are possessed by violence and frenzy. Their souls explode like the colors and voices and emotions. Do they forget themselves and show their true faces? Nobody knows. The important thing is to go out, open a way, get drunk on noise, people, colors. Mexico is celebrating a fiesta. And this fiesta, shot through with lightning and delirium, is the brilliant reverse to our silence and apathy, our reticence and gloom.

6   According to the interpretation of French sociologists, the fiesta is an excess, an expense. By means of this squandering the community protects itself against the envy of the gods or of men. Sacrifices and offerings placate or buy off the gods and the patron saints. Wasting money and expending energy affirms the community's wealth in both. This luxury is a proof of health, a show of abundance and power. Or a magic trap. For squandering is an effort to attract abundance by contagion. Money calls to money. When life is thrown away it increases; the orgy, which is sexual expenditure, is also a ceremony of regeneration; waste gives strength. New Year celebrations, in every culture, signify something beyond the mere observance of a date on the calendar. The day is a pause: time is stopped, is actually annihilated. The rites that celebrate its death are intended to provoke its rebirth, because they mark not only the end of an old year but also the beginning of a new. Everything attracts its opposite. The fiesta's function, then, is more utilitarian than we think: waste attracts or promotes wealth, and is an investment like any other, except that the returns on it cannot be measured or counted. What is sought is potency, life, health. In this sense the fiesta, like the gift and the offering, is one of the most ancient of economic forms.

7   This interpretation has always seemed to me to be incomplete. The fiesta is by nature sacred, literally or figuratively, and above all it is the advent of the unusual. It is governed by its own special rules, that set it apart from other days, and it has a logic, an ethic and even an

economy that are often in conflict with everyday norms. It all occurs in an enchanted world: time is transformed to a mythical past or a total present; space, the scene of the fiesta, is turned into a gaily decorated world of its own; and the persons taking part cast off all human or social rank and become, for the moment, living images. And everything takes place as if it were not so, as if it were a dream. But whatever happens, our actions have a greater lightness, a different gravity. They take on other meanings and with them we contract new obligations. We throw down our burdens of time and reason.

8   In certain fiestas the very notion of order disappears. Chaos comes back and license rules. Anything is permitted: the customary hierarchies vanish, along with all social, sex, caste, and trade distinctions. Men disguise themselves as women, gentlemen as slaves, the poor as the rich. The army, the clergy, and the law are ridiculed. Obligatory sacrilege, ritual profanation is committed. Love becomes promiscuity. Sometimes the fiesta becomes a Black Mass. Regulations, habits and customs are violated. Respectable people put away the dignified expressions and conservative clothes that isolate them, dress up in gaudy colors, hide behind a mask, and escape from themselves.

9   Therefore the fiesta is not only an excess, a ritual squandering of the goods painfully accumulated during the rest of the year; it is also a revolt, a sudden immersion in the formless, in pure being. By means of the fiesta society frees itself from the norms it has established. It ridicules its gods, its principles, and its laws: it denies its own self.

10   The fiesta is a revolution in the most literal sense of the word. In the confusion that it generates, society is dissolved, is drowned, insofar as it is an organism ruled according to certain laws and principles. But it drowns in itself, in its own original chaos or liberty. Everything is united: good and evil, day and night, the sacred and the profane. Everything merges, loses shape and individuality and returns to the primordial mass. The fiesta is a cosmic experiment, an experiment in disorder, reuniting contradictory elements and principles in order to bring about a renascence of life. Ritual death promotes a rebirth; vomiting increases the appetite; the orgy, sterile in itself, renews the fertility of the mother or of the earth. The fiesta is a return to a remote and undifferentiated state, prenatal or presocial. It is a return that is also a beginning, in accordance with the dialectic that is inherent in social processes.

11   The group emerges purified and strengthened from this plunge into chaos. It has immersed itself in its own origins, in the womb from which it came. To express it in another way, the fiesta denies society as an organic system of differentiated forms and principles, but affirms it as a source of creative energy. It is a true "re-creation," the opposite of the "recreation" characterizing modern vacations, which do not entail any rites or ceremonies whatever and are as individualistic and sterile as the world that invented them.

12   Society communes with itself during the fiesta. Its members return to original chaos and freedom. Social structures break down and new relationships, unexpected rules, capricious hierarchies are created. In the general disorder everybody forgets himself and enters into otherwise forbidden situations and places. The bounds between audience and actors, officials and servants, are erased. Everybody takes part in the fiesta, everybody is caught up in its whirlwind. Whatever its mood, its character, its meaning, the fiesta is participation, and this trait distinguishes it from all other ceremonies and social phenomena. Lay or religious, orgy or saturnalia, the fiesta is a social act based on the full participation of all its celebrants.

13   Thanks to the fiesta the Mexican opens out, participates, communes with his fellows and with the values that give meaning to his religious or political existence. And it is significant that a country as sorrowful as ours should have so many and such joyous fiestas. Their frequency, their brilliance and excitement, the enthusiasm with which we take part, all suggest that without them we would explode. They free us, if only momentarily, from the thwarted impulses, the inflammable desires that we carry within us. But the Mexican fiesta is not merely a return to an original state of formless and normless liberty: the Mexican is not seeking to return, but to escape from himself, to exceed himself. Our fiestas are explosions. Life and death, joy and sorrow, music and mere noise are united, not to re-create or recognize themselves, but to swallow each other up. There is nothing so joyous as a Mexican fiesta, but there is also nothing so sorrowful. Fiesta night is also a night of mourning.

14   If we hide within ourselves in our daily lives, we discharge ourselves in the whirlwind of the fiesta. It is more than an opening out: we rend ourselves open. Everything—music, love, friendship—ends in tumult and violence. The frenzy of our festivals shows the extent to which our solitude closes us off from communication with the world. We are familiar with delirium, with songs and shouts, with the monologue . . . but not with the dialogue. Our fiestas, like our confidences, our loves, our attempts to reorder our society, are violent breaks with the old or the established. Each time we try to express ourselves we have to break with ourselves. And the fiesta is only one example, perhaps the most typical, of this violent break. It is not difficult to name others, equally revealing: our games, which are always a going to extremes, often mortal; our profligate spending, the reverse of our timid investments and business enterprises; our confessions. The somber Mexican, closed up in himself, suddenly explodes, tears open his breast and reveals himself, though not without a certain complacency, and not without a stopping place in the shameful or terrible mazes of his intimacy. We are not frank, but our sincerity can reach extremes that horrify a European. The explosive, dramatic, sometimes even suicidal

manner in which we strip ourselves, surrender ourselves, is evidence that something inhibits and suffocates us. Something impedes us from being. And since we cannot or dare not confront our own selves, we resort to the fiesta. It fires us into the void; it is a drunken rapture that burns itself out, a pistol shot in the air, a skyrocket.

✧ Evaluating the Text

1. What factors contribute to the popularity of fiestas in Mexico, especially in relationship to the Mexican national character, as described by Paz? In what way are people's experiences of time during the fiesta period qualitatively different from their experience of time during the rest of the year?

2. How does Paz's use of economic information as to the cost and frequency of fiestas help explain the extraordinary importance they play in Mexican life?

3. In what sense does a fiesta provide an opportunity for the solitary individual to be "at once resolved and redeemed"? What do you think Paz means by this?

4. How do Paz's comparisons between Mexican attitudes toward celebrations, life, and death with those of Europeans and North Americans make it easier for his readers to understand his analysis?

✧ Exploring Different Perspectives

1. In what way does the ritualized spectacle of the fiesta described by Paz play a role similar to the escapist atmosphere of the shopping mall described by Richard Keller Simon in "The Shopping Mall and the Formal Garden"?

2. Compare the expenditures for purposes of renewal in "Fiesta" with those described by Harold Miner in "Body Ritual Among the Nacirema."

✧ Extending Viewpoints through Writing and Research

1. Have you ever been at a party that came close in spirit to the Mexican fiesta, when people use the occasion to renew friendships, get drunk together, and discover kinships? If so, describe your experiences and discuss the similarities and differences in terms of the emotional transformation that such celebrations encourage.

2. To what extent do celebrations such as weddings, baptisms, bar mitzvahs, Mardi Gras in New Orleans, and vacations serve much the same function in the United States as fiestas do in Mexico?

Richard Keller Simon

The Shopping Mall and the Formal Garden

---◆---

Richard Keller Simon is professor of English at California Polytechnic State University, San Luis Obispo, and director of the Humanities Program. He is the author of The Labyrinth of the Comic *(1986) and* Trash Culture: Popular Culture and the Great Tradition *(1999), in which the following selection first appeared. In addition to being a vital feature of modern culture, the contemporary shopping mall updates and incorporates garden designs of the past to create a self-enclosed world devoted to consumption.*

Before You Read

Consider what lessons you learn about consumer society from the shopping mall.

---◆---

1   The contemporary shopping mall is a great formal garden of American culture, a commercial space that shares fundamental characteristics with many of the great garden styles of Western history. Set apart from the rest of the world as a place of earthly delight like the medieval walled garden; filled with fountains, statuary, and ingeniously devised machinery like the Italian Renaissance garden; designed on grandiose and symmetrical principles like this seventeenth-century French garden; made up of the fragments of cultural and architectural history like the eighteenth-century irregular English garden; and set aside for the public like the nineteenth-century American park, the mall is the next phase of this garden history, a synthesis of all these styles that have come before. But it is now joined with the shopping street, or at least a sanitized and standardized version of one, something never before allowed within the garden. In this latest version of the earthly paradise, people live on the goods of the consumer economy peacefully, pleasurably, and even with sophisticated complexity, for although their pleasure comes from buying and everything is set up to facilitate that pleasure, the garden itself is no simple place. Nordstrom has come to Eden. There were dangers and temptations in the very first garden, of course, and the delights dangled before us have

been equally powerful. We have moved from the knowledge of good and evil to the joys of shopping.

2   Visitors learn the meanings of consumer society at the mall, not only in the choices they make in their purchases but also in the symbol systems they walk through, just as visitors to those earlier gardens were invited to learn about the meanings of their own times from the pastoral adventures presented to them. Like the formal garden, the shopping mall is a construct of promenades, walls, vistas, mounts, labyrinths, fountains, statues, archways, trees, grottoes, theaters, flowering plants and shrubs, trellises, and assorted reproductions from architectural history, all artfully arranged. Some of these features, such as the mount, have undergone technological or economic modification. The mount—the manmade earthworks designed to present a vista of the garden to the visitor and typically reached by path or staircase— was a standard part of garden design from the Middle Ages to the eighteenth century. This has been replaced by the escalator, which rises at key points in the enclosed central parts of the mall, where it presents a similar vista of the space to the visitor, who is now lifted dramatically from the floor below by unseen forces without any effort on his or her part. And this, in its turn, is only the modification of a standard feature from Italian Renaissance gardens, the elaborate hydraulic machinery or automata that engineers had devised to move statues about in striking dramatic tableaux. Now in the mall it is the visitors who are moved about by the escalators, becoming themselves the actors in a tableau we might title "modern shopping." Combining the mount with the automata, the mall then encloses this machinery in two or three stories of space, topped with skylights. The result is something like Houston's Galleria Mall, a massive, three-story, enclosed mall topped with skylights. This, in turn, is an updated version of Henry VIII's great garden at Hampton Court, where a mount was topped by a three-story glass arbor surrounded by figures of the king's beasts and royal crown. We have dispensed with the beasts and crown; joggers now run on the roof of the Galleria. But the mount in the king's garden allowed the visitor to look both inside and outside of his garden; the escalator within the enclosed mall of the Galleria, by contrast, only allows the visitor to look at the inside space.

3   Similarly, the labyrinth—the maze of pathways or hedges that confounded the visitor's attempts to find an easy way out and was a favorite device of Renaissance gardens—is now the cleverly laid out pattern of aisles with department stores, which can be designed to discourage the visitor's easy exit. Shoppers simply cannot find a way out. A decade ago Bloomingdale's in the Willow Grove Mall in suburban Philadelphia received so many complaints from irate shoppers lost in its mazes that finally small, discreet exit signs were posted. What might have originated in the mazes of the early Christian Church, which peni-

tents traveled on their knees while praying at particular points, was first moved outside into the garden, where it was secularized, and has now become thoroughly commodified, a journey in which purchases have replaced prayers. Buy enough and we will let you out.

4   Played against the maze and labyrinth in the Renaissance garden were the axial and radial avenues that began as extensions of hallways of the palace and ended in suitably grand natural vistas. Played against the department store maze in the mall are the axial and radial avenues that begin as extensions of hallways of one anchor department store and end in the grand vistas of the entrances to other anchor department stores.

5   The kitchen garden, that area of the formal garden closest to the house and set aside for the production of food, has become the food court, that area of the mall set aside for the consumption of food. The statues—the assorted imitations of Greek and Roman models, portraits of contemporary royalty, or stylized representations of the ancient virtues—have become mannequins decked out in fashionable clothing, the generalized imitations of consumers in their most beautiful, heroic, and changeable poses, portraits of contemporary anonymous life that we should see as stylized representations of the modern virtues: pose, flexibility, nubility, interchangeability, emotional absence. The generalized faces on the statues are now the empty faces of the mannequins. And the various architectural antiquities that became a feature of eighteenth-century English irregular gardens—the miscellaneous copies of Greek temples, Gothic ruins, Japanese pagodas, Roman triumphal arches, and Italian grottoes—are now represented not so much by the miscellaneous architectural reproductions that appear seasonally in the mall, as in the Easter Bunny's cottage or Santa's Workshop, but much more profoundly by many of the stores themselves, which present idealized versions of architectural and cultural history to the consumer: the Victorian lingerie shop, the high modernist fur salon, the nineteenth-century Western goods store, the Mexican restaurant, the country store designed as a red barn, the dark bar designed as a grotto. Also present in smaller details—in the grand staircase, the wall of mirrors, the plush carpeting, the man playing the white grand piano—are echoes of the 1930s movie set; in the merry-go-round, the popcorn cart, and the clown with balloons, the echoes of funland. The eighteenth-century garden included such historical reproductions in an effort to make sense of its past and to accommodate its cultural inheritances to new situations. One can say the same about the mall's inclusion of historical recollections. If we judge this to be playful and parodic, then we can also call the space postmodern, but if it is only a nostalgic recovery of history, we cannot. This can be a tricky thing. The mall's appropriation of history into idealized spaces of consumption can be a nostalgia or parody, or both at the same time.

6   The Stanford Shopping Center near Paló Alto presents such a parodic and nostalgic bricolage of cultural and architectural history: Crabtree and Evelyn with its images of eighteenth-century life; Laura Ashley with its images of Romantic and early Victorian life; Victoria's Secret, the late Victorian whore-house with overtones of French fashion; Banana Republic, the late Victorian colonial outfitter; the Disney Store with its images of 1940s art; and The Nature Company, closest to the sixteenth century and the rise of science in its stock of simple instruments and decor of simple observations of nature. One walks through the images of history just as one did in the formal garden, but now they can be appropriated through the act of consuming. One buys images but learns "history." It is a clean, neat, middle-class version of history without the homeless of a downtown big city, and thus a retreat from the frenzy of urban life and of contemporary history, which is exactly what the formal garden was designed to be. To one side is an alley devoted to food: a lavishly idealized greengrocer, a pseudo-Italian coffee bar, and Max's Opera Café, a reproduction of a grand nineteenth-century cafe in Vienna—but what one finds when one wanders inside is not real or ersatz Vienna, but a glorified Jewish deli. Here the history of central Europe is rewritten as it might have been.

7   In one Renaissance garden a grotto dedicated to Venus and voluptuous pleasure was juxtaposed with one dedicated to Diana and virtuous pleasure. In another a Temple of Ancient Virtue was contrasted with one representing Modern Virtue. In a similar manner the visitor to the modern garden at Stanford is presented with choices between Victoria's Secret, the shop of voluptuous pleasure, and Westminster Lace, the shop of virtuous pleasure and chastity, but he or she does not have to choose between the Temple of Modern Virtue, the modern shopping center itself, or the Temple of Ancient Virtue, the remnants of the gardens of the past, because the mall artfully combines both.

8   We are almost at an end of our catalogue of garden elements. In fact, the only standard feature of garden design not present in the modern mall, either in original or in modified form, is the hermitage ruin, a favorite eighteenth-century architectural device designed to allow the visitor to pretend to be a hermit, to be alone and to meditate. There are only two places where a visitor can be alone in the mall: in the lavatories and in the clothing store changing room, but even there one can find surveillance cameras. Meditation and isolation are not virtues encouraged by the modern garden because, interestingly enough, given the opportunity, too many consumers will not meditate there at all, but try to steal whenever they can.

9   The shopping mall is, of course, quite an imperfect paradise, but the fault does not lie so much with the garden as with the shopping street it has come to assimilate. It is true that there are very few trees in these postmodern gardens, and those that do appear are typically confined in antipastoral concrete planters, but such subordination of

nature has occurred before in garden history. Plants were incidental to the Renaissance garden, where visitors instead were expected to direct their attention to the grottoes, fountains, and various mechanical automata.

10   By bringing the mundane world of commerce into the garden, along with its attendant ills, the mall appears to be inverting the fundamental purposes of many of those earlier gardens as places of repose and contemplation, of escape from the mundane world. Conspicuous consumption has replaced quiet repose. But many of the great styles of garden history have been practical, if not precisely in this way, for example, the *ferme ornée* or eighteenth-century ornamented working farm with its fields, kitchen gardens, orchards, and pastures placed beside the more decorative and formal elements of the garden. These were gardens that had their practical commercial aspects. But although the mall is a far more commercial place than the practical garden, the shift has not so much destroyed the garden—for most of history a space set aside for the rich—as adapted it to new social and economic realities, and it thus can be seen as the appropriate garden for a consumer-oriented culture. In the formal gardens of the past, where nature was rearranged to fit the aesthetic taste of the period, one walked through the landscape contemplating the vistas and approaching the beautiful. In the shopping mall, where nature is similarly rearranged to fit the commercial needs of the period, one walks through the landscape, now contemplating not the vistas of nature, which have been completely blocked out, but rather the vistas presented by the entrances to the anchor department stores, and now approaching not the beautiful but rather the commodities by means of which one can become beautiful. These are practical times. The aristocrat who walked down the path of the garden admired the flowers and smelled their scents; the consumer who walks down the path of the shopping mall buys the flower scents in bottles and then smells like the flower or the musk ox. The focus has shifted from the individual in reverie facing an artificial version of nature to the individual in excitement facing a garden of consumer products. In the eighteenth century the visitor to the garden was expected to feel the elevation of his or her soul. It is unlikely that the visitor to the modern mall has a comparable experience.

✧ Evaluating the Text

1. How does the modern shopping mall incorporate features of gardens of the past for a single-minded purpose: consumption? What are some of these features and what function do they serve?

2. Why is it significant that, of all past garden features, only the hermitage (a place to be alone in which to meditate) is not included in the shopping mall of today?

3. How do the worlds one can enter in the shopping mall re-present past eras in a commercialized form?

✦ Exploring Different Perspectives

1. Compare the attitudes toward consumerism as portrayed by Simon with the extreme indulgences of the Mexican fiesta as described by Octavio Paz.

2. What complementary perspectives are offered by Simon and Harold Miner in "Body Ritual Among the Nacirema"?

✦ Extending Viewpoints through Writing and Research

1. Analyze how the layout, architecture, and specialty boutiques of the shopping mall you frequent are designed to create a fantasy dimension in which you will spend time and money.

2. To what extent do Web sites attempt to create a virtual mall with the same purpose as the shopping mall as described by Simon?

Nabil Gorgy

Cairo Is a Small City

◆

Nabil Gorgy was born in Cairo in 1944 and studied civil engineering at Cairo University. After working as an engineer in New York City, he returned to Cairo, where he now runs his own art gallery. His interests in mysticism, Egyptology, and Sufi traditions are reflected in his novel The Door *(1981). His collection of short stories is* The Slave's Dream and Other Stories *(1991). In "Cairo Is a Small City," translated by Denys Johnson-Davies (1983), an upper-class Egyptian engineer falls victim to an age-old Bedouin tradition.*

Before You Read

Notice the way Gorgy begins to infuse the story with ancient cultural traditions before we find out what happens.

◆

1   On the balcony of his luxury flat Engineer Adil Salim stood watching some workmen putting up a new building across the wide street along the centre of which was a spacious garden. The building was at the foundations stage, only the concrete foundations and some of the first-floor columns having been completed. A young ironworker with long hair was engaged in bending iron rods of various dimensions. Adil noticed that the young man had carefully leant his Jawa motorcycle against a giant crane that crouched at rest awaiting its future tasks. "How the scene has changed!" Adil could still remember the picture of old-time master craftsmen, and of the workers who used to carry large bowls of mixed cement on their calloused shoulders.

2   The sun was about to set and the concrete columns of a number of new constructions showed up as dark frameworks against the light in this quiet district at the end of Heliopolis.

3   As on every day at this time there came down into the garden dividing the street a flock of sheep and goats that grazed on its grass, and behind them two bedouin women, one of whom rode a donkey, while the younger one walked beside her. As was his habit each day, Adil fixed his gaze on the woman walking in her black gown that not so much hid as emphasized the attractions of her body, her waist being tied round with a red band. It could be seen that she wore green plastic slippers on her feet. He wished that she would catch sight of him on

475

the balcony of his luxurious flat; even if she did so, Adil was thinking, those bedouin had a special code of behaviour that differed greatly from what he was used to and rendered it difficult to make contact with them. What, then, was the reason, the motive, for wanting to think up some way of talking to her? It was thus that he was thinking, following her with his gaze as she occasionally chased after a lamb that was going to be run over by a car or a goat left far behind the flock.

4   Adil, who was experienced in attracting society women, was aware of his spirit being enthralled: days would pass with him on the balcony, sunset after sunset, as he watched her without her even knowing of his existence.

5   Had it not been for that day on which he had been buying some fruit and vegetables from one of the shopkeepers on Metro Street, and had not the shopkeeper seen another bedouin woman walking behind another flock, and had he not called out to her by name, and had she not come, and had he not thrown her a huge bundle of waste from the shop, after having flirted with her and fondled her body—had it not been for that day, Adil's mind would not have given birth to the plan he was determined, whatever the cost, to put through, because of that woman who had bewitched his heart.

6   As every man, according to Adil's philosophy of life, had within him a devil, it was sometimes better to follow this devil in order to placate him and avoid his tyranny. Therefore Engineer Adil Salim finally decided to embark upon the terrible, the unthinkable. He remembered from his personal history during the past forty years that such a temporary alliance with this devil of his had gained him a courage that had set him apart from the rest of his colleagues, and through it he had succeeded in attaining this social position that had enabled him to become the owner of this flat whose value had reached a figure which he avoided mentioning even in front of his family lest they might be upset or feel envy.

7   Thus, from his balcony on the second floor in Tirmidhi Street, Engineer Adil Salim called out in a loud voice "Hey, girl!" as he summoned the one who was walking at the rear of the convoy. When the flock continued on its way without paying any attention, he shouted again: "Hey, girl—you who sell sheep," and before the girl moved far away he repeated the word "sheep." Adil paid no attention to the astonishment of the doorman, who had risen from the place where he had been sitting at the entrance, thinking that he was being called. In fact he quietly told him to run after the two bedouin women and to let them know that he had some bread left over which he wanted to give them for their sheep.

8   From the balcony Adil listened to the doorman calling to the two women in his authoritative Upper Egyptian accent, at which they came to a stop and the one who was riding the donkey looked back at him.

Very quickly Adil was able to make out her face as she looked towards him, seeking to discover what the matter was. As for the young girl, she continued on behind the flock. The woman was no longer young and had a corpulent body and a commanding look which she did not seek to hide from him. Turning her donkey round, she crossed the street separating the garden from his building and waited in front of the gate for some new development. Adil collected up all the bread in the house and hurried down with it on a brass tray. Having descended to the street, he went straight up to the woman and looked at her. When she opened a saddlebag close by her leg, he emptied all the bread into it.

9   "Thanks," said the woman as she made off without turning towards him. He, though, raising his voice so that she would hear, called out, "And tomorrow too."

10   During a period that extended to a month Adil began to buy bread which he did not eat. Even on those days when he had to travel away or to spend the whole day far from the house, he would leave a large paper parcel with the doorman for him to give to the bedouin woman who rode the donkey and behind whom walked she for whom the engineer's heart craved.

11   Because Adil had a special sense of the expected and the probable, and after the passing of one lunar month, and in his place in front of the building, with the bread on the brass tray, there occurred that which he had been wishing would happen, for the woman riding the donkey had continued on her way and he saw the other, looking around her carefully before crossing the road, ahead of him, walking towards him. She was the most beautiful thing he had set eyes on. The speed of his pulse almost brought his heart to a stop. How was it that such beauty was to be found without it feeling embarrassed at ugliness, for after it any and every thing must needs be so described? When she was directly in front of him, and her kohl-painted eyes were scrutinizing him, he sensed a danger which he attributed to her age, which was no more than twenty. How was it that she was so tall, her waist so slim, her breasts so full, and how was it that her buttocks swayed so enticingly as she turned away and went off with the bread, having thanked him? His imagination became frozen even though she was still close to him: her pretty face with the high cheekbones, the fine nose and delicate lips, the silver, crescent-shaped earrings, and the necklace that graced her bosom? Because such beauty was "beyond the permissible," Adil went on thinking about Salma—for he had got to know her name, her mother having called her by it in order to hurry her back lest the meeting between the lovers be prolonged.

12   Adil no longer troubled about the whistles of the workers who had now risen floor by floor in the building opposite him, being in a state

of infatuation, his heart captured by this moonlike creature. After the affair, in relation to himself, having been one of boldness, to end in seeing or greeting her, it now became a matter of necessity that she turn up before sunset at the house so that he might not be deprived of the chance of seeing her. So it was that Engineer Adil Salim fell in love with the beautiful bedouin girl Salma. And just as history is written by historians, so it was that Adil and his engineering work determined the history of this passion in the form of a building each of whose columns represented a day and each of whose floors was a month. He noted that, at the completion of twenty-eight days and exactly at full moon, Salma would come to him in place of her mother to take the bread. And so, being a structural engineer, he began to observe the moon, his yearning increasing when it was in eclipse and his spirits sparkling as its fullness drew near till, at full moon, the happiness of the lover was completed by seeing the beloved's face.

13   During seven months he saw her seven times, each time seeing in her the same look she had given him the first time: his heart would melt, all resolution would be squeezed out of him and that fear for which he knew no reason would be awakened. She alone was now capable of granting him his antidote. After the seventh month Salma, without any preamble, had talked to him at length, informing him that she lived with her parents around a spring at a distance of an hour's walk to the north of the airport, and that it consisted of a brackish spring alongside which was a sweet one, so that she would bathe in the first and rinse herself clean in the other, and that there were date palms around the two springs, also grass and pasturage. Her father, the owner of the springs and the land around them, had decided to invite him and so tomorrow "he'll pass by you and invite you to our place, for tomorrow we attend to the shearing of the sheep."

14   Adil gave the lie to what he was hearing, for it was more than any stretch of the imagination could conceive might happen.

15   The following day Adil arrived at a number of beautifully made tents, where a vast area of sand was spread out below date palms that stretched to the edge of a spring. Around the spring was gathered a large herd of camels, sheep and goats that spoke of the great wealth of the father. It was difficult to believe that such a place existed so close to the city of Cairo. If Adil's astonishment was great when Salma's father passed by him driving a new Peugeot, he was yet further amazed at the beauty of the area surrounding this spring. "It's the land of the future," thought Adil to himself. If he were able to buy a few *feddans* now he'd become a millionaire in a flash, for this was the Cairo of the future. "This is the deal of a lifetime," he told himself.

16   On the way the father asked a lot of questions about Adil's work and where he had previously lived and about his knowledge of the

desert and its people. Though Adil noticed in the father's tone something more than curiosity, he attributed this to the nature of the Bedouin and their traditions.

17   As the car approached the tents Adil noticed that a number of men were gathered under a tent whose sides were open, and as the father and his guest got out of the car the men turned round, seated in the form of a horse-shoe. With the father sitting down and seating Engineer Adil Salim alongside him, one of the sides of the horse-shoe was completed. In front of them sat three men on whose faces could be seen the marks of time in the form of interlaced wrinkles.

18   The situation so held Adil's attention that he was unaware of Salma except when she passed from one tent to another in the direction he was looking and he caught sight of her gazing towards him.

19   The man who was sitting in a squatting position among the three others spoke. Adil heard him talking about the desert, water and sheep, about the roads that went between the oases and the *wadi*, the towns and the springs of water, about the bedouin tribes and blood ties; he heard him talking about the importance of protecting these roads and springs, and the palm trees and the dates, the goats and the milk upon which the suckling child would be fed; he also heard him talk about how small the *wadi* was in comparison to this desert that stretched out endlessly.

20   In the same way as Adil had previously built the seven-storey building that represented the seven months, each month containing twenty-eight days, till he would see Salma's face whenever it was full moon, he likewise sensed that this was the tribunal which had been set up to make an enquiry with him into the killing of the man whom he had one day come across on the tracks between the oases of Kharga and Farshout. It had been shortly after sunset when he and a friend, having visited the iron ore mines in the oases of Kharga had, instead of taking the asphalt road to Assiout, proceeded along a rough track that took them down towards Farshout near to Kena, as his friend had to make a report about the possibility of repairing the road and of extending the railway line to the oases. Going down from the high land towards the *wadi*, the land at a distance showing up green, two armed men had appeared before them. Adil remembered how, in a spasm of fear and astonishment, of belief and disbelief, and with a speed that at the time he thought was imposed upon him, a shot had been fired as he pressed his finger on the trigger of the revolver which he was using for the first time. A man had fallen to the ground in front of him and, as happens in films, the other had fled. As for him and his friend, they had rushed off to their car in order to put an end to the memory of the incident by reaching the *wadi*. It was perhaps because Adil had once killed a man that he had found the courage to accept Salma's father's invitation.

21   "That day," Adil heard the man address him, "with a friend in a car, you killed Mubarak bin Rabia when he went out to you, Ziyad al- Mihrab being with him."

22   This was the manner in which Engineer Adil Salim was executed in the desert north-west of the city of Cairo: one of the men held back his head across a marble-like piece of stone, then another man plunged the point of a tapered dagger into the spot that lies at the bottom of the neck between the two bones of the clavicle.

✧ Evaluating the Text

1. How is the engineer, Adil Salim, characterized? What incidents reveal these character traits most clearly? How does he see himself? To what does he attribute his success and affluence?

2. Under what circumstances does the engineer first meet the Bedouin girl? What is his attitude toward her?

3. After reading the story, discuss the significance of the title, especially as it sheds light on the surprising consequences for the engineer. To what extent does the title suggest that the Cairo of the Bedouins and the Cairo of the engineer, although seemingly very different, are basically the same?

✧ Exploring Different Perspectives

1. How does the protagonist in Gorgy's story and Liza Dalby in "Kimono" come into contact with older traditional ways of seeing the world, albeit with very different consequences?

2. Compare as cultural markers for female attractiveness the Bedouin girl in Gorgy's story with the allure of the bound foot as described by Valerie Steele and John S. Major in "China Chic: East Meets West."

✧ Extending Viewpoints through Writing and Research

1. In a short essay, discuss Gorgy's attitude toward ancient cultural traditions as they emerge in the story.

2. Adil's actions and reactions indicate that he is in love. What actions and reactions of your own or someone you know serve as surefire signs of being in love?

3. For a firsthand account of Bedouin customs, see http://www.sherryart.com/women/bedouin.html.

Liza Dalby

Kimono

◆

Liza Dalby received a doctorate in anthropology from Stanford University. Dalby, who is fluent in Japanese, became the only non-Japanese ever accepted by geishas during a yearlong residence in Kyoto. The profession of geisha originated in the eighteenth century. As their popularity grew, geisha became society's fashion arbiters, and their sophisticated style had a great impact on the art, music, and literature of nineteenth-century Japan. The world of the geisha offers a unique glimpse into a disciplined and glamorous way of life that is quintessentially Japanese. Dalby is the author of Kimono: Fashion in Culture *(1993). Her latest work is* The Tale of Murasaki *(2000). This piece, a chapter drawn from her book* Geisha *(1998), provides insight into the social codes embodied in the kimono, the traditional costume worn by geisha.*

Before You Read

Consider what you know about the kimono and what it suggests about Japanese cultural values to you.

◆

1   A month after I returned to the United States, I was invited to appear on the "To Tell the Truth" television show because of my odd distinction of being the only non-Japanese ever to have become a geisha. The object for the panelists would be to guess the identity of the real "geisha anthropologist," so I had dressed myself and the two women pretending to be me in cotton kimono. As we walked through the program's format during rehearsal, each of us was to announce, "My name is Liza Crihfield," then step ten paces to our seats facing the panel at stage left. The director shook her head in dismay before we even took our places. "Stop," she called. "You've just given it away."

2   After my year-long training as a geisha, the technique of walking gracefully in a kimono had become second nature. The two poseurs, though they had diligently studied my research proposal in order to anticipate questions from the panel, could not, in an afternoon, master the art of walking. It was quite obvious who was who before we even opened our mouths.

3   Repeatedly I showed them the technique of sliding one foot, pigeon-toed, in front of the other with knees slightly bent. I tried to convey how the shoulders should have a barely perceptible slope, how

the arms should be carried gracefully, close to the body. We tried to minimize the contrast. They made great efforts to mimic an authentic movement, while I attempted to recreate the clumsiness of my own first experience in wearing kimono. Even so, on the show the next day, none of the panelists except Bill Cullen was fooled a bit. I am convinced that our body language had "told the truth."

4   Learning to wear kimono properly was one of the most difficult aspects of my geisha training. But it was essential so that I could fit without awkwardness into a group of geisha. No one gives geisha formal lessons in how to wear kimono. Most of them have learned how to move gracefully in kimono by virtue of their practice of Japanese dance. Awkward gestures are noticed immediately by the watchful mothers, who seldom fail to utter a reproof to a fidgety maiko.

5   When I lived in Pontochō, the sardonic old auntie who worked at the Mitsuba invariably had some critical remark when I checked in for okāsan's approval of my outfit before going off to a teahouse engagement. I usually managed to put together a feasible color combination of kimono, obi, and *obi-age* (the sheer, scarf-like sash that is tied so as to be barely visible above the obi), but it was many months before I could proceed on my way to a party without something having to be untied and retied properly. Only when I reached the point where I could put on the entire outfit in less than twenty minutes by myself did I finally win the grudging respect of the old auntie who tended the inn.

The Language of Kimono

6   Wearing kimono is one of the things that distinguishes geisha from other women in Japan. Geisha wear their kimono with a flair just not seen in middle-class ladies who, once or twice a year, pull out their traditional dress to attend a wedding, a graduation, or perhaps a retirement ceremony. They are uncomfortable in the unaccustomed garment, and it shows.

7   To the untutored eye, the kimono a geisha chooses are much the same as those any other Japanese woman might wear. The resplendent trailing black robe with deep reverse décolletage is the geisha's official outfit, but she actually wears it infrequently. Her usual garment is an ankle-length, medium-sleeve silk kimono in slightly more subdued colors than those other women wear. The subtle differences in sleeve openings, in color, or in the manner of tying the obi that set a geisha apart are not immediately obvious, even to many Japanese. But together with her natural way of wearing the outfit, such cues are visible to an observer who is sensitive to the language of kimono. A connoisseur will know the wide vocabulary of elements that varies according to the region, class, age, and profession of the wearer. He or she will be able to recognize a geisha easily.

8   The elements of the kimono costume in fact constitute a social code. This was revealed to me when I inadvertently mixed up some of them early in my geisha career, before I had acquired an appropriate wardrobe from the taller geisha in the neighborhood. In the beginning, the only kimono I owned was one that Yuriko, my well-to-do middle-aged friend in Tokyo, had given me. It was a lovely burnt orange color with a pattern of weeping willow branches in brown shot with gold. She had worn it a few times many years ago, before she had married. Now the colors were inappropriate to her age, and besides, she told me, she never wore kimono any more. She doubted she could even tie the obi by herself.

9   When okāsan first asked me to help her out at a party at the Mitsuba so I could see the geisha's side of the affair, I gladly agreed and planned to wear my only kimono. As she helped me put it on, she remarked that, lovely as it was, it would be entirely unsuitable in the future. It was the sort of thing a stylish bourgeois young lady might wear, not a geisha. It would have to do for that evening, though. She loaned me a tea-green obi with a pale cream orchid dyed into the back and gave me an old obi-age sash that she had worn as an apprentice many years ago.

10   The obi-age was of sheer white silk with a pattern of scattered fans done in a dapple-effect tie-dying technique called *kanoko*. Okasan slipped it over the pad that held the back loop of the obi secure, and as she tied it in the front she said, "Here is a trick for keeping the front knot in place. All the geisha tie their obi-age this way." She made a little loose slipknot in one end, making sure the red fan pattern showed at the front of the knot, then drew the other end through. The effect was of a simply knotted sash, but without the bulk of both ends tied together. She smoothed and tucked this light sash down behind the top of the obi, so that only a glimpse of the red and white was visible. At the time, I was reminded of letting a bit of lace show at the neckline of a blouse. Since the obi-age is technically considered part of the "kimono underwear," my thought was more apt than I first realized.

11   Still wearing this outfit, I went out after the party. Later that evening I met a pair of college teachers at a nearby bar. We struck up a conversation, and I told them a bit about the circumstances of my being in Japan. The bartender, half listening in, finally exclaimed, "Aha, now I realize what was bothering me about you. You said you were a student, and I could tell that you're an unmarried young lady from a proper family. Your kimono is perfectly appropriate. But I think it's your sash, something about the way it's tied, that struck me as odd for a young lady—something too much like a geisha about it." As I had not yet said anything about the precise subject of my study, I was astounded at the acuity of the man's eye.

12   Incongruent as it was, my outfit that evening expressed my odd position rather well. Not exactly an *ojōsan*, a demure young lady, not yet a geisha, I was attired in disparate elements of each style, so I presented an odd aspect to someone with a perspicacious eye for dress. The bartender had received all the messages my outfit conveyed but was puzzled at the totality, as well he might have been.

Kimono Wearers

13   *Mono* means "thing," and with *ki-* from *kiru*, "to wear," kimono originally meant simply "a garment." Not all things to wear are kimono, however. Today, the relevant distinction is between *yōfuku*, "Western apparel," and *wafuku*, "native apparel": kimono. Western clothes, following all the latest fashion trends, are what most Japanese women wear most of the time. Some women don't even own a kimono, and many, like my friend Yuriko in Tokyo, have forgotten how to wear those they have tucked away in the Japanese equivalent of cedar chests. Few if any social occasions in Japan now would exclude a woman because she was not dressed in kimono.

14   Most women own a black kimono dyed with the family crest that they will pull out of a drawer for a few highly formal occasions. This garment was probably the main item in their wedding trousseaux. Families are encouraged to buy their young daughters the gaudy, long-sleeved *furisode*-style kimono for New Year, so a woman often has one of these packed away from her girlhood as well. Such occasional use means that most Japanese women are nearly as unaccustomed to the proper manner of wearing kimono as a foreigner would be. They sigh with relief when they can finally unwind the stiff obi from around their waists and slip back into comfortable Western clothes.

15   As my eye became educated to the niceties of kimono, I was more and more struck by how many women who put one on fail to achieve a graceful demeanor. A good time to view masses of kimono is the New Year holiday. Young girls, who trudge to school in loafers all year, suddenly mince about in traditional *zōri* that match their long-sleeved kimono. Arms swinging, knees pumping up and down as they do in skirts, the girls flock on the streets like pinioned flamingos. Colorful and clumsy, they brighten the bleak January streets briefly before donning their familiar blue and white school uniforms again at the end of holidays. Women over fifty generally feel more at home than this in kimono. They probably wore the traditional dress as children and feel a pang of nostalgia when they put it on.

16   Middle-class women of means are now rediscovering the conspicuous display afforded by kimono. The wearing of wafuku, as opposed to the Cacharel skirts and Dior blouses of their friends, has become a fashionable hobby. A woman who would blanch at spending two hundred dollars on a dress could easily justify spending five times as much on a

kimono. After all, a kimono is an investment. It won't go out of style, it can accommodate thickening midriffs without alteration, and it can be passed on to one's daughters. In the status game, it is difficult to spend more than a thousand dollars on even the most skillfully tailored Western dress. But with kimono, one can easily wear thousands of dollars on one's back without looking too obvious. The expensive yet understated possibilities of kimono are ideally suited to this aspect of fashion one-upmanship.

17   Yet the wearing of kimono is not without problems in modern Japan. Aside from the matter of expense, kimono inherently belong to a different style and pace of life. That life still thrives here and there, but usually under special circumstances—as are found, for example, in the geisha world. Few would call the beautiful kimono a practical garment for modern living.

Floors versus Chairs

18   The kimono was once part of a cultural totality that embraced every aspect of daily life. The garment was influenced by, and in turn it influenced, canons of feminine beauty that enhanced some parts of the body (nape, ankle, and hip) and concealed others (waist, legs, and bosom). Not surprisingly, the kimono flatters a figure found most often in Japanese women: a long waist and long thigh but small bust and short calf. Cultural notions of ideal beauty seem to influence actual physical characteristics, however; as Western notions of long-legged, big-bosomed glamour have affected postwar Japan, amazingly, such physical types seem to have blossomed. The cultivation of this new type of figure does not bode well for the kimono.

19   The wearing of kimono was also perfectly integrated into the arrangement of living space in the traditional Japanese home. Much of the activity of daily life was conducted close to the floor, on low tables where people knelt, not sat, to accomplish tasks. To Japanese, a shod foot treading the floor inside the house would be as gauche as shoes on a Westerner's dining room table. Floors were clean enough to permit trailing garments, and the wives of wealthy men let their robes swirl about their feet as they glided down polished halls from one tatami mat room to another. The trailing hem contributed to the overall balance of the outfit, creating an effect of elegance. Again, nowadays one must look to the geisha's formal kimono to see what that style was like. Ordinary modern kimono are adjusted, by a fold at the waist, to reach only the ankle. The line, rather than flowing, is somewhat stiff and tubular.

20   The integration of cultural elements that formed the whole of which kimono was a part has now fragmented. The single most nefarious artifact in this respect is the chair. Chairs are antithetical to kimono, physically and aesthetically.

21   Women who wear kimono of course sit on chairs, but the garment is poorly adapted to this posture; it is designed for sitting on the floor. When Americans sit on the floor, this implies a greater degree of relaxation than does sitting on a chair. Not so in Japan. A chair is comfortable and relaxed compared to the straight-spine posture required to sit properly on the tatami floor. There are two different verbs meaning "to sit" in Japanese, depending on whether it is on the floor or in a chair. If in a chair, then one literally "drapes one's hips" there.

22   When, out of determination to show the Japanese that we understand etiquette, we Westerners endure a tea ceremony or traditional banquet sitting on the floor, after thirty minutes our knees are jelly and our legs so benumbed they refuse to obey our brain's directive to stand. We are consoled that young Japanese have much the same problem. Part of the exhaustion we feel is due to the gradual slumping of our unsupported backs. Skirts ride up, pants become constricting, narrow belts bite into our waists. But the kimono that became disheveled and kept us perched uncomfortably at the edge of a chair now offers back support with the obi, and it turns out to be almost comfortable in the posture for which it was designed.

23   The back view of a kneeling kimono-clad woman shows off the garment to its best advantage. The obi often has a large single design woven or painted on the back part, which forms a large, flat loop in the common style of tying known as *taiko* (drum). This flat drum, not quite a square foot in area, is framed by the contrasting color of the kimono. I have often been struck by the artfulness of a seated figure, Japanese style. In a chair, the drum of the obi is not only hidden from view, it is a positive nuisance, as it prevents one from sitting back.

24   The fact that the back view of a kimono-clad figure is such an aesthetic focus has to do, I think, with the way a traditional Japanese room is arranged and how a woman in public (such as a geisha) moves and is viewed on a social occasion. At a banquet, low, narrow tables are laid end to end, forming a continuous row that parallels three sides of the room. People sit on individual flat square cushions along the outer edge of this U-shaped arrangement. In effect, everyone sits next to someone, but nobody sits across from anyone else.

25   The seating positions are hierarchical: the places of highest status are in front of the alcove, and the lowest are those closest to the entrance. People usually have a keen sense of where they stand vis-à-vis one another's status in Japan, so the problem of where they sit is solved with a minimum of polite protestation. When everyone has taken a seat, the banquet can begin. After it has started, however, people leave their original places to wander across the center of the room, squatting temporarily in front of different personages to make a toast or have a short conversation. This center space is a no-man's-land,

ringed as it is by the prescribed statuses of the proper seats on the other side of the tables. Here more relaxed conviviality can occur.

26　　When geisha attend upon a banquet, they often move into the center free space, kneeling for a few minutes across from one guest after another. As they do so, their backs are turned toward an entire row of tables on the other side of the room. The first time I was a guest at a traditional banquet, I noticed the beauty of the backs of the geisha as they talked with other guests. Upon reflection, it hardly seems accidental that the view from that particular vantage point was so striking.

✧ Evaluating the Text

1. In what way does the kimono serve as a complex signaling system that embodies and communicates traditional Japanese values?

2. Dalby says that "chairs are antithetical to kimono, physically and aesthetically." What does she mean by this, and how does this insight provide a glimpse into a traditional world that modern Japanese remember somewhat nostalgically?

3. What insights do you gain from this account as to why Dalby went to Japan to learn to be a geisha?

✧ Exploring Different Perspectives

1. Compare and contrast the constraints of wearing kimono with those of the "lotus" foot described by Valerie Steele and John S. Major in "China Chic: East Meets West" as symbols of femininity and social status.

2. Compare the meaning of veiling alluded to by Nabil Gorgy in "Cairo Is a Small City" with that of the kimono.

✧ Extending Viewpoints through Writing and Research

1. To what extent do elegant outfits such as a ball gown or white tie and tails perform the same function in Western culture that the kimono does in Japan?

2. To what extent does the kimono enforce a very specified gender role for women? What physical and psychological constraints does it impose? Why would it be unlikely to catch on in the United States?

Valerie Steele and John S. Major

China Chic: East Meets West

◆

Valerie Steele is chief curator of the Museum at the Fashion Institute of Technology (FIT). Steele organized a major exhibition at FIT to coincide with the 1999 publication of China Chic: East Meets West. *She is the editor of* Fashion Theory: The Journal of Dress, Body, and Culture *and has also written* Paris Fashion: A Cultural History *(1998) and* Fashion and Eroticism *(2000). A recent work is* Fashion, Italian Style *(2003). John S. Major is director of the China Council of the Asia Society. He is the author of* Heaven and Earth in Early Han Thought *(1993) and* The Silk Route: 7,000 Miles of History *(1996). The following essay, from* China Chic, *examines foot binding in the context of China's political, economic, and cultural history and its correspondence to fashions in the West.*

Before You Read

Consider how foot binding in China (accomplished through dwarfing the foot by dislocating its bones) was a symbol of fashion just as high-heeled shoes are in the West today.

◆

1   Foot binding lasted for a thousand years. It apparently began in the declining years of the Tang dynasty and it persisted in remote areas of China until the middle of the twentieth century. Yet despite its manifest significance within Chinese history, foot binding has been the subject of surprisingly little scholarly research. Recently, however, scholars such as Dorothy Ko have begun to explore the subject—with surprising results. As Ko points out, "It is natural for modern-day reformers to consider footbinding a men's conspiracy to keep women crippled and submissive, but this is an anachronistic view that finds no support in the historical records."[1]

2   Many of the sources on which our understanding of foot binding are based are themselves highly problematic. Western missionaries attacked the "barbaric" practice of foot binding, but they did so within the context of a prejudiced and ignorant denunciation of many other aspects of Chinese civilization. Most of the Chinese literature on the subject was written by men, who often emphasized the erotic appeal of foot binding. For a better understanding of foot binding, it is necessary

to search for evidence of what Chinese women themselves thought about the practice. It is also necessary to place foot binding within its (changing) historical context. As Ko puts it, "Foot binding is not one monolithic, unchanging experience that all unfortunate women in each succeeding dynasty went through, but is rather an amorphous practice that meant different things to different people . . . It is, in other words, a situated practice."[2]

3   What did foot binding signify to the Chinese, and why did they maintain the practice for so long? Although historians do not know exactly how or why foot binding began, it was apparently initially associated with dancers at the imperial court and professional female entertainers in the capital. During the Song dynasty (960–1279) the practice spread from the palace and entertainment quarters into the homes of the elite. "By the thirteenth century, archeological evidence shows clearly that foot-binding was practiced among the daughters and wives of officials," reports Patricia Buckley Ebrey, whose study of Song women reproduces photographs of shoes from that period. The Fujian tomb of Miss Huang Sheng (1227–43), for example, contained shoes measuring between 13.3 and 14 cm. (5¼ to 5½ inches), while the Jiangxi tomb of Miss Zhou (1240–74) contained shoes that were 18 to 22 cm. (7 to 8⅝ inches) long.[3] Over the course of the next few centuries foot binding became increasingly common among gentry families, and the practice eventually penetrated the mass of the Chinese people.

4   Foot binding generally began between the ages of five and seven, although many poorer families delayed beginning for several years, sometimes even until the girl was an adolescent, so they could continue to benefit from her labor and mobility. First-person accounts of foot binding testify that the procedure was extremely painful. The girl's feet were tightly bound with bandages, which forced the small toes inward and under the sole of the foot, leaving only the big toe to protrude. Then the heel and toe were drawn forcefully together, breaking the arch of the foot.

5   This was the most extreme type of foot binding. However, many girls apparently had their feet "bound in less painful styles that 'merely' kept the toes compressed or limited the growth of the foot, but did not break any bones."[4] Nevertheless, there is no doubt that foot binding was a radical form of body modification. As early as the Song dynasty, Che Ruoshui made perhaps the first protest against foot binding. He wrote: "Little children not yet four or five *sui* [i.e. five to seven years old], who have done nothing wrong, nevertheless are made to suffer unlimited pain to bind [their feet] small. I do not know what use this is."[5]

6   In fact, foot binding served a number of uses. To begin with, as Ebrey suggests, by making the feet of Chinese women so much smaller than those of Chinese men, it emphasized that men and women were

different. Then, too, since only Chinese women bound their feet, the practice also served to distinguish between Chinese and non-Chinese. An investigation of the political situation suggests why this might have been thought desirable. At the time when foot binding began (in the late Tang) and spread (in the Song), China was in bad shape. Various foreign peoples who lived along the frontiers repeatedly raided and invaded China, sometimes conquering sizeable portions of Chinese territory and establishing their own dynasties on land that the Chinese regarded as properly theirs—as the Khitans did in the northeast when they defeated the Tang and established the Liao dynasty (907–1125), as the Tanguts did in the west when they established the XiXia Kingdom, and again as the Jürchens did in the north when they established the Jin dynasty (1115–1260) to succeed the Khitan Liao.

7   Although the Chinese managed to establish the Song dynasty in 960, after the turmoil that accompanied the fall of the Tang, it occupied only a portion of what had been Chinese territory, and even that portion decreased dramatically. Chinese men must often have been reminded of their military inferiority in the face of the aggressive "barbarians" encroaching from the north. Did they, perhaps, feel reassured about their strength and masculinity when they compared themselves to their crippled female counterparts? It may be possible to infer something of the sort when we analyze Song erotic poetry, devoted to the charms of tiny feet and a hesitant gait.

8   The suggestion that the spread of foot binding in the Song may have been related to the perceived need on the part of the Chinese gentry to emphasize the distinctions between men and women, Chinese and non-Chinese is strongly supported by Ebrey's analysis. "Because the ideal upper-class man was by Sung times a relatively subdued and refined figure, he might seem effeminate unless women could be made even more delicate, reticent, and stationary," she writes. In other words, anxieties about masculinity and national identity, rather than the desire to oppress women, *per se*, contributed to the spread of foot binding. "But," Ebrey adds, "we must also come to grips with women's apparently eager participation." A crucial element here, she argues, was the competition between wives and concubines. Chinese mothers may have become enthusiastic proponents of foot binding because small feet were regarded as sexually attractive, yet unlike the other tricks used by courtesans and concubines, there was nothing "forward" or "immodest" about having bound feet.[6]

9   The spread of foot binding during the Song dynasty also coincided with a philosophical movement known as Neo-Confucianism, which placed a pronounced ideological emphasis on female inferiority. (In Neo-Confucian metaphysics, the *yang* male principle was seen as superior to the *yin* female principle in both a cosmological and a moral sense.) Moreover, as already seen, political developments in the Song

contributed to the demise of the great aristocratic families and the corresponding proliferation of gentry families, whose social and economic position was much more insecure, and whose predominant social function was to serve as bureaucrats. Members of this new class may have been especially receptive to foot binding, because the practice simultaneously provided reassurance about their social status, proper gender relations, and Chinese identity.

10   Foot binding may have been reassuring to the Chinese, but it did not prevent the Mongols from becoming the first foreigners to conquer all of China. Genghiz Khan unified the Mongols, and Kublai Khan established the Yuan dynasty (1279–1368). Similar anxieties about sexual and racial boundaries appeared again several centuries later toward the end of the Ming dynasty, when the Chinese began to be threatened by the Manchus. Moreover, when the Manchus succeeded in conquering China and establishing the Qing dynasty in the mid-seventeenth century, they passed edicts ordering Chinese men to shave their foreheads and Chinese women to cease foot binding.

11   The resulting "hysterical atmosphere" was "full of sexual overtones," since both cutting men's hair and unbinding women's feet were perceived by Chinese males almost as a symbolic mutilation or castration, which might even be worse than death. As Ko points out, "Although no one openly advocated footbinding, the very establishment of the Manchu dynasty created a need to reemphasize the differences between 'we' and 'they' and between 'he' and 'she.' The ban on footbinding, thus doomed from the start, was rescinded in 1668, four years after its promulgation."[7]

12   Contrary to popular belief, it was not only the wealthy who bound their daughters' feet. By the Qing dynasty, the majority of Chinese women had bound feet—peasants included—although there did exist variations in the degree and type of foot binding. According to one Qing observer, "The practice of footbinding is more widespread in Yangzhou than in other places. Even coolies, servants, seamstresses, the poor, the old, and the weak have tiny feet and cramped toes."[8] Manchu women, however, did not bind their feet, nor did members of other ethnic minority groups. Indeed, under the Qing, Manchu women were specifically forbidden to bind their feet, which is intriguing, since it implies a desire to do so.

13   Because foot binding is usually interpreted today as a gruesome example of women's oppression, it is important to stress that women who experienced the practice rarely perceived it in those terms. Indeed, Ko has unearthed considerable evidence that many Chinese women felt proud of their bound feet, which they regarded as beautiful and prestigious. Foot binding was a central part of the women's world. The rituals surrounding foot binding were female-exclusive rituals, presided over by the women of the family, especially the girl's

mother, who prayed to deities such as the Tiny Foot Maiden and the goddess Guanyin. According to Ko, these rituals "and the beliefs behind them help explain the longevity and spread of the custom."

> For all its erotic appeal to men, without the cooperation of the women concerned, footbinding could not have been perpetuated for a millennium. In defining the mother–daughter tie in a private space barred to men, in venerating the fruits of women's handiwork, and in the centrality of female-exclusive religious rituals, footbinding embodied the essential features of a woman's culture documented by the writings of the women themselves.[9]

Women wrote poems about lotus shoes and they exchanged them with friends. Proverbs emphasized women's control over foot binding: "A plain face is given by heaven, but poorly bound feet are a sign of laziness."[10]

14   Good mothers were supposed to bind their daughters' feet tightly so they could make advantageous marriages, just as they made their sons study hard so they could pass their examinations. The Victorian traveler Isabella Bird visited China and reported that "The butler's little daughter, aged seven, is having her feet 'bandaged' for the first time, and is in torture, but bears it bravely in the hope of 'getting a rich husband' . . . The mother of this suffering infant says, with a quiet air of truth and triumph, that Chinese women suffer less in the process of being crippled than foreign women do from wearing corsets!"[11]

15   Indeed, Chinese and westerners alike not infrequently compared foot binding with corsetry, debating their relative injuriousness and irrationality. Yet measurements of existing corsets and lotus shoes indicate that both the sixteen-inch waist and the three-inch golden lotus were only achieved by a minority of women. Writing at the turn of the century, the sociologist Thorstein Veblen used foot binding (as well as such western fashions as corsets and long skirts) as examples of what he called "conspicuous leisure," because they supposedly indicated that the wearer could not perform productive labor. Yet, contrary to popular belief, neither bound feet nor corsets prevented women from working and walking; most Chinese women worked very hard, albeit usually at home. Moreover, although foot binding was believed to ensure female chastity by, literally, preventing women from straying, in fact women were far more restricted by social and legal constraints.

16   Although for many centuries most Chinese men and women approved of foot binding, the practice eventually ceased to be valorized as a way of emphasizing the beauty and virtue of Chinese women and/or the virility and civility of Chinese men. Writing in the early nineteenth century, the novelist Li Ruzhun attacked foot binding on the grounds that it oppressed women. His novel *Flowers in the Mirror*

included a satirical sequence about a country where women ruled and men had their feet bound.

17   Missionary efforts undoubtedly played a role in the demise of foot binding, as the Chinese were made aware that Westerners thought the practice was "barbaric," unhealthy, and oppressive to women. The Chinese girls who attended mission schools were taught that foot binding was bad. More significantly, however, growing numbers of young Chinese men (and a few educated Chinese women) began to reinterpret foot binding as a "backward" practice that hindered national efforts to resist western imperialism.

18   Chinese reformers began to discuss whether China could be strengthened *vis-à-vis* the West, if only Chinese women became stronger physically. This, in turn, seemed to depend on the elimination of what was increasingly regarded by progressive Chinese as the "feudal" practice of foot binding. Organizations such as the Natural Foot Society were founded, and struggled to change the idea that unbound female feet were "big" and ugly. Indeed, it was apparently difficult to convince the Chinese that foot binding was any more "unnatural" than other kinds of bodily adornment, such as clothing, jewelry, hairstyles, or cosmetics.[12]

19   There is even some evidence that the introduction of western high-heeled shoes, which give the visual illusion of smaller feet and produce a swaying walk, may have eased the transition away from the bound foot ideal. Manchu shoes were another alternative to lotus shoes in the early years of the anti-foot-binding movement, although with the rise of anti-Manchu nationalism at the time of the 1911 Revolution, this style disappeared.

20   Foot binding had never been mandated by any Chinese government. Indeed, various Qing rulers had sporadically attempted to abolish foot binding, without success. After the Qing dynasty was overthrown and a republic was declared, foot binding was outlawed. Laws alone would not have sufficed to end the practice, however, had it not already ceased to claim the allegiance of significant segments of the Chinese population, but once foot binding began to be regarded as "backward," modern-thinking Chinese increasingly attacked the practice.

21   Older brothers argued that their sisters should not have their feet bound, or should try to let their feet out—a process that was itself painful and only partly feasible. Sometimes husbands even abandoned wives who had bound feet, and looked for new, suitably modern brides. Obviously, these developments took place within the context of broader social change. The new generation of educated, urban Chinese increasingly argued that many aspects of traditional Chinese culture

should be analyzed and improved. Women, as well as men, should be educated and should participate in athletic activities. Arranged marriages should be replaced by love matches. The Chinese nation should modernize and strengthen itself.

NOTES

1. Dorothy Ko, *Teachers of the Inner Chambers: Women and Culture in Seventeenth-Century China* (Stanford: Stanford University Press, 1994), p. 148.
2. Dorothy Ko, "The Body as Attire: The Shifting Meanings of Footbinding in Seventeenth Century China," *Journal of Women's History* 8.4 (1997), p. 15.
3. Patricia Buckley Ebrey, *The Inner Quarters: Marriage and the Lives of Chinese Women in the Sung Period* (Berkeley: University of California Press, 1993), pp. 38–39.
4. Feng Jicai, *The Three-Inch Golden Lotus*, trans. David Wakefield (Honolulu: University of Hawaii Press, 1994), p. 236.
5. Cited in Ebrey, *The Inner Quarters*, p. 40.
6. Ebrey, *The Inner Quarters*, pp. 42–43.
7. Ko, *Teachers of the Inner Chambers*, p. 149.
8. Ibid., p. 263.
9. Ibid., p. 150.
10. Ibid., p. 171.
11. Isabella Bird, *The Golden Chersonese and the Way Thither* (first published London, 1883; reprinted, Singapore: Oxford University Press, 1990), p. 66.
12. Ko, "The Body as Attire," pp. 17–19.

✧ Evaluating the Text

1. What is the practice of foot binding? What political and social meanings did it communicate within the context of Chinese culture at the time it was practiced?

2. Why do Steele and Major draw a distinction between Western condemnation of foot binding and what the practice meant to Chinese women at the time?

✧ Exploring Different Perspectives

1. In what respects does the kimono both constrain and define the geisha as described by Liza Dalby—as did footbinding for Chinese women in previous eras?

2. How do the rituals described by Harold Miner in "Body Ritual Among the Nacirema" define sought-after cultural values as bound feet did in ancient China?

✧ Extending Viewpoints through Writing and Research

1. What do the kind of shoes you wear say about you? What are your favorite styles, heel heights, and colors? Given the choice between

a pair of fashionable or comfortable shoes, which would you buy? Alternatively, compare the meanings communicated by various traditional shoe types—including moccasins, sandals, mules, boots, and clogs—and their modern variants.

2. The so-called "lotus foot" (named because the walk of a woman whose foot was bound was thought to resemble the swaying of the lotus plant in the wind) captivated the Chinese imagination such that the foot took on the role of a sexual object. In what way do "shoes that have no relationship to the natural foot shape" (high heels) communicate the same psychological meaning in the West?

3. An illustrated Web site on foot binding is available at http://www. ccds.charlotte.nc.us/History/China/04/hutchins/hutchins.htm.

Why is this modern photo of a young woman wearing high-heeled boots ironic in light of Steele and Major's analysis?

Connecting Cultures

◆

Harold Miner, "Body Ritual Among the Nacirema"

Are the rituals Germaine Greer discusses in "One Man's Mutilation Is Another Man's Beautification" in Chapter 2 really so different from those discussed by Miner, and if so, why?

Mary Brave Bird, "The Granddaddy of Them All"

How does the use of piercing and mutilation in the sun dance differ from the way it is used by Germaine Greer in "One Man's Mutilation Is Another Man's Beautification" in Chapter 2?

Jennifer Fisher, "Nutcracker Nation"

To what extent has the use of chopsticks as described by Guanlong Cao in Chapter 2 ("Chopsticks") been assimilated in American culture in much the same way as Tchaikovsky's ballet?

Octavio Paz, "Fiesta"

In what sense are the fiestas in Mexico and weddings in Japan (as described by Nicholas Bornoff in "The Marriage Go-Round" in Chapter 3) designed as rituals intended to attract abundance?

Richard Keller Simon, "The Shopping Mall and the Formal Garden"

What similar marketing techniques are employed by shopping malls as described by Simon and advertisers who target children as discussed by Eric Schlosser in "Kid Kustomers" in Chapter 6?

Nabil Gorgy, "Cairo Is a Small City"

How does the concept of reciprocity work in Gorgy's story and in David R. Counts's "Too Many Bananas" in Chapter 7?

Liza Dalby, "Kimono"

How does clothing serve an ideological purpose in Dalby's account and in Elizabeth W. Fernea and Robert A. Fernea's analysis in "A Look behind the Veil" in Chapter 3?

Valerie Steele and John S. Major, "China Chic: East Meets West"

In what way did foot binding symbolize sought-after attributes as extreme thinness does in America according to Susan Bordo (see "Never Just Pictures" in Chapter 3)?

Pronunciation Key

$\blacklozenge$

The pronunciation of each of the following names is shown in parentheses according to the following pronunciation key.

1. A heavy accent ' is placed after a syllable with the primary accent.
2. A lighter accent ´ is placed after a syllable with the secondary accent.
3. The letters and symbols used to represent given sounds are pronounced as in the examples below.

a	bat, nap	o	box, hot
ā	way, cape	ō	boat, go
â	dare, air	ô	ought, order
ä	art, far	oi	voice, joy
		oo	ooze, rule
b	cabin, back	ou	loud, out
ch	beach, child		
d	do, red	p	pot, paper
		r	read, run
e	bet, merry	s	see, miss
ē	equal, beet	sh	show, push
e.	learn, fern		
		t	tell, ten
f	fit, puff	th	thin, path
g	give, go	th	that, smooth
h	how, him		
		u	up, butter
i	pin, big	ù	put, burn
ī	deny, ice	ü	rule, ooze
j	jam, fudge		
k	keep, kind	v	river, save
		w	west, will
l	love, all	y	yes, yet
m	my, am	z	zeal, lazy
n	in, now	zh	vision, measure
ng	sing, long		

ə occurs only in unaccented syllables and indicates the sound of

a   in alone
e   in taken
i   in pencil
o   in gallop
u   in circus

FOREIGN SOUNDS

a   as in French *ami*
Y   as in French *do;* or as in German *über*
œ   as in French *feu;* or as in German *schön*
N   as in French *bon*
H   as in German *ach;* or as in Scottish *loch*
R   as in Spanish *pero;* or as in German *mare*

Examples

Hanan al-Shaykh   (hä´ nän´ al shāk´)
Gayatri Devi   (gā a´ trē de´ vē)
Nawal El Saadawi   (na´ wäl´ əl sä dou´ wē)
Tomoyuki Iwashita   (tō mō yü´ kē i wä shē´ tä)
Mahdokht Kashkuli   (mə dōkt´ käsh kü´ lē)
Shirley Saad   (shừr´ lē säd)
Ngũgĩ wa Thiong'o   (nə goo̅´ gē wä tē ong´ō)

Credits

◆

Hanan al-Shaykh, "The Persian Carpet" from *Modern Arabic Short Stories,* translated by Denys Johnson Davies (Washington, DC: Three Continents Press, 1988). Copyright © 1988 by Denys Johnson Davies. Reprinted by permission of the translator.

Gloria Anzaldúa, "Cervicide" from *Borderlands/La Frontera: The New Mestiza* by Gloria Anzaldúa. Copyright © 1987, 1999 by Gloria Anzaldúa. Reprinted by permission of Aunt Lute Books.

Mary Brave Bird with Richard Erdoes, "The Granddaddy of Them All" from *Ohitika Woman.* Copyright © 1993 by Mary Brave Bird and Richard Erdoes. Used by permission of Grove/Atlantic, Inc.

Susan Bordo, "Never Just Pictures" from *Twilight Zones: The Hidden Life of Cultural Images from Plato to O. J.* Copyright © 1997 by University of California Press. Reprinted by permission.

Nicholas Bornoff, "The Marriage Go-Round" from *Pink Samurai.* Copyright 1991 by Nicholas Bornoff. Reprinted by permission of the author.

Christy Brown, "The Letter 'A'" from *My Left Foot.* Copyright © 1955 by Christy Brown. Reprinted by permission of Martin Secker & Warburg, Ltd.

Guanlong Cao, "Chopsticks" from *The Attic: A Memoir of a Chinese Landlord's Son.* Copyright © 1996 by University of California Press. Reprinted by permission.

Raymonde Carroll, "Money and Seduction" from *Cultural Misunderstandings: The French-American Experience.* Copyright © 1988 by University of Chicago Press. Reprinted by permission.

Sucheng Chan, "You're Short, Besides!" from *Making Waves: An Anthology of Writings by and About Asian Women* (Boston: Beacon Press, 1989). Copyright © 1989 by Asian Women United of California. Reprinted by permission.

Stephen M. Chapman, "The Prisoner's Dilemma" from the *New Republic* (March 8, 1980). Copyright © 1980 by The New Republic, LLC. Reprinted by permission.

John Cheever, "Reunion" from *The Stories of John Cheever* by John Cheever. Copyright © 1978 by John Cheever. Used by permission of Alfred A. Knopf, a division of Random House, Inc.

Photo Credits

◆————————————◆

Key Search Terms Index

◆

CHAPTER 4

Workplace Confrontations + Styles of Male and Female Assertion	Deborah Tannen
Low-Wage Workers + Single Mothers on Welfare	Barbara Ehrenreich
California Water Dependence + Poor Resource Planning	Gerald W. Haslam
Immigrant Labor + Mexican-Americans	Victor Villaseñor
Money and the Ladakhis + Impact on Agricultural Societies	Helena Norberg-Hodge
Corporate Disillusionment + Japanese Salaryman	Tomoyuki Iwashita
Investor Greed + Paper Replicas in Funeral Rites	Catherine Lim

CHAPTER 5

African-American Equality + Civil Rights	Martin Luther King Jr.
Finding One's Roots + Authentic Names	Itabari Njeri
Native-American Schooling + Government Abuses	Mary Crow Dog
Plantation-Era Racism + Class Prejudices	Kate Chopin
Chicano Identity + Higher Education	Richard Rodriguez
Success, Sex, and Money + French and American Attitudes	Raymonde Carroll
Being an Orphan + Poverty in Iran	Mahdokht Kashkuli
Life as an Untouchable + India's Caste System	Viramma

CHAPTER 6

"Quick Fix" Culture + Addictions	Philip Slater
Beef Industry + Environmental Impact	Jeremy Rifkin
Marketing for Children + Product Tie-Ins	Eric Schlosser
Survival in Prison + Dictatorship in Chile	Luis Sepulveda
Middle Eastern Punishments + Pros and Cons of Incarceration	Stephen Chapman
Code of Military Conduct + Soldier's Conscience	Panos Ioannides
Disenchanted Red Guards + Cultural Revolution	Rae Yang

CHAPTER 7

Autism + Causes and Treatment   Temple Grandin
Illegal Immigrants + Life on the   Gloria Anzaldúa
  U.S.-Mexican Border
Thai Immigrants + American Individualism   Poranee
                                                    Natadecha-Sponsel

Voodoo + Social Control in Haiti   Gino Del Guercio
Colonialism's Effects + Kenya   Ngũgĩ wa Thiong'o
Conversations in Japan + Formal and   Kyoko Mori
  Informal
Barter Economy + Traditional and Modern   David R. Counts

CHAPTER 8

Cleansing Rituals + Cross-Cultural   Harold Miner
Sun Dance + Lakota   Mary Brave Bird
Nutcracker Ballet + Stagings   Jennifer Fisher
Mexican Fiestas + Expenditure   Octavio Paz
Shopping Malls + Formal Gardens   Richard Keller Simon
Bedouins + Justice and Revenge   Nabil Gorgy
Kimono + Ceremony and Symbolism   Liza Dalby
Foot Binding + Cultural Meanings   Valerie Steele
                                                    and John S. Major

Geographical Index

◆

Index of Authors and Titles

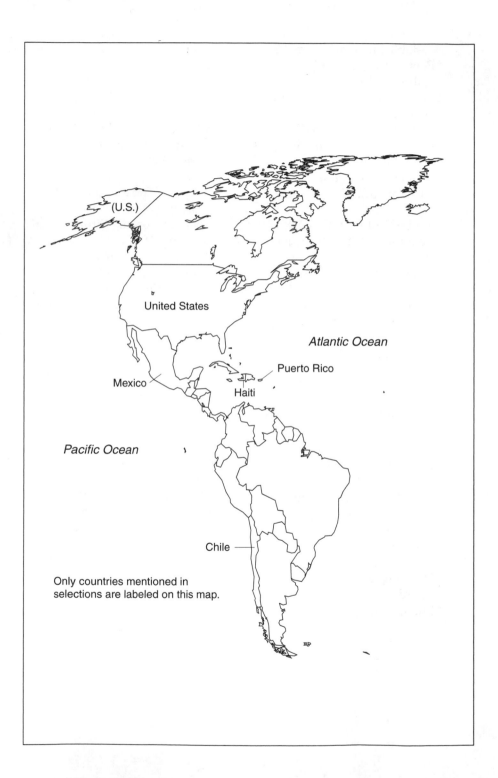

(U.S.)

United States

Atlantic Ocean

Mexico

Puerto Rico

Haiti

Pacific Ocean

Chile

Only countries mentioned in
selections are labeled on this map.

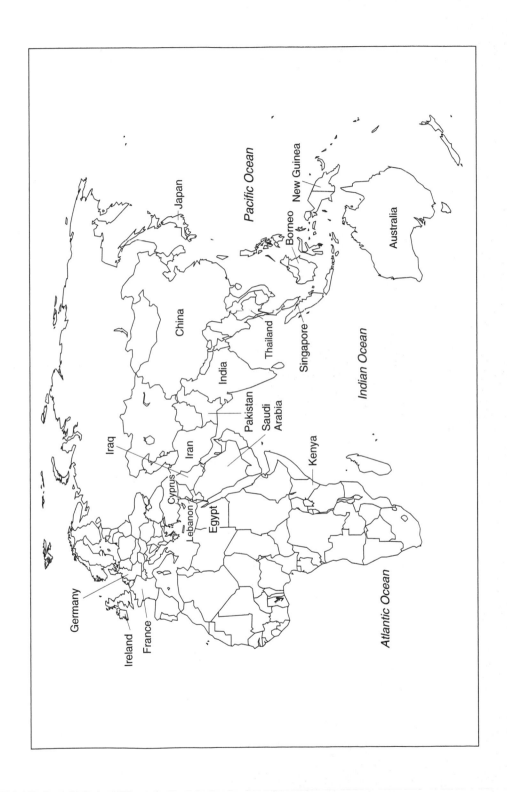